Protest Cultures
A Companion

Protest, Culture and Society

General editors:

Kathrin Fahlenbrach, Institute for Media and Communication, University of Hamburg
Martin Klimke, New York University, Abu Dhabi
Joachim Scharloth, Technische Universität Dresden, Germany

Protest movements have been recognized as significant contributors to processes of political participation and transformations of culture and value systems, as well as to the development of both a national and transnational civil society.

This series brings together the various innovative approaches to phenomena of social change, protest and dissent which have emerged in recent years, from an interdisciplinary perspective. It contextualizes social protest and cultures of dissent in larger political processes and socio-cultural transformations by examining the influence of historical trajectories and the response of various segments of society, political and legal institutions, on a national and international level. In doing so, the series offers a more comprehensive and multi-dimensional view of historical and cultural change in the twentieth and twenty-first centuries.

Protest Cultures

A Companion

Edited by
Kathrin Fahlenbrach, Martin Klimke,
and Joachim Scharloth

berghahn
NEW YORK · OXFORD
www.berghahnbooks.com

First published in 2016 by
Berghahn Books
www.berghahnbooks.com

Library of Congress Cataloging-in-Publication Data

Protest cultures : a companion / edited by Kathrin Fahlenbrach, Martin
    Klimke, and Joachim Scharloth.
        pages cm. -- (Protest, culture and society ; 17)
    Includes bibliographical references.
    ISBN 978-1-78533-148-0 (hardback : alk. paper) -- ISBN 978-1-78533-
    149-7 (ebook)
    1. Protest movements--History. 2. Demonstrations--History. I. Fahlenbrach,
    Kathrin, editor. II. Klimke, Martin, editor. III. Scharloth, Joachim, editor.
    HM881.P76 2016
    303.48'4--dc23
                            2015035794

British Library Cataloguing in Publication Data

A catalogue record for this book is available from the British Library

ISBN 978-1-78533-148-0 hardback
ISBN 978-1-78533-149-7 ebook

Contents

Part III: Morphology of Protest: Media

Part IV: Morphology of Protest: Domains of Protest Actions

Part V: Morphology of Protest: Re-Presentation of Protest

Part VI. Pragmatics of Protest: Protest Practices

Figures

Tables

Acknowledgments

The conceptualization and production of this book took many years, and we would like to express our sincerest gratitude to all the contributors for their wonderful collaboration, as well as their patience and trust in this project. We would also like to acknowledge the kind support of the whole team at Berghahn Books and would like to especially thank Marion Berghahn, Ann Przyzycki DeVita, Adam Capitanio, and Chris Chappell for their enduring support and for gently guiding us through the process. Special thanks also go to Thea Brophy, Sylvia Landau, Marie Harder, Johannes Schmid, and Laura Heeder for all their organizational and editorial efforts.

Kathrin Fahlenbrach, Martin Klimke, Joachim Scharloth

Introduction

Kathrin Fahlenbrach, Martin Klimke,
and Joachim Scharloth

Perspectives and Motivations

In today's globalized public sphere, protest is a ubiquitous phenomenon. Expressions of protest are no longer only articulated by social movements or political groups (like NGOs or trade unions), but also by youth movements, grassroots initiatives, individual citizens, intellectuals, or artists. Also institutionalized branches of social movements have become serious political players both on the domestic and international level.[1] Furthermore, protest actions have become performances in the public sphere, showcasing dissent and advocating for a change of the rules, habits, or values of society. Thereby protesting groups today tend to create more fluid and temporary networks based on digital online media.[2] This goes along with a broader dissemination of protest forms and practices especially in Western societies.

This book is an attempt to offer both a theoretical and methodological introduction into the scholarly analysis of protest cultures. It offers a survey of relevant concepts and perspectives of research dealing with cultural aspects of protest communication and actions. While research on protest is still dominated by sociological approaches, we favor a cultural studies approach that considers protest on a general basis as a form of contesting communication by the use of different media and strategies and in the broad context of different social and cultural institutions and actors. Hence "protest cultures" are considered as a multilayered phenomenon that emerges in the interplay from different social, communicative, and historical actors, processes, and semiotic forms. Accordingly protest cultures are understood as not only internal effects (e.g. ideologies and collective identities) but also external effects (e.g. influence on cultural values) of protest performed by specific social movements. While research on the cultural impacts of protest[3] still mostly focuses on social movements as key actors, we believe that it is time to recognize that the structure of social movements not only generally shifted toward rather "lose connections"[4] in globalized public spheres, but that protest cultures today have become a relevant part of mainstream culture in Western societies.

The interest in such a broader cultural perspective on protest came about as a result of the three editors' shared interest in a particular set of protest movements during the 1960s and 1970s. Coming together more than ten years ago, as young scholars from different disciplinary backgrounds, we soon realized the need for a broader interdisciplinary dialogue on social movements and phenomena of dissent, and the benefit it could yield on our own work. Exactly this dialogue was held in an institutional framework first as part of a Interdisciplinary Research Forum on Protest Movements (2002–5), then as part of a Marie Curie Conference and Workshop Series, "European Protest Movements since the Cold War: The Rise of a (Trans-)national Civil Society and the Transformation of the Public Sphere after 1945" from 2006–10 funded by the European Union. Designed as an interdisciplinary training series for young scholars, this initiative soon established itself as an international, transdisciplinary research network with more than 250 affiliated researchers from over 35 countries.

Utilizing approaches from sociology, political science, and media studies, its events analyzed the aesthetics and lifestyles of peace and protest cultures as well as the institutional and social impact of protest. The initiative also explored the impact protest movements had on transformations of the public sphere in general and on the emergence of a (trans-)national civil society in particular, thereby paving the way for substantial changes in domestic and international systems. More specifically, we examined how globalization processes, human rights discourses, and the emergence of international NGOs (INGOs) influenced established politics, transnational exchange, and international relations since World War II.

What emerged from this framework was not only a plethora of independent and cross-disciplinary research networks and working groups, follow-up projects, and publications, but also—as we had hoped—a desire among its participants to try to capture some of the wealth of methodological and theoretical approaches in this area through a reference work with a broader, decidedly cultural as well as interdisciplinary perspective.[5] This is what we have brought together in this book.

In many ways, the design of this volume reflects the fact that current research on protest, dissent, and social movements is not confined to traditional academic boundaries anymore.[6] Narrow, disciplinary approaches have long been superseded by a broad-based debate about the multifaceted efficacy and significance of protest in today's world, whether it be on the domestic or the international level; a fact that has progressively been captured by the respective scholarly handbooks in the field.[7] This shift is due to the fact that the so-called new social movements of the 1970s and 1980s have now increasingly become the object of historical analysis in the wake of a tremendous wave of scholarship on the 1960s and, in particular, the metaphorical "1968." In many cases, the social movement scholarship these movements themselves generated (social movement theory, history from below, etc.) has become a well-established feature of the academy that has been complemented by other perspectives that transcend political science, sociology, and history, and also include media and communication studies.[8]

The emergence of modern mass media in the twentieth century in particular changed the communication of protest in a fundamental way. Social, political, or habitual forms of protest with the aim of changing society came to depend on the use of mass media and, more recently, on digital network media. At the same time, protest corresponded to the desire of the mass media for a constant supply of spectacular images. As a consequence, protest agents and the media gradually established a mutual interdependence in the last century.[9] Political protest traditionally developed professionalized strategies of symbolic communication to influence political decision-making and public opinion.[10] Social movement theory distinguished these "instrumental" strategies of protest from more "expressive" articulations of dissent. This distinction has, however, become untenable. In today's media-dominated societies, symbolic actions and events have also become politically relevant instrumental strategies.

Expressive forms of protest have also become integral parts of popular culture. The media, fashion, and advertising industries regularly absorb new expressions and symbolic signs used by protest actors. As a result, these expressions of protest impact the habitus and lifestyle in a society. Protest cultures also often form the building blocks of social milieus that create the grassroots level from which other political actors and movements emerge (e.g., the environmental movement of the 1970s and 1980s in the wake of the student movement and counterculture of the 1960s).[11] Protest actors, in turn, have begun to use subversive techniques and guerrilla strategies to resist the smooth integration of protest into popular culture. With the rising importance of the Internet, we can observe the emergence of new kinds of protest cultures that address specific audiences by creating alternative media or networks and news services online, largely ignoring traditional mass media.

Since a coherent and comprehensive overview of the cultural dimension of protest remains a gap in the research on social movements, this companion seeks to examine the cultural elements of protest communication, including the methods and approaches to investigate them. It widens the perspective to protest phenomena in general, a term much more appropriate to cover the various cultures of dissent worldwide.

Overview

Based on our understanding of protest cultures sketched above, this companion uses systematic distinctions that examine basic cultural structures, often integrating different, sometimes even antagonistic, actors and practices. After an introduction to relevant perspectives in the research on protest cultures in part 1, subsequent parts deal with the *morphology* and *pragmatics* of protest communication. Both distinctions are based on the common premise that relevant social realities emerge during performative acts of communication. More specifically, protest is understood here basically as a form of contentious communication implying different rules and conventions; at the same time, the meanings of protest communication evolve in a discursive and public process in which very different actors and institutions are involved.

Accordingly, we distinguish four aspects in the morphology of protest cultures: *constructing reality* (Part 2), including ideologies, identities, or narratives; *media* (Part 3), including/covering different kinds of media such as the body, alternative media, or images; different *domains of protest actions* (Part 4), such as the public sphere, everyday life or cyberspace; and finally, *re-presentations of protest* (Part 5), including witness and testimony, media coverage, as well as archives.

The pragmatics of protest are analyzed in Parts 6, 7, and 8, which introduce significant performative action types and practices and their constitutive contexts. By recognizing a broad spectrum of different protest agents (including mass media, or other established actors), we wish to overcome the close focus on social movements as agents of protest (even though they are still considered relevant ones). As key aspects in the pragmatics of protest, we distinguish protest practices (part 6), reactions to protest actions (part 7), and long-term consequences of protest (part 8). Accordingly, we not only consider the performance of contesting actions (in different contexts) relevant for the emergence and societal effects of protest cultures, but also the reactions evoked in different contexts and actors (e.g., established politics or advertisement). Furthermore, looking at long-term consequences of protest (e.g., changing gender roles or the diffusion of symbolic forms), we understand protest cultures as a historical process, dynamically affected by different, even contrasting interests, motivations, and practices of the actors involved.

In the following, we give a more detailed overview of each of these parts. The first part, "Perspectives on Protest," provides systematic and classic definitions of protest and an overview of the academic disciplines engaged in the research of protest cultures. It assembles a number of articles about different possibilities of conceptualizing and highlighting different aspects of protest in various disciplines. One of the most prevalent is to view protest as an integral part of social movements (Donatella Della Porta) as well as to explore dimensions and functions of protest cultures in social movements (Dieter Rucht). Another perspective deals with protest as a constitutive element of sub- and countercultures (Rupa Huq), not necessarily aiming at political change, but at performing minor cultural practices and antihegemonic cultural discourses. However, as Huq argues, the term "subcultures" requires a critical revision in protest research, given that the interrelations between hegemonic and minor cultural practices and discourses have become highly ambivalent. As Jana Günther shows, protest can also be framed as symbolic politics, a strategic use of signs to meet society's requirements of political orientation, which can of course have a substantial impact on policy. Moreover, protest can be displayed by ostentatious expressive forms in everyday life, manifesting itself in individual lifestyles (Nick Crossley). Along with the redefinition and widening of the concept of art, many forms of protest can clearly be viewed as artistic expressions. As TV Reed points out, this includes both the role of artistic artifacts used within movements as symbolic forms as well as protest events themselves understood as artistic texts. In addition, a constitutive element of every public expression of protest is its articulation in specific media of communication. Taking into account different dimensions of media, protest is therefore generally viewed by Kathrin Fahlenbrach as a media phenomenon.

The second part, "Morphology of Protest: Constructing Reality," reflects on the most relevant forms and functions that come into play when protest is being performed. This morphology of protest takes its cue from mechanisms of the sociosemantic ideologies, identities, as well as motivations and frames that shape the agenda and criticism of protesters. Ruth Kinna (ideologies) and David A Snow (frames, framing processes) introduce these prominent concepts by closely interrelating the cognitive and the cultural understanding of protest, including protesters as well as their addressees and the general public. These dynamics also shape the meaning-making process of protest communications in a *longue durée* and its remembrance in cultural memory, as Lorena Anton explains. With the term of *narratives,* Jakob Tanner inserts another relevant distinction that is useful to analyze more precisely the strategies of assigning meaning to protest in communication. An integral element of this is the construction of utopias (Laurence Davis) as well as the production of images of the self with the aim to generate collective identities among protesters (Natalia Ruiz-Junco and Scott Hunt). Considering the role of emotion (Deborah B Gould) and commitment (Catherine Corrigall-Brown), we also take a closer look at motivational aspects in the practices performed during protest actions.

The third part, "Morphology of Protest: Media," then covers the different symbolic forms and media through which protest is being uttered in different media. Following a broad and multidimensional understanding of media, we define media as communicative forms that relate different areas and actors of communication, which includes the body and its semiotic expressions as well as visual, linguistic, and multimodal media and their relevant genres in protest communication (e.g., posters, humor, or political songs). Such a broader perspective also includes specific forms of protest expressions, such as violence as a medium of protest communication. Starting with an analysis of the body (Andrea Pabst), its aesthetic presentation and its movement patterns (dance, Eva Aymamí Reñé), this section discusses different modalities and forms of actions like violence (Lorenzo Bosi) and parody and humor (Marjolein 't Hart), as well as contentious aesthetical forms in fashion (Nicole Doerr) and design (Tali Hatuka). Additional media of protest explored in this section are: alternative media (Alice Mattoni), graffiti (Johannes Stahl), posters and placards (Sascha Demarmels), images (Kathrin Fahlenbrach), typography and text design (Jürgen Spitzmüller), as well as political music and protest songs (Beate Kutschke). Each of these chapters offers a systematic introduction into the specific qualities of the respective media and how they are typically involved in protest communication and culture.

Articles in part 4, "Morphology of Protest: Domains of Protest Actions" discuss the specificities of different domains of protest actions, such as the public sphere (Simon Teune), urban spaces (Tali Hatuka), everyday life (Anna Schober), and the Internet (Paul G Nixon and Rajash Rawal). They demonstrate that the specific (technological, semiotic, public, or urban) infrastructures of the different spaces and domains have a significant influence on how protest is being articulated and performed. The articles in part 5, "Morphology of Protest: Re-Presentation of Protest," reflect on forms and functions of the re-presentations of protest (events) from the perspective of witnessing (Eric G Waggoner), media coverage (Andy Opel), and the long-term storage of sources in archives (Hanno Balz)—all widely focusing on representing protest performed by others.

The next three parts of the book examine the "Pragmatics of Protest" by looking at specific action types and the contextual conditions that shape them, as well as the interactive effects that derive from performing protest practices. Under the heading of part 6 "Pragmatics of Protest: Protest Practices," specific culturally shaped action types and their performative rules are investigated. Among those are linguistic performances like uttering (Constanze Spiess), street protest (Matthias Reiss), as well as speech acts like insult and devaluation (John Michael Roberts) and public debating (Mary E Triece). Another focus of part 6 is on strategies of protest actions performed by different actors, specifically focusing on artistic and entertaining practices of protest. This includes the strategies used in media campaigns (Johanna Niesyto) or theatrical protest (Dorothea Kraus). Anna Schober discusses cinema as a social and discursive space for mediating protesting themes and values. Subsequent chapters demonstrate different practices of hiding, masking, and the rule-breaking in protest: Helena Flam and Åsa Wettergren examine different ways of civil disobedience, Freia Anders explores the practice of creating temporary autonomous zones, while Sebastian Haunss looks at concepts of mummery. Further protest practices analyzed here include the recontextualizing of cultural signs (David Eugster), clandestine actions (Gilda Zwerman), as well as violent protest practices (Peter Sitzer and Wilhelm Heitmeyer).

Pragmatics as defined above also consists of the reactions to protest by those who are addressed and by the general public, which is its witness. This perspective, which has not yet been sufficiently addressed in protest research, is unfolded on a general scope in part 7 "Pragmatics of Protest: Reactions to Protest Actions," oscillating between refusal, suppression, and control while also including the selective assimilation of protest forms and strategies in mainstream culture. The articles in this section therefore cover the reactions to protest deriving from political and institutional confrontation (Lorenzo Bosi and Katrin Uba), from which one of the most prevailing is suppression of protest discourse and censorship (Brian Martin). They also discuss cultural conflicts in the discursive field (Nick Crossley), reflect on the transformation that goes with the assimilation of protest codes in advertisement and, hence, in mainstream culture (Rudi Maier), and categorize corporate reactions against protest campaigns (Veronika Kneip).

Feedback from social institutions also has a substantial impact on protest which can lead to changes and processes of institutionalization of protest cultures. The articles in the part 8, "Pragmatics of Protest: Long-Term Consequences," deal with the long-term consequences protest can have either on the biographies of the activists themselves (Marco Giugni) or on societal roles, exemplified by the change of gender roles (Kristina Schulz), by the creation of new milieus (Michael Vester), as well as by a rising awareness of conflicts and the diffusion of symbolic forms within a society (Dieter Rucht). As a significant example, Sabine Elsner-Petri discusses the public discourse rules on political correctness as a long-term outcome of protest cultures in many Western countries.

Given the complexity and scope of all of these aspects and the general topic at hand, this volume cannot claim to be either complete or canonical. Especially during the last decade, protest cultures have constantly changed their forms, media, and practices, and we certainly cannot cover all of them. However, we hope that the individual contributions and the book as a whole inspire not only further interdisciplinary discussion, but also a deep appreciation of protest as a multilayered cultural phenomenon that warrants our attention not only as citizens but also as scholars.

Notes

1. See Maria Stephan and Erica Chenoweth, "Why Civil Resistance Works: The Strategic Logic of Nonviolent Conflict," *International Security* 33 (2008): 7–44; Erica Chenoweth and Maria J Stephan, *Why Civil Resistance Works: The Strategic Logic of Nonviolent Conflict* (New York, 2011); Thomas Olesen, *Power and Transnational Activism* (Abingdon, Oxon, 2011); Kathrin Fahlenbrach et al., eds, *The Establishment Responds: Power, Politics, and Protest Since 1945* (New York, 2012).
2. This tendency is for example observed and analyzed in Eva Horn and Lucas Marco Gisi, eds, *Schwärme—Kollektive ohne Zentrum. Eine Wissensgeschichte zwischen Leben und Information* (*Masse und Medium 7*; Bielefeld, 2009); Howard Rheingold, *Smart Mobs. The Next Social Revolution* (Cambridge, MA, 2002); Jan-Hendrik Passoth, Birgit Peuker, and Michael Schillmeier, eds, *Agency without Actors? New Approaches to Collective Action* (London, 2012); Eugene Thacker, "Networks, Swarms, Multitudes. Part One," *Ctheory* (18 May 2004), http://www.ctheory.net/articles.aspx?id=422.
3. Cf. Britta Baumgarten, Priska Daphi, and Peter Ullrich, *Conceptualizing Culture in Social Movement Research* (New York, 2014).
4. This tendency is currently investigated in a graduate school at the University of Hamburg, dealing with "loose connections" in both urban and digital spaces, directed by Urs Stäheli and Gabriele Klein. Cf. "Loose Verbindungen. Kollektivität im urbanen und kollektiven Raum" [Loose Connections. Collectivity in the Urban and in the Digital Space], http://www.wiso.uni-hamburg.de/fileadmin/sowi/soziologie/Staeheli/Lose_Verbindungen_Programm.pdf.
5. See, for example, the publication series "Protest, Culture, and Society" (Berghahn Books, www.protest-publications.org), the Social Movements Research Network at the Council for European Studies at Columbia University (http://councilforeuropeanstudies.org/research/research-networks/social-movements), or the Institut for Protest and Bewegungsforschung (http://protestinstitut.eu/).

6. Given that relevant areas of protest research and its cultural implications are treated intensively in this companion, we avoid a detailed research overview in this introduction.

7. See representatively Bert Klandermans and Suzanne Staggenborg, eds, *Methods of Social Movement Research* (Minneapolis, MN, 2002); David A Snow, Sarah Anne Soule, and Hanspeter Kriesi, eds, *The Blackwell Companion to Social Movements* (Malden, MA, 2004); Donatella Della Porta, Hanspeter Kriesi, and Dieter Rucht, eds, *Social Movements in a Globalizing World* (London, 2009); Bert Klandermans and Conny Roggeband, eds, *Handbook of Social Movements Across Disciplines* (New York, 2010); Jeff Goodwin, *The Social Movements Reader: Cases and Concepts* (Chichester, 2012); David A Snow et al., eds, *The Wiley-Blackwell Encyclopedia of Social and Political Movements* (Malden, MA, 2013); Jacquelien van Stekelenburg, Conny Roggeband, and Bert Klandermans, eds, *The Future of Social Movement Research: Dynamics, Mechanisms, and Processes* (Minneapolis, MN, 2013).

8. Representative examples of this kind of integrative scholarship on "1968" include, most recently Joachim Scharloth, *1968: Eine Kommunikationsgeschichte* (Paderborn, 2011); Timothy Brown, *West Germany and the Global Sixties: The Antiauthoritarian Revolt, 1962–1978* (Cambridge, 2013). Timothy Brown and Andrew E Lison, eds, *Sound and Visions. Counterculture and the Global 1968* (New York, 2014); Stefanie Pilzweger, *Männlichkeit zwischen Gefühl und Revolution. Eine Emotionsgeschichte der bundesdeutschen 68er-Bewegung* (Bielefeld, 2015).

9. See Kathrin Fahlenbrach, Erling Sivertsen, and Rolf Werenskjold, eds, *Media and Revolt: Strategies and Performances from the 1960s to the Present* (New York, 2014).

10. See, for example, Nicole Doerr, Alice Mattoni, and Simon Teune, *Advances in the Visual Analysis of Social Movements* (Bradford, 2013).

11. Sven Reichardt, Detlef Siegfried, eds, *Das alternative Milieu: antibürgerlicher Lebensstil und linke Politik in der Bundesrepublik Deutschland und Europa 1968–1983* (Göttingen, 2010); Sven Reichardt, *Authentizität und Gemeinschaft: linksalternatives Leben in den siebziger und frühen achtziger Jahren* (Berlin, 2014).

Part I

Perspectives on Protest

Chapter 1

Protest in Social Movements

Donatella Della Porta

Protest: A Definition

Protest includes *nonroutinized* ways of affecting political, social, and cultural processes. Especially from the 1960s on, survey research recognized that a "new set of political activities has been added to the citizens' political repertoire."[1] Among "unconventional" forms of political participation, social science research listed signing petitions, lawful demonstration, boycotts, withholding of rent or tax, occupations, sit-ins, blocking traffic, and wildcat strikes. This expansion of the repertoire of political participation was indeed a long-lasting characteristic of democratic politics. More than two decades later, analyses of the World Value Surveys polls confirmed that "many of these forms of activity, such as petitions, demonstrations, and consumer boycott, are fairly pervasive and have become increasingly popular during recent decades. Protest politics is on the rise as channel of political expression and mobilization."[2]

The very spread of protest opened a debate about the possibility to consider it as a nonroutine or nonconventional repertoire. While more and more frequently used by a broad range of actors, it is however still true that law-and-order coalitions, time and again, challenged the legitimacy of forms of action that are still often based on the disruption of everyday routines and often rules and regulation. Not by chance, new waves of protest are repressed with vigor even in democracies.[3]

Another characteristic of protest is it being relational. As social movement studies have stressed, typical of protest is the use of *indirect* channels to influence decision makers, setting in motion a process of persuasion mediated by mass media and powerful allies. As Michael Lipsky noted, "protest is successful to the extent that other parties are activated to political involvement."[4]

Different typologies of protest have been suggested. Protest can be more or less radical in nature, ranging from more conventional petitioning to more conflictual blockades, and including a number of episodes of violence. Forms of protest can also be distinguished according to the logic, or modus operandi, which the activists assign them: logic of numbers, logic of damage, or logic of testimony.[5]

Protest as a Strategic Option

Research on social movements has analyzed the choices between forms of protest as strategic options that take into account a multiplicity of objectives, balancing the need to keep members' commitment with that of gaining the support of the public and influencing public decision makers.[6] For social movements, given their lack of material resources to invest in material selective incentives, it is particularly important to find tactics, which are also suitable for realizing internal aims. For the labor movement, strikes had more than a simply instrumental function,[7] and this is also true of occupations for the student movement, both reinforcing collective identity and reciprocal solidarity. In the most recent wave of protest, the camps have emerged as forms of protest endowed with very high prefigurative capacity. In Tahir Square, Placa del Sol, or Sintagma Square—and the thousands of other squares occupied for weeks or months all over the globe—the occupation of a public square is much more than just a disruptive tactic, allowing instead to experiment with new practices of democracy and new forms of social relations.[8]

Actions that are well-suited to strengthen internal solidarity might however, under some conditions, reduce external support. If radical, direct actions tend to maintain rank-and-file support, they however risk alienating potential allies as the more peaceful and institutional a course of unconventional political action is (petitioning, for example), the greater the level of public approval (as opinion polls have shown). The camps of the Indignados movements acquired such a strong identification capacity that police evictions brought about serious crises.

Mass media is extremely relevant to propagate the movement messages but also very difficult to please for outsiders.[9] Research on protest coverage has demonstrated,[10] in order to obtain media coverage, action must involve a great many people, utilize radical tactics, or be particularly innovative. At the same time, however, research has also time and again confirmed that the mass media tends to stigmatize political violence as deviant, criminal behavior. While new technologies (of the Web 1.0 and Web 2.0 type) have undoubtedly increased the capacity of social movement organizations, and even single activists to communicate, difficulty remains in expanding the public audience to beyond those who are already sympathetic.[11]

Some forms of action may also cause an escalation in repression and alienate sympathizers. In particular, violence polarizes the social conflicts, transforming "relations between challengers and authorities from an open, many-sided game into a bipolar one in which people are forced to choose sides, allies defect, bystanders retreat and the state's repressive apparatus swings into action."[12]

The choice of form of action is instrumental, and as mentioned, protest has also a prefigurative function for social movement activists. The aims do not justify the means, and much of the debate inside social movements is about not only the efficacy but also the meaning and symbolic value. Stressing the euphoria and pleasures involved in protest, James Jasper observes indeed that "tactics represent important routines, emotionally and morally salient in these people's lives."[13]

Repertoire and Historical Changes

Beyond instrumental and ethical concerns, the choice of forms of action is also constrained in time and space. Charles Tilly has used the concept of a *repertoire of collective action* to define the differences in the types of contentious actions widespread in particular historical periods.[14] His research pointed first of all at the order that could be found in what was mainly considered as disorder, and the political struggles readable in what authorities presented as disturbance. As he noted, repertoires are made by a repetition of a limited number of actions and aim at political effects.

Stressing the role of ordinary people in making history, he looked at the evolution of contentious politics in France and Great Britain, marked by a deep change, developing between the end of the eighteenth century and the beginning of the nineteenth century. Before then, protest was present in European history: peasants burned down mills in protest against increases in the price of bread; citizens dressed up in order to mock their superiors; funerals could be turned into the occasion for denunciations of injustice. These contentious gatherings had some characteristics in common: they were *parochial* scope, addressed mainly local actors or the local representatives of national actors, and relied on *patronage*—"appealing to immediately available power holders to convey grievances or settle disputes, temporarily acting in the place of unworthy or inactive power holders only to abandon power after the action."[15]

The new repertoire of European protest, which developed toward the end of the eighteenth century—involving actions such as strikes, electoral rallies, public meetings, petitions, marches, insurrection, and the invasion of legislative bodies—was instead *national*, "though available for local issues and enemies, it lends itself easily to coordination among many localities," and *autonomous*, as "instead of staying in the shadow of existing power holders and adapting routines sanctioned by them, people using the new repertoire tend to initiate their own statements of grievances and demands."[16] Additionally, if in the past, people used to participate as members of pre-constituted communities, in the modern repertoire, they participate as representatives of particular interests.

The concept of repertoire points is the specific, historically bound characteristics of protest: it is in fact finite in its forms that are constrained in both time and space. In fact, repertoires are reproduced over time, because they are what protesters "know how." The forms of action used in one protest campaign tend to be adopted and adapted in subsequent ones, as activists imitate what happened in previous waves of protest. Traditions are in fact transmitted from one generation of activists to another. For instance, the public march developed out of the practice of holding electoral banqueting and then evolved through the institutionalization of specific rituals and structures such as the closing rally and the stewarding of marches.[17]

Rooted in the shared political cultures of the activists, repertoires contain the options known and considered practicable, while excluding others. The repertoire of contentions is then "something like the theatrical or musical sense of the word; but the repertoire in question resembles that of commedia dell'arte or jazz more than that of a strictly classical ensemble: people know the general rules of performance more or less well and vary the performance to meet the purpose at hand."[18]

Repertoires are however also innovated, through experiments with new forms and new combination of old ones. Forms of actions—especially successful ones—are imported from other movements, countries, and generation. The European history of contentious testifies for the generalization of some forms of action (such as strike or road blocks) from specific social and political groups to most of them. In addition, each new generation introduces specific forms in the repertoire, or adapts old ones.[19] The rituals of marches has for instance changed over time adapting to modern (or "postmodern") times: from those oriented to show unity and organization to more theatrical ones, giving space to a colorful expression of diversity and subjectivity.

Imported from the premodern repertoire, forms of protest like charivari or "Katzenmusik" found at times their place also in contemporary conflicts.

Cycles and Opportunities

Action produces action, as protest events tend indeed to cluster in time. As Beissinger observed, in his analysis of the nationalist conflicts that developed with the breakdown of the Soviet Union, in order to understand protest one has to consider that "events and the contention over identity which they represent are not distributed randomly over time and space. Their appearance is structured both temporally and spatially."[20] So, protests come in chains, series, waves, cycles, and tides "forming a punctuated history of heightened challenges and relative stability."[21] This means that events are "linked sequentially to one another across time and space in numerous ways: in the narrative of the struggles that accompany them, in the altered expectations that they generate about subsequent possibilities to contest; in the changes that they evoke in the behavior of those forces that uphold a given order, and in the transformed landscape if meaning that events at times fashion."[22] In Beissinger's words, waves of protest, as "modular phenomenon," proceeds as "increasing number of groups with less conducive structural preconditions are drawn into action as a result of the influence of the prior successful example of others."[23]

Similarly, cycles of protest have been defined as phases of heightened contention that develop across the social and political system. As Tarrow notes, they include "a rapid diffusion of collective action from more mobilized to less mobilized sectors; a quickened pace of innovation in the forms of contention; new or transformed collective action frames; a combination of organized and unorganized participation; and sequences of intensified inter-actions between challengers and authorities which can end in reform, repression and sometimes revolution."[24]

As economic cycles, also protest cycles are expected to follow a path upward, followed by a peak and then a decline. In Tarrow's words, they proceed "from institutional conflict to enthusiastic peak to ultimate collapse. After gaining national attention and state response, they reached peaks of conflict that were marked by the presence of movement organizers who tried to diffuse the insurgencies to a broader public. As participation was channeled into organizations, the movements, or part of them, took a more political logic—engaging in implicit bargaining with authorities. In each case, as the cycle wounded down, the initiative shifted to elites and parties."[25]

The recurrent dynamic of ebb and flow is inherent in the notion of the cycle. Cycles spread through demonstration affects, as "by demonstrating the vulnerability of the authorities the first movements to emerge lower the cost of collective action for other actors."[26] They however also involve competition as "the victories they obtain undermine the previous order of things, provoking counter-mobilization."[27] Victories, even if contested, spread protest to new groups: spin-off movements imitate the first-riser ones, so expanding the range of claims.[28]

Besides ebbs and flows, forms of protest tend to change along the cycle. In the initial stages of protest the most disruptive, but not often violent tactics, come to the fore; also new forms are invented by the new collective actors, while those who remobilize from previous cycles of protest bring in their traditional repertoires.[29] As protest spreads, elites tend however to react with a variable mix of repression and cooptation that often initiates, as the same time, processes of radicalization and institutionalization.

In some moments, such as during the cycles of protests of the 1970s, especially in countries as Italy or Germany, protest forms tended to radicalize, in some cases up to the formation of clandestine political organizations.[30] Radicalization was often gradual, evolving during interactions on the streets of movements, countermovements, and the police. At the outset of protest, violent action was limited in its presence, small in scope and unplanned, developing mainly as an unforeseen result of direct action such as sit-ins or occupations. As protest increased, violent forms of action initially spread more slowly than nonviolent ones, taking the form of clashes between demonstrators and police or counterdemonstrators. Starting out as occasional, such episodes, nonetheless, tended to be repeated and to acquire on a ritual quality. During this process, small groups began to specialize in increasingly extreme tactics, built up specialized structures for violent action, and occasionally went underground. The very presence of these groups contributed to a demobilization. The final stages of the cycle thus saw both a process of institutionalization and a growing number of violent actions.

Following Tilly and Tarrow's early contributions, in social movement studies protest events have been mainly studied as aggregated collective action. Protest has been considered as a "dependent variable" and explained on the basis of political opportunities and organizational resources. An opening up of political opportunities has been quoted to account for the emergence of protest cycles. Collective actors tend in fact to mobilize above all when and where they perceive the possibility of success[31]: so the opening of channels of access tends to moderate the forms of protest, while closing them down induces radicalization.[32]

Beyond temporal variations, there are however also specificities of national protest repertoires, that cross-national research has in fact singled out and linked to more stable political characteristics. So, protest is more moderate in countries characterized by functional division of power, territorial decentralization, and an inclusive political culture.[33] In Mediterranean Europe, France and Germany, absolutism and the late introduction of universal suffrage led to a divided and radicalized labor movement. In the smaller, open-market countries in Great Britain and Scandinavia, on the other hand, where no experience of absolutism and universal suffrage was introduced early, inclusive strategies produced a united and moderate labor movement.[34] In Italy, continuously repressed unions were more eager to support mass protests, even of the most disruptive type.[35]

Research on protest cycles has also stressed the importance of physical and symbolic interactions between protesters and the police, and therefore of the policing of protest, influenced by national democratic history.[36] In Italy during the 1970s, radical tactics emerged in the course of an escalation of the use of force in the policing of marches and demonstrations.[37] The interventions of the police and carabinieri became increasingly determined while extreme left and right groups clashed with ever more lethal weapons: stones, molotov cocktails, spanners, and eventually guns. Later on the prevalence of de-escalation in police strategies reflected the routinization of some protest forms, as well as the legitimation of some protest actors. Recent protests show some countertendencies, especially when new actors and forms of action enter the scene. The militarization of police training and equipment is having most visible effects in the policing of some protest events, especially since (post-9/11) issues of security are coupled with "zero tolerance" doctrines, even for petty crimes or disturbances of public order. The war on terrorism had a strong impact on the policing of protest, as well as individual freedom at the national and transnational levels. Particularly delicate in this respect have been transnational protest events, which have a high visibility and unite activists from different countries.[38]

Eventful Protest

In a recent essay on Charles Tilly's enormous contribution to research on repertoires of protest, Sidney Tarrow described his initial work as moved by a "structuralist persuasion," inherited from Barrington Moore Jr.[39] Among the structural precondition for the development of social movements (as sustained campaigns of protest mobilized by ad hoc associations) are long-term structural changes such as the increasing power of the state, parliamentarization of national politics, urbanization, and proletarization. Tilly himself commented that "in those distant days," "method meant statistical analysis," and explanation "ignores transformative processes."[40]

Even if focusing on normal, everyday events, in later work Tilly stressed more and more eventful histories over event-counting.[41] Explaining the evolution of repertoires of protest, he moreover added to external circumstances (among which regime and opportunity structures), also the history of contentious politics itself.[42] In a similar vein, concepts such as transformative events or "eventful protest" have been coined to stress the effects of protest on the social movements and the activists themselves. Protest events tend in fact to fuel mechanisms of social change: during protests, organizational networks develop; frames are bridged; personal links foster reciprocal trust. Especially during some protest events, collective experiences develop through the interactions of different individual and collective actors, which with different roles and aims take part in them.[43]

In his work on the history of the French labor movement in the eighteenth and nineteenth century, William H Sewell has defined the concept of *eventful temporality*.[44] Differently from teleological temporality, which explains events on the basis of abstract transhistorical processes "from less to more" (urbanization, industrialization, etc.), and from "experimental temporality," comparing different historical paths (revolution versus nonrevolution, democracy versus nondemocracy), *"Eventful temporality* recognizes the power of events in history."[45] According to Sewell, events are a "relatively rare subclass of happenings that *significantly transform structure*"; an eventful conception of temporality is "one that takes into account the transformation of structures by events."[46] Events have transformative effects in so far as they "transform structures largely by constituting and empowering new groups of actors or by re-empowering existing groups in new ways."[47] Some protest events put in motion social processes that "are inherently contingent, discontinuous and open ended."[48]

With reference to eventful temporality, the concept of *transformative events* has been developed to single out events with a high symbolic (and not only) impact. As McAdam and Sewell observed, "no narrative account of a social movement or revolution can leave out events ... But the study of social movements or revolutions—at least as normally carried out by sociologists or political scientists—has rarely paid analytic attention to the contingent features and causal significance of particular contentious events such as these."[49] The two scholars therefore called for analysis of the ways in which events "become turning points in structural change, concentrated moments of political and cultural creativity when the logic of historical development is reconfigured by human action but by no means abolished."[50]

Moments of concentrated transformations have been singled out especially in those highly visible events that end up symbolizing entire social movements—such as the taking of the Bastille for the French revolution or the Montgomery Bus Boycott for the American civil rights movement. It is particularly during protest cycles that some events (e.g., the contestation of the Iran Shah in Berlin in 1967, or the Battle of Valle Giulia in Rome in 1968) remain impressed in the memory of the activists as emotionally charged events, but also represent important turning points in the evolution of the organizational structures and strategies of the movements. The history of each movement and of contentious politics in each country always includes some particularly "eventful" protests.

In the conception of eventful protest,[51] Della Porta puts the focus on the internal dynamics and transformative capacity of protest, looking however at a broader range of events than those included under the label of transformative event. Her assumption is that protests have cognitive, affective and relational impacts on the very movements that carry them out. Through protest events, new tactics are experimented with, signals about the possibility of collective action are sent,[52] feelings of solidarity are created, organizational networks are consolidated, and sometimes public outrage at repression is developed.[53] Protest is therefore, in part at least, a "byproduct" of protest itself, as conflicts do produce social capital, collective identity, and knowledge that is then used to mount collective mobilization.

A study on transnational protests, such as EU countersummits and the European social forums,[54] reflected in particular on what makes protest *eventful* by distinguishing *cognitive* mechanisms, with protest as an arena of debate: *relational* mechanisms, which bring about protest networks, and *emotional* mechanisms, through the development of feelings of solidarity "in action." Although the most varied people use protest every day, it is still a type of event that tends to produce effects, not only on the public authorities or public opinion, but also (possibly mainly) on the movement actors themselves. These effects are all the more visible in some specific forms of protest that require long preparatory processes, in which different groups come together (e.g., transnational campaigns), stress the relevance of communication (e.g., social forums), and are particularly intense from the emotional point of view (e.g., symbolic and physical struggles around the occupied sites). These kinds of protest are especially "eventful," that is, they have a very relevant cognitive, relational, and emotional impact on participants and beyond participants. Long-lasting events (or chains of events, such as campaigns), inclusive communicative arenas, and free spaces are forms of protest that seem particularly apt to create relational, cognitive, and emotional effects on protesters. The transnational character of recent protest, as well as the internal heterogeneity of recent waves of mobilization (with "movement of movements" as its self-definition), have added values to the relevance of those relational, cognitive, and affective mechanisms that make protest eventful.

Donatella Della Porta is professor of sociology in the Department of Political and Social Sciences at the European University Institute, where she directs the Center on Social Movement Studies (Cosmos). She also directs a major European Research Council project, Mobilizing for Democracy, on civil society participation in democratization processes in Europe, the Middle East, Asia, and Latin America. Her very recent publications include: *Can Democracy Be Saved?* (Cambridge, 2013); *Clandestine Political Violence* (Cambridge, 2013); and *The Wiley-Blackwell Encyclopedia on Social and Political Movements* (edited with D Snow, B Klandermans, and D McAdam (Chichester, 2013). In 2011, she was the recipient of the Mattei Dogan Prize for distinguished achievements in the field of political sociology.

Notes

1. Samuel H Barnes et al., *Political Action* (London, 1979), 149.
2. Pippa Norris, *Democratic Phoenix: Reinventing Political Activism* (New York, 2002), 221.
3. See for example, Donatella Della Porta, Abby Peterson, and Herbert Reiter, eds, *The Policing of Transnational Protest* (Aldershot, 2006), on the repression of the global justice movements, and David Waddington and Mike King, "Contemporary French and British Urban Riots: An Exploration of the Underlying Political Dimensions," in *Violent Protest, Contentious Politics and the Neoliberal State,* ed. S Seferiades and H Johnston (Aldershot, 2012), 119–32, on the repression of anti-austerity protests, the indignados, and occupy movements.
4. Michael Lipsky, *Protest and City Politics* (Chicago, 1965), 1.
5. Donatella Della Porta and Mario Diani, *Social Movements: An Introduction* (Oxford, 2006), chapter 7.
6. Lipsky, *Protest and City Politics,* 163; Thomas R Rochon, *Between Society and State: Mobilizing for Peace in Western Europe* (Princeton, NJ, 1988), 109.
7. Rick Fantasia, *Cultures of Solidarity: Consciousness, Action, and Contemporary American Workers* (Berkeley, 1988).
8. Jeffrey S Juris, "Reflections on #Occupy Elsewhere: Social Media, Public Space, and Emerging Logics of Aggregation," *American Ethnologist* 39, no. 2 (2012): 259–79; Paolo Gerbaudo, *Tweet and the Streets* (London, 2012).
9. Todd Gitlin, *The Whole World Is Watching: Mass Media in the Making and Unmaking of the New Left* (Berkeley, 1980).

10. John McCarthy, Clark McPhail, and Jackie Smith, "Images of Protest: Dimensions of Selection Bias in Media Coverage of Washington Demonstrations, 1982 and 1991," *American Sociological Review* 61 (1996): 478–99.
11. Donatella Della Porta, *Can Democracy Be Saved? Participation, Deliberation and Social Movements* (Oxford, 2013).
12. Sidney Tarrow, *Power in Movement: Social Movements, Collective Action and Politics* (Cambridge, 1994).
13. James M Jasper, *The Art of Moral Protest: Culture, Biography and Creativity in Social Movements* (Chicago, 1997), 237.
14. Charles Tilly, *From Mobilization to Revolution* (Reading, MA, 1978).
15. Charles Tilly, *The Contentious French* (Cambridge, MA, 1986), 391–92. Emphasis in the original.
16. Ibid.
17. Pierre Favre, *La Manifestation* (Paris, 1990).
18. Ibid.
19. James M Jasper, *The Art of Moral Protest: Culture, Biography and Creativity in Social Movements* (Chicago, 1997), 250.
20. Mark R Beissinger, *Nationalist Mobilization and the Collapse of the Soviet State* (Cambridge, 2002), 16.
21. Ibid.
22. Ibid., 17.
23. Mark R Beissinger, "Structure and Example in Modular Political Phenomena: The Diffusion of Bulldozer/Rose/Orange/Tulip Revolutions," *Perspectives on Politics* 5, no.2 (2007): 266.
24. Sidney Tarrow, *Power in Movement: Social Movements, Collective Action and Politics* (Cambridge, 1994), 153.
25. Ibid., 168.
26. Donatella Della Porta, "Protest, Protesters and Protest Policing," in *How Movements Matter,* ed. M Giugni, D McAdam, and C Tilly (Minneapolis, MN, 1999), 66–96.
27. Ibid.
28. Ibid.
29. Alessandro Pizzorno, "Political Exchange and Collective Identity in Industrial Conflict," in *The Resurgence of Class Conflict in Western Europe,* ed. C Crouch and A Pizzorno (New York, 1978), 277–98.
30. Donatella Della Porta, *Clandestine Political Violence* (Cambridge, 2013).
31. Tarrow, *Power in Movement.*
32. Della Porta, *Clandestine Political Violence.*
33. Hanspeter Kriesi, Ruud Koopmans, Jan-Willem Duyvendak, and Marco Giugni, *New Social Movements in Western Europe* (Minneapolis, MN, 1995).
34. Gary Marks, *Union in Politics: Britain, Germany and the United States in the Nineteenth and Early Twentieth Century* (Princeton, 1989), 14–15 passim.
35. Sidney Tarrow, *Democracy and Disorder: Protest and Politics in Italy, 1965–1975* (Oxford, 1989); Donatella Della Porta, *Movimenti Collettivi e Sistema Politico in Italia* (Rome, 1996).

36. Donatella Della Porta and Herbert Reiter, eds, *Policing Protest: The Control of Mass Demonstration in Western Democracies* (Minneapolis, MN, 1998); Robert J Goldstein, *Political Repression in 19th Century Europe* (London, 1983).
37. Della Porta, *Clandestine Political Violence.*
38. Donatella Della Porta, Abby Peterson, and Herbert Reiter, eds, *The Policing of Transnational Protest* (Aldershot, 2006).
39. Sidney Tarrow, "Charles Tilly and the Practice of Contentious Politics," *Social Movement Studies* 7 (2008): 225–46, 226.
40. Charles Tilly, *Explaining Social Processes* (Boulder, 2008), 2.
41. Tarrow, "Charles Tilly and the Practice of Contentious Politics."
42. Charles Tilly, *Contentious Performances* (Cambridge, 2008).
43. Donatella Della Porta, "Eventful Protests, Global Conflicts," *Distinktion. Scandinavian Journal of Social Theory* 9, no. 2 (2008): 27–56.
44. William H Sewell, "Three Temporalities: Toward an Eventful Sociology," in *The Historic Turn in the Human Sciences,* ed. TJ McDonald (Ann Arbor, 1996), 245–80.
45. Ibid., 262.
46. Ibid. Emphasis added.
47. Ibid., 271.
48. Ibid., 272.
49. Doug McAdam and William H Sewell, "It's About Time: Temporality in the Study of Social Movements and Revolutions," in *Silence and Voice in the Study of Contentious Politics,* ed. R Aminzade et al. (Cambridge, 2001), 89–125, 101.
50. Ibid., 102.
51. Donatella Della Porta, "Eventful Protests, Global Conflicts."
52. Aldon Morris, "Charting Futures for Sociology: Social Organization; Reflections on Social Movement Theory: Criticisms and Proposals," *Contemporary Sociology* 29 (2000): 445–54.
53. David Hess and Brian Martin, "Repression, Backfire, and the Theory of Transformative Events," *Mobilization* 11 (2006): 249–67.
54. Donatella Della Porta and Manuela Caiani, *Social Movements and Europe* (Oxford, 2009).

Recommended Reading

Della Porta, Donatella. *Can Democracy Be Saved? Participation, Deliberation and Social Movements.* Oxford, 2013. The text stresses the role of social movements in developing alternative conceptions of democracy, pointing at participation and consensus building.

Della Porta, Donatella, and Manuela Caiani. *Social Movements and Europe.* Oxford, 2009. Using data from claims analysis, interviews with movement organizations' representatives, and surveys with protesters, this volumes addresses different paths of Europeanization of contentious politics.

Della Porta, Donatella, Abby Peterson, and Herbert Reiter, eds. *The Policing of Transnational Protest.* Aldershot, 2006. Looking at transnational protest events—including anti-EU countersummits—the authors point at the relations between contentious politics and the policing of collective mobilization.

Norris, Pippa. *Democratic Phoenix: Reinventing Political Activism.* New York, 2002. The broad range of data reported in this volume indicates the increase in unconventional forms of political participation and their relevance for democratic developments.

Tarrow, Sidney. *Power in Movement: Social Movements, Collective Action and Politics.* Cambridge, 1994. In this classical work, the author looks at the ways in which contentious and noncontentious politics interact.

Chapter 2

Protest Cultures in Social Movements

Dimensions and Functions

Dieter Rucht

Protest Cultures: A General Introduction

Protest cultures can be seen as a kind of software, including the protesters' themes, motives, arguments, narratives, frames, and symbolic expressions. However, it would be wrong to strictly separate the cultural aspects of protest from its hardware such as its physical manifestation. For example, a huge crowd participating in a protest rally is in itself a symbol indicating a widely shared and publicly expressed concern. By its very size, such a protest, whatever its specific content may be, carries a message. Even more so, the purposive physical arrangement of the protesters may be a telling message when they encircle an object such as a military camp or when numerous bodies are arranged as a peace symbol. These considerations, in line with general definitions of culture,[1] suggest a wide concept of protest cultures that include all aspects that are intended to carry meaning as opposed to mere technical aspects (e.g., the means of transport to bring the protesters together) or structural patterns that only become visible in the aggregate of many protests, for example, their distribution over time and place.

Dimensions of Protest Cultures

Protest cultures can be identified at various levels, ranging from the micro to the macro. At the most concrete level, each group exhibits its own culture, especially when the group stabilizes and repeatedly engages in acts of protest. The group may develop and use specific protest techniques, slogans, and habits that distinguish it from other protesters. For example, protest marches are often subdivided into segments or formally designated blocks with specific collective identities that sometimes are only being identifiable for insiders (for example, when groups use flags with specific colors). Yet even a handful of protesters who meet only once cannot avoid to exhibit elements of the broader culture insofar as they try to link their concern to general values or apply a specific form of action that is part of a known and learned repertoire. The group's messages only "work" if they are decoded by other actors, including the protesters' target groups, on the basis of a (partly) shared cultural background.[2] Accordingly, the protesters' outfit looks familiar or strange to bystanders; their message is met with sympathy, disinterest, or aggression; the form of protest is perceived as boring or spectacular. Particularly when protest is practiced by large groups and has become routinized, protest cultures are likely to loose their challenging character. Eventually, they may become part and parcel of a broader political culture and normal politics. Just consider that quite a number of constitutional rights as well as various contemporary political parties have their origins in social movement struggles.

Some of these general considerations can be illustrated by the manifestations on the first of May. Whereas at a first glance every May Day protest seems to promote basically the same cause, a closer look reveals significant differences across time and place. Two separate May Day rallies in Germany in the 1920s, organized on the same day in the same city by the Social Democrats and the Communists, respectively, had a similar shape but different slogans. Two May Day protests in the divided city of Berlin in the 1950s and 1960s not only had different slogans but also differed widely in their physical form. While the Westerners were gathering in a rather amorphous crowd, the Easterners, in a distance of only a few hundred meters from the western event, marched in accurate rows. And even in the reunited Berlin of the early 2000s, the May Day demonstrators were far from having a unified and uniform performance that could be seen as an expression of one and the same protest culture. In fact, ignoring a few minor gatherings, there were separate marches or rallies organized by the trade unions, the left radicals (with three different marches starting at different points of time on the same day, each representing a specific ideological strand), and the right radicals who, in turn, provoked a left counterdemonstration. Each of these gatherings was characterized by its own slogans, banners, speakers, kind of music, and so on. Considering these differences in the same city, it comes as no surprise that the May Day demonstrations differ widely across countries. In Copenhagen, for example, they resemble a large and relaxed family picnic, while in Istanbul they occur in a tense atmosphere with the demonstrators facing large contingents of police in riot gear. From the example of May Days, it follows that protest cultures may vary considerably over places, times, and groups even when they put forward the same or a similar cause. Variation is likely to increase when comparing different matters of protest.

Functions of Protest Cultures

Protest cultures have many facets, which, for the purpose of analytical clarification, can be attributed to a few basic dimensions. First, aside from vandalism that often comes without an explicit message, every collective protest expresses a concern, a problem, or a critique that is the driving, though not sufficient, factor to engage in joint action. This concern may relate to local or global matters, express a minority or a majority position, refer to material or immaterial goods, envisage a short- or a long-term perspective, and aim at a minor political change or a fundamentally different societal order. Each society has its own spectrum of protest themes in a given period, as one could see when comparing, for example, a predominantly agrarian society with an advanced industrial society. Also, when considering a given nation-state at one point in time, it is likely that rural areas are generally marked by a set of protest themes that differ from those in big cities. Especially ethnic and/or cultural minorities who strive for more autonomy or even segregation from a given nation-state are keen to exhibit their distinctive (protest) culture.[3]

A second important protest dimension is the social background of the participants. Farmers and students, to mention only two groups, have different social environments, ways to speak, and channels to articulate their demands and exert pressure. Accordingly, their protest cultures are distinct, notwithstanding that in rare cases these groups may jointly act as it occurred, for example, in protests against nuclear facilities in some countries.

Third, protest cultures tend to reflect the activists' ideological leaning. As a rule, groups with radical ideologies are inclined to apply radical means, while the opposite holds for groups that, though being critical on specific issues, by and large accept the given structure of society. Some societies in some periods are marked by deep ideological cleavages. Two polarized camps may engage in a bitter struggle that can ultimately lead to a civil war, as it happened in Spain around the mid 1930s. Other societies rest on a broad ideological consensus so that conflicts tend to be moderated or restricted to less central issues, as exemplified by most Scandinavian countries throughout the nineteenth and twentieth century.

Often closely related to the ideologies are, fourth, the preferred forms of action. These may be more instrumental or more expressive, moderate or radical, spontaneous or calculated, an isolated action or part of a sustained campaign, aiming at broad but less demanding participation or at high-risk activities for which only few people are ready to engage. Also, they may rely mainly on symbols or on elaborated arguments, targeting directly an opponent or rather appealing to third parties including the broad public.

Role of Context for Protest Cultures

These variations underline the crucial role of context for shaping protest cultures.[4] First, almost all kinds of protest occur in a specific setting. The selection of time and place matters. Some protests are scheduled at a symbolic date, for example the anniversary of a historic event (e.g., the Hiroshima Day on August 6), and therefore planned in advance. Other protests are a spontaneous expression of anger or other kinds of emotions,[5] triggered by a shocking and unexpected event. This may be the beating or killing of a demonstrator or a disaster such as a nuclear accident. Moreover, the physical setting influences protest cultures. Outdoor protests differ from indoor protests insofar as, for example, the former generally allow more people to participate, give more flexibility to move freely around, and can be watched by bystander publics. In many countries, outdoor protests are submitted to a legal permitting procedure that may imply specific restrictions such as nominating a minimum number of marshals, remaining distant from a particular building or event, or following a prescribed route. Also the selection of a specific site facilitates or restricts certain forms of protest. While, for example, a large square accommodates an amorphous crowd, a march through narrow streets forces the participants to line up so that not all of them are physically close and can watch each other. In addition, the selection of place can carry a highly symbolic baggage. Organizers may deliberately choose a particular city such as the capital or a specific site, for example, an embassy or a war memorial. Moreover, the range and constellation of physically present actors have an influence on protest cultures. Direct confrontation with counterdemonstrators may lead to increasing aggression on both sides. The presence of a large and impressive police contingent could intimidate the protesters or, on the contrary, stir anger on the side of the protesters. The presence of media, especially television, is also likely to impact protest because it stimulates performative and spectacular actions.

Second, most acts of protest are not isolated incidences but part of larger campaign or social movement with its own traditions and behavioral patterns.[6] These put a stamp on each movement-specific event. Generally speaking, the more a protest is embedded in a larger campaign or movement, the less likely are erratic and unexpected behaviors. For some movements or movement organizations, it is obligatory that their activities remain within the legal boundaries while others are inclined to test and even transgress such confines.

Third, as mentioned above, every protest relates to the broader political culture. Against such a backdrop, the protest appears as a confirmation of or a challenge to this culture, a matter of routine or a shock, a signal for widespread dissatisfaction or a desperate outcry of a few dissenters. Accordingly, the broader public may embrace, reject, or simply ignore the protest.

Protest Cultures in a Long-Term Perspective

When looking at protest cultures over long periods of time, one can observe remarkable traits of both continuity and discontinuity. On the one hand, some general forms of protest, for example, the workers' strike, were introduced already in the eighteenth or nineteenth century and have not dramatically changed since then.[7] Still, we can identify changes in some respects. Strikes that were unregulated in earlier times gradually tended to become legalized and institutionally channeled. Accordingly, today's so-called wildcat strikes are the exception rather than the rule. The same applies to machine breaking and occupations of factories. One important reason for this was the establishment of trade unions and their withdrawal from straight anti-Capitalist stances. On the other hand, new forms of protest such as civil disobedience have been introduced only in the twentieth century. While in its early times civil disobedience has been regarded as threat to the public order and therefore sanctioned severely, nowadays a more relaxed attitude prevails on the side of the judiciary and the general public opinion. Finally, also new substantive problems or new technologies have an impact on the protest repertoire and protest cultures. Cross-border problems, for example climate change, fostered cross-border mobilization. New information and communication technologies offered not only additional channels for mobilization but also new forms of protest, as various forms of cyber protest including the so-called hacktivism demonstrate.

In sum, protest cultures are a multifaceted phenomenon that is strongly influenced by numerous factors, especially its context. Protest cultures, in turn, through their aggregate effects, also shape the broader political culture[8] as well as the institutional design of political regimes.

Dieter Rucht is professor emeritus of sociology at the Free University of Berlin. He was codirector of the research group "Civil Society, Citizenship and Political Mobilization in Europe" at the Social Science Research Center Berlin. His research interests include political participation, social movements, political protest, and public discourse. Among his recent books in English are: *The World Says No to War: Demonstrations against the War on Iraq* (Minneapolis, MN, 2010), coedited with Stefaan Walgrave; and *Meeting Democracy: Power and Deliberation in Global Justice Movements* (Cambridge, 2013), coedited with Donatella Della Porta.

Notes

1. See Roger M Keesing, "Theories of Culture," *Annual Review of Anthropology* 3 (1974): 73–97.
2. Ann Swidler, "Culture in Action: Symbols and Strategies," *American Sociological Review* 51 (1986): 273–86.
3. An illustrative case is the protest culture of the Basque country. See Jesus Casquete, "From Imagination to Visualization: Protest Rituals in the Basque Country," Discussion Paper SP IV 2003-401, Wissenschaftszentrum Berlin für Sozialforschung WZB (2003): 1–37.
4. Rhys H Williams, "The Cultural Contexts of Collective Action: Constraints, Opportunities, and the Symbolic Life of Social Movements," in *The Blackwell Companion to Social Movement Research,* ed. DA Snow, SA Soule, and H Kriesi (Oxford, 2004), 91–115.
5. On the role of emotions in the context of protest movements, see Jeff Goodwin, James M Jasper, and Francesca Polletta, "Emotional Dimensions of Social Movements," in *The Blackwell Companion to Social Movement Research,* ed. DA Snow, SA Soule, and H Kriesi (Oxford, 2004), 413–32.
6. A general overview is provided by John Lofland, "Social Movement Culture," in *Protest,* ed. J Lofland (New Brunswick, 1985), 219–39. For the example of the U.S. labor movement, see Rick Fantasia, *Cultures of Solidarity: Consciousness, Action, and Contemporary American Workers* (Berkeley, CA, 1988). For the New Left in the United States, see Harry C Boyte, "Building a New Culture," in *The Backyard Revolution,* ed. HC Boyte (Philadelphia, PA, 1980), 167–208. For the U.S. women's movement, see Verta Taylor and Nancy Whittier, "Analytical Approaches to Social Movement Culture: The Culture of the Women's Movement," in *Social Movements and Culture,* ed. H Johnston and B Klandermans (Minneapolis, MN, 1995), 163–87.
7. Charles Tilly, From Mobilization to Revolution (Reading, 1978), 159–71.

8. See Jennifer Earl, "The Cultural Consequences of Social Movements," in *The Black-well Companion to Social Movement Research,* ed. DA Snow, SA Soule, and H Kriesi (Oxford, 2004), 508–30.

Recommended Reading

Casquete, Jesus. "From Imagination to Visualization: Protest Rituals in the Basque Country." Discussion Paper SP IV 2003–401, Wissenschafts-zentrum Berlin für Sozialforschung WZB (2003): 1–37. This article describes the extent and cultural forms of protest in the Basque country, which are strongly influenced by the regionalist movement struggling for more autonomy or even separation from the Spanish nation-state.

Johnston, Hank, and Bert Klandermans, eds. *Social Movements and Culture.* Minneapolis, MN, 1995. A good collection of articles investigating cultural aspects of social movements from various angles, including theoretical, empirical, and methodological perspectives. Most articles rely on a constructionist paradigm.

Swidler, Ann. "Culture in Action: Symbols and Strategies." *American Sociological Review* 51 (1986): 273–86. This article examines in general terms the relationship between culture and action, emphasizing variation across time and historical situation. It argues that culture shapes and constrains the tool kit of habits, skills, and styles from which people construct strategies of action.

Chapter 3

Protest in the Research on Sub- and Countercultures

Rupa Huq

Defining Protest and Subculture

The concept of protest is closely linked to the notion of subculture—both are bound up in ideas of the oppositional and unofficial. Hebdige has explained: "spectacular subcultures express forbidden forms (transgressions of sartorial and behavioural codes, law-breaking etc.)."[1] Subculture succeeded in becoming popularized unlike most sociological theory: the pop weekly *NME* gave Hebdige's *Subculture*[2] highly favorable review. The fact that subculture has come of age is evidenced in the way it now commands its own secondary texts and readers alongside the primary sources themselves.[3]

Subcultures are groups that seek to differentiate themselves from dominant culture with distinct attitudes and lifestyles. The idea was most influential at the time of the Centre for Contemporary Cultural Studies (CCCS) studies of the 1970s, which can be seen as a political project: a last sixties-idealist flourish that saw "youth as a metaphor for social change."[4] Class, youth, and ideology were ever-present in these studies written against a backdrop of sixties political struggles (student unrest, radical antiwar politics, etc.). Protest has also been linked to moral panic and the theory of deviance amplification first popularized by Stanley Cohen.[5]

Subculture is a diversion from the powerlessness of the young: a heady mix of idealism and hedonism. Youthful idealism is often seen as a norm: if the young are not marching then who are? Yet the youth-led, class-focused old territorial subcultural studies are looking woefully inadequate to deal with modern-day protest mobilizations and social networks. More recently, even though subculture was often seen as the opposite of parent culture and a rejection of family values, many original participants of groups such as punk, hip-hop, mod, and goth are now parents themselves.

Given the large academic shadow of youth culture and subculture, numerous critiques have accumulated, particularly of Birmingham CCCS subcultural studies, suggesting that subculture has now run its course as a concept. Indeed the adjectives "postsubcultural,"[6] and the variant "post Birmingham"[7] are repeatedly emphasized by twenty-first-century neosubculturalists. Other alternatives include various micro communities, scenes, and tribes. The evolution of this concept suggests to some extent that we are living in post political times.

Specific Disciplinary Approach and Significance of Protest Research within the Discipline

The concept of subculture was established by theorists of the twentieth-century Chicago School who were interested in deviance.[8] In the United Kingdom, the Birmingham CCCS in the 1970s revisited this in a body of work that forms British academia's most sustained engagement with youth culture. Hall and Jefferson's *Resistance through Rituals,* a multiauthored volume saw authentic subcultural identity as a cohesive and collective cultural resistance to the dominant order.[9] Protest was present in the CCCS studies, but the youth doing this were seen as symbolically resisting the dominant order and winning subcultural space, rather than manning the barricades directly.

The CCCS, as befitting their British base, were preoccupied with social class and working-class subjugation within structures for youth as seen in, for example, the book title *Working Class Youth Culture* by Mungham and Pearson.[10] Murdock and McCron declare: "subcultural styles can therefore be seen as coded expressions of class consciousness transposed into the specific context of youth and reflective of the complexity in which age acts as a mediation both of class experience and of class consciousness."[11] Works like Paul Willis's celebrated school-to-work transition study, Learning to Labour,[12] documented small-scale rebellions on a micro level (classroom and factory floor) rather than on the streets, which is what the popular imagination associates with protest.

The skinheads were a classic group that subcultural theorists saw as mounting their own form of protest in the face of their traditional working-class communities declining with diminishing industry and employment opportunities. Clarke described how they were engaged in "symbolic defence of (threatened) territory."[13] This was seen as part of a "magical attempt to recover community" by "dispossessed inheritors." Skinhead style was identified as a particularly potent example of exemplifying the working-class community as a defensively organized collective. Their cropped hair braces and boots were seen as signifying working-class and masculine identity, while their racist attacks on "scapegoated outsiders"[14] were seen as inevitable. Any questioning of why skinhead aggression targeted powerless immigrants instead of the authorities responsible for their situation is unexplored. This means that it is excused as much as explained. Similarly, football hooliganism[15] was interpreted as representing the working-class youths' attempts to win back control of their game in an attempt to retrieve the disappearing sense of community. Even "Paki-bashing" was an understandable form of political and economic struggle by the heroic working classes.[16] Willis's "lads"[17] are sexist, racist, and homophobic, even talking about the joys of rape—but this celebration of white male heterosexual power seems to be cancelled out by their supposed working-class subordination. As Cohen later observed in his 1980 reprint, "those same values of racism, sexism, chauvinism, compulsive masculinity and anti-intellectualism, the slightest traces of which are condemned in bourgeois culture, are treated with deferential care … when they appear in subculture."[18]

By the 1990s, some argued that subculture had run out of steam with talk of a generation X or slackers: tertiary-educated, jobless, bored middle-class dropouts with the relative security of a position to drop out from[19] lacking the subcultural drive of earlier generations. The late 1980s and early 1990s saw the new moral panics of rave with some subcultural characteristics tightly bonded, high visibility, fringe-delinquent working-class group. UK legislation threatening to criminalize rave lifestyles in the Criminal Justice Act and Public Order Act of 1994 was seen at the time as injecting some radicalism into the movement.[20] Rave contained multiple paradoxes. Its anonymous stars and lack of strict fashion code are not really spectacular subculture. Thornton's idea of "subcultural capital"[21] borrows from Bourdieu's work on cultural distinction[22] and a (Stanley) Cohenite approach to the media. However, a body of postsubcultural studies began to emerge.

Research Traditions

Subcultural studies has been informed by traditions including Marxism, Gramsci's theory of hegemony, and Chicago School studies of urban microsociology grounded in U.S. behavioural social science.[23] The Frankfurt

School's (Marxist) vision of a mass society and French structuralist political theory were also crucial influences. Hebdige for example drew on semiotics and the Lévi Straussian concept of "style as bricolage," mixing meanings to signify resistance to, and the subversion of, traditional norms, and again shows how objects can be appropriated in subtle protest. For Hebdige, "style in subculture is pregnant with significance. Its transformations go 'against nature' interrupting processes of 'normalisation' ... our task becomes like Barthes', to discern the hidden messages inscribed in code on the glossy surfaces of style, to trace them out as 'maps of meaning' which obscurely re-present the very contradictions they are designed to resolve or conceal."[24] The punk use of the Nazi symbol the swastika and the humble safety pin as a fashion statement is an example of this: the historical moment at which its use occurred—that is, the relative recentness of the war—also increased its shock value.

Althusser's work on ideological state apparatuses playing out the political and ideological domination of one class over others and Gramscian notions of hegemony[25] were further building blocks of subcultural theory that saw a divide between parent culture and dominant culture. In this way, subcultures are subordinate but autonomous; there is acceptance of one's situation but a simultaneous rejection of it through the adoption of styles that represent a refusal to accept the values of the dominant culture. The Foucaldian concepts of knowledge, power, and the control of the body were also influential in Hebdige's writing on youth surveillance and display.[26]

By the 1980s, Marxism was out of fashion, confirmed by the collapse of state Communism in the former Eastern Bloc.[27] Further research seemed to construct youth as a problem to be treated in a problem-solving manner. Examples included unemployment[28] and youth training.[29] Lynne Chisholm commented that "since the mid-seventies youth unemployment has cut a swathe through young people's landscapes, leaving an open wound filled with broken transitions, massive disillusionment and smouldering resentment."[30] Hebdige declared, "In the current recession, the imaginary coherence of subculture seems about to dissolve under the pressure of material constraints."[31] Youth were no longer harbingers of social change but victims of it. Meanwhile protest did continue, for example, in the 1981 People's March for Jobs, 1984–85 miner's strike, and in the popular pressure group CND (Campaign for Nuclear Disarmament). Protests around acid house and rave were the next major conflict from the late 1980s to mid 1990s.

Research Results and Positions

Subcultural theory has received manifold criticism even from some of its own authors like Dick Hebdige and Angela McRobbie. Its "fetishism of resistance"[32] is clearly problematic. Gary Clarke critiqued the CCCS for concentrating on spectacular subcultures and its methodological short-comings.[33] Ethnography, when it does occur, is then used not to illustrate but to validate or confirm preordained political positions. Cohen's retrospective criticism included the point that in subcultural theory, "the symbolic baggage the kids are being asked to carry is just too heavy ... the interrogations are just a little forced."[34] Class mobility or any recognition of varying degrees of subcultural affiliation were not allowed for in the blunt instrument of subculture. Far from being unproblematic, coherent, and sovereign, identity itself is constructed and multifaceted, with subcultural membership being only one aspect. In addition, conformist youths were largely ignored in these studies. This is exemplified by the overidentification of Willis with the lads at the expense of the activities, opinions, voices of less rebellious classmates identified (by the lads) as the "ear' oles" (also young, white, working-class males) who are described disparagingly.[35]

McRobbie and Garber claimed at the time that "female invisibility in youth subcultures then becomes a self-fulfilling prophecy, a vicious cycle ... the emphasises in the documentation of these phenomenon [sic], on the male and masculine, reinforce and amplify our conception of the subcultures as predominantly male."[36] Jon Savage has argued that the impact/influence of gay culture on British postwar youth culture present from Teddy Boys to acid house and beyond is a further CCCS omission.[37] The sparse relevant studies of British blacks tended either to sympathize with black youth as victims of racism or to objectify them as a source of white stylistic fetishization/appropriation.[38] Hebdige mapped a phantom history of race relations since the war implicitly sees white youth subcultural styles on one side or other of a symbolic acceptance or refusal of black culture.

Most subcultural studies have been concerned with working-class youth who have tended to fascinate middle-class academics, despite the fact that many postwar subcultural and protest movements have sprung from decidedly middle-class origins, for example, mod and punk contrived by middle-class students in art school classrooms[39] and the 1960s hippies and anti-Vietnam student radicals.[40] Frith has written about an over-romanticism of working-class resistance: "There has always been a tendency for sociologists (who usually come from middle class, bookish backgrounds) to celebrate teenage deviancy, to admire the loyalties of street life."[41] In a direct criticism of the later book *Common Culture*,[42] Harris comments "[Paul] Willis has found out almost nothing about the political views of young people directly ... once again the respondents provide the innocent data and the analysts provide the politics for them."[43] Despite the engagement of cultural studies, academics in antiracism, and feminism as individuals,[44] paradoxically the identification with working-class youth could blind the authors to some of the less attractive features of working-class youth cultures, for example, racism and sexism.

Perhaps the main result of the initial subculturalists and protesters is that they grew old. Subculture is always mentioned interchangeably with youth culture. There is now a sub-branch of subcultural studies concerned principally with the aging of participants including punks, mods, or goths.[45] It could be argued that youth is now a word devoid of all meaning.[46] Cultural critic Toby Young has claimed: "the cult of youth ... [is] a modern invention which like most contemporary phenomena came complete with built-in obsolescence and has now had its day."[47] Cohen stated in the introduction to the second edition of *Folk Devils and Moral Panic* that the original was out of date the moment it appeared.[48] This is an unavoidable occupational hazard with this type of research, which tended to view things as snapshots rather than adopting a more longitudinal view. Old protesters adopt their tactics into later life—the term "grey power" describes the growing assertiveness of pensioners in making their demands as befits the demographically aging societies of the Western world. Rather than thinking in terms of the sociology of youth and the sociology of aging as two discrete categories, perhaps it would be more useful to consider protest cultures and youth culture within a broader sociology of life course.

Connections to Other Approaches and Disciplines

In the 1980s, Stuart Hall discussed how moral panic surrounding muggers was frequently a coded way of talking about black youth. Postcolonial studies is another niche of cultural studies area that overlaps with subculture with well-known exponents including the original Birmingham CCCS member Paul Gilroy with his theorization of the Black Atlantic.[49] After long being at best an adjunct to black youth, with the exception of mentions of Paki-bashing as referred to above, a number of studies have gone some way to redressing the balance by addressing the subject of Asian youth outside the narrow parameters of racism studies.[50] Recent decades have seen a transition of the public perception of Asians from migrants to settled population and recognition of subdivisions within this category, for example,

Muslims, Hindus, Sikhs, and so on. Active sites of youth culture research have been the Scandinavian nations who have spawned *Young: The Nordic Journal of Youth Research,* where some of this research has appeared.[51] As well as comprehensive studies of the United Kingdom, light has been shed on the United States. Maira's (2003) American-based Indian subcontinent diaspora fieldwork covered three U.S. universities where music including bhangra, Hindi film music, and crossover club sounds were consumed. The edited collection of Sharma et al.[52] was a landmark in addressing young Asians through the filter of music-making processes and political lyrics. Protest-wise, one chapter looked at the potential effects of the 1994 Criminal Justice and Criminal Justice and Public Order Act, that is, UK anti-rave legislation.

More recent approaches drawing on subcultural theory knit together cultural studies and political protest in a reoriented theory of social movements. The journal *Social Movement Studies* was launched in 2002 with a mission statement that ambitiously declared that it would be "not merely dazzled by current movements, but rather attentive to how the social forces and practices that generate them vary across time and place ... recognize the increasingly key role that social movements play as the dynamic and oppositional forces within socio-global socio-economies."[53] It also claimed to be interdisciplinary and even to "exist at the intersection of academic and activist inquiry into social movements, especially as (we may like to think that) there is no necessary disjunction between the two." The journal's first edition included a forceful argument for combining theories of social movements and subcultures, as critics of the CCCS, though numerous, have not successfully proposed many viable alternatives.[54]

Two concurrent and, at times overlapping, postclass conceptions that have been invoked as an explanation for youth culture formations are the theory of postmodern tribes/neotribalism[55] and the individualization thesis of Beck and Giddens.[56] Maffesoli talks of "a new (and evolving) trend ... in the growth of small groups and networks," and the "growing detachment from the abstract general public sphere."[57] Bauman's neotribes are formed as concepts rather than integrated social bodies constructed with an inevitable inconclusiveness with membership easily revocable and divorceable from long-term obligations. Like neotribal paradigms, individualization theory is synonymous with the diversification of late twentieth-century lifestyle trajectories. It essentially rests on the prerequisites of a general shift in emphasis from a work-based to leisure-based society as part of a wider loosening of traditional structure(s) in the increasingly flexible contemporary post-Fordist society. Some aspects of individualism and neotribal theory can be attacked for the same reasons as subcultural study was: claims are often made with little empirical evidence and to state that class has ceased to exist and that youth identities and choices are progressively widening for all young people seems somewhat of an exaggeration. Encouragingly, however, the concept of reflexive biography,[58] intrinsic to individualism, may lend itself better to considering female youth culture than the structural approach of traditional subcultural studies located in groupings around football or street corners, which can be partly held responsible for producing understandings of male youth culture as the norm.

Arguably, the most informed generation ever has also been painted as the most depoliticized youth. Much cited in 2001 was the statistic that more young people voted in the TV reality show *Big Brother* eviction that took place in the same week as the UK General Election. Turnouts subsequently rose from 2001's all-time low of 59 percent to 65 percent. Disconnection from UK Westminster politics from the public at large probably peaked in 2009 when a series of corruption scandals related to expense claiming rocked the UK Parliament. There is an argument that voluntary alienation from the political system is an option in itself, borne of rational choice theory.[59] Such arguments aside, there is much evidence against the contention that young people are engaged in causes that have wider consequences than ballot-box participation once every five years. Youth involvement in protest movements of playful, technologically sophisticated, media-savvy direct action that first surfaced in the United Kingdom in examples such as the raver's defense mounted in opposition to the Criminal Justice and Public Order campaigns of 1994[60] have been termed part of a new politics. The original criminal justice cause was expanded by protesters to include a broadened agenda of global justice and anticorporate demands. Numerous commentators make the point that these new concerns are global in nature, encompassing a broad human rights agenda including environmental sustainability, aid to the developing world, debt cancellation, ethical consumerism, and fair trade. Nash argues enthusiastically for "the potential for moving the concerns of global politics away from traditional struggles over sovereignty."[61]

There are some suggestions of double standards too in good involvement and bad involvement in protest. Cunningham and Lavalette[62] cite UK government hypocrisy in clamping down on pupils involved in school strikes against the war in Iraq in spring 2003 as students were only following the instruction of their own citizenship-teaching, which impresses the principle of political participation upon pupils' teachings of political participation. The same can be said of the student protesters of 2010 or rioters of August 2011 in British cities. Social media was seen as helpful in the case of the Arab Spring for enabling protesters to connect with one another. Technology has been a key driver of modern protest. McRobbie and Garber noted "the 'culture of the bedroom'—experimenting with make-up, listening to records, reading the mags, sizing up boyfriends, chatting, jiving."[63] However home-based leisure and more privatized culture (e.g., social networking web sites and the cult of the iPod) and protest (organizing e-petitions) is a significant phenomenon of the twenty-first century that applies to both genders, as Lincoln has recently shown.[64] The occupy and anti-Capitalism movements have also been vocal with young people among their ranks in recent years. National leaders too have utilized popular music figures in trying to win office. For instance, U.S. President Obama's success in the 2008 and 2012 election has been attributed in parts to the participation of Bruce Springsteen and Stevie Wonder in his campaigns. Both were youth icons once.

Conclusions

Subcultural studies have evolved from the Chicago School from the 1920s and 1950s, via the Birmingham CCCS, who invested great hope in the youth as political agents of social change in the 1970s, to the position now with postsubcultural critics. Bennett and Harris,[65] in their edited collection, include chapters on bedroom cultures and goth. The volumes of Hodkinson and Deicke, as well as Muggleton and Weinzierl cover similar ground.[66] New paths of inquiry are forever developing, making grand theories and linear models of subculture and protest increasingly redundant in the culturally pluralist, multimedia twenty-first century, characterized arguably by uncertainty and globalization.[67] Accordingly, there has been a growth in comparative perspectives on youth and subculture stressing their global dimension. Nilam and Feixia offer a comprehensive collection including chapters on hip-hop in Senegal, Muslim youth in Indonesia, subcultures in postrevolutionary Iran, and neo-Nazi French skinheads, among others. In their conclusion, they argue that transnationalism is the defining feature for the next generation. They explore transnational networks and technological advance behind current social activism in Barcelona and Lisbon termed "new, new" social movements for their wider European and global dimensions.[68] Lukose meanwhile has updated Salman Rushdie's metaphor "Midnight's Children" for postindependence India to its contemporary thriving Capitalist economy and its youth who are termed "Liberalization's children."[69] Contrasts are made between the globalization of old, which implicated Coca Cola and Disney to its more plural, networked twenty-first-century update. Eastern European subcultures have been examined by Pilkington and Roberts[70] who look at youth trajectories before and after the fall of Communism in countries of the former Soviet Union that now have

EU membership. Between them, these titles show the way that subcultural locations are multiple and multifaceted.

Minority communities of all persuasions once seen as passive and quiescent are getting more and more active and emancipated. All over Europe, such assertive groupings include the rise of a politicized Islam led by charismatic imams and followed by youths who adopt religious identities that their parents frequently downplayed. This was seen in the oppositions to the Danish cartoons and the repugnant actions of Andreas Brevik in Norway who claimed that his mass shootings of Socialist Party youth activists were a reaction to Islamism. These conflicts present dilemmas for secular liberals. Some of the old strategies and slogans adopted by antiracist campaigning seem outdated when mixed-race has become such a significant category. Allen and Maceyassert: "The equation of race with black-white relations is inadequate for dealing with the European context."[71] In Kingston, South London, the main minority is South Korean, a category which sees itself as neither. The new mobile EU citizens underline the cultural pluralism of Europe. Old traditions of radical struggles around the politics of equality, social justice, and redistribution that once underpinned subcultural theory and protest are constantly being challenged with technology and social networking as seen in the Arab Spring of 2011, which included youth mobilizations. Finally, at the time of writing, a further new line of inquiry seems to have developed around aging youth cultures.[72] It seems that the onset of adult responsibilities may blunt some of the more radical edges of former subcultural devotees, but this area remains one to be continued.

Rupa Huq is Member of Parliament for Ealing Central and Acton, London. Until 2015 she was a senior lecturer in sociology at Kingston University. Her research interests are clustered around urbanism/suburbanism, youth studies, ethnicity, and subcultures. She is author of *Beyond Subculture: Youth, Pop and Identity in a Post-Colonial World* (London, 2006), *On the Edge: the Contested Cultures of English Suburbia* (London, 2013), and *Making Sense of Suburbia through Popular Culture* (London, 2013).

Notes

1. Dick Hebdige, *Subculture: The Meaning of Style* (London, 1979), 91–92.
2. Ibid.
3. Ken Gelder and Sarah Thornton, eds, *The Subcultures Reader* (London, 1997); Ken Gelder, ed., *The Subcultures Reader* (New York, 2005); Steve Redhead, Justin O'Connor, and Dereck Wynne, eds, *The Clubcultures Reader: Readings in Popular Cultural Studies* (Oxford, 1997).

4. John Clarke et al., "Subcultures, Cultures and Class," in *Resistance Through Rituals: Youth Subcultures in Post-War Britain,* ed. S Hall and T Jefferson (London, 1976), 17.

5. Stanley Cohen, *Folk Devils and Moral Panic: The Creation of the Mods and Rockers* (London, 1972).

6. Andy Bennett and Keith Harris, *After Subculture: Critical Commentaries Subcultural Theory* (Palgrave, 2004); David Muggleton and Rupert Weinzierl, *The Post-Subcultures Reader* (Oxford, 2003).

7. Sarah Thornton, *Club Cultures: Music, Media, and Subcultural Capital* (Oxford, 1995).

8. Albert Cohen, *Delinquent Boys: The Culture of the Gang* (Chicago, 1955); Milton Gordon, "The Concept of the Sub-Culture and Its Application," in *The Subcultures Reader,* ed. K Gelder and S Thornton (London, 1997), 40–43.

9. Stuart Hall and Tony Jefferson, eds, *Resistance through Rituals: Youth Subcultures in Post-War Britain* (London, 1976).

10. Geoff Mungham and Geoff Pearson, eds, *Working Class Youth Cultures* (London, 1976).

11. Graham Murdock and Robin McCron, "Age and Class: The Career of a Confusion," in *Working Class Youth Cultures,* ed. G Mungham and G Pearson (London 1976), 206.

12. Paul Willis, *Learning to Labour: How Working Class Kids Get Working Class Jobs* (Farnborough, 1977).

13. John Clarke, "The Skinheads and the Magical Recovery of Community," in *Resistance through Rituals: Youth Subcultures in Post-War Britain,* ed. S Hall and T Jefferson (London, 1976), 99–102.

14. Clarke, "Skinheads and the Magical Recovery of Community," 102.

15. For example, see Peter Marsh, *Aggro: The Illusion of Violence* (London, 1978); Ian Taylor, "Soccer Consciousness and Soccer Hooliganism," in *Images of Deviance,* ed. S Cohen (Harmondsworth, 1971).

16. For example, in Hebdige, *Subculture*; Gus Pearson, "'Paki-Bashing' in a North-East Lancashire Cotton Town: A Case Study in Its History," in *Working Class Youth Cultures,* ed. G Mungham and G Pearson (London, 1976), 48–81.

17. Willis, *Learning to Labour.*

18. Cohen, *Folk Devils and Moral Panic,* xxvii.

19. For example, see Steven Best and Douglas Kellner, "Beavis and Butt-Head: No Future For Postmodern Youth," in *Youth Culture: Identity in a Postmodern World,* ed. J Epstein (Oxford, 1998), 74–99; Jonathan Epstein, "Introduction: Generation X, Youth Culture and Identity," in *Youth Culture: Identity in a Postmodern World,* ed. J Epstein (Oxford, 1998), 1–23.

20. Rupa Huq, "The Right to Rave: Opposition to the Criminal Justice and Public Order Act 1994," in *Storming the Millennium: The New Politics of Change,* ed. T Jordan (London, 1999), 15–33; John Hutnyk, "Repetitive Beatings or Criminal Justice?," in *Dis-orienting Rhythms: The Politics of the New Asian Dance Music,* ed. S Sharma, A Sharma, and J Hutnyk (London, 1996), 156–89; George McKay, *Senseless Acts of Beauty: Cultures of Resistance since the Sixties* (London, 1996); George McKay, *DIY Culture: Party and Protest in Nineties Britain* (London, 1998).

21. Thornton, *Club Cultures.*

22. Pierre Bourdieu, *Distinction: A Social Critique of the Judgment of Taste* (London, 1984).

23. Cohen, *Delinquent Boys*; Robert K Merton, "Social Structure and Anomie," *American Sociological Review* 3, no. 5 (1938): 672–82; William F Whyte, *Street Corner Society* (Chicago, 1955).
24. Hebdige, *Subculture,* 18.
25. Luis Althusser, "Ideology and the State," in *Lenin and Philosophy and Other Stories* (London, 1971); and Antonio Gramsci, *Selections from the Prison Notebooks,* ed. and trans. Q Hoare (London, 1971).
26. Dick Hebdige, *Hiding in the Light: On Images and Things* (London, 1988).
27. Angela McRobbie, *Postmodernism and Popular Culture* (London, 1994), 38.
28. For example, Pramod Junankar, ed., *From School to Unemployment? The Labour Market for Young People* (London, 1988); Kenneth Roberts, *School-Leavers and Their Prospects: Youth in the Labour Market in the 1990s* (Oxford, 1984); Claire Wallace, *For Richer, for Poorer: Growing Up in and out of Employment* (London, 1987). Steven Waller and Len Barton, eds, *Youth, Unemployment and Schooling* (Milton Keynes, 1986).
29. Dan Finn, *Training Without Jobs: New Deals and Broken Promises* (London, 1987); Robert G Hollands, *The Long Transition: Class, Culture and Youth Training* (London, 1990).
30. Lynne Chisholm, "A Sharper Lens or a New Camera? Youth Research, Young People and Social Change in Britain," in *Childhood, Youth and Social Change: A Comparative Perspective,* ed. L Chisholm, P Büchner, H Krüger, and P Brown (London, 1990), 33–57, 42.
31. Hebdige, *Hiding in the Light,* 35.
32. Douglas Kellner, *Media Culture: Cultural Studies, Identity and Politics* (London, 1994), 37.
33. Gary Clarke, "Defending Ski-Jumpers: A Critique of Theories of Youth Subcultures," in *On Record: Rock, Pop and the Written Word,* ed. S Frith and A Goodwin (London, 1990), 81–96.
34. Cohen, *Folk Devils and Moral Panic,* pxv.
35. Willis, *Learning to Labour,* 14. "The term 'ear'ole' itself connotes the passivity and absurdity of the school conformists for the lads. It seemed that they are always listening, never doing." Asian youth are taken to be "ear'oles" by extension, which explains why they are so disliked. Willis, *Learning to Labour,* 49.
36. Angela McRobbie and Jenny Garber, "Girls and Subcultures: An Exploration," in *Resistance through Rituals: Youth Subcultures in Post-War Britain,* ed. S Hall and T Jefferson (London, 1976), 177–88.
37. Jon Savage, "Tainted Love: The Influence of Male Homosexuality and Sexual Difference on Pop Music and Culture since the War," in *Consumption, Identity and Style: Marketing, Meanings and the Packaging of Pleasure,* ed. A Tomlinson (London, 1990), 153–70.
38. For example, Mike Brake, *The Sociology of Youth Culture and Youth Subcultures: Sex, Drugs and Rock 'n' Roll* (London, 1980); Hebdige, *Subculture*; Simon Jones, *Black Culture, White Youth: From Jamaica to U.K.* (London, 1988).
39. Simon Frith and Howard Horne, *Art into Pop* (London, 1987); Brian Longhurst, *Popular Music and Society* (Cambridge, 1994).

40. Hippiedom did attract a passing interest in some published studies: Kenneth Leech, *Youthquake: The Growth of a Counter-Culture through Two Decades* (London, 1973); Frank Musgrove, *Ecstasy and Holiness; Counter Culture and the Open Society* (London, 1974). Clarke et al. do include "counterculture" as a subsection, but this movement is largely dismissed, not seen to have the same function as supposedly all-pervasive, working-class subculture for the reason that "they [hippies] inhabit a dominant culture ... they represent a rupture inside [it]" (Clarke et al., "Subcultures, Cultures and Class," 9–74, 57–71).

41. Simon Frith, "The Sociology of Youth," in *Sociology: New Directions,* ed. M Haralambos (Ormskirk, 1985), 303–68.

42. Paul Willis, *Common Culture: Symbolic Work at Play in the Everyday Lives of Young* (Milton Keynes, 1990).

43. David Harris, *From Class Struggle to the Politics of Pleasure: The Effects of Gramscianism on Cultural Studies* (London, 1992), 169.

44. As pointed out by Martin Barker and Anne Beezer, eds, *Reading into Cultural Studies* (London, 1992).

45. Paul Hodkinson, "Ageing in a Spectacular 'Youth Culture': Continuity, Change and Community amongst Older Goths," *The British Journal of Sociology* 62, no. 2 (2011): 262–82; Andy Bennett and Paul Hodkinson, eds, *Ageing and Youth Cultures: Music, Style and Identity* (New York, 2012).

46. Pierre Bourdieu, "La 'jeunesse' n'est qu'un mot," in Pierre Bourdieu *Questions de Sociologie* (Paris, 1984), 143–54.

47. Toby Young, "The Shock of the Old," *New Society 14*, no. 3 (1986), 17-18.

48. Cohen, *Folk Devils and Moral Panic,* i.

49. Paul Gilroy, *The Black Atlantic: Modernity and Double Consciousness* (London, 1993).

50. Muhammad Anwar, *Ethnic Minorities and the British Electoral System: A Research Report* (Warwick, 1998); Les Back, *New Ethnicities and Urban Culture: Racisms and Multiculture in Young Lives* (London, 1996); Ghazala Bhatti, *Asian Children at Home and School: An Ethnographic Study* (London, 1999); Marie Gillespie, *Television, Ethnicity and Cultural Change* (London, 1995); Sanjay Sharma, Ashwani Sharma, and John Hutnyk, eds, *Dis-orienting Rhythms: The Politics of the New Asian Dance Music* (London, 1996).

51. For example, the article Rupa Huq, "From the Margins to the Mainstream? Representations and Realities of British Asian Youth in Music," *Young: The Nordic Journal of Youth Research* 11, no. 1 (2003): 29–48.

52. Sharma, Sharma, and Hutnyk, *Dis-orienting Rhythms.*

53. Tim Jordan, "Social Movement Studies: Opening Statement," *Social Movement Studies: Journal of Social, Cultural and Political Protest* 1, no. 1 (2002): 5–6.

54. Greg Martin, "Conceptualizing Cultural Politics in Subcultural and Social Movement Studies," *Social Movement Studies: Journal of Social, Cultural and Political Protest* 1, no. 1 (2002): 73–88.

55. Michel Maffesoli, *The Time of the Tribes: The Decline of Individualism in Mass Society,* trans. D Smith (London, 1996); Zygmunt Bauman, *Legislators and Interpreters: On Modernity, Post-Modernity and Intellectuals* (Cambridge, 1987).

56. Ulrich Beck, *Risk Society: Towards a New Modernity* (London 1992); Anthony Giddens, *Modernity and Self-Identity: Self and Society in the Late Modern Age* (Stanford, CA, 1991).
57. Maffesoli, *The Time of the Tribes,* 40–46.
58. Beck, *Risk Society,* 130–31.
59. Nick Couldry, "Culture and Citizenship: The Missing Link?," *European Journal of Cultural Studies* 9, no. 3 (2006): 321–39.
60. Huq, "The Right to Rave."
61. Kate Nash, "Global Citizenship as Showbusiness: The Cultural Politics of Make Poverty History," in *Media, Culture and* Society 30, no. 2 (2008): 167–81.
62. Steve Cunningham and Michael Lavalette, "'Active Citizens' or 'Irresponsible Truants'? School Student Strikes Against the War," *Critical Social Policy* 24, no. 2 (2004): 255–69.
63. McRobbie and Garber, "Girls and Subcultures."
64. Siân Lincoln, *Youth Culture and Private Space* (Basingstoke, 2012).
65. Bennett and Harris, *After Subculture.*
66. Paul Hodkinson and Wolfgang Deicke, *Youth Cultures: Scenes, Subcultures and Tribes* (Oxon, 2007); Muggleton and Weinzierl, *The Post-Subcultures Reader.*
67. For example, individualization thesis of Germany (Beck, *Risk Society: Towards a New Modernity*), Northern European youth transitions literature (Johan Fornäs, Ulf Lindberg, and Ove Sernhede, *In Garageland: Rock, Youth and Modernity* [London, 1995]; Johan Fornäs and Goran Bolin, *Youth Culture in Late Modernity* [London, 1995]; the respected *Young: The Nordic Journal of Youth Research*), studies from Australia (Johanna Wyn and Rob White, *Rethinking Youth* [London, 1996]) and America (Jonathan S Epstein, ed., *Youth Culture: Identity in a Postmodern World* [Oxford, 1998]; Henry A Giroux, *Fugitive Cultures: Race, Violence and Youth* [New York, 1996]; Henry A Giroux, *Channel Surfing: Race and the Destruction of Today's Youth* [Basingstoke, 1997]): all ostensibly taking about the same category of young people.
68. Pam Nilam and Carles Feixia, eds, *Global Youth? Hybrid Identities, Plural Worlds* (Oxon, 2006).
69. Ritty A Lukose, *Liberalization's Children: Gender, Youth, and Consumer Citizenship in Globalizing India* (Durham, NC, 2009).
70. Hilary Pilkington, *Russia's Youth and Its Culture: A Nation's Constructors and Constructed* (London, 1994); Hilary Pilkington, *Russia's Skinheads Exploring and Rethinking Subcultural Lives* (Oxon, 2012); Ken Roberts, *Youth in Transition: Eastern Europe and the West* (Basingstoke, 2009).
71. Sheila Allen and Marie Macey, "Race and Ethnicity in the European Context," *The British Journal of Sociology* 41, no. 3 (1990): 375–93.
72. For example, the edited collection of Bennett and Hodkinson, *Ageing and Youth Cultures: Music, Style and Identity,* which includes chapters on goths, mods, and hip-hop.

Recommended Reading

Clarke, Gary. "Defending Ski-Jumpers: A Critique of Theories of Youth Sub-cultures." In *On Record: Rock, Pop and the Written Word*, edited by S Frith and A Goodwin, 81–96. London, 1990. The book discusses the relationship between subculture and young people.

Hall, Stuart and Tony Jefferson, eds. *Resistance through Rituals: Youth Subcultures in Post-War Britain*. London, 1976. Classic edited collection of essays on the political nature of 1970s subcultures.

Huq, Rupa. *Beyond Subculture: Youth, Pop and Identity in a Post-Colonial World*. London, 2006. The book offers a postmillennial look at youth culture with a focus on minority ethnic youth—a category that was sidelined by 1970s subculturalists.

Redhead, Steve. *The End of the Century Party: Youth and Pop towards 2000*. Manchester, 1990.

Chapter 4

Protest as Symbolic Politics

Jana Günther

In the last fifteen years or so, the understanding of what symbolic politics is has not been uncontroversial, even though it is often used in scholarly debate. Even if, at first glance, the term symbolic politics seems to be a simple definition of symbolic action geared toward the dissemination of politics or the political, one can surely felicitously argue about the understanding of symbols and politics per se and herein about the scope of the concept of symbolic politics.[1]

Expanding the debate to include the perspective of symbolic politics in protests may lead to further confusion. But, it may also create an opportunity to address a number of hopefully fruitful interdisciplinary considerations. Among the interesting questions are: What exactly is the political? How is the concept of symbolic politics handled in the respective scientific discourses? And, how can the concept of symbolic politics be understood in the context of protest action?

This chapter aims both to present the discourse on the concept of symbolic politics and to locate sociological points of reference in order to approach the symbolic politics of protest action. In the process, a more useful and applicable concept of symbolic politics in general will be discussed.

General Definitions

At first, it seems indisputable that symbols are directly relevant to protest movements, that is that specific symbols function within a respective movement and also serve to present the movement to nonparticipants in the general public. Symbols are consciously employed during moments of public theatralization and for consolidation efforts within the protesting social group. In the following, it is argued that the collective staging of protests represents a conscious act to influence the struggle for the interpretation of symbols. Therefore, such symbolic politics aim to raise the level of visibility of those utilizing them, to gain recognition, and to achieve political change. To illustrate this argument, various forms of public protest will be discussed, for example, rallies, demonstrations, and symbolically expressive actions.

On the Difference between Signs and Symbols

In reference to semiotics, originally formulated by Charles Sanders Peirce in the late nineteenth century, it is especially important for the analysis of symbolic politics to use a hermeneutic understanding of symbols that differentiates between signs and symbols. Signs denote specific objects or circumstances. The user of the sign uses the sign as a signifier for the thing which is being signified, that is, which he or she aims to describe. If the sign or significatum clearly and distinctly represents a specific thing, then one can speak of denotation.[2]

Symbols are signs sui generis, that is, all symbols are signs, but not all signs are symbols.[3] As specific signs, symbols refer to a specific object, but the meaning thereof can be interpreted differently by each member of a community. The interpretation of symbols is thus always at least a bit ambiguous. Interpretations are not singular and a result from its specific use on part of its individual interpreters. This means that signs become symbols only after a process of interpretative connotation. Symbols can therefore be understood as hermeneutic phenomena. The interpretation of symbols results from the experiences or life worlds of the interpreter and his or her "knowledge, experiences, principles, and emotions."[4] Symbols can neither mask simple reality, because they, so to speak, actually constitute reality. Nor do they provide us with a comprehensive picture of reality, for the outcome of interpretation differs from individual to individual and from group to group.

In the political context, symbols point in a concentrated manner to the specific meanings and emotions, which are created and developed by the members of a group utilizing them.[5] Through the identifying process with symbols, a form of collective or common identity is fostered. This identity forms self-understanding within a group by giving order to the various convictions. In the process, it serves to preserve and defend this self-understanding.

This supports the argument that political symbols function in a dual manner with regard to the constitution of social protests. On the one hand, they fulfill the specific purposes of integration relevant to protest action. On the other hand, the process of connotation and perhaps ultimately of denotation of political symbols becomes a battleground in itself among vertically opposed social groups. Similar struggles to connote specific political symbols occur on the horizontal level as well. This can be exemplified through recent developments in European political movements: specific symbols, previously connoted by leftist milieus and movements, are now increasingly being connoted by radical right-wing groups. For instance, "autonomous nationalists" display red flags and the image of Che Guevara[6] in a seemingly conscious appeal toward anti-imperialist arguments and to illustrate an "anti-capitalistic embellishment of their rejection of globalization."[7]

Role in Protest Cultures

Protest action and other forms of protest are specific aspects of social movements. Spontaneous protests often herald the formation of social movements. In other instances, protests are purposefully propagated and organized by movement protagonists.

In the first case, protests occur in an *eruptive manner* and *without an underlying strategy,* that is, as riots, bread riots, or revolts. In the second case, protests are *strategically initiated* by a more or less organized and defined group of stakeholders. Of course, protests do not necessarily lead to politically motivated movements. It should also not be assumed that strategically initiated protests or protest movements are always borne of democratic claims based on principles of enlightenment and emancipation, as a number of studies regarding right-wing extremist protests clearly illustrate.[8] Furthermore, it must be mentioned that, in addition to collective protests, *individual protest action* and the *politics of refusal,* for example, the refusal to pay taxes as a component of civil disobedience (e.g., in the spirit of Henry David Thoreau), fall into a more general category of protest. In the context of this analysis of symbolic politics, this type of protest is not addressed in detail. Instead, the chapter focuses explicitly on protests within social movements as a type of collective action.[9]

The preconditions for collective protest include not only a state of relative deprivation of a particular social group, but also the understanding that the respective injustice or problem is not considered to be inevitable or unalterable. In order to mobilize potential protesters, most often a guilty party or enemy of the articulating group must be identified, and a possible solution to the grievances must be formulated.[10] Through this consensus mobilization, as Bert Klandermans writes, enough potential for mobilization emerges for the formation of a social movement, which can then result in a persistence of mobilization for protest action.[11] "As action mobilization builds on the results of consensus mobilization, the first step accounts for the result."[12]

Two factors are essential for successful strategic protest action. First, protest action must be coordinated. Second, resources must be available to the coordinators of the action, for example, for the production and dissemination of placards and leaflets. Regarding coordination, the protesting groups must carry out specific organizational tasks, including planning and possibly dealing with authorities pertaining to the location and time of the action, its route and progression, its speakers and slogans, and so on. Regarding the resources necessary for protest action, it is important to note that the costs involved should not be underestimated. These include, for example, costs for staging, amplification, musicians, and the like.[13]

For action mobilization, a crucial factor is found in the context in which the action is to take place and the situational conditions thereof. Such context includes scandals, explosive media reports, recent policy decisions, and the reaction of police or other authorities toward demonstrative protests.[14] The mobilization potential can also be increased through targeted exaggeration, dramatization in the media,[15] provoking collective fear, or referring to the common, for example, cultural, background of the potential protesters. Also, the credibility of the movement's claimed grievance and the reputations of the coordinating persons and organizations contribute greatly to the level of mobilization potential. In many cases, movement organizations hearken to past successes or refer to prominent, credible, and recognized personalities in support of their concern, so that they can gain legitimacy in the public sphere and win the trust of potential protesters. Political demands are often supported by referring to expert opinions or documentary images.[16] Also, it is important for the success of the protest action that the chances for change are presented in an optimistic manner prior to the beginning of the action or campaign.[17] Moreover, political actions and campaigns strive to fulfill a dual function, namely to resonate both externally and internally. Regarding external resonance, actions are intended to raise the awareness of an issue among bystanders and in the public sphere in order to win over more supporters and increase political pressure. Regarding internal resonance, political campaigns and actions generate social relations among the participants and therewith foster a sense of internal conformity or community. Klandermans writes: "Movement organizations not only supply sources of identification, they also offer all kinds of opportunities to enjoy and celebrate the collective identity: marches, rituals, songs, meetings, signs, symbols, and common codes."[18]

The mobilization efforts on the part of social movements—action mobilization—carry in themselves symbolic elements and take place under the premises of symbolic strategies of dissemination. In the context of this tension, however, to what extent can one speak of symbolic politics?

Research Traditions and Perspectives: Symbolic Politics and Protest

Symbolic politics as a term carries a rather negative connotation in the German and English language scientific discourses. This perspective, also existent in everyday thinking, assumes that politics disseminated through the media follows merely the logic of theatrics and is thus devoid of substance. This perception of symbolic politics results from the understanding that the political is comprised of making policy, that is, the institutional actions within the realm of the state. Similar to Murray Edelman (1985) and Ulrich Sarcinelli (1987), who speak of an "illusion versus political reality,"[19] Thomas Meyer refers in general to the illusoriness of political processes in the context of how mass media functions. It is not entirely coincidental that terminology from the realm of the performing arts, such as staging, performance, and aestheticization, is used to define the specific medial logic of symbolic politics.

The approach of symbolic politics from above[20] strives deliberately to separate well-grounded public discourse from political reality in the sense that it serves not to address the substantive political process, which is oftentimes difficult to relate to the public, but rather to portray this process through the media in a targeted manner. In doing so, this form of symbolic politics utilizes reductionist and simplified political imagery, such as specific symbols, rituals, and other commonly understood schemas, in a seemingly intentional manner in order to relate political decision-making processes to the general public.

Edelman's point of reference is the obfuscation of real conditions by politicians and political institutions. Through his perspective, the logic of the staging of politics for the public sphere is omnipresent. This logic is strengthened through the market-based character of the mass media. For Edelman, public processes always contain a specific dramaturgy and schematization, while the parallel political and policy decision-making processes—that is, the processes that directly influence the members of society—remain hidden.[21] In this sense, Meyer and Andreas Dörner use the terms "placebo politics"[22] and "political placebo,"[23] respectively, to denote a form of top-down politics focused on influencing on a discursive level the opinions of the public concerning the societal and policy decisions at hand. This form of politics seems to be deployed only to gain public support by calming the electorate and setting trends of thought. For Meyer, "symbolic politics from above" are thus politics of empty symbolism without any relation to reality. They involve strategic action alone, address no substantive arguments, and are aimed at merely influencing the perception of the electorate.

Meyer develops a positive counterpart to this rather dismaying understanding of symbolic politics, namely "symbolic politics from below." This form does not strive to replace real political actions with symbolism. Instead, the goal of bottom-up symbolic politics is to unmask the staged as-if politics and to reveal the underlying injustice or issue.[24] This expansion of the concept of symbolic politics, the perspective of which stems from outside of the institutionalized context, allows for a tangible viewpoint toward approaching the use of symbolic politics within the context of protest action. Nonetheless, Meyer's symbolic politics from below as a strategy to reveal reality represents only one side of the coin.

In summary, the approaches from above and from below are based on the following assumptions: that actual politics or decision-making on the part of the political elite occur backstage and are thus not witnessed by the public; and that a form of theater or pseudopolitics is played out in front of the backdrop to mask the events, that is, the real political negotiation processes, behind it.[25] The only conceptual difference between these approaches is in their assessment of symbolic politics either as a necessary instance for the dissemination of information via the media or as a conscious masking of reality.

Sarcinelli's analysis of symbolic politics is concerned as well with the institutionalized form or business of politics. He begins his analysis by discussing the functioning of the modern media society. As he ascertains, it is not possible for each individual to directly access political reality in a modern pluralistic society. Citing empirical studies, Sarcinelli argues that politicians—at least those interested in retaining support for their actions—are dependent on the dissemination of symbolic surrogates of their politics which, in turn, generate a medially constructed reality.[26] Nonetheless, Sarcinelli understands this to be only a partial description of symbolic politics. He argues elsewhere that his concept should not be seen as limited to include only this surrogate function of medial influence on reality. Accordingly, symbolic politics should be recognized as an "indispensable phenomenon within political communication."[27]

This approach toward the concept of symbolic politics evokes two analytical dilemmas. First, from a political science perspective, its applicability to institutional mechanisms in the context of representation and dissemination alone appears to be too limited. Meyer's understanding of symbolic politics as from below implies that symbolic political action can also take place outside of representative institutional politics. On the other hand, his argument that this involves an unmasking of as-if politics seems to be reductionist. In my point of view, in contrast, political action should be understood as symbolic praxis per se. Gerhard Göhler argues, "Politics always concerns symbols and cannot be adequately grasped without the symbolic dimension."[28] This certainly includes protest action, for symbols are used here as well to define and address political goals, friend–enemy schemas, and courses of action. Indeed, the symbolic dimension seems especially important to protest action, because the goals thereof are to win over as large a group of supporters as possible and then to subsequently mobilize this group over the long term. As they are described by Edelman, the phenomena of ritualization and myth are also mechanisms of staging, which are utilized by protagonists of social movements.

The second dilemma is made clear when the concept of symbolic politics is approached from a sociological perspective in general and from a constructivist perspective in particular. Through this perspective, symbolic politics gain meaning in the sense that they represent social action. The constructivist position argues that only one reality exists, and that this reality continuously emerges via social interaction. Through this perspective, symbolic politics cannot be limited in definition to a specific form of politics. Instead, politics on the whole are understood as symbolic, as is the case with all other phenomena.[29] Thus, a debate regarding the functionality of specific forms of symbolic politics seems in the end to be of little use. In light of the constructivist viewpoint,[30] the postulated assumption or the analytical schema of multiple realities, that is, of a stage and a backstage, seems obsolete. This standpoint is akin to Erving Goffman's 1969 study of everyday communication. "In this respect, symbolic politics are not a political novelty."[31]

Nevertheless, as Göhler[32] and Sarcinelli[33] make clear, symbols do possess a specific consolidating function toward reality. This functional element of symbolic politics appears to be especially meaningful within the context of political action.

Protest as a Struggle for Symbolic Power

Pierre Bourdieu's sociological perspective of symbolic power is helpful to better understand symbolic protest action.[34] In his analysis, Bourdieu references a central concept of Ernst Cassirer's philosophy of symbolic forms. For Cassirer, the semiotic sphere of symbolic forms provides the key for understanding both structure and actions and objectivity and subjectivity in the social world.[35]

Bourdieu expands upon Cassirer's idealist philosophy of symbolic forms to include the elements of power and societal control. As Karl Marx did, Bourdieu argues that economic capital produces social classes. In order to more completely grasp the social dimension, though, Bourdieu introduces the concepts of social and cultural capital. Furthermore, social and cultural capital can be transferred to symbolic capital, which, in turn, is perceived as legitimate structuring mechanisms. For Bourdieu, this is the symbolic power that structures social reality. According to their economic, cultural, and social capital, individuals occupy specific positions in the social space and fortify their positions through their respective symbolic power. As Bourdieu argues, such positioning is determined through habitus as a structured and structuring structure. Habitus constitutes social reality and social positioning in the form of patterns of perception. Habitus functions as a distinguishing feature in society (articulated by lifestyle) and steers the perception of belonging or nonbelonging. It can also effectuate the acceptance of differing positions of unequally distributed power within the structured whole. Common patterns of perception produced in this manner provide for the basis for political and social control. They are thus not transcendental in character, as Cassirer understood them, but rather result from political struggles for symbolic power.[36]

In her study on the staging of protest in the students' movement of the late 1960s,[37] Kathrin Fahlenbrach analyzes the connection between habitus and lifestyle in relation to mobilization. She argues that "not only social, cultural, and political conflict situations" form the starting point for the emergence of social movements, but more importantly the "individual experience of collectively shared problems."[38] In this context, she defines protest movements as habitually stabilized conflict systems. Therewith, great importance is placed in the "visual-expressive symbols of protest" for the inner workings of protest movements.

As Göhler states, these in part highly symbolic codes function not only in a consolidating manner. They also play a significant role in the struggle for interpretive power vis-à-vis the dominating culture. Regarding symbolic politics, this means that the group in possession of the most symbolic capital, with which it asserts its power, also supplies the "governing symbols as exclusive interpretive offers."[39] As Dörner writes, this group has the "power to definitively establish its descriptions, its terminology, and its interpretations."[40]

Accordingly, strategic protest action forces exactly those struggles of interpretative power and appellatively generates symbolic strategies to these ends.

Collective Self-Presentation as Theatralization

In his 1959 study, *Primitive Rebels. Studies in Archaic Forms of Social Movement in the 19th and 20th Centuries,* Eric Hobsbawm finds significance in symbolism in both archaic and modern movements.[41] He stresses the importance of rituals for movements, even though he concludes that archaic movements placed great weight on rituals, whereas modern "social movements outside such old-fashioned circles tended to adopt ritual chiefly for the more utilitarian purpose of security against the blows of their enemies."[42] Rituals can be defined as the use of symbols and symbolic gestures in a recurring and prestructured chain of actions.[43] Similarly, Edelman notes that slogans and phrases in a militant atmosphere aid to "bring people with widely-differing motives and views to concentrate their protests toward one common issue."[44] The collective self-representation is articulated mainly in public protest actions.[45]

Collective self-representation occurs mainly in the context of a specific logic of theatralization. In her analysis of the semiotics of the performing arts, Erika Fischer-Lichte distinguishes four integral aspects of the concept of theatralization. First, performance describes an act of presentation of voice and body to a viewing public and is composed of the ambivalent interaction between all participating factors. Second, staging is defined as a specific mode of the use of signs during the production of the performance. Third, embodiment results from the presentation of the material. Fourth, perception references the audience and its observing function and perspective. Taken together and each in its own specific way, all four of these aspects determine the theatralization of an event. The staging of the production is especially important in cases in which a protest action aims to create a certain effect through theatralization.[46] As such, it is an aesthetic process, and its effects can be understood as aesthetic reality. As an aesthetic category, the staging of the action relates directly to the aspect of perception. Fischer-Lichte's terminology applies to all forms of staging, including those in the political theater.[47]

In its complexity and interaction between protagonists and the viewing public, the act of collective self-representation in the public sphere is the actual performance. The organizers of demonstrative protest action seemingly always at least attempt to plan their actions prior to their taking place and, in the process, stage them in order to have the best possible effect both inward and outward. In this sense, the protagonists utilize ritualized forms of interaction, which are recognized both in the respective milieus from which the movement stems and as "visually-expressive symbols of protest" in the public sphere.[48] The mass of people, staged through their innumerable nonverbal forms of expression, obtains therewith its embodiment. Specific forms of expression found in protest actions can include: the number of demonstrators; the demonstration's route, use of space and objects, its formation, style of marching, and banners; the demonstrators' types of clothing, insignias, and flags; and the use of specific acoustic forms of expression and gestures. All of this influences the perceptions of both the public viewing the protest action and its participants.

With the entry into the public space and the conscious visualization of the symbolic body mass, expressively and habitually based schemas are stimulated, and habitual patterns of identity are activated.[49] The protesters actively struggle for visibility and, to put it bluntly, they reach for symbolic power. Therefore, symbolic politics play a large role in protest action.

Street Protest as a Pure Form of Symbolic Politics

The large social movements in the last two hundred years, among them the voting rights' and workers' movements, were closely linked to the struggle for demonstrative forms of expression on the streets and in the public space. As Fahlenbrach states, they "represent up until today the oldest and most important form of public protests" and "exhibit historically established ritualistic qualities which are, even in the era of mass media, absolutely essential for the successful formation of a movement."[50] Street protests are especially attractive for protest action because they are accessible to all. As mundane as this may seem at first glance, in the streets there exist few, if any, boundaries with regard to social context. The streets are in no way an exclusive location of power for the elite. In this sense, they function as a tribunal and as a medium of expression. In the streets, it can come to tumult, angry crowds, provocative jaunts, and riots.[51] According to Dieter Hoffmann-Axthelm, public space per se was first established through ritual and riot. In the early cities, public space existed only on the margins, and it was the procession that "opened the areas of the city which had been previously comprised of closed, private, and impassable agglutinations."[52]

Public forms of protest action or, in general, the representation of the "symbolic body mass" follow the logic of theatralization discussed above. "From the self-constitution of its protagonists to the interaction with its opponents and the viewing public, street protest is a process of disseminating symbols."[53] These include the "feelings, mindsets, and the sense of connection" of the protesters. Signs, symbols, and whole symbolic actions are "culturally and socially determined codes" within the context of "articulation and mobilization both of views and mindsets and of belonging and non-belonging."[54]

Thomas Balistier classifies three specific forms of demonstrative action: political rallies, demonstrations, and symbolically expressive actions.[55] Additionally, he formulates three "modes of escalation," which occur within the context of these forms of action.[56] First, escalation can be achieved through a large number of participants in the demonstrative action. Through bystanders, eyewitnesses, and participants, the fact of the action is immediately inscribed in reality. Demonstrative forms of protest are a symbol of freedom of expression. They serve to mold the political discussion in the sense that they visualize the significance of their political statements through the presentation of the mass of their supporters. More often than not, the size of a demonstrative action determines the seriousness to which others give the political will expressed by the action. Balistier defines the second specific mode of escalation as the presentation and expressivity of the demonstrative protest, that is, the respective orchestration of the performance. He defines the third mode of escalation as the forcing of escalation, that is, the tendency or attempt to transform an appellative demonstration into direct action. The mass falls apart, it leaves the ritual terrain, it is an element of strategic theatralization on part of the coordinators of the protest, or it culminates in a direct expressive action, a change in the route of the action, or the development of more violent forms of protest.

Balistier understands rallies, as a specific form of street protest, to be mainly highly organized and ritualized events.[57] In the context of the specific design of the action at hand, they are organized as singular events or as part of a more multifaceted demonstration. The majority of these are organized by large organizations or associations.

A demonstration, as defined by Balistier and others, can be understood as a difficult medium between procession and riot. A procession is a cyclical event, whereas a riot is an eruptive and spontaneous collective action geared toward immediate change. As Hoffmann-Axthelm writes, "the riot first reaches its goal when the Bastille is destroyed, when blood, fire, defenestration, and the destruction of furniture and files illustrate irreversibility."[58] Demonstrations are also forms of action initiated by protagonists to publicly decry grievances and ultimately to achieve change. In their staging, demonstrations are symptomatically similar to processions, that is, through rituals, mass, location, route, and the signs portrayed by the participants. Both forms intend to convince the viewing and greater public of the legitimacy of their aims. Demonstrations strive to symbolically take possession of a specific space or location by means of its body mass. They have temporal and geographic dimensions, and sometimes, forms of protest are chosen that consciously stretch or somehow otherwise alter the normal length or route. Through demonstrations, many demands are not achievable in the short term. Nonetheless, by means of a certain level of perseverance, protesters can symbolize the ability to persevere, and thus also illustrate the seriousness of the issue. Most demonstrations take place on foot, wherein the participants form groups or blocs. The expressive culmination of protest is most often the acoustic and visual staging of the demonstration. The instruments applied are flags, banners, lights, torches, placards, and orchestrated formations, among them uniforms or uniform-like clothing (e.g., the so-called black bloc in anti-Fascist demonstrations or the white bloc regarding British suffragettes). Accordingly, the symbols used in demonstrations are specific and manifold and vary according to context and milieu.

According to Balistier, a demonstration escalates in form when it moves from an appellative to a direct form of action.[59] Escalating situations can emerge when a demonstration leaves its scheduled route, comes to a halt, does not disperse at its conclusion, or becomes violent. After this transformation process, a demonstration mutates into a direct action. A demonstration is thus a closed movement with a beginning and an ending, its medium of action is the street, and the central element of the demonstration is composed of the demonstrators, its bystanders, and other nonparticipants who become aware of the demonstration.

Symbolically expressive actions are specialized forms of staging that not only correlate to the specific logic of the situation with regards to the issues being protested, but also develop along the lines of a more-or-less complex plot. The intention, goals, feelings, and mind-sets of the protesters are thus staged via the action. A specific dramaturgy and aesthetics emerge in the process. Examples of symbolic-expressive actions are picketing, vigils, chaining to objects at symbolically relevant locations, heckling at political events, and disruptions in the public space.

The categorical boundaries between such demonstrative protest actions are not clear-cut. Even members of the institutionalized elite sometimes take part in symbolically expressive actions on the local level. When the demonstrative form of action does not offer a perspective for change in the substance of its grievance, sometimes further steps toward escalation are taken on the part of participants in order to increase political pressure. This can lead to specific forms of direct action, to militant action. The respective action, including the handling of the conflict and the interaction with opposing forces and the viewing public, is a symbolically laden process in itself. Some examples are violence in symbolic locations of power, targeted conflicts with the authorities or police, and attacks against prominent personalities.

It can be concluded that rallies, demonstrations, and symbolically expressive actions are means of articulation of social movements. In this sense, they theatralize oppositional interpretations of existing conditions. These forms seem to be especially attractive and efficient because they draw breath from the creative power and inventiveness of their participants. The formula seems to be that the level of success amounts to more protesters for the cause, thus increasing its legitimacy in society and its political power. Demonstrative and direct actions may have differing profiles of theatralization, but decisive is their symbolic character with which they attempt to influence the perception of the viewing and general public.

As discussed above and in social movement research, the forms of convincing others within a specific milieu or scene function by means of two dimensions of mobilization. The exact conditions, with their problems, injustices, and dangers, are problematized, the political and substantive spheres of a movement's opponents are addressed, and alternatives are presented. Because it is difficult to logically present complex issues for the public, understanding reality is often reduced to only those elements deemed to be essential. The opposing spheres are consolidated therewith in the form of specific persons, institutions, or objects. Because it is hardly an easy task to convince one's opponents, appeals toward good faith reasoning are often replaced by theatrical staging against the arrogance of power of the elite.

All of these forms function along strategic lines of symbolic politics. They serve the reduction and dissemination of political goals both inward and outward. Symbolic politics steer and reproduce the consolidation of a collective identity. In the best-case scenario, they help develop social movements with the ability to sustain protest actions over long periods of time.

Conclusion:
Is There a Link between Frames and Symbolic Politics?

In accordance to Sarcinelli's understanding,[60] symbolic politics are composed of a specific mixture of information and emotion, intend to trigger identification based on sentiment, mobilize group consciousness, and create political boundaries. As Sarcinelli postulates in the context of institutionalized politics, this logic also seems applicable to public protest. In the field of medial attention, protest movements are especially dependent on a reduction to the visual. The symbolic politics of protest movements—in the larger sense, the struggle for symbolic interpretative authority—serve as a simplification and reduction of a political claim. Over the course of protest, they form and propagate the establishment of a collective identity through symbols, rituals, and other commonly understood schemas.

In doing so, "symbolic politics from below," as Meyer describes, do not expose or debunk institutional symbolic politics in the classical sense, but rather utilize the same modes. For the "formation of a body mass" in public protest actions, as Fahlenbrach states, the use of these modes is even absolutely necessary.

Within the collective cultural and symbolic systems of a milieu or movement, the cognitive schemas form the basis for systems of the individual and collective action and thus function in an indispensable way. In the context of protests, these cognitive schemas have a mobilizing function as well.

When one agrees that symbolic politics are an essential element of social movements and are also fundamental for mobilization processes, then it is necessary to expand the political science approach to include sociological approaches to movements. In the interdisciplinary sense, the specific frame approach within movement research could be very important to this debate on the whole. At the center of this complex and multifaceted methodological approach toward the "framing processes,"[61] as found, for example, in Goffman's analysis of frames,[62] is the argument that symbolically disseminated patterns of interpretation or cognitive frames of meaning are absolutely important to mobilization in social movements.

Jana Günther is research assistant at Dresden University of Technology and PhD candidate at Humboldt University of Berlin, Germany. She was scholarship holder of the Hans Böckler Foundation. Her research interests are the sociology of social protest, early women's movement in Germany and Great Britain, and laboring feminism. She is coeditor of the German journal for feminist political science *Femina Politica*.

Notes

My special thanks go to William Hiscott (†) for his valuable hints and his great help with the translation.

1. Gerhard Göhler, "Symbolische Politik—Symbolische Praxis: Zum Symbolverständnis in der deutschen Politikwissenschaft," in *Was heißt Kulturgeschichte des Politischen?*, ed. B Stollberg-Rilinger (Berlin, 2005), 57.
2. Ibid., 65–66.

3. Ibid., 66.
4. Ibid.
5. Murray Edelman, *Politik als Ritual: Die symbolische Funktion staatlicher Institutionen und politischen Handelns* (Frankfurt, 1990), 9.
6. "Front National verwendete Che-Guevara-Foto: 15.000 Euro Strafe," *Der Standard,* 9 June 2008. http://derstandard.at/?url=/?id=3341060
7. Thomas Grumke, "Rechtsextremismus in Deutschland—Begriff—Ideologie—Struktur," in *Erlebniswelt Rechtsextremismus,* ed. S Glaser and T Pfeiffer (Schwalbach, 2007), 26.
8. Wilhelm Heitmeyer, "Right-Wing Extremist Violence," in *International Handbook of Violence Research,* ed. W Heitmeyer and J Hagan (Dordrecht, 2003), 399*ff.*
9. David A Snow, Sarah A Soule, and Hanspeter Kriesi, "Mapping the Terrain," in *The Blackwell Companion to Social Movements,* ed. DA Snow, SA Soule, and H Kriesi (Malden, MA, 2007), 6.
10. Dieter Rucht, "Politischer Protest in der Bundesrepublik Deutschland: Entwicklungen und Einflussfaktoren," in *Politische Partizipation zwischen Konvention und Protest: Eine studienorientierte Einführung,* ed. B Hoecker (Opladen, 2006), 200.
11. Bert Klandermans, "The Demand and Supply of Participation: Social-Psychological Correlates of Participation in Social Movements," in *The Blackwell Companion to Social Movements,* ed. DA Snow, SA Soule, and H Kriesi (Malden, MA, 2007), 369–70.
12. Ibid., 370.
13. Rucht, "Politischer Protest in der Bundesrepublik Deutschland," 201.
14. Ibid., 201–2.
15. Kathrin Fahlenbrach, *Protestinszenierungen, Visuelle Kommunikation und kollektive Identitäten in Protestbewegungen* (Wiesbaden, 2002), 144.
16. Sigrid Baringhorst, "Strategic Framing—Deutungsstrategien zur Mobilisierung öffentlicher Unterstützung," in *Handbuch Politisches Marketing. Impulse und Strategien für Politik, Wirtschaft und Gesellschaft,* ed. VJ Kreyher (Baden-Baden, 2004), 81.
17. William Gamson and David Meyer, "The Framing of Political Opportunity," in *Comparative Perspectives on Social Movements: Political Opportunities, Mobilizing Structures, and Cultural Framings,* ed. D McAdam, JD McCarthy, and MN Zald (Cambridge, 1996), 278.
18. Klandermans, "The Demand and Supply of Participation," 367.
19. Andreas Dörner, *Politischer Mythos und symbolische Politik: Sinnstiftung durch symbolische Formen Formen am Beispiel des Hermannsmythos* (Opladen, 1995), 45.
20. Thomas Meyer, *Die Inszenierung des Scheins: Voraussetzungen und Folgen symbolischer Politik; Essay-Montage* (Frankfurt, 1992), 62-63
21. Edelman, *Politik als Ritual,* XII.
22. Meyer, *Die Inszenierung des Scheins,* 55.
23. Dörner, *Politischer Mythos und symbolische Politik,* 53.
24. Meyer, *Die Inszenierung des Scheins,* 62-63.
25. Hans-Georg Soeffner and Dirk Tänzler, "Figurative Politik. Prolegomena zu einer Kultursoziologie politischen Handelns," in *Figurative Politik: Zur Performanz der Macht in der modernen Gesellschaft,* ed. H-G Soeffner and D Tänzler (Opladen, 2002), 18.

26. Ulrich Sarcinelli, *Symbolische Politik* (Opladen, 1987).
27. Ulrich Sarcinelli, *Politische Kommunikation in Deutschland: Zur Politikvermittlung im demokratischen System* (Wiesbaden, 2009), 126–27.
28. Göhler, "Symbolische Politik," 57–58.
29. Ibid., 60.
30. Peter L Berger and Thomas Luckmann, *Die gesellschaftliche Konstruktion der Wirklichkeit* (Frankfurt, 1988).
31. Ulrich Sarcinelli, "Aufklärung und Verschleierung: Anmerkungen zur Symbolischen Politik," in *Kunst, Symbolik und Politik,* ed. Ansgar Klein (Opladen, 1995), 334.
32. Göhler, "Symbolische Politik."
33. Sarcinelli, *Symbolische Politik.*
34. Pierre Bourdieu, *Zur Soziologie der symbolischen Formen* (Frankfurt, 1974).
35. Dörner, *Politischer Mythos und symbolische Politik,* 47.
36. Göhler, "Symbolische Politik," 63
37. Fahlenbrach, *Protestinszenierungen, Visuelle Kommunikation und kollektive Identitäten in Protestbewegungen,* 43*ff.*
38. Ibid., 85.
39. Göhler, "Symbolische Politik," 64
40. Dörner, *Politischer Mythos und symbolische Politik,* 49.
41. Eric John Hobsbawm, *Primitive Rebels: Studies in Archaic Forms of Social Movement in the 19th and 20th Centuries* (Manchester, 1959), 150.
42. Ibid., 161.
43. Fahlenbrach, *Protestinszenierungen, Visuelle Kommunikation und kollektive Identitäten in Protestbewegungen,* 112.
44. Edelman, *Politik als Ritual,* 123.
45. Fahlenbrach, *Protestinszenierungen, Visuelle Kommunikation und kollektive Identitäten in Protestbewegungen,* 112.
46. Fischer-Lichte, "Inszenierungsgesellschaft? Zum Theater als Modell, zur Theatralität von Praxis," in *Inszenierungsgesellschaft,* ed. H. Willems/M. Jurga, 86-87.
47. Erika Fischer-Lichte, *Ästhetik des Performativen.* (Frankfurt/M., 2004), 86–87f.
48. Fahlenbrach, *Protestinszenierungen, Visuelle Kommunikation und kollektive Identitäten in Protestbewegungen,* 111.
49. Ibid., 148.
50. Kathrin Fahlenbrach, "Protest-Räume—Medien-Räume Zur rituellen Topologie der Straße als Protest-Raum," in *Straße als kultureller Aktionsraum,* ed. SM Geschke (Wiesbaden, 2009).
51. Roland Roth, "Die Macht liegt auf der Straße: Zur Bedeutung des Straßenprotestes für die neuen sozialen Bewegungen," in *Straße und Straßenkultur: Interdisziplinäre Beobachtungen eines öffentlichen Sozialraumes in der fortgeschrittenen Moderne,* ed. H-J Hohm (Konstanz, 1997), 196.
52. Dieter Hoffmann-Axthelm, "Straße: Ritus und Aufruhr," in *Ästhetik und Kommunikation* (Berlin, 1997), 16.
53. Thomas Balistier, *Straßenprotest: Formen oppositioneller Politik in der Bundesrepublik Deutschland zwischen 1979 und 1989* (Münster, 1996), 28.
54. Ibid., 28*ff.*

55. Ibid., 34*ff.* Translator note: *Kundgebungen* (rallies), *Demonstrationen* (demonstrations).
56. Balistier, *Straßenprotest,* 41.
57. Ibid., 34*ff.*
58. Hoffmann-Axthelm, "Straße," 17–18.
59. Balistier, *Straßenprotest,* 50.
60. Sarcinelli, "Aufklärung und Verschleierung," 332.
61. David A Snow, "Framing Processes, Ideology, and Discursive Fields," in *The Blackwell Companion to Social Movements,* ed. DA Snow, SA Soule, and H Kriesi (Malden, MA, 2007), 380*ff.*
62. Erving Goffman, *Frame-Analysis* (London, 1974).

Recommended Reading

Fahlenbrach, Kathrin. *Protestinszenierungen, Visuelle Kommunikation und kollektive Identitäten in Protestbewegungen.* Wiesbaden, 2002. This publication, *Staging of Protest—Visual Communication and Collective Identities in Protest Movements,* is a broad empirical and actor-centered study about protest mobilization in 1968 with regard to Pierre Bourdieu's habitus theory.

Fischer-Lichte, Erika. *Ästhetik des Performativen.* Frankfurt, 2004. *The Aesthetics of Performance,* is oriented toward cultural studies and includes ideas about performance, corporality, spectacle, and enactment, which are useful to describe moments of political staging in protest mobilization.

Meyer, Thomas. *Die Inszenierung des Scheins: Voraussetzungen und Folgen symbolischer Politik; Essay-Montage.* Frankfurt, 1992. *Staging the Illusion: Preconditions and Consequences of Symbolic Politics* is a summary of essays about symbolic politics. After a social historical introduction, he defines and compares specific types of political symbols and symbolic politics.

Chapter 5

Protest and Lifestyle

Nick Crossley

Introduction and Definitions

It is commonly claimed that protest and social movement activity, that is, expression of opposition to the activities of government and other elites, is increasingly interwoven with lifestyle; that is, with the ways in which individuals live out their everyday lives, their consumption activities, the ways in which they dress, the ways in which they communicate, and their self-identifications. This interweaving of protest and lifestyle, as explored in the literature, has a number of sometimes overlapping aspects, which this entry unpacks.

Protest and Lifestyle. A Definition

The first and perhaps most obvious way, in which lifestyle and protest overlap is in contexts where protests are about lifestyle. This arises when, for example, social movements campaign against the damage or threat to specific lifestyles affected by wider social (including political and economic) changes. The claims of indigenous movements, whose ways of life have been and are affected by dominant settler groups, and/or the demands of large corporations with an economic interest in their territory, are obvious examples of this. Languages, forms of dress, rituals, and many other such practices of indigenous cultures can be eclipsed as the political and/or economic dominance of outsiders facilitates their cultural dominance too and/or generates a social environment in which indigenous lifestyle can no longer survive. Indigenous movements often resist this, effecting protest around lifestyle and ways of life more generally.

A less obvious but no less important example, at least in terms of recent academic debate, comes from debates on new social movements and also the anticorporate or global justice movement, which appears to have overtaken and subsumed new social movements both in practice and in recent social movement theory. Many of the classic accounts of the new social movements, from Touraine, through Habermas to Melucci, center upon lifestyle.[1] Each argues, albeit in different ways, that the dominant terrain of struggle for social movements in the West began to shift, around the 1970s, from the workplace to the domains of everyday life, identity, and lifestyle. This shift, they maintain, was an effect of wider social changes that effectively pacified and institutionalized working-class unrest (qua class unrest), incorporating it within the political system and simultaneously fragmenting its solidaristic bases of support, but only at the price of greater impingement by the state, private business interests, and various professional agencies, upon what were previously considered private or relatively autonomous domains of everyday life. Touraine's references to the "programmed society" and Habermas's to "colonization of the lifeworld" clearly bring this tension and dynamic to the foreground.[2] And both writers, along with Melucci,[3] argue that the emergence of new social movements was a response to this impingement upon everyday life and lifestyle. Somewhat like indigenous movements, new social movements emerged in response to the threat to traditional ways of life posed by the impingement of new, alien economic-political forms upon them, and more especially in relation to perceived growing restrictions upon the capacity for self-determination in relation to lifestyle caused by that impingement.

The distinction that these writers make between new and (by implication) old social movements has been widely contested.[4] This is not the place to engage with these debates, but it is significant that a key observation to emerge from them concerns the significance of lifestyle issues in labor movement politics, past and present. While labor parties in the middle of the twentieth century may have campaigned on relatively narrow utilitarian issues, the unions and other key players in the labor movements had and have engaged a much wider range of issues, many of which center upon quality of life and lifestyle.

The emergence of what is now usually referred to as the global justice movement, since the late 1990s, has arguably shifted the terrain of movement struggle somewhat, away from that described by the theorists of new social movements. In particular, there has been a noticeable resurgence of labor movements, working alongside so-called new social movement groups.

More significantly, there has been an increasing alignment between groups and networks across continents, as protesters from the Global North, South America, Asia, and Africa have identified common ground and begun, in varying degrees, to coordinate their efforts. Moreover, many of the economic issues that new social movement theories regarded as resolved have begun to resurface, provoking renewed critique and protest. Prominent among the many concerns and grievances raised by this movement, however, is the threat to cherished lifestyles and identities posed (in the view of activists) by neoliberal forms of (global and national) economic governance, and also by the policies of major economic corporations. Every aspect of our lives is increasingly subject to the logic of the market and thus the power of large corporations, it is argued, threatening our autonomy and the very social frameworks that give meaning to our lives.[5]

Specific Disciplinary Approaches.
Habermas: Colonization of the Lifeworld?

Though by no means the only theoretical possibility, Habermas's account of the colonization of the lifeworld provides a useful way of thinking about the underlying processes and tensions involved here.[6] Habermas claims that the crisis tendencies of the economy, identified in Marxist social theory, have only been contained, insofar as they have, through expansion of both economic (market) relations and the state bureaucracy into areas of life once free of their influence. This is damaging for Habermas because these areas of life, which he dubs "the lifeworld," are the spaces within the social world where identities, moral orientations, and meanings are constructed through linguistic exchange or what he calls "communicative action." As such, the lifeworld is essential to both social integration and the personal, psychological integration of all members of society. Colonization of the lifeworld threatens this because economic transactions and bureaucratic systems, which cannot do the work of communicative action, nevertheless tend to displace and inhibit it. They cannot generate and sustain meanings, norms, and identities. They tend rather to destroy the communicative fabric that sustains these essential aspects of human life. Colonization therefore tends to threaten both social integration and psychological well-being. New social movements are, among other things, a reaction against this process for Habermas.

In some cases, new social movements are conservative in orientation, even sometimes reactionary. They seek to defend established and traditional lifestyles, even to recoup past lifestyles, in response to the threat posed by the advance of an expanding economy and state into the domain of everyday life. In other cases, however, they exploit the opportunities created by this shake up, seeking not only to remoralize the lifeworld, rescuing it from the systemic logic of state and economy, but also re-forming it in accordance with new, emergent moral forms. They seek to re-form lifestyles as well as to defend their autonomy from the twinned logics of the market and state bureaucracy. In these cases, they are progressive in orientation.

The most obvious example of this, perhaps, is feminism, which has sought to challenge dominant patterns of gender relations and inequalities, not only in the workplace but in all areas of social life. As the famous feminist slogan puts it: "the personal is political." Feminism, at least in many of its manifestations, does not seek to defend traditional lifestyles but rather to challenge and change them.

Much of Habermas's work on this matter was written in the late 1970s and early 1980s. He is reflecting upon the welfare societies of Western Europe as they took shape between 1950 and 1980. From the contemporary point of view, though this perspective remains salient, the balance of forces within the colonization of the lifeworld has arguably shifted.[7] State intervention has been, in some respects, drawn back, and the economy is in the driving seat. It was not the new social movements who rose to prominence as the cracks in the welfare society widened. It was the neoliberals. And the consequence of that has been greater economic colonization. Moreover, through the mediation of such global players as the International Monetary Fund, the World Bank, and major corporations, colonization has arguably gone global. The logic of the market is penetrating new areas of life both within and across nations. It is this, no doubt, which generates a basis of solidarity and unification between the new social movements of the Global North and the various movements of the Global South within the context of the global justice movement. The effects differ in type and severity, but the cause, according to the analyses of at least some activists, is the same.

These contemporary trends have been picked up by a number of contemporary theorists, most notably Michael Hardt and Antonio Negri.[8] As the title of their first book, *Empire,* suggests, there is a level of continuity between their argument and that of Habermas. They explore and criticize the taking over of everyday life by alien forces. Where Habermas's argument centers upon the increasing impingement of the state upon lifestyles, however, Hardt and Negri focus upon large multinational corporations. As this suggests, moreover, they open their focus beyond the implicitly national parameters of Habermas's argument to locate contemporary protest in its (increasingly) international context.

A Clash of Lifestyles

A variation on the theme of "lifestyles under threat" is the case where different lifestyles and cultures clash and impact negatively upon one another. A significant strand within the global justice movement, for example, is focused upon the link between consumption patterns in Western societies and economic exploitation in the developing world, or again, between Western consumption and environmental degradation. Anti-sweatshop campaigns and fair-trade initiatives are the most obvious example of this. It is lifestyles in both the West and the developing world that are at issue in these campaigns. One of the key criticisms of the economic exploitation of labor in the developing world centers upon its impact upon the lives and lifestyles of workers. Low wages and long hours often mean that workers have no opportunity to develop a life or lifestyle outside of work. Of course, the contrast between this situation and the Western lifestyles it both funds and services is also therefore a key rhetorical lynchpin for some campaigners.

The rise in Islamic terror groups may also be seen, in some part, through this lens. Although it would be naïve to adopt the view that Islamic-based terror is premised entirely upon a clash of cultures (and thus lifestyles) or indeed upon the perceived threat to Islamic culture posed by Westernization, the movement clearly does issue a call to a particular form of religious adherence on behalf of its followers and identifies both a threat to Islam, as a way of life, and a need to universalize that way of life in its rhetoric.[9] Even Islamic terrorism is a lifestyle movement in this respect, and the point no doubt applies to other fundamentalist-inspired forms of protest and political action (violent or otherwise). Moreover, a shared faith, expressed and maintained through a shared lifestyle, is the basis upon which events across many of the political and geographical divides of the Middle East, from Iraq, Afghanistan, and Iran to Israel and Palestine, can be linked into a single political discourse and ideology. Faith and lifestyle form a basis of collective identity that, in turn, forms a basis for collective action. For this reason, lifestyle expressions of faith, not least in dress and physical appearance, have become a part of this complex political configuration.

Research Perspectives: Lifestyle, Tradition, and Critical Thought

Lifestyle functions in this account as a good, which is threatened and defended but perhaps also as a lens through which social life is viewed and a benchmark against which deprivations are measured and assessed.[10] EP

Thompson's perceptive analysis of "the moral economy of the crowd" offers a useful insight here.[11] Observing the considerable local political volatility of eighteenth-century England, Thompson notes that is was not hardship per se that triggered collective outbursts and hostility. Hardship was endemic, and people accepted and endured even its harshest forms in many instances. Violent outbursts were more often triggered by violations of local norms and customs. Such customs afforded a collective sense of justice, and their violation, accordingly, was perceived to be unjust. It was this perceived injustice, and not hardship as such, which triggered protest in Thompson's view. As such, even minor infractions with only minor consequences might provoke a riot. Collective ways of life gave rise to a collective sense of morality, a collective definition of reality, rooted in custom and practice, and not only were all hardships experienced relative to the expectations embodied in these collective ways of life, but violation of those expectations in any way was experienced as a threat and prompted a response.

Lifestyle as a Precondition of Protest and Mobilization

It is important to stress, having focused in some detail upon the strains and grievances which provoke protests, that a great deal of research on social movements since the 1970s has argued that strains or grievances are not sufficient, in and of themselves, to generate protests and social movements.[12] This is not the place to list or discuss the other key factors that movement analysts have deemed important for turning grievance into protest.[13] However, we should briefly mention the considerable importance that has been attached to social networks and to collective identity. Protest, it is argued, is much more likely where aggrieved populations are already connected to one another.[14] This draws us again toward lifestyle because our social networks are very much a part of the structure of our everyday lifestyle. Our networks comprise the people we routinely interact with, forming bonds, identities, and definitions of our life situation. And networks are a more effective mechanism of mobilization still where networked actors share a collective identity, which already (i.e., prior to any suggestion of protest or unrest) unites them on both cognitive and emotional levels.

Much work on the black civil rights movements in the United States during the 1950s and 1960s, for example, has claimed that black churches and colleges played a central role in recruitment and solidarity building.[15] Many activists in the struggle did not become involved as individuals. They became involved in blocks, through their church or college, that is, through their existing networks and the solidarity embedded therein. Moreover, in this process, places of worship, rituals, and organizational aspects of the church were reconfigured as mechanisms of movement mobilization, recruitment, and organization. Given the level of segregation in American society at the time, these networks were clearly black networks. The collective identity as black mapped directly onto the membership of local networks. This too has been cited as a factor shaping and facilitating protest—an argument supported by the fact that protest was more marked in areas of higher segregation.[16] Protest, in other words, found its foothold in the mundane practices and spaces of everyday life: lifestyle.

Lifestyles which Inhibit Protest and Mobilization

If lifestyle can be a precondition of mobilization, then it can also be an inhibiting factor. Habermas, for example, refers to what he calls "civil privatism"; that is, a lifestyle characterized by a relative lack of interest in public and political matters.[17] Privatized citizens vote in elections, but on a relatively instrumental (rather than solidaristic) basis. More importantly, their involvement in political life is more or less restricted to this one practice. They have no involvement in politics beyond voting in elections and no wish for greater involvement. Their life is centered around their family and home. Habermas identifies various sociological studies from the 1950s and early 1960s, which suggested that this lifestyle of civil privatism was becoming prominent.[18]

Whatever the merits and problems of this account, it is interesting insofar as it relates the proclivity to protest to lifestyle. It suggests that citizens' relations to many of the public issues that they might protest about are mediated through lifestyles, which either inhibit or encourage that possibility. Lifestyles can open citizens up to political issues but also close issues off, as in civil privatism. Lifestyle can be a bubble that we live in, cutting us off from much of what is going on outside of our bubble. Moreover, even where interest in political issues is aroused, lifestyle involves commitments, constraints, and a degree of inertia, which might prevent that interest from being converted into action. Engaging with protest, unless an actor does so regularly, entails breaking with routines and habits, which is often difficult. Moreover, actors' time and other resources are often spoken for, making a deviation from the usual costly, inconvenient, and difficult. This compounds the tendency to free riding, which may already inhibit willingness to become involved.[19]

Protest as a Lifestyle

Civil privatism has an counterpart, however, in what we might call the protest lifestyle and career.[20] For many of those who become involved in protest and social movements, doing so can become a matter of identity and lifestyle. They adopt an activist identity and an activist lifestyle. They campaign regularly on a host of issues, and often move across a range of groups and movements in the course of their activist career. Protest is not a break from routine for these activists. It is a part of their routine. At the risk of trivializing (which I do not intend), they follow political events and causes, offering their collective support, as other people follow football teams, through thick and thin, whatever the wider level of support or interests in the population, and across a range of campaigns.

This commitment to political involvement can have a considerable impact upon other aspects of the activist's life, including family and work. A number of studies suggest, for example, that many serious activists seek out work that allows them the flexibility to sustain their campaigning activities.[21] In extreme cases, this may mean refusing to engage in the labor market at all, such that the activist is free to engage in sustained actions and to endure the prison sentences that sometimes follow them.

In contrast to the civilly privatized, who largely insulate themselves from potential matters of protest and political concern, these activists are plugged in and seek political engagement out. They may insulate themselves from other issues and live in their own bubble (as we all do), but through the events they attend and the various forms of mass media they use, they involve themselves in national and world events.

Lifestyle as Protest

A further aspect of this, which may exist in relative detachment from it, involves the various ways in which aspects of lifestyle may in themselves constitute a form of protest. From the cultivation of appearance, through different consumption patterns, to attempts to construct an entirely alternative lifestyle, lifestyle can be a site and/or means of protest and struggle.

In some cases, this may be symbolic. In an otherwise very conventional piece of political sociology, for example, Parkin notes how some male middle-class supporters of the UK's Campaign for Nuclear Disarmament (CND) in the 1960s grew and used beards as a way of indicating role distance from what were their often very respectable occupations.[22] The beard, albeit in a gentle way, symbolized dissent and a left-leaning political orientation. It signified, at least as far as the bearded pacifists were concerned, that although their jobs often situated them firmly within the establishment, they were, on another level, outsiders to that establishment and not squares or conformist functionaries. To give another example, it has been argued that the recent trend for veiling among Muslim women, both in the East and the West, is symbolic of a rejection of Western lifestyles, a means of publicly indicating dissent.[23] The dreadlocks cultivated by some environmentalist protesters is a further example still.

Of course appearance and all visible markers of dissent do not simply position those involved against something. They facilitate the formation of collective identities among activists, which in turn enhance the conditions for further, more traditional forms of protest activity. As Durkheim argued at the very dawn of sociology, appearance is one of the most basic ways in which social groups establish their existence and cultivate esprit de corps.[24] The logic here is similar to that through which youth subcultures create a collective identity and presence through clothing and fashion. Adherents express their political identity through their appearance and also draw support and comfort from others who do the same. They mutually confirm and reinforce their adherence to particular protest discourses through their appearance.

A slightly different example of the politics of dress comes from the various feminist debates on dress and fashion in the 1970s.[25] Many Western feminists of the 1970s refused to dress in styles coded as conventionally feminine and refused to cultivate physical beauty, at least as conventionally defined. Many reasons were offered for this. There was a symbolic rejection of the patriarchal order and symbolic embrace of feminism as an identity and movement. At the same time, however, feminists argued that conventional female attire and the preoccupation with beauty effectively constituted women as sexual objects within a societal beauty contest, which both pitted women against one another and subordinated them (sexually, as objects) to men.[26] How women appeared and were seen, it was argued, was integral to the ways in which they were defined and treated. It positioned them (negatively) in society. The adoption of different dress codes was therefore a form of direct action against what was perceived as a mechanism of oppression. It was akin to hunt sabotage or the prevention of land clearance through treetop occupation. Finally, it was argued that many female forms of clothing were impractical and inhibited women's agency. High heels, for example, are difficult to walk in and inhibit movement. Likewise, a woman wearing a skirt has to be mindful of how she sits and moves if she wishes to avoid exposing her underwear, in a way that is not true of trousers. In this context, the politics of appearance was clearly complex and multifaceted.

Beyond the symbolic dimension, lifestyle and particularly consumption choices have been deemed by some as a more practical and effective means of seeking to change particular aspects of society than the more traditional means: for example, marches, petitions, occupations. Boycotting certain goods in one's consumption practices, for example, if enough people become involved, can reduce demand for those goods to a point where manufacturers cease to make them or at least cease to make them in the ways objected to by protesters. Anti-sweatshop protests are a clear example of this kind of protest. The converse of this is the "buycott," where campaigners elect to buy specific kinds of goods. Campaigns around fair-trade products are the most obvious recent example. The logic here is much the same as for the boycott. If purchasing specific goods channels resources to companies deemed to do good work, then it allows those companies to do more good. And this creates a market incentive for other companies to emulate them. The more people buy fair-trade products, for example, the greater the incentive for economic agents who trade with the developing world to do so under a fair-trade banner and in accordance with fair-trade norms.

At the extreme of the lifestyle as protest continuum, we find, in the context of the anti-Capitalist movement, the growth of social centers, that is, communal living arrangements, often in squatted properties, whose participants experiment with lifestyles in an effort to arrive at alternatives that involve fewer compromises with the system, as perceived by them, and which prefigure arrangements which it is imagined might be much more widespread in a future, better world. This concept of prefiguration, which is key to many contemporary movement debates, has a somewhat ambiguous relation to protest. On one level, prefigurative politics represents a move away from protest, toward active attempts to bring about change more directly and from within. On another level, however, social centers have an important role to play within the context of protest campaigns, both as resources that support their members' more overt protest activities and as working examples of alternative ways of living and working, which can be used for educative purposes and have a strong symbolic value.

Nick Crossley is professor of sociology at the University of Manchester, United Kingdom. He has a particular interest in the role of social networks in the mobilization of protest and other forms of collective action. He published a book on social movements, *Making Sense of Social Movements* (New York, 2002), with the Open University Press, and his most recent book is *Towards Relational Sociology* (London, 2012).

Notes

1. Alain Touraine, *The Voice and the Eye* (New York, 1981); Jürgen Habermas, *The Theory of Communicative Action,* vol. 2 (Cambridge, 1987); Alberto Melucci, *Nomads of the Present* (London, 1989); and Alberto Melucci, *Challenging Codes* (Cambridge, 1996).
2. Touraine, *The Voice and the Eye*; Habermas, *The Theory of Communicative Action.*
3. Melucci, *Nomads of the Present*; Melucci, *Challenging Codes.*
4. For example, Gemma Edwards, "Habermas and Social Movements: What's New?," in *After Habermas,* ed. N Crossley and J Roberts (Oxford, 2004), 113–31; Gemma Edwards, "Habermas, Activism and Acquiescence: Reactions to Colonization in UK Trade Unions," *Social Movement Studies* 6, no. 2 (2007): 111–30; Graig Calhoun, "New Social Movements of the Early Nineteenth Century," in *Repertoires and Cycles of Contention,* ed. M Traugott (Durham, 1995), 173–216; and Kenneth Tucker, "How New Are the New Social Movements?," *Theory, Culture and Society* 8, no. 2 (1991): 75–98.
5. For example, Naomi Klein, *No Logo* (London, 2000); George Monbiot, *Captive State* (London, 2000).
6. Habermas, *The Theory of Communicative Action.*
7. Nick Crossley, "Even Newer Social Movements," *Organisation* 10, no. 4 (2003): 287–305.
8. Michael Hardt and Antonio Negri, *Empire* (Cambridge, MA, 2000); Michael Hardt and Antonio Negri, *Multitude* (Harmondsworth, 2004).
9. James Corbin, *The Base* (London, 2003); Lawrence Wright, *The Looming Tower* (London, 2006).
10. See Gemma Edwards, "The Lifeworld as a Resource for Social Movement Participation and the Consequences of Its Colonization," *Sociology* 42, no. 2 (2008): 299–316, for a discussion of the lifeworld as a resource for protest.
11. Edward P Thompson, *Customs in Common* (Harmondsworth, 1993).
12. See Donnatella Della Porta and Mario Diani, *Social Movements* (Oxford, 1999); and Nick Crossley, *Making Sense of Social Movements* (Maidenhead, 2002).
13. See Della Porta and Diani, *Social Movements*; Crossley, *Making Sense of Social Movements.*
14. See Della Porta and Diani, *Social Movements*; Crossley, *Making Sense of Social Movements*; Nick Crossley, "Social Networks and Extra-Parliamentary Politics," *Sociology Compass* 1, no. 1 (2007): 222–36.
15. Aldon D Morris, *Origin of the Civil Rights Movement* (New York, 1984); Doug McAdam, *Political Process and the Development of Black Insurgency, 1930–1970* (Chicago, 1982).
16. McAdam, *Political Process and the Development of Black Insurgency.*
17. Jürgen Habermas, *Legitimation Crisis* (Boston, 1975).
18. Ibid.
19. For the classic account of free riding, see Mancur Olson, *The Logic of Collective Action* (Cambridge, MA, 1971).

20. This is as in the interactionist sense outlined by Becker; Howard S Becker, *Outsiders* (New York, 1963).
21. Doug McAdam, *Freedom Summer* (New York, 1988); Doug McAdam, "The Biographical Consequences of Activism," *American Sociological Review* 54 (1989): 744–60; James Downton and Paul Wehr, *The Persistent Activist* (Boulder, 1997).
22. Frank Parkin, *Middle Class Radicalism* (Manchester, 1968).
23. Arlene E MacLeod, "Hegemonic Relations and Gender Resistance," *Signs* 17, no. 3 (1992): 533–57.
24. Emile Durkheim, *Elementary Forms of Religious Life* (New York, 1915).
25. See Lynn Walter, "The Embodiment of Ugliness and the Logic of Love," *Feminist Review* 36 (1990): 103–26; Elizabeth Wilson, *Adorned in Dreams* (London, 1985); and Elizabeth Wilson, "Deviant Dress," *Feminist Review* 35 (1990): 67–74.
26. Walter, "The Embodiment of Ugliness and the Logic of Love."

Recommended Reading

Downton, James, and Paul Wehr. *The Persistent Activist.* Boulder, 1997. This is an excellent ethnographic account of a group of activists for whom protest is engrained in their lifestyle.
Edwards, Gemma. "Habermas and Social Movements: What's New?" In *After Habermas,* edited by N Crossley and J Roberts, 113–31. Oxford, 2004. This presents an excellent introduction to Habermas, with a good account of his continued relevance.
Klein, Naomi. *No Logo.* London, 2000. This may be a bit dated now but still is a great insider account of the anti-Capitalist movement that began to take shape in the late 1990s/early 2000s, and of the concerns over lifestyle that motivated some of those who became involved in it.
Melucci, Alberto. *Nomads of the Present.* London, 1989. This remains a classic statement of why lifestyle is important in relation to protest and social movements.

Chapter 6

Protest as Artistic Expression

TV Reed

General Definition of Protest Art

In order for the concept of protest as artistic expression to come into existence, two major tendencies had to converge. From one direction, a significant cohort of artists and art critics had to spawn a conceptual frame that argued that art was fundamentally political. And, from another direction, there had to be recognition among social movement activists that protest involves an inescapably aesthetic dimension. The process of convergence of these two intellectual force fields has been under way for over one hundred years and continues to evolve.

The phrase protest as artistic expression raises a number of interesting definitional challenges; all three key words protest, artistic, and expression are complicated, contested terms. However, by linking these key words to the context of social movements, the definitional problems are lessened somewhat, or at least shifted.

Protest, from the Latin *protestare,* suggests etymological roots in publicness and witness. To engage in protest is to offer public witness. Many dictionaries stress the oppositional side of protest, protesting against. But protest, as the prefix "pro" suggests, can also be presentational, putting forth a positive alternative or creative vision.

Of the many definitions of social movements extant in the literature, scholars interested in the relation of movements to artistic expression have stressed movements as forces leading to public display or dramatic action, in contrast to focusing on such issues as organizational structures, or material resources. In a multifaceted definition of social or protest movements,

Charles Tilly notes that the "repertoire" of social movements includes: "creation of special purpose associations and coalitions, public meetings, solemn processions, vigils, rallies, demonstrations, petition drives, statements to and in public media, and pamphleteering."[1] Note how many of the elements of this repertoire involve dramatic public action. Indeed, elsewhere, Tilly even more forcefully emphasizes "repeated public displays" as the heart of movements.[2] Tilly's definition is certainly contested, but it serves this context well in that it moves us toward the claim that to *stage* protest is to enter into the domain of the arts, a fact that is arguably more important than ever in the increasingly media-saturated contemporary world.

The term "artistic" and the phrase "artistic expression" are also problematic. Recent art history has stretched the boundaries of what counts as art, blurred the line between high art and popular culture, and stressed art process over art product. Where expression might once have implied simply putting forth an already formed art object, an emphasis on process stresses that an art text, as opposed to a static art work, is always becoming. This suggests that artistic expression in a movement context is (re)defined by the context. Thus, art works are not simply expressed in a protest context but are created or re-created by such contextualization.

To speak of protest as artistic expression is, therefore, to invoke two related phenomena: on the one hand it is to speak of the (fluid) role of artistic texts in movements, on the other it is to speak of protest events themselves as artistic texts.[3]

General Function of Protest Art

In social movements over the centuries, theater, and the more recent closely related form known as performance art, have demonstrated a natural affinity. But that affinity has had to be actively nourished. From medieval carnival to twentieth-century radical professional theater by such practitioners as Brecht, Boal, Fugard, and many others, dramatic form has surely influenced activists, sometimes directly, more often indirectly.

Protest marches and demonstrations have a long history that ties them to other forms of public drama. The parade and pageant form, for example, were drawn upon and refined by labor activists in nineteenth-century Europe and the United States, and by the suffragettes (women's voter rights activists) in the early twentieth century.[4] In 1912, for example, the anarcho-syndicalist Industrial Workers of the World (IWW) staged an event in New York's Madison Square Garden in support of striking silk mill workers in the textile town of Paterson, New Jersey. In an unprecedented collaboration, modernist dramatist Eugene O'Neill helped direct more than a thousand actual mill workers in the play, and modernist artist John Sloan painted a 200-foot-long backdrop to the set. The "Paterson Pageant" was staged in five episodes: the workers going to work, entering the mill, and then rushing out a little later when the strike was called; picketing and police clubbing in front of the mill; a reenactment of the funeral procession of a textile striker shot by police agents; the strikers, the majority of whom were women, sending their children to the safety of "strike mother" supporters in surrounding cities; and finally, a strategic strike meeting that ends with a rousing rendition of the *Internationale* sung by the 1,200 striker-actors and much of the audience.

The blurring of the line between theater and protest is made possible by a larger process over the last century or more to undermine a strong tradition, particularly in the West, of viewing artistic expression as individualized—the myth of the isolated artist creating out of the shear genius of their muse is deeply embedded in popular consciousness and has also proven difficult to dislodge from art history and aesthetic theory. It is not coincidental, however, that a de-emphasis on individuality and a greater awareness of art as socially produced and socially consumed in our most recent, modern and postmodern period has come at the same time as a rise in aesthetic self-conscious and aesthetically rich forms of social movement protest.

Cultural critic Walter Benjamin, in one of his best-known essays, "The Work of Art in the Age of Mechanical Reproduction" (1935), was among the first to examine the new configuration emerging between art and politics. With the spectacle of Nazism very much on his mind, Benjamin warned against what he called "the aestheticization of politics," the artful expression of state power, and argued that such forces must be countered by "the politicization of aesthetics," the libratory use of art in radically democratic struggle. When Benjamin made these observations, new forms of politicized aesthetics were very much in play. Modernist movements in the arts, from at least the mid nineteenth century, struggled to find ways to escape the commercial nexus. For decades, this approach led to ever more formalistic, self-referential, and desperate attempts to isolate art from social life and therefore market reductionism. By the end of the nineteenth century, these efforts, exemplified by phrases like "art for art's sake" and movements like decadence and aestheticism, had played out a certain logical extreme of alienation from social life, of escape into a putatively pure aesthetic realm.

By the 1920s, and following the horrors of World War I, isolation for the sake of art had failed both society and the arts. In the twenties, a host of avant-garde modernist movements arose with a different conceptualization of the relation between art and social life. Movements including Dada, Futurism, Constructivism, and Surrealism, among others, came to attack the very idea of art, and began clearing the way for understanding art not as aside from social praxis, but as the very model of critical social praxis. Artistic movements known collectively as the avant-garde explicitly raised the question of how the arts could be political interventions. Like Benjamin, many avant-gardists argued that the art object had been so deeply compromised by Capitalism that even the most complexly alienating formalisms were simply products for bourgeois consumption. In response, they argued, only political struggle tied to deeply antiformalist moves could restore the power and integrity of art by destroying the institution of art.

The avant-garde developed a repertoire that both directly and indirectly entered the vocabulary of social protest. On the one hand, a variety of kinds of protest art emerged. On the other hand, protest movements directly employed radical aesthetics in their public actions. A key element of this development was critique of the notion deeply embedded in the West of art as individual expression. The avant-garde, beginning in the early twentieth century and continuing in waves decade after decade, expanded the definition of art as collective social action and moved the individual artist down from aesthetic heaven to everyday life on Earth. This move also included a blurring of the line between so-called high art or fine art and popular forms. By denying the art object what Benjamin called its "aura," through such resolutely demystifying creations as Duchamp's ready-mades, including most scandalously a urinal as objet d'art, avant-gardists open the territory for art to enter ever more directly into the realm of the political.[5] The agent of these art-political interventions ranges from individuals acting outside any movement organization, to collective actions involving the entirety of a protesting group.

In the mid twentieth century, the Situationists in France offered one of the most compelling theoretical discourses connecting the politics of form to forms of politics.[6] Their critique of the "society of the spectacle" served as inspiration for a generation of student revolutionaries who more broadly than ever before brought avant-garde expression out into the streets in mass protest. A slogan found often on the walls of buildings in Paris during the May 1968 student-worker protests, "all power to the imagination," encapsulates the sense that social change does not so much require artfulness as become an art form itself. In the wake of May 1968, and the 1960s more broadly, it became more or less expected that social movements would have an element of dramaturgy, of dramatic staging, but the degree, nature, and meaning of these stages was and remains much debated. From one angle, the goal of Situationist-inspired protest is to turn everyday life into a form of artistic expression, or artistic enactment. This strategy has been pursued at varying scales, ranging from seemingly utopian calls for the dissolution of the art/life binary, to somewhat more modest calls for the creation of temporary zones of relatively free, creative action.

One can connect this strand of action backward in time to the medieval carnivals in which social hierarchies were (temporarily) turned upside down, a tradition Mikhail Bakhtin argued continues in the modern era through forms of the "carnivalesque in literature and the arts as a form of subversion of authority."[7] In the late twentieth and early twenty-first century, this tradition was carried on by a number of less totalizing but similar positions, from the prefigurative politics of 1960s movements analyzed by Wini Breines that emphasized movement communities as models for future society, though the expressly carnival-like Reclaim the Streets movement in Britain and elsewhere, to Temporary Autonomous Zones (Hakim Bey) in the global justice movement.

Role of Art in Protest Cultures

More modest than the protest as total art of the avant-gardists, but of equal or greater importance, has been the role of what we can call collectively the protest art forms. Virtually every form of art has been drawn into the circle of protest over the last several decades. Graphic arts, particularly in the form of protest posters, have been of great importance to movements. Both professional artists and amateur activist designers have been involved in producing poster art to advertise movement events and protest signs for use in marches and other events.[8] And the form has recently found new life and greater ease of dissemination via digital media like the World Wide Web. For reasons discussed above, protest theater and its cousin performance art have been crucial influences shaping protest actions as drama, including for several decades now protest puppetry in the form of giant papier-mâchè figures first brought into modern protest via German artist Peter Schumann's "Bread and Puppet Theatre."[9] Numerous other arts might also be spoken of in similar terms: protest painting, protest poetry, protest dance, protest films, protest photography, and so forth. Indeed, given the trend discussed in the previous section, the world has moved from a situation where the words "art" and "politics" were seen as anathema to each other, to a situation, especially since the social movements of the 1960s, when art and protest are so entwined that it is impossible to imagine the art world without political art.

In talking about the protest arts, it is useful to make a distinction between movement-based and movement supportive forms, recognizing a

Figure 6.1. Giant puppet of Iraqi mother holding a dead or injured child in her arms, at antiwar rally, Judkins Park, Seattle, Washington, 27 October 2007. © Joe Mabel under GNU Free Documentation License.

graduated scale from these two poles. By the former, I mean art that emerges from within social movement groups themselves, and by the latter, I mean work by professional artists who use their medium for protests in sympathy with social change. These supportive forms can be more or less directly linked to social movements, but they are not part of movement organizations themselves.

Among the many forms of protest art, no doubt the best known and the only one to have entered public discourse as a common phrase is "protest music." But another, equally important, ubiquitous form of protest is graphic art, especially posters. Poster art promoting movement activities and ideas have been particularly prominent since the early twentieth century when inexpensive mass production techniques allowed them to be widely distributed. Posters have changed in style, mode of production, and method of distribution over the years, from laboriously handmade silk-screened images stapled to trees or telephone poles to images made and circulated instantaneously across the world by computer. But their basic functions have remained the same. Movement posters are designed, as are the military ones they sometimes mimic, primarily as recruitment and educational devices. They aim to tell a story quickly, dramatically, and primarily visually. They must condense often quite complex ideas and ideological positions into a few images and words. Poster imagery can even speak to audiences of limited literacy.

The visual language of the contemporary protest poster originates in a number of sources, including most ironically the modern military recruitment and war propaganda posters prominent in World War I and World War II. Parodying the military poster has been particularly attractive to antiwar activists for obvious reasons; the famous "Uncle Sam Wants You" poster of World War I, for example, has been parodied in dozens of ways aimed to undermine its prowar message. Movement posters have also drawn techniques from the high art world. Sometimes this is simply the use of certain colors, tones, or styles. Posters in the 1960s often used the psychedelic style of the 1960s rock concert poster, while the ones from the Iraq antiwar effort borrowed the forms of graffiti artist and AIDS activist Keith Haring. Some professional artists directly offer their talents to the movement, while at other times, influence from the art world may take the form of recontextualizing a famous artwork. For example, there are many variations of Picasso's protest antiwar painting *Guernica*. A poster (originally a mural) entitled "Iraqnica" for example, seeks to link the Fascist bombing of the Spanish town for which Picasso's painting is named to the bombing of Iraq.[10] The piece may also serve as a reminder that art itself has become a commodity, with works like those of Picasso, a long time Communist, now hanging on the walls of the very corporations he detested, and peace activists' critique of the military-industrial-media complex behind recent wars in the Middle East.

A related visual art form, the protest mural, grew out of a modernist mural art movement that flourished most profoundly in early twentieth-century Mexico, led by with three great artists Diego Rivera, José Clemente Orozco, and David Alfaro Siqueiros. Their work, especially Rivera's, was itself deeply political, but in addition invented a visual language used by subsequent muralists tied directly to protest movements like the Chicano Power movement in the United States, and Sandinistas in Nicaragua. Murals serve a function similar to posters, but usually on a grander scale and with less temporally limited content. Murals can be integrated as permanent parts of neighborhoods, where passersby are confronted with literally larger than life images of protest.[11]

Similar stories of forms moving from art world to protest arenas could be told of many other mediums, including film (both fiction and documentary), poetry, photography, and dance (as both expressive form and street protest tactic).

Theoretical and Empirical Research

Scholarly discourse on protest as artistic expression is at once expansive and modest. It is expansive because there are many fields that touch on this research area. But there is no single discipline, or even interdiscipline, that lays full claim to this particular field. And the specific role of the arts in social movement protest remains undertheorized and underinvestigated. Art historians and aestheticians; ethnic, gender, and cultural studies scholars; performance studies specialists; and a few social scientists (sociologists, political scientists, and anthropologists, primarily) have made some forays, but nothing very definitive or comprehensive yet exists. Each of these arenas of analysis has something to contribute, but a full approach will require works of synthesis. For the most part, the role of art as protest has been subsumed under more general concern to define and analyze movement cultures.

The new confluence of work on culture and movements has had to work against traditional limitations in the various social sciences, humanities, and cultural studies fields that have made major contributors to this literature. By the turn of the twenty-first century, a few scholars had begun to synthesize the most relevant portions of the social science and the cultural studies traditions. This work was pioneered by European new social movement theorists like Melucci, Ingelhart, Touraine, Lauclau and Mouffe, and

Habermas, among others, who, beginning in the 1970s, looked increasingly to ideological and cultural factors downplayed by previous movement scholars. In the United States, the empirical tradition was expanded from within by sociologists like Verta Taylor and Nancy Whittier, Doug MacAdam, and Steven Beuchler, who sought various ways to document the impact of culture. Despite these developments, significant tensions continue to exist among movement theorists on questions of culture in general and the role of artistic protest in particular.

A solid body of recent work has laid important groundwork for research on protest as artistic expression, but the body of empirical work remains thin. For many social scientists, the cultural turn went far enough, without going into the even softer domain of artistic expression. The U.S. social science approaches to social movements with the best resources for such a move are no doubt those growing out of phenomenological and symbolic interactionist traditions. In particular, the frame analysis approach, which has long lead the way in analyzing ideological representation within and around movements, and dramaturgical approaches have perhaps the deepest affinity and most to offer. Dramaturgical analysis treats public action as ritual and identity as performance in ways that obviously resonate with the art as life approach to radicalism. More generally, if all public action involves a degree of performance on the social stage, then clearly art-inspired actions that draw upon particular aesthetic theories and artistic practices add a degree of self-consciousness about such engagements that could further (or hinder) movements.

Dramaturgical analysis has been applied to social movements by Robert D Benford and Scott A Hunt who argued that "social movements can be described as dramas in which protagonists and antagonists compete to affect audiences' interpretations of power relations in a variety of domains."[12] This approach remains relatively naïve about the nature of performance, and recent, more sophisticated work in performance studies might well be deployed to add greater complexity to sociological forms of dramaturgical analysis, perhaps by utilizing particular aesthetic traditions of performance to designate a typology of protest drama. A different kind of philosophical sophistication could emerge from further work examining Habermas's heuristic "ideal speech situation" as deeply dramatic in nature, and linking that concept to those crucial moments of public culture at the center of much protest activity.

Research Gaps and Open Questions

The most important cultural impact of a social movement may not come from particular cultural values or aesthetic interventions, but from its overall structure. Several movement scholars have attempted to view the overall structure of movements as messages, symbolic actions, direct theory, or social texts that speak beyond their particular issues. All movements, even relatively quietistic ones in democratic societies that normalize certain kinds of protest, offer some degree of symbolic challenge to the dominant order just by the fact of their existence outside electoral political activity. While obviously the degree and kind of symbolic challenge offered by particular movements varies immensely, the challenge is in some an aesthetic question, a question of cultural form. Wini Breines has analyzed, for example, how the prefigurative politics of the New Left movement of the 1960s was embodied in their movement culture as it sought to enact within itself the radically different values and forms it sought to create in the wider world.[13] Feminist scholar Noël Sturgeon has offered a deeper semiotic reading of the organizational structures (like small-scale affinity groups and consensus process) of the antinuclear direct action movement of the 1980s. She argues that movement structures not only *expressed* movement values, but also embodied the movement's theories about social change. Sturgeon offers the innovative term "direct theory" to characterize the way in which the movement's organizational form embodied a point-by-point theoretical and symbolic alternative to the dominant order's notions of legitimate power.[14] Italian movement theorist Alberto Melucci has written of the "symbolic challenge of movements," in which movement cultural codes counter the cultural codes of the dominant society through a sometimes direct, sometimes indirect, semiotic warfare.[15] TV Reed, in *Fifteen Jugglers, Five Believers,* argued that movements both create new social texts and are themselves texts. Movements are at once sites from which particular alternative stories about the culture emerge, and a kind of metanarrative about an alternative way to live in the wider world.[16] Though differing in emphasis and case study examples, all of these theorists have shown how movement cultures deploy alternative aesthetics that become formally rich messages of resistance and embodiments of alternative social arrangements.

The notion of social movements as cultural texts is not synonymous with the art-as-life-as politics approach in the Situationist tradition. That tradition has met with severe critique by activists who see it as self-indulgence far removed from concrete material grievances, or who connect avant-gardism to undemocratic vanguardist politics.[17] And theorists of the avant-garde in general have become increasingly aware of ways in which the make it new philosophy of modern and postmodern artists may be less a critique of Capitalism than a part of it, feeding new styles back into exhausted markets. Avant-gardism has increasingly announced its own death in order to avoid this type of consumption,[18] but the problem remains that the systems criticized by art-political radicals seem able to absorb critique and even turn into their advantage, as in the example of radical punk subcultures that saw their style turned into fashion only weeks after arriving on the public stage.

Nevertheless, as Doug McAdam notes, "Given the entrenched political and economic opposition movements are likely to encounter, it is often true that their biggest impact is more cultural than narrowly political and economic."[19] One key reason for this is that cultural institutions tend to be relatively more open, relatively less defensive, than these other realms. Indeed, since at least the rise of modernism in the arts, innovation has been an imperative in much cultural production. Thus while revolution at total art can hardly be said to have met with total success, the very active search for new aesthetic and cultural forms has sometimes played to the advantage of movements. While the particular successes and limits of various cultural code transgressions matters, there is also a more general level on which the extrainstitutional nature of movements and the contestatory nature of their cultural practices constitute an ongoing message that the status quo is open to change.

John Lofland has offered a schema for measuring movement culture intensity that, whatever one thinks of its particulars, provides a useful starting point for thinking about the range of kinds of movement cultures and use of artistic texts in movement contexts.[20] Lofland divides the terrain of movement culture into six dimensions: values, objects (material culture), stories, occasions (particular rituals, events), roles (specialized to create, perform, and disseminate movement ideas and values), and personae (modelers of movement identities). He further suggests that each of these elements be examined for intensity across six qualities: sharing (how widely the elements are held in common), distinctiveness (how close or distant from mainstream culture or other movement cultures), scope (narrow to wide focus of cultural alternatives offered), elaboration (degree of complexity of interaction among cultural elements), quantity (sheer volume of objects, forms, ideas), and expressiveness (degree of emotional depth evoked in group members). A model like this can generate a continuum between extremes of strong and weak movement cultures, and help isolate the impact of degrees of movement culture strength on other aspects of movement activity.

Alongside any schema for measuring movement culture intensity, it is also important to look at the functions of cultural and aesthetic forms within movements. Reed has identified ten primary functions (functions that overlap and interact in various configurations) as follows:

1. *Encouragement:* individuals feel strength of the group. Poetry read in mass rallies can move one out of the individual self to feel the strength of the group.
2. *Empowerment:* individuals feel their own strength. A movement text can empower an individual to feel more deeply his or her own personal commitment.
3. *Harmonizing:* cultural forms can sometimes cut across lines of age, class, region, even ideology, providing a sense of overarching connection that, at least for a time, subordinates differences.
4. *Internal communication:* express or reinforce movement values, ideas, tactics, and so on. Movement aesthetic texts provide information in compact, often highly memorable and emotionally charged ways, both to educate new recruits and to refocus veterans.
5. *External communication:* express movement values, ideas, tactics, and so on to potential recruits, opponents, and undecided bystanders. Movement cultural texts can often be a more effective and affective means of promoting movement ideas to people outside the movement. Poster art has played a particularly important role in this regard, as have traveling movement culture groups like the Student Nonviolent Coordinating Committees "Freedom Singers" or the feminist art movement's "Guerrilla Girls."
6. *Enact movement goals:* art that actively intervenes directly to achieve values. Examples here might include eco-active art that helps restore an ecosystem, or a movement mural that improves the appearance in a neighborhood.
7. *Historicizing:* invent, tell, and retell the history of movement. This might range from an epic poem about the movement to a self-produced documentary about an action like Indymedia's "This Is What Democracy Looks Like: The Battle of Seattle."
8. *Transform affect:* set a new emotional tone (i.e., diffuse tension from anger to focused resistance, or from fear to calm resolve), or redirect attention of group (i.e., a song or giant puppet signaling a new stage of a demonstration).
9. *Critique movement ideology:* challenge dominant ideas, values, tactics, or undercut tendencies toward dogma by evoking emotions and meanings not reducible to narrowly ideological terms (as in a poem written to parody ideological rigidity in the movement).
10. *Give pleasure:* provide respite from the rigors of movement work through aesthetic joy in art texts *not* tied to movement work.

Culture in movements is, of course, never purely the creation of a movement. Various mainstream cultural forces continue to play through movement cultures, both because it is neither possible nor desirable to invent a full culture out of hand (not every element of mainstream culture is ideologically tainted) and because it is impossible to remain isolated from the continuing flow of mainstream culture (even deeply separatist movements maintain some reliance on the dominant system). Conversely, the mid-movement adoption of some elements of a movement culture by the mainstream may require it to reshape itself to retain its otherness (i.e., punk fashion undermining the protest function of punk clothing).

Conversely, one way to keep mainstream culture at bay is through appropriation via parody. Movements frequently take elements of mainstream culture and put a movement twist on them. The most common form is the appropriation and parody of mainstream music found in many movements. It is also present in *AIDS Coalition to Unleash Power*'s use of mainstream advertising techniques, a practice elaborated into a full-fledged movement unto itself in the form of groups like Adbusters, and others of the culture jamming school of social action.[21]

The cultural study of social movements also needs to take cognizance of various relationships between and among *movement cultures* (with their relatively well-defined, ideologically self-conscious but usually narrow core constituencies), *cultural and aesthetic formations* (with their more diffuse, less ideologically conscious but often broader constituencies), and *subcultures* (with their more or less political elements mediating between these other two). Because subcultures are treated elsewhere in this volume, I want to conclude with a few remarks on how movement cultures interact with cultural formations.

Cultural and aesthetic formations begin in the arts or in other intellectual circles and diffuse slowly into wider cultural circles.[22] Like movement cultures, they can have a wide or a narrow agenda in terms of opposition to dominant cultural forms, but unlike them, their first concern is usually thought of as aesthetic, rather than political (though often their work includes questioning the aesthetic/political dichotomy). Often, through a preceding process of movement culture diffusion, formations have some part of their origins in social movements, but generally they do not know of or acknowledge those origins. Cultural formations are at times virtually coextensive with a movement culture, as was the case with what Michael Denning has called the "cultural front" formation that emerged out of the radical labor and Communist movements in thirties America, or with many ethnic revival movements. On some occasions, parts of a cultural formation can be absorbed fully into a social movement (as with those European

Dadaists who joined the Communist movement). But usually the process is more mixed, as in the case of rap music, wherein you have a range from more overtly political message rap to implicitly oppositional forms to co-opted commercial modes.

Denning also makes a useful distinction between cultural politics and aesthetic ideologies when discussing cultural formations. The former he uses to name the complex of political and institutional affiliations, "the politics of letterheads and petitions, the stances taken by artists and intellectuals," and the history of the cultural-political institutions in which the new formation is embedded. Aesthetic ideologies, on the other hand, refers to the politics of form, the actual aesthetic practices, the forms, styles, genres, and conventions that emerge to embody the cultural politics.[23] Depending on the degree of autonomy insisted upon by the artists and intellectuals involved, the cultural politics and the aesthetic ideologies range from close alignment to considerable disjunction. Some politically committed artists have seen their art as a weapon in the struggle, some equally committed ones have insisted that their politics and their art are fully separable, and most have found positions between these poles. Frequently within the same cultural formation, there are a number of different aesthetic ideologies that need to be sorted out and judged by specific aesthetico-political criteria. Judging forms ranging from ephemeral works of "agit-prop" to complex works of art by the same criteria has often led to dismissive evaluations of all political art. In the 1930s, the cultural front contributed significantly to both major works of art like "Citizen Kane" and ephemeral works designed only for a very specific audience of workers on a picket line. Similarly, the cultural formations of the 1960s produced both street theater works meant to do their work for a few days, and contributed to the creation of brilliant works of literary art by Toni Morrison that will be read for hundreds of years.

One crucial dimension of the role of high art (as opposed to more purely instrumental cultural forms) in movements is to critique and transcend ideology. Complex aesthetic texts are always both ideological and in excess of ideology, and their role in and around movements can be to remind activists, who often are tempted by the pressures of political struggle into ideologically reductive positions, that the full lived complexity of cultural life cannot be reduced to any ideological system.

The central paradox is that the energies of radical movement cultures and aesthetic forms they generate have their greatest impact when they are *diffused* in less overtly ideological ways into the larger social arena via cultural movements. But that impact is largely *defused* (rendered ineffective) unless self-consciously ideological social movements continue their work. This ongoing, irresolvable, and creative tension between defusion and diffusion should be a key point of study for the aesthetic analysis of movements. We need to analyze more fully the processes by which movements help create contexts of cultural reception in relation to the production of alternative aesthetic cultures. The work on movement cultures is suggestive in this regard, but far more work needs to be done.

TV Reed is Lewis A and Stella E Buchanan distinguished professor of American studies and English at Washington State University in Pullman. His scholarly interests include interdisciplinary cultural theory, digital culture, environmental justice cultural studies, and the role of culture in social movements. His key social movement publications include *Fifteen Jugglers, Five Believers: Literary Politics and the Poetics of American Social Movements* (Berkeley, CA, 1992), and *The Art of Protest: Culture and Activism from the Civil Rights Movement to the Streets of Seattle* (Minneapolis, MN, 2005). He is the web editor/manager of *culturalpolitics.net*.

Notes

1. Charles Tilly, *Social Movements, 1768–2004* (Boulder, CO, 2004), 53.
2. Charles Tilly, "From Interactions to Outcomes in Social Movements," in *How Social Movements Matter*, ed. M Giugni, Doug McAdam, and Charles Tilly (Minneapolis, MN, 1999), 253–70.
3. For an analysis of movements as texts, see TV Reed, *Fifteen Jugglers, Five Believers: Literary Politics and the Poetics of Social Movements* (Berkeley, CA, 1992).
4. Susan G Davis, *Parades and Power* (Berkeley, CA, 1988), provides a rich history of eighteenth- and nineteenth-century protests, pageants, and marches.
5. The standard analysis of this tradition remains, Peter Burger, *Theory of the Avant-Garde* (Minneapolis, MN, 1984).
6. Ken Knabb, ed., *The Situationist Anthology* (Berkeley, CA, 1981); and Tom McDonagh, ed., *Guy Debord and the Situationist International: Texts and Documents* (Boston, 2004), provide a good sampling of Situationist writings, while their theory, practice, and influence are covered by Greil Marcus, *Lipstick Traces: A Secret History of the Twentieth Century* (Cambridge, MA, 1990); and Sadie Plant, *The Most Radical Gesture: The Situationist International in a Postmodern Age* (New York, 1992).
7. See Michail Bakhtin, *Rabelais and His World* (Bloomington, IN, 1965); and Peter Stallybrass and Allon White, *The Poetics and Politics of Transgression* (Ithaca, NY, 1988).
8. For the brilliant display of graphics in protest actions against HIV/AIDS, see Douglas Crimp and Adam Ralston, *AIDS DemoGraphics* (Seattle, 1990); for continuing work in the rich field of feminist and antiracist art, see Maura Reilly and Linda Nochlin, eds, *Global Feminisms: New Directions in Contemporary Art* (Buffalo, NY, 2007).

9. From the extensive literature on radical theater and performance art see, for example, James M Harding and Cindy Rosenthal, eds, *Restaging the Sixties: Radical Theaters and Their Legacies* (Ann Arbor, MI, 2006); and Jan Cohen-Cruz, ed., *Radical Street Performance: An International Anthology* (London, 1998). For a brief history of political puppetry see http://www.rogueruby.com/radpup.html.

10. The image of "Iraqnica" can be found at http://www.cyberhumanisme.org/matiere/tousterriens/gulfwarII/source/iraqnica.html.

11. On political murals, see Eva Cockcroft and Holly Barnet-Sanchez, eds, *Signs from the Heart: California Chicano Murals* (Venice, CA, 1990); Shifra Goldman, *Dimensions of the Americas: Art and Social Change in Latin America* (Chicago, 1994); and Alicia Gaspar de Alba, *Chicano Art inside/outside the Master's House: Cultural Politics and the CARA Exhibition* (Austin, TX, 1998).

12. Robert D Benford and Scott A Hunt, "Dramaturgy and Social Movements: The Social Construction and Communication of Power," *Sociological Inquiry* 62, no. 1 (1992): 36–55.

13. Wini Breines, *Community and Organization in the New Left, 1962–1968: The Great Refusal* (New Brunswick, 1989).

14. Noël Sturgeon, "Theorizing Movements: Direct Action and Direct Theory," in *Cultural Politics and Social Movements,* ed. M Darnovsky, Barbara Epstein, and Richard Flacks (Philadelphia, PA, 1995), 35–51.

15. Melucci's ideas can be found in compact form in "The Symbolic Challenge in Contemporary Movements," *Social Research* 52 (1985): 781–816, and in more elaborated form in his book, *Challenging Codes* (Cambridge, 1996).

16. Reed, *Fifteen Jugglers, Five Believers.*

17. For a summary of critiques of the Situationism, see Sadie Plant, *The Most Radical Gesture* (New York, 1992).

18. See, Paul Mann, *The Theory-Death of the Avant-Garde* (Bloomington, IN, 1991).

19. Doug McAdam, "Culture in Social Movements," in *Social Movements: Perspectives and Issues,* ed. SM Buechler and F Kurt Cylke (Mountain View, CA, 1997), 473–86.

20. John Lofland, "Charting Degrees of Movement Culture," in *Social Movements and Culture,* ed. H Johnston and B Klandermans (Minneapolis, MN, 1995), 188–216.

21. Naomi Klein discusses both the power and the limits of "culture jamming" as a social change strategy in *No Logo* (New York, 1999), especially 279–309.

22. Raymond Williams develops the notion of "formations" in *Marxism and Literature* (Oxford, 1977), and *The Sociology of Culture* (New York, 1981). Michael Denning in his book *The Cultural Front* (London, 1998) makes brilliant use of the "formation" concept in a 1930s social movement context.

23. See Michael Denning, *The Cultural Front* (New York, 1997), xix–xx.

Recommended Reading

Cockcroft, Eva, and Holly Barnet-Sanchez, eds. *Signs from the Heart: California Chicano Murals.* Venice, CA, 1990. Traces one of the most important examples of the mural form used in social protest.

Crimp, Douglas, and Adam Ralston, eds. *AIDS DemoGraphics.* Seattle, 1990. Offers images and analysis of the brilliant use of graphic art—posters, signs, buttons, sticker, T-shirt designs, and more—in the movement to bring AIDS to greater public awareness.

Harding, James M, and Cindy Rosenthal, eds. *Restaging the Sixties: Radical Theaters and Their Legacies.* Ann Arbor, MI, 2006. Includes historical roots and recent late twentieth-century use of theater as a mode of social protest.

Reed, TV. *The Art of Protest: Culture and Activism from the Civil Rights Movement to the Streets of Seattle.* Minneapolis, MN, 2005. Broad survey of various art forms (including music, drama, poetry, film, murals) as used in various U.S. social movements from the 1950s to the 2000s.

Chapter 7

Protest as a Media Phenomenon

Kathrin Fahlenbrach

General Definitions of Protest as a Media Phenomenon

Medium/Media

Considering protest as a media phenomenon requires, as a first step, taking into account basic dimensions of medium and media. In most general terms, a medium is something in between two or more entities, relating to the transmission of physical, technical, biological, and/or sociocultural information. Accordingly, different general definitions of medium/media might be discerned: physical media (e.g., the transmission of sound or light), technical media, implying a technical apparatus (e.g., in medical media instruments or broadcasting media), biological media, referring to the senses by which information data are received and processed (e.g., visual media, acoustic media, or audiovisual media), and sociocultural media, relating to conventions of communications (e.g., media as genres).[1] This selective list already demonstrates the relevance of different media in human communication. Even media that act as physical or biological transmitters can be part of human communication, whether in face-to-face communication or via technically based media.

Focusing more specifically on communication media, there are further ways to distinguish general categories, as proposed by media scholar Harry Pross.[2] He defines (1) *primary media* of communication, which include no technical devices, neither for the production nor the reception of information. Accordingly, they are restricted to biological and sociocultural media dimensions of human communication, such as facial expression, gestures, and spoken language; (2) *secondary media* involve technical devices for the production, but not the reception of information, such as written language or press media; and (3) *tertiary media* afford technological devices or apparatuses both for the production and reception of information, such as broadcasting media or computer-based media of communication. Media technologies are considered in media and communication studies as a key aspect in human communication.[3]

Other definitions of media focus more specifically on *mass media,* as technologically based media of human communication, but also take into account their social and cultural dimensions. Media scholars Schmidt and Zurstiege,[4] for example, distinguish four dimensions of communication media, which are all part of mass media: (1) *media technologies* for the production and reception of mass media products (e.g., TV studios and TV sets); (2) *semiotic systems* as communicative devices (e.g., linguistic, visual, or multimodal signs and codes); (3) *institutions* that manage, finance, and juristically represent media technologies and media products; this includes the social organization of a media institution (e.g., editorial office, management department, etc.); (4) the *media products* as results of the interaction by the previously mentioned dimensions of mass media (e.g., books, journals, movies, or TV shows). A relevant societal effect of mass media is their establishment of a dispersive public sphere. In contrast to local public spheres, based on distinct places[5] physically accessible for a broad public (e.g., the market place of a city), mass media generate a public space beyond such distinct localities, based on discourses.[6] However, mass media public spheres are shaped by the economic, political, and social power of single institutions and hence also act as arenas of discursive conflicts and struggles.[7] They allow those entering the restricted public arena as producers and distributors of information to diffuse their interests in a broad public in order to influence collective opinions, knowledge, memory, and sometimes even the actions of institutions and individuals in a society.

In fact, the asymmetrical situation of public spheres established by mass media has been changing with the rise of online media. Generally, all of the dimensions mentioned by Schmid and Zurstiege[8] also apply to online media as another category of technically based communication media. However, a general difference between them has to be acknowledged, in that online media differ from mass media by establishing an interactive relation between communicators. While in mass media individual institutions and actors distribute information to a broad audience (*one-to-many*), online media provide a bidirectional communication channel between senders and receivers of information data (*many-to-many*).

Media of Protest—Protest as a Medium

Considering the former definitions of medium/media allows some general aspects of protest as a media phenomenon to be discerned. Applying Pross's model, protest communication involves primary, secondary, and tertiary media.

1. *Primary media of protest*: face-to-face-communication and physical staging has been shown to be one of the most relevant aspects of both articulating protest and of mobilizing participants and public support. This includes first of all body performances[9] in all forms of public protest actions during demonstrations or the staging of "image events."[10] In the first case, the formation of a collective body serves as a symbol of contestation that is being manifested at a specific time and place.[11] As "action mobilization,"[12] the contesting collective body is performed in order to make a political statement and execute public pressure on their addressees. While acting collectively in situ as an embodied symbol of contestation, primary media of body language are used, such as shouting and singing, but also the rhythmic choreography of movements by running or walking as a medium of protest communication toward audiences. In the second case, primary media are restricted in fact to the bodily performance of small groups of activists or even individuals in a staged image event,[13] for example by disguising their body and performing in a symbolic way. This is often the case in staged image events, professionally organized by NGOs. Other, more artistic ways of protest performances, which are based on primary media are happenings,[14] dance,[15] or theater.

2. *Secondary media of protest*: protest cultures, from their very beginnings, have used written language (e.g., slogans on placards, written or printed pamphlets, or manifests),[16] images in the form of drawings, paintings, or photographs,[17] as well as music (live performances with instruments, e.g., during demonstrations or at oppositional festivals).[18] While secondary protest media are received and processed by our senses, their production includes technological devices such as instruments for writing or drawing, the camera, or the computer. This further implies technologies of reproduction for producing placards, leaflets, flyers, such as print technologies in graphics and press, computer copying, and so on.

3. *Tertiary media of protest*: as is outlined more specifically in the following, across the history of protest cultures, mass media as well as online media has taken on a key role in protest communication during the history of protest cultures. Technological devices and apparatuses are elementary tools for all actors included in protest communications for producing, distributing, and receiving contentious information: protest actors, their

directly accused addressees, the media institutions as indirect addressees, and the public sphere, including the audiences.

To provide, as a first step, a more specific phenomenological distinction between different aspects of mass media and online media in protest communication, the four dimensions introduced above[19] are applied in the following paragraph: (1) media institutions, (2) media technologies, (3) media as semiotic systems, and (4) media products.

As four dimensions of *Mass media* one can distinguish: (1) *Institutions* of mass media: these are public or private broadcasting organization and media companies as producers and providers of media products, but also national and international public institutions that guide and control them. In protest communication, these institutions follow economic and political criteria in their selection of information about protest events and movements. Activists and protest movements typically have no direct access to these institutions and decision makers. It is, rather, by addressing the selective criteria of news production in their public articulation of protest that they can sometimes influence their decisions (cf. 3: semiotic systems). Furthermore, they can relate their communication directly to individual journalists or representatives of media institutions as gate keepers. Depending on the closeness of a movements' aims and claims to the political profile and the values of a given media institution, they might have easier access to their public by personal contact.[20] (2) *Technologies of mass media:* These are for instance broadcasting stations, print presses, and electronic and digital channels of distribution which are provided and managed by the before mentioned public and economic institutions. Hence protest movements have limited access to such technologies. Only in building alternative mass media (e.g., journals or radio stations)[21] can they establish and manage their own technological infrastructure. Such activities have widely been replaced by the contentious use of online media (cf. below). In order to achieve broad public attention and visibility,[22] they are however still dependent on hegemonic mass media to disperse information about their aims and motifs via established technological infrastructures. (3) *Semiotic systems of mass media*: Dispersive public spheres have been introduced before as discursive spaces. As such, they are structured by communicative codes and signs, by semiotic knowledge and practices shared by those who enter these spaces.[23] This includes linguistic, visual, and multimodal (e.g., in audio-vision) codes and signs, as well as body language, expressive habits, and interaction styles,[24] performed in visual/audiovisual media. In their media products (e.g., TV shows, series, articles, features, advertisements, etc.), mass media and their institutions significantly determine the public use and meaning of such codes and signs. Protest movements and activists are hence confronted with hegemonic semiotic systems that they can either adapt strategically (cf. below), confront provocatively, or ignore.[25] Relevant aspects of standard semiotic systems that guide media coverage of protest are news values[26] that might be adapted by protesters in their public self-representation and articulation of protest. It is on this level of communication that the interrelation between protest movements and mass media has generated conventional standards in Western societies since the mid twentieth century.[27] Since discovering the news worthiness of protest performances, especially in visual and audiovisual mass media, paralleled by the chance to represent their own Western and democratic values, print media and TV tend to regularly cover protest events. Mass media possess, particularly in visual representation of protest, standardized semiotic codes and patterns related to recurrent media frames (e.g., those of confrontation, injustice, or democracy). (4) *Mass media products:* Products in the mass media that matter for protest communication include journalistic genres like news, features, or comments in press and TV. The only way for protesters to influence these products is mostly to address semiotic codes and signs of news coverage. Another option is to distribute alternative products via their own channels.

As four dimension of online-media one can distinguish: (1) *Institutions* in online media: The spectrum of institutions in online media is more heterogeneous than in mass media. Of course, the institutional providers of basic technological infrastructures (see below) are restricted to established media companies, often acting on a global market (e.g., providers of online access or of social web platforms, or telecommunication services) as well as national and international public institutions that determine general juristic and economic rules in online communication (e.g., at the European Commission or at U.S. Department of Homeland Security). At the same time, their institutional power has been minimized by the fact that nonestablished companies, noncommercial and political groups, and private users can spread software devices for public use (media technologies). On this basis, they can build hypertext infrastructures (e.g., web sites, blogs, social web networks) and use them to distribute media products (e.g., online videos) that they select or produce according to their specific interests and motifs (e.g., biographical, entertaining, or political). Accordingly, online media offer a high range of possibilities for protesters to establish alternative infrastructures and institutions (e.g., "indymedia") that allow them to manage information distribution both within and without their networks. Yet, they are still dependent on hegemonic media institutions that provide them with basic infrastructure and determine the general juristic and economic rules and limits of protest communication (e.g., rules on authorship for online sources or censorship of radical right-wing movements). (2) *Technologies of online media*: The hegemonic institutions of online media are at the same time restrict and enable protest movements and activists to build their own public spheres. On the one hand, activists use commercial technologies of social networks and online platforms (e.g., Facebook, Twitter, or YouTube) in order to quickly distribute information to their participants (such as a call for participation at a demonstration or a smart mob), to direct addressees of their claims (e.g., online petitions to public institutions or companies) or to mass media (such as press information). More generally, activists are dependent on computer technology provided by media companies, including all types of apparatuses as necessary hardware, to participate in online communication at all (e.g., personal computer, tablet, or mobile phone). On the other hand, hacktivist movements (e.g., *Anonymous*) and other independent programmers and collectives established new standards of do-it-yourself technologies in protest cultures by providing users with alternative software devices and online platforms to exchange and spread information (cf. WikiLeaks). Consequently, technological skills are relevant resources for contentious communication in online media.

(3) *Semiotic codes and signs in online media*: In the interactive realm of the Internet, the public spheres of online media and their semiotic codes and signs are much less dominated by hegemonic media institutions than in mass media public spheres. In contrast, a "participatory culture"[28] has been established in online media that is widely shaped by codes and practices of individualism, authenticity, and do-it-yourself. Given the virtual character of online communication, it has been shown that there is a growing relevance of communicating in an authentic way (e.g., in the so-called Blogosphere[29]). This might result, for example, in a more extensive use of affective language, pictorial emoticons, or images. At the same time, the participatory culture is coined by individual, ironical, and partly subversive recontextualization[30] and resemiotization[31] of codes and signs established in hegemonic public spheres. A prominent example is the production and dissemination of mash-up videos that recompose sequences from well-known movies or TV series, giving them a new meaning. Such popular practices have their roots in protest culture and more specifically in oppositional culture-jamming-practices like adbusting.[32] Linguistic, visual, or multimodal signs and codes, once established by the contested systems (e.g., the political system or the economic system) are adapted and subversively recoded with oppositional meanings.[33] Semiotic rules and forms guiding political campaigns or ads for example are simulated and distributed with contentious messages via online platforms, social media, or on web sites. The most efficient adbusting campaigns gain public attention both on the Internet and in the mass media (e.g., the campaign of the anticorporate group *Adbusters* against Dow Chemical

in 2003[34]), what is mostly achieved by viral guerilla tactics in spreading a subversive spot or image.

(4) *Products of online media*: Relevant *products* of online media resulting from online communication by institutions and users who are involved in the external or internal representation of protest are journalistic articles, features, and news published on online releases of journals and TV stations, as well as their contextualization by hypertexts, including video uploads. Some of these institutional web sites also imply interactive platforms that allow readers and viewers to leave their comments, comments which themselves contribute to the framing of protest coverage. For the internal self-representation and communication of protesters, relevant media products are: web sites and blogs that present relevant information, opinions, claims, and links, as well as mailing lists, online petitions, online videos, tweets, and Facebook messages (cf. Cyberprotest).[35]

Role of Protest as a Media Phenomenon in Culture and in Protest Culture

Protest as a media phenomenon as described above continues to occupy and influence Western culture, including social hierarchies and roles, cultural values and norms, as well as cultural practices.

In premodern, feudal societies, protest has been performed solely on the basis of primary media: contesting bodies that formed a mass, confronting a sovereign with the rage of the people. As Koopman[36] states, this has been the era of direct protest, addressed toward a personified power (such as a monarch or a lord). But as a relevant effect of the Enlightenment and social modernization of Western societies, power dispersed since the seventeenth century into complex systems, for example, of politics, economy, and education, generated what Foucault called a "structural power."[37] As he went on to argue, such structural power is effectively executed since the seventeenth century in discourses and cultural practices that regulate social life in public (e.g., education styles in school or punitive sanctions in prison) and private (e.g., sexuality). This is a relevant reason why the practice of directing protest to a single person in possession of power became irrelevant. Instead, protest in modern times is being addressed *indirectly* against institutions accused of being responsible for a crisis or problem[38] and by directing the mass media as a transmitter of protest. Obviously, with the rise of mass media technologies, the public sphere changed radically as a place of contentious communication. Consequently, protest as a media phenomenon changed its cultural forms and impacts.

Mass media established a virtual form of public spheres in early modern societies that were the result of social change. Even more than this, they enabled the development of a new social and democratic order. In premodern Western societies, the public sphere was a local and physical one: places within a city, usually the market place, that have been used for public meetings, announcements, or political acclamations. At such places, the public sphere was established by the physical encounter of people being there at the same time.

After the invention of the printing press by Johannes Gutenberg around 1440, public spheres have been released more and more from such local and temporal fixation and have been broadened into discursive spaces into which audiences and communicators might enter into at different places and times. The mass production and distribution of books, journals, and magazines that followed Gutenberg's invention gave rise to public spheres that encompassed audiences and communicators across social and local borders.[39] Acting as a promoter for broad education and literacy in Western societies, the printing press was not only a result of the Enlightenment, but also a key factor in social change, namely the change from aristocratic to democratic societies in Europe. As such, it initiated not only the spreading of knowledge and information. It provided revolutionaries and protesters with new media for contestation. In the upheavals and revolutions of people in feudal societies during the eighteenth century, especially in France and Germany, the printing press was used to produce leaflets and bulletins as secondary media to mobilize people on the streets. During the French Revolution, such media helped the contesting actors address their followers and inform and mobilize even more people to participate at upheavals like the storming of the Bastille. Hence, these print media were used as early alternative media, generating a temporally limited virtual public sphere, closely linked with the local public sphere and its physical places of contestation, but also widening it. With the later inventions of mass media technologies in the nineteenth and early twentieth century, like photography, film, and broadcasting, the cultural forms of contestation and their impact on culture in society changed eminently.

Protest cultures in the early era of mass media in late nineteenth and early twentieth century still restricted their contentious communication to primary and secondary media: the labor movement or the women's movement of this time articulated their protest by collectively marching into the streets or, in front of factories, enhancing their symbolic performance via the use of flags and placards. More than in the upheavals at the edge of modernity, they used local public places as symbolic places. Although they no longer addressed a distinct personal power, but a political and economic system of power, including the values and norms being established in society and culture (e.g., gendered values), they formed a collective body of contestation that symbolically occupied significant public spaces of urban metropoles such as Berlin or London. In the early democracies of France or Germany (Weimar Republic), this symbolic presence already could be used as a political resource by the activists. However, in many European countries, mass media were strongly controlled by political institutions, and also guided by commercial interests that contrasted with the emancipative claims of workers or women. Hence, these movements hardly had any chance to enter the mass media public sphere. Yet some profited from mass media technologies when using them to produce and spread their own, oppositional print media (e.g., in the German labor movement journal *Vorwärts*).[40] While the cultural impact of these movements was, over the long term, based on their political and institutional effects (e.g., the implementation of voting rights for women or the limitation of labor time for workers), the cultural impact of protest movements increased significantly with their growing public visibility in mass media.

A historic change in the interrelation between protest movements and mass media institutions can be observed in the late 1960s.[41] At this time, several moments of cultural, social, and media change came together and created new potential for protesters to gain in public visibility and also impact on public spheres and on culture. At this time, mass media expanded their technological and economic range of infrastructures and products. A rising media economy aimed to produce and sell media technologies and media products in ever-growing markets beyond the borders of nation states. As a result, public spheres were widened across national borders. Movies, lifestyle and fashion magazines, advertisements, TV shows, and photographs have been increasingly produced and offered for international markets since the mid twentieth century. This widening of mass media public spheres was accompanied by an attendant dominance of commercial interests and motifs. This also affected journalism that covered political events and actors. Since this time, news and political coverage have to be not only informative but entertaining. Reinforced by a growing competition for public attention, selective criteria evolved to evaluate the attractiveness of information for audiences in terms of spectacle, human touch, visuality, or local/national relevance.[42] This has been accompanied since the 1960s by a cultural change that promoted in Western societies "postmaterial values"[43] such as hedonism, individuality, and autonomy. Protest movements in the late 1960s echoed this cultural change and were even a relevant part of it. Antiauthoritarian movements, student movements, or the new feminist movement have been agents of a cultural change toward postmaterial cultural values, identities, and cultural practices. All these factors—change of mass media, general cultural change in Western societies, and change of protest cultures—provided new conditions for protest as a media phenomenon and its cultural impacts. On the one hand, new forms and media of protest have been generated that influenced protest cultures until today. The body has been used as a primary medium in new expressive forms of symbolic performances. In sit-ins, go-ins, teach-ins, and other public happenings, it was not only the mass of a collective body of contestation that made an argument, but also the very form of its staging and its reference to the symbolic meaning of the place where it takes place. Furthermore, with rising mass media attention, such performances also addressed the dispersive public sphere.

As secondary media, not only placards and flags have been used (as classical media of contestation), but a broad range of new symbols and images, including photographs and pictures from the press (e.g., depicting victims of Vietnam War). Contentious imagery has been used both at public places during demonstrations or happenings, and in alternative media (journals, magazines, pamphlets, etc.). Furthermore, contentious imagery on posters was put in private rooms and even onto an individual's body when printed on T-shirts and other clothes. This blending of protest communication in public and private spheres, and of political and expressive claims around hedonistic and emancipative ideas of identity, provided strong news values for media coverage. Even in negative framing,[44] the spectacular and symbolic image character of their self-representations offered these movements regular attention by the mass media in many Western countries. As a consequence, not just local public spheres and alternative media, but also mass media were addressed in a strategic fashion. It was the close interrelation between general cultural change, change to the mass media public sphere—implying a significant upgrading of images in public communication—and change in protest cultures, that offered the chance to new social movements to get visible in broad public.[45] This visibility was used both as a political resource to change public opinions and to mobilize further sympathizers and participants.

Since the new social movements in the late 1960s, protest cultures professionalized their strategies to enter mass media at the semiotic level of symbolic self-representation and also by addressing single gate keepers in the media institutions (see above). Hence protest in the late 1960s, in its different mediated forms, also had a significant impact on subsequent protest cultures. This is also the case for cultural practices and protest in online media today. Subversive and Situationist tactics of happenings and guerilla communication continue to be employed when activists call for participation in smart and flash mobs or in virally spreading adbusting campaigns.[46]

Another historic change in protest as a media phenomenon can be considered in the rising use of online media. While the new options for contentious communication provided by the Internet have been sketched above, the cultural impact is also substantial. Most significantly, the barrier to participate in contentious communication has been lowered for a broad public by the wide spreading of online petitions and the gathering of online support. While the public acceptance of protest and the will to participate has been widened in many countries and cultures around the globe, not only in Western countries, but also in Africa or Asia[47]—the commitment to a specific movement and its collective identity is often lowered.

As has been stated by several scholars however,[48] the dominant use of online media by protesters did not result, until now, in a decrease in demonstrations and protest actions in local public places. In contrast, it seems that physical actions and the use of the body as a primary medium even gained new relevance in a globalized public sphere of contestation. Given the tendency of lower commitment in online communication, physical actions allow activists to visually and bodily manifest the existence of their network and its impact.

Research Perspectives

Until the early 1990s, protest as a media phenomenon has been widely ignored in research. Up to then, the pioneering study of Gitlin, first published in 1977,[49] had a unique position in exploring the complex interrelation between protest and mass media. The study investigates the framing of the student movement in the U.S. mass media and its effects for the internal and external representation of the movement.

It was only around 1990 that protest as a media phenomenon received a broader interest in research, focusing first of all on the impact of mass media for social movements. With the establishment of social movement theories such as resource mobilization theory or framing theory and the professionalization of media strategies by NGOs and activists (e.g., in the peace movement or the environmental movement), scholars began to investigate the interrelation between mass media and social movements. Apart from empirical case studies,[50] this includes systematic approaches dealing with the media strategies of protest actors,[51] and interrelations between protest movements and the media in public spheres.[52]

In subsequent studies, two general perspectives evolved that were valid until recently: (a) research on the representation of protest by mass media, and (b) research dealing with the strategic address of mass media rules and gate keepers by activists in order to receive public visibility as a relevant political resource.[53] Both perspectives generally share a focus on social actors in protest communication, be it protesters and their organizations, or representatives and institutions in mass media. This scope on different actors and their interests in protest communication as well as their infrastructures and resources characterizes the foremost sociological research that widely dominates the examination of protest as a media phenomenon so far, while studies in other disciplines are rather scarce.

Since the two influential studies by Gitlin[54] and McAdam,[55] who investigated mass media coverage of the Black Power movement, the representation of protest in mass media is mostly analyzed via framing theory. Based on research in cognitive psychology,[56] sociology,[57] media studies,[58] and other disciplines, framing theory has been applied to social movement research, for example, by Snow.[59] *Frames* are understood as guiding cognitive schemata that structure our knowledge in order to make sense of the world. In recent framing theory in media and communication research, the works of SD Reese[60] and Entman[61] have been central in exploring how social phenomena are constructed by the media, subsequently affecting the audience's interpretation. Entman[62] argued that all framings will contribute to (1) a definition and a limitation of the problem, (2) an identification of the cause to the problem, (3) a basis for moral judgment, and (4) a suggestion of solutions. Media framing in reverse can change further framings in the news. This reflexive discursive dynamic of media framing significantly affects the public representation of protest movements and actions. It is relevant that, as Gamson and Wolfsfeld,[63] Gamson,[64] and other scholars have demonstrated, the interaction between social movements and mass media occurs via frames as culturally, ideologically, and cognitively based patterns of interpretation. Media framing is manifested in the way mass media contextualize, interpret, and evaluate protest news by comments and pictures, and also by the selective presentation of speakers and actors. Framing theory distinguishes media frames that either legitimize or delegitimize protest actions.[65] This might include frames that marginalize and trivialize activists, or which polarize protesters and police by framing one part of them as aggressive and the other as peaceful.

Research dealing with mass media strategies by social movements in order to receive public visibility as a relevant political resource often investigate how they address news values and single gate keepers in the media. Rucht[66] provides a more general perspective. He distinguishes four basic attitudes of movements toward mass media: (a) the explicit *abstention* from entering the mass media public sphere and (b) the building of *alternative* media; (c) the *attack* of mass media, implying a fundamental critique of their infrastructure, their ideologies, and their contents; and (d) the *adoption* of the mass media rules and their selective criteria of news coverage. Rucht's distinction of the four attitudes implies a historical perspective on different kinds of social movements that are either more self-oriented and often differ more radically from the established common sense in a society (e.g., anarchist movements); and externally oriented movements that share a broader common sense with their context (e.g., peace movement, feminist movement).

Another approach, considering the reflexive interrelation between social movements and mass media has been proposed by Koopmans.[67] In his ecological approach, he determines mass media public sphere as an ecological system with public attention as a restricted resource that different actors are fighting for (e.g., political representatives, organizations, companies, etc.). As per the rules of mass media, only those actors are successful in getting this resource, those who adequately anticipate the reactions of their addressees. By selective attention, performed by mass media and the audience, a balance of discursive power is being established. This balance reinforces the most adaptive actors and weakens the nonadaptive ones. And this, when the criteria of selective attention change, also implies historical change.

While all these approaches manifest the asymmetrical disposition of protest movements in a mass media public sphere, research on protest as a media phenomenon gained new perspectives with the rise of the Internet. Since the beginning of the twenty-first century, broad attention is given to the impact of ICT (Information Communication Technology) and different online media for protest communication.[68] Accordingly, research in the framing and representation of protest by hegemonic actors decreased. The Internet is considered as a new resource of mobilization, providing movements and activists with an increased public power. As the hegemonic relations in the discursive and political field of contentious communication grow more complex and the limits between producers, distributors, and receivers of protest information become increasingly blurred, it is obvious that scholars strive for more integrative approaches when dealing with protest as a media phenomenon today. In recent years, some volumes and studies have been presented, advocating for multidimensional perspectives that recognize the close interrelation between contentious media practices by activists, mass media, and audiences. Cammaerts, Mattoni, and McCurdy[69] propose the concept of *mediation* for conceptualizing the fact that protest communication is being mediated today along the blurred borders between activists and audiences, producers, and users of contentious communication, but also between online and mass media. Accordingly, protest as a media phenomenon cannot be analyzed adequately anymore by strictly distinguishing actors striving for resources (public, political, etc.) and others striving to achieve them by the use of different strategies. Rather, it has to be acknowledged that protest communication in the age of the Internet is a fluid and context-dependent process that can hardly be predicted. In this process, power positions between once hegemonic and nonhegemonic actors might change immediately.[70] This includes the potential of single forms of protest, be it demonstrations, symbols, or images, generated in the close interaction, for example, between activists, users, mass media, and the audiences. In an often unforeseeable manner, single pictures or videos get worldwide attention, providing local activists immediately with a strong resource of mobilization. Accordingly, Cammaerts, Mattoni, and McCurdy consider symbolic and discursive elements in their model of mediation of protest communication.

From a media studies approach, it could be said that, apart from technological media (such as tertiary media), primary and secondary media received a new importance in the age of the Internet: both the bodily performances of protest actions by collective masses and by individual activists (primary media), and their representation in photographs, graffiti, videos, and so on, as well as the use of masks, flags, and symbols (as secondary media) might gain quicker public attention than during the period when only mass media dominated the public sphere. Hence, symbolic material provides a growing potential for protest mobilization in a public sphere increasingly characterized by the participatory culture of the Internet.

Research Gaps

Given recent developments, further research and more systematic approaches are needed, ones that consider the implications of specific kinds of media and the different symbolic forms of protest in several public spheres. It seems that media literacy is of growing relevance, not only for social movements and activists, but also for researchers of protest. This implies the consideration of current media technologies and practices. To give an example: media-based protest practices like adbusting, flash mobbing, or the viral dispersion of Internet memes are being adapted by advertisement (guerilla advertising) and software providers that offer users to participate in such practices just for entertainment (*know your meme*).[71] Hence, media practices might change from the contentious to the affirmative. Accordingly, together with a more specific acknowledgment of media technologies, the dynamically changing semiotics of the different media forms have to be recognized more specifically in protest research. This also implies a broadening of the scope of media understanding by investigating the use of primary (body language) and secondary media (like images, written language, etc.) in different, yet interrelated, public spheres: the local public sphere of the street, as well as virtual public spheres established by online and mass media. The Internet is a hybrid medium that connects diverse kinds of media into multimodal hypertexts. Given that it has also attained a key relevance in also relating different public spaces, the media literacy in knowing technological preconditions and semiotic codes of media practices by different actors is of growing importance for research.

Sociological and historical research has established fundamental approaches to study the actor-based resources, strategies, and interrelations in protest communication. Media studies could contribute more to investigate the technological and semiotic impact of different kinds of media for contentious communication. This implies systematic analyses of codes and signs in specific media products as they are created by different producers, like activists, journalists, or users on the Internet. As far as specific linguistic, image-based, or acoustically created artifacts or media products are concerned, methods from linguistics, literary studies, image studies, and music studies could contribute to an interdisciplinary investigation of the material and semiotic character of protest as a media phenomenon. Furthermore, discourse analysis and cultural studies provide important approaches to investigate the discursive conflicts and power relations between different actors involved in contentious communication.[72] Accordingly, a public sphere might be understood as an arena of contestation, where hegemonic and nonhegemonic actors fight for accomplishing their readings of a conflict, including its identification, interpretation, and solution. Following Hall,[73] the discursive dynamic of these struggles can be explored by observing the coding and decoding of contentious messages across media and the areas of different actors involved. Again, this would allow for a more integrative investigation of protest as a media phenomenon without isolating specific actors or media.

The complexity and the interrelatedness of technologies, semiotics, actors, and institutions in protest as a media phenomenon calls for more interdisciplinary research, combining approaches and methods from sociology, history, media and cultural studies, and humanities.

Kathrin Fahlenbrach is professor for media studies at the Department for Media and Communication at the University of Hamburg, Germany. Relevant areas of her research include media and visual codes in protest communication, cognitive and affective aesthetics of film and television, metaphors, and icons in media culture. She is author of the book *Protest-*

inszenierungen. Kollektive Identitäten und visuelle Kommunikation in Protest-bewegungen (Opladen, 2002) and editor of *Media and Revolt. Strategies and Performances from the 1960s to the Present.* (New York, 2014) (together with Rolf Werenskjold and Erling Sivertsen), as well as of *Embodied Metaphors in Film, Television, and Video Games: Cognitive Approaches* (London/New York 2016). Together with Martin Klimke and Joachim Scharloth, she is editor of the book series "Protest, Culture, and Society" at Berghahn Books (New York).

Notes

1. Cf. Roland Posner, "Nonverbale Zeichen in öffentlicher Kommunikation," *Zeitschrift für Semiotik* 7, no. 3 (1985): 237–71.
2. Harry Pross, *Publizistik: Thesen zu einem Grundcolloquium* (Neuwied, 1970).
3. For example, Marshall McLuhan, *The Gutenberg Galaxy. The Making of Typography* (Toronto, 1964); Marshall McLuhan, *Understanding Media. The Extensions of Men* (New York, 1964); Vilém Flusser, *Into the Universe of the Technical Images* (Minneapolis, MN, 2011).
4. Siegfried J Schmidt and Guido Zurstiege, *Orientierung Kommunikationswissenschaft. Was sie kann, was sie will* (Reinbek, 2000).
5. Michel De Certeau, *The Practice of Everyday Life* (Berkeley, CA, 1984).
6. Stuart Hall, "Encoding and Decoding," in *Media and Cultural Studies,* ed. MG Durham and DM Kellner (Malden, MA, 2001), 166–76.
7. Stuart Hall, *Representation. Cultural Representation and Signifying Practices* (London, 1993); Chris Barker and Dariusz Galasínski, *Cultural Studies and Discourse Analysis. A Dialogue on Language and Identity* (London, 2001).
8. Schmidt and Zurstiege, *Orientierung Kommunikationswissenschaft.*
9. Andrea Pabst, "Bodies and Bodily Protest: A Plea for a 'Thinking through the Body' in Social Movement Research," in *Between the Avant Garde and the Everyday: Subversive Politics in Europe, 1958 to the Present,* ed. TS Brown and L Anton (New York, 2011), 191–200.
10. John W Delicath and Kevin M De Luca, "Image Events, the Public Sphere, and Argumentative Practice: The Case of Radical Environmental Groups," *Argumentation* 17 (2003): 315–33.
11. Cf. Kathrin Fahlenbrach, *Protestinszenierungen. Visuelle Kommunikation und kollektive Identitäten in Protestbewegungen* (Wiesbaden, 2002); Pabst, "Bodies and Bodily Protest."
12. Bert Klandermans, *The Social Psychology of Protest* (Oxford, 1997).
13. Delicath and De Luca, "Image Events, the Public Sphere, and Argumentative Practice."
14. Cf. Bernd Jürgen Warneken, ed., *Massenmedium Straße. Zur Kulturgeschichte der Demonstrationen* (Frankfurt, 1991); Matthias Reiss, ed., *The Street as Stage. Protest Marches and Public Rallies since the Nineteenth Century* (Oxford, 2007).

15. Cf. Eva Aymamí-Reñé, "Kissing the Cactus. Dancing Gender and Politics in Spain" (unpublished dissertation, 2008); and in this volume.
16. Cf. Joachim Scharloth, *1968. Eine Kommunikationsgeschichte* (Paderborn, 2011).
17. Antigoni Memou, *Photography and Social Movements. From Globalization of the Movement (1968) to the Movement against Mobilization (2001)* (Manchester, 2013).
18. Cf. Beate Kutschke and Barton Norton, eds, *Music and Protest* (New York, 2013);
19. Schmidt and Zurstiege, *Orientierung Kommunikationswissenschaft.*
20. Todd Gitlin, *The Whole World Is Watching. Mass Media and the Making and Unmaking of the New Left* (Berkeley, CA, 2003); Dieter Rucht, "The Quadruple 'A': Media Strategies of Protest Movements since the 1960s," in *Cyber Protest: New Media, Citizens and Social Movements,* ed. W Van den Donk, BD Loader, PG Nixon, and D Rucht (London, 2004), 29–57; Ruud Koopmans, "Movements and Media: Selection Processes and Evolutionary Dynamics in the Public Sphere," *Theory and Society* 33, no. 3–4 (2004): 367–91.
21. Cf. Alice Mattoni, *Media Practices and Protest Politics: How Precarious Workers Mobilize* (Farnham, England, 2012).
22. Cf. Nicole Doerr, Alice Mattoni, and Simon Teune, eds, *Advances in the Visual Analysis of Social Movements* (Bingley, UK, 2013).
23. Hall, *Representation*; Peter Ludes, Winfried Nöth, and Kathrin Fahlenbrach, "Critical Visual Theory," *Triple C. Communication, Capitalism, and Critique: Journal for a Global Sustainable Information Society* 12, no. 1 (2014).
24. Erving Goffman, *Frame Analysis: An Essay on the Organization of Experience* (New York, 1974).
25. Cf. Rucht, "The Quadruple 'A.'"
26. Johan Galtung and Mari H Ruge, "The Structure of Foreign News. The Presentation of the Congo, Cuba and Cyprus Crises in Our Norwegian Newspapers," *Journal of Peace Research* 2, no. 1 (1965): 64–91; Paul Brighton and Dennis Foy, *News Values* (Thousand Oaks, CA, 2007).
27. Cf. Katrin Fahlenbrach, Erling Sivertsen, and Rolf Werenskjold, eds, *Media and Revolt. Performances and Strategies from the 1960s to the Present* (Oxford, 2014).
28. Henry Jenkins, *Convergence Culture—Where Old and New Media Collide* (New York, 2006); Jean Burgess and Joshua Green, *YouTube. Online Video and Participatory Culture* (Cambridge, 2009).
29. Cf. Michael Keren, *Blogosphere. The New Political Arena* (Plymouth, 2006); Adrienne Russel and Nabil Echchaibi, *International Blogging. Identity, Politics, and Networked Publics* (New York, 2009).
30. Michele Knobel and Colin Lankshear, "Remix: The Art and Craft of Endless Hybridization," *Journal of Adolescent & Adult Literacy* 52, no. 1 (2008): 22–33.
31. Rick Iedema, "Resemiotization," *Semiotica* 137, no. 1–4 (2001): 23–39.
32. Kalle Lasn, *Culture Jam: How to Reverse America's Suicidal Consumer Binge—And Why We Must* (New York, 2000).
33. Cf. Siegrid Baringhorst, Verena Kneip, and Johanna Niesyto, eds, *Political Campaigning on the Web* (Bielefeld, 2009).
34. Cf. Kathrin Fahlenbrach, "Protest in Television. Visual Protest on Screen," in *Media and Revolt. Strategies and Performances from the 1960s to the Present,* ed. K Fahlenbrach, R Werenskjold, and E Sivertsen (New York, 2014), 234–50.

35. Cf. W Lance Bennett, "New Media Power: The Internet and Global Activism," in *Contesting Media Power: Alternative Media in a Networked World,* ed. N Couldry and J Curran (Lanham, MD, 2003); Wim Van de Donk, Brian D Loader, Paul G Nixon, and Dieter Rucht, eds, *Cyber Protest: New Media, Citizens and Social Movements* (London, 2004).

36. Koopmans, "Movements and Media."

37. Michel Foucault, *Discipline and Punish. The Birth of Prison* (New York, 1979).

38. Cf. Koopmans, "Movements and Media."

39. Cf. McLuhan, *The Gutenberg Galaxy.*

40. Via agit-prop cinema, activists in the Russian Revolution even produced movies to mobilize people affectively.

41. Fahlenbrach, Sivertsen, and Werenskjold, *Media and Revolt.*

42. Cf. Galtung and Ruge, "The Structure of Foreign News"; and Brighton and Foy, *News Values.*

43. Ronald Inglehart, *The Silent Revolution* (Princeton, NJ, 1977).

44. Cf. Gitlin, *The Whole World Is Watching.*

45. Cf. Fahlenbrach, *Protestinszenierungen.*

46. Cf. Baringhorst, Kneip, and Niesyto, *Political Campaigning on the Web.*

47. Cf. Lusike Lynete Mukhongo, "Negotiating the New Media Platforms: Youth and Political Images in Kenya," *Triple C. Communication, Capitalism, and Critique: Journal for a Global Sustainable Information* Society 12, no. 1 (2014): 328–41.

48. For example, Rucht, "The Quadruple 'A'"; Marion Hamm, "Proteste im hybriden Kommunikationsraum: Zur Mediennutzung sozialer Bewegungen," *Forschungs-journal Neue Soziale Bewegungen* 19 (2006): 77–90.

49. Gitlin, *The Whole World Is Watching.*

50. For example, Doug McAdam, "The Framing Function of Movement Tactics. Strategic Dramaturgy in the American Civil Rights Movement," in *Comparative Perspectives on Social Movements. Political Opportunities, Mobilizing Structures, and Cultural Framings,* ed. JD McCarthy and MN Zald (Cambridge, 1996); Douglas M McLeod, "Communicating Deviance: The Effects of Television News Coverage of Social Protest," *Journal of Broadcasting and Electronic Media* 39, no. 4 (1995): 4–19.

51. For example, Rüdiger Schmitt-Beck, "Über die Bedeutung der Massenmedien für Soziale Bewegungen," *Kölner Zeitschrift für Soziologie und Sozialpsychologie* 42, no. 4 (1990): 642–62; William A Gamson and Gadi Wolfsfeld, "Movements and Media as Interacting Systems," *Annals of the American Academy of Political and Social Science* 528 (1993): 114–25.

52. Dieter Rucht, "Öffentlichkeit als Mobilisierungsfaktor für soziale Bewegungen," in *Öffentlichkeit, öffentliche Meinung, soziale Bewegungen,* ed. F Neidhardt (Opladen, 1994), 337–59; Jürgen Gerhards, *Neue Konfliktlinien in der Mobilisierung öffent-licher Meinung. Eine Fallstudie* (Opladen, 1993).

53. For example, Rucht, "The Quadruple 'A'"; Koopmans, "Movements and Media"; Patrick McCurdy, "Social Movements, Protest, and Mainstream Media," *Sociology Compass* 6, no. 2 (2012): 244–55. In a similar way, McCurdy distinguishes in his research overview between "representational" and "relational" research.

54. Gitlin, *The Whole World Is Watching.*

55. McAdam, "The Framing Function of Movement Tactics."
56. Frederic C Bartlett, *Remembering: A Study in Experimental and Social Psychology* (Cambridge, 1932).
57. Goffman, *Frame Analysis*.
58. Gaye Tuchman, *Making News: A Study in the Construction of Reality* (New York, 1978).
59. David A Snow and Robert D Benford, "Ideology, Frame Resonance, and Participant Mobilization," *International Social Movement Research* 1 (1988): 197–217.
60. Stephen D Reese, Oscar H Gandy, and August E Grant, *Framing Public Life: Perspectives on Media and Our Understanding of the Social World* (Mahwah, NJ, 2001); Stephen D Reese, "The Framing Project: A Bridging Model for Media Research Revisited," *Journal of Communication* 57 (2007): 119–41.
61. Robert M Entman, "Framing Bias: Media in the Distribution of Power," *Journal of Communication* 57 (2007): 163–73.
62. Robert M Entman, "Framing: Towards a Clarification of a Fractured Paradigm," *Journal of Communication* 43, no. 4 (1993): 51–58.
63. Gamson and Wolfsfeld, "Movements and Media as Interacting Systems."
64. William Gamson, "Bystanders, Public Opinion, and the Media," in *The Blackwell Companion to Social Movements,* ed. D Snow, SA Soule, and H Kriesi (Malden, MA, 2006), 242–61.
65. Recent studies based on framing approaches are presented in Fahlenbrach, Sivertsen, and Werenskjold, *Media and Revolt*. Many of these studies are focused on visual framing of protest in mass media (e.g., Stuart Hilwig, "Constructing a Media Image of the Sessantotto: The Framing of the Italian Protest Movement in 1968"; Antigoni Memou, "Revolt in Photos: The French May 68 in the Student and Mainstream Press"; Erling Sivertsen and Rolf Werenskjold, "Photos in Frames or Frames in Photos? The Global 1968 Revolts in Three Norwegian Dailies").
66. Rucht, "The Quadruple 'A.'"
67. Koopmans, "Movements and Media."
68. Bennett, "New Media Power: The Internet and Global Activism"; Van de Donk, Loader, Nixon, and Rucht, *Cyber Protest*.
69. Bart Cammaerts, Alice Mattoni, and Patrick McCurdy, eds, *Mediation and Protest Movements* (Bristol, 2013).
70. Significant examples are the revolutions in North Africa after 2010 (Arab Spring) or in Ukraine in 2013 ("Euromaidan").
71. Cf. Stefka Hristova, "Visual Memes as Neutralizers of Political Dissent," *Triple C. Communication, Capitalism, and Critique: Journal for a Global Sustainable Information Society* 12, no. 1 (2014): 265–76.
72. Hall, *Representation. Cultural Representation and Signifying Practices*; Barker and Galasínski, *Cultural Studies and Discourse Analysis*; Ludes, Nöth, and Fahlenbrach, "Critical Visual Theory."
73. Hall, *Representation. Cultural Representation and Signifying Practices*; Hall, "Encoding and Decoding."

Recommended Reading

Cammaerts, Bart, Alice Mattoni, and Patrick McCurdy, eds. *Mediation and Protest Movements*. Bristol, 2013. Cammaerts, Mattoni, and McCurdy offer in their approach to *mediation* of protest a helpful method to analyze the manifold and collective dynamic in protest communication, including not only activists, but also audiences and different users of protest communication in mass media and on the Internet.

Fahlenbrach, Kathrin, Rolf Werenskjold, and Erling Sivertsen, eds. *Media and Revolt. Strategies and Performances from the 1960s to the Present*. New York, 2014. This presents a spectrum of studies on protest performed in and by press, television, film, and photography, with a strong emphasis on framing theory.

Gitlin, Todd. *The Whole World Is Watching. Mass Media and the Making and Unmaking of the New Left*. Berkeley, 2003. This is pioneer work and, until today, one of the most influential studies on the interplay between protest movements, especially the student movement of the 1960s and mass media.

Mattoni, Alice. *Media Practices and Protest Politics: How Precarious Workers Mobilize*. Farnham, 2012. This offers relevant insights into different media practices of activists today, focusing on the precarious workers movement in Italy, both in mainstream and in alternative media.

Van de Donk, Wim, Brian D Loader, Paul G Nixon, and Dieter Rucht, eds. *Cyber Protest: New Media, Citizens and Social Movements*. London, 2004. This is another influential volume and one of the first to have broadly analyzed the impact of computer and online media for protest movements.

Part II

Morphology of Protest

Constructing Reality

Chapter 8

Ideologies/Cognitive Orientation

Ruth Kinna

General Definition of the Term

Ideology is typically associated with the classification of belief systems and the construction of social meaning, the development of political traditions— formal ideologies—and their function. In protest movement literature, the significance of ideology as a discrete area of analysis is contested. At the heart of the debate is an argument about the role ideology plays in mobilizing action: in encouraging or securing the alignment of social movement organizational values with nonmovement belief systems and/or in shaping and reshaping activist understandings. Some scholars argue that emotions play a key role in this process; ideology focuses attention on what individuals know, or think they know about the world—on cognitive factors—in forging alignments and orienting actions.

The term ideology was coined by Antoine Destutt de Tracy in the eighteenth century and first used to describe a system of classification useful for the construction of a science of ideas. Under Marx's influence, ideology came to be associated with political obfuscation and the distortion of reality, rooted in class interest and the legitimation of particular political practices. Karl Mannheim's sociological analysis pointed to a more nuanced conception. Ideology described a complex set of beliefs—rational and irrational, conscious and unconscious—which shaped individuals' knowledge of the world and were malleable to a range of outlooks. Mannheim argued that ideologies provided important psychological supports for particular social groups and that they were open to "utopian" challenge. He also shared de Tracy's interest in classification. Charging intellectuals with the task of rising above the partial and subjective ideological positions present in society at any given time, he held open the possibility of providing nonevaluative interpretations of the social world.

Clifford Geertz dubbed these dominant usages of the concept "pejorative," linking them to two alternative—not necessarily incompatible—perspectives on social determination: interest theory, in which ideology is associated with struggles for power advantage and strain theory, which casts ideology as a safety valve or social comfort in periods of upheaval or disruption. Both, he argued, treated ideology as an evaluative concept, "an entity in itself—an ordered system of cultural symbols."[1] Indeed, Mannheim's call for the formulation of *nonevaluative* interpretation illustrated this weakness. For in pitting ideology against reality, analysts of ideology raised irresolvable methodological issues about objectivity and the boundary lines between truth and belief.

Geertz identified the limitation of these approaches in their narrow functionalism. Interest theorists focused their attention on the causes of ideology and strain theorists on its effects, but both described ideology as a phenomenon that served a particular role in political systems and neither could explain the relationship between the structures that supported ideology and the attitudes they incited. Both neglected the complexity of the social processes through which cultural systems are shaped and the role that ideology plays within them.[2]

Drawing on philosophies of language and mind and on literary criticism, Geertz suggested that ideology was not so much a factor in the social construction of knowledge as it was concerned with the vehicles of conception or meaning, principally the metaphors used in the construction of social reality. The campaign against the 1947 Taft-Hartley Act, which restricted U.S. labor movement action, illustrated his point. The union's description of the act as a "slave labor law" was misunderstood by interest and strain theorists as an attempt to deceive or excite opinion. In fact, Geertz argued, the ideological import of the slogan "drew its power from its capacity to grasp, formulate, and communicate social realities that elude the tempered language of science ... mediate more complex meanings than its literal reading suggests."[3] The slogan was an ideological metaphor that derived its expressive power from the images it evoked and its rhetorical force from the ways in which discussants mapped these images to existing social realities.[4] For Geertz, the study of ideology did not properly lie in the analysis of perceptions or their manipulation, but with the processes of symbolic formulation.

General Cultural Functions

While Geertz suggested that mainstream approaches to ideology were narrowly functional, he did not deny that ideology fulfilled an important cultural role. On the contrary, the point of his analysis was to provide a better insight into the relationship between the causes and effects of ideology. He saw ideology as a special kind of map, "a template or blueprint for the organization of social and psychological processes," patterning the translation of symbols into principles, values, goals and ideals, and shaping responses to events or behaviors in a reasoned way.[5] An important aspect of this view is that ideology is an extrinsic source of information, and not something hidden in the realm of consciousness. Conceptualized in this way, ideology is an instrument for cognitive orientation (understood to describe experiential practices and behaviors, as well as learning or knowledge) particularly in moments of social dislocation, where individuals become temporarily disoriented, and established institutionalized guides to behavior are weakened or put into abeyance.

Using Geertz's insights, contemporary political theorists have also drawn on linguistic philosophy to examine the operation of ideology. For Michael Freeden, ideologies are a form of Wittgensteinian language game "whose meaning and communicative importance can only be determined by noting their grammar ... their conventional employment in a social context, and the degree of acceptability of the rules by which they play."[6] Here too, ideologies are maps, but maps whose intelligibility depends on shared understandings. Similarly, ideological traditions can be thought of as family resemblances: constellations of ideas that usually share certain features in common, but which might also include atypical elements. Ideological traditions do not exist apart from or outside cultural systems, but play a particular role in processes of symbolic formulation, articulating norms and values and patterning ideas, both conceptually and through collective political actions.

Role in Protest Cultures

The value of ideology in social movement research is contested. However, there is a consensus that interest in the concept was rekindled in the 1980s as part of an attempt to bring ideas back in to the study of mobilization. Ideas had always played some role in social movement research, but as DA Snow argues, in resource mobilization and process/opportunity accounts, the role was narrowly construed. Ideas were treated as generic grievances, and mobilization conceptualized as an expression of perceived injustice. The possibility that grievances were described by ideas, and that they might be understood or interpreted in different ways, was downplayed and so, too, was the significant effect that interpretation might have on the process of mobilization. However, as scholars turned their attention to the interpretative processes that mediated the relationship between meaning and mobilization, research refocused on the concept of ideology.[7]

Theoretical and Empirical Research Perspectives

In recent social movement literature, ideology has been discussed in the context of frame theory. In Zald's work, ideology operates at a "micro and social psychological level" as a methodological tool for examining processes of socialization and—"on meso and macro levels"—for analyzing the relationship between social movements and other political organizations: political parties, interest groups, government bodies, and bureaucratic institutions.[8] He classifies social movement activity as ideologically structured action (ISA). And pointing to a fundamental change in the "intellectual conditions of the social sciences and ... on the ground in the world of social movement related phenomena,"[9] he suggests that ISA both reflects this shift and offers a framework of analysis best suited to capturing its complexity.

For Zald, ISA deepens understanding of social movement activity and, especially, frame theory. Oliver and Johnston also focus on this relationship and suggest that there is an analytical distinction between ideology and framing, which frame theorists have wrongly neglected. They explain this neglect with reference to the negative connotations of the concept. Echoing Geertz, they argue that mainstream approaches to ideology are "pejorative." Yet ideology, they contend, can be cast in positive terms, and they point to three applications. Ideology provides a tripartite account of action, proceeding from diagnosis, to prognosis, and finally to the rationale legitimizing and motivating the action. It helps analyze the ways in which individuals understand the world and steer their behaviors. As Zald also suggests, it can be deployed to examine the interrelationship of movement and antimovement positions.[10] Bringing these ideas together, Oliver and Johnston define ideology as "a system of meaning that couples assertions and theories about the nature of social life with values and norms relevant to promoting or resisting social change."[11] To study ideology, they continue, "is to focus on systems of ideas which couple understandings of how the world works with ethical, moral, and normative principles that guide personal and collective action."[12]

Turning to the relationship between frames and ideology, Oliver and Johnston argue that "framing points to process, while ideology points to content."[13] Their view—hotly contested by Snow—casts framing as a process through which movement entrepreneurs market or present messages to maximize their appeal to movement activists and outsiders, and ideology as the belief systems within which framing operates and is coded. To underscore the distinction, they suggest that shared frames are subject to ideological dispute. To illustrate, they argue that both parties to the abortion debates of the 1970s adopted a civil rights frame *ideologically*: either to stress the unborn's right to life or the mother's choice.[14]

Oliver and Johnston's treatment of framing appears to dovetail with Geertz's understanding of ideology. Just as Geertz understands ideology as cultural map, they talk about frames as the "template" that facilitates the negotiation of everyday culture. Yet, their description of the frame is not Geertz's ideology relabeled, since the interpretative role seems to rest on intentionality rather than expressive power, rhetorical force, or as Freeden argues of political ideologies, the articulation of shared meanings. In ordinary life, framing occurs "tacitly by subtle linguistic and extralinguistic cues." In social movements, it is deliberate and "calls attention to the ways in which movement propaganda reflects both the frames of the writers and their perceptions of their targets."[15] Moreover, in tracing the disciplinary roots of frame theory to cognitive psychology and linguistics and ideology to political theory, Oliver and Johnston suggest a clear and sharp divide between the two. Frames, they suggest, refer to "the cognitive process wherein people bring to bear background knowledge to interpret an event or circumstances and locate it in a larger system of meaning." In contrast, ideology describes the "content of whole belief systems." Underscoring the division, they tie each concept to specific research agendas: the study of frames to the analysis of movement organizations and actors and the study of ideology to the origin of ideas "their interrelations and consistency."[16]

In sum, while Oliver and Johnston's discussion of the pejorative connotations of ideology appears to chime with Geertz's, their desire to strip ideology of its negativity points to an evaluative treatment rather than an understanding of symbolic formulation. And their attempt to distinguish the politics of ideology from the cognition of framing runs counter to recent developments in political theory, where the cultural turn has encouraged analysts to probe the links between linguistic practices, norms, and cognition when reflecting on the complex ways in which individuals orientate themselves politically. In pointing to a disciplinary and conceptual space between ideology and framing, they veer toward a formal concept of ideology, rather one that is rooted in culture. And they view framing as a form of extrinsic manipulation, stimulating an intrinsic, unconscious cognitive process.

Research Gaps and Open Questions

The open questions about ideology in social movement research turn on its conceptualization and on the research agendas to which competing concepts are linked. There is a consensus that ideology plays a role in social movement research, but little agreement about its definition or applications. Snow argues that ideology and framing describe "different aspects and dimensions of the complex of symbolic, ideational, and intersubjective factors associated with movement mobilization and dynamics."[17] Ideologies are resources for frames—once the theoretical clarity and empirical value of framing is recognized and the difficulty of determining the precise analytical value of ideology is acknowledged.[18] Questions about the relationship between cause and effect, to use Geertz's terms, and the special properties of social movements as sites for ideological action, are difficult to resolve for as long as the concept of ideology itself remains contested.

Ruth Kinna teaches political theory at Loughborough University, United Kingdom. Her research interest focuses on radical politics, particularly anarchism, and she works on historical and contemporary themes. She is the editor of the *Continuum Companion to Anarchism* (London, 2012), coeditor of *Libertarian Socialism: Politics in Black and Red* (Basingstoke, 2012) and *Anarchism and Utopianism* (Manchester, 2009), and the author of *The Beginner's Guide to Anarchism* (London, 2009).

Notes

1. Clifford Geertz, "Ideology as a Cultural System," in *The Interpretation of Cultures: Selected Essays by Clifford Geertz* (London, 1975), 196.
2. Ibid., 212–13.
3. Ibid., 210.
4. Ibid., 213.
5. Ibid., 216.
6. Michael Freeden, *Ideology a Very Short Introduction* (Oxford, 2003), 43.

7. David A Snow, "Framing Processes, Ideology, and Discursive Fields," in *The Blackwell Companion to Social Movements,* ed. DA Snow, SA Soule, and H Kriesi (Oxford, 2007), 382–83.
8. Mayer N Zald, "Ideologically Structured Action: An Enlarged Agenda for Social Movement Research," *Mobilization* 5, no. 1 (2000): 2.
9. Mayer N Zald, "Mobilization Forum: New Paradigm? Nah! New Agenda? I Hope So," *Mobilization* 5, no. 1 (2000): 33.
10. Pamela E Oliver and Hank Johnston, "What a Good Idea! Ideology and Frames in Social Movement Research," *Mobilization* 5, no. 1 (2000): 43.
11. Ibid.
12. Ibid., 44.
13. Ibid., 45.
14. Ibid., 39.
15. Ibid., 45.
16. Ibid.
17. Snow, "Framing Processes, Ideology, and Discursive Fields," 405.
18. David A Snow and Robert D Benford, "Mobilization Forum: Clarifying the Relationship Between Framing and Ideology," *Mobilization* 5, no. 1 (2000): 59.

Recommended Reading

Freeden, Michael. *Ideology: A Very Short Introduction.* Oxford, 2003. This provides a concise statement of the complex analysis presented in *Ideologies and Political Theory: A Conceptual Approach* (Oxford, 1996), the benchmark for the analysis of ideology in contemporary political theory.

Geertz, Clifford. "Ideology as a Cultural System." *The Interpretation of Cultures: Selected Essays.* London, 1975, 193–229. This essay outlines his highly influential understanding and the significance of his anthropology to its conceptualization.

Chapter 9

Frames and Framing Processes

David A Snow

General Definition of Frames and Their General Cultural Function

Frames are material or linguistic interpretive devices that help to render meaningful and understandable the things, objects, or events they bound and encompass. Frames do this interpretive work by performing three core functions. First, they focus attention by punctuating or bracketing what in our sensual field is relevant and what is irrelevant, what is in-frame and what is out-of-frame, in relation to the object of orientation. In the case of photos and paintings, whether and how they are seen depends in part on whether and how, and with what, they are enframed. The mere act of framing itself is an act of signification in that it designates the object as meriting focused attention and perhaps even contemplation. Second, frames function as articulation mechanisms in the sense of tying together the various punctuated elements of the scene so that one set of meanings rather than another is conveyed, or, in the language of narrativity, one story rather than another is told. Thus, whether baton-wielding police officers clubbing protesters are seen as riotous or responsible social control agents, depends in part on which of the other elements of the scene are enframed and accented. And third, frames sometimes perform a transformative function by reconstituting the way in which some objects of attention are seen or understood, as relating to each other or to the actor. Examples of this transformative function abound, as in the de-eroticization of the sexual in the physician's office, the transformation or reconfiguration of aspects of one's biography, as commonly occurs in contexts of religious conversion, and in the transformation of routine grievances or misfortunes into injustices or mobilizing grievances in the context of social movements and protest.

Given the focusing, articulation, and transformative functions of frames, it is arguable that they are fundamental to interpretation, so much so that few, if any, objects, things, utterances, gestures, actions, experience, or events could be meaningfully understood apart from the way they are framed.

The analysis of frames and associated processes has been conducted in relation to various activities and social categories (e.g., artwork, advertising, face-to-face interaction, gender, talk) in a variety of domains of social life (e.g., culture, organizations, politics, public policy). To date, however, few areas of substantive inquiry in the social sciences have generated the volume of theorization and empirical research on frames and framing processes as the study of collective action and social movements.

Function of Frames in Protest Cultures

Framing, within the context of social movements and protest, refers to the signifying work or meaning construction engaged in by movement adherents (e.g., leaders, activists, and rank-and-file participants) and other actors (e.g., adversaries, institutional elites, media, and countermovements) relevant to the interests of movements and the challenges they mount in pursuit of those interests.[1] The concept of framing within the collective action context is beholden to Erving Goffman's *Frame Analysis*[2] and is rooted in the symbolic interactionist and constructionist principle that meanings do not naturally or automatically attach themselves to the objects, events, or experiences we encounter, but arise, instead, through interpretive processes mediated by various contextual factors. Applied to all varieties of social phenomena, including civil disturbances, social movements, and politics in general, the idea of framing problematizes the meanings associated with relevant events, activities, places, and actors, suggesting that those meanings are typically contestable and negotiable, and thus open to debate and differential interpretation.

Research Perspectives

The link between framing and social movements was first noted in an experimental study of the conditions under which authority is defined as unjust and challenged[3] and then developed more fully in a 1986 article that offered a systematic conceptualization and elaboration of "frame alignment processes."[4] Since then, there has been a rapid proliferation of research on framing and social movements, with much of the work congealing into what is now called the framing perspective on social movements.[5] The analytic appeal and utility of this perspective is based largely on the conjunction of three factors. The first is the relative neglect of the relationship between meaning and mobilization, and the role of interpretative processes in mediating that relationship, by the dominant perspectives on social movements that emerged in the 1970s; the second is the rediscovery of culture and the so-called discursive turn in the social sciences that occurred during the 1980s; and the third is the development of a conceptual architecture or scaffolding that has facilitated more systematic theorization and empirical assessment of framing processes and effects.

Within the scholarly research on framing and related processes in relation to social movements, there are a number of concepts that can be thought of as cornerstone concepts and processes in that they provide a conceptual architecture that has stimulated much of the research exploring the relevance of framing to mobilization both empirically and theoretically. These key concepts or processes include: collective action frames, master frames, core framing tasks, frame alignment processes, frame resonance, and discursive processes and fields.[6]

These concepts have been applied and explored in relation to a variety of events and settings. For example, a study of the electoral success of the Northern League in Italy in comparison to a number of competing groups in the same region in the early 1990s finds analytic purchase in drawing on the concept of master frames and linking it to political opportunity.[7] The study reveals that different master frames—which are collective action frames that come to function like master algorithms in the sense that they color and constrain the orientations and activities of other movements within particular periods—helped to account for the electoral success of the Northern League, but not independent of the political context and particularly the political opportunity structure. In another study exploring the relationship between ideology and framing processes in relation to Islamic terrorist movements, it argued that the monolithic application of the concept of ideology to Islamic terrorist movements, as many national leaders have done, is of questionable analytic utility because it not only ignores ideological variation and flexibility among these movements, but also glosses over the ways in which ideas, beliefs, and values—the stuff of ideology—and various on-the-ground social events are strategically linked together via the discursive mechanisms of frame articulation and elaboration and the core framing tasks of diagnostic, prognostic, and motivational framing. It is through these processes, it is argued, that elements of Islamic ideology and events are linked together in ways that have helped to justify and inspire Islamic terrorist movements and their activities.[8] Another study examined frame variation and the factors that account for it by conducting a comparative study of how the Fall 2005 French riots, were framed, diagnostically and prognostically across a diverse set of actors (e.g., media, French Government, French opposition, riot participants, and international actors) in six countries (Canada, England, France, Germany, the Netherlands, and the United States).[9] A fourth illustrative study extends understanding of frame resonance by showing how feminist framing in the abortion debates, from 1970–1994, in the United States and Germany varied in terms of whether it was culturally or institutionally resonant or radical, and how such differences were affected by different discursive opportunity structures in the two countries.[10] And a final study shows how two framing mechanisms—articulation and elaboration—work together to affect cultural revitalization and fabrication, two important forms of cultural change.[11]

Together, the above illustrative studies show the analytic utility of a number of key framing concepts and processes—master frames, resonance, frame articulation, and elaboration, and the core framing tasks of diagnostic, prognostic, and motivational framing. They also suggest how framing processes and the resultant collective action or master frames are connected to other key concepts or processes—ideology, political opportunity structures, discursive opportunity structures, and law—in ways that both constrain and facilitate framing processes. In doing so, these and a plethora of other studies,[12] highlight the importance of interpretive frames and framing processes to understanding the dynamics of movement mobilization and protest.

David A Snow is distinguished professor of sociology at the University of California, Irvine. His research interests include collective behavior and social movements; changes in cognitive orientation and interpretive perspective with an emphasis on framing processes, conversion, and identity work; and socioeconomic marginality in urban contexts with an emphasis on homelessness. His recent publications most relevant to protest and social movements include *The Blackwell Companion to Social Movements* (Oxford, 2004), with S Soule and H Kriesi; *Readings on Social Movements: Origins, Dynamics, and Outcomes* (Oxford, 1997, 2010), with D McAdam; *A Primer on Social Movements* (Norton, 2010), with Sarah Soule; and the *Wiley-Blackwell Encyclopedia of Social and Political Movements* (Oxford, 2013), with D Della Porta, B Klandermans, and D McAdam.

Notes

1. Robert D Benford and David A Snow, "Framing Processes and Social Movements: An Overview and Assessment," *Annual Review of Sociology* 26 (2000): 611–39; William A Gamson, Talking Politics (New York, 1992); David A Snow et al., "Frame Alignment Processes, Micromobilization, and Movement Participation," *American Sociological Review* 51 (1986): 464–81; David A Snow, "Framing Processes, Ideology, and Discursive Fields," in *The Blackwell Companion to Social Movements,* ed. DA Snow, S Soule, and H Kriesi (Oxford, 2004), 380–412.
2. Erving Goffman, *Frame Analysis* (New York, 1974).
3. William A Gamson, Bruce Fireman, and Steven Rytina, *Encounters with Unjust Authority* (Homewood, IL, 1982).
4. Snow et al., "Frame Alignment Processes, Micromobilization, and Movement Participation."
5. For a recent overview of the range of research on framing and social movements, see David A Snow, Robert D Benford, Holly J McCammon, Lyndi Hewitt, and Scott Fitzgerald, "The Emergence, Development, and Future of the Framing Perspective: 25+ Years since 'Frame Alignment'," *Mobilization: The International Quarterly Review of Social Movement Research*, 19 (2014): 23-45.
6. Benford and Snow, "Framing Processes and Social Movements"; Snow, "Framing Processes, Ideology, and Discursive Fields."
7. Mario Diani, "Linking Mobilization Frames and Political Opportunities: Insights from Regional Populism in Italy," *American Sociological Review* 61 (1996): 1053–69.
8. David A Snow and Scott C Byrd, "Ideology, Framing Processes, and Islamic Terrorist Movements," *Mobilization: An International Journal* 12 (2007): 119–36.
9. David A Snow, Rens Vliegenhart, and Catherine Corrigall-Brown, "Framing the French 'Riots': A Comparative Study of Frame Variation," *Social Forces* 86 (2007): 385–415.
10. Myra Marx Ferree, "Resonance and Radicalism: Feminist Framing in the Abortion Debates of the United States and Germany," *American Journal of Sociology* 109 (2003): 304–44.
11. David A Snow, Anna E Tan and Peter D Owens, "Social Movements, Framing Processes, and Cultural Revitalization and Fabrication," *Mobilization: The International Quarterly Review of Social Movement Research*, 18 (2013): 225-242.
12. For examples, see Benford and Snow, "Framing Processes and Social Movements"; Snow, "Framing Processes, Ideology, and Discursive Fields," and "The Emergence, Development, and Future of the Framing Perspective: 25+ Years since 'Frame Alignment'."

Recommended Reading

Benford, Robert D, and David A Snow. "Framing Processes and Social Movements: An Overview and Assessment." *Annual Review of Sociology* 26 (2000): 611–39.

Goffman, Erving. *Frame Analysis*. New York, 1974.

Snow, David A. "Framing Processes, Ideology, and Discursive Fields," in *The Blackwell Companion to Social Movements*, edited by DA Snow, S Soule, and H Kriesi, 380–412. Oxford, 2004.

Chapter 10

Cultural Memory

Lorena Anton

General Definitions and Cultural Functions of Cultural Memory

In Greek mythology, memory—the goddess Mnemosyne—was the mother of the muses, thus having complete power over time, imagination, and all cultural activities. Since then, ordinary people as well as scholars have been intrigued and preoccupied with the power and place of memory, in its different types and forms. In recent years, the study of memory, in its sociocultural aspects and collective manifestations, has determined the apparition of a transdisciplinary domain of social research, generally known as memory studies.[1]

Grosso modo, cultural memory is understood as the social memory of collectivities (i.e., individual memories collectively shared) transmitted via cultural artifacts, and in this form, available to people to construct and (re)define their relation to the past, the present, and, sometimes, the future. Its appearance as a concept in the social sciences and humanities is generally related to the writings of the French sociologist Maurice Halbwachs[2] and of the German art historian Aby Warburg,[3] although others too contributed to the beginning of the field in almost the same period.[4] Warburg, following the writings of Durkheim, used the term "social memory" to analyze artworks as "repositories of human history." For Halbwachs, remembering was socioculturally framed, as the individual is a social being. Thus, memory is collective, as people acquire and construct it as members of a group and always recall their memories in this context.

As a research domain, memory studies began to take off in the 1980s, after the memory work surrounding the Holocaust had become an international affair. From history to psychology, through sociology, anthropology, or cultural studies, the study of shared recollections and collective mnemonic practices became of growing interest for social scholars. Bit by bit, new memory sites were opened to public inquiry and recollection, as post-Communist Europe, post-totalitarian South America, or post-genocide Africa started to come to term with their troubled pasts. Nowadays, the memory discourse is present more than ever. Its cultural functions—of creating and sustaining self-image, historical consciousness, or group affiliation, or ensuring an equilibrium between past, present, and future—are intrinsically linked to individual and social identity, historical traumas, or redistributive justice, thus becoming a powerful tool in ethnic, national, or international politics.

Role of Cultural Memory in Protest Cultures

For protest cultures, cultural memory could be a powerful operational category of analysis, as it is always the complex phenomenon of remembering, which determines a group's identity, thus making future collective claims possible. At the same time, a divided memory over the same past can trigger opposite collective manifestations. One of the most recent European examples in this case is Tallinn's *Bronze Soldier* affair, dating from April 2007. Following the delocalization of a World War II commemoration site from the center of Estonia's capital to an ordinary cemetery in the city, a powerful street protest, initiated by the Russian community, erupted in the city. Soon, it became the catalyst of a more complicated, international debate about remembrance of World War II and the Soviet Union's role in the Baltic States (and Eastern Europe).[5] An influential tool in ethnic or national construction, cultural memory becomes thus an important instrument in protest starting. The "politics of memory"[6] can go hand in hand with the politics of protest, as the past—a foreign country[7]—is always recollected in the present.

The mere idea of protesting identity can also be inherited and transmitted via cultural memory. In short, some societies are more open to social movements than others, as they have a long established tradition of challenging the establishment—take, for example, France and its social history of fighting for individual and human rights. For French society, to protest is to continue living in a post-French Revolution or, more recently, a post-May 1968 society. This past is highly (re)valorized, debated almost daily, and thus transmitted from generation to generation through sites of memory, which continually fuel national pride in a "French protest culture," as the actual memory is no longer vivid or, as Nora puts it, "There are *lieux de mémoire*, sites of memory, because there are no longer *milieux de mémoire*, real environments of memory."[8]

Using the Memory Approach: Research Perspectives

In order to better analyze the intersubjectivities between cultural memory and different arenas of contestation, one of the most challenging theoretical apparatuses is the "dynamics of memory approach," which analyzes memory as a continuous process of negotiation between different actors involved both in the recollected past and in the present of remembrance.[9] By not reducing cultural memory to a mere instrument of elite manipulation or group hegemony, the dynamics of memory approach locate social remembering in "the space between an imposed ideology and the possibility of an alternative way of understanding experience."[10] Thus, memory analysis is open to the way the past is brought into the present—individually remembered but socially framed, collectively shared but shaped by different politics of the self or the Establishment—by the use of narrative and as well as non-narrative means (such as bodily reflexes, common emotions, shared silence, etc.). To sum up, memory work is thus recognized as a flexible phenomenon that could incorporate and, at the same time, determine controversy and even conflict, as it contributes daily to the construction and interpretation of present realities.

The selection and interpretation of all these nuances make the analysis of cultural memory even richer, especially when researching into social movements and protest cultures. Protest, as cultural memory, is intersubjective. This intersubjectivity is developed both between the members of a protesting group as well as between different protesting generations, which reclaim and make use of a certain protest culture. Protest logics are always related to the memory of a past protest or a present social inequality, and usually develop in parallel with certain politics of memory concerning past events in order to legitimize present claims. Sometimes the beginning of an entire protest culture is constructed upon the cultural memory of another one. At others, certain politics of memory determine the social construction of reality, thus directly influencing the apparition and manifestation of different protest cultures. To take a case study, (most of) the *protest movements for abortion rights* all over the world developed generally in the late 1960s, indirectly related to the eruption of *women's movements* and subjectivity as a contesting argument, a phenomenon that formed the core of the 1968 protests. In the United States, the Roe vs. Wade controversy determined numerous movements and street protests, but the controversy was—and still is—always discussed starting from the point of view of an American cultural memory related either to religion or to individual rights (of the child to be vs. the women's)—both frameworks directly inherited and continually transmitted, in general, in American society.

On the other side of the Atlantic, in Communist Europe for instance, abortion controversies were either related to Communist gender equality, as long as the Soviet model dictated it, or to different national demographic policies, supported by powerful propaganda campaigns. In Ceauşescu's Romania, for example, where reproduction control (1966–89) is considered to have represented one of the most repressive political demographies in twentieth-century Europe, protesting for abortion rights was unimaginable in the public sphere, as from the late 1960s on, the pronatalist state constructed a social tradition of maternity (as a Socialist value and source of national pride). Along with the banning of abortion on demand, the construction of the cultural memory of the large Romanian family determined the banning of (legitimate) protest concerning proabortion rights in the public arenas of Romanian Communist society. This was not the case in spring 2012, when a highly controversial legislative project proposed the creation of significant barriers (compulsory biased counseling at pregnancy crisis counseling offices and a so-called reflection period of five days) for women seeking an abortion. For the very first time since the end of Ceauşescu's political demography (December 1989), the abortion issue was back in the limelight. Civil society, as well as the medical profession, immediately protested against such control over women's bodies and decisions and, more than once, former pronatalist biopolitics were recalled.

Research Gaps and Open Questions

The multitude of approaches to researching into cultural memory are the strength and, at the same time, the weakness of memory studies as a field of social inquiry. Nevertheless, its high transdisciplinarity, although sometimes contested, enables a fine analysis of the researched phenomena, a fact which can only benefit correlated research on protest cultures. In questions like *why* and *how* a protest culture is formed in a specific time and space, cultural memory can thus offer pertinent insights. More case studies in this direction would enrich the understanding of protest and social movements, as well as of their separate or intersubjective histories in the twentieth century.

Lorena Anton is Marie Curie-CIG Fellow at University of Bucharest, Romania. Her current research interests include memory of state Socialism in Europe, and European past and present politics of reproduction (with special regard to Eastern Europe). Recent publications include "Politics of Reproduction in a Divided Europe: Abortion, Protest Movements and State Interventions after the Second World War," with Yoshie Mitobe and Kristina Schulz, in *The "Establishment" Responds: Power and Protest during and after Cold War*, ed. K Fahlenbrach et al. (Basingstoke, 2012); and *Between the Avant-garde and the Everyday: Subversive Politics in Europe from 1957 to the Present*, with Timothy Brown (Oxford, 2011).

Notes

1. For an up-to-date characterization of the field per se, as well its classical categories of analysis (collective memory/social memory/cultural memory, etc.), see especially Jeffrey K Olick and Joyce Robbins, "Social Memory Studies: From Collective Memory to the Historical Sociology of Mnemonic Practices," *Annual Review of Sociology* 24 (1998): 105–40; Barbara Misztal, *Theories of Social Remembering* (Maidenhead, PA, 2003); and Jeffrey K Olick et al., eds, *The Collective Memory Reader* (Oxford, 2011). Also, for cross-disciplinary developments of the field, see especially Paul Connerton, *How Societies Remember* (Cambridge, 1989); and Paul Connerton, *How Modernity Forgets* (Cambridge, 2009); Paul Antze and Michael Lambek, eds, *Tense Past: Cultural Essays in Trauma and Memory* (London, 1996); Kerwin Lee Klein, "On the Emergence of Memory in Historical Discourse," *Representations* 69 (2000): 127–50; Jacob J Climo and Maria G Cattel, *Social Memory and History: Anthropological Perspectives* (New York, 2002); Jöel Candau, *Anthropologie de la mémoire* [*Anthropology of Memory*] (Paris, 2005); and Astrid Erll et al., eds, *Cultural Memory Studies: An International and Interdisciplinary Handbook* (Berlin, 2008); as well as the dedicated journal published by Sage, *Memory Studies*, (http://mss.sagepub.com/).
2. Maurice Halbwachs, *Les cadres sociaux de la mémoire* (Paris, 1994).
3. Aby Warburg, *Das Schlagenritual: Ein Reisebericht* (Berlin, 2011).
4. See, for example: the French historian Marc Bloch, who used the term "collective memory" in 1925, and later in his book on feudal society (*La Société Féodale/ Feudal Society*, Paris 1939), the British psychologist Frederick C Bartlett, who established that remembering is socially framed (*Remembering: A Study in Experimental and Social Psychology* [Cambridge, 1932]), or the British anthropologist Edward E Evans-Pritchard, who developed the notion of "structural-amnesia" in his famous study of the Nuer (*The Nuer: A Description of the Modes of Livelihood and Political Institutions of a Nilotic People*, Oxford 1940).
5. For the Russian community, the Estonian Bronze Soldier was the symbol of all the unknown heroes who died "in the Great War against fascism." For the Estonian community, World War II also meant the beginning of the Soviet occupation. For

a larger analysis of Europe's politics of memory via its Communist past in the Baltic States, see Eva C Onken, "The Baltic States and Moscow's 9 May Commemoration: Memory Politics in Europe," *Europe Asia Studies* 59 (2007): 23–46.

6. The very concept of politics of memory appeared in the social sciences (following older concepts of collective identity and politics of identity) in order to analyze the ways in which power and politics influence, and often dictate, the memory boom of one past or another. In short, the notion of politics of memory in the public sphere could be associated, on a larger scale of interpretation, with that of strategy with regard to the social remembering of individuals, groups, or an entire society. It implies, in fact, an actor who is developing a memory project, either at a transnational, national, or organizational level. "Simply stated, it is who wants whom to remember what, and why" (Alain Confino, "Collective Memory and Cultural History: Problems of Method," *American Historical Review, Vol. 102, No. 5* (1997): 1386–1403). For details, see especially Andreas Huyssen, *Present Pasts: Urban Palimpsests and the Politics of Memory* (Stanford, CA, 2003); Patrick Garcia, "Politiques de la mémoire," *Eurozine Review,* 7 March 2006, www.eurozine.com/pdf/2006-07-03-garcia-fr.pdf ; Luisa Passerini, *Memory and Utopia: The Primacy of Intersubjectivity* (London, 2007); and Richard N Lebow et al., eds, *The Politics of Memory in Postwar Europe* (Durham, NC, 2006).

7. David Lowenthal, *The Past Is a Foreign Country* (Cambridge, 1999).

8. Pierre Nora, "Between Memory and History: Les lieux de mémoire." *Representations,* no. 26 (1989): 7.

9. For an exhaustive description of the dynamics of the memory approach, see Misztal, *Theories of Social Remembering,* 67–74.

10. Susannah Radstone, "Working with Memory: An Introduction," in *Memory and Methodology,* ed. S Radstone (Oxford, 2000), 1–24.

Recommended Reading

Lebow, Richard N, et al., eds. *The Politics of Memory in Postwar Europe.* Durham, NC, 2006. A volume of collected articles about the actors and politics involved in the memory work of Postwar Europe, this study offers interesting analyses of the legacies of World War II in different national contexts and their interconnections with an international memory debate on historical traumas.

Misztal, Barbara. *Theories of Social Remembering.* Maidenhead, 2003. The book is an excellent study of the history and development of social memory research. It surveys and explains the classic texts in the evolution of the domain, offering at the same time a refreshing approach to the non-paradigmatic, transdisciplinary, centerless field of memory studies.

Nora, Pierre, ed. *Les lieux de mémoire [Realms of memory].* 5 vols. Paris, 1984–92. This collection of essays is generally considered to be the first major contemporary study to critically inquire the complicated relation between history and memory, taking as a case study modern France, a modernity in which—according to Nora, the editor—"we speak so much about memory because there is so little of it left." "Between Memory and History: Les lieux de mémoire." *Representations*, no. 26, Special Issue: Memory and Counter-Memory (1989): 7.

Passerini, Luisa. *Memory and Utopia: The Primacy of Intersubjectivity.* London, 2007. The author discusses cultural memory as an intersubjective phenomenon shared by generations, which thus primarily influences the construction of reality and history—in this case, that of Europe and its making.

Chapter 11

Narratives

Jakob Tanner

Protest cultures articulate themselves in social movements. Narratives constitute an important vehicle for mobilization, and they are also indispensable to the historical analysis of such movements. This double issue is outlined first ("General Definition of Narratives and Their Role in Protest Movements"). Subsequently, we trace the displacement from a social sciences approach to a cultural analysis of social movements ("Theoretical Approaches: Cultural Analysis of Narratives in Protest Movements"). "Research Gaps and Open Questions" documents current controversies and deals with new, innovative departures.

General Definition of the Narratives and Their Role in Protest Movements

Narratives are linguistic and discursive phenomena; they are distinct, however, from language (as analyzed for instance by linguistics and historical semantics) and from discursive dispositives (the objects of discourse analysis) by a sequential logic and a consecutive mode of producing meaning. Narratives are subject to a specific dramaturgy. They develop an initial situation, and they structure a diegetic space in which charges of emotion, imputed causation, moments of suspense, and reversals can be generated and (usually) a climax constructed. Finally, the story leads up to a moral lesson, often as its poignantly delivered message—or else it loses itself in a variety of allusions, ambiguities, and surprises. Narrative theories developed across the disciplines distinguish between stories, plots, and narration, as well as their different meaning effects.[1] The techniques of emplotment thrive on a warehouse of stories contained in the cultural memory of society.

Patricia Ewick and Susan Silbey note, "Narratives are fluid, continuous, dynamic, and always constructed interactively—with an audience and within a context—out of the stuff of other narratives."[2] This phrasing refers to a flexible narrative pragmatics that ties in with the work of Soviet literary theorist Mikhail M Bakhtin, according to whom language primarily derives meaning from its performative dimensions. Narration is seen as a process, and narrative forms are analyzed in view of their openness toward social heteroglossia.[3] From this perspective, the effects of narrative structures result above all from complex interaction with an audience, which in turn is conditioned by specific reading, listening, and viewing habits, and with its own political expectations that may miss the story's explicit meaning. Hence, subtext and unconscious effects come to the fore.[4] Similarly, Fredric Jameson questions the clarification and transparency effect of true stories by analyzing narratives as socially symbolic actions, which constitute the specific mode of production of the political unconscious.[5] Moreover, narratives are media-bound.[6] In the age of mass media, instrumental strategies and expressive manifestations of social movements forcefully interpenetrate one another. With the emergence of new image media (illustrated magazines, film, and television), the status of visual narratives has become much enhanced during the twentieth century. Just as viscourses and discourses mutually support the production of knowledge in the natural sciences, one can also observe in social movements a mutual translation and elucidation of iconographic representations, musical choreographies as well as linguistic narrative patterns. Synesthetic phenomena (such as the 1960s countercultural stories combining pictures, music, texts, gestures, practices, and substances, e.g., drugs) also refer to new emotional regimes. Thus, emotional conjunctures and narrative dynamics are intertwined.

The analysis of protest culture and narrative structure brings ideas into play that also concern the chapters on iconography (Fahlenbrach), motivation (Corrigal-Brown), framing (Snow), and emotion (Gould), and particularly "narrative emotions."[7] Focusing on the discursive construction and narrative self-presentation of social movements, one may heuristically distinguish two levels of study: On the one hand, stories belong to the effective means of mobilization of such movements; they refresh the moral resources of protest, offer meaningful possibilities of identification, and generate (partially unintended) potential meanings. Since the 1960s, this increasingly includes the interventions of experts using scientific narratives in the media struggle for conclusive authority. On the other hand, historiography and the various human sciences (sociology, political science, social psychology, and other disciplines concerned with social protest) use narrative patterns that are sometimes explicitly interrogated, but frequently remain implicit in order to explain the dynamics of social movements and the mechanisms of their internal integration and political intervention. Both levels are connected and mutually intertwined. Often social activists distinguish themselves *post festum* as scholarly analysts who are able to resort to remembered knowledge, which only partly exists in documented form. In such cases, history and memory fuse together. Conversely, the social sciences have produced representations of protest cultures that barely take note of the partisan view, the participants' own interpretations of events. In both cases, there are difficult problems of group loyalty and analytical distance, which the history of social movements has had to deal with since its beginnings.

Theoretical Approaches: Cultural Analysis of Narratives in Protest Movements

Since the end of the 1950s, social history and historical sociology have (re-) discovered social movements as a research topic.[8] As new, empirically and quantitatively oriented methodologies, they were opposed to the hermeneutics of the humanities. Instead of telling colorful stories, historians and sociologists were urged to explain historical phenomena through social relations in interdisciplinary collaborations with social psychology, geography, ethnology, and so on, thereby using an abstract, theory-guided vocabulary. But despite their distancing themselves from grassroots meanings and narrative historism, the "historical social sciences" were in turn dedicated to the metanarrative of modernization. This enabled them to comprehend social movements as the product and indicator of social change.[9] Protest generally became an indispensable ingredient of occidental rationalization.[10] These movements voice political demands and moral claims to shaping policy, which makes them the main protagonists of a sustained, long-term social process of emancipation and democratization. Labor history as a privileged area of research in the 1970s reveals some effects of this premise: as a result, the self-image of the organized labor movement converges ideally with the interpretation of its historical relevance and simultaneously with the overall development curve of society. These three narrative levels are homologized, and they mutually reinforce each other and blend into a single, great, modern metanarrative of the—despite many setbacks—ultimately heroic struggle of the labor movement and of the progressive democratizing of society.[11] Hence, the following critical position toward ideologies may be articulated: if the contemporary actors under consideration were not able to adequately define their situation and task, then, in retrospective interpretation, they displayed a false consciousness, which in turn can be read as the result of the influence of various hegemonic (national, colonial, culture-industrial, etc.) narratives of ruling classes.

Ideological criticism of this kind is strongly opposed by a structural-functionalist approach. The latter stipulates that social movements in different social subsystems generate perturbations that, depending on their strength of resonance, trigger processes of systemic adaptation and communicational learning. Niklas Luhmann, in his analyses, resorts to medical metaphors and claims, for instance, that protest movements enhance the defensive forces of the social immune system.[12] With this theory, academic analysis departs from the self-image of the protest's protagonists. Having considered themselves to be in opposition to and resisting social developments, they are now forced to recognize themselves as an early warning contrivance that effectively maintains the system. Thus, social movements generally become feedback loops that adaptive, complex, and functionally differentiated social systems actually depend on. It is no coincidence that this explanation's central category, that of function, derives from physiology, which since the interwar years has developed narratives of a "Wisdom of the Body" based on homeostatic self-regulation.

Since the late 1970s, the dynamic of the *cultural turn* began to assert itself in the historical sciences. Discourse analysis, postcolonialism, and post-structuralism held sway. Issues related to story patterns and narrative schemata moved center-stage in methodology and theory. Discourse theorists like Hayden White consider narrative as "a particularly effective system of discursive meaning production"[13] and demonstrate the "operations of moral consciousness in the achievement of narrative fullness."[14] White usefully distinguishes between a historical discourse that describes (i.e., narrates) and a discourse that tells (i.e., narrativizes).[15] The latter fuses *true story* and *real story,* which enables the tradition of a "shared reality."[16] White's premise is a "performance model of discourse," and he conceives of discourse "as an apparatus for the production of meaning rather than as only a vehicle for the transmission of information."[17] A narrative discourse is clearly distinct from a chronicle through its performative effects and signification, as there is a displacement from the *noema* (cognition) to the *poiesis* (i.e., practical action).[18] The emphasis on the importance of narrative patterns for the representation of social reality revealed the deficits of the social historical and sociological approaches. They were forced into the defensive on two sides. On the one hand, it was proclaimed that historiography had returned to narrative. Traditional social history did not really meet this challenge productively. It insisted that a scientific explanation of social change differed from (and had to be different from) narrative historiography and maintained a skeptical, defensive stance. On the other hand, the grand master narratives of social history that had legitimated the meaning of empirical analyses lost their plausibility. What remained from the point of view of the critics was a naïve historical realism devoted to the phantasma of social progress and yielding to the desire for a clearly laid out, closed history, a *histoire totale*.

Critics of metanarratives, such as Jean-François Lyotard, explain the latter's secular success with the difficulties of achieving a synchronous representation of history or of social movements. Diachronic narrative promises one solution to this problem by distributing the problems arising on the axis of diachrony. Arranging contradictory elements in a temporal order defuses the potential brisance of their simultaneous presence and explains away all disaccords. Such a temporal extension may, however, occur in two opposing ways. "One flows counter the stream, towards an origin, the other goes with the flow towards a destination." Hence, "one of these stories forms ... the mythic narratives (récits) indispensable to traditional communities, the other the narratives of emancipation."[19] Unlike the myths fixed to an origin, these modern metanarratives seek legitimacy "in an attainable future, i.e., in an idea yet to be realized."[20] The nineteenth and twentieth centuries witnessed various reactionary social movements that couched themselves in mythical perceptions of reality. The many progressive movements, however, derived their motivating and mobilizing force from stories narrating a temporalized utopia. They are open to what is yet to come (or, as in Romance languages, to the *avénir* or *avenire*).

Such an approach makes it possible to understand social movements as narrative experiments. This corresponds with Pierre Bourdieu's view. His thesis of a critical moment prevents a continuous conception of history.[21] The critical event disrupting existing structures and establishing new ones lets the unimaginable irrupt the expected course of events, thereby marking the starting point of a completely new history. For this reason, social movements oscillate in their self-image between narrative determination and situational openness. They use the level of familiarity and hence decodability of established narrative forms to mobilize campaigns, while simultaneously betting on an unexpected turn of events. This double bind is constitutive of all activist movements. In the same way, intrinsic and extrinsic interpretations oscillate between formal routine (as a prerequisite of political efficiency) and innovative creativity (as a condition of the possibility of social change).

Research Gaps and Open Questions

Confronted with approaches reifying a "homo narrans"[22] or narration as explanatory super categories,[23] the historical and cultural examination of protest cultures is well advised to extrapolate the insights of politico-social history, while simultaneously orienting itself toward new topics in cultural theory. In his introduction to the German translation of Hayden White's *Tropics of Discourse*,[24] Reinhart Koselleck, an early exponent of historical semantics, divides the study of the conditions of potential history into one question directed at factual issues and another directed at narratives.[25] In this manner, history as an "imaginary construct" can be brought together with fact-based methods of reconstruction. This makes it possible to describe social movements in categories derived from the analysis of narrative performance, while retaining an excess of meaning and therefore allowing for new interpretations. A particularly interesting approach of social history that utilizes a visual display has been developed by Charles Tilly. He considers social movements as the main actors of a history of democratization and de-democratization. Written into a matrix with the two axes of democracy and state capacity, history, as emerging out of the struggles between (collective) activists, appears as a complex, spiraling curve.[26] To all intents and purposes, protest activists have indeed been aware of this analytical pattern, in imagining the strenuously fought for ascendancy of their movement as a metaphorical upward spiral. A study placing visual narratives center-stage might also be informed by Otto Neurath's concept of isotypes. To the Austro-Marxist Neurath, with his motto "words divide, images unite," icons ought to become a new medium for the mobilization and communication of social movements.[27]

From the same perspective, but concerned with linguistic narratives, Francesca Polletta, in her studies on storytelling and social movements in the nineteenth and twentieth centuries,[28] reaches two important conclusions. First, the narratives' mobilizing potential does not depend on their moral certitude, but on their allusions and ambiguities. This allows story recipients to become discursive coproducers. They are quasi-invited to complement, to vary, and to elaborate the narratives further. Second, the effectiveness of these narratives does not result from their formal attributes or coherent content, but from the situational use made of them. This makes it necessary to consider social conventions and performative rules that regulate who may tell which stories, when and how. Hence, the focus of the historical study shifts from the form and content analysis of political propaganda to "storytelling as a form of movement culture." This poses the fundamental question of how protest movements deal with the problem of ignorance, incertitude, and incompletion, which opens up a wide and fascinating area of future research. The latter would have to include, among others, the virulently dadaistic and surrealistic forms of expression in social movements,[29] as well as the role that media ensembles, rhetorical tropes, icons, visual narratives, but also music and rhythm,[30] play in this process.

Jakob Tanner is professor emeritus for contemporary history at Zurich University. A main focus of his research lays in the entanglement of sociocultural change and the perception of societal problems. He has published a book and several articles on historical anthropology (2004, with Lynn Hunt: 2007, 2009) and the history of social movements (labor movement, suffragettes, ecological movements, rebellion around 1968). He recently published a book on the history of Switzerland in the twentieth century.

Notes

Translated by Henry M Taylor.

1. Noël Carroll, ed., *The Poetics, Aesthetics, and Philosophy of Narrative* (Malden, MA, 2009); Alain Rabatel, *Homo Narrans: pour une analyse énonciative et interactionelle du récit*, 2 vols. (Limoges, 2008); Raphaël Baroni, *La Tension Narrativ: Suspense, Curiosité et Surprise* (Paris, 2007); Mieke Bal, ed., *Narrative Theory: Critical Concepts in Literary and Cultural Studies*, 4 vols. (London, 2007); Emma Kafalenos, *Narrative Causalities* (Columbus, OH, 2006); Paul Ricoeur, *Time and Narrative*, 3 vols. (Chicago, 1984–90).
2. Patricia Ewick and Susan Silbey, "Narrating Social Structure: Stories of Resistance to Legal Authority," *American Journal of Sociology* 108 (2003): 1328–72.
3. Michail M Bachtin, *Autor und Held in der ästhetischen Tätigkeit* (Frankfurt, 2008); Michail M Bachtin, *Die Ästhetik des Wortes* (Frankfurt, 1979); Pam Morris, *The Bakhtin Reader: Selected Writings of Bakhtin, Medvedev and Voloshinov* (London, 1997).
4. Charles Baxter, *The Art of Subtext: Beyond Plot* (Saint Paul, MN, 2007).
5. Fredric Jameson, *The Political Unconscious: Narrative as a Socially Symbolic Act* (Ithaca, NY, 1981).
6. Christoph Schmitt, ed., *Erzählkulturen im Medienwandel* (Münster, 2008); Marie-Laure Ryan, ed., *Narrative across Media: The Languages of Storytelling* (Lincoln, NE, 2004).
7. Martha C Nussbaum, *Love's Knowledge. Essays on Philosophy and Literature* (New York, 1990), 286–313.
8. Regarding earlier approaches see Robert Michels, *Soziale Bewegungen zwischen Dynamik und Erstarrung: Essays zur Arbeiter-, Frauen- und nationalen Bewegung* (Berlin, 2008).
9. Joachim Raschke, *Soziale Bewegungen. Ein historisch-systematischer Grundriss* (Frankfurt, 1987).
10. Dieter Rucht, *Modernisierung und neue soziale Bewegungen: Deutschland, Frankreich und USA im Vergleich* (Frankfurt, 1994); Roland Roth and Dieter Rucht, eds, *Die Sozialen Bewegungen in Deutschland seit 1945: Ein Handbuch* (Frankfurt, 2007).
11. Peter Brandt, *Soziale Bewegungen und politische Emanzipation. Studien zur Geschichte der Arbeiterbewegung und des Sozialismus* (Bonn, 2008).

12. Niklas Luhmann, *Protest: Systemtheorie und soziale Bewegungen*, ed. K-U Hellmann (Frankfurt, 1997).
13. Hayden White, *The Content of Form. Narrative Discourse and Historical Representation* (Baltimore, 1987), x.
14. Ibid., 22.
15. Ibid., 2.
16. Ibid., 1.
17. Ibid., 42.
18. Ibid.
19. Jean-François Lyotard, "Memorandum über die Legitimität," in *Postmoderne und Dekonstruktion. Texte französischer Philosophen der Gegenwart*, ed. P Engelmann (Stuttgart, 1997), 49–56.
20. Jean-François Lyotard, "Randbemerkungen zu den Erzählungen," in *Postmoderne und Dekonstruktion. Texte französischer Philosophen der Gegenwart*, ed. P Engelmann (Stuttgart, 1997), 54–75.
21. Pierre Bourdieu, *Homo Academicus* (Frankfurt, 1988), 254–303.
22. Rabatel, *Homo Narrans*.
23. Donald E Polkinghorne, *Narrative Knowing and the Human Sciences* (Albany, NY, 1988).
24. Hayden White, *Tropics of Discourse* (Baltimore, 1985).
25. Reinhart Koselleck, "Einführung," in *Auch Klio dichtet oder Die Fiktion des Faktischen. Studie zur Tropologie des historischen Diskurses*, ed. H White (Stuttgart, 1991), 1–6.
26. Charles Tilly, "Astonishing Switzerland," in *Swiss Political Science Review* 15, no. 2 (2009): 321–31.
27. Otto Neurath, *Gesammelte bildpädagogische Schriften* (Vienna, 1991).
28. Francesca Polletta, *It Was Like a Fever: Storytelling in Protest and Politics* (Chicago, 2006); Francesca Polletta, "Storytelling in Social Movements," in *Culture, Social Movements, and Protest*, ed. H Johnston (Surrey, 2009), 33–53.
29. Klaus Brigleb, *1968. Literatur in der antiautoritären Bewegung* (Frankfurt, 1993).
30. Robert Miklitsch, *Roll over Adorno. Critical Theory, Popular Culture, Visual Media* (Albany, NY, 2006).

Recommended Reading

Bal, Mieke, ed. *Narrative Theory: Critical Concepts in Literary and Cultural Studies*. 4 vols: Vol. 1: *Major Issues in Narrative Theory*; Vol. 2: *Special Topics*; Vol. 3: *Political Narratology*; Vol. 4: *Interdisciplinarity*. London, 2007. Offers a broad and multifarious overview of all aspects of narrative theory and storytelling techniques.

Jackson, Bruce. *The Story Is True: The Art and Meaning of Telling Stories*. Philadelphia, PA, 2007. Explains from different angles how people make sense out of their life course, and how truth claims and personal experience are intertwined with the practice of storytelling.

Polletta, Francesca. *It Was Like a Fever: Storytelling in Protest and Politics.* Chicago, 2006. Describes storytelling as a mobilizing factor in social movements and explains the impact of framed narratives on social movements as an effect of their ambiguity and ambivalence.

Ryan, Marie-Laure, ed. *Narrative across Media: The Languages of Storytelling.* Lincoln, NE, 2004. Analyzes the interference between narrative models and media theory. The study asks the question of whether and how new media transform rhetorical strategies and affect the formation of social movements.

Chapter 12

Utopia

Laurence Davis

The term "utopia" refers to a no place (*outopia*) that is a good place (*eutopia*). The apparent elusiveness of the concept thus immediately raises a number of puzzling questions for those concerned with its role in protest cultures. How might one reach such a good place if it cannot be located on a map of the world? Is utopia accessible only by means of the faculty of imagination, and if so, what possible *political* functions might it perform in the very imperfect real world in which we all must live?

Utopia and Its Critics

According to anti-utopian critics of utopia, it is precisely this quality of ahistorical and antipolitical abstraction from existing reality that renders utopias either hopelessly impractical, or dangerously idealistic, or both. The latter objection (dangerous idealism) was expressed with particular vehemence by influential post-World War II liberal thinkers such as Karl Popper, Isaiah Berlin, Michael Oakeshott, and Friedrich Hayek, all of whom equated utopia with the quest for impossible perfection, and then concluded from this premise that it raised the specter of totalitarianism. Of particular concern was the gap that utopian abstraction necessarily opened up between ends and means. Berlin expressed the point by posing the following rhetorical question: if it is possible to attain a final solution to all human ills, then what price could be too high to pay for such a goal? Those convinced they had discovered the only true path to ultimate salvation would also believe they had a license to do away with the liberty of choice of others, provided they did so in the name of utopia. This, according to Berlin, was the faith of Lenin, Trotsky, and Mao, and the justification for the slaughter of millions in wars or revolutions: "gas chambers, gulag, genocide, all the monstrosities for which our century will be remembered—are the price men must pay for the felicity of future generations."[1]

The former objection (hopeless impracticality) was articulated most forcefully and influentially from a very different political perspective by Marx and Engels in *The Communist Manifesto*. In part III of the *Manifesto*, under the heading "Critical-Utopian Socialism and Communism," Marx and Engels lampooned utopian Socialists such as Saint-Simon, Fourier, and Robert Owen for conjuring up utopian castles in the air abstracted from the realities of the modern class struggle between proletariat and bourgeoisie, "historical action is to yield to their personal inventive action, historically created conditions of emancipation to fantastic ones, and the gradual, spontaneous class-organization of the proletariat to an organization of society specially contrived by these inventors."[2] According to Marx and Engels, the utopian Socialists deserved praise for articulating imaginative criticisms of existing society that contributed to the enlightenment of the working class, but their significance bore an inverse relationship to the historical development of that class. In short, like their anti-utopian liberal counterparts, Marx and Engels condemned utopianism because of its apparent quality of abstraction from existing historical and political reality.

Insofar as these criticisms are valid, then it would appear that utopia has very little value for contemporary protest movements. Moreover, whatever value it does have would be more than outweighed by its potential dangers.

Against this view, I draw an original distinction in this essay between two very different types of utopian impulse, only the first of which is vulnerable to some of the criticisms outlined above. The first I refer to as "transcendent" utopia, the second as "grounded" utopia. What chiefly distinguishes the two, I contend, is their degree of abstraction from existing reality.

Transcendent and Grounded Utopias

As the prefix "u" in utopia suggests, some utopias are constructs of the perfectionist ethical imagination that abstract from existing reality in a transcendent fashion. They thus posit a dichotomous opposition between the ideal and the real, ought and is, in which utopianism and realism confront one another as irreconcilable opposites.

In her essay "A Non-Euclidean View of California as a Cold Place to Be," Ursula K Le Guin refers to such utopias as "Euclidean" utopias. A reaction of reason and will against, away from, the here and now, the Euclidean utopia is quite literally nowhere. Pure abstract and static end, or goal, it ceases to be utopia as soon as we reach it. It can thus speak only in the future tense—the language of progress—and is inherently uninhabitable.[3] As the histories of Capitalist, industrial, and colonial development make all too clear, it is also potentially highly destructive of what is.

The focus of the non-Euclidean utopia, by contrast, is on the temporally extended present, the right here, right now inhabited by living, breathing human beings. Paradoxically, it is such that if it is to come, then it must exist already. In fact, according to Le Guin, it has existed already, as a feature of many of the so-called primitive societies crushed under the wheels of European Capitalism and technological progress. Its essence was and is a form of society in which human beings are at peace with themselves and their natural environment. Animated by a generous spirit of place rather than an exclusive and aggressive spirit of race, Le Guin's habitable utopia is concerned primarily not with the continuous advance of technology and ever-expanding economic growth, but with preserving its existence. It has a modest standard of living, conservative of natural resources, and a political life based upon consent.[4]

The distinction I wish to draw between transcendent and grounded utopias draws upon and extends Le Guin's analysis. In particular, I want to emphasize the distinction between utopias associated with the imagination of and/or quest for perfection in some impossible future (transcendent utopia), and those associated with the encouragement of greater imaginative awareness of neglected or suppressed possibilities for qualitatively better forms of living latent in the present (grounded utopia). Rather than abstracting from the ostensibly irredeemably corrupt social practices of our world in order to pass final moral judgements on them, the latter helps to shape existing social practices by converting the given confines of the here and now into an open horizon of possibilities. It does so in part by illuminating the heterodox and the extraordinary in the seemingly ordinary, and by reminding us that past, present, and future all contain multiple possibilities far in excess of concretely realized actualities.

Role in Protest Cultures

From the perspective of participants in protest cultures seeking radical democratic social change, transcendent utopias are of little value. This is because they depict or enact a static vision of society in which change seems neither desirable nor possible. They thus reproduce the dichotomous division between actual real and impossible ideal that they seek to challenge, and disempower those who engage in protest precisely in order to reject predetermined assumptions about what should be desired and what can be attained.

Grounded utopias, by contrast, both emerge organically out of and contribute to the further development of, historical movements for social change. As a result, they are emphatically not fantasized visions of perfection to be imposed upon an imperfect world, but an integral feature of that world representing the hopes and dreams of those consigned to its margins. Part and parcel of dynamic and open-ended processes of struggle, and grounded in immediate everyday needs, they challenge dominant conceptions of reality not by measuring them against the transcendent ethical standard of a fixed vision of an ideal society, but by opening a utopian space for thinking, feeling, debating, and cultivating the possibility of historically rooted (and thus historically contingent) alternative social relations.

Grounded utopias can take a variety of forms. In their fictional literary guise, they are intended to fire the imagination by engaging the reader in a complex dialogue about what is, what might be, and the relationship between the two. They are thus neither purely escapist fantasies, nor narrowly didactic constructions meant to secure the reader's unquestioning assent to a particular sociopolitical agenda, but thought experiments that invite the reader to participate in a time-sensitive journey of the utopian imagination complete with fundamental moral conflict, meaningful choice, and continuing change, by the end of which she or he may return to the nonfictional present with a broader perspective on its latent emancipatory possibilities. In their most grounded forms—notable recent examples of which include Starhawk's *The Fifth Sacred Thing* and Le Guin's *Always Coming Home*—such literary utopias evoke a strong sense of place and recall the lived experience of active participants in contemporary social movements resisting systems of oppression and domination. They may also serve as a source of inspiration for, and a catalyst for critical reflection by, these same movement activists, as in the case of Le Guin's *The Dispossessed* (itself inspired by the rebellions of 1968) and the anarchist-influenced contemporary alter-globalization movement.

Grounded utopias are by no means restricted to fictional literary creations, however, nor even to the other species of written work typically analyzed by students of utopian social and political theory. They may be expressed in an almost endless variety of forms, from unorthodox lifestyles to experiments in alternative education. Within the context of protest cultures, one may detect the distinctive traces of grounded utopianism in practices ranging from neighborhood assemblies and climate camps, to direct actions arising out of participatory democratic campaigns, to high points of revolutionary struggle. What all such (nonliterary) instances of grounded utopianism share in common is their creation of utopian spaces in concrete social or political practices meant to cultivate the possibility of alternative social relations.

Consider by way of an illustrative example the case of contemporary grassroots movements of farmers or landless people (such as the Zapatistas in Mexico) reclaiming the right to use common land to meet their subsistence needs. In the face of the currently dominant consensus that there is no alternative to market-driven corporate globalization, these very diverse grass-roots movements demonstrate by their very existence that another world is possible. Their grounded utopianism consists not in some sort of blueprint-style embodiment of the way the world should be—few if any movement participants would make such extravagant claims—but rather in stubbornly living lives at odds with the relentlessly homogenizing and destructive logic of global Capitalism. By daring through collective action to reclaim the power and responsibility for organizing their own lives, the individuals who make up these movements contest dominant understandings of what is possible and open up utopian spaces for imagining and practicing peaceful, ecologically sustainable, egalitarian, and radically democratic alternative ways of living.

Research Gaps and Open Questions

In closing, I want to acknowledge the need for extensive additional theoretical and empirical research work on the subject matter that I have explored in this essay. To date, the now well-established scholarly field of utopian studies has focused primarily on three broad varieties of utopianism: literary utopias, utopian theory, and communal experiments. By comparison, the study of the relationship between utopia and social movements has been relatively neglected. There is, in particular, a pressing need for interdisciplinary research that successfully combines philosophical analysis of the concept of utopia with an empirical understanding of social movement processes.

In any such research, the student of utopia will need to steer a careful course between two epistemological extremes: on the one hand, the Scylla of capitulation to dominant understandings of political possibility; and on the other hand, the Charybdis of reinforcing the prevailing association between utopia and deeply problematic ideas about human perfectibility. One of my primary aims in this essay has been to facilitate balanced scholarship of this sort, both by drawing an analytical distinction between transcendent and grounded utopias, and by arguing the case for the far greater explanatory power of the latter with respect to contemporary protest cultures.

Laurence Davis is college lecturer in government at University College Cork, Ireland. A series editor of the *Contemporary Anarchist Studies* book series published by Bloomsbury Press, he has taught politics at a wide range of universities in Ireland and the United Kingdom, including Oxford University, Ruskin College, University College Dublin, the National University of Ireland Galway, and the National University of Ireland Maynooth, where he cocreated the MA in community education, equality, and social activism. His publications include *Anarchism and Utopianism* (Manchester, 2014), coedited with Ruth Kinna; *The New Utopian Politics of Ursula K Le Guin's The Dispossessed* (Lexington Books, 2005), coedited with Peter Stillman.

Notes

1. Isaiah Berlin, *The Crooked Timber of Humanity,* ed. Henry Hardy (London, 1991), 16.
2. Karl Marx and Friedrich Engels, "The Communist Manifesto (1848)," in *Karl Marx: Selected Writings,* ed. D McLellan (Oxford, 1977), 244.
3. Ursula K Le Guin, "A Non-Euclidean View of California as a Cold Place to Be," in *Dancing at the Edge of the World: Thoughts on Words, Women, Places,* ed. UK Le Guin (New York, 1989), 81.
4. Ibid., 84, 93, 96.

Recommended Reading

Bammer, Angelika. *Partial Visions: Feminism and Utopianism in the 1970s.* New York, 1991. A ground-breaking study of the relationship between feminism and utopianism in the 1970s.

Cox, Laurence. "Building Utopia Here and Now: Left and Working-Class Utopias in Ireland." *Ecopolitics Online Journal* 1, no. 1 (2007): 123–32. A very helpful consideration of the relationship between utopia and contemporary Irish left and working-class social movements.

Davis, Laurence, and Ruth Kinna, eds. *Anarchism and Utopianism.* Manchester, 2014. The first book-length study of the relationship between anarchism and utopianism.

Fournier, Valérie. "Utopianism and the Cultivation of Possibilities: Grassroots Movements of Hope." In *Utopia and Organization,* edited by M Parker, 189–216. Oxford, 2002. Explores the utopian dimension of grassroots alternatives to neoliberal globalization.

Stillman, Peter. "'Nothing Is, but What Is Not': Utopias as Practical Political Philosophy." In *The Philosophy of Utopia,* edited by B Goodwin, 9–24. London, 2001. An exceptionally thoughtful analysis of utopian literature as a form of practical political philosophy.

Chapter 13

Identity

Natalia Ruiz-Junco and Scott Hunt

General Definition of the Term

Social movement groups attach meanings to symbols, narratives, and other cultural objects through social interactions. They engage in social interaction with members of their own group as well as those from other social movements, countermovements, authorities, and larger publics. Intermeshed with cultural frameworks and ideologies, identity is a crucial product of this meaning construction and at the same time facilitates the creation of distinctive protest cultures.

Since the 1980s when Jean Cohen famously put an end to a debate in the field that pitted identity against strategy in the explanation of social movement dynamics, much has been written about identity in social movements.[1] The new literature focusing on identity focused most of the attention upon the concept of collective identity.[2] While a variety of definitions of collective identity exist depending on the theoretical perspective taken, some of them have been especially important in capturing the imagination of scholars.

Melucci introduced one of the most influential definitions in the history of the concept, arguing that collective identity is "an interactive and shared definition produced by several individuals ... and concerned with the orientations of action and the field of opportunities and constraints in which the action takes place."[3] Melucci provided an important directive when he made clear that social movements should be viewed as dynamic forms of doing and being together, as actors engaged in answering both the question of what to do and simultaneously the question about what can be done. With these ideas, Melucci significantly contributed to the view that identities are emergent constructs.

A fundamental distinction is commonly made between collective and individual identity. Individual identity has received comparatively much less attention from researchers than collective identity.[4] In addition, identity has been commonly studied as a threefold structure. For example, Gamson examines identity in terms of "organizational," "movement," and "solidary group"[5]; Jasper distinguishes between identities that are "organizational," "tactical," and "activist"[6]; and Johnston, Laraña, and Gusfield refer to "individual," "collective," and "public" identities.[7] The existence of multiple classifications signals the difficulties of developing a coherent theoretical system that can encompass the empirical reality that amounts to what we call "identity" in social movements. The exuberance of classifications suggests a complex web of activity that involves identity attributions and announcements at a variety of identity levels, from personal, small group, organizational, and public.[8]

General Cultural Functions

An important function of identity is to increase the probability that people will participate in social movements. Alberto Melucci pointed out that involvement in social movements was related to identity construction: "The propensity of an individual to become involved in collective action is thus tied to the differential capacity to define an identity, that is, to the differential access to resources that enable him to participate in the process of identity building."[9]

Some scholars emphasize that participation in social movements is possible when the personal or individual identities of movement participants blend with the collective identities of the movement groups.[10] In the framing literature, this process is known as alignment; framing studies focus on understanding alignment from the perspective of individual and collective identities among movement group members, and also on understanding the framing of personal experience in the construction of activist identities.[11]

In addition, identity also functions to reinforce participation among those who are already members of social movements and identify with the group. Bert Klandermans describes this dialectic logic as follows: "Collective identity appears to foster action preparedness, action preparedness produces action participation, and in its turn, action participation strengthens collective identity."[12]

Role in Protest Cultures

In a comprehensive review, Polletta and Jasper point out that the social movement literature uses identity-based explanations to account for: (1) the start of protest when the reasons behind it cannot be simply assumed as preexisting in the social structure, (2) the reasons for actors to engage in collective action when those reasons do not reside in economic gains, (3) the election of movement tactics, and (4) the culturally based consequences of collective action.[13]

In some circumstances, as the above suggests, collective identity is often the very thing contested politically and culturally by social movements. This is commonly discussed today in terms of identity politics. Bernstein emphasizes that while every movement organization is involved with collective identity construction, many leading contemporary movements are contests over collective identities in the public sphere and thus move identity to the forefront of our study of the political.[14]

Theoretical and Empirical Research Perspectives

Like a mythical hydra, the concept of identity in the social movement literature has many facets. The most influential concept to emerge out of the interpretivist theoretical approach in social movements is identity work. The concept of identity work remains a useful tool for those scholars analyzing what people do in their everyday lives, the meanings that these actions have for them, and what they try to accomplish following those actions.

Identity work—"the range of activities individuals engage in to create, present, and sustain personal identities that are congruent with and supportive of the self-concept"[15]—is a concept initially coined at the individual level, but its reach expands to the collective level in empirical studies. These are questions the identity work concept can help clarify at both levels of analysis: Why social movement actors react with indignation to certain attacks against their group? Why do they share tears and laughter when working together toward a common goal? Why do they use certain words and not others to speak about the issues that motivate their collective action?

One of the most influential theoretical perspectives applied to the study of identity in social movements is framing. Within this orientation, it is generally assumed that we should study identity along with framing processes. However, sociologists working with this perspective note that recruitment on the basis of identity varies substantially, with some movements employing framing profusely to aid in identity work, and some others flourishing in their "consensus formation," [16] thus doing less identity work at the beginning of their mobilization.[17]

Finally, if theoretical perspectives have commonly emphasized collective identity as a single entity, empirical analysis has revealed a different reality leading sociologists to argue that "any particular movement, indeed, probably any movement organization, has a multiplicity of collective identities."[18] To illustrate, a movement organization may attempt to brand a particular collective identity for public consumption, emphasize slightly different elements of their collective identity to sympathetic allies, and stress still different elements to its members. At the same time, a movement organization may have to engage a social identity of the group that is attributed by media and other agents external to the movement. To maintain a sense of integrity or authenticity, movement organizations seek to maintain ostensible consistency between these various collective identity constructs. However, within an organization, a multiplicity of understandings of the group's identity may exist. This variation in internal collective identity constructs may go unnoticed by the actors themselves, or they may recognize some internal differences but not see them as problematic. At times, however, these internal differences in who we think we are become the focus of serious disputes that may be resolved with a greater common understanding of the group's collective identity or with enhanced factionalism or even dissolution.

Research Gaps and Open Questions

While the work on collective and individual identity in movement scholarship has produced some solid theoretical and empirical moorings, we believe that there remains some open questions that could push this body of work even further.

First, what is the relationship between identity work and each of the dimensions of framing outlined in the literature—that is, "punctuating," "attributional," and "articulatory" dimensions.[19] Specifically, there is a need to investigate the relationship between these dimensions of framing and identity construction processes at the collective and individual level. Even though the three aspects of framing mentioned above are likely to vary case by case, researchers should expect to discover several patterns of identity work within each framing dimension.

Research should also focus on the cultural processes involved in identity-making. As two scholars of social movements point out, "We still know little about the cultural building blocks that are used to construct collective identities."[20] This task remains unfinished. To address it, we suggest that we must advance beyond the triad of the cognitive, the moral, and the emotional to discuss the truly cultural. What does this ask of us as analysts? It requires us to attend to cultural processes without losing sight of the intertwined nature of attachment analyzed in our empirical work. As Melucci put it, "There is no cognition without feeling and no meaning without emotion."[21] Indeed, the literature must refocus the understanding of identity work in cultural terms, and must expand to fully include emotions in this inquiry.

Probably, the most pressing unresolved question in the literature regarding identity and protest cultures brings us back to an old but still challenging topic in social theory, that of agency and structure. Can social movement actors liberally frame their social worlds without attending to preexisting and overarching protest cultures? Are movement actors free to weave meanings at their whim, or are they totally constrained by worldviews, ideologies, and taken-for-granted meanings? We believe these relations should be studied further.

Natalia Ruiz-Junco is assistant professor of sociology at Auburn University. Her research interests include social movements, social theory, identity and emotions. She has recently published in *Current Perspectives in Social Theory*, *Journal of Contemporary Ethnography*, *Sociology Compass*, and *Studies in Symbolic Interaction*.

Scott Hunt is full professor in the School of Justice Studies at Eastern Kentucky University. His current research interests include the connection between pathological gambling, crime, and the criminal justice system; violence against migrant women; natural law theory; religion's influence on the history of criminal justice; identity construction; and social movement cultures. He is coauthor (with Pamela Wilcox and Kenneth Land) of *Criminal Circumstance: A Dynamic Multicontextual Criminal Opportunity Theory* (New York, 2003). Hunt has been published in several journals, including *Deviant Behavior*, *Symbolic Interaction*, *The Sociological Quarterly*, *Perspectives on Social Problems*, *Sociological Inquiry*, and *Journal of Criminal Justice and Popular Culture*. He was editor of the *Journal of Contemporary Ethnography* from 2004 until 2009.

Notes

1. Jean L Cohen, "Strategy or Identity: New Theoretical Paradigms and Contemporary Social Movements," *Social Research* 52 (1985): 663–716.

2. Since the inception of identity studies in social movements, however, a lingering question remains: "whether identity is really 'collective.'" See Jeffrey Broadbent, "Identity Dynamics: Motivations and Movement Mobilizations in the United States and Japan," in *Economic and Political Contention in Comparative Perspective*, ed. M Kousis and C Tilly (Boulder, CO, 2005), 48.

3. Alberto Melucci, "The Process of Collective Identity," in *Social Movements and Culture*, ed. H Johnston and B Klandermans (Minneapolis, MN, 1995), 44. See also Verta Taylor and Nancy E Whittier, "Collective Identity in Social Movement Communities: Lesbian Feminist Mobilization," in *Frontiers in Social Movement Theory*, ed. A Morris and C Mueller (New Haven, CT, 1992), 104–29.

4. See, for example, Kendal L Broad, "Institutional Selves in Social Movements: The Rhetorical Production of FTM/Transmen," *Research in Political Sociology* 13 (2004): 225–55; Rebecca E Klatch, "The Development of Individual Identity and Consciousness among Movements of the Left and Right," in *Social Movements. Identity, Culture, and the State*, ed. DS Meyer, N Whittier, and B Robnett (New York, 2002), 185–201.

5. William A Gamson, "Commitment and Agency in Social Movements," *Sociological Forum* 6 (1991): 27–50; see also William A Gamson, "Constructing Social Protest," in *Social Movements and Culture*, ed. H Johnston and B Klandermans (Minneapolis, MN, 1995), 85–106.

6. James M Jasper, *The Art of Moral Protest* (Chicago, 1997).

7. Hank Johnston, Enrique Laraña, and Joseph R Gusfield, "Identities, Grievances, and New Social Movements," in *New Social Movements: From Ideology to Identity*, ed. E Laraña, H Johnston, and JR Gusfield (Philadelphia, PA, 1994), 3–35.

8. Scott A Hunt, Robert D Benford, and David A Snow, "Identity Fields: Framing Processes and the Social Construction of Movement Identities," in *New Social Movements: From Ideology to Identity*, ed. E Laraña, H Johnston, and JR Gusfield (Philadelphia, PA, 1994), 185–208.

9. Alberto Melucci, "Getting Involved: Identity and Mobilization in Social Movements," *International Social Movement Research* 1 (1988): 343.

10. See David A Snow and Doug McAdam, "Identity Work Processes in the Context of Social Movements: Clarifying the Identity/Movement Nexus," in *Self, Identity and Social Movements*, ed. S Stryker, TJ Owens, and RW White (New York, 2000), 41–67.

11. Natalia Ruiz-Junco, "Losing Neutrality in Your Everyday Life: Framing Experience and Activist Identity Construction in the Spanish Environmental Movement," *Journal of Contemporary Ethnography* 40 (2011): 713–33.

12. Bert Klandermans, "Politicized Collective Identity: Collective Identity and Political Protest," *Advances in Group Processes* 22 (2005): 163.

13. Francesca Polletta and James M Jasper, "Collective Identity and Social Movements," *Annual Review of Sociology* 27 (2001): 284.

14. See Mary Bernstein, "Identity Politics," *Annual Review of Sociology* 31 (2005): 47–74.

15. David A Snow and Leon Anderson, "Identity Work among the Homeless: The Verbal Construction and Avowal of Personal Identities," *American Journal of Sociology* 92 (1987): 1348.

16. Bert Klandermans, "The Formation and Mobilization of Consensus," *International Social Movement Research* 1 (1988): 173–96.
17. Snow and McAdam, "Identity Work Processes in the Context of Social Movements," 56.
18. Scott A Hunt and Robert D Benford, "Collective Identity, Solidarity, and Commitment," in *The Blackwell Companion to Social Movements,* ed. D Snow, SA Soule, and H Kriesi (Oxford, 2004), 450.
19. Robert D Benford and David A Snow, "Framing Processes and Social Movements: An Overview and Assessment," *Annual Review of Sociology* 26 (2000): 611–39.
20. Francesca Polletta and James M Jasper, "Collective Identity and Social Movements," *Annual Review of Sociology* 27 (2001): 299.
21. Melucci, "The Process of Collective Identity," 45.

Recommended Reading

Cohen, Jean L. "Strategy or Identity: New Theoretical Paradigms and Contemporary Social Movements." *Social Research* 52 (1985): 663–716. Classic argument that signals a shift in the field toward greater acceptance of social movement perspectives focusing on identity.

Hunt, Scott A, and Robert D Benford. "Collective Identity, Solidarity, and Commitment." In *The Blackwell Companion to Social Movements,* edited by D Snow, SA Soule, and H Kriesi, 433–457. Oxford, 2004. Reviews the connections between the concept of collective identity and the related concepts of solidarity and commitment.

Melucci, Alberto. "The Process of Collective Identity." In *Social Movements and Culture,* edited by H Johnston and B Klandermans, 41–63. Minneapolis, MN, 1995. An influential definition of collective identity with a focus on process.

Snow, David A, and Doug McAdam. "Identity Work Processes in the Context of Social Movements: Clarifying the Identity/Movement Nexus." In *Self, Identity and Social Movements,* edited by S Stryker, TJ Owens, and RW White, 41–67. New York, 2000. Applies the concept of identity work in social movement contexts distinguishing several identity construction processes.

Chapter 14

Emotion

Deborah B Gould

General Definitions

Etymologically, emotion and movements (in the sense of protest) are related. Emotion, meaning a physical moving, stirring, agitation, comes from the Old French *emouvoir,* meaning stir up, and from the Latin *emovere,* meaning move out, remove, agitate, from *ex-* meaning out and *movere* meaning to move.[1] Movement comes from the postclassical Latin *movementum,* meaning motion, and earlier, *movimentum,* meaning emotion, rebellion, or uprising.[2] The verb "to move"—which means to affect with emotion and to prompt or impel toward some action—links emotion and movements and suggests a frequent accompaniment.[3] We might expect, then, that studies of social movements and other forms of protest politics would foreground the role of emotion in mobilization. History shows, however, that scholars of protest have been and continue to be ambivalent about emotion.

Emotion: General Cultural Functions and Role in Protest Cultures

The collective behavior literature from the late nineteenth and early to mid-twentieth century tended to pathologize those who engage in contentious politics, viewing collective protest not as struggles over power but rather as the emotionally driven working out of participants' psychic distress. In this view, protest emerged when a structural strain—for example, an economic depression—disrupted the normative order and provoked feelings like alienation and anxiety, leading individuals to turn toward rash, frenzied, disruptive group behavior. Individuals engaged in protest not because they had political grievances but because social changes made them psychologically unstable and emotionally overwrought, leading them toward irrational behavior.[4]

Distinguishing itself from this earlier collective behavior literature, the new field of social movement studies that emerged in the 1970s responded to the former's disparaging portrayals of protest and protesters by adopting paradigms that assumed, even if implicitly, the rationality of protesters. Resource mobilization and political process models, for example, posit that participants in collective action are ordinary actors in the polity who, blocked from engaging in routine interest group politics, unite and prudently turn to extrainstitutional politics to press their demands. This embrace of rational actor models usefully countered the classical paradigms' depictions of protesters as impulsive, irrational deviants, but it simultaneously entailed an evacuation of emotion from research into contentious politics. In light of prevailing understandings that oppose emotion to reason, acknowledging that protesters might be motivated by feelings risked painting activists as irrational, so scholars in this new field expelled emotion, replacing the unthinking and irrational psychological misfit with the dispassionate and calculating rational actor. Whereas in the classical models we had protesters who felt their grievances deeply but never cognitively assessed them, in the now-dominant models, we have rational actors who coolly calculate their grievances and pursue a strategic course of action, all the while apparently devoid of anger, fear, joy, pride, shame, hope, or any other emotion.[5]

Emotion in Protest Cultures: Research Perspectives

This is the terrain on which an emotional turn in the study of social movements has occurred. In the late 1990s, in an effort to offer a corrective to the assumption of rational actors in the reigning political process model but without resurrecting the problems presented by the classical collective behavior models, a number of social movement scholars began to explore the emotional dimensions of mobilization and demobilization. Where the earlier collective behavior literature coded institutional politics as the realm of reason and maligned protest as driven by emotion and thus unreason, and where, in response, the next generation of scholars assumed movement actors' rationality and wrote emotion out of their accounts, scholars in the emotional turn offer a multifaceted picture of human beingness that, without denying the reasoning capabilities of movement actors, posits emotion as a ubiquitous feature of social life. Challenging the pitting of emotion against reason, this literature instead posits emotion as a motivational force and a crucial means by which we as human beings come to know and understand ourselves and our contexts, our interests and commitments, our needs, and our options in securing those needs. Scholars accordingly cannot ignore emotion or relegate it to one arena (e.g., protest) that can then be disparaged and dismissed.[6]

This turn toward emotion in the study of protest not only challenges the rationalist ontology that prevails in much of the literature, but it also enhances our understanding of the workings of key concepts in the field. The factors that movement scholars deem important for mobilization have force precisely because of the feelings that they elicit, stir up, amplify, dampen: opening political opportunities, for example, might be an important factor in the emergence of a social movement but only to the extent that an emotional charge attaches to those openings; a collective action frame successfully mobilizes only when emotionally resonant. Even more than improving existing models, in foregrounding emotion this research points us toward a largely unexplored arena for analyzing crucial sources of activism, and blockages as well. Political opportunities might be tightly closed, but indignation and desperation might combine to encourage mobilization, or the sheer pleasure of engaging in contentious politics might generate a willingness to protest despite the small odds of success. Conversely, political opportunities might be opening, but fear, a paralyzing sense of hopelessness, or an overriding numbness might impede mobilization.

A focus on emotion also provides insight into why participants continue their involvement in activist formations when they could easily take the proverbial free ride and rely on others to do the work. Activist contexts, as sites where world-making occurs, generate strong feelings among participants—for example, marvel at being part of a collectivity, euphoria and camaraderie from being in an action together, feelings of fulfillment that derive from taking part in something larger than oneself, a sense of freedom to become the self you want to be. Once experienced, the desire to feel those feelings again may be strong and that might sustain participation. As well, activist contexts are crucial sites of meaning-production in the realm of emotion: they not only offer a language for people's often amorphous, inchoate, nontransparent affective states, they also provide an emotional pedagogy of sorts, a guide for what and how to feel and for what to do in light of those feelings. Stories from women's consciousness-raising groups show that feminists challenged individualized understandings of what many women were experiencing as depression and, pointing to the social origins of that feeling state, renamed it anger. Their interpretive emotion work encouraged women to understand themselves and their situations in new ways and indeed to feel differently, and then to act differently as well.

Attending to emotion may also illuminate aspects of movement decline. To understand why internal conflicts sometimes fracture movements, for example, we may need to explore their emotional undercurrents, the often unstated and unacknowledged, but nevertheless forceful, feeling states that often shape the texture, tonality, intensity, velocity—the very content and character—of such conflicts. Internal conflicts do not always destroy movements, but they can become extremely difficult to navigate when feelings such as betrayal, nonrecognition, resentment, and mistrust are in play.

In short, then, foregrounding emotion helps to illuminate what it is like to participate in protest politics and enhances our understanding of the emergence, sustainability, and decline of activist formations.

An important open question for scholars in the field is how to characterize emotion. Renewed interest in emotion spans the disciplines, and as a result, definitions have proliferated. For those studying social movements and other forms of protest politics, one central unresolved question is the relationship between emotion and reason. Haunted by the earlier collective behavior literature, which often equated emotionality with irrationality, scholars in the emotional turn sometimes have tamed emotion conceptually, strongly linking it to cognition and rationality.[7] Assuming thought-emotion continuity allows scholars to fend off the specter of irrationality, but what aspects of political action and inaction are missed if we ignore, for example, bodily experience and nonconscious forms of knowing and sense-making; the often ambivalent and contradictory nature of our feelings; the inconsistencies and noncoherences within our thoughts and between our cognitive and felt responses to the world? While it is true that political feelings sometimes flow unambiguously and predictably from one's cognitive processing, such a rationalist perspective masks the way that feelings—political and otherwise—frequently diverge from our reasoning selves. We might know that our government has authorized torture of prisoners, and we might even be outraged, but feeling overwhelmed in the face of this information, having anxiety about engaging in activism, or desiring to block out the world's problems might be what shapes our responses, or nonresponses, to this knowledge.

Political emotion is often less tied to conscious, cognitive, rational assessments and more ambiguous, ambivalent, contradictory, noncoherent, undisciplined, and surprising than we would like to believe. If we pursue cultural theorist Lauren Berlant's claim that nonrationality is "at the heart of the political,"[8] we can open our analyses to inquiries into how the less-than-fully conscious, inchoate, contradictory, indeterminate aspects of human emotion shape political action and inaction.[9]

Deborah B Gould is associate professor of sociology at the University of California, Santa Cruz. Her scholarly interests are in contentious politics and political emotion. Her first book, *Moving Politics: Emotion and ACT UP's Fight Against AIDS* (Chicago, 2009) won the "Distinguished Contribution to Scholarship Award" from the American Sociological Association's Political Sociology Section (2010) and the "Ruth Benedict Book Prize" from the American Anthropological Association (2010). Other recent publications include articles in *The Sociological Quarterly, Contexts,* and *Contemporary European History,* as well as a chapter in *Methods of Exploring Emotions,* ed. H Flam and J Kleres (Routledge, 2015).

Notes

1. Online Etymology Dictionary, s.v. "emotion," at http://www.etymonline.com/ index.php?search=emotion&searchmode=none.
2. Oxford English Dictionary Online, s.v. "movement," at http://dictionary.oed.com/ cgi/entry/00317198?single=1&query_type=word&queryword=movement&first=1 &max_to_show=10.
3. Online Etymology Dictionary, s.v. "move," at http://www.etymonline.com/index. php?term=move.
4. For a succinct and lucid analysis of different classical models of protest, including collective behavior models, see Doug McAdam, *Political Process Model and the Development of Black Insurgency, 1930–1970* (Chicago, 1982), chapter 1.
5. For a critique of the rationalist bias in these models, see Jeff Goodwin, James M Jasper, and Francesca Polletta, "Return of the Repressed: The Fall and Rise of Emotions in Social Movement Theory," *Mobilization* 5, no. 1 (2000): 65–84.
6. Texts in the emotional turn are proliferating; a few that helped to launch it are: Ronald Aminzade and Doug McAdam, "Emotions and Contentious Politics," in *Silence and Voice in the Study of Contentious Politics,* ed. R Aminzade et al. (Cambridge, 2001), 14–50; Jeff Goodwin, James M Jasper, and Francesca Polletta, eds, *Passionate Politics: Emotions and Social Movements* (Chicago, 2001); and James M Jasper, "The Emotions of Protest: Affective and Reactive Emotions in and around Social Movements," Sociological Forum 13, no. 3 (1998): 397–424.
7. See, for example, Jasper, "The Emotions of Protest"; and Jeff Goodwin, James M Jasper, and Francesca Polletta, "Introduction: Why Emotions Matter," in *Passionate Politics: Emotions and Social Movements,* ed. J Goodwin, J Jasper, and F Polletta (Chicago, 2001), 13.
8. Nonrationality differs from irrationality: the nonrational is beside, or to the side of, rather than within, conscious, cognitive sense-making; the term irrational usually means that which is contrary to such processes, connoting that which goes against one's interests as well as that which is (therefore) illogical, crazy, senseless, unfounded, and unreasonable.
9. See Lauren Berlant, "Unfeeling Kerry," *Theory & Event* 8, no. 2 (2005).

Recommended Reading

In social movement studies, texts for further reading include:

Emirbayer, Mustafa, and Chad A Goldberg. "Pragmatism, Bourdieu, and Collective Emotions in Contentious Politics." *Theory and Society* 34 (2005): 469–518.

Flam, H. & King, D. (Eds.) (2005) *Emotions and Social Movements.* Routledge, London.

Goodwin, Jeff, James M Jasper, and Francesca Polletta, eds. *Passionate Politics: Emotions and Social Movements.* Chicago, 2001.

Gould, Deborah B. *Moving Politics: Emotion and ACT UP's Fight against AIDS.* Chicago, 2009.

In Marxist literary theory, see:

Williams, Raymond. *Marxism and Literature.* Oxford, 1977.

In cultural studies, see works by Lauren Berlant including "Unfeeling Kerry." *Theory & Event* 8, no. 2 (2005); and "The Epistemology of State Emotion." In *Dissent in Dangerous Times,* edited by A Sarat, 46–78. Ann Arbor, MI, 2005.

Chapter 15

Commitment

Catherine Corrigall-Brown

Humans are fundamentally social and, therefore, become embedded in a multitude of relationships. A person is committed to a group, cause, or relationship to the extent that they are fully invested in it and feel a sense of loyalty and belonging to it. Individuals with these feelings of personal commitment come to see the group or cause as an extension of the self.[1] Feelings of commitment impel people to remain in a relationship, cause, or group over time,[2] and a committed individual pursues a consistent line of activity even at the expense of other potential activities and interests.[3] In this chapter, I examine commitment within a specific context, social movements and contentious politics.

General Definition of the Term

Commitment is a multidimensional construct. Based on the work of Meyer and Allen,[4] Klandermans outlines three dimensions of commitment, which can be directed at a group, a relationship, or a cause.[5] First, there is an affective dimension: an emotional attachment that results from rewarding participatory experiences. Second, individuals can become normatively committed to a cause, group, or relationship. This commitment is the result of long-term socialization processes that generate values and beliefs congruent with those of the organization. Finally, individuals can feel a sense of continuance commitment, which is an obligation to remain in the organization or cause over time. This type of commitment is based on the perceived costs associated with leaving the cause or group. When individuals invest more and when the alternatives are poor, they will develop continuance commitment.

General Cultural Functions and Role in Protest Cultures

A feeling of personal commitment is significant for both initial and continued participation in social movements. Individuals become involved in groups to which they feel a sense of commitment. Personal commitment is then further strengthened through continued participation in social movements because engaging in social movement groups, activities, and causes can help to create feelings of attachment to the issues, organizations, and other participants. Once created, however, movement commitment does not endure by itself. It must be maintained through interaction with other members and the organizations as a whole. The more rewarding these interactions, the more likely it is that individuals will sustain their commitment and participation over time.[6] However, disappointing participatory experiences weaken commitment, and this weaker commitment leads to less active participation over time.

Engagement in ritual activity within groups is particularly important for fostering feelings of commitment.[7] Rituals are symbolic embodiments of the beliefs and feelings of a group. As such, they bring like-minded individuals together on a regular basis, rejuvenating the emotional bonds and relational ties that strengthen affective commitment and keep people integrated into the group. Collective rituals remind participants of their basic moral commitment to the group and reinforce a sense of solidarity within the group.[8] These rituals may be as simple as informal conversations between members but are often more complex events such as prayer meetings, rallies, and attendance at consciousness-raising groups.[9]

Theoretical Perspectives and Empirical Research

The United Farm Workers (UFW) illustrate the significance of both social interaction and ritual activity in the creation of commitment among group members. The UFW is an organization that fights for labor rights for migrant farm workers in the United States. Leaders of the UFW were able to create and maintain commitment among the membership in part because many participants lived communally at the union headquarters at La Paz. This living arrangement involved high levels of intense social interaction that enabled individuals to create and maintain strong relationships with one another. The long working hours and rigorous campaigns also contributed to solidifying friendships within the organization.[10]

Ritual interaction, in the form of weekly meetings, strengthened the social ties created in the UFW. Group meetings were based on the shared Catholic experience of many of the group members and were also inspired by African American, Protestant church culture. They included singing, speeches, witnessing, prayer, and other ritualized activities. In addition, the celebration of holidays, such as Cesar Chavez's birthday, Mexican Independence Day, and weddings, brought together individuals living at La Paz. Finally, community was intentionally created and sustained through activities such as caring for communal gardens.[11]

Organizations can be critical to the development of commitment among group members. There are many dimensions of organizational structure or group context that can facilitate or hinder the development of commitment among participants. Hirsch's study of the Columbia Divestment Campaign illustrates the significant role of group context in creating and sustaining commitment over time.

In the early 1980s, a Columbia student group was formed to stop their university from investing in companies that conducted business in South Africa. From 1981 to 1985, the group struggled to attract widespread support. However, in 1985, a dramatic 3-week blockade on campus attracted several hundred student participants.[12] The organizers were able to create feelings of intense commitment among the participants over the course of the blockade through the use of four main techniques: consciousness-raising, collective-empowerment, polarization, and collective decision making.

Collective decision making was a particularly important means of fostering commitment in this campaign. At one point, the university administration threatened to expel U.S. students and deport international students involved in the protests. Group leaders conducted intense discussion sessions, sometimes lasting four to five hours, and group participants worked to create a consensus about what course of action would be taken. Because committed protesters often felt bound by group decisions made during discussions, even when those decisions were contrary to their personal preferences, their individual commitment and participation was sustained for most members, despite difficult circumstances.

Social interaction, engagement in ritual activities, and collective decision making within organizations all aid in the creation and maintenance of commitment within social movements. This personal commitment is very important for social movement groups and causes because it helps to maintain the participation of individuals over time. Indeed, Zurcher and Snow find that an individual's continued participation in a movement or cause over time "is largely a function of the extent to which the individual's dispositions, interests, and world view become linked to the goals, ideology, and internal requirements of the movement as an organized collectivity."[13] In effect, whether a participant remains active or leaves is largely dependent on whether he or she becomes committed to the movement or organization. Individuals who are more committed tend to remain active longer and are more likely to engage in more intense and consistent ways.

Catherine Corrigall-Brown is assistant professor in the Department of Sociology at the University of British Columbia, Canada. Her research focuses on participation in social movements, coalitions, and framing. This research has appeared in journals such as *Social Forces* (2007), *Sociological Perspectives* (2009), the *International Journal of Comparative Sociology* (2011), and *Mobilization* (2010), as well as in her book *Patterns of Protest: Trajectories of Participation in Social Movements* (Stanford, CA, 2012). She is currently working on a cross-national comparative project examining the funding of the global environmental movement.

Notes

1. Rosabeth M Kanter, *Commitment and Community: Communes and Utopias in Sociological Perspective* (Cambridge, 1972).
2. Bert Klandermans, *The Social Psychology of Protest* (Oxford, 1997).
3. Howard Becker, "Notes on the Concept of Commitment," *American Journal of Sociology* 66 (1960): 32–40.
4. John P Meyer and Natalie J Allen, "The Measurement and Antecedents of Affective, Continuance and Normative Commitment to the Organization," *Journal of Occupational and Organizational Psychology* 63 (1990): 1–8.
5. Klandermans, *The Social Psychology of Protest*.
6. Ibid.
7. James Downton and Paul Wehr, *The Persistent Activist: How Peace Commitment Develops and Survives* (Boulder, CO, 1997); Verta Taylor and Nancy E Whittier, "Analytical Approaches to Social Movement Culture: The Culture of the Women's Movement," in *Social Movements and Culture,* ed. H Johnston and B Klandermans (Minneapolis, MN, 1995), 163–87.
8. James M Jasper, "The Emotions of Protest: Affective and Reactive Emotions in and around Social Movements," *Sociological Forum* 13, no. 3 (1998): 397–424.
9. Rick Fantasia, *Cultures of Solidarity: Consciousness, Action, and Contemporary American Workers* (Berkeley, CA, 1988); Eric L Hirsch, "'Sacrifice for the Cause.' Group Processes, Recruitment, and Commitment in a Student Social Movement," *American Sociological Review* 55, no. 2 (1990): 243–54; and Sharon E Nepstad, "'Persistent Resistance' Commitment and Community in the Plowshares Movement," *Social Problems* 51, no. 1 (2004): 43–60.

10. Catherine Corrigall-Brown, *Patterns of Protest: Trajectories of Participation in Social Movements* (Stanford, CA, 2012).
11. Ibid.
12. Eric L Hirsch, "Sacrifice for the Cause: Group Processes, Recruitment, and Commitment in a Student Social Movement," *American Sociological Review* 55, no. 2 (1990): 243–54.
13. Louis A Zurcher and David A Snow, "Collective Behavior: Social Movements," in *Social Psychology: Sociological Perspectives,* ed. M Rosenberg and RH Turner (New York, 1981), 447–82.

Recommended Reading

Downton, James, and Paul Wehr. *The Persistent Activist: How Peace Commitment Develops and Survives.* Boulder, CO, 1997. This book provides a theoretical and empirical examination of commitment in the peace movement.

Hirsch, Eric L. "Sacrifice for the Cause: Group Processes, Recruitment, and Commitment in a Student Social Movement." *American Sociological Review* 55, no. 2 (1990): 243–54. This article examines of the role of organizations in fostering commitment within the Columbia Divestment movement.

Kanter, Rosabeth M. *Commitment and Community: Communes and Utopias in Sociological Perspective.* Cambridge, 1972. Kanter's book is a series of in-depth case studies of commitment in utopian communities.

Klandermans, Bert. *The Social Psychology of Protest.* Oxford, 1997. This book provides a broader conceptualization of social movement participation and the importance of commitment for individual participants.

Part III

Morphology of Protest

Media

Chapter 16

Body

Andrea Pabst

General Definition of the Term

The body has never been a topic of the natural sciences alone.[1] Its diverse
cultural meanings have been discussed, for instance, by philosophers, psy-
choanalysts, anthropologists, and sociologists. There is thus no one single
definition of the body as such. General studies that try to map the field of a
sociology of the body usually proceed by adding adjectives to the body like
"disciplined," "dominating," "mirroring," or "communicative"[2]; use combi-
nations like the body "and social (dis)order," "and identities," "in health and
disease," "and technologies," "in consumer culture"[3]; and/or critically consult
classical authors and approaches of sociology.[4] Sociological approaches of the
body can thus be broadly distinguished as structuralist, system-theoretical,
post-structuralist, constructivist, and structuration approaches. Embodied
social theory is moreover influenced by psychoanalysis, by phenomenology,
or in particular in a German context, by philosophical anthropology.

The diversity of such studies and the broad range of sociological perspectives show that the human body can be broadly understood as a hybrid of
social, technological, cultural and natural components that are mutually
intertwined in manifold ways.

General Cultural Functions

The specific cultural functions attributed to the body depend on the respective theoretical approach. From a structuralist perspective, the body is

Figure 16.1. Putting oneself at stake: "manufactured vulnerability."
© Photo by Betty Pabst.

Figure 16.2.
Reducing vulnerability:
tools against physical
and political repression.
© Photo by Betty Pabst.

understood, for instance, as a symbol of social structures[5] or as something that must be controlled to not become a threat for social order.[6] In systems theory following Niklas Luhmann, the cultural functions of the body depend on the respective communication over it.[7] Michel Foucault's understanding of bodies as discourses can be seen as an already classical approach of post-structuralism. Here power relations determine the respective cultural functions of the body.[8] According to constructivism, the body structures interaction, in particular face-to-face-interaction.[9] Structuration theory tries to integrate structuralist and constructivist assumptions by defining the body as a product and producer of society.[10]

Role in Protest Cultures

The prominence of the body in social and cultural theories is owed not least to diverse liberation movements such as the ones undertaken by feminists, gays, lesbians, and queers, the black civil rights movement, anti-AIDS activists, and the disability rights or the anti-psychiatry movements, which raised awareness about bodies' different needs and about discrimination based on embodiment. Those activists and the movements they started were often part of academia themselves, and thus they helped to develop and establish systematic social and cultural research on bodies. Beyond traditional liberation movements, one can think of further protests in which the *issue* itself is the body—parts of it or particular bodies. For instance, some pro-life activists understand every abortion as murder, and racists attack people because of another skin color. When the body is the issue, it is not necessarily and not always only its physical being that is at stake. Often the body stands as a *symbol* as well: skin color is seen as a signifier of worth by racists. Feminists have claimed that the right of women to control their own bodies is a basic human right, which often meant and still can mean the right to be seen as human beings at all. Black civil rights movements not only claimed that "black is beautiful," but also fought for recognition and for abandoning discrimination based on skin color. In a similar vein, disability rights' activists demand the recognition of needs of disabled people without degrading them to second-class status. Some people suffering from psychiatric treatment are protesting against the ongoing intoxication of their bodies with psychotropics.

What is at stake is not only the physical body, but also the sociocultural meanings it stands for: when female, queer, black, disabled, sick bodies are seen as less valuable, this obviously has consequences for the respective individual or group of people. Those social and political consequences can sometimes be life-threatening. In any case, they affect the person as such because we cannot leave our bodies behind. Furthermore, bodies can be the *means* of protest cultures: pictures of dead fetuses shown by pro-life activists, women wearing T-shirts saying "I had an abortion," anti-AIDS campaigners staging die-ins to draw attention to the mortal disease or self-immolations are just some brief examples.

Whether the body is at issue in the protest itself, or whether it is used as a means or a symbol, it always has consequences for the respective embodied self as such: the *experience* of embodiment in protest thus plays a crucial role. Activists might encounter bodily harm due to their protest through their own actions or through those of others. Trauma and emotional harm are embodied experiences, too. But beside those experiences of violence, protest can be also a joyous, irritating, motivating, strengthening, or overwhelming experience that will be bodily remembered as such.

Theoretical and Empirical Research Perspectives

Most of the studies on embodiment and protest consider more than only one perspective of those roles of the body in protest cultures mentioned above. This is due to the fact that they all analyze those topics in relation to a certain protest movement, tactic/strategy, or event. Up to now, there are only a few monographs that focus primarily on embodiment and protest: Allen Feldman's study on violence in Northern Ireland, Patrick Anderson's research on hunger as a means of protest, or Brett Lunceford's book on nudity in protest.[11]

In her study of left-wing militant activists in Sweden between 1996 and 1999, Abby Peterson devotes one chapter to the militant body.[12] She explores three dimensions of militant bodies: vulnerable, massed, and moralized/self-disciplined bodies. Speaking about vulnerable bodies, she refers in particular to Brian Doherty's study on manufactured vulnerability.[13] Kevin Michael DeLuca also refers to the vulnerability of protesters and shows how they make use of it.[14] He focuses on how the body itself becomes the argument.

A contribution that particularly emphasizes the meaning of embodied experience of protest is Lisa Blackman's study of anti-psychiatric activism, namely the work of the Hearing Voices Network that tries to enable voice hearers to live with their embodied experience of voice hearing rather than being treated with psychotropics.[15] Jeffrey Juris points to the significance of experiencing existing networks by performing street protests.[16]

When it comes to the connection of social stratification, embodiment, and protest, it is especially the *gender dimension* that has been referred to in existing scholarship. Barbara Sutton reflects upon the naked protest of a woman at the 2003 World Social Forum in Porto Alegre, and the ambivalence this entails between contesting and affirming the stereotypical image of women.[17] In her research on women's bodily resistance in Argentina, Sutton reveals diverse dimensions of women's *poner el cuerpo* (giving the body/putting the body at stake) that transform the suffering female bodies into bodies of resistance, as in the case of the mothers of the Plaza de Mayo or women who suffered (sexualized) torture engaging in public shaming performances to denounce rapists.[18] Orna Sasson-Levy and Tamar Rapoport explore how the Cartesian dualism of body and mind works in movements: while the mixed gender movement, "The 21st Year," used the body as a medium for "carrying the movement's political message" in the case of the women-only movement, "Women in Black," "the body never remained unmarked or taken for granted: the body was the message."[19] In a similar vein, Wendy Parkins describes how the body itself became the argument in the British suffragette movement: "Suffragettes did not simply act to 'become' citizens or act 'like' citizens, they 'acted' citizenship."[20] Moreover, she refers to the undermining of feminine images by the highly self-disciplined, almost military suffragettes' bodies that made the hunger strike an important tool of suffragettes' protest. Referring to the use of the body as a means of protest, Margaret L Laware describes women's bodies in protests against the placement of nuclear missiles in Great Britain as "rhetorical topos."[21]

Jasbir K Puar and Amit S Rai give an example of the embodiment of protesters by their *opponents*.[22] Drawing on Foucault, they show how after 9/11 terrorists have been constructed as sexual perverts with a failed heterosexuality and a hybrid gender; as monsters that have to be quarantined to save the population as such (biopolitics); and as individuals who have to be corrected.[23] Puar and Rai show how this increased the violence against queers and specifically queers of color in the United States.

Research Gaps and Open Questions

Following Bourdieu, Nick Crossley for instance suggests the terms "radical habitus" and "taste of contention" but does not elaborate on the corporeality of these terms regarding protest.[24]

While protest research deals extensively with the question of collective identity, the collective body is still under-theorized. Peterson's heuristic of massed bodies is a rare example of an approach to the relation between the collective and the individual body in protest. This under-theorization is certainly due to the wide lack of social research on collective bodies and embodiment in general. In this regard, applying the embodied social theory of Bourdieu and in particular his differentiation between class/group and individual habitus or the Foucauldian perspective of bio-power that deals with the regulation of collective bodies in the sense of populations might be helpful starting points.

Furthermore, the relations between embodied experiences and the instrumentalization of the body for protest have thus rarely been addressed.

When it comes to the question of social stratification, there are mostly references made to the connection of embodied protest and gender. What is still missing is systematic research regarding these questions in regards to class, race, disability, or age.

Last but not least, it seems that most of the scholars who research the connection of embodiment/bodies and protest chose kinds of activism that they somehow sympathize with or are generally speaking seen as left-liberal. Without a doubt, research on protesting bodies and embodied protest could be thus broadened topically as well.

Andrea Pabst did her doctor's degree in sociology at Trier University, Germany. Her main fields of research are political sociology, with a focus on protest and violence, sociology of the body as well as sociology of knowledge. She published a couple of articles on the body in protest, as for instance: "Protesting Bodies and Bodily Protest—A Plea for a 'Thinking through the Body' in Social Movement Research," in *Between the Avant Garde and the Everyday: Subversive Politics in Europe, 1958–2008,* ed. L Anton and T Brown (New York, 2011). Together with Florian Heßdörfer and Peter Ullrich, she coedited the book *Prevent and Tame. Protest under (Self-)Control* (Berlin, 2010). Together with Martin Endreß, she published the article "Violence and Shattered Trust: Sociological Considerations," in: *Human Studies,* March, 36, 1, (2013), 89–106.

Notes

1. For critical comments and corrections, I would like to thank André Bank and Rosalie Metro.
2. Arthur W Frank, "For a Sociology of the Body: An Analytical Review," in *The Body. Social Process and Cultural Theory,* ed. Mike Featherstone, Mike Hepworth, and Bryan S Turner (London, 1991), 36–102.
3. Mariam Fraser and Monica Greco, *The Body. A Reader* (New York, 2005).
4. For example, Chris Shilling, *The Body and Social Theory* (London, 1993); and Nick Crossley, *The Social Body. Habit, Identity and Desire* (London, 2001).

5. Cf. Mary Douglas, *Natural Symbols: Explorations in Cosmology* (Harmondsworth, 1970).

6. Cf. Bryan S Turner, *The Body and Society. Explorations in Social Theory* (Oxford, 1984).

7. Cf. Bero Rigauer, "Die Erfindung des menschlichen Körpers in der Soziologie. Eine systemtheoretische Konzeption und Perspektive," in *Body Turn. Perspektiven der Soziologie des Körpers und des Sports,* ed. Robert Gugutzer (Bielefeld, 2006), 57–79.

8. Cf., for example, Michel Foucault, *The History of Sexuality Vol. 1: The Will to Knowledge* (London, 1976).

9. Cf., for example, Erving Goffman, *The Presentation of Self in Everyday Life* (London, 1969).

10. Cf. Pierre Bourdieu, *The Logic of Practice* (Cambridge, 1990), 110.

11. Allen Feldman, *Formations of Violence: The Narrative of the Body and Political Terror in Northern Ireland* (Chicago, 1991); Patrick Anderson, *So Much Wasted: Hunger Performance and the Morbidity of Resistance* (Durham, NC, 2010); Brett Lunceford, *Naked Politics: Nudity, Political Action, and the Rhetoric of the Body* (Lanham, MD, 2012).

12. Abby Peterson, *Contemporary Political Protest: Essays on Political Militancy* (Aldershot, 2001), 69–101.

13. Brian Doherty, "Manufactured Vulnerability: Eco-Activist Tactics in Britain," *Mobilization* 4, no. 1 (1999), 75–89.

14. Kevin Michael DeLuca, "Unruly Arguments: The Body Rhetoric of Earth First!, ACT UP, and Queer Nation," *Argumentation and Advocacy* 36 (1999), 9–21.

15. Lisa Blackman, "Psychiatric Culture and Bodies of Resistance," *Body & Society* 13, no. 2 (2007), 1–23.

16. Jeffrey Juris, *Networking Futures. The Movements against Corporate Globalization* (Durham, NC, 2008).

17. Barbara Sutton, "Naked Protest: Memories of Bodies and Resistance at the World Social Forum," *Journal of International Women Studies* 8, no. 3 (2007), 139–148.

18. Barbara Sutton, "Poner el Cuerpo: Women's Embodiment and Political Resistance in Argentina," *Latin American Politics and Society* 49, no. 3 (2007); Barbara Sutton, *Bodies in Crisis: Culture, Violence, and Women's Resistance in Neoliberal Argentina* (New Brunswick, 2010), 161–90.

19. Orna Sasson-Levy and Tamar Rapoport, "Body, Gender, and Knowledge in Protest Movements. The Israeli Case," *Gender & Society* 17, no. 3 (2003): 398.

20. Wendy Parkins, "Protesting Like a Girl: Embodiment, Dissent and Feminist Agency," *Feminist Theory* 1, no. 1 (2000): 63.

21. Margaret L Laware, "Circling the Missiles and Staining Them Red: Feminist Rhetorical Invention and Strategies of Resistance at the Women's Peace Camp at Greenham Common," *NWSA Journal* 16, no. 3 (2004): 32*ff.*

22. Jasbir K Puar and Amit S Rai, "Monster, Terrorist, Fag: The War on Terrorism and the Production of Docile Patriots," *Social Text* 20, no. 3 (2002). 117–148.

23. Ibid., 121.

24. Nick Crossley, "From Reproduction to Transformation: Social Movement Fields and the Radical Habitus," *Theory, Culture & Society* 20, no. 6 (2003). 43–68.

Recommended Reading

Anderson, Patrick. *So Much Wasted. Hunger, Performance, and the Morbidity of Resistance.* Durham, NC, 2010. Anderson outlines what he calls the "politics of morbidity" by referring to three different cases of self-starvation and their respective political economy: the anorectic in the clinic, the fasting body in the gallery, and the hunger striker in the prison.

Feldman, Allen. *Formations of Violence. The Narrative of the Body and Political Terror in Northern Ireland.* Chicago, 1991. Feldman's study on violence in Northern Ireland and the respective formations of the body is still one of the most far-reaching, in-depth studies of the connection of embodiment and protest. Feldman analyzes how the protest on the streets is paralleled to the protests by prisoners. In both forms, the body is seen not only as a means but as a real weapon.

Lunceford, Brett. *Naked Politics: Nudity, Political Action, and the Rhetoric of the Body.* Lanham, MD, 2012. Focusing on the animal rights organization PETA, so-called lactivists who protest for the right to breastfeed in public, and the "World Naked Bike Ride," Lunceford draws a map of meanings nudity symbolizes and how nudity is used in protest.

Chapter 17

Dance as Protest

Eva Aymamí Reñé

General Definition of the Term. What Are Dance Studies?

Dance is a meaning-making creative art form that explores choreography and moving bodies. Dance studies look into the concept of corporeality, the study of bodies through a consideration of bodily reality. The body is considered not as a natural but as a socially constructed entity, a tangible category of cultural experience. Hence, dance studies investigate the study of movement and the choreographies of the body including formal ideologies, critical theory, aesthetic concepts, and technical attributes.

In the early 1920s, dance studies began to be considered as an academic discipline in the United States and in Europe, but it was not until the 1960s that dance theory was taught and researched at university level. The three main categories of study were: (1) the aesthetic meaning behind dance, or semiotics; (2) choreology, that is, movement analysis and description; and (3) the sociological aspect, regarding the role of dance in society and culture.

From the 1960s to 1980s, a first generation of dance scholars[1] channeled the discipline toward the development of crucial tools for the study of dance, specifically in movement analysis. This first generation was initiated in the modern dance studio; they adapted and engaged with methods of formal analysis from their graduate trainings in anthropology, literary studies, and musicology. In the late 1980s, a second generation of dance scholars[2] emerged who considered movement analysis to be too restrictive for the study of dance. Instead, they no longer concerned themselves with the study of the dance work and the artist biography but also contemplated the study of movement and the body as an extension of social practice and how dances engaged with their social, historical, and political contexts. As Mark Franko describes in his article on the study of the history of the discipline, "Dance and the Political: States of Exception," this new generation[3] brought a methodological debate into dance studies. Following the central debates of contemporary scholars in other fields, this second generation borrowed methodology and theory from cultural studies, gender studies, and post-structuralism. These debates demonstrated that dance studies is an interdisciplinary field, as they illustrated that it both borrowed from and informed other disciplines.

General Cultural Functions

Currently, the study of dance mostly concentrates on the sociological aspect: regarding the role of dance in society and culture. Dance scholars focus on the way in which dance creates social and cultural meanings. Understanding dance as a culturally constructed phenomena allows to acknowledge the multivoiced character of dance in culture.

Corporeality is the central element of dance studies. As a vast reservoir of signs and symbols, bodies not only pass meaning along, they also create choreographies of signs. Through performing, bodies can reproduce as well as produce social meanings and cultural values. For instance, scholar Susan Foster, in her study of three protest movements in different times, *Choreographies of Protest*,[4] considers how bodies in public demonstrate protest movements.[5] Foster wants to frame new perspectives on individual subjects and collective actions, bringing the discipline to an interdisciplinary field that will be used as methodology and theory for other disciplines when studying the body and movement. Indeed, there is not an established category of the body, but rather the question is what and how bodies are constructing, resisting, and how these values shape embodiment.

As dance ethnographers[6] claim, a primary way of knowing and understanding the world comes through conceptions of our bodies and through movement experiences delivered by society; culture is embodied.[7] Citizens create movement (produce and reproduce it), and with these actions participate in the making and the transmission of culture. As studied in sociology and anthropology, social systems produce certain bodies and movements, but it is a main current in dance studies to simultaneously understand the body and its capacity to create certain social values. The comprehension of dance as simultaneously productive and reproductive of cultural values is echoed by Cynthia Novack,[8] who remarks that dance can simultaneously reflect and resist cultural values, noting the example of the ballerina who "embodies and enacts stereotypes of the feminine while she interprets a role with commanding skill, agency and a subtlety that denies stereotype."[9]

Role in Protest Cultures

There is still a debate regarding how dance can effectively be used as a means of protest. On the one hand, dance is tacitly political because it conveys identities and ideologies that have political implications. Ideologies are means by which individual identities are maintained to larger group forma-tions. Indeed, dance can perform and retain the effects of political power, and with the same gesture resist them. And it is this capacity for resistance that makes dance a powerful form of social protest. For instance: discourses of dance—through movement, body image, and technique are often rooted in ideas of natural gender differences. Conversely, dance performances are places to reproduce these standardized values but also places to resist them. Choreographer Eduard Lock's "Human Sex" (1985) dance video is often used as an example of oppositional gender values. (See Figure 17.1.) In this piece, Lock focuses much of his choreographic attention on the female dancer Lecavalier, whose physicality is muscularly androgynous and whose performance is brutal and risky. Lecavalier dances topless with a tutu and a moustache painted on her face. This piece has had multiple readings, and it continues being an important reference for feminine critics.[10]

On the other hand, of the 198 methods of protest described in *The Politics of Nonviolent Action,* Gene Sharp identifies "theatre and music," "symbolic public acts"—such as symbolic exhibitions and marches—and "physical interventions"—characterized by the intervention of physical bodies, such as sit-ins, walk-ins, and occupations—among other methods of nonviolent protest. While Sharp identifies performances as one method of protest, the difference he establishes between performances, symbolic acts, and physical interferences remains more ambiguous. Thus, if we approach the body as a reservoir of signs and symbols, the physical body itself, either in a performance or in a street demonstration, is a symbolic public act. What matters in this discussion is that beyond these technical differences on pro-test methods, the body remains as an articulate matter that evidences the central role of physicality on the construction of individual subjectivities and social identities.

Consequently, dance can exercise protest by performing identities cir-cumscribed to a larger community, by confronting ideologies, and by sym-bolic acts of protest. The role of dance in protest cultures has been often

Figure 17.1. La La La Human Steps, *Human Sex*, 1985.
© La La La Human Steps.

articulated as resistance. Borrowing from De Certeau's concept, resistance is embedded in the practices of everyday life: the tricks, deceits, and simulations through which the common citizen expresses their ways of consumption, which are articulated as choices of resistance. In De Certeau's *The Practice of Everyday Life,*[11] the ordinary individual belongs to a silent majority that unconsciously is the creator of cultural resistance based on the ability to invent everyday practices. The choices of consumption of everyday life, what De Certeau names tactics, are little places for resistance in the dominant grid of power. And dance can be part of these tactics of everyday life consumption.

In order to ground this analysis, this chapter turns to an analysis of the treatment of dance under dictator Franco's regime in Spain, which will illustrate how dance can be articulated as resistance toward the dominant values of a regime. Addressing existing tensions in the construction of national and gender identity under the dictatorship in Spain, this case articulates how the embracing of modern dance can be conceived as symbolic action of resistance to the dictatorial values of the regime.

After the end of the Spanish Civil War in 1939, General Francisco Franco established a dictatorship in Spain that lasted until his death in 1975. Spanish society lived under a very conservative regime, which infused society with traditional values. With the aim to create a folkloric dance to unify a divided country, the Feminine Section of the Spanish *Falange* [12]—a feminine institution born in 1934 to serve the ideals of Franco's regime— shaped a selective way to interpret and collect the folkloric dances of all Spain. After a close study of the way these dances were collected,[13] it has been claimed that these dances were re-created and reenacted according to the conservative values of the Catholic Church, which was the moral justification of the Fascist dictatorship. In this way, the regime created a specific standardized folklore that conveyed its ideals of a culturally united nation. This illustrates Franko's claim that dances are tacitly political.

Figure 17.2. Coros y Danzas, Group of the Women's Branch of the Falange (Sección Femenina), Madridejos (Toledo), Spain, Joaquin Diaz Gonzalez.

Upon Franco's death in 1975, the new vocabulary of modern dance broke with the categorization of what folkloric dance symbolized for the performing arts scene and represented a way to refuse and resist the traditional values in folkloric dances that the regime promoted. For instance, two years after the dictator Franco died in Spain in 1977, the *Grup Estudi Anna Maleras* (Study Group Anna Maleras) presented among other choreographies, *Guernika'37* at the First Dance Festival (Mostra de Dansa) organized by the Catalan government. With the name and year of the Basque city that was bombed by the Fascists during the Spanish Civil War (1936–39), this short piece reminded Spanish audiences of the horror of civil war at a time when civil society and politicians had agreed to forget the horrors of the recent dictatorship that governed the country (from 1939 to 1975). Unlike folkloric dances, modern dance is allowed to speak of forgotten memories, and with them to challenge the imposed oblivion of that time.

Theoretical and Empirical Research Perspectives

While there is still a certain interest in producing studies on movement analysis, in the last thirty years, dance scholars have made significant contributions to cultural analysis of movement and dance, positioning their research in relation to more extensive issues of social and philosophical theory.

The works of Roland Barthes and Michel Foucault articulate cultural criticism on the ways of interpretation. Dance scholar Susan Foster draws from Barthes and Foucault's argument that reading and dancing are forms of body imprinting, she explains "[these authors] have attempted to rethink the issue of representation, and doing so they have called into question the nature of the subject [and the body] who engages in the act of representation." Foster's[14] choice of reading and writing as metaphors for interpreting dance, treating dance pieces as texts, serves as an example of incorporating critical theory in dance studies and giving it much needed discursive relevance.

The feminist problematization of gender pushes for an interrogation of the relationship between biological versus cultural constructions of bodies. The use of Butler's "performativity"[15] opens up new connotations to daily representations of class and gender, by discussing the process of socialization by means of which gender and sexuality identities, for example, are produced through regulating practices. Her theorization slightly departs from Ervin Goffman's presentation of the individual in every day life.[16] However, if Goffman articulates a volatile subject that exists in between these performative interactions, that can choose which role or mask to use in each contact interaction, then Butler's performativity denies the existence of this subjectivity in between performances and claims that the subject or the individual does not exist but in the performative actions, who creates and constructs her/his individuality through these processes. It is this concept of constant recreation and construction of identity that can articulate a way of resistance, when challenging values of gender constructed through history and politics, and when contemporary choreographers play and oppose these standardized constructions through their pieces.

More recently, dance scholars have analyzed the component of protest and resistance in performances. For example, Giersdorf and Chakravorty, among others, have made deep studies of how dance contests social matters. Pallabi Chakravorty, in her dance ethnography *Bells of Change, Kathak Dance, Women and Modernity in India,* analyzes the tension between modernity and tradition in contemporary women in India through the evolution of Kathak dance and how women find agency in this patriarchal ideology of a caste identity, by creating their own dance company to perform as women in a mostly male-dominated discipline. In a similar way, Giersdorf, in his article on two German choreographers over the treatment of East Germania, illustrates how the comparison brings to surface the concepts of making dances.[17] He explains, "A comparison of Waltz's production to Jo Fabian's choreographic representation of East German identity in his piece *Pax Germania* further illuminates these deficiencies in her (Waltz) work. Whereas Waltz reduces bodies to responding objects in her display of East German identity, Fabian re-creates the actual transformation process for East German citizens on the bodies of the dancers as well as through the audience members."[18] One dance is just responding movements to several stimulations, and the other is an embodied response to the social changes occurring in East Germany after the fall of the Berlin Wall in 1989.

Research Gaps and Open Questions

How dance can contest its social times remains still as an open question for researchers. As the second generation of dance scholars raised, more studies appeared on the social and political implications of the body and movement. On the other hand, it is still understudied how these physical interferences can be articulated as protest.

In *Critical Moves,* Randy Martin advocates incorporating critical theory in dance study to create a critical approach to dance.[19] With an emphasis on the interdependence of dance and politics, Martin illustrates how the study and practice of dance can reanimate prospects for progressive politics and social change. On the other hand, from a different perspective, Susan Foster opens a new possibility for dance studies in analyzing the interaction of physical bodies in public acts of protests, such as sit-ins and march-ins. In her article *Choreographies of Protest,* Foster articulates from a dance studies perspective an analysis of how physical interferences create protest in relation to a changing structure of power.[20] In this way, Foster hopes to contribute to the theoretical discussion of social movements, showing how dance studies are themselves a form of social theory. New pieces and texts may provide enlightenment as to how dance pieces on the stage or physical bodies in public acts can create a motor for social change.

Eva Aymamí Reñé is a lecturer of dance at the Music and Performing Arts Department, Anglia Ruskin University, United Kingdom. A Fulbright scholarship recipient, she holds a master's degree in culture and performance from University of California, Los Angeles, and a PhD in dance studies at University of Surrey, United Kingdom. Eva continues her research in dance as a corporeal language to speak of gender, memories, and silence in post-Franco Spain.

Notes

1. For example, Janet Adshead-Lansdale, Marcia Siegel, Judy Lynne Hanna, and Stephanie Jordan.
2. For example, Susan Foster, Cynthia Novack, Mark Franko.
3. Mark Franko, "Dance and the Political: States of Exception," *Dance Research Journal* 38, no. 1–2 (2006): 13–18. Franko names them "contextualists" in opposition to the first generation of dance scholars—the formalists.
4. Susan L Foster, "Choreographies of Protest," *Theatre Journal* 55, no. 3 (2003): 395–412.
5. "The possibility of a body that is written upon but that also writes, moves critical studies of the body in new directions. It asks scholars to approach the body's involvement in any activity with an assumption of potential agency to participate in or resist whatever forms of cultural production are underway." Susan L Foster, *Corporealities: Dancing Knowledge, Culture and Power* (London, 1995), 15.
6. Adrienne Kaeppler, Pallabi Chakravorty, and Cynthia Novack among others.
7. Cynthia Novack, *Sharing the Dance: Contact Improvisation and American Culture* (Madison, WI, 1990).
8. Ibid.
9. Ibid., 181.
10. Victoria Thoms, "Reading Human Sex: The Challenges of a Feminist Identity through Time and Space," *European Journal of Women's Studies* 13, no. 4 (2006): 357–71.
11. Michael De Certeau, *The Practice of Everyday Life* (Berkeley, CA, 1988).
12. This was a feminine institution born in 1934 to serve the ideals of Franco's regime on the indoctrination of women.
13. Estrella Casero-Garcia, *La España Que Bailó Con Franco: Coros y Danzas De La Sección Femenina* (Madrid, 2000).
14. Foster, Susan Leigh. *Reading Dancing: Bodies and Subjects in Contemporary American Dance* (Berkeley, 1986) xx.
15. Judith Butler, *Bodies That Matter: On the Discursive Limits of "Sex"* (New York, 1993).
16. Erving Goffman, *The Presentation of Self in Everyday Life* (Garden City, NY, 2002).

17. Jens R Giersdorf, "Border Crossings and Intra-National Trespasses: East German Bodies in Sasha Waltz's and Jo Fabian's Choreographies." *Theatre Journal* 55, no. 3 (2003): 413–32.
18. Giersdorf, "Border Crossings and Intra-National Trespasses," 424.
19. Randy Martin, *Critical Moves: Dance Studies in Theory and Politics* (Durham, NC, 1998).
20. Foster, "Choreographies of Protest."

Recommended Reading

Foster, SL. *Reading Dancing: Bodies and Subjects in Contemporary American Dance.* Berkley, CA, 1988. Departing from contemporary semiotics and post-structuralism criticism, this book offers four models of representation that are illustrated with historical examples of contemporary choreographers.

Franko, M. *Dancing Modernism/Performing Politics.* Bloomington, IN, 1995. Presents a critical revision of modern dance history by emphasizing the evolution of the concept of feminism.

Taylor, D. *The Archive and the Repertoire: Performing Cultural Memory in the Americas.* Durham, NC, 2003. Taylor challenges the assumption that performance is an ephemeral entity that disappears, in contrast to the materiality of the archive, which endures. Taylor commits instead to the idea of performance as a repertoire of embodied knowledge, which can transmit cultural memory.

Chapter 18

Violence/Militancy

Lorenzo Bosi

General Definition of the Term

If violence is not an intrinsic feature of movement protest, it is neither rare, particularly in today's world.

Protest can incorporate different forms of violence, including such actions as verbal and physical confrontation, striking, operating a free store, erecting barricades, rioting, attacks on property (sabotage), squatting, blowing up buildings, arson, bodily assaults, holding of an individual against his expressed will, clashing with the police, public self-immolation, hunger striking, murdering, bombing, to mention only a few. Violent repertoires are indiscriminately scattered across the political spectrum, including left-wing[1] and right-wing militants[2], militant feminists,[3] militant animal rights advocates,[4] white supremacists,[5] antiglobal activists,[6] abortion opponents,[7] militant hactivists,[8] nationalists and ethnonationalists,[9] environmentalists,[10] students,[11] and religious militants.[12]

We need to remember that violence is culture-dependent. So what would be violent for one society can be perceived as nonviolent in another one or in another historical period of the same society. The emergence and worldwide development of the Internet has challenged, for example, the same definition of violence as a strategic use of physical force. Hactivism, activism on the Internet, can use different strategic means in order to materially damage property for spreading its message without adopting physical force, but still be perceived as a violent action, for example, hacking, defacing web pages, e-mail floods, viruses and worms, and data theft or destruction.[13] Whether anticipated, threatened, or actual,[14] violence is a particular confrontational repertoire of action oriented at inflicting material damage to individuals and/or property with the purpose to influence several audiences. Media and new technologies are the way militant groups can spread their messages and intensify their voice.

General Cultural Functions

While violence is used instrumentally by social movement participants as a means to affecting or resisting political, social, and cultural changes, militants and their leaders know very well that it is almost impossible to defeat national or transnational policing in a conventional military sense. For this reason, violence should be understood as a means of communication to influence several audiences in order to draw the institutions to sit at the conference table to negotiate on the activists' terms. "The cultural and emotional effects that ... [violence] produces are more important than the material damage."[15] Violence is an oppositional performance of militant actors geared to different audiences, such as political and social institutions, elites and pressure groups, countermovements, political parties, the mass media, and the general public. It is most of the time symbolic rather than primarily strategic. But violence, as other repertoires of protest, has not only external targets, it serves as well to create and stabilize militant identities. It has an internal movement building dimension. As Abby Peterson tells us in reference to contemporary militant groups, "more and more it is what the activists *do* which makes them militant and their politics radical, not what they *say*."[16] Violence in this sense is an end in itself. Within militant groups, violence has the power to make individuals see themselves as members of something, to foster a mentality of embattlement, to effect their sense of self-affirmation and achievement. It is perceived from militants as a way of reclaiming dignity for themselves and to reject what they feel as their own long-subordinate position, real or not.

Stories, political culture's mentalities, modes of behavior, and narratives, which are part of the social movement culture, are opportunity structures that connect the militants' past to their present situation and can justify individual and collective violence. In devising violent actions, militants draw on options that conform to their cultural frames of meaning and are congruent with their ideological visions with which they make sense of their life. So you would aspect, for example, militant pacifist committing actions of civil disobedience that can slightly damage physical properties, but it would be difficult to see these militants bodily assaulting or murdering anyone. On the other hand, militant activists with their repertoires of protest are always looking to construct new meanings. Having said that, this does not mean that violent repertoires are only dependent on certain ideologies. The opposite is true. Groups with radical ideologies adopt violent repertoires only when political opportunities trigger escalation.[17]

Theoretical and Empirical Research Perspectives

More often than not, social scientists treat violence as if it is detached from surrounding instances of political action, and they consequently see outbreaks of violence as signs of structural strain, material deprivation, or individual and social pathologies. Though differing in their specifics, early scholars on the topic have seen people engaging in violence as a result of frustrated expectations when a wide process of social and cultural breakdowns occur in a social system.[18] By contrast, those few social movement scholars who have engaged with this particular topic have countered breakdown explanations with rationalist approaches, which have de-exceptionalized violence, by locating it within the wider social context and within the movement dynamics as one among many possible tactics that leaders can adopt.[19] Some of these scholars advocate the so-called resource mobilization theory and therefore consider violence as a means to pursue social political goals instead of the result of symptoms of strains or psychological characteristics.[20] Other scholars, advocates of the so-called political process theory, while drawing its rationalist framework from resource mobilization theorists, see violence as an outcome of the interaction between institutional political actors and protest. Violence is here embedded in a complex web of sociopolitical relations, involving multiple actors.[21] For political process theorists, closed political opportunities to protest facilitate the escalation of violent repertoires, especially during the declining phase of mobilization.[22] Scholars employing social networks to explain movement participation have as well particularly stressed the importance of preexisting networks to understand why individuals join militant violence.[23] Recently, a range of studies have suggested that violence emerges as a result from diverse processes of social interaction. They have proposed a relational approach to study violence.[24] In response to the cultural turn in the social sciences, framing theory and new social movement theory helped to bring back discourse, ideology, symbolism, attitudes, manners of communication, identity formation, and framing processes as potential causal factors that motivate individuals to movement participation and to violence as well. Potential militants are drawn into action by the force of their ideas and by their identity. They are not passive actors influenced from social forces, but rather the creators of conditions.

Since the 1990s, the collective action literature, drawing once again on social psychology, has also begun to rediscover and to take into serious consideration the importance of emotions.[25]

Research Gaps and Open Questions

The social movement's literature has dedicated scant attention to violent forms of political action.[26] However, in recent years, a growing number of social movement scholars have turned their attention toward violent phenomena, and at the same time, more and more studies on militant groups and violent conflicts have adopted a social movement perspective. For furthering our understanding of violence, research requires in the future to respond to key questions, which so far remain unanswered from the literature:

1. Which are the political cultures that encourage groups to decide to adopt strategies involving violence repertoires?
2. Which are the facilitating factors that encourage activists to move in or out of militancy?
3. How much does the decline of a cycle of protest encourage violence repertoires on the fringes of a movement?
4. How much do new contextual opportunities for violence arise from the global dimension of international political and economic governance?
5. How are strategic choices made about targets?
6. How do social movements change when political violence appears?
7. To what extent does engagement in violent activities strengthen an organization's appeal within some segments of a social movement?
8. What kind of government policy facilitates individual and collective disengagement from militancy?
9. Which are the sociopolitical impacts of violence if contrasted with nonviolent strategies?
10. Which are the biographical consequences of militant violent protesters?

In the literature that deals with violence and militancy, there exists a general failure to undertake primary research. This has left the most of the studies deeply removed from their research subject.[27] We need instead to interact and engage in our fieldwork research with violent militants if we are looking to understand and explain this social phenomenon within its specific context. This obviously poses important ethical and methodological challenges for the researcher and his/her work, which we need to be aware of if we want to defend the scientific credibility of our analysis. Francesca Polletta, in 2006, was the section editor of a relevant forum in the journal, *Mobilization,* titled "Mobilization Forum: Awkward Movements."[28]

The research on violence falls mainly into one of two groups: separate monographs on the history of violent groups or studies of violence in general. There exist only few systematic comparative studies on violence, be it cross-national or cross-temporal. Case studies on the subject have produced inductive and descriptive accounts that are difficult to integrate into broader general analysis because of the lack of common theoretical framework. An additional issue, however, is that the in-depth comparative studies that do exist compare only those violent organizations that have similar ideologies and political purposes. Comparative research on cases where the nature of the demands behind the violence is different has been absent, despite the fact that these would enable analysts to open up the possibility of testing the validity of a wide spectrum of theoretical propositions generated by the literature on social movements. Future studies should address, then, those types of militant actors with which we are not usually familiar and look as well at those geographical areas, other than the ones traditionally addressed from collective action scholars, in order to facilitate cumulative knowledge and challenge prevailing assumptions.[29]

Lorenzo Bosi is assistant professor at the Institute of Humanities and Social Sciences at the Scuola Normale Superiore, Italy. He is a political sociologist pursuing comparative analysis into the cross-disciplinary fields of social movements and political violence. Since January 2014 he is the principal investigator for the Italian team on a project titled, "Living with Hard Times: How European Citizens Deal with Economic Crises and Their Social and Political Consequences." He is also convener of the European Consortium of Political Research (ECPR) Standing Group on Political Violence, and head of the "Moveout-network." He has published in several journals of political and sociological studies. He is co-editor of *Dynamics of Political Violence* (Ashgate, 2014), of *Political Violence in Context* (ECPR Press, 2015), of *The Dynamics of Radicalization: A Relational Comparative Perspective* (Oxford University Press, 2015), and of *The Consequences of Social Movements* (Cambridge University Press, 2016).

Notes

1. Gilda Zwerman, Patricia Steinhoff, and Donatella Della Porta, "Disappearing Social Movements: Clandestinity in the Cycle of New Left Protest in the US, Japan, Germany and Italy," *Mobilization* 5 (2000): 83–100.

2. Bert Klandermans and Nonna Mayer, *Extreme Right Activists in Europe: Through the Magnifying Glass* (London, 2006).

3. Jessica Rosenberg and Gitana Garofalo, "Riot Grrrl: Revolutions from Within," *Signs: Journal of Women in Culture and Society* 23 (1998): 811–41.

4. James Jasper and Jane Poulsen, "Fighting Back: Vulnerabilities, Blunders and Countermobilization by the Targets in Three Animal Rights Campaigns," *Sociological Forum* 8 (1993): 639–57.

5. Rory McVeigh, *The Rise of the Ku Klux Klan: Right-Wing Movements and National Politics* (Minneapolis, MN, 2009).

6. Jeffrey Juris, "Violence Performed and Imagined. Militant Action, the Black Bloc and the Mass Media in Genoa," *Critique of Anthropology* 25, no. 4 (2005): 413–32.

7. Dallas Blanchard, *The Anti-Abortion Movement and the Rise of the Religious Right* (New York, 1994).

8. Tim Jordan, *Activism! Direct Action, Hacktivism and the Future of Society* (London, 2002).

9. Lorenzo Bosi, "Explaining Pathways to Armed Activism in the Provisional IRA, 1969–1972," *Social Science History* 36, no. 3 (2012): 347–90.

10. Bran Taylor, "The Tributaries of Radical Environmentalism," *Journal for the Study of Radicalism* 2, no. 1 (2008): 27–61.

11. Mark Boren, *Student Resistance: A History of the Unruly Subject* (New York, 2001).

12. Scott Appleby, *The Ambivalence of the Sacred: Religion, Violence, and Reconciliation* (Lanham, MD, 2000).

13. Tim Jordan, *Activism! Direct Action, Hacktivism and the Future of Society* (London, 2002).

14. Abby Peterson, *Contemporary Political Protest* (Aldershot, 2001), viii.

15. Donatella Della Porta, "Research on Social Movements and Political Violence," *Qualitative Sociology* 31, no. 3 (2008): 221–31.

16. Peterson, *Contemporary Political Protest*, viii.

17. Lorenzo Bosi, "The Dynamics of Social Movements Development: The Northern Ireland's Civil Rights Movement in the 1960s," *Mobilization* 11, no. 1 (2006): 81–100.

18. Ted R Gurr, *Why Men Rebel* (Princeton, NJ, 1970).

19. Lorenzo Bosi, "État des savoirs et pistes de recherche sur la violence politique," *Critique Internationale* 54, no. 1 (2012): 171–89.

20. Charles Tilly, *From Mobilization to Revolution* (Reading, MA, 1978).

21. Bosi, "The Dynamics of Social Movement Development."

22. Donatella Della Porta, *Political Violence and the State* (New York, 1995).

23. Bosi, "Explaining Pathways to Armed Activism in the Provisional IRA," 347–90; Lorenzo Bosi and Donatella Della Porta, "Micro-Mobilization into Armed Groups:

The Ideological, Instrumental and Solidaristic Paths," *Qualitative Sociology* 35 (2012): 361–83.

24. Eitan Alimi, Lorenzo Bosi, and Charles Demetriou, *The Dynamics of Radicalization: A Relational Perspective* (Oxford, forthcoming).

25. Jeff Goodwin and Steven Pfaff, "Emotions Work in High-Risk Social Movements: Managing Fear in the U.S. and East German Civil Rights Movement," in *Passionate Politics,* ed. J Goodwin, J Jasper, and F Polletta (Chicago, 2001), 282–302.

26. This development is represented, inter alia, by Eitan Alimi, Lorenzo Bosi, and Charles Demetriou, "Relational Dynamics and Processes of Radicalization: A Comparative Framework," *Mobilization* 18, no. 1 (2012): 7–26; Bosi, "Explaining Pathways to Armed Activism in the Provisional IRA"; Bosi and Della Porta, "Micro-Mobilization into Armed Groups"; Chares Demetriou, "Political Violence and Legitimation: The Episode of Colonial Cyprus," *Qualitative Sociology* 30, no. 2 (2007): 171–93; Della Porta, *Political Violence and the State*; Della Porta, "Research on Social Movements and Political Violence"; Jeff Goodwin, "A Theory of Categorical Terrorism," *Social Forces* 84 (2006): 2027–46; Jeroen Gunning, "Social Movement Theory and the Study of Terrorism," in *Critical Terrorism Studies: A New Research Agenda,* ed. R Jackson, MB Smyth, and J Gunning (London, 2009), 157–77; Charles Tilly, *The Politics of Collective Violence* (Cambridge, 2003); Robert White, "From Peaceful Protest to Guerrilla War: Micromobilization of the Provisional Irish Republican Army," *American Journal of Sociology* 94 (1989): 1277–1302; Zwerman, Steinhoff, and Della Porta, "Disappearing Social Movements," 83–100.

27. Bosi, "Explaining Pathways to Armed Activism in the Provisional IRA."

28. Francesca Polletta, "Mobilization Forum: Awkward Movements," *Mobilization* 11, no. 4 (2006): 475–78.

29. Bosi and Della Porta "Micro-Mobilization into Armed Groups"; Alimi, Bosi and Demetriou, *The Dynamics of Radicalization.*

Recommended Reading

Alimi, Eitan, Lorenzo Bosi, and Chares Demetriou. "Relational Dynamics and Processes of Radicalization: A Comparative Framework." *Mobilization* 18, no.1 (2012): 7–26. Instead of focusing on why radicalization happens, this article looks to answer how and when questions. It builds on the relational tradition in the study of social movements and contentious politics by expanding on a mechanism-process research strategy. Three ethnonational episodes of radicalization are examined: the enosis-EOKA movement in Cyprus (1950–59), the Provisional Irish Republican Army in Northern Ireland (1969–72), and the Fatah-Tanzim in Palestine (1995–2001).

Bosi, Lorenzo, and Donatella Della Porta. "Micro-Mobilization into Armed Groups: The Ideological, Instrumental and Solidaristic Paths." *Qualitative Sociology* 35 (2012): 361–83. It seeks to improve our understanding of how individuals join armed groups. It focuses on those former activists who have joined the Provisional Irish Republican Army and Red Brigades. Three general paths are singled out: the ideological path, the instrumental path, and the solidaristic path. Each of these is characterized by complex interactions between the individual motivations for involvement (micro-level), the networks that facilitate the recruitment process (meso-level), and the effects of repression on individuals (macro-level).

Bosi, Lorenzo, Charles Demetriou, and Stefan Malthaner, eds. *Dynamics of Political Violence.* Farnham, 2014. It examines the ways in which violence emerges and develops from episodes of contentious politics. By considering various such episodes, it focuses on the dynamics that shape processes of radicalization and violence escalation. Specifically, it features studies that converge around four process dynamics that are particularly germane to processes of radicalization: dynamics of movement-state interaction; dynamics of intramovement competition; dynamics of meaning formation and transformation; and dynamics of diffusion.

Della Porta, Donatella. *Political Violence and the State.* New York, 1995. It is a comparative work of two cycles of political violence in Germany and Italy from the 1960s to the 1990s. It presents the relation between social movements actors and the state in the process of radicalization.

Wood, Elisabeth. *Insurgent Collective Action and Civil War in El Salvador.* Cambridge, 2003. Building on ethnographic fieldwork and oral histories, Wood looks to understand which circumstances and with which motivations rural people mobilize for social change. She combines collective action theories and theories of revolution.

Chapter 19

The Role of Humor in Protest Culture

Marjolein 't Hart

General Definition of the Term and Cultural Functions

Humor belongs to the rich instruments of communication and can be used as such in social protest. Puns, punch lines, and jokes can articulate discontent; cartoons can visualize injustice. Thanks to the jesting packing, they express these views in an attractive way. Another advantage is that humor tends to disarm the opponent, as to react in a serious way to a joke is generally not done. Usually, jokers can express risky ideas without directly being held responsible. Criticism expressed in a joking manner is also more difficult to refute by rational arguments. Furthermore, as jokes invite to laugh *with* one another, humor appeals to all-human feelings, and in this way, it can lower political barriers.[1] At the same time, humor bolsters up community building and brings about a sense of belonging together, as sharing humor creates a bond. In tense political confrontations, jokes can also lower stress and reduce fear. In addition, humorous protest usually attracts considerable media coverage, which may lead to wider political support and improved resource mobilization.

Typical devices of humor are jokes, cartoons, humorous chants, absurd theater, carnival-like festivities. Another humorous device with a long tradition is the parody and satire. All too often, authorities faced difficulties in punishing the authors and publishers, as parodies and satires are never explicitly clear about the object of their wit, even though the butt is often unmistakable to the public at large.[2]

Humor can attract large audiences, but there are limits, as humor is always strongly context-bound. In fact, most jokes are contained along social, ethnic, or gendered lines.[3] Jokes, then, can bring people together, but they can also shock, hurt, and exclude. In order for humor to be successful in bringing down existing barriers, the joker should be able to play with the codes of more than one world.[4]

Role in Protest Cultures

In particular a number of new social movements have learned to appreciate these powers of humor. In the 1960s, the reinvention of Marxism coincided with an emerging youth subculture (happenings) next to an already existing subversive tradition in the arts. Formats of the absurd theater transformed into a new repertoire of protesters in among, above all, the student and peace movements. Their comical performances and funny chants surprised the authorities and attracted an enormous audience. Once arrested, the protesters could continue to mock the state institutions. In the late 1960s, the German student movement exploited the court proceedings in ridiculing the absurdity of the state, combining radical criticism with theatrical devices again.[5]

Figure 19.1. Postcard from the Dutch Peace Movement, 2004.
© De Brandnetel/Omslag.

Figure 19.2. Army of clowns at the main gate of the Büchel air base, 30 August 2008. Photographed, uploaded to Wikimedia Commons, and released into the public domain by Buroll.

What was new in these decades was the application of humor in an age in which media coverage was fast and widespread, in an age in which having sense of humor had come to be regarded as a virtue, and not least also among the higher classes in the Western world.[6] The playful performances of the new social movements were to some degree an innovation in protest culture, in particular the emphasis on the absurdity of the state. Yet much of the actual humorous repertoire itself was not new.

Carnival-like festivities in the past had offered room for comparable social protest before. During carnivals, for example, former ranks and hierarchies disappeared, and familiar contacts were allowed between different social groups and classes. The articulation of the idiomatic "world turned upside down" in parades was a funny and subversive way to play with established rules and hierarchies.[7]

A similar ritualized setting that allowed for political criticism in a funny way was the jester in a royal court. Like the participants in carnivals, he did not have to fear punishment, as his peculiar position carried immunity.[8] Somewhat comparable to the jester are the present-day cartoonists and other professional joke-makers. They can freely express themselves as long as they remain within strict boundaries: the context of a newspaper or the confines of a theater performance. Cartoons prove extremely valuable, as they can reach numerous uneducated and semi-literate sections of the population. Cartoons can also foster a shared identity among the uprooted, by recognizing their hardships and complaints, and transforming these into political demands.[9] Their criticism becomes problematic once they step outside these boundaries, when for example cartoons are deliberately reprinted outside their context or when jokes are retold in front of a different public. The controversy around the Muhammad cartoons serves as a perfect example.[10]

For several of the more recent, left-wing, autonomous groups in Western Europe, humor forms part and parcel of their sphere and is central to their alternative political identity. For them, humor not only is a way of framing protest, but is in itself a protest against the existing establishment, which is viewed as vertical, petrified, closed, and humorless. By their playful acts, they want to show they belong to a different world, one that is horizontal, human, and open.[11]

Several of these more recent protest movements use the devices of former carnival, with their painted faces, masks, or costumes. Most outspoken in this regard are the parades of the gay and lesbian movement. Although always joyful events, the participants nevertheless criticize the typical heterosexual norms, using humorous inversions of gendered roles.[12]

Laughing together forms a bond, as sharing emotions in general does. But humor in itself does not create a collective identity. Certainly, it may give a playful twist to that identity, but the political aims of a movement must be clear in order to be able to bring a humorous message in a successful way, with political effect. Gays and lesbians hold parades to bolster up their feeling of community, but the movement already enjoyed a certain collective identity.

Good examples of political jokes that are not necessarily linked to a political movement are the jokes circulating in some authoritarian regimes. Perhaps no other country harbored so many anticommunist jokes as the Soviet Union, yet in themselves they were no sign or proof of existing or rising opposition. Such jokes may well boost up morale and break down isolation, but the laughter remain isolated events as long as no existing movement will reap it in a political follow-up.[13]

Much of the social protest is not only aimed against the opponent, also the audience is important. The response from the public varies strongly, depending also upon the kind of humor used. Research has showed that in political debates, self-deprecating humor is best appreciated, whereas vicious and insulting humor is usually less valued, regardless of the political persuasion of the onlookers.[14] A political movement that has been extremely successful in using self-deprecating humor are the Mexican Zapatistas, in no small respect thanks to Marcos's specific use of humor.[15]

To conclude, life is full of incongruities and contradictions. Social protest is a natural reaction to them. Humor typically thrives thanks to those incongruities and contradictions. Most of the existing social protest is deadly serious, and it should be. But if applied in a heedful way, humor can bring energy to social movements, make it fun to be involved, draw in new members, attract usually more media coverage, and thus well serve the serious causes of social protest in the end again.

Research Perspectives and Open Questions

While the impact of humor in protest movements and its possible contribution to their resilience or success is a rather understudied phenomenon in general, a number of issues deserve attention here. Strongly underrepresented are studies on the role of humor in non-Western protest movements.[16] The expansion of the Internet facilitates the spread of protest methods, also the humorous ones. In the Arab Spring of 2011, for example, members of the Egyptian 6 April Youth Movement learned from Serbian activists how to attack authorities and police forces in a funny, disarming way.[17] How such templates of action can be shared across different cultures and continents, despite the fact that humor is usually strongly context-bound, is an open question. Finally, also the role of gender needs more attention. The long established myth that women have no sense of humor has been fostered by the male-dominated discourse and by the fact that women often laugh about different things than men. Yet, in all-women organizations, humor serves likewise to counteract authorities and other critics of the movement.[18]

Marjolein 't Hart is head of the History Research Department at the Huygens Institute for the History of the Netherlands, Royal Academy of Arts and Sciences in The Hague, and professor of history at the VU University Amsterdam. She has published widely on the history of state formation and contention, among others, *The Making of a Bourgeois State. War, Politics and Finance during the Dutch Revolt* (Manchester, 1993). Together with Dennis Bos, she edited *Humour and Social Protest* (Cambridge, 2007).

Notes

1. Christie Davies, *Jokes and Their Relation to Society* (Berlin, 1998), 176; Alexander Rose, "When Politics Is a Laughing Matter," *Policy Review* 59 (2001–2): 59–71.
2. MM Bakhtin, *Rabelais and His World* (Bloomington, IN, 1984), 452–54; Anton C Zijderveld, "Jokes and Their Relation to Social Reality," *Social Research* 35 (1968): 286–311; for an example John Reed, *Snowball's Chance. A Novel* (New York, 2002).
3. Giselinde Kuipers, *Good Humor, Bad Taste. A Sociology of the Joke* (Berlin, 2006); Janet Holmes and Meredith Marra, "Over the Edge? Subversive Humour between Colleagues and Friends," *Humor* 15 (2002): 65–87; Barbara Plester and Mark Orams, "Send in the Clowns: The Role of the Joker in Three New Zealand IT Companies," *Humor* 21 (2008): 253–81.
4. See for example Nancy Levi Arnez and Clara B Anthony, "Contemporary Negro Humor as Social Satire," *Phylon* 29 (1968): 339–46.
5. M Lane Bruner, "Carnivalesque Protest and the Humorless State," *Text and Performance Quarterly* 25 (2005): 136–55; Simon Teune, "Humour as a Guerilla Tactic: The West German Student Movement's Mockery of the Establishment," in *Humour and Social Protest,* ed. M 't Hart and D Bos (Cambridge, 2007), 115–32; Jörgen Johansen, "Humor as a Political Force, or How to Open the Eyes of Ordinary People in Social Democratic Countries," *Philosophy and Social Action* 17, no. 3 and 4 (1991): 23–29.
6. Rod A Martin, *The Psychology of Humor: An Integrative Approach* (Burlington, MA, 2007), 24.
7. Peter Burke, *Popular Culture in Early Modern Europe* (London, 1978), 187–204; Emmanuel Le Roy Ladurie, *Carnival in Romans* (New York, 1979).
8. Anton Zijderveld, *Reality in a Looking Glass: Rationality through an Analysis of Traditional Folly* (London, 1982), 207. Compare the immunity position of the joker in various societies in Mary Douglas, "The Social Control of Cognition: Some Factors in Joke Perception," *Man* 3 (1968): 361–76.
9. Michael Cohen, "'Cartooning Capitalism': Radical Cartooning and the Making of American Popular Radicalism in the Early Twentieth Century," in *Humour and Social Protest,* ed. M 't Hart and D Bos (Cambridge, 2007), 35–58; Nicola Pizzolato, "Revolution in a Comic Strip: Gasparazzo and the Identity of Southern Migrants in Turin, 1969–1975," in *Humour and Social Protest,* ed. M 't Hart and D Bos (Cambridge, 2007), 59–76.
10. P Lewis, ed., "The Muhammad Cartoons and Humor Research: A Collection of Essays," *Humor* 21 (2008): 1–46, with contributions by Christie Davies, Giselinde Kuipers, Paul Lewis, Rod A Martin, Elliott Oring, and Victor Raskin.
11. Sorensen, "Humor as a Serious Strategy of Nonviolent Resistance to Oppression," 176; Cristina Flesher Fominaya, "The Role of Humour in the Process of Collective Identity Formation in Autonomous Social Movement Groups in Contemporary Madrid," in *Humour and Social Protest,* ed. M 't Hart and D Bos (Cambridge, 2007), 243–58; Patrick Gun Cuninghame, "'A Laughter That Will Bury You All': Irony as Protest and Language as Struggle in the Italian 1977 Movement," in *Humour and Social Protest,* ed. M 't Hart and D Bos (Cambridge, 2007), 153–86.

12. Anna Lundbergh, "Queering Laughter in the Stockholm Pride Parade," in *Humour and Social Protest,* ed. M 't Hart and D Bos (Cambridge, 2007), 169–87.
13. Christie Davies, "Humour and Protest: Jokes Under Communism," in *Humour and Social Protest,* ed. M 't Hart and D Bos (Cambridge, 2007), 291–305; Kathleen Stokker, "Quisling Humor in Hitler's Norway: Its Wartime Function and Postwar Legacy," *Humor* 14 (2001): 339–57.
14. Amy Bippus, "Factors Predicting the Perceived Effectiveness of Politicians' Use of Humor during a Debate," *Humor* 20 (2007): 105–21.
15. Thomas Olesen, "The Funny Side of Globalization: Humour and Humanity in *Zapatista* Framing," in *Humour and Social Protest,* ed. M 't Hart and D Bos (Cambridge, 2007), 21–34.
16. See for example Oscar Verkaaik, "Fun and Violence: Ethnocide and the Effervescence of Collective Aggression," *Social Anthropology* 11 (2003): 3–22.
17. Valentine M Moghadam, *Globalization and Social Movements: Islamism, Feminism, and the Global Justice Movement* (2nd ed., Plymouth, 2012).
18. Krista Cowman, "Doing Something Silly: The Uses of Humour by the Women's Social and Political Union, 1903–1914," in *Humour and Social Protest,* ed. M 't Hart and D Bos (Cambridge, 2007), 259–74; Janet Bing, "Liberated Jokes: Sexual Humor in All-Female Groups," *Humor* 20 (2007): 337–66.

Recommended Reading

Bruner, M Lane. "Carnivalesque Protest and the Humorless State." *Text and Performance Quarterly* 25 (2005): 136–55. This discusses recent humorous protest movements.
Kuipers, Giselinde. *Good Humor, Bad Taste. A Sociology of the Joke.* Berlin, 2006. Explains the limits of jokes because of different social and cultural contexts.
Sorensen, Majken Jul. "Humor as a Serious Strategy of Nonviolent Resistance to Oppression." *Peace & Change* 33 (2008): 167–90. Offers an excellent example of the power of humor in social protest.
't Hart, Marjolein, and Dennis Bos, ed. *Humour and Social Protest.* Cambridge, 2007. Contains contributions on the role of humor in protest movements from the early modern period to the present day with a helpful introduction by 't Hart.

Chapter 20

Fashion in Social Movements

Nicole Doerr

Characteristic Features of Fashion in Social Movements

Fashion is a symbolic way used by activist groups to struggle for an inclu-
sion into public life, art, and politics, a media that creates cultural meaning outside linguistic signs yet that is bound within cultural connotations.[1]
While EU officials celebrated the "year of Eastern enlargement" in 2005,
Serbian feminist activist Tanja Ostojić posed in a pair of EU flag–colored
panties, titled "After Corbet."[2] Ostojić's EU panties poster, quoting Gustave
Corbet's *L'origine du monde,* was to protest the exclusive character of EU
Eastern enlargement, with harsh border controls and travel restrictions for
noncitizens. Activist fashion speaks where it quotes and yet breaks with the
cultural conventions that constitute good taste for fashion.[3]

General Cultural Functions of Fashion in Social Movements

From a Bourdieusian sociology of fashion,[4] fashion produced by activists
communicates the public sphere by breaking with the symbolic codes that
constitute legitimate costumes and the *habitus* of public expression. Ostojić's
poster, for example, provoked media critiques in its subtle rebuke of high
culture habitus as a basically arbitrary, and artificial distinction to bad taste.[5]
In its mixing of differences of taste in a single act of activist art, the panties poster reveals and reverses the symbolic relationship between high art
(Corbet) and low culture as a political struggle about fetish, taste, and the

distinct meaning of European culture. Hannah Arendt shows that long before the French revolution, those who feared labor movements, and later protesters themselves, used fashion as a tool to symbolize and mobilize solidarity in a struggle for recognition into the public sphere.[6] Arendt discusses the *sans culotte* as a symbol for a struggle for equal recognition and distinction by laborers who previously had no place to speak in public and created their own costume as a way of mutual recognition, and distinction.[7]

State of Research in Related Social Movement Research

Like French revolutionaries, other political movements such as ecologists and feminists, the 68 movement, and pacifists have all provoked the public producing their own fashions.[8] In 1922, Dadaist Hannah Höch outraged Weimar critiques with her "memorial for an important lace shirt"—a persiflage of the then conventional habit of nationalists to stage veteran memorials in public and private places. To protest against traditional gender clothing and limits of equal education for women like herself, Russian avant-gardist Varvara Stepanova created a unisex pilot uniform—a metaphor for flying and Communist modernity. In 1968, media artist Valie Export photographed her "Action pants: Genital panic" to reverse the image of female passivity with her naked genital triangle.[9] Like these historical examples, Tanja Ostojić, and other activist collectives across Europe today produce fashion to provoke the public and reimagine it as feminist performance space to stake the claim for radical democracy in the EU.

Activist fashion, interestingly, is politically effective where it combines distinct personal experiences and professional skills to reinvention conventions of traditional left activism.[10] Alice Mattoni's (2008) study on the Italian fashion collective "Serpica Naro" gives a good example of the political effectiveness of fashion that communicates protest.[11] Created in 2005 in Milan, Italy, Serpica Naro involved around two hundred professional fashion workers, journalists, graphic designers, and activists to launch a large international media hoax that made public the issue of precarious labor contracts.[12] Serpica Naro organizers, themselves local autonomous and left libertarian activists, protested the worsening local conditions of underpaid work in the fashion and creative industry in the broader context of a global sweatshop network producing for the Milanese fashion industry.[13]

Serpica Naro's DIY fashion parade was successful and received a wide media response as its organizers knew how to turn its members' pluralist experiences and skills into effective collective action. Right before the

Milanese global fashion week in 2005, Serpica Naro journalists launched a large amount of media hype in order to promote "young upcoming Japanese fashion designer Serpica Naro"—a personality that was in fact invented. Serpica Naro graphic designers created a fake Serpica Naro homepage. Serpica Naro fashion artists held a fashion defilé, parading as models in special designs designed for themselves: precarious employees in dresses to hide a pregnancy, flex workers wearing superhero costumes, and dresses suitable for precarious chain workers in the fashion business. The activists' provocative show received press coverage in Italy and reached a wide international media, including fashion magazines and European TV channels.[14]

While most analysts of social movements focus on text-based methods of analysis, activist fashion tells stories through performative fashion parades or, also, through textual experiments outside conventional media. "Ten years ago one would have asked what can be subversive about sewing and knitting," writes Insa Freudenschuss in her report about the Innsbruck-based Radical Sewing Circle.[15] The Radical Sewing Circle is a group that introduced U.S.-based craftivism to Central Europe.[16] Freudenschuss defines craftivism as "the appropriation of handcraft by activists spread from the U.S. and imitated by a growing global movement that includes 'do it yourself' (DIY) Lifestyle-individualists, anti-sweatshop activists and autonomous handcraft work."[17] Members of the Radical Sewing Circle take feminist text literally. They hold public meetings and workshops to knit and refashion the public spaces that surround them. They discuss conventional media practices that legitimize sexist adverts, violence against women, or reproduce traditional images of feminity. Radical Sewers, like Christine Pavlic, play on text and taste when they drill and sew feminist slogans into public park benches.[18]

Telling stories to people outside protest movements, Stephanie Müller notes, is typical of many current craftivist groups that aim to break with conventional codes of protest and professional fashion design.[19] In a similar way to the Radical Sewing Circle, groups have emerged in Berlin, Milan, Geneva, and Paris, calling themselves such names as Pilotki femzine fashion project, Serpica Naro, or also Stich'n Bitch.[20] Communicating over shared blogs such as the Serpica Naro homepage,[21] fashion collectives have started to organize joint transnational conferences, performances, and DIY fashion parades, such as the "Multiforma" workshop in Geneva in 2009, inviting U.S and Latin American craftivist collectives to join them.[22] Regarding their political messages, several of the above groups and other European fashion collectives share their critique of restrictive immigration policies, precarity, and global Capitalism in the fashion business.

Research Gaps and Open Questions

Analysts of political participation and cultures of protest may find it interesting to explore further that participants in fashion collectives are people previously not engaged in classical political forms of activism such as parties, unions, or social movement organizations. Women in their twenties, thirties, or forties start fashion groups as students of graphic design, photo journalism, or fashion without necessarily being involved previously in activist groups as a way to get engaged into politics that relates to their everyday life and struggle for social justice in a global perspective.[23] Other fashion collectives emerge in existing anarchist or feminist groups whose members discover DIY fashion as a way to communicate efficiently to the public, or, also, break group-internal gender dominance.[24] The Berlin DIY fashion project, "Pilotki," for example, was both. "Pilotki" emerged within the environment of a Central Eastern European youth media project called "Plotki—Rumours from around the Bloc."[25] Through their transnational contacts, a number of Plotki participants discovered feminism.[26] To finance the printing of their first "Plotki fem-zine," this group produced feminologist uniforms with the screen print *je suis immigrée* (*I'm an immigrant*) and the group's logo of a woman pilot.[27] Pilotki uniforms played with the seriousness of soviet women pilots to turn victim images of immigrants into uniforms symbolizing autonomy and creativity. Pilotki unisex uniforms were inspired by Russian avant-garde women artists like Stepanova, but they had their uniform elements from caro bags sewed into them. Global caro bags are a symbol of free migration according to Plotki femzine members, who created their uniforms of (second hand) workers' dresses, overalls, and cleaners' and nurse skirts. Pilotki uniforms symbolized agency and attempted to tell stories of struggle of exploited (precarious) immigrant workers—stories of everyday life connecting personal experiences by a number of Plotki members themselves with historical social movements symbolizing the potential of change. What needs to be explored is how and when images of fashion help activists to recall condensed aesthetic sentiments of heroic activism to mobilize imaginaries for future collective action across cultural boundaries.[28]

Another open question is the use of fashion as a practice of radical democratic communication inside social movements: social and political movements used fashion to speak to an *outside* media public sphere.[29] But fashion serves groups also as a practical media to communicate more democratically *within* both translation and local movement groups. Personal experiences with exclusive decision-making in editorial boards of fashion magazines, publishing houses, global firms, or the academia serve fashion creators as a source of inspiration to democratize communication in their own groups. Serpica Naro designers, for example, use the U.S. craftivist bible, *Handmade Nation*[30] as a practical tool to advertise democratic communication inside and outside their own group. In fact, Serpica Naro founders see fashion production as an internal participatory media to create more visibility of the groups' own pluralism, gender equality, and internal difference, similar as other collectives.[31] Several other groups use DIY photography as an experimental media to communicate mutual proposals without risking to validate one over another or reproducing distinct codes.[32] For transnational groups in particular, DIY photography is also a practical media to communicate and decide: Plotki femzine members use pictures to share their fashion ideas over e-mail, as members live in different cities.[33] Local and transnational groups use participatory fashion workshops that encourage participants to develop their own communicative skills in pluralist ways. As demonstrated by Stephanie Müller, a workshop invites participants to bring their favorite clothes, texts, or images and to discuss fashion, feminism, and political issues.

Drawing lessons from such communicative experiments, all of the above groups try to spread democratic experiments beyond their own groups, in DIY fashion defiles, exhibitions, and fan zines. Transnational public spheres based on face-to-face communication are critical network spaces that facilitate communication within fashion groups in Europe and beyond the European context. In Western Europe, a particularly vibrant transnational public for fashion creators is the local "LaDIYfests," while in Central and South Eastern Europe, queer feminist festivals such as the "Rdece Zore—Red Dawns" in Ljubljana also are important events for networking. LaDIYfests, festivals, and DIY exhibitions bring together third wave feminist and queer groups with musicians, students, and fashion creators who produce their own music, films, texts, or media such as "grrrlzines."[34] Some fashion collectives also turn art exhibitions into "transnational exhibition publics"[35] that allow current fashion producers to learn by showing each others' work and build on the work of past women artists, musicians, and producers of fashion (see, for example, the exhibition "Lost and Found").[36]

This contribution has explored the transformative potential of fashion in movements and in broader symbolic struggles about style, taste, and public speech. By using their own personal and professional experiences as a cultural source, fashion groups question established taste and familiar codes of public communication inside movements and the larger public sphere. Communicating fashion within movements and outside them, activists have invented methods to remake participatory democracy beyond the classical tradition of discourse politics and deliberation in past and present social movements. More than that, fashion groups treated members' different competencies as *complex equalities*,[37] thereby avoiding the dominance of singular skills and experiences.

Nicole Doerr is assistant professor of international relations at Mount Holyoke College, Massachusetts. She was a Marie Curie postdoctoral fellow at Harvard University and at UC Irvine. Doerr's work examines social movements and democracy in transnational and multilingual settings in Europe, the United States, and South Africa. Her comparative focus explores questions of discourse, deliberative democracy and culture, multilingualism, migration and inequality, gender, and intersectionality. Doerr recently edited an issue of *Research on Social Movements, Conflict and Change* on "Visual Analysis of Social Movements" with Alice Mattoni and Simon Teune. Her current book project, *Political Translation—A Critique of Democracy, Deliberation and Inequality in Social Movements*, delivers an empirical comparison of multilingual and monolingual deliberation in the United States and Europe.

Notes

1. Cf. Roland Barthes, *Système de la mode* (Paris, 1967).
2. Stephanie Müller, "Do You Read Me? Ein Gruppenexperiment von Stephanie Müller mit Christina Sofie John, Mirjam Stutzmann, Laura Theis und Tina Täsch," in *Handbook of Critical Crafting*, ed. V Kuni et al. (Forthcoming).
3. Diana Crane, *Fashion and Its Social Agendas: Class, Gender, and Identity in Clothing* (Chicago, 2000); Angela McRobbie, "Fashion as a Culture Industry," in *Fashion Cultures: Theories, Explorations and Analysis,* ed. S Bruzzi and P Church Gibson (London, 2000), 253–63.
4. Pierre Bourdieu, *La distinction: critique sociale du jugement* (Paris, 1979).
5. Ibid., 250.
6. Hannah Arendt, *The Human Condition* (Chicago, 1958).
7. Ibid., 218.
8. Wendy Parkins, "Taking Liberty's, Breaking Windows: Fashion, Protest and the Suffragette Public," *Continuum* 11, no. 3 (1997): 37–46; Anna Schober, *Blue Jeans: Vom Leben in Stoffen und Bildern* (Frankfurt, 2001).
9. Müller, "Do You Read Me?," 9.
10. Cf. Francesca Polletta, "Culture and Movements," *The Annals of the American Academy of Political and Social Science* 619, no. 1 (2008): 78–96.
11. Alice Mattoni, "Serpica Naro and the Others. The Media Sociali Experience in Italian Struggles Against Precarity," *Portal* 5, no. 2 (2008): 2–24.
12. Ibid.
13. Ibid.

14. Nicole Doerr and Alice Mattoni, "Public Spaces and Alternative Media Practices in Europe: The Case of the EuroMayDay Parade against Precarity," in *The Revolution Will Not Be Televised?" Media and Protest Movements,* ed. Rolf Werenskjold, Kathrin Fahlenbrach, and Erling Sivertsen (New York, forthcoming), 386–405; Nicole Doerr, "Politicizing Precarity, Producing Visual Dialogues on Migration: Transnational Public Spaces in Social Movement," *Forum Qualitative Social Research* 11, no. 2 (2010): art. 30.

15. My translation: http://www.basis-wien.at/avdt/htm/182/00073142.htm.

16. See also Red Chidgey, Jenny Gunnarsson Payne, and Elke Zobl, "Rumours from around the Bloc: Gossip, Rhizomatic Media, and the Plotki Femzine," *Feminist Media Studies* 9, no. 4 (2009): 477–91.

17. My translation: http://www.basis-wien.at/avdt/htm/182/00073142.htm.

18. Müller, "Do You Read Me?"

19. Ibid.

20. Chidgey, Payne, and Zobl, "Rumours from around the Bloc"; Mattoni, "Serpica Naro and the Others."

21. "Serpica Naro," http://www.serpicanaro.com.

22. "Genève—Uniforme," http://www.serpicanaro.com/lab/geneve-uniforme-2009.

23. Anna Voswinckel, "Gossip. A fanzine," *Plotki femzine* 1, no. 3–4 (2006). http://www.plotki.net/cms/index.php?option=com_content&task=view&id=398&Itemid=31.

24. Chidgey, Payne, and Zobl, "Rumours from around the Bloc"; Mattoni, "Serpica Naro and the Others."

25. "Plotki: Rumours from around the Bloc," http://www.plotki.net.

26. Voswinckel, "Gossip. A fanzine."

27. Chidgey, Payne, and Zobl, "Rumours from around the Bloc."

28. Doerr, "Politicizing Precarity, Producing Visual Dialogues on Migration."

29. Anna Schober, *Ironie, Montage, Verfremdung: Aesthetische Taktiken und die politische Gestalt der Demokratie* (Munich, 2009).

30. Faythe Levine and Cortney Heimerl, *Handmade Nation: The Rise of DIY, Art, Craft, and Design* (New York, 2008).

31. Mattoni, "Serpica Naro and the Others."

32. Müller, "Do You Read Me?"

33. Chidgey, Payne, and Zobl, "Rumours from around the Bloc."

34. Elke Zobl, *The Global Grrrl Zine Network: A DIY Feminist Revolution for Social Change* (Vienna, 2003).

35. Marion von Osten, "Eine Frage des Standpunktes. Ausstellungen machen," *Olympe: Feministische Arbeitshefte zur Politik* 19 (2006): 59–72.

36. "Doing beyond Gender: Lost & Found," http://www.doingbeyondgender.net/cms/de/178/?c=Art_Exhibition.

37. Francesca Polletta, *Freedom Is an Endless Meeting—Democracy in American Social Movements* (Chicago, 2002).

Recommended Reading

Chidgey, Red, Jenny Gunnarsson Payne, and Elke Zobl. "Rumours from around the Bloc: Gossip, Rhizomatic Media, and the Plotki Femzine." *Feminist Media Studies* 9, no. 4 (2009): 477–91. This raises theoretical questions for feminist media studies based on a fine empirical case study of fashion and protest culture in a Central and Eastern European queer feminist group embedded in transnational alternative media networks.

Kuni, Verena, and Sonja Eismann, Elke Gaugele Elke Zobl *Handbook of Critical Crafting* (forthcoming). This explores the practice of critical crafting, grounding this concept in a series of case studies on fashion producers that form part of transnational social movement networks.

Levine, Faythe, and Cortney Heimerl. *Handmade Nation: The Rise of DIY, Art, Craft, and Design*. New York, 2008. This offers a fascinating overview of the emergence of the movement of DIY craftivism in the United States.

Schober, Anna. *Blue Jeans. Vom Leben in Stoffen und Bildern*. Frankfurt, 2001. This provides an excellent cultural historical analysis of blue jeans as a symbol of popular fashion connoting social and political change.

Chapter 21

Action's Design

Tali Hatuka

General Definition of the Term

Design, as defined by the Oxford English Dictionary, is "a plan or scheme conceived in the mind" and intended for subsequent execution, or the pre-liminary idea that is to be carried into effect by action. In this sense, an act of protest is a design—a planned event envisioned in the minds of its organizers—with two purposes: an external purpose in which protesters confront a target and thereby enhance the impact of their political message, and an internal purpose in which protesters confront themselves, thereby intensifying emotional and political solidarity among participants. At the heart of both purposes is a scheme—a designed action with social, spatial, and material dimensions. In other words, as a call for attention to a particular ideology, the action of protest is, first and foremost, a planned display whereby protesters design and use their available means to express beliefs and ideas.

Role in Protest Cultures

To further illustrate what the design of a protest entails, we delineate a few interconnected defining factors such as symbolic and communication practices, the forms of human gathering, and order and surveillance, all of which contribute to the dissent's physical and cultural significance (Table 21.1).

Generally, the design of an action assumes a relationship of interaction among participants. The connection between leaders, participants, and viewers during the event is carefully planned, with particular physical/spatial relationships. For example, a speaker standing in a center of a circular space would project a message of being part of the crowd, emerging from it, as opposed to a speaker standing on a high podium at the edge of a rectangular space, evoking a distinct hierarchy and theatricality. While spatial proportions and building masses affect participants' movements and their symbolic meaning, it is also the case that the physical setting of a protest—whether held in an institutional space like a civic square, in a leisure place like park, or in the city streets—is often modified by the installation of a stage, microphones, flags, and posters, which reinforce the visual and textual symbols of the event. In terms of designing a protest, the choice of location is also closely connected to the expected and desired number of participants, which depends on the space's attributes of surveillance and control.

In addition to the effect of space on the form of human gathering, timing and scale are also critical to defining the action's design. By timing, we mean whether an event is held during the day or night, whether it is short or long, repetitive or singular. By scale, we mean the size of a place and the number of people it can host (scale of place) and whether the protest takes place at the local, national, or global level (scale of protest), as well as their interrelationships. These two factors, timing and scale, have a crucial impact on the choice of place for the action. Thus, for example in a case of a mass congregation, a monumental space contributes to transforming the individual into an anonymous participant, an integral part of a unified entity. When this same place is empty, the scale and physical features of its space are a continuous reminder of the regime's power as well as action's monumentality.

In an action's production of symbols and strategies, the media is a critical component that influences political decision-making and public opinion, thus acting as a decisive participant in protest. For this reason, the design of an action must include a way to engage with the media to attract attention. In fact, advocates of social change have now come to depend on the use of media. At the same time, protest activities have helped fill the media's need for a steady supply of spectacular images and stories, thus creating an interdependent relationship that must be acknowledged as part of an event's design.

Order is another key component of a protest, designating two interrelated systems: the order of the assembly and the order of the space. The order of the assembly and its ritual performance components (i.e., marching, gathering, singing, clothing, even the scheduled timing and length of the event) represent the way participants see themselves either as supporters or protesters against social order, all within the culture of their society.[1]

This order has a dual role: it is a mechanism for constructing meaning and for interpreting social reality, and it is a device for negotiating between the state and the citizen. The order of the assembly takes place within the arrangement of a physical space, which includes the setting's topography, boundaries, traffic movements, and building uses (i.e., governmental, commercial, or residential). The space's setting and design, defined by architects and authorities, are representations of the civic identity of the society. For example, when protesters march together, they aim to reclaim or symbolically possess their city, or particular public spaces in the city. They modify (temporarily) the daily hum of urban life with dynamic vocal and visual messages through which they challenge the established social order identified with the dominant powers. Thus, the form of a march and its route are critical to attracting spectators and additional participants. As such, marching in the main plaza of a city or passing by government buildings indicates the intention of the protesters to communicate with officials and challenge or sway their decisions. Marching in residential areas or gathering at nongovernmental venues outside of the center indicates the group's intention to protest far from the hegemonic powers, as a contraposition to them. By extension, the group can then be seen as imposing their order over whatever space they occupy.

The well-known example of the Mothers of Plaza de Mayo in Argentina, marching in circles, reveals how an innovative act emerges from both the space's design (the paved circle around the monument) and the legal limitations of protesting against the regime. This example shows how groups appropriate space by redefining its access, appearance, and representation, and reclaim the space by using some of its physical attributes, modifying its cultural origin. Another example is the Israeli "Women in Black" who temporarily appropriate "informal public spaces" throughout Israel every Friday afternoon.[2] These relatively small groups have the power to decide their own spatial configuration, performance acts, and means of action. However, in a case of large assemblies, it is the powers (i.e., the political parties or institutions) that define the spatial configuration of the crowd by planning the size of the space to best suit the number of people assembling, enhancing the sense of togetherness and solidarity among participants, both reinforcing the crowd's perception of its own power and reassuring those in power.

Surveillance practices, in use in most public spaces, are an integral part of the planning of any protests. Some of the space characteristics are modified temporarily to fit the order of the action, with barriers, blocked routes, and adjusted traffic rules controlling the order of the crowd's movement. In addition, police attempt to maintain this order through additional means of surveillance, such as cameras and secret agents in a crowd, to remain alert

Figure 21.1. Forms of gatherings, Buenos Aires, 2006. © Photo by Tali Hatuka.

Figure 21.2. Forms of gatherings, London, 2007. © Photo by Tali Hatuka.

to any form of violence that might occur. Yet, in many assemblies, there is direct coordination between the organizers (activists or political powers) and the police.[3] This coordination is often seen as desirable by both sides, with the first seeing it as a means of keeping safe and the latter as a means of maintaining civil order.

Surveillance is also empowered by modern technology and is clearly the most effective means of achieving what Foucault has called "docile bodies," citizens targeted by power control.[4] Furthermore, the increased media attention provides additional surveillance, controlling events simultaneously from above and on the ground. However, one must be careful when using these terms, as surveillance and enforced order *can* be challenged through sociopolitical agencies, as in the case of the Mothers of Plaza de Mayo, who operated under a military coup. The order's significance, of both assembly and space, is that it serves as a means of control, but it can also become a means of liberation and mediation.

There is also the question of overdesign and aestheticizing of the action that is often associated with totalitarian regimes. This was evident with the Nazi party, which relied on carefully contrived architectural orchestration and lighting, as in the 1934 Zeppelin Field event masterminded by the architect Albert Speer. Speer directed a battery of 130 antiaircraft searchlights in the night sky to create his famous "cathedral of light." By developing the sublime in Nazi Germany, argues Leach,[5] the architecture set the scene for an aesthetic celebration of the violence that underpinned Fascist thinking, thereby enlisting architectural aesthetics to serve political power and increase the tensions between ideologies and ethics.

These parameters—symbolic meaning, scale and the form of gathering, order, and surveillance—along with cultural and functional definitions, play a crucial role in the design of a protest's action and in producing meaning (see Table 21.1). It is these parameters that frame a protest's form (i.e., design or structure) and practice (i.e., enactment). Being flexible and dynamic, these parameters express citizens' negotiations among themselves and with the regime, thus making the logic of how they are put together crucial to how they work, and to that which their designs enable them to accomplish.[6]

Research Gaps and Open Questions

Protests are designed and planned actions, with event physicality affecting both the participants' movement and performance as well as the socio-spatial definition of the protest. However, the relationship between protest and space has not been studied in depth. In part, the reason for this derives

Table 21.1. Matrix of Action's Design

Parameters of action design	Symbolic and communication practices	Forms of gathering	Order and surveillance
Form	Influences ritual performance components	Subjective to social norms, configurations of appropriation	Negotiates with authorities/permits
Scale	Affects interaction among participants (internal)	Affects size of assemblies (small/large, formal/informal)	Affects order of assembly and order of space
Media	Boosts message and impact (external)	Defined in expectation of possible media coverage	Contributes to control practices
Place	Impacts rhythm and symbols on action's message	Affects event's form and scale	Impacts control management (by participants)

from the historical and theoretical development of protest analysis in the social sciences, in which culture, behavior, reasoning, and mobility have been the main parameters rather than the physical and formal settings of the protest itself. The physical implications of protest in the architecture of civic squares has not received much attention, nor has the use of the public arena. Recent studies have addressed the role of built spaces in constructing a national identity,[7] focusing on architecture as a cultural artifact within intricate power geometries.[8] Particular attention has been paid to the architectural concept of buildings as mediators between civic society and its urban image.[9] Yet, addressing questions such as what makes citizens choose protest, or why do they choose a particular form of protest and how do they use space, expand the theoretical understanding of the relationship between the action's meaning and the action's physicality.

Tali Hatuka is an architect, urban planner, and head of the Laboratory of Contemporary Urban Design in the Department of Geography and Human Environment at Tel Aviv University. Hatuka works primarily on social, planning, and architectural issues, focusing on the relationships between urban regeneration and development, violence, and life in contemporary society. Her recent book, *Revisioning Moments: Violent Acts and Urban Space in Con-*

temporary Tel Aviv was published both in English (Austin, TX, 2010) and Hebrew (Tel Aviv, 2008). Her work has been published in a wide range of journals, including the *Journal of Urban Design International, the Journal of Architecture, the Journal of Architecture and Planning Research, Planning Perspectives, Political Geography,* and *Geopolitics.*

Notes

1. Don Handelman, *Models and Mirrors: Towards an Anthropology of Public Events* (Cambridge, 1990).
2. Tova Benski, "Breaching Events and the Emotional Reactions of the Public: Women in Black in Israel," in *Emotions and Social Movements,* ed. H Flam and D King (New York, 2005), 57–78.
3. For further reading on situations when these agreements are violated by violence, see Tali Hatuka, "Negotiating Space: Analyzing Jaffa Protest's Form, Intention and Violence, October 27th 1933," *Jerusalem Quarterly* 35 (2008): 93–106; Aysegul Baykan and Tali Hatuka, "Politics and Culture in the Making of a City-Center: The Case of Taksim Square, Istanbul," *Planning Perspectives* 25, no. 1 (2010): 49–68.
4. Michel Foucault, *Discipline and Punish* (New York, 1995).
5. Neil Leach, *The Anaesthetics of Architecture* (Cambridge, 1999).
6. Handelman, *Models and Mirrors,* 16.
7. Sibel Bozdoğan, *Modernism and Nation Building: Turkish Architectural Culture in the Early Republic* (Seattle, 2001); Abidin Kunso, *Behind the Postcolonial* (London, 2000); Lawrence J Vale, *Architecture, Power and National Identity* (New Haven, CT, 1992).
8. Lisa Findley, *Building Change* (London, 2005); Kim Dovey, *Framing Places* (London, 1999).
9. Richard Sennett, *The Spaces of Democracy* (Ann Arbor, MI, 1998).

Recommended Reading

Canetti, Elias. *Crowds and Power.* New York, 1962. Reviews the way crowds form, develop, and dissolve, using the taxonomy of mass movement as a key to the dynamics of social life.

D'Arcus, Bruce. *Boundaries of Dissent: Protest and State Power in the Media Age.* New York, 2006. On the media role and its contribution to the scale and boundaries of protest.

Findley, Lisa. *Building Change.* London, 2005. Illustrates the relationships between power, space, and architecture.

Goffman, Erving. *Interaction Ritual: Essays in Face-to-Face Behavior.* New Brunswick, NJ, 2005. Examines public events' design and organization as a means to understand the ritual in relation to the world within which it is created and practiced.

Mayo, James M. "Propaganda with Design: Environmental Dramaturgy in the Political Rally." *Journal of Architectural Education* 32, no. 2 (1978): 24–32. Addresses the link between the form of space and the design of protest.

Chapter 22

Alternative Media

Alice Mattoni

General Definition of the Term

Alternative media are channels of communication, existing in places, situations, and contexts different from the realm of mainstream and corporate media, which spread content opposed to the dominant system of meanings and whose creation is sustained through face-to-face interactions and/or computer-mediated communication among nonmedia professionals. Be it transnational, national, or local, alternative media production takes place outside and beyond the profit logic of corporate media. Alternative media circulation is lower than mainstream media. The presence of small audiences, however, is a peculiarity rather than a problem: it is not possible to measure the success of alternative media simply by assessing the extent of their diffusion.[1] Indeed, the sites of alternative media channels are multiple, and the places of alternative media content are dispersed in a variety of technological means: from posters to radio, from television to theater, and from graffiti to stickers.[2] Alternative media constitute an "area of cultural production" where various forms of alternative media practices and products, which have a different degree of radicalization, intertwine.[3] In other words, alternative media is a field of social interactions, communication, and mediation with an intrinsic transformative power directed toward the realms of media, society, and culture.

General Cultural Functions

Alternative media perform at least two different tasks when it comes to general cultural functions. On the one side, they have an impact on the level of circulation and diffusion of alternative media messages. On the other, they have an impact on the level of processes leading to the production of alternative media channels and contents.

As for circulation and diffusion, the presence of alternative media in societies contributes to the diversification of information sources available to citizens. Therefore, the very existence of alternative media provides the opportunity of aiming at cultural diversity and constitutes a counterbalance to a usually homogeneous mainstream and corporate media. As they are outside the profit logic of the market, indeed, alternative media often draw attention to issues, citizens, and facts that do not meet the newsworthy criteria of mainstream and corporate media, who follow profit market logics. Moreover, alternative media sustain the diffusion of meanings, codes, and languages, presenting new cultural values in the public sphere.[4]

As for processes behind the production of alternative media channels and contents, the impact is at the micro level of citizens and their perception of the media at large. When citizens engage in development of alternative media, they learn how to produce their own narratives about themselves and the social realities in which they are embedded. This process in turn enhances the citizens' understanding of the constructed nature of media narratives and renders visible the mechanism of naming realities on which media power rests.[5] The awareness of media power that citizens gain poses a challenge to mainstream and corporate media, whose accounts and reports cease to be seen as transparent and unbiased representations of social realities. In a way, then, citizens who engage in the creation of alternative media channels and texts increase their media literacy and ability to interpret mediated cultural representations, often based on stereotypes.

Role in Protest Cultures

The role of alternative media is even more important with regard to protest cultures. Social movements are producers of alternative systems of meanings and include new codes and languages that reconstruct and/or reappropriate social realities.[6] Alternative media, therefore, become an area of cultural production where flows of communication related to alternative systems of meaning emerge and diffuse. Alternative media are one of the sites in which social movements express the knowledge and culture they have developed before, during, and after mobilizations. They hence become the place where social movements meet critical audiences and, also due to this encounter, explore, discuss, and refine alternative systems of meanings. Finally, alternative media are sites in which activists, in defining their protest cultures, name themselves and elaborate the boundaries of their (collective) identity.

Yet protest cultures and social movements intertwine with different types of alternative media. Two dimensions seem particularly relevant: persistence over time and the social movement affiliation of alternative media. For persistence over time, there are well-established and long-lasting alternative media outlets whose presence in the public sphere transcends a single wave of mobilization. In other cases though, alternative media are episodic and ephemeral outlets whose existence is strictly linked to a well-defined moment of protest. As for the affiliation of alternative media, there are mono-affiliated alternative media strictly embedded in one specific type of activist group, and in contrast, there are multi-affiliated alternative media linked to a diverse and fluid social movement coalition. Four types of alternative media derive from the combination of the two dimensions and play a different role in protest cultures. Long-lasting and mono-affiliation alternative media usually attract small audiences of activists belonging to a specific protest culture. Such alternative media support communication flows within the activist group and have a role in the development of its collective identity. Long-lasting and multi-affiliation alternative media refer instead to a composite and changing coalition of activist groups that recognize themselves as being in a common and broad system of meaning, despite internal differences. Alternative media, in this case, function as a space of dialogue and hybridization among different protest cultures. Ephemeral and mono-affiliation alternative media aim at precise objectives during mobilizations, like explaining the reasons behind a protest event or providing the coverage of a mobilization from the point of view of a single activist group. Ephemeral and multi-affiliation alternative media though are protest-related media that involve a composite social movement coalition in the management of information and communication related to mobilizations.

Theoretical and Empirical Perspectives

Literature on alternative media had a marginal role in media studies till the end of the 1990s and only gained larger recognition in recent years when monographs and special issue journals on the topic flourished. Research on alternative media is organized along two theoretical perspectives: the one looking at alternative media as products and the one looking at alternative media as processes.

As for approaches taking into consideration alternative media as products, the focus is on contents and messages expressed through alternative media. The meanings they spread constitute, indeed, an alternative to mainstream media texts.[7] Focusing only on the textual level, we can also find messages criticizing the dominant system of meanings within those media, which cannot be strictly defined as alternative media, like progressive press, that has been labeled "critical media."[8]

There are, then, approaches interested in the processes of production behind alternative media. The development of alternative media channels and the creation of alternative media texts empower citizens taking part in such processes. In looking for new means through which to express their own voices and desires, citizens have an active role in the construction of their own subjectivities. The expression "citizen media"[9] refers to the empowerment potential that lies at the heart of alternative media production processes. In the same line, the expression "community media"[10] stresses the crucial role of citizens' participation in the making of small-range alternative media based at the local level of communities.

In between the two theoretical perspectives, other approaches consider both the product and the processes leading to the product, as well as the messages and the social interactions behind the creation of messages. Some authors consider as alternative those media that reach a certain degree of alternativeness at the product and/or content level.[11] Other authors instead consider those media as alternative that attain a certain degree of alternativeness both on the product and the process level. For instance, "radical media"[12] are progressive media deeply intertwined with social movements produced through horizontal social relations that spread messages oriented toward political change. In the same vein, "democratic media activism"[13] creates alternative media channels and content to alter power asymmetries that exist in the mediascape and in so doing democratize the media according to participatory processes of production.

Although different theoretical interpretations are at work, authors drawing upon such a holistic approach look at alternative media as a whole set of processes and products. In summary, content, aesthetics, and physical support are three relevant dimensions when considering alternative media as a product, while distribution, social relations, and communication processes are three relevant dimensions when considering the processes of creation behind alternative media.[14]

At the theoretical level, a high degree of conceptual multiplicity characterizes the field of alternative media, where scholars employ concurrent expressions, belonging to diverse areas of research and relying on a number of schools of thought. On the empirical level, instead, the alternative media field seems to suffer from a convergence toward the investigation of alternative media of Western societies linked to progressive social movements.[15] Moreover, with the raising of information and communication technologies, and especially web platforms and internet applications, scholars tend to focus more and more on alternative media created in online and virtual environments, such as informational web sites,[16] or on social networking sites like Facebook and Twitter in which activists publish their radical messages, leaving aside other forms of alternative media that continue to exist, like the radio and theatrical performances, which are often combined with new technological means.

Research Gaps and Open Questions

Research on alternative media is a rich field of study of which many aspects have been already analyzed. There are, however, some relevant research gaps concerning alternative media audiences,[17] and there is little evidence about the path that alternative system of meanings follow after having been produced. More research is hence needed to grasp interactions between alternative media and their audiences,[18] and alternative media and mainstream media.[19] In addition, one of the outcomes of social movements is the knowledge they produce while engaging in social practices oriented toward mobilization.[20] Some scholars stress that social movements studies often neglect considering this point, despite it being crucial in understanding the production of social movements' cultures.[21] This remark singles out yet another research gap in alternative media studies, as little is known about how activists involved in social movements perceive the broad range of alternative media. Furthermore, to investigate how alternative media practitioners perceive and evaluate alternative media is particularly important to construct well-informed theories about contemporary alternative media cultures within and beyond protest cultures.

Another research gap concerns the so-called web 2.0 platforms and applications,[22] which includes social networking and content sharing web sites, such as Facebook, Twitter and YouTube. These applications are online mainstream and profit-oriented media that activist groups and individual activists increasingly employ to diffuse oppositional and radical cultures. Although there is a growing body of literature concerning the use of social networking and content sharing websites during protests, specific research about what happens to alternative media content and messages when they are spread through web 2.0 applications and platforms is needed. In a similar vein, changes at the level of creative and collective processes of production behind alternative media have not been extensively investigated as to how they intertwine with such applications and platforms.

Alice Mattoni is assistant professor at the Insitute of Humanities and Social Sciences, Scuola Normale Supereiore and a research fellow at the Centre on Social Movement Studies (Cosmos), hosted in the same institution. Amongst her recent publications are *Spreading Protests. Social Movements in Times of Crisis*, co-edited with Donatella Della Porta (ECPR Press, 2014); *Advances in the Visual Analysis of Social Movements,* co-edited with Nicole Doerr and Simon Teune (Emerald, 2013); *Media Practices and Protest Politics. How Precarious Workers Mobilise* (Ashgate, 2012).

Notes

1. Alfonso G Dagron, "The Long and Winding Road of Alternative Media," in *The SAGE Handbook of Media Studies,* ed. JDH Downing et al. (Thousand Oaks, CA, 2004), 41–46.
2. John DH Downing, *Radical Media: Rebellious Communication and Social Movements* (Thousand Oaks, CA, 2001).
3. Chris Atton, *Alternative Media* (London, 2001).
4. Clemencia Rodríguez, *Fissures in the Mediascape. An International Study of Citizens' Media* (Creskill, NJ, 2001).
5. Nick Couldry and James Curran, *Contesting Media Power: Alternative Media in a Networked World* (Lanham, MD, 2003).
6. Alberto Melucci, *Challenging Codes: Collective Action in the Information Age* (Cambridge, 1996).
7. Couldry and Curran, *Contesting Media Power.*
8. Christian Fuchs, "Alternative Media as Critical Media," *European Journal of Social Theory* 13, no. 2 (2010): 173–92.
9. Rodríguez, *Fissures in the Mediascape.*
10. Kevin Howley, *Community Media: People, Places, and Communication Technologies* (Cambridge, 2005); Martine Hackett, "Community Radio and Television," in *Encyclopedia of Activism and Social Justice,* ed. GL Anderson and KG Herr (Thousand Oaks, CA, 2007).
11. Joshua D Atkinson, *Alternative Media and Politics of Resistance* (New York, 2010).
12. Downing, *Radical Media.*
13. William K Carroll and Robert A Hackett, "Democratic Media Activism through the Lens of Social Movement Theory," *Media Culture Society* 28, no. 1 (2006): 83–104; Robert A Hackett and William K Carroll, *Remaking Media: The Struggle to Democratize Public Communication* (London, 2006).
14. Atton, *Alternative Media.*

15. Chris Atton, "Current Issues in Alternative Media Research," *Sociology Compass* 1, no. 1 (2007): 17–27.
16. Kate Coyer, "If It Leads It Bleeds: The Participatory Newsmaking of the Independent Media Centre," in *Global Activism, Global Media*, ed. W De Jong, M Shaw, and N Stammers (London, 2005); Donatella Della Porta and Lorenzo Mosca, "Global-net for Global Movements? A Network of Networks for a Movement of Movements," *Journal of Public Policy* 25, no. 1 (2005): 165–90; Douglas Morris, "Globalization and Media Democracy: The Case of Indymedia," in *Shaping the Network Society: The New Role of Civil Society in Cyberspace*, ed. D Schuler and P Day (Cambridge, MA, 2004).
17. John DH Downing, "Audiences and Readers of Alternative Media: The Absent Lure of the Virtually Unknown," *Media Culture Society* 25, no 5 (2003): 625–45.
18. Ibid.
19. Atton, "Current Issues in Alternative Media Research."
20. Ron Eyerman and Andrew Jamison, *Social Movements* (Cambridge, 1991).
21. Laurence Cox and Alf G Nilsen, "Social Movement Research and the 'Movement of Movements': Studying Resistance to Neoliberal Globalisation," *Sociology Compass* 1, no. 2 (2007): 424–42.
22. Danah M Boyd and Nicole B Ellison, "Social Network Sites: Definition, History, and Scholarship," *Journal of Computer-Mediated Communication* 13, no. 1 (2007): 210–30.

Recommended Reading

Atton, Chris. *Alternative Media*. London, 2002. This offers a comprehensive literature review on the topic and presents a holistic model of interpretation for investigating different degrees of alternativeness in alternative media.

Couldry, Nick, and James Curran, eds. *Contesting Media Power: Alternative Media in a Networked World*. Lanham, MD, 2003. This discusses alternative media as challenges to mainstream and corporate media power. It presents empirical case studies that consider the (sometimes contradictory) interactions between alternative media and the state, the market, civil society, and religion.

Downing, John. *Radical Media: Rebellious Communication and Social Movement*. Thousand Oaks, CA, 2001. A seminal study on alternative media. The author discusses a variety of technological supports and communication channels that function as radical media and sustain progressive protest cultures.

Rodríguez, Clemencia. *Fissures in the Mediascape: An International Study of Citizens' Media*. Creskill, NJ, 2001. This introduces the concepts of "citizen media," grounding this concept in extensive fieldwork on social interactions behind the production of alternative media channels and content.

Chapter 23

Graffiti

Johannes Stahl

There have been perennial attempts to get rid of it, but graffiti is a permanent and immortal accompany of cultural history. The term originally comes from the Greek *graphein* for writing. During the centuries, it saw a change in meaning from the renaissance Italian *sgraffiti* (as an official decorative technique for scratching into fresh plaster) toward the mid nineteenth century, when French publications focused on graffiti as illegal, scriptural, or pictural use of public walls. In our contemporary use, the term also can label an art form, which—claimed as such since a central essay by French photographer and writer Brassai in the 1930s—has developed an own pictural grammar and reached worldwide extension after forceful impulses out of New York and Philadelphia since the 1970s.

Asides the continuing flood of well-pictured books, some basic research has been done. But still the item is remaining in an open field where sociological, linguistic, psychological, art, historical, and design researchers compete for dominance. Recently, many studies are focusing on the artists as a special group in society (more on a personal level than from statistic bases).[1] A second important field has recently been opened in design theory, trying to put in relation the roots of graffiti, special developments, and impact on everyday picture worlds.[2] The most important gap (due to the rather temporary careers in the art world) is that up to now, deep-going studies on graffiti as art in close connection with developments in contemporary art still are lacking.

The use of graffiti as a medium of protest has often been claimed, and the intensity of this contribution changed with the times. Before taking this functional definition as a special medium for protest in closer focus, it is worth paying attention to other ways to approach the phenomenon. Some theories claimed the factor of occupation as central for graffiti: marking territory and changing its appearance may mean discussing society and power. Another factor of graffiti is claiming a public identity. This matches with the main group of adolescent boys who make graffiti and with the ongoing public impact on names, (trade)marks, and public visibility. In following this argumentation, these marks are not exclusively meant as protest, but also as embellishment.

A closer look on the protest impact graffiti shows this history is a very old one. It appears in political notes on the walls of Pompeji, in French and German revolutionary caricatures of the nineteenth century, and since World War I can both be seen in photographic documents and on walls. It can be supposed that graffiti has been a continuous factor in the history of protest. Especially the French 1830s caricatures frequently repeat the antiroyal pear caricature. In the satirical daily paper *La Caricature,* graphic designers like Auguste Bouquet argued by street urchins, drawing the caricature at the walls, claiming this protest was a point of view shared by possibly the whole people—and thus giving it the shape of a multimedia campaign. As a special protest culture, graffiti comes closer into sight during oppressing regimes like the Third Reich. The Austrian AEIOU (*Austria est*

Figure 23.1. Auguste Bouquet: *Voulez Vous faire Vos ordures plus loin, polissons!* (Make your shit elsewhere, you pigs!) Lithograph, *La Caricature* Nr. 115, 17. January 1833.

in orbis ultimo, engl. Austria will be the last in the world) as a traditional formula for the Austrian Empire and its everlasting existence became—differently interpreted—a secret spell for a free Austria and was placed at walls as a protest sign against the Nazi usurpation. The Lothringian Cross as its equivalent in France and many political symbols from the non-Nazi world are now—if they have survived the times—protected as valuable historical documents.

A strange museification in a different context can be seen in the Amsterdam subway station, Nieuwe Markt. Graffiti and barricades from the squatters who fought the construction of the subway are now part of a historical documentation, which now decorates the subway walls. Reading *Wij blijven hier wonen* (we stay housing here) at the remains of a formerly squatted house might well be recognized as a sort of cynical official comment toward an expelled culture that had one of its bases in the Nieuwe Markt quarter.

The 1970s and 1980s squatters' movement was a part and result of some political attempts to gain more direct influence in political systems, may it be the dictatorship in Greece, Spain, Portugal, or the constitutional democracies. Whether it was the general term of counterculture,[3] which had some influence on art production, the occupied universities in 1960s Europe, media emancipation questions, or ethnic movements such as Black Panthers in the United States, graffiti was regarded as an appropriate means to articulate a position that, in concerns of media presence, was inferior, but could stand for a much larger number of people. Rather often, the argumentation claimed the right to do so (nevertheless graffiti was not a human right) because other forms of expression were occupied by the media majority.

Jean Baudrillard went so far to claim New York graffiti as an uproar of signs, thus connecting European conceptions of political radicalism with a culture that had its own origins with a strong accent on linguistic thinking.[4] Thus, claiming something like an unaware protest, he disregards Norman Mailor's more empirical interpretation of their own cultural impulses the spray can youngsters had,[5] and which can be found up to more recent investigations.[6]

Nevertheless, in Europe some rather intense discussions about graffiti as a protest medium had been connected to the Sprayer von Zürich since the late 1970s. Claiming his spray can drawings are an individual and artistic protest against the architectural devastations of the urban environment or ecological catastrophes,[7] the phantom, which since 1979 was discovered as Swiss artist Harald Naegeli, was a key figure of this European discussion. His vivid spray can drawings animating the concrete surface of the Swiss bank capital were widely acclaimed by a variety of art reviews, but in his hometown created a political argument about their role in public order—

Figure 23.2. Harald Naegeli: "The Dance of Death for Fish," spray can drawings on 200 km alongside the Rhine, Bonn 1987. © Photo by Johannes Stahl.

even if they were accepted as art. This discussion became an example for many similar graffiti cases since then, especially when Naegeli went to jail for half a year in 1984. Following a continuing boom in presenting American graffiti as an art form, integrated like rap or break dance in hip-hop lifestyle, a more analytical aspect of their protest elements became inferior to the visual arguments of presentation.

Meanwhile, the jurisdiction on and prosecution of graffiti has become sharper, accompanied by wider surveillance of public space. Following this, the term graffiti has been joined and partly replaced by less argued terms like street art or urban art. Nevertheless, the main kernel, the noncommanded and partly nonpermitted public expression, has remained quite similar. A look toward the walls today shows visual protest notes in pictural or written form has not at all disappeared. But compared with other key impacts in the amount of tagging, pieces, or stenciled pictures, the political protest seems to have diminished and obviously uses other media.

Johannes Stahl is working as an author, curator, and cultural advisor. He taught at the universities of Bonn and Halle/Saale and at the academies of Fine Arts in Mainz and in Halle/Saale. His working focus is on public art, graffiti, art education, art loan schemes, installations, and questions of spatiality in different media. His recent publications include: *Der interaktive*

Blick. Über Kunst, Wirkungsräume und Mitspieler (Münster, 2011) and a theory reader with collection catalog on CD: *Giveaways. Catalogue Artothek im Bonner Kunstverein/Hochschule für Grafik und Buchkunst Leipzig*, coedited with Joachim Penzel (Bonn, 2002).

Notes

1. Julia Reinecke, *Street-Art: Eine Subkultur zwischen Kunst und Kommerz*, 2nd ed. (Bielefeld, 2012).
2. Staffan Jacobson, *Den spraymålade bilden: graffitimåleriet som bildform, konströrelse och läroprocess* (Lund, 1996); Daniela Krause and Christian Heinicke, *Street Art. Die Stadt als Spielplatz* (Berlin, 2006).
3. Theodore Roszak, *The Making of a Counter Culture. Reflections on the Technocratic Society and Its Youthful Opposition* (Berkeley, CA, 1968).
4. Jean Baudrillard, *Kool Killer oder die Revolution der Zeichen* (Berlin, 1978). First in *Interferences* 3 (1975): 26–27.
5. Norman Mailor, *The Faith of Graffiti* (New York, 1973); Nancy McDonald, *The Graffiti Subculture: Youth, Masculinity and Identity in London and New York* (Basingstoke, 2004).
6. Craig Castleman, *Getting Up: Subway Graffiti in New York* (Cambridge, 1984).
7. Harald Naegeli *Mein Revoltieren, mein Sprayen* (Bern, 1979).

Recommended Reading

Derwanz, Heike. *Street Artists. Karrieren auf dem Kunst- und Designmarkt.* Paderborn, 2013. It is a brilliant new study, with an overview of research up to now.

Mailor, Norman. *The Faith of Graffiti.* New York, 1973. Offers an early, clear, and basic anthropological view.

Naegeli, Harald, *Mein Revoltieren, mein Sprayen: Dokumentation von Fotos, Zeichnungen u. Texten.* Bern, 1979. It is the first artist-run publication about the activities of Naegeli and his collaborators, with a confessional character and stringent form.

Stahl, Johannes. *Street Art.* Königswinter, 2009. Offers a new and revised approach twenty years after the doctorate thesis of the author. English, French, and Spanish editions are also available.

Chapter 24

Posters and Placards

Sascha Demarmels

General Definition of the Term

A poster is a printed paper, placed in public which adheres to a certain format.[1] Whereas in Germany this format is at least A3 size (standard paper size of 27.9 cm × 42 cm), in Switzerland the so-called Weltformat (128 cm × 90.5 cm) is the standard.[2] The size often depends on the billboards, the official spots to place posters. In the United Kingdom, there are billboards available from four sheets of paper (101.6 cm × 152.4 cm) to 96 sheets.[3] In the United States, however, 9' 7" × 21' 7" (292.1 cm × 657.86 cm) and 10' 5" × 22' 8" (317.5 cm × 690.88 cm) are common formats for poster panels (framed posters in commercial and industrial areas), and bus shelter posters are 4' × 6' (121.92 cm × 182.88 cm).[4] Recently, billposting has become no longer restricted to billboards alone. For example, very big posters are hung on buildings in times of renovations. That is called Building Wrap.[5] The posting is carried out and regulated by an official billposting company. They hang and remove the posters and organize the changing of the billboards.

It is essential that the poster be hung in a central public area where people cannot help but see it. Thus, one can reach lots of people and be guaranteed the message gets to the masses.[6] However, the viewing time has been reduced from 30 to 1.5 seconds since 1940.[7] That means the struggle for attention has been getting harder for the last fifty years.[8] Today, communication with the public does not use posters exclusively anymore but utilizes different channels.[9] In advertising, this is called media-mix: the same campaign appears in different media like on posters, in papers, and on television.[10]

The codes that can be used in poster communication are basically verbal and visual: pictures, lettering, and color.[11] As for the pictures, printing technology is very important. In 1796, the first step was taken by the invention of the lithography, which allowed for printing pictures in black and white.[12] At the end of the nineteenth century, color lithography brought an aesthetic revolution to the art of poster designing.[13]

Besides the codes, text elements are also essential components of posters. They have been established in the advertising research (see below), but can be used to describe posters in general. Because posters are very large in scale, typography has to be large and pictures cannot hold many details, so that the poster can be read from a distance—there is no use for too detailed of text elements as there are in (paper) advertisements. The main text blocks are the headline (as some kind of title to a poster), the copy or body copy (the main text in several lines as a text block), the slogan, and the logo.[14] However, there are more differences between product and political advertising.[15]

A placard is very similar to a poster and sometimes even used as a synonym. One differentiation is that placards are often more solid because they are made of cardboard. Further, they are not hung up on walls but brought to a demonstration and held in the air, affixed to a stick. For this purpose, they are often not printed but painted by hand. Moreover, there are fewer pictures on placards than on posters, where pictures play a decisive role.

In contrast to other media types, wallpaper is, in fact, less large-scale and has more text in smaller typography. Essentially, it is a newspaper hung up on a wall. Flyers can be seen as the parents of the poster we have today.[16] They have a smaller format and are not hung up but distributed on the streets.[17] And then there are political postcards.[18] They are not very frequent nowadays, but they do have a modern equivalent in the so-called e-cards. You can find them on web sites of political parties and movements for sending via e-mail. They usually consist of a fitting visual motif and/or a slogan. And there is a digital equivalent for the poster, too: public screens in the out-of-home area.[19] All these means of communication are used for advertising products as well as political and social issues. The functions of these media do not change much nor does their general role in culture.

General Cultural Functions

The main goal of posters is to share information, advertising for products and events, political and also social issues. It is about directing attention and persuading people to buy or vote for something. Sometimes the persuasion is very similar to propaganda. Thus, wars have been important in the evolution of posters because they were used in an attempt to communicate and manipulate in as efficient a manner as possible.[20] There have been times when political posters were banned from public life because people were overwhelmed by the effect the posters had on them.[21]

The high potential of posters lies especially in the visual aspect. Therefore, multimodality and emotionalization are important research fields (see below).[22] As for art posters, made by actual artists, it is also about aesthetics. Posters are ahead of their time and can absorb actual styles immediately.[23] In this case, posters serve as a vehicle for aesthetic change. They bring art from the museums and galleries out to the streets and to the average person.[24]

Role in Protest Cultures

When Martin Luther started the reformation, he not only had the translated bible printed in a large edition but he also had the possibility of printing pamphlets—comparable with today's flyers—with the new invented printing press. This fact helped him to win his revolution. Without the pamphlets, he probably would not have been capable of communicating with the broad masses.[25]

For protest movements, it was always important to have a means of communication not only to gain the masses but also to communicate at low expense and nevertheless be efficient in communicating. For example, in the 1980s in Switzerland, the youth movement printed their posters with a copy machine. That was cheap and very effective. With the posters they advertised for alternative culture events. This alternative culture was at that time punk, which itself can be seen as a protest against the existing aesthetic standards. "The posters always vexed the general public's habits of seeing."[26] So protest can be manifested already in the poster itself, in the visual part of it, before the content of its verbal text has been read.

Generally, billposting is done officially by some agency; illegal billposting is possible though and often used by protest movements. This reduces costs and draws even more attention to the posters and to the (political) statement.

Yet another form of protest in the area of posters is the so-called adbusting (busting of advertisements). Adbusters alter posters in public to change their message and appeal for a critical view of consumerism. Founder Kalle Lasn wants to get individuals to think critically about advertising.[27] There are several groups of adbusters, often originating in the street art community, who also communicate about their artwork on the Internet via blogs or videos on YouTube.[28] The terms guerilla communication and subvertising (from subversive and advertising) are often used in the context of adbusting. They often attract a lot of attention, sometimes even in the classical media.

So, in addition to being effective for communication without costing too much, the role of the poster in protest cultures is to attract interest and to wrap political statements in an aesthetical way. With new signs and perhaps new visual language, there is high potential for recruiting people who may want to be part of the new movement.

Theoretical and Empirical Research Perspectives

As mentioned above, posters are used for advertising. Besides, posters can also be read as art.[29] There are many illustrated books with art historic claims. They assemble posters made by (famous) artists. Then there are collections with posters from a certain area, for example, with political or social posters ("Kunst und Propaganda,"[30] "Political Posters in central and eastern Europe 1945–95,"[31] "Breaking the Rules. Posters from the turbulent 1980s in Switzerland,"[32] "Political and Social Posters of Switzerland"[33]). In these books, the images are central. They are discussed in regard to aesthetics and art history as well as their social functions. Often there are considerations about political behavior too.

Another approach comes from the media sciences with the question of how posters affect recipients and their behavior. This is, though, more technical, and these studies include reflection on the context of posters (city vs. country, traffic situation, and so on).[34] Usually, there are no further thoughts on the visual or verbal contents of posters.

In linguistics, there is a tradition of advertising analysis (mostly about product advertisements in papers), which can be transferred to posters and to the political domain. At first, there were studies about headlines and slogans. It was often in the context of advertising language being a special language. There are also studies comparing the verbal and the visual text in reference to their extent and alignment.[35] In recent years, the concept of multimodality has boomed.[36] There, the visual and verbal texts are analyzed together as a whole. Multimodality means that a text is encoded with different semiotic codes, for example, with pictures and words. There are also studies dealing with different styles of typography.[37]

Because pictures are, like text blocks, a substantial element of posters, they should be examined, therefore, not primarily from an artistic perspective, but rather from the perspective of their communicative function. In this context, emotionalization—the arousal of emotions in the recipients—seems to be important. If one wants to advertise for (or against) something (products, political action), one has to gain attention and persuade the target audience. Therefore, emotionalization strategies are often used. They have also not changed much over the years and are similar in different cultures.[38]

Figure 24.1. Appeal for public participation in a Labor Day demonstration and speech (in Europe on May 1st). Poster, anonymous, Museum für Gestaltung Zürich, Plakatsammlung. Franz Xaver Jaggy. © ZHdK.

Research Gaps and Open Questions

Altogether, posters have not gained much attention in the social sciences and humanities. Most collections are viewed as art rather than analyzed for their context within a certain political movement. Other branches of science do not take posters into account at all. There have been a few studies conducted on election posters in Germany, and there are some books about political movements that include posters.[39] Posters are seen very frequently in our everyday lives. It is a major advantage of this medium that it does not stand out but is being perceived unconsciously. That may be the reason why it is not analyzed that much. Perhaps in the current age of online and offline digital communication, it is also seen as an ancient medium not worth much notice. New media, such as television or the Internet, seem to be more favored subjects of research nowadays.

In regard to protest movements, it would be interesting to investigate the status in current movements like, for example, the occupy movement. Though professional posters are not that cheap anymore, posters and placards can be fabricated at low-cost if necessary. The question would be whether this medium is still attractive to the target group, and perhaps, if this target group is still on the streets, where the posters are hung. Nowadays, a lot of interaction takes place via the Internet where, with social media like Facebook, Twitter, and blogs, there lies a great possibility for immediate exchange and equal participation.

Sascha Demarmels is professor for professional communication at Lucerne University of Applied Sciences, Switzerland. She is a linguist, and one of her main research topics is comprehensibility. Her recent publications include: *Ja. Nein. Schweiz. Schweizer Abstimmungsplakate im 20. Jahrhundert* (Konstanz, 2009), which compares historical political posters in Switzerland, focusing on emotionalization strategies; "Nachhaltigkeits-Marketing in der Strombranche: Abstrakte Begriffe verständlich kommuniziert?," in *Nachhaltigkeit in der Wirtschaftskommunikation,* ed. M Nielsen et al. (Wiesbaden, 2013) with Anja Janoschka; and "Die Wirkung von Verständlichkeit in der Marketingkommunikation für erklärungsbedürftige Güter," in *Wert und Werte der Marketingkommunikation,* ed. T Schirl and J Tropp (Cologne, 2013) with Dorothea Schaffner.

Notes

1. Johannes Kamps, *Plakat* (Tübingen, 1999), 3.
2. Anita Kühnel, "Ein Jahrhundert im Weltformat," in *Ein Jahrhundert im Weltformat*, ed. B Evers (Berlin, 2001), 9*ff.*
3. "Outdoor Advertisement for Posters, Banners, Print and Productions, Leaflets," http://www.apexoutdoor.co.uk/specials.shtml.
4. "Burkhart Advertizing: Outdoor Advertising Display Options," http://www.burkhartadv.com/ofh_display.html.
5. "Outdoor Advertisement for Posters, Banners, Print and Productions, Leaflets," http://www.apexoutdoor.co.uk/specials.shtml.
6. Kamps, *Plakat*, 4.
7. Thomas Schierl, *Text und Bild in der Werbung. Bedingungen, Wirkungen und Anwendungen bei Anzeigen und Plakaten* (Cologne, 2001), 264.
8. Sascha Demarmels, "Funktionen des Bildstils von politischen Plakaten: Eine historische Analyse am Beispiel von Abstimmungsplakaten," *Themenheft zu IMAGE 3* (2006): 93–125.
9. Schierl, *Text und Bild in der Werbung*, 64.
10. Jim Surmanek, *Media Planning: A Practical Guide*, 3rd ed. (Lincolnwood, 1995), 49*ff.*
11. Bernd Evers, ed. *Ein Jahrhundert im Weltformat: Schweizer Plakate von 1900 bis zur Gegenwart* (Berlin, 2001), 7.
12. Armin Leutert, *Allgemeine Fachkunde der Drucktechnik* (Baden, 1993), 17.
13. Bernhard Dens^{ch}er, "Bilder und Worte: Wissenschaftliche Forschung und Literatur zur Geschichte der Plakatkunst" (1992), Deutsches Historisches Museum: http://www.dhm.de/ausstellungen/kkv/BilderUndWorte.htm.
14. For example, Achim Zielke, *Beispiellos ist beispielhaft oder: Überlegungen zur Analyse und zur Kreation des kommunikativen Codes von Werbebotschaften in Zeitungs- und Zeitschriftenanzeigen* (Pfaffenweiler, 1991); and Nina Janich, *Werbesprache: Ein Arbeitsbuch*, 3rd ed. (Tübingen, 2003).
15. Demarmels, "Funktionen des Bildstils von politischen Plakaten."
16. Frank Kämpfer, *Der rote Keil. Das politische Plakat. Theorie und Geschichte* (Berlin, 1985), 13.
17. For example, Jörn Münkner, "Illustrierte Flugblätter, Zeitungsreklame, Grossraumplakate: Vormoderne und moderne Formen dynamisierter Wahrnehmung in publizistischen Medien," in *Moderne deutsche Texte*, ed. M Wierzbicka, M Sieradzka, and J Homa (Frankfurt, 2005), 239–52; and Jannis K Androutsopoulos, "Die Textsorte Flyer," in *Textsorten. Reflexionen und Analysen*, ed. K Adamzik (Tübingen, 2000), 175–206.
18. Hajo Diekmannshenke, "Poltik-Postkarten: Proaganda, Wahlwerbung, politische Kommunikation," in *Strategien politischer Kommunikation. Pragmatische Analysen*, ed. H Girnth and C Spiess (Berlin, 2006), 97–120.
19. Sascha Demarmels, "Die Tradition des politischen Plakates im Zeitalter des Internets. Politische Werbung gestern und heute," *Internet-Zeischrift für Kulturwissenschaft* 16 (2006), http://www.inst.at/trans/16Nr/07_1/demarmels16.htm; Sascha

Demarmels, "Code- und Medienwandel. Eine exemplarische Betrachtung am Beispiel von politischen Plakaten," *Kodikas/Codes: Art Semioticas* 29, no. 4 (2007), 397–410; and Sascha Demarmels, "Als ob die Sinne erweitert würden … Augmented Reality als Emotionalisierungsstrategie," *IMAGE* 16 (2012): 29–46.

20. Jean-Charles Giroud, *Les Artistes Suisse et L'Affiche. Un Siècle de Fascination et de Confrontation* (Neuchâtel, 2001), 130.

21. Kai Artinger, *Das politische Plakat – Einige Bemerkungen zur Funktion und Geschichte,* ed. Deutsches Historisches Museum (Berlin, 2000), 19.

22. Sascha Demarmels, "Emotionalisierungs-Strategien auf Schweizer Abstimmungsplakaten im 20. Jahrhundert," in *Unmitte(i)lbarkeit. Gestaltung und Lesbarkeit von Emotionen,* ed. P Michel (Zürich, 2005), 287–317; Sascha Demarmels, "Konvergenz und Divergenz im Text-Bild-Design von politischen Plakaten," in *Textdesign und Textwirkung in der massenmedialen Kommunikation,* ed. KS Roth and J Spitzmüller (Konstanz, 2007), 143–60; Sascha Demarmels, "Die Beeinflussung von Bügerinnen und Bürger durch Emotionalisierung in der Politik," in *Multilingualism – Applied Linguistics Approaches,* ed. H Cölfen, J ten Thier, and C Spiegel (Duisburg, 2008), 39–51.

23. Willy Rotzler, Fritz Schärer, and Karl Wobmann, *Das Plakat in der Schweiz* (Schaffhausen, 1990), 14–15.

24. Edwin Lüthy, *Das künstlerische politische Plakat in der Schweiz* (Basel, 1920), 3.

25. Mark U Edwards, *Printing, Propaganda, and Marthin Luther* (Minneapolis, MN, 2005), 1.

26. Bettina Richter, *Poster Collection. Breaking the Rules. Posters from the Turbulent 1980s in Switzerland* (Zürich, 2007), 5.

27. Kalle Lasn, *Culture Jam. How to Reverse America's Suicidal Consumer Binge—and Why We Must* (New York, 2000).

28. See for example, "Adbusters Culturejammer Headquarters," http://www.adbusters.org.

29. Martin Henatsch, *Die Entstehung des Plakates: Eine rezeptionsästhetische Untersuchung* (Hildesheim, 1995).

30. Hans-Jörg Czech and Nikola Doll, *Kunst und Propaganda im Streit der Nationen 1930–1945* (Dresden, 2007).

31. James Aulich and Marta Sylvestrová, *Political Posters in Central and Eastern Europe 1945–95* (Manchester, 1999).

32. Museum für Gestaltung, ed., *Poster Collection. Breaking The Rules: Posters from the turbulent 1980s in Switzerland* (Zürich, 2007).

33. Willy Rotzler and Karl Wobmann, *Political and Social Posters of Switzerland. A Historical Cross-Section* (Zürich, 1985).

34. Martial Pasquier, *Plakatwirkungsforschung: Theoretische Grundlagen und praktische Ansätze* (Freiburg, 1997).

35. Schierl, *Text und Bild in der Werbung.*

36. Gunther Kress and Theo van Leeuwen, *Reading Images: The Grammar of Visual Design* (London, 1996); Gunther Kress and Theo van Leeuwen, *Multimodal Discourse: The Modes and Media of Contemporary Communication* (New York, 2001); Harmut Stöckl, *Die Sprache im Bild—Das Bild in der Sprache. zur Verknüpfung von Sprache und Bild im massenmedialen Text: Konzepte. Theorien. Analysemethoden* (Berlin, 2004).

37. Susanne Wehde, *Typographische Kultur: Eine zeichentheoretische und kultur-geschichtliche Stude zur Typographie und ihrer Entwicklung* (Tübingen, 2000); Jürgen Spitzmüller, "Typographie," in *Einführung in die Schriftlinguistik*, ed. C Dürscheid (Göttingen, 2006), 207–38.
38. Sascha Demarmels, "Die Darstellung des Bösen auf politischen Plakaten," in *Visuelle Stereotypen*, ed. T Petersen and C Schwender (Cologne, 2008); Sascha Demarmels, *Ja. Nein. Schweiz.—Schweizer Abstimmungsplakate im 20. Jahrhundert* (Konstanz, 2009); Marion G Müller, *Politische Bildstrategien im amerikanischen Präsidentschaftswahlkampf 1828–1996* (Berlin, 1997).
39. Christina Holtz-Bacha and Eva-Maria Lessinger, *Wahlwerbung als Indikator politisch-kulturellen Wandels: Erfahrungen aus einer Langzeituntersuchung*, ed. H Bohrmann et al. (Wiesbaden, 2000), 273–79; Gerd Langguth, ed., *Politik und Plakat. 50 Jahre Plakatgeschichte am Beispiel der CDU* (Bonn, 1995); Eva-Maria Lessinger and Markus Moke, "'Ohne uns schnappt jeder Kanzler über …' Eine Studie zur Rezeption von Plakatwerbung im Bundestagswahlkampf 1998," in *Wahlkampf in den Medien—Wahlkampf mit den Medien*, ed. C Holtz-Bacha (Opladen, 1999).
40. Aulich and Sylvestrová, *Political Posters in Central and Eastern Europe 1945–95*, 1.
41. Czech and Doll, *Kunst und Propaganda im Streit der Nationen 1930–1945*, 11.

Recommended Reading

Aulich, James, and Marta Sylvestrová. *Political Posters in Central and Eastern Europe 1945–95*. Manchester, 1999. James Aulich and Marta Sylvestrová provide a broad collection of the Soviet posters that had "a decisive political and cultural status"40 and are now looked at from an art historical as well as a politic and sociological perspective.

Chiu, Melissa, and Zheng Shengtian, eds. *Art and China's Revolution*. New York, 2008. Melissa Chiu and Zheng Shengtian assemble in their volume essays from historians, art historians, and artists and invert for once the question about posters and politics by asking how the regime of Mao Zedong influenced the development of aesthetics from the 1950s to the 1970s in China.

Czech, Hans-Jörg, and Nikola Doll. *Kunst und Propaganda im Streit der Nationen 1930–1945*. Dresden, 2007. Hans-Jörg Czech and Nikola Doll allow, with their catalog to an exhibition at the German Historical Museum, a comparison between visual political statements of different states like Italy, Soviet Union, Germany, and the United States from 1930 to 1950. This comparison quarries well-known facts and interpretations but also shows differences, for example between "persuasive strategies of democratic and totalitarian regimes."41

Museum für Gestaltung, ed. *Poster Collection. Breaking the Rules: Posters from the Turbulent 1980s in Switzerland*. Baden, 2007. The poster collection from the Museum für Gestaltung takes a look at the youth movement of the 1980s in Zurich and the new expressivity in the graphic design influenced by the punk movement that led to new innovative visual expressions.

King, David. *Red Star over Russia: A Visual History of the Soviet Union from 1917 to the Death of Stalin. Posters, Photographs and Graphics from the David King Collection*. London, 2009. David King presents the rise and fall of the Soviet Union from 1917 to the death of Stalin, creating the big picture by stringing posters, photographs, and verbal texts from historical relevance. Posters are not in the center but in the midst of these historical processes.

Chapter 25

Images and Imagery of Protest

Kathrin Fahlenbrach

General Definitions of Images and Imagery

Providing a general definition of images requires differentiation between several distinctive criteria. Three of them will be explained in the following: (1) There are different *types of images* from a phenomenological point of view. (2) Images have specific *semiotic characteristics*, closely combined with their cognitive and affective qualities. And, (3) they might fulfill specific *communicative and rhetoric functions* for those creating, distributing, and receiving them.

(1) *Types of images*: Starting with the first criterion, one might refer to art historian William J Mitchell, who states that there is no single or even ontological definition of an image, but that there exists a wide spectrum of images.[1] This could be, for example, composed still pictures in painting or photography, statues, visual symbols and pictograms, moving pictures as in film, but also mental and inner pictures like dreams or memories. All together, they build a "family of images."[2] Regarding the wide scope of image phenomenona, Mitchell proposes a useful typology by discerning *graphic images* (pictures, statues, designs), *optical images* (mirrors, projections), *perceptual images* (based on visual sensation during viewing), and *mental images* (dreams, memories, ideas, fantasies, etc.). Thereby, perceptual and mental images produced in one's mind can be distinguished from *manifest images,* materialized in a specific graphic medium, be they still or moving ones. From a broader perspective, body performances can also be considered as manifest images. These are for example, nonverbal signs of communication as gestures, body postures, mimic emotion expression that

imply a conventional or even symbolic use. Furthermore, on a more collective scope (audio-)visual staging include performative actions and events in public spaces.[3] All these phenomena can act as visual signs in social communication as part of imagery in a broader sense.

(2) *Semiotic characteristics of images*: In the aforementioned typology, what Mitchell considers as a most general semiotic quality of images in a closer sense is their likeness, resemblance, or similitude with the depicted object as the common criterion for most image types. While he concentrates in this on images as composed pictures, Charles S Peirce offers a broader approach. In his semiotic theory of human culture, Peirce distinguished icons from symbols and indices.[4] Accordingly, the likeness of the iconic sign, for example, a realistic painting or photograph as composed pictures, is considered as distinctive for visual signs. However, not all visual signs are iconic, meaning based on resemblance with the represented. There are *visual symbols,* based on arbitrary conventions (such as traffic signs); and *visual indices,* that have a causal relation to the represented object (such as pictograms or nonverbal signs like emotion expression). With regard to their likeness and similarity, images are often characterized as being more natural than symbolic signs (such as arbitrary signs of language). In contrast, Umberto Eco argues that the iconicity of visual signs or images is also based on conventions, on iconic codes that guide the cognitive recognition of an image as being similar to the represented object by culturally learned rules and schemata.[5]

Another significant semiotic criterion put forward by philosophers and scholars is their affective quality, that is, that images are often affectively experienced. There are both semiotic and psychological explanations for this criterion. Roland Barthes is one of the most influential philosophers to have argued that the meaning of images as conventionally weak signs is determined more *connotatively* than *denotatively.*[6] Hence the commonly established meaning of a picture or a visual sign is rather loose, and thus depends much on its communicative framing (e.g., by language). Its specific visual structure furthermore initiates associations that allow viewers to combine them with their subjective memories and mental images. Barthes characterizes the sensorial and affective impact that photos might initiate in their viewer as "punctum," a moment of immediate understanding and visual evidence.[7]

There are also many psychological explanations for the affective qualities of pictures. One of the most prominent ones is their close connectedness with the limbic center in the brain, being responsible for the quick activation of emotional responses by visual emotional cues.[8] Strong visual emotional cues are, for example, emotional facial expressions or innate reflexes to images of children or injured people. Furthermore, there are primary visual gestalt elements, for example, the color and the size of depicted visual elements and their spatial proportions in an image that trigger embodied associations and mental images based on innate brain structures.[9] Both the likeness of iconic pictures and their affective qualities are a relevant precondition for their evidence: the more iconic and similar a visual depiction of a represented reality, and the more it immediately makes sense to our senses and affects, the stronger its appeal to viewers of objectively documenting it. Obviously, this especially concerns photographic images that have often been discussed as being physical traces of the depicted reality.[10]

(3) *Communicative and rhetoric functions of images*: Given these specific semiotic and affective qualities, it is obvious that visual signs and images can be used strategically in order to guide viewers' attention and emotions, and maybe even attitudes, habits, and behavior. Hence, a third criterion for defining images is their communicative function in visual rhetoric.[11] This includes using images for creating a fictional illusion (e.g., in cinema), convincing viewers (e.g., in election campaigns or political photojournalism), persuading them (e.g., in advertising), appealing morally to their social consciousness (e.g., in political adbusting), or making them consider and reflect on a given area (e.g., in visual arts or in contentious imagery). Classical strategic forms of visual rhetoric are, for example: visual hyperboles, symbols, metaphors, or metonymies (examples are given below).

Images and Imagery of Protest

From a general perspective, there are two basic categories of images and imagery of protest: images of protest being produced and distributed by activists and those being selected, produced, and distributed by other actors, for example, in the mass media; in other words: the visual self-representation of protesters and their visual representation by others.[12] Accordingly, both the different social and discursive practices are at stake when categorizing contentious imagery and its different visual types. While the visual representation of protest in mass media necessarily leads to a discussion of rules and criteria of media coverage,[13] this chapter primarily concentrates on the different types of images and visual signs in self-representation of protesters.

Considering types of imagery in protest cultures, a broad spectrum might be observed, including (1) *manifest protest images* as composed (still and moving) pictures of protest, produced by activists themselves or depictions of their protest, done by others (e.g., mass media), (2) *(audio-)visual protest performances,* as well as (3) *mentally contentious imagery,* meaning the collective visual knowledge and memory in a culture.[14]

Among the most traditional visual manifestations of contentious imagery are visual symbols. Social movements like the French Revolution or later the workers movement in the nineteenth century produced visual symbols that were put on flags, placards, or leaflets. Examples are the cockade and the Phrygian cap of the French Revolution or the fist, and the red flag of the labor movement. From a semiotic point of view, they are based on arbitrary conventions established in a protest culture. Accordingly, visual protest symbols represent the common ideology of a movement in an abstract, though at the same time, visually evident way. The fist, for example, is in the first instance an iconic picture of a powerful human gesture, indicating the affront of an enraged person; by convention of the labor and the Socialist movement, it is at the same time a symbol that acts metonymically as a symbolic *pars pro toto* for the rage and strong collective will of the workers to fight for their rights. The media for visual protest symbols are broad. Today, symbols like the one of the anarchist movement, or of Anonymous, are seen not only on placards or flags, but also on buttons/badges, clothes, or on online sites.

Another relevant type of protest images is photographic pictures. Movements sometimes use photos from the mass media, especially press photographs depicting (a) victims of a conflict or (b) role models or spokespeople of a movement. Significant for (a) are, for example, the press pictures made by journalists during the Vietnam War, as they have been used by the peace movement in the 1960s and 1970s on placards and posters in order to mobilize the public morally and affectively against the war and for the aims of the peace movement.[15] Representative for (b) are the press pictures of Che Guevara or Ho Chi Minh as used as symbolic icons supposed to reinforce the collective identity and commitment of the student movement in the 1960s. This implies the genesis of a collective visual knowledge and memory, as well as mental contentious imagery in a protest culture.

Certainly the relevance of professional press pictures for social movements has diminished since this era, and activists use and distribute much more frequently photographs made by themselves or by amateurs.[16] With the growing importance of the Internet and other information and communication technology (ICT) for internal and external mobilization of movements, do-it-yourself-images often enjoy higher credibility than professional ones. These include images being made by protesters for example during demonstrations and in confrontations with the police. Such pictures often act as relevant documents for accusing their opponents and mobilizing further protest.[17] Like protest symbols, they are put on placards during demonstrations, though also distributed by mobile technologies and the Internet.

In the history of protest cultures, a broad arsenal of manifest contentious images has developed, which movements and activists distribute internally and externally as symbolic tools of public mobilization. While the use of photographs mostly addresses the selection rules of mass media,[18] other visuals more explicitly distance themselves from mass media imagery. These include illustrations, cartoons, graffiti, and many others that are used in different media as placards, leaflets or posters, clothes, walls, in alternative print media, or in online videos.[19]

Finally, bodily staged protest performances are some of the most relevant elements in contentious imagery: protest actions performed on the street, in public space, but also documented in online videos. From a historical point of view, the bodily staging of protest actions in public spaces has grown in parallel with the rise of visual and audiovisual mass media. The workers movement or the women's movement in the nineteenth century performed collective demonstrations in the street in terms of action-mobilization.[20] The sheer number of participants alone made a strong argument for political change. Here, the homogenous mass of demonstrators attains symbolic qualities as a visual and collective body of contestation, representing the upheavals of a whole social class or group (metonymy). While action mobilization remains a strong element of demonstrations, its bodily staging has since been highly differentiated, echoing the growing need to not only address a local public, but also gain the attention of the mass media.[21] On the one hand, the arsenal of visual tools has been widened.[22] Looking at placards and flags as traditional tools, one can detect a broad spectrum of established and new protest symbols, such as masks (e.g., the Guy Fawkes mask of Anonymous) and disguises (e.g., as clowns or as parodies of political representatives).

Rooted in the tradition of Situationist and guerilla communication of the 1960s,[23] the bodily staging, on the other hand, also implies collective performances based on visual symbols. Protesters represent a collective body of living images that make the contested situation or conflict visually evident, such as human chains, star marches, sit-ins, or death-ins.[24] Furthermore, social movements, and especially professionalized NGOs, stage public image events[25] with a more selected number of activists that perform visual narratives: they tell a story in a performative way that is addressed first of all to mass media in order to achieve their attention and provide them with both attractive images and a catchy narrative (cf. examples below).

The rising dominance of the Internet in protest communication has also initiated specific online forms of visual protest performances, such as smart mobs.[26] Using social web applications like Twitter and Facebook, activists organize spontaneous local actions in order to fill public urban spaces with a symbolically acting crowd. Such a collaborative action might work in a similar fashion to the denial of service attacks practiced by hacktivists in blocking the established rules and routines, and thereby making them publicly visible in a subversive way.[27]

Role of Images and Imagery in Protest Cultures

The relevance of imagery for protest cultures has exponentially increased since the mid twentieth century, when visibility in mass media became a significant resource for political action—both in the traditional political establishment and in protest cultures.[28] In democratic societies, mass media are not only the dominant sphere for political opinion building. The media also serves as a crucial interface between the political establishment and the people; it remains essential for every political actor to become visible in the public sphere. At the same time, this public sphere has become more and more differentiated by the growing number of mass media providers (in television and print) and, nowadays, by the increasing role of online forums (such as blogs, online magazines, or video platforms). Accordingly, the challenge for political actors increases to become visible to a broad public. Consequently, a key function of images for protesters consists in their potential for both (1) *external* and (2) *internal mobilization,* which goes along with specific strategies in visual rhetoric, following at the same time *instrumental* and *expressive* functions. Both aspects will be explored in the following.

(1) External mobilization by protest images: Protest imagery produced by activists and movements themselves is often addressed *externally* toward the mass media. These are focused by their very nature on pictures that make a conflict or situation evident. As has been demonstrated by several scholars,[29] social movements, and especially professionalized NGOs, respond to clearly established *news values*[30] when strategically aiming to get their protests in the news: providing the media with visually attractive, or even spectacular (still or moving) images, or visual protest performances, as well as with pictures of speakers or otherwise individual representatives of a movement.

Photographs of single people allow mass media to reduce the complexity of a network of activists with their specific aims and motifs. Looking at the facial expressions and body language of an individual depicted on a photograph always implies affects, sometimes even empathy or antipathy. Hence, such images provide an emotional approach to a movement, which is part of their news value. Prominent spokespeople of the civil rights movement like Martin Luther King Jr. and Angela Davis, or Daniel Cohn-Bendit of the French student movement, were ideal objects for such a visual personalization. Their images offer the viewer not only expressive emotions, but a charisma that transports the ideology of these movements in both a symbolic and affective way. Some of these pictures even achieved the status of media icons: pictures that are widely distributed because of their visual attractiveness by mass media, by the movements themselves (e.g., on posters or buttons/badges), and across various other channels of media culture (e.g., in arts, movies, and advertisements).[31] Accordingly, media icons of protest demonstrate the close interrelation between protest movements and mass media in image politics.[32]

This is one of the reasons why, however, in recent years social movements (e.g., the antiglobalization movement, Anonymous, or occupy) have become skeptical about presenting single spokespeople to the media, while also generally negating leadership. In contrast, symbolic pictures of their followers and participants as representatives are distributed on the Internet and in mass media: pictures of individual anonymous activists wearing masks, costumes, or posing in a symbolically intriguing way. This includes pictures of single protesters in confrontation with their antagonists (mainly the police[33]), or protesters depicted as victims (e.g., injured demonstrators[34]). These photographs provide the mass media and the viewers with an affective perspective to a conflict and, furthermore, with archetypical visual narratives, for example, "hunter vs. prey," "offender vs. offended," or just "good vs. bad." From a semiotic perspective, these types of visual personalization can be called *metonymies*: the depiction of one activist or spokespeople as a symbolic pars pro toto for the whole movement. As a rhetorical element, it makes evident the identity, aims, and motifs of a movement in a simplified way.

Visual metaphors of protest are another strategically used form of visual rhetoric. In a classical understanding, metaphors are built on the similarity between two different semiotic entities like words or visual motifs, generating a symbolic meaning that surmounts their individual ones. A metaphor like "death of democracy" figuratively draws a comparison between democracy and a living person whose life is threatened. The consequences of that threat, for example, as caused by censorship or political despotism, is highlighted in the concrete image of a dying or dead body. This provides a broad spectrum of symbolic visualizations when distributed in protest campaigns against antidemocratic politics[35]: corresponding metaphoric imagery includes pictures of demonstrations and visual performances that represent a dying or even a dead person (cf. above: die-in) called "Democracy" (e.g., written on her front); her face is often pale and sometimes her mouth stitched up, indicating censorship as the cause of her death. Other metaphoric depictions show coffins or graves with the name "Democracy" put on the inscriptions, together with the date of her death. Such metaphorical representations address their viewer not only cognitively, but also emotionally and bodily, activating vital fears of death and violation of one's own human body. Activating such associations by a picture or body performance and using them to stand for the state of a democracy makes immediately evident to viewers the threatening character of the situation, in a physical and affective way.[36]

Another strategic instrument of contentious visual rhetoric is the recontextualization and remediation of existent imagery and their underlying codes and rules in culture jamming practices in the political and economic public sphere. Mostly used for anticorporate campaigns,[37] this instrument aims to get public attention by using the very surfaces and signifiers of hegemonic imagery of placards or clips in advertisements, but attributing oppositional meanings to them. So doing the appeal for consumerism gets changed into an appeal for anticonsumerism and moral consciousness— while using the same visual signs and rules of the offended system. Based on guerilla communication from the late 1960s and applied to anticonsumerist movements in the age of global economies by Kalle Lasn,[38] this instrument aims not only to confront and provoke the companies accused. It also addresses the consumers and appeals for a change of their minds and habits in everyday life.[39] Furthermore, culture jamming activists like the *Adbusters,* by using viral techniques of distribution on the Internet, but also more traditional sites of advertisement or political election campaigns in public spaces, often insert their subverted imagery into the very same contexts where the public is used to receive the hegemonic ones. This is to provoke reflection on the rules that govern these places.

(2) Internal mobilization by protest images: Apart from their *instrumental function* to externally mobilize public attention as a relevant resource for oppositional action, as for exerting public pressure on political or economic representatives, the described protest imagery also provides an *expressive function* of *internal mobilization*. It has been shown that collective identity is a relevant resource for social movements.[40] This implies not only identification with its single aims and motifs, but also the feeling of being part of it as a social group, sharing ideologies, attitudes, values, habits, and even emotions. These are often rooted in similar biographical experiences of a conflict, crisis, or threat. Obviously, commitment to a movement and the will to commonly fight for their aims increases with the appropriation of a collective protest identity. It goes together with collectively shared mental

images of the self and includes *mental imagery of contestation*,[41] a collective visual knowledge. And as such, it generates diachronically from the common protest images and bodily protest performances, including shared expressive habits such as clothing, gestures, and other forms of body language. To conclude, the forms of contentious imagery described, as well as their public staging and distribution, fulfill *internally* the relevant *expressive* function to enhance the commitment. They mobilize activists and sympathizers cognitively and affectively as members of a social group who share a collective identity.

Theoretical and Empirical Research Perspectives

Both theoretical and empirical research on contentious imagery is still scarce. However, the relevance of images has been recognized in social movement research for a while by several researchers, both in terms of symbolic resources used by activists to mobilize public opinion and in terms of a visual framing of protests by the mass media. These are often considered as stereotypical and negative.[42] Generally spoken, these two perspectives are of great significance for research on protest imagery: (a) studying the creation, performance, framing, and distribution of contentious imagery by protesters, and (b) studying its visual selection, creation, framing, and distribution by established institutions and actors such as mass media, governments, or companies. However, the investigation of visual self-expression of protesters and of external visual representations,[43] incorporates further different disciplinary and theoretical perspectives (even if they are sometimes intertwined):

Functional perspectives focus on the institutionally and socially based interests and motifs of collective actors in their production and public distribution of protest images. Without looking necessarily at the visual character of pictures, such studies first of all analyze the institutional and social backgrounds of their production and distribution by different actors. Consequently, this touches all literature concerned with the interrelation between social movements and mass media, as hegemonic providers of public images of protest.[44] Another focus of social movement research consists of the restricted and alternative preconditions and channels of activists for contentious communication.[45] In this, the implications of ICT and Internet as oppositional arenas of contestation have increasingly become the focus of research.[46]

Most frequently, research on contentious imagery refers to *framing perspectives*. A relevant paradigm in social movement research,[47] it is used to explain how different actors, especially mass media and social movements themselves, frame the public understanding and evaluation of protest actions and events by their selection and design of contentious imagery. This also implies a functional look at the leading ideologies, worldviews, and values of mass media. However, framing approaches also consider more concrete visual criteria when analyzing the use of specific motifs (e.g., confrontations between activists and police, injured demonstrators, or policemen, etc.), their interrelation with comments or slogans, and how they frame the interpretation and evaluation of the depicted protest. Several analyses of the mass media's visual framing of protests[48] show how they use images to implicitly delegitimize, or legitimize it. Other scholars investigate visual framing practices by social movements, for example, analyzing strategic counter-framings. These are often performed by professional NGOs like Greenpeace[49] or Attac in order to import oppositional frames into the mass media by providing them with contentious visual narratives that coincide with general values of a media provider and a broader public (e.g., the denial of injustice and violence, when exerted toward weaker persons[50]).

Little research has been done so far in applying semiotic and aesthetic perspectives on the analysis of contentious imagery as well as the guiding codes and rules of their staging. This includes research questions such as: how do different actors actually design and compose still or moving images of protest for performances?, how do they stage their intentions and their messages by the use of culturally established symbols and iconographies?, what are the implications of contentious imagery for internal and external mobilization by its visual qualities in terms of color, visual composition, body posture, facial expressions, etc.?

Some studies explore the history of protest symbols[51] and of visual performances of protest.[52] There are also case studies on current movements and their specific visual expressions.[53] Only few systematic models have been proposed for a visual analysis of contentious imagery. An influential approach of image events is developed by Delicath and DeLuca.[54] Using the example of environmental groups, they demonstrate instrumental strategies of visually staging protest performances in order to achieve mass media attention.

Looking at the expressive functions of contentious imagery for collective identities, Fahlenbrach[55] presents a model relating the analysis of embodied and affective qualities of visual protest performances with socially established expressive codes of a given protest milieu and its *habitus*.[56] An integrative model for visual analysis of contentious imagery is further proposed by Doerr and Teune.[57] They closely relate the identification of different forms of visual expressions (e.g., symbols or photographs) and their shaping in different media (e.g., a print journal or online platform), resulting in changing appearances and impacts of the visuals. Such a specific distinction of visual and media forms is combined with different perspectives to interpret protest images such as identity or framing. While this leads to a more concrete analysis of the visual types and semiotic qualities of contentious imagery, other recent studies refer to approaches from art history and semiotics, in order to investigate even more specifically their visual characteristics. A promising approach from such a perspective is the application of art historian Panofsky's method of iconology to analyze the composition and contextualization of motifs of contestation by Daphi, Le, and Ullrich.[58] Accordingly, images of protest are closely analyzed in the canonic three-step-method of Panofsky: (a) the formal analysis of a picture, (b) the detection of denotative and conventional meanings, and (c) its contextualization with regard to historically shaped symbolic, but also to current communicative discourses and frames. Combining visual and semiotic analysis of protest images with discourse analyses allows a close functional relation to be drawn between the very visual creation and aesthetics of the images and the ideologically and strategically based intentions of their creators and distributors in protest communication.

Research Gaps

As has been shown, there is still a lack in research when dealing in a more specific fashion with semiotic and visual-aesthetic features of protest imagery as expressions of social, ideological, and political interests, motifs, and strategies of different actors in protest communication. Similarly, few attempts have been made so far in the field of visual rhetoric of protest[59] to investigate classical and contemporary forms as to how they strategically use visual signs and codes in different kinds of imagery and their materialization in different media.

This also invites a more distinct investigation of subversive imagery as in culture jamming. The recontextualization and resemiotization[60] of collective visual knowledge and specific visual signs and codes of hegemonic imagery becomes increasingly important in the age of online communication. As arenas of contestation and contentious imagery, public spheres of the Internet transgress not only national and cultural borders.[61] They are also hybrid spaces, combining different channels and media. This implies the constant mixing and recontextualization of semiotic codes and signs, once significant for specific media (e.g., press photography and private photography, fiction film, and documentary). Subversive media practices of remixing, as in adbusting, have broadly been adapted by Internet users and result in popular practices like the production of amateur mash-up videos or funny visual memes.[62] Consequently, scholars confronted with protest practices in the realm of the Internet have to develop a differentiated semiotic and visual-aesthetic knowledge and understanding of the ever-changing rules and conventions of contentious imagery.

Kathrin Fahlenbrach is professor for media studies at the Department for Media and Communication at the University of Hamburg, Germany. Relevant areas of her research include media and visual codes in protest communication, cognitive and affective aesthetics of film and television, and metaphors and icons in media culture. She is author of the book *Protestinszenierungen. Kollektive Identitäten und visuelle Kommunikation in Protestbewegungen* (Opladen, 2002) and editor of *Media and Revolt. Strategies and Performances from the 1960s to the Present.* (New York, 2014) (together with Rolf Werenskjold and Erling Sivertsen), as well as of *Embodied Metaphors in Film, Television, and Video Games: Cognitive Approaches* (London/New York 2016). Together with Martin Klimke and Joachim Scharloth, she is editor of the book series "Protest, Culture, and Society" at Berghahn Books (New York).

Notes

1. William JT Mitchell, *Iconology. Image, Text, Ideology* (Chicago, 1987).
2. Ibid., 9.
3. As mentioned later, these are called "image events" by Delicath and DeLuca (2003).
4. Charles S Peirce, *Peirce on Signs: Writings on Semiotic* (Chapel Hill, NC, 1991).
5. Umberto Eco, *A Theory of Semiotics* (Bloomington, IN, 1979).
6. Roland Barthes, *Image Music Text* (London, 1977); Roland Barthes, *Camera Lucida* (New York, 1981).
7. Barthes, *Camera Lucida,* 26.
8. Allan Paivio, *Imagery and Verbal Processes* (New York, 1978); Paul Ekman, *Emotions Revealed. Understanding Faces and Feelings* (London, 2003).
9. Bruce E Goldstein, *Sensation and Perception,* 9th ed. (Belmont, CA, 2014).
10. Cf. Mitchell, *Iconology.*
11. Joachim Knape, ed., *Bildrhetorik* (Baden-Baden, 2007).
12. Nicole Doerr, Alice Mattoni, and Simon Teune, eds, *Advances in the Visual Analysis of Social Movements* (Bingley, UK, 2013).
13. Cf. Nicole Doerr and Simon Teune, "The Imagery of Power Facing the Power of Imagery. Toward a Visual Analysis of Social Movements," in *The Establishment Responds. Power, Politics, and Protests since 1945,* ed. K Fahlenbrach et al. (London, 2012), 43–55.

14. Aleida Assmann, *Cultural Memory and Western Civilization. Arts of Memory* (Cambridge, 2011); Doerr and Teune, "The Imagery of Power Facing the Power of Imagery."

15. Kathrin Fahlenbrach and Laura Stapane, "Visual and Media Strategies of the Peace-Movement," in *The Euromissiles Crisis: NATO Double-Track Treaty, the Peace Movement, and the Transatlantic Alliance of the 1980s,* ed. C Becker-Schaum et al. (forthcoming).

16. Cf. Antigoni Memou, *Photography and Social Movements. From Globalization of the Movement (1968) to the Movement against Mobilization (2001)* (Manchester, 2013).

17. Tina Askanius, "Protest Movements and Spectacles of Death. From Urban Places to Video Spaces," in *Advances in the Visual Analysis of Social Movements,* ed. N Doerr, A Mattoni, and S Teune (Bingley, UK, 2013), 105–33.

18. Kathrin Fahlenbrach, *Audiovisuelle Metaphern. Zur Körper- und Affektästhetik in Film und Fernsehen* (Marburg, 2010); Memou, *Photography and Social Movements.*

19. Cf. Jasmina Gherairi, *Persuasion durch Protest. Protest als Form erfolgsorientierter strategischer Kommunikation* (Wiesbaden, 2015).

20. Bert Klandermans, *The Social Psychology of Protest* (Oxford, 1997).

21. Cf. Kathrin Fahlenbrach, Erling Sivertsen, and Rolf Werenskjold, eds, *Media and Revolt. Performances and Strategies from the 1960s to the Present* (Oxford, 2014).

22. The spectrum of recent protest forms has been documented and carefully analyzed in Gherairi, "Persuasion durch Protest!" as communicative elements of protest rhetoric.

23. Cf. Alexander Holmig, "Die aktionistischen Wurzeln der Studentenbewegung: Subversive Aktion, Kommune I und die Neudefinition des Politischen," in *Handbuch 1968. Zur Kultur- und Mediengeschichte der Studentenbewegung,* ed. M Klimke and J Scharloth (Stuttgart, 2007), 107–19.

24. Cf. Fahlenbrach and Stapane, "Visual and Media Strategies of the Peace-Movement."

25. John W Delicath and Kevin M DeLuca, "Image Events, the Public Sphere, and Argumentative Practice: The Case of Radical Environmental Groups," *Argumentation* 17 (2003): 315–33.

26. Cf. Howard Rheingold, *Smart Mobs. The Next Social Revolution* (Cambridge, 2002).

27. There is a wide spectrum between *flash mobs* as humorous actions, performed by Internet users without any political or social implications and *smart mobs* as forms of collective contestations. The borders between them are fluid. Cf. Rheingold, *Smart Mobs.*

28. Cf. Kathrin Fahlenbrach, "Protest in Television: Visual Protest on Screen," in *Media and Revolt. Performances and Strategies from the 1960s to the Present,* ed. K Fahlenbrach, E Sivertsen, and R Werenskjold (Oxford, 2014), 234–50.

29. For example, Todd Gitlin, *The Whole World Is Watching. Mass Media and the Making and Unmaking of the New Left* (Berkeley, CA, 2003); Rüdiger Schmitt-Beck, "Über die Bedeutung der Massenmedien für Soziale Bewegungen," *Kölner Zeitschrift für Soziologie und Sozialpsychologie* 42, no. 4 (1990): 642–62; Dieter Rucht, "The Quadruple 'A': Media Strategies of Protest Movements since the 1960s," in *Cyber Protest: New Media, Citizens and Social Movements,* ed. W van den Donk et al. (London, 2004), 29–57.

30. Johan Galtung and Mari H Ruge, "The Structure of Foreign News. The Presentation of the Congo, Cuba and Cyprus Crises in Our Norwegian Newspapers," *Journal of Peace Research* 2, no. 1 (1965): 64–91.

31. The most prominent media icon stemming from the student movement is certainly the Che Guevara portrait of press photographer Alberto Korda; Cf. Stefan Lahrem, "Che. Eine globale Protestikone des 20. Jahrhunderts," in *Das Jahrhundert der Bilder. Bildatlas 1949 bis heute*, ed. G Paul (Göttingen, 2008), 234–42.

32. Cf. also Christian Lahusen, *The Rhetoric of Moral Protest. Public Campaigns, Celebrity, Endorsement, and Political Mobilization* (Berlin, 1996).

33. Gitlin, *The Whole World Is Watching*; Rolf Werenskjold, "The Revolution Will Be Televised: The Global 1968 Protests in Norwegian Television News," in *Between Prague Spring and French May. Opposition and Revolt in Europe 1960–1980*, ed. M Klimke and J Scharloth (Oxford, 2011), 177–99.

34. Cf. Askanius, "Protest Movements and Spectacles of Death."

35. Metaphoric images and visual performances have been used, for example, in protests against the arrest of members of Pussy Riot in Russia in March 2012, or in Turkey during the occupation of the Gezi Park in 2013.

36. Cf. Fahlenbrach, *Audiovisuelle Metaphern*.

37. Kalle Lasn, *Culture Jam: How to Reverse America's Suicidal Consumer Binge—And Why We Must* (New York, 2000); Siegrid Baringhorst, Verena Kneip, and Johanna Niesyto, eds, *Political Campaigning on the Web* (Bielefeld, 2009).

38. Lasn, *Culture Jam*.

39. Cf. Baringhorst, Kneip, and Niesyto, *Political Campaigning on the Web*; Siegrid Baringhorst et al., *Unternehmenskritische Kampagnen. Politischer Protest im Zeichen digitaler Kommunikation* (Wiesbaden, 2010).

40. Klandermans, *The Social Psychology of Protest*.

41. Kathrin Fahlenbrach, *Protestinszenierungen. Visuelle Kommunikation und kollektive Identitäten in Protestbewegungen* (Wiesbaden, 2002).

42. Gitlin, *The Whole World Is Watching*.

43. Doerr, Mattoni, and Teune, *Advances in the Visual Analysis of Social Movements*, xii.

44. Early examples would be Gitlin, *The Whole World Is Watching*; Schmitt-Beck, "Über die Bedeutung der Massenmedien für Soziale Bewegungen".

45. For example, Nicole Doerr, "Politicizing Precarity, Producing Visual Dialogues on Migration: Transnational Public Spaces in Social Movements," *Forum Qualitative Social Research* 11, no. 2 (2010): art. 30; Alice Mattoni, *Media Practices and Protest Politics: How Precarious Workers Mobilize* (Farnham, 2012).

46. For example, Baringhorst et al., *Unternehmenskritische Kampagnen*; Askanius, "Protest Movements and Spectacles of Death."

47. David A Snow and Robert D Benford, "Ideology, Frame Resonance, and Participant Mobilization," *International Social Movement Research* 1 (1988): 197–217; Bert Klandermans, "Framing Collective Action," in *Media and Revolt. Performances and Strategies from the 1960s to the Present*, ed. K Fahlenbrach, E Sivertsen, and R Werenskjold (Oxford, 2014), 41–58.

48. Gitlin, *The Whole World Is Watching*; Rolf Werenskjold, "The Dailies in Revolt. The Global 1968 Revolts in Major Norwegian Newspapers," *Scandinavian Journal of History* 33, no. 4. (2008): 417–40; Erling Sivertsen and Rolf Werenskjold,

"Photos in Frames or Frames in Photos? The Global 1968 Revolts in Three Norwegian Dailies," in *Media and Revolt. Performances and Strategies from the 1960s to the Present*, ed. K Fahlenbrach, E Sivertsen, and R Werenskjold (Oxford, 2014), 126–46; Stuart Hilwig, "Constructing a Media Image of the *Sessantotto:* The Framing of the Italian Protest Movement in 1968," in *Media and Revolt. Performances and Strategies from the 1960s to the Present*, ed. K Fahlenbrach, E Sivertsen, and R Werenskjold (Oxford, 2014), 109–25; Juliane Riese, "On Dynamic Processes of Framing, Counterframing, and Reframing: The Case of the Greenpeace Whale Campaign in Norway," in *Media and Revolt. Performances and Strategies from the 1960s to the Present*, ed. K Fahlenbrach, E Sivertsen, and R Werenskjold (Oxford, 2014), 283–99.

49. Riese, "On Dynamic Processes of Framing, Counterframing, and Reframing."

50. Askanius, "Protest Movements and Spectacles of Death."

51. Gottfried Korff, "Symbolgeschichte als Sozialgeschichte? Zehn vorläufige Notizen zu den Bild- und Zeichensystemen sozialer Bewegungen in Deutschland," in *Massenmedium Straße. Zur Kulturgeschichte der Demonstrationen*, ed. BJ Warneken (Frankfurt, 1991), 17–37.

52. Matthias Reiss, ed., *The Street as Stage. Protest Marches and Public Rallies since the Nineteenth Century* (Oxford, 2007).

53. Nicole Doerr and Alice Mattoni, "Public Spaces and Alternative Media Practices in Europe: The Case of the EuroMayDay Parade against Precarity," in *Media and Revolt. Performances and Strategies from the 1960s to the Present*, ed. K Fahlenbrach, E Sivertsen, and R Werenskjold (Oxford, 2014), 386–405; Priska Daphi, Anja Le, and Peter Ullrich, "Images of Surveillance. The Contested and the Embedded Visual Language of Anti-Surveillance Protests," in *Advances in the Visual Analysis of Social Movements*, ed. N Doerr, A Mattoni, and S Teune (Bingley, UK, 2013), 54–80; Askanius, "Protest Movements and Spectacles of Death."

54. Delicath and De Luca, "Image Events, the Public Sphere, and Argumentative Practice."

55. Fahlenbrach, *Protestinszenierungen.*

56. Pierre Bourdieu and Pierre Boltanski, *Photography. A Middle-Brow Art* (Cambridge, 1990).

57. Doerr and Teune, "The Imagery of Power Facing the Power of Imagery. Toward a Visual Analysis of Social Movements."

58. Daphi, Le, and Ullrich, "Images of Surveillance."

59. Lahusen, *The Rhetoric of Moral Protest. Public Campaigns, Celebrity, Endorsement, and Political Mobilization*; Gherairi, "Persuasion durch Protest!"

60. Rick Iedema, "Resemiotization," *Semiotica* 137, no. 1–4 (2001): 23–39.

61. Cf. Simon Cottle and Libby Lester, eds, *Transnational Protest and the Media* (New York, 2011).

62. Stefka Hristova, "Visual Memes as Neutralizers of Political Dissent," *Triple C. Communication, Capitalism, and Critique: Journal for a Global Sustainable Information Society* 12, no. 1 (2014): 265–76.

Recommended Reading

Doerr, Nicole, Alice Mattoni, and Simon Teune, eds. *Advances in the Visual Analysis of Social Movements*. Bingley, 2013. This is the first encompassing volume on recent methods and approaches to visual analysis of protest communication.

Fahlenbrach, Kathrin. *Protestinszenierungen. Visuelle Kommunikation und kollektive Identitäten in Protestbewegungen*. Wiesbaden, 2002. This presents an integrative approach to the visual analysis of protest, relating embodied and affective aspects of visual protest performances with the expressive codes of a protest milieu. This is exemplified by an analysis of the German student movement around 1968.

Memou, Antigoni. *Photography and Social Movements. From Globalization of the Movement (1968) to the Movement against Mobilization (2001)*. Manchester, 2013. This provides fundamental insights into the role of photography in protest communication, while analyzing, for example, the student movement in Paris in May 1968, the Zapatista rebellion, or the anti-Capitalist protests in Genoa in 2001.

Chapter 26

Typography and Text Design

Jürgen Spitzmüller

General Definition of the Terms

While typography (from Greek τύπος "letter, sign" + γράφειν "carving, writing") originally denoted the technique to produce printed texts with movable type (as opposed to woodcut, lithography, etc.), the term nowadays more generally refers to "the visual attributes of written, and especially printed, language"[1] and "is concerned with how letterforms ... are organized visually regardless of how the letters are produced."[2]

Usually, two typographic levels are distinguished: micro-typography, which includes the choice and arrangement of typefaces, emphasizing, and everything else that concerns the one-dimensional scope of a line, and macro-typography, which includes the two-dimensional placement of letters and paragraphs on the page, the handling of images and the like, as well as the overall layout up to cover design and media/material choices.[3]

Text design focuses on the practice of text creation. The concept stresses that the appearance of a text might be the result of a deliberate action that aims at specific effects. The term was coined by H-J Bucher in order to raise the media researchers' awareness of creative text production strategies.[4] The concept includes typography, but it also considers the text's content, its organization (argumentation strategies, coherence, etc.), as well as the linguistic and stylistic choices. Text design thus attempts to "close the gap between layout and text, page design and utterance design, content and form."[5] An equivalent term, proposed by K Schriver, is document design, which is defined as "the act of bringing together prose, graphics, illustration, photography and typography for purposes of instruction, information, or persuasion."[6]

General Cultural Functions

The main functions of typography can be subsumed to either text organization or contextualization. The former category includes attempts to enhance the readability of a text by specific typographic choices as well as attempts to ease text navigation (by emphasizing specific parts, adding headings, paragraph breaks, whitespace, running headers, etc.). The latter category, which is most important for protest research, bundles all cases where typographic elements serve as indexes or cues that evoke interpretive frames and thereby co-construct the context of interpretation. Typographic elements might be perceived as indexes of specific text genres, eras, cultures, or social groups, of subcultural orientation, ideologies,[7] and so on. It is assumed that these ascriptions are not necessarily conscious to the discourse actors. Hence, the use of typography, even if it follows social conventions, might not always be as intentional as the text design concept implies.[8]

Role in Protest Cultures

Text design and typography play a crucial role within processes of social negotiation, as signifiers of social identities and ideologies. Political propaganda is a case in point: verbal and argumentative strategies are framed by sociosemiotically connoted symbols, images, typefaces, colors, and so on. In the light of this, it is not surprising that protest propaganda relies on text design as well. In fact, typographic means have been used that way right from the beginning of printing. The German Protestant movement systematically used blackletter typefaces as an identity signal and roman typefaces as stigmata both in antipapist pamphlets and in canonical texts (such as the Luther Bible).[9] This "typographical manifesto"[10] constituted, together with the choice of the vernacular (as opposed to the clerical Latin), an ideological text design strategy proper. Similar strategies can be observed in other protest movements throughout the centuries. As far as modern protest cultures are concerned, it appears that most groups developed and use specific visual forms in their written propaganda, on posters, flyers, T-shirts, banners, stickers, and so on. Graffiti, the "anarcho typography" current in punk culture and the use of both blackletter type and nationalist symbols by neonationalists (but also, in deliberate opposition, in anti-Fascist propaganda) are prominent examples.[11]

Furthermore, in the wake of advertisement, dedicated typographical protest cultures, often driven by professional typesetters, emerged in the twentieth century. Some of these groups (the Italian Futurism, Swiss/

German Dadaism, the American grunge, and guerilla typography[12]) attempted to establish an alternative typography that deliberately breaks the traditional norms of typesetting. Others aimed at criticizing Capitalism by means of "antiadvertisement" (or "subvertisment") that tries to redefine commercial propaganda by parodying logos, layouts, and slogans of major companies. A prominent exponent of the latter strategy is the culture jamming movement that is part of the antiglobalization culture, with its currently most active group, the adbusters network, founded by a former advertising manager in the late 1980s and allegedly consisting of 100,000 members worldwide (as of 2013).

Theoretical and Empirical Research Perspectives

Beyond academic design theory proper,[13] research into text design and typographical communication is still in its infancy. Consequently, basic work still needs to be done. However, many scholars meanwhile set out to explore the field and provide both theoretical and empirical input. Many of them assemble under the label "social semiotics," a research strand that emerged from critical discourse analysis.[14] The aim of these researchers is to provide a comprehensive theory of multimodal communication and to reconstruct socially rooted semiotic patterns. Further frameworks and empirical analyses are provided by linguistic stylistics, a discipline that increasingly focuses on social issues.[15] Also, there is an increasing interest of sociolinguistics in writing practices and visual communication.[16] Besides these linguistic disciplines, other disciplines from different fields of philology and media research started to explore the field as well.[17]

Research Gaps and Open Questions

Because of the research situation outlined above, many questions are open, and many gaps need to be filled. Most importantly, a comprehensive theory that bundles the diverse suggestions and attempts is still missing. Researchers need to query a broad and highly heterogeneous range of disciplines and attempts in order to set up a theoretical framework for their own purpose.

As far as protest research is concerned, much empirical work is still required until protest communities' text design strategies can be generally evaluated. The range of fundamental questions concerns the sociosemiotic values attributed to given graphic elements within protest communities, the actual use of such elements, patterns, conventions, policies and prescriptions of visual protest propaganda, graphic stereotypes, metadiscursive negotiations of graphic practices, as well as identity work and "othering" by means of visual communication. To this end, particularly interdisciplinary attempts are required.

Jürgen Spitzmüller holds the chair of Applied Linguistics at the University of Vienna, Department of Linguistics. His main research interests are located in the fields of language ideology research, visual and scriptal communication as well as discourse analysis. His latest publications cover a monograph presenting a sociolinguistic theory of graphic variation, *Graphische Variation als soziale Praxis. Eine soziolinguistische Theorie skripturaler 'Sichtbarkeit'* (Berlin, 2013); a textbook introducing linguistic discourse analysis, *Diskurslinguistik. Eine Einführung in Theorien und Methoden der transtextuellen Sprachanalyse* (Berlin, 2011); and recent papers primarily cover discourse theory and multimodal scriptality.

Notes

1. Robert Waller, *The Typographic Contribution to Language. Towards a Model of Typographic Genres and Their Underlying Structures* (PhD thesis, University of Reading, 1987), 5.
2. Sue Walker, *Typography and Language in Everyday Life: Prescriptions and Practices* (London, 2001), 2.
3. For a detailed classification, see Hartmut Stöckl, "Typography: Body and Dress of a Text—A Signing Mode between Language and Image," Visual Communication 4, no. 2 (2005): 204–14.
4. See Hans-Jürgen Bucher, "Textdesign—Zaubermittel der Verständlichkeit? Die Tageszeitung auf dem Weg zum interaktiven Medium," in *Textstrukturen im Medienwandel,* ed. EWB Hess-Lüttich, W Holly, and U Püschel (Frankfurt, 1996), 31–59.
5. See ibid., 33; my translation.
6. Karen A Schriver, *Dynamics in Document Design* (New York, 1997), 10.
7. For details, see Jürgen Spitzmüller, "Floating Ideologies: Metamorphoses of Graphic 'Germanness,'" in *Orthography as Social Action: Scripts, Spelling, Identity and Power,* ed. A Jaffe et al. (Berlin, 2012), 255–88.
8. See ibid.
9. See John Lewis Flood, "Humanism, 'Nationalism,' and the Semiology of Typography," in Italia ed Europa nella linguistica del Rinascimento: confronti e relazioni. Atti del convegno internazionale Ferrara, Palazzo Paradiso, 20-24 marzo 1991, 2nd vol., ed. M Tavoni et al. (Ferrara, 1996), 179–96.
10. Ibid., 187.
11. See Spitzmüller, "Floating Ideologies."

12. See Susanne Wehde, *Typographische Kultur. Eine zeichentheoretische und kultur-geschichtliche Studie zur Typographie und ihrer Entwicklung* (Tübingen, 2000), 390–413, for Futurism and Dada; see Brenda Danet, *Cyberpl@y: Communicating Online* (Oxford, 2001), 289–44, for guerilla typography.
13. For an overview, see Waller, "The Typographic Contribution to Language"; and Walker, *Typography and Language in Everyday Life*.
14. See Ron Scollon and Suzie Wong Scollon, *Discourses in Place. Language in the Material World* (London, 2003).
15. See Nikolas Coupland, *Style. Language Variation and Identity* (Cambridge, 2007).
16. See Mark Sebba, *Spelling and Society. The Culture and Politics of Orthography around the World* (Cambridge, 2007).
17. See Danet, *Cyberpl@y.*

Recommended Reading

Jaffe, Alexandra et al., eds. *Orthography as Social Action: Scripts, Spelling, Identity and Power.* Berlin, 2012. A recent collection of articles on diverse sociolinguistic and sociopolitical implications of variation in writing, which gives a good overview on the current sociolinguistic research on scriptal variation. Some chapters also focus on typography.

Spitzmüller, Jürgen. *Graphische Variation als soziale Praxis. Eine soziolinguistische Theorie skripturaler Sichtbarkeit.* Berlin, 2013. Provides a sociolinguistic theory of graphic variation (with a major focus on typography) and case studies on the use of typography as a means of genre, ideology, and identity construction.

Stöckl, Hartmut. "Typography: Body and Dress of a Text—A Signing Mode between Language and Image." *Visual Communication* 4, no. 2 (2005): 204–14. This article outlines a sociostylistic theory and classification of typography and provides a solid framework for the analysis of typographic design.

Van Leeuwen, Theo. "Towards a Semiotics of Typography." *Information Design Journal* 14, no. 2 (2006): 139–55. Van Leeuwen outlines a sociosemiotic approach to the analysis of typography that stands in line with the general sociosemiotic theory of communication.

Chapter 27

Political Music and Protest Song

Beate Kutschke

General Definition of Political Music

As the term "political music" indicates, there is music we consider to be related to politics. But how does music relate to politics? Imagine the scenario that a composer wants to write a piece of political music—a hymn, for instance, that praises the French Revolution or a march that aims at motivating a social group to fight against unemployment. She will face a serious problem: she cannot easily 'make' music, as a sign configuration,[1] that refers to nonmusical issues such as politics. Whereas, in verbal language, conventions determine which words (the signifier[s]) refer to which phenomena or concepts (one or several signifieds), such conventions are rather rare or nonexistent in music.[2] We understand music (as a sign system) not on the basis of abstract conventions, but *similarities* and what we call *associations*:[3] consciously or unconsciously, we observe or construct features that are shared by a sound configuration (a motive, a rhythmic pattern, or a chord progression) on the one hand, and another sound configuration (of the same piece or another piece) and/or non-musical phenomena (motion, color, shape, structure, etc.) on the other.[4] We attribute to the former the function to refer to the latter, and transfer our associations evoked by the former to the latter. Moreover, grammar in the verbal-language sense does not exist in music. Because of the specific ways that music is used and understood as a sign system, we cannot use it to formulate arguments. There are no logical operators in music that can negate something—for example, in the manner of various antinuclear icons that depict a nuclear sign radiation symbol being crossed out. Therefore, the composer of political music will have to deal with the difficulty of expressing her message in an equivocal medium. In this light, the question arises: how can she ensure that her hymn hailing the French Revolution will not be mistaken as a paean to the monarchy? How can she clearly express resentment over unemployment instead of projecting solidarity with the employer class?

There are essentially three strategies for using music effectively despite its equivocality in political contexts: (1) The composer complements the musical piece with less ambiguous *verbal language* that defines the political message: a text to which the music is set and/or a title and/or commentary in the score (the latter perform their function only if the title and commentary are known by the composition's addressees, the performers and audiences alike). (2) The composer might trust that the *context* in which her composition is performed will clearly define its political orientation. Her hymn on the French Revolution will be recognizable as approving in nature if performed during an event celebrating the anniversary of the revolution. The composer's march against unemployment will receive its political determination when a group of angry-looking, poorly dressed people, equipped with some posters reading "More jobs!," hum or whistle the march's melody. (3) Most importantly, the composer chooses musical means to which Western listeners usually attribute an "expression"[5] that corresponds with the mood of the political camp whose ideas, ideologies, critiques, and aspirations she wants to support. In order to hail and affirm the existing political system she uses musical means to which we respond with positive feelings. In contrast, protest music with which engaged composers aim at criticizing the current state and supporting the change of the political system tends to be "negative" and marked by tension. This "expression" is produced by means of unresolved dissonances and harsh timbres to which listeners usually attribute discontentment, conflict and anger—that is, emotions protesters themselves often feel. Other protest music has march-like, agitated rhythms that correspond with the activists own energetic mental and bodily state.

Why, however, is music performed in political contexts? What ends does political music serve? Music for state-*affirmative* and state-*critical* purposes operates in part differently, and it thus makes sense to discuss both types separately.

General Cultural Functions of Political Music in State-Affirmative Contexts

In order to maintain power, rulers aim at making their power manifest to the citizens who are for their part expected to submit to them. To this end, the former organize political ceremonies that generate what Bourdieu has called "symbolic power,"[6] meaning the power to change the world through the use of signs (instead of physical power).[7] Music, together with other signs such as clothes, gestures, insignia, and speeches, serves as an important factor in the creation of "symbolic power". To give an example, the ceremony and festive procession through Paris on the occasion of the celebration of the French military victory of Steinkerque on 3 August 1692 included the parade of the king, the music of the Grande Écurie (the wind ensemble used for royal occasions), the deployment of the Swiss Guards, the proclamation of the peace treaty, and the performance of the "Te Deum" (H. 146) that Marc Antoine Charpentier had composed for this event.[8] Whereas the Grand Écurie—through its high social status and the heroic-military music it performed—served the king and his ministers to demonstrate the French state's power to the witnessing aristocrats, bourgeois, and crowd, the sacred "Te Deum"—its music and its lyrics[9]—was supposed to suggest that the French military's war and Louis XIV's reign had divine blessing. In order to achieve this, in addition to the hymn's pompous opening movement, "Prélude,"[10] whose *stile di tromba* (full orchestra, trumpets, and timpani) the listening French citizens could again identify as signifying the king's financial, cultural and general capacities, the devotional parts (featuring a solo singer accompanied by an organ) evoked an individual, Louis XIV, who submitted himself to higher—here: divine—powers and, in doing this, received divine support. These cognitive-associative procedures of the listeners generated Louis XIV's "symbolic power," a kind of power that is essentially based on sign interpreters who have been willing to understand the signs—here: music—in a way that confirmed their—subjective—belief in another individual's physical power, which made them to submit to and support this individual.[11]

In the twentieth century, performative, ritualistic practices contributing to the generation of "symbolic power" have hardly changed. During the ceremony marking the first inauguration of Barack Obama on 20 January 2009, that, still today, serves to "magically" transform a normal human being into a superhuman individual of global power, the two main musical agenda items, the well-known American patriotic folk song[12] "My Country, 'Tis of Thee" and John Williams's arrangement of Aaron Copland's "Air and Simple Gifts" for classical quartet aimed at multiple identity generation with the United States. The following properties of the music and its creators advanced the nationalist-patriotic ideals: drawing on a Shaker—that is, an *authentic* American–folk tune, Aaron Copland's "Simple Gifts"[13] was used by the inauguration's organizers to remind the listeners of the US-American nation's founding myth: the settlement of religiously persecuted groups in North America, the high esteem of religious freedom and work ethic. Both Copland and Williams[14] are *truly* American composers, holding up the American field of composition against Europe's perceived historical superiority (Bach, Mozart, Beethoven, Schubert, Wagner, Schönberg, and so forth). In completion to this, the performers—the black soul singer Aretha Franklin, the Chinese American cellist Yo-Yo Ma, the Venezuelan American pianist Gabriela Montero, the Israeli American violinist Itzhak Perlman, and the African American clarinetist Anthony McGill—epitomized the United States's self-image of a multicultural, tolerant nation. The organizers of the inauguration obviously expected that the audiences in front of the Capitol and the television would produce the same associations with the state's origins and key values.

Even more than democracies, authoritarian regimes such as the Third Reich and the Soviet Union put the weight on music's assumed performative quality, that is, its impact on the world through purely semiotic means. On the one hand, they employ beautiful—sometimes cheerful, sometimes glorious—propaganda music to make their citizens believe in the paradisiacal conditions that the authoritarian state promises to bring about. On the other hand, nowhere more so than in dictatorships do rulers fear music's equivocal character. They do this because, depending on the specific context of a composition's performance, listeners do in fact understand a composition as supporting their own subversive, state-critical attitude. State officials, however, searching for the subversive messages in the abstract sound configurations alone instead of the combination of several factors—the performance context, the composition and, first and foremost, the associations and constructions of similarities by the listeners—achieve no more than a mere reading of the musical tea leaves.

The Role of Music in Protest Cultures, Exemplified by the Protest Song

Like the composers and organizers of state-affirmative political music performances, the composers and organizers of performances of protest music, that is, state-critical music, want to shape their audiences' opinions regarding the state's actions—yet in a critical way. Songs in the context of—overt—protest usually criticize the existing social conditions by means of their pithy lyrics and thus help to convey the protesters' grievances; they demand change and negotiations with opposing political groups, mostly state officials and groups in power (workers vs. employers, environmental activists vs. industry, feminists vs. the patriarchal society, New-Leftist students vs. the establishment). The lyrics of "Die Wacht am Rhein" ("The Guard at the Rhine"), for instance, that became the West German protest hymn of the mid-1970s not only criticized the French and West German governmental plans to build a chemical factory and a nuclear power plant in the rural winegrowing region Alsace/Baden, but also offered explanations to the citizens. Furthermore, they invited them to join the civil solidarity campaign that had organized itself to fight the industrial plans. Often sung together, protest songs, like pro-state music, serve to build solidarity and make protesters feel part of a strong community. They not only spiritually uplift the singing activists, but also support the formation of a collective identity. Which role, though, does the music (independent of the lyrics) play?

Like political music in state-affirmative contexts, the success of a protest song heavily depends on associations the listeners generate on the basis of observed similarities between the song and other music and/or contextual knowledge that contributes to its "meaning."[15] Regarding the melody, the singer-songwriter Walter Mossmann in "Die Wacht am Rhein" wisely avoided alienating the people of Baden, a majority of whom traditionally elected the Christian Democratic—that is, a right-oriented, conservative, and anti-Communist—party, by drawing on the musical language of the German Socialist–Communist workers song tradition of the 1920s and 1930s. Instead he enabled associations with a variety of traditions, including the Christian one. The melody is said to originally be a Christian chorale that Florence Reece, a wife of a National Miner's Union leader in Kentucky, adapted in order to accompany a poem that she had written to support her husband's fight in the coal miner strikes of 1931 in Harlan County.[16] Mossmann, however, appropriated the song not directly from Reece, but from Pete Seeger who had popularized it in the context of the American student and protest movements of the 1960s. In musicological terms, Mossmann created a contrafactum or parody: he substituted the text of a given piece of music with another. In doing so, he stimulated a wide variety of associations that the tune had "inherited" throughout its history: the Christian-Protestant protest tradition, starting with Martin Luther, the spirit of the old American workers movement and the union fights in the 1930s, and the optimistic striving of the student and protest movements of the 1960s.[17]

To stimulate these associations, the tonality played an important role. The ancient key, known as the Dorian or Aeolian mode[18] of this originally Christian hymn, is usually associated by Western listeners with ancient or archaic times. It evokes the cruel religious wars that had taken place in Europe from the reformation till the mid-seventeenth century. Mossmann, by the way, was fully aware of the song's similarity to ancient chants and even claimed to have *intensified* this reference by varying the melody. "Except for the activist cadence with leading tone g sharp [Mossmann finishes the song with a modern dominant-tonic cadence, characteristic for major-minor-tonality, instead of a typically-Dorian minor dominant, as in the version of Seeger], the modified melody has more clearly become Dorian than the old version [of Seeger/Reece[19]]. ... In the church hymnbook, there are in fact numerous Dorian chorales ... What do people associate with the memories of these melodies in the church mode [Dorian]? The avowal, the consciousness of the togetherness of the community [or congregation], the feeling of higher right for which [however] people do not make allowance in this vale of tears."[20] In other words, the composition's close connection to the Christian-Protestant tradition should implicitly sanctify the protesters' actions. Even though these intentions might not have been consciously recognized by most listeners, the composers and performers of "Die Wacht am Rhein" could hope that the listeners would carry out the desired procedures: observing similarities between one musical piece ("Die Wacht am Rhein"), on the one hand, with another piece and its extra-musical contexts, on the other; and understanding (unconsciously) the former as a signifier referring to, and thus "meaning,"[21] the latter.

Theoretical and Empirical Research Perspectives

The investigation of political music belongs naturally to two disciplinary fields: musicology, on the one hand, and sociology and political sciences on the other. In musicology, the history of various genres of political music, especially protest song, has been extensively investigated (workers movement, rock music, folk music, French revolution, avant-garde music).[22] More recently, "music and protest" has developed into a musicological research field on its own. In this context, researchers have moved beyond the narrow focus on Western cultures to investigate "music and protest" in other areas of the globe.

Despite these fruitful achievements, thus far protest music as music, that is, not as lyrics, has only started to be analyzed in detail.[23] Which role have musical means played in which contexts to support the activists' expression of dissent? Regarding this question, the investigation of the similarities of protest music with music that was composed in dictatorships and which the dictatorial state authorities consider to be subversive appears to be most promising. In addition to the analysis of music, recent research results from sociopolitical fields—a deeper understanding of protest techniques, the mechanism of the performative subversion of sign systems, and the significance of the bodily presence during demonstrations—have not been applied yet to political, especially protest music. More concretely, the interplay of music, on the one hand, and protest as sociopolitical activity and its various dramaturgies, on the other, has not been systematically explored yet. During which phase of protest—a demonstration for instance—is which music played? In which respects is music as a protest "tool" similar to or distinct from other protest "tools"? To what degree does the participation of the body in the performance of music including protest songs effectively play out in the context of demonstrations and political upheaval?

Beate Kutschke has taught at various universities in and outside Germany: among those, the Technical University Dresden, the University of Arts in Berlin, the Harvard University and the University of Hong Kong. In addition to numerous articles collections and journals, she has published two monographs on modern music: one concerning the end of history in the works of Theodor W Adorno and Wolfgang Rihm (2002) and the other on the New Left and West German and U.S.-American avant-garde music of the 1960s and 1970s (2007). She edited *Musikulturen in der Revolte* (Stuttgart, 2008), and coedited *Music and Protest in "1968"* (Cambridge, 2013) with Barley Norton. The latter received the Ruth Solie Award of the American Musicological Society in 2014.

Notes

1. I use "sign" instead of "symbol" because, in English as in other Western languages, the word "symbol" is not only used as a synonym for "sign" (in a semiotic sense), but also to refer to a multitude of concepts not compliant with semiotic theories.
2. Conventions determine, for instance, that the word "house," the signifier, refers to concrete houses or the concept of house, the signified.
3. Associations are based on the observation of similarities and the construction of structural analogies: since in a former context this or that music served to demonstrate this and that, a similar musical style serves to do the same in the current context.
4. The significance of similarities in the understanding of music does not mean that conventions do not play any role. They indeed influence on which of the numerous similarities between phenomena (such as the similarity shared by all phenomena of "being a phenomenon") we focus our attention. For more details on music as a sign system and the role of conventions as well as on the construction of similarities, see Beate Kutschke, "Music and Other Sign Systems" in *Music Theory Online* 20:4 (2014), http://www.mtosmt.org/issues/mto.14.20.4/mto.14.20.4.kutschke.pdf.
5. What we call the "expression of music" is not an emotive property of the music, but the emotions that we, the listeners, experience while listening to the music and ascribe to it.

6. Pierre Bourdieu, *Language and Symbolic Power* (Cambridge, 1991), 113–16.

7. Regarding the use of the words "sign" and "symbol" see footnote 1.

8. Cf. Catherine Cessac, *Marc-Antoine Charpentier* (Portland, OR, 1995), 175.

9. "We praise thee, O God/ we acknowledge thee to be the Lord/ ... O Christ ... Thou sittest at the right hand of God ... O Lord, save thy people/ and bless thine heritage."

10. Today, the Prélude serves as the Eurovision opening hymn.

11. The power of the ruler is not his own—physical—power, but the effect of the power demonstration of his entourage, his army, courtiers and government who generate and maintain his power by behaving as it were his personal power that rules them.

12. The lyrics of "My Country, 'Tis of Thee" revolve around the ideal of liberty, the pilgrimage myth, Christian faith, love of nature, and the power of music.

13. "Simple Gifts" is the seventh section of Copland's ballet *Appalachian Spring*.

14. The composer of *Star Wars, Jaws,* and *Schindler's List* has won several Oscars and Grammies.

15. Music—like any other sign system—does not *possess* meaning. What we call "meaning" is the mental effect of attributing to a thing or phenomenon the function to serve as a signifier referring to a signified. Furthermore, what we call an "association" is basically the same as what we call the "meaning" of a phenomenon: that is, the process of attributing the function to serve as signifier. Nonetheless, we use the words "meaning" and "association" differently. If we are sure that other sign users share our attribution we call it "meaning" while, using the word "association," we indicate that we are aware that our attribution is most likely subjective, that is, will not be shared by other sign users.

16. Which music Reece had in mind when she set her verses to it, could not be verified yet and is principally difficult to verify because of the rather unspecific shape of the refrain—upward motion from scale degree one to five and back again, omitting the second tone—that can be found in this way or the other in countless chorales and folk songs. Reece mentioned the Baptist hymn "Lay the Lily Low" and the hymn "I'm Going to Land on that Shore." Some folklorists and musicologists have believed that the model could have been the British ballad "Jack Munro" (or "Jack Munroe" or "Jackie Frazer"; see The Mudcat Café).

17. For scores see Walter Moßmann, "Die Wacht am Rhein," in *Alte und neue politische Lieder,* ed. W Moßmann and P Schleuning (Reinbek, 1978), 18–80.

18. The melody does not include the sixth tone of the scale and is as such equivocal.

19. The fact is however that both Seeger's and Mossmann's versions of the song are both Dorian and Aeolian in equally ambiguous measure. Whereas Seeger uses exclusively minor chords (i, iv, and v), Mossmann underscores the ancient, Christian-Protestant, and folk song character by harmonizing the melody by the typical Dorian chord set: i, IV, and v. At the same time, however, he weakens this reference by the V (dominant) at the penultimate chord. Mossmann's changes of the melody, the avoidance of the second tone of the scale, and thus creation of a twice-gapped scale, does not increase the similarity with the Dorian mode, but with Appalachian tunes; see Ralph Lee Smith and Madeline MacNeil, *Songs and Tunes of the Wilderness Road* (Pacific, MO, 1999), 20; Mary O Eddy, *Ballads and Songs from Ohio* (New York, 1939), viii.

20. Moßmann, "Die Wacht am Rhein," 65–66.
21. Regarding the concept of "meaning," see footnote 16.
22. See list of references of Hanns-Werner Heister, "Politische Musik," in *Die Musik in Geschichte und Gegenwart*, Vol. 7, ed. L Finscher (Kassel, 1997), 1661–82, and key words "political music" and "protest song" in the music bibliography RILM.
23. The conference "Protest Music in the Twentieth Century," held in November 2013, has shed new light on the multitude of phenomena that will require more in-depth investigation in the future (for the conference program see http://www.luigiboccherini. org/images/Programme%20Protest.pdf).

Recommended Reading

A comprehensive list of titles on protest music is indicated in the English musicological bibliography RILM (Répertoire International de Littérature Musicale), http://www.rilm.org.

Adlington, Robert. *Composing Dissent: Avant-garde Music in 1960s Amsterdam.* Oxford, 2013. Analyzes in depth protest music in the Netherlands around 1968.

Drott, Eric, *Music and the Elusive Revolution: Cultural Politics and Political Culture in France, 1968–1981.* Berkeley, CA, 2011. Analyzes in depth protest music in France around 1968.

Eyerman, Ron, and Andrew Jamison. *Music and Social Movements.* Cambridge, 1998. Investigates protest music from the sociological perspective.

Kutschke, Beate, and Barley Norton, eds. *Music and Protest in 1968.* Cambridge, 2013. Presents a comprehensive picture on the relationship between social protest and musical expression in different countries across the globe around 1968.

Peddie, Ian, ed. *The Resisting Muse: Popular Music and Social Protest.* Aldershot, 2006. The contributors, situated in a wide range of disciplines, focus on post-1975 popular music.

Perone, James E. *Music of the Counterculture Era.* Westport, CT, 2004. Provides a comprehensive survey about its development in the context of the U.S.-American countercultural movements.

Robb, David, ed. *Protest Song in East and West Germany since the 1960s.* Rochester, NY, 2007. Traces back the West and East German protest song scene since the 1960s to the combat songs of the early twentieth century and the 1948 song tradition.

Part IV

Morphology of Protest

Domains of Protest Actions

Chapter 28

The Public Sphere

Simon Teune

General Definition of the Term

The concept of the public sphere designates an array of social sites and arenas where political and aesthetic concerns are negotiated and public opinion is formed. The idea encompasses settings potentially accessible by anyone—spaces, institutions, and practices—in which meaning is produced collectively. Instances of the public sphere are mass media, assemblies, or encounters in the public space[1] as well as platforms connecting people through the Internet. Both public sphere and the German term *Öffentlichkeit* that influenced the English concept include at least two semantic layers: (1) a spatial reference to arenas of contention and the public space and (2) the collective that is concerned, an audience or simply the public. The normative call for inclusivity and transparency that adds to these semantic levels resonates stronger in the German term.

The dominant interpretation of the public sphere goes back to basic ideas of enlightenment. While the public sphere is a recent notion, its historical antecedent "public opinion" (*opinion publique* in French) was then introduced as a corrective to the state. It emerged from the idea that pieces of art and political decisions are to be scrutinized in the public use of reason by an audience of free and equal citizens.[2] This rationalist perspective on the public sphere is continued most prominently in Jürgen Habermas's political theory. His seminal book on the "structural transformation of the public sphere"[3] and subsequent works spurred discussion on the issue among Anglo-American scholars.[4] In order to develop his concept of the public sphere and its function in a democracy, Habermas identifies sites and media of the bourgeois public sphere in the eighteenth and nineteenth century. Although he stresses that the commodification of information and the power-ridden structural transformation associated to this development has led to a demise of the bourgeois public sphere, Habermas sticks to the basic idea of the public sphere as an arena for free exchange that allows emphasizing citizens' needs vis-à-vis the bureaucratic state and a market-regulated economy.

The rationalist take on the public sphere has been criticized because it is considered to take the specific context of the liberal representative system as a general model, which in effect excludes those who have no access to the canonical sites of the public sphere, lack the required competencies, or find other ways to express themselves.[5] The institutionalization of a rule of reason by bourgeois men who claim to form the public would then be a form of distinction from other social groups. Habermas's affirmative reference to bourgeois journals and coffeehouse discussions is deemed problematic as it tends to undervalue public exchange in the labor movement as found in strikes and sports associations that developed in opposition to a bourgeois public sphere.[6] Therefore, the bourgeois public sphere is confronted with counter-publics as alternative ways of organizing experience.

Beyond the conceptual use of public sphere that refers to its functional position in society, the plural term "publics" (*Öffentlichkeiten* in German) is commonly used to grasp the multitude of levels and arenas of public exchange that are networked to a certain degree but may also be detached by issue, social group, and so on. Emerging from the critique of the bourgeois public sphere, the idea of counter-publics is of particular interest for the study of protest movements. In opposition to dominant publics, that is mainly commercial and public mass media, counter-publics include those arenas in which deviant interpretations of social and political problems are discussed and alternative information is made available.

General Cultural Functions

The public sphere as a site of contention is interpreted in different ways. Rationalist thinkers underline the dialogic function of public reasoning from which the better argument emerges victorious: in an equal exchange among people with different positions, political and aesthetic matters are evaluated and norms justified. It is this nonpartisan procedure that forms the basis for a communicative power "exercised in the manner of a siege"[7] to influence the political and economic system. Critics of the rationalist perspective on the public sphere prefer the idea of an "agonistic public sphere"[8] in which irreconcilable positions continue to exist. As a consequence, public exchange is a constant struggle over hegemony. While certain positions are taken for granted, others have to be brought in over and over again. These opposed assumptions connect to different ideas about political representation. On the one side, the public sphere is conceived of as a mediating system that potentially represents all affected. Considered that public deliberation is inconclusive, the public sphere provides an arena to bring in and discuss new arguments. In this line of thought, the public sphere is a corrective that feeds in the political process of liberal democracies. On the other side, the public sphere is seen as a remedy to the limits of the representative system in the context of increased complexity and diversity. Open to anyone, it guarantees individual self-expression and the "right not to be represented."[9] Dependent on how the public sphere is conceptualized, the exchange and controversy that takes place is associated with different results. In the rationalist interpretation, the public sphere can be seen as a locus of integration into a community. In the public use of reason, participants of deliberation agree on a procedure and negotiate underlying norms. Arguing publicly is an exercise in assuring oneself of the own community and the way in which it should develop. Scholars stressing diversity and the continuity of incompatible positions emphasize public exchange as a way of self-assertion and empowerment. It allows highlighting differences and inequalities.

Role in Protest Cultures

In the domain of protest, the concept of the public sphere can be applied from two perspectives. (1) The public sphere is considered as a contextual factor to and a target for protest events and the individuals involved. In this perspective, protest is part of public discourse and a resource that is used to feed alternative views and formerly hidden issues into the public sphere. As a form of communication, protest intervenes in a public environment where it aims at reaching more or less specific target groups such as fellow citizens, allies, or adversaries, political or corporate decision makers. (2) Protests themselves or gatherings of the groups, organizations, and networks that make them happen can be regarded as public spheres. In such meetings, political activists express themselves, discuss different interpretations, and create a community. Alternative media and other forms of exchange have the same effect. Thus, these phenomena constitute an alternative public.[10]

If the emphasis is on the public sphere as a context for protest movements, at least two aspects of their environment come into play. First, there are the physical conditions for the staging of protest, associated with the concept of public space. Second, protest in contemporary societies cannot be understood without reference to commercial and public mass media. Mass media coverage is crucial both as a mediator and an amplifier to protests. Even in countries where the media are controlled by the state, a regime cannot evade their effect as soon as protests are covered beyond its sphere of influence. As a matter of fact, mass media are the primary source for most citizens to gather information about protests, to understand, and to evaluate demonstrators' intentions.

Activists do certainly not rely solely on mass media to get their message across. This leads to the second perspective on protest and the public sphere. While protesters try to shape the way mass media report on their activities, they also have means of their own to spread ideas. They produce their own media—journals, web sites, or images—and they create insurgent spaces to broaden the basis for their protest. To some extent, this production aims at influencing the environment: mass media, decision-makers, and fellow citizens, directly. But these exchanges can also be understood as expressions of an alternative public sphere that constitutes a community of challengers. Protests, congresses, and gatherings are instances for this community to meet and discuss their strategies and ideas.

Given the reference to the nation state and a common emphasis on nationally bound mass media, scholars used to confine the public sphere within national borders. However, the growing importance of both supranational communities such as the European Union and transnational media such as CNN or Al-Jazeera has spurred a broader use of the term public sphere.[11] A transnational public sphere is considered both an expression and a precondition of a transnational community. On the one hand, protest movements aim at attracting resonance in transnational public spheres. For instance, attention in other countries will improve the situation of protesters who are marginalized in their domestic context. On the other hand, activists contribute to the creation of transnational publics in transnational mobilizations, publications, and other forms of exchange.

Theoretical and Empirical Research Perspectives

From the onset, scholars have considered the public perception of protest a basic feature to understand the dynamics of contentious politics. In their account of collective behavior, Turner and Killian hold that the effects of political protest "depend largely on the influence of *mediating* publics that interpret and evaluate particular instances of collective behavior."[12] It is this intermediate function of the public sphere that has attracted most scholarly interest. However, only few scholars studying protest in the framework of social movements integrate the idea of the public sphere explicitly.[13] Nevertheless, researchers have tried to translate the relationship of protest and public exchange into measurable concepts.

In their actual research, scholars tend to focus on mass media coverage that is tacitly equated with the public perception of protest. In the tradition of political process theories, scholars have underscored the relevance of mass-mediated publics for protests to influence the state and other target groups. As Koopmans argues "it is no longer the co-present public that counts most, but the mass audience."[14] Notwithstanding the selection bias in media coverage, printed commercial mass media are a well-established source to understand the public perception of protest.

In a narrow sense, protest itself is a matter of public debate. As Della Porta argues, the limits of acceptable protests and legitimate policing of dissenters are negotiated publicly in liberal democracies.[15] To understand activists' chances of success, protest messages have been located in a wider setting. In terms of content, protesters are confronted with culturally and temporally contingent discursive opportunities that inhibit or facilitate mobilizations for a certain issue.[16] Once they are represented in the mass media, activists are part of a broader societal discourse. Their utterances and those of relevant actors such as decision-makers and journalists are linked in the claims analysis method.[17]

Beyond mediation through mass media, protest is a way to visualize dissent in the public space. Several authors have underlined the street as the stage for protest[18] or the appropriation of space in social movements, especially when analyzing urban movements. Even if the space available for the expression of protest is thought to be shrinking through privatization and state repression, activists are creative in recapturing the streets. In fact, the right to protest is closely connected to the right to the city, to using and shaping public space.

Alternative spaces, activist media, as well as other arenas and infrastructures of exchange, can be analyzed as part of an alternative public sphere.[19] The branch of research focusing on counter-publics has grown with the emergence of the Internet, which is widely considered an important opportunity for activists to spread their message with low costs in a "virtual public sphere."[20] However, a dense analysis of contentious events has to acknowledge the fact that protests take place in a "hybrid space of communication"[21] that connects one-to-one and one-to-many communication as well as online and offline activities. Research in alternative publics that concentrates on one medium risks falling short of the dynamics that shape internal exchange as well as the impact that such counter-publics may have on a wider societal level.

Research Gaps and Open Questions

While sporadic studies have been published on the issue, the internal dynamics of protest publics continues to be understudied. Protest events can be seen as assembly publics that allow forming a community and fortify participants' beliefs. Few studies reconstruct these transient publics, their emergence, and functions empirically.[22] While the experience of protest is an important instance of self-assertion and performing community, it is usually too short to establish lasting bonds with fellow protesters and too limited in terms of content. Both socializing and discussion take place in group meetings and other assemblies such as conferences. If the focus is at how dissidents develop their own critique in continuous discussions, these are the events that have to be studied.

As laid out before, protests are part of a complex interplay of different arenas for public exchange. A superordinate concept that is considered an outcome of these exchanges and central for the political process is the notion of public opinion. So far, scholars know little about the interplay of protest mobilizations and public opinion. To what extent are protests dependent on public opinion, for instance influencing mobilizing efforts and forms of action? And how can the impact of contentious episodes on publicly shared attitudes be explained? While the former question is tackled in the concept of discursive opportunity structures, scholars interested in the outcomes of social movements found the combination of protests and concordant public opinion to be likely to promote change.[23]

This article illustrated that the focus on arguments and textual discourse prevalent in public sphere theory has also been dominant in attempts to understand the relation of protest and the public. It is open to future research to explore the role of nontextual elements in the constitution of a public sphere. Having identified an "iconoclasm" in public sphere theory,[24] scholars are just beginning to locate images in the framework of the public sphere. This seems of particular interest to understand the specific situation of protest in an environment that is dominated by the logics of public and commercial mass media. On the one hand, the opportunity to communicate complex messages is extremely limited in protest events. On the other hand, rational arguments tend to pass only as a side effect in a media environment that privileges dissemination over dialogue, image over reason, and dissent over consensus.[25] Delicath and DeLuca hold that protesters facing this challenge rely on image events in which their criticism is condensed in a symbolic visual expression, for instance a coffin carried in a demonstration, to compensate for their structural underrepresentation in mass-mediated discourse.[26] The production, diffusion, and reception of such images belong to a worthwhile field of research.

Simon Teune is a sociologist based in Berlin. He is a co-founder of the Institute for Protest at Berlin and the co-director of the research area Social Movements, Technology and Conflicts at the Center for Technology and Society, Technische Universität Berlin. Teune's research focuses on the cultural embedding of protests and social movements, their media resonance, and their link to visual culture. He is coeditor of *Nur Clowns und Chaoten?* (Frankfurt, 2008), a book that unpacks the media event of the Heiligendamm protests; editor of *The Transnational Condition. Protest in an Entangled Europe* (New York, 2010); and coeditor of *Advances in the Visual Analysis of Social Movements,* vol. 35, of *Research in Social Movements, Conflict and Change* (Bingley, 2013).

Notes

1. This distinction is made in Jürgen Gerhards and Friedhelm Neidhardt, "Strukturen und Funktionen moderner Öffentlichkeit: Fragestellungen und Ansätze," in *Öffentlichkeit, Kultur, Massenkommunikation,* ed. S Müller-Doohm and K Neumann-Braun (Bielefeld, 1991), 49–56.
2. See Peter U Hohendahl, ed., *Öffentlichkeit. Geschichte eines kritischen Begriffs* (Stuttgart, 2000).
3. Jürgen Habermas, *The Structural Transformation of the Public Sphere. An Inquiry into a Category of Bourgeois Society* (Cambridge, 1993).
4. Craig Calhoun, ed., *Habermas and the Public Sphere* (Cambridge, 1992).
5. For a summary of the criticism see Nancy Fraser, "Rethinking the Public Sphere: A Contribution to the Critique of Actually Existing Democracy," in *Habermas and the Public Sphere,* ed. C Calhoun (Cambridge, 1992), 109–42.
6. See Oskar Negt and Alexander Kluge, *Public Sphere and Experience: Toward an Analysis of the Bourgeois and Proletarian Public Sphere* (Minneapolis, MN, 1993).
7. Jürgen Habermas, *Between Facts and Norms. Contributions to a Discourse Theory of Law and Democracy* (Cambridge, 1996), 486.
8. Chantal Mouffe, "For an Agonistic Public Sphere," in *Democracy Unrealized. Documenta 11 Platform 1,* ed. O Enwezor et al. (Ostfildern, 2002), 87–96.
9. Alberto Melucci and Leonardo Avritzer, "Complexity, Cultural Pluralism and Democracy: Collective Action in the Public Space," *Social Science Information* 39 (2000): 507–27.

10. Ulla Wischermann's analysis of the women's rights movement is a rare study combining both perspectives on the public sphere: *Frauenbewegungen und Öffentlichkeiten um 1900. Netzwerke Gegenöffentlichkeiten Protestinszenierungen* (Königstein, 2003).

11. Nancy Fraser, "Special Section: Transnational Public Sphere: Transnationalizing the Public Sphere: On the Legitimacy and Efficacy of Public Opinion in a Post-Westphalian World," *Theory Culture Society* 24 (2007): 7–30; Thomas Olesen, "Transnational Publics: New Spaces of Social Movement Activism and the Problem of Global Long-Sightedness," *Current Sociology* 53 (2005): 419–40.

12. Ralph H Turner and Lewis M Killian, *Collective Behaviour* (Englewood Cliffs, NJ, 1987), 205, emphasis in original.

13. The canonical *Blackwell Companion to Social Movements,* for instance, includes a chapter which covers the field without making the public sphere a central issue: William Gamson, "Bystanders, Public Opinion, and the Media," in *Blackwell Companion to Social Movements,* ed. DA Snow, SA Soule, and H Kriesi (Malden, MA, 2004), 242–61.

14. Ruud Koopmans, "Movements and Media: Selection Processes and Evolutionary Dynamics in the Public Sphere," *Theory and Society* 33 (2004): 368.

15. Donatella Della Porta, "Protest, Protesters, and Protest Policing: Public Discourses in Italy and West-Germany from the 1960s to the 1980s," in *How Social Movements Matter,* ed. M Giugni, D McAdam, and C Tilly (Minneapolis, MN, 1999), 66–96.

16. Myra M Ferree et al., *Shaping Abortion Discourse. Democracy and the Public Sphere in Germany and the United States* (Cambridge, 2002), chapter 4; Ruud Koopmans and Susan Olzak, "Discursive Opportunities and the Evolution of Right-Wing Violence in Germany," *American Journal of Sociology* 110 (2004): 198–230.

17. Ruud Koopmans and Paul Statham, "Political Claims Analysis: Integrating Protest Event and Political Discourse Approaches," *Mobilization* 4 (1999): 203–22.

18. Matthias Reiss, ed., *The Street as Stage. Protest Marches and Public Rallies since the Nineteenth Century* (Oxford, 2007).

19. Robert Asen and Daniel C Brouwer, eds, *Counterpublics and the State* (Albany, NY, 2001).

20. Lauren Langman, "From Virtual Public Spheres to Global Justice: A Critical Theory of Internetworked Social Movements," *Sociological Theory* 23 (2005): 42–74; see also Wim van de Donk et al., eds, *Cyber Protest: New Media, Citizens and Social Movements* (London, 2004); Thomas Olesen, *International Zapatismo: The Construction of Solidarity in the Age of Globalization* (London, 2005).

21. Marion Hamm, "Proteste im hybriden Kommunikationsraum: Zur Mediennutzung sozialer Bewegungen," *Forschungsjournal Neue Soziale Bewegungen* 19 (2006): 77–90.

22. For instance Wischermann, *Frauenbewegungen und Öffentlichkeiten um 1900.*

23. Marco Giugni, *Social Protest and Policy Change* (Lanham, MD, 2005); Felix Kolb, *Protest and Opportunities: The Political Outcomes of Social Movements* (Frankfurt, 2007).

24. Cara A Finnegan and Jiyeon Kang, "'Sighting' the Public: Iconoclasm and Public Sphere Theory," *Quarterly Journal of Speech* 90 (2004): 377–402.

25. Kevin M DeLuca and Jennifer Peeples, "From Public Sphere to Public Screen: Democracy, Activism, and the 'Violence' of Seattle," *Critical Studies in Media Communication* 19 (2002): 125–51.
26. John W Delicath and Kevin M DeLuca, "Image Events, the Public Sphere, and Argumentative Practice: The Case of Radical Environmental Groups," *Argumentation* 17 (2003): 315–33.

Recommended Reading

Delicath, John W, and Kevin M DeLuca. "Image Events, the Public Sphere, and Argumentative Practice: The Case of Radical Environmental Groups." *Argumentation* 17 (2003): 315–33. Offers the notion of image events to understand the staging of protest as a way to argue in the mass-mediated public sphere.

Ferree, Myra M, et al. *Shaping Abortion Discourse. Democracy and the Public Sphere in Germany and the United States.* Cambridge, 2002. Provides an analytical concept to understand public discourse on conflicting issues highlighting the differences between Germany and the United States.

Koopmans, Ruud. "Movements and Media: Selection Processes and Evolutionary Dynamics in the Public Sphere." *Theory and Society* 33 (2004): 367–91. Explains interactions between social movements and their target groups as mediated by the public sphere and dependent on discursive opportunities.

Rucht, Dieter. "Öffentlichkeit als Mobilisierungsfaktor für soziale Bewegungen." In *Öffentlichkeit, öffentliche Meinung, soziale Bewegungen,* edited by F Neidhardt, 337–58. Opladen, 1994. Introduces the concrete use of the concept of the public sphere for the analysis of social movements and their dynamics.

Chapter 29

Public Space

Tali Hatuka

General Definition of the Term

Public space as a product of socio-spatial relations is always under construction.[1] The word public—defined as the opposite of private—is that which is open to general observation or knowledge, and thus public actions are performed and carried out in full view, without concealment. Social and anthropological theories consider public to be the domain of people, united by sociability and a constructed normative order. Space has multiple meanings, yet when associated with public it denotes an area or extension of an area. Thus, public space indicates affiliations between the public and space, creating a physical area for open interactions and practices. Consequently, public space is a place that belongs to the people as a whole, affecting or concerning the culture of a community or a nation. This sense of belonging makes public space: (1) a sphere of multiplicity and plurality and (2) a significant location for cultures to negotiate, protest, modify, and present their values and traditions.

Public space has raised much discussion about its role and contribution to public life. Anthony Giddens[2] argues that understanding the manner in which human activity is distributed in space is fundamental to analysis of public life. Ervin Goffman[3] used the concepts front and back to illustrate a fundamental divergence in social spatial activity. For Goffman, a front region is composed of those places in which we put on a public on-stage performance, acting out stylized, formal, and socially acceptable activities, while a back region is an area where we are behind the scenes, where we prepare ourselves for public performance, or where we can relax into less formal modes of behavior.

These spatial differences of public space are a key concern in architecture and planning, disciplines engaged in transforming the concept of public life into a physical reality. If we wish to define public space without imposing aesthetic criteria, we are compelled to include all spaces between buildings for public use. In architecture and urban planning, public space indicates such components as streets, squares, alleys, and parks. These spaces, though they are part of the collective assets of citizens, are usually under the control of the local authority, which is responsible for their maintenance. In the contemporary reality of cities, this authoritarian control can include gates, surveillance cameras, and other restrictions that limit the public's actions within these spaces. These surveillance practices alter the interplay between property (as a parcel of owned space) and people by regulating their use and accessibility, becoming a means of excluding some people and classes of people from otherwise publicly accessible property.[4]

Over the last few decades, there has been a growing critique regarding the impoverishment of contemporary civil life. Scholars have pointed out the significance of public experience, beyond the private sphere, for the self-development of men.[5] These writings address public space as a social relations' product—relations that are often conflicting and unequal, without romanticizing the concept of public space as an empty free space equally accessible to all.

General Cultural Functions

Of all the various types of public spaces, three key urban typologies have received significant attention from architects, town planners, and social groups—the square, the street, and the park, all arenas for dissent.

Traditionally, the square is created by a grouping of houses around an open space, which affords a high degree of control over the inner space and facilitates a ready defense against external attacks. This kind of courtyard has symbolic value and was, therefore, chosen as the model for the construction of numerous holy places (agora, forum, mosque courtyard, etc.). This spatial pattern became a model for public and private developments, with many houses being built around central courtyards or atriums.[6] Today, the secular civic square, around which government and cultural buildings are located, is the modern equivalent to a holy place. These civic squares recruit architectural elements, such as scale, symmetry, monumental buildings, and symbolic icons, to place the individual in a meaningful social hierarchy that promulgates implicit power relationships.

Unlike the square, the street is the product of a settlement's expansion. It provides a framework for the distribution of land and gives access to individual plots. More functional than the square (which, by virtue of its size and arrangement of buildings, is more attractive and often monumental), the street serves as a channel of traffic and movement, with the residential street used mainly by residents, and the commercial (sometimes pedestrian) street used as a bustling public arena for the city's inhabitants and visitors—thus serving as the socioeconomic vein of a city.

Unlike the street and square, the urban park is a relatively recent development that emerged in the nineteenth century due first to the allocation, in Europe, of royal land for public use; and, second, to the creation of non-utilitarian, landscaped urban areas with woodlands and pastures designated for public recreation. Owned and maintained by the local government, the urban park, with varying uses and scales, exists as a modern typology in cities all over the world.

These physical definitions of the square, street, and the park have often been challenged, not only with reference to epistemology, but also on the grounds that urban form is itself bound by historical and social processes and by hegemonic power structures. That is, economic relations and forces of production, as well as social, political, and cultural histories, have an impact on the form of space and its meaning.[7] One of the social strategies that significantly affects public space is protest. This is a strategy by which political powers and citizens alike manifest their ideology in public.

Role in Protest Cultures

As a planned ideological action, a protest expresses a conviction of wrong or injustice.[8] Since protesters are seen as unable to correct the objectionable situation directly by their own daily efforts, this action is intended to draw attention to grievances, to provoke the taking of ameliorative steps by some target group. As such, protesters depend upon a combination of sympathy and fear to move the target group to action on their behalf. In attempting to achieve this purpose, protesters carefully plan their event, taking into account the action's public location, which affects the attention the action receives as well as its meaning.

As suggested, the square, the street, and the park have a significantly different use value and spatial definition from one another (Table 29.1). All play a significant role in terms of the impact of the protest and its visual representations. Thus, protests that take place in a square, which is a pause or extension within the city's network, are often static congregations that use or challenge a space's symbolic value. The enclosed space increases a sense of ritual and solidarity. In contrast, protests that take place along streets, defined as the city's structural movement network, are often more dynamic, with active marching. In this latter type of action, traffic in the street halts, and the march paralyzes the city's network, enhancing the impact by drawing viewers and passersby. Still other conditions are created when a protest takes place in a park, which is often an isolated piece of nature in the midst of the bustling urban nature of the city's network. This protest is often a large-scale activity, a festive event, in which the detached nature of the park creates minimal interference for the daily dynamics of the city.

Figure 29.1. Gathering in the square, London, 2007. © Photo by Tali Hatuka.

Figure 29.2. Taking the streets, Athens, 2007. © Photo by Tali Hatuka.

Figure 29.3. Assembling at the edges of the village, Bakaa el Garbia [Israel], 2009. © Photo by Tali Hatuka.

These basic spatial differences play a significant role in the public experience of space and the social meaning of the protest. Yet, these voids, or spaces, in the city are defined by the built form surrounding them, which also carries significant meaning. Public institutions such as governmental buildings, transit hubs, private consumption spaces such as malls, or labor buildings such as factories with their adjacent public space often become sites or even targets of contestation. In some cases, the design of the action itself may carry a *counter-meaning* to the representation of the building or institution as a part of the protest's performance and the message's craft. In that sense, it is impossible to separate the built form from space, and they should be seen together. Furthermore, many protests use various spatial qualities to enhance their impact (e.g., marching in the streets and congregating in the square, in front of a governmental building). Moreover, particular account should be paid to the fact that cities differ significantly from each other in terms of scale, planning, social rules, and cultural traditions, all of which affect the public spaces' accessibility to dissent. This is particularly true for laws that govern public space and that allow or prevent its use for protests (often through negotiation and permits with authority).

Table 29.1. Public Space's Role and Meanings in Protest Culture: The Square, the Street, and the Park

	Square	Street	Park
Use	Meeting	Traffic/movement channel	Recreation
Key value/ Concern	Symbolic	Functional	Leisure
Spatial definition within the city	A pause within the city network	The city network	An isolated, enclosed pause within the city network
Influence of protests	Static congregations, challenged symbols displayed in space; enclosure that increases the sense of ritual and solidarity	Dynamic marching, crowd's growth, enhancing impact by affecting accidental viewers, paralyzing city's network	Large-scale events, festival-oriented, minimal interference of the daily dynamic of the city

As a secular ceremony, the protest is intended to strengthen the existing cultural-ideological construction of a group or a society. In this context, public spaces are viewed as forums for voicing disagreements, or as physical locations for resolving them.[9] As such, a protest is a mode of action that contributes to the reciprocal interactions between space and social practice, with the symbolism and iconography of public spaces constantly defined and re-created by users. As Henri Lefebvre argues,[10] social space is a social product, so that any transitions in the form of social relations must entail the production of a new space. This process of the appropriation and transformation of space has become a focal issue in much of the literature on politics and space, and on how societies negotiate their identity and claims through modifying their modes of operation.[11] In other words, the appropriation—or possession of space during protests challenges the established social order identified in, or with, a particular space.

Theoretical and Empirical Research Perspectives

With increasing interest in the spatial dimensions of protests, there is a growing body of research in geography, anthropology, and architecture and planning, concerning the relationships between public space and protest. Most of this literature employs an interdisciplinary perspective, yet there are significant differences in their initial disciplinary reference points of observation. Thus, in general terms, architecture and planning focuses on the impact of built space and the physicality of dissent; geography gives much more weight to the territorial and control strategies used during dissent; and, sociology and anthropology deals with the meanings associated with the settings and locations of rituals and ceremonies.

On the role of built spaces in constructing a sociopolitical identity, scholars such as Sibel Bozdoğan, Kim Dovey, Lisa Findley, Abidin Kunso, and Lawrence Vale[12] have focused on the built space as a cultural artifact within intricate power geometries. Particular attention has been paid to the architectural concept of buildings as mediators between civic society and its urban image. These researchers see the public space as a spatial-cultural phenomenon and insist on the need to envisage it as representing power relations in a specific cultural arena, that is, in relation to the groups that affect the space's design and definitions. Detailed studies that address the relationships between specific public spaces and dissent can be found in relation to Plaza de Majo (Buenos Aires), Rabin Square (Tel Aviv), and Tiananmen Square (Beijing), to name a few.[13]

Significant attention has been given to the control of public space, and the way it influences concepts of publicity, citizenship, and democracy. For example, Donald Mitchell and Lynn A Staeheli[14] aim at understanding how modes of access and possibilities for association in publicly accessible space vary with individuals and classes of people, and with the role public spaces play in shaping democratic possibilities. Bruce D'Arcus examines how public and private space is symbolically mediated, and the way power and dissent are articulated in the contemporary media.[15]

On the symbolic and political uses of space, Murray Edelman and Anthony Giddens[16] have both pointed out that a setting is actively involved in social interaction; Nicholas Entrikin[17] has commented that the control over the meanings of setting is an important expression of power.[18] More directly, Ervin Goffman has studied symbolic interaction in public space, and Don Handelman has examined public events' design and organization as a means of understanding the ritual in relation to the world within which it is created and practiced.[19]

Research Gaps and Open Questions

The above perspectives share the assumption that the socio-spatial array of the city forces us to adjust to particular social contexts, behavioral codes, and political regulations. However, at the same time, this spatial array also provides us with a space in which to negotiate, oppose, and resist. This particular dialectic of constraint and freedom is what makes public spaces so crucial to political dissent, so strategic as a tool allowing people to negotiate their claims. Will the role of public space as a significant location and as the material of dissent diminish? What civic role will public space play in the future with the development of information and communication technologies (ICTs)? It is true that ICTs contribute to social movements (though they also contribute to information overload, misinformation, access restriction, and predominance of use by elites). However, it is not expected that these technologies will replace direct actions; rather, they will continue to complement and enhance them.[20]

Tali Hatuka is an architect, urban planner, and head of the Laboratory of Contemporary Urban Design in the Department of Geography and Human Environment at Tel Aviv University. Hatuka works primarily on social, planning, and architectural issues, focusing on the relationships between urban regeneration and development, violence, and life in contemporary society.

Her recent book, *Revisioning Moments: Violent Acts and Urban Space in Contemporary Tel Aviv*, was published both in English (Austin, TX, 2010) and Hebrew (Tel Aviv, 2008). Her work has been published in a wide range of journals, including the *Journal of Urban Design International*, the *Journal of Architecture*, the *Journal of Architecture and Planning Research*, *Planning Perspectives*, *Political Geography*, and *Geopolitics*.

Notes

1. Doreen B Massey, *For Space* (London, 2005), 9.
2. Anthony Giddens, *The Constitution of Society: Outline of the Theory of Structuration* (Berkeley, CA, 1984).
3. Erving Goffman, *Relations in Public: Microstudies of the Public Order* (New York, 1971).
4. There is extensive literature on these issues; see, for example, the works of Don Mitchell, *The Right to the City: Social Justice and the Fight for Public Space* (New York, 2003), especially 1–12; Sharon Zukin, *The Culture of Cities* (Cambridge, MA, 1996), 1–48.
5. In particular, see the work of Richard Sennett, *The Conscience of the Eye: The Design and Social Life of Cities* (New York, 1990); Richard Sennett, *The Fall of Public Man* (New York, 1977); Ali Madanipour, ed., *Whose Public Space?: International Case Studies in Urban Design and Development* (London, 2010); Ali Madanipour, *Public and Private Spaces of the City* (London, 2003); Don Mitchell, "The End of Public Space? People's Park, Definitions of the Public, and Democracy," *Annals of the Association of American Geographers* 85(1995): 108–33; Zukin, *The Cultures of Cities*.
6. Rob Krier, *Urban Space* (New York, 1979), 19–20.
7. Manuel Castells, "The New Historical Relationship Between Space and Society," in *Designing Cities,* ed. AR Cuthbert (Malden, MA, 2003), 59–68.
8. Ralph H Turner, "The Public Perception of Protest," *American Sociological Review* 34, no. 6 (1969): 815–31.
9. Don Handelman, *Models and Mirrors: Towards an Anthropology of Public Events* (Cambridge, 1990), 10–21.
10. Henri Lefebvre, *The Production of Space* (Oxford, 1991), 68–168.
11. See for example John A Agnew, *Place and Politics: The Geographical Mediation of State and Society* (Boston, 1987); Denise Cosgrove and Stephan Daniels, eds, *The Iconography of Landscape: Essays on the Symbolic Representation, Design, and Use of Past Environments* (Cambridge, 1988); Don Mitchell, "Iconography and Locational Conflict Form the Underside," *Political Geography* 11, no. 2 (1992): 152–69.
12. Sibel Bozdoğan, *Modernism and Nation Building: Turkish Architectural Culture in the Early Republic* (Seattle, 2001); Lisa Findley, *Building Change* (London, 2005); Kim Dovey, *Framing Places* (London, 1999); Abidin Kunso, *Behind the Postcolonial* (London, 2000); Lawrence J Vale, *Architecture, Power and National Identity* (New Haven, CT, 1992).

13. Tali Hatuka and Rachel Kallus, "The Architecture of Repeated Rituals," *Journal of Architectural Education* 61, no. 4 (2008): 85–94; Wu Hung, *Remaking Beijing: Tiananmen Square and the Creation of a Political Space* (Chicago, 2005); Susan Torre, "Claiming the Public Space: The Mothers of Plaza de Mayo," in *Gender, Space, Architecture,* ed. J Rendell, B Penner, and I Borden (London, 2000), 140–5.

14. Donald Mitchell and Lynn A Staeheli, *The People's Property? Power, Politics, and the Public* (New York, 2008).

15. Bruce D'Arcus, *Boundaries of Dissent: Protest and State Power in the Media Age* (New York, 2006).

16. Anthony Giddens, *Central Problems in Social Theory: Action, Structure, and Contradiction in Social Analysis* (Berkeley, CA, 1979).

17. Nicholas J Entrikin, *The Betweenness of Place: Towards a Geography of Modernity* (Baltimore, MD, 1991).

18. Murray Edelman, *The Symbolic Uses of Politics* (Urbana, IL, 1964).

19. Erving Goffman, *Interaction Ritual: Essays in Face-to-Face Behavior* (New Brunswick, NJ, 2005); Goffman, *Relations in Public.*

20. Martha McCaughey and Michael D Ayers, eds, *Cyberactivism: Online Activism in Theory and Practice* (New York, 2003).

Recommended Reading

Carmona, Matthew, Tim Heath, Taner Oc, and Steve Tiesdell. *Public Places, Urban Spaces.* Amsterdam, 2010. Provides a general overview of the complex and interacting dimensions of urban spaces and design.

Dovey, Kim. *Framing Places.* London, 1999. Analysis of architecture and public spaces with a focus on power and meaning.

Madanipour, Ali. *Public and Private Spaces of the City.* London, 2003. Reviews the role and meaning of public and private space, and relationships between them.

Vale, Lawrence J. *Architecture, Power and National Identity.* New York, 2008. Explores the role of formal institutional buildings in defining power and identity.

Chapter 30

Everyday Life

Anna Schober

The everyday has to do with repetition, the ordinary, the slow rhythms of work, and the various paths one uses to traverse the city one happens to live in. It is usually opposed to the exceptional situation—such as the celebration, the holiday, or the revolution.

In modernity, everyday life acted as a reference point for a variety of different areas of intervention: for politics in a more narrow sense, for social reform, for philosophy, for new scientific branches such as sociology or psychology, but also for the arts or for the various public actions of the citizens. And paradoxically, this ordinary, everyday life thereby became repeatedly defined as a site from which extraordinary change, upheaval, and even revolution could arise.

The Everyday and the Political

This new focus on everyday life is linked to the profound political upheavals that characterized the French Revolution. Claude Lefort[1] investigated this transformation from traditional to modern societies. He demonstrated that in traditional societies the king occupied the central place of power, and a combination of his natural and his supernatural body linked the people to this center. With the revolutions toward democracy in the eighteenth and nineteenth centuries, however, this central place of power became empty and a variety of protagonists (and their emblems) could now offer themselves to occupy it temporarily. Even if—as the various authoritarian regimes in the twentieth century show—there was a constant threat to fill this central space of power with the figure of a new leader again, as part of these transformations a discourse gained ground, spreading the concept that power is permanently owned by nobody and that the exercise of power needs a periodic contest in the form of elections.

As a consequence of these transformations, the ways in which human connectivity was set in form changed: on the one hand, a whole modern body of politics in a more narrow sense—containing parties and the parliament—emerged. But on the other hand, this stage of politics was surrounded by and directed toward a newly emerging broader public political sphere. Here, agendas could be raised as well as voters recruited, and pressure and urgency could be channeled toward the stage of politics in a more narrow sense. But at the same time, in this broader political sphere, also new collective bodies—explicitly political movements such as the working-class movement but also other grassroots and subcultural groups—could gain visibility and presence, staging novel political demands and/or incorporating utopian visions.

This sphere of the political is a "space of appearance," as Hannah Arendt calls it.[2] Here every phenomenon of perception—be it an object, a gesture, a notion, a song, or a charismatic person—can potentially be politicized and used to protest against prevailing worldviews. With this, various elements of the everyday gained a new role: red carnations or the cloth cap, for example, came to signify the revolutionary working class; everyday gestures such as walking through the city were transformed into new political means such as demonstrations; and particular people could be seen as representatives of a particular version of a new life. This transformation went together with a symbolic restructuring, where objects became interpreted as carriers of creed and become things that set people in motion, and at the same time, their meaning is nevertheless open for interpretation in a new way. And simultaneously individuals, too, can temporarily become representatives of broader political wills. Politicization thus means a questioning and challenging of accustomed attributions and assignments, for example of bodies and spaces, by generating a new kind of public presence for which everything at hand and potentially everybody can be deployed.[3]

The everyday thus became a reservoir for potential politicization. At the same time, however, the activities, emanating from the now emerging apparatus of politics in a more narrow sense—parties, the parliament, but also related bureaucracies and institutions—focused on the everyday in a new way too: all of these entities now introduced strategies to reform or to better the everyday and to bridge the gap between experts and broader audiences. In doing so, they tried to extend their radius of action and control. Hence, everyday living conditions, in modernity, have been always already politicized via these various interventions.[4]

Everyday and Everybody

In her book *The Human Condition,* Hannah Arendt mentions the curious fact that the workers, when they entered the stage of history as the Sans Culottes of the French Revolution, did so by distinguishing themselves via their clothes and were satisfied with being named according to their external appearance. To her, it seemed as if they were wearing a new costume in order to celebrate their emergence and to distinguish themselves from all the others.[5] This reference indicates two issues that are important in respect to the abovementioned politicization of the everyday in modernity: the appearance of the worker as one of the central figures for modern protest movements and the importance that tangible and visible presence plays in this process. Both issues can be explained with reference to the already mentioned historical transformation, which however also included a change in the regime of perception.

This new form of perception emerging in modernity is dominated by a persistent, eventful, subjectivized way of seeing and an evidential paradigm.[6] This means that the gaze is attentive for all that is visible—it is at the same time distracted and fixed upon details. At the same time, images or objects were revaluated by becoming a central factor in the constitution, reproduction, and contesting of social practices: they acquire the ambivalent double function of simultaneously uniting social circles and of acting as markers of difference toward other social circles and occasionally even work as means of political provocation.[7]

As part of the new formation of collectivity and how this collectivity was staged and perceived, the way audiences were addressed also changed. The various interventions into the public sphere no longer represent the extraordinary or the unusual person—the king, the god, the muse—but the ordinary, the everybody, the common man or the common woman.[8] Hence, modern discourses even need this reference in order to present themselves as authentic, true, and universal. So even if such figures of the common men, the common women, or the everybody usually appear with an always different face and under an always different name, they nevertheless assume the always similar function of universalizing a discourse and linking it closely to reality. Thereby, they act as central—psychologically affective and politically effective—linking elements between modern social-reform discourses and the self-performances of consumers and protesters. And because of the special antagonisms in the Western world in the nineteenth and first half of the twentieth century, it so happened that in this period the worker became the model for such an everybody. In recent decades, other figures such as the migrant or the ethnic other have often taken over this function.

The Everyday in Focus: Critique and Revolution

Especially in the decades before and after the Russian revolution, approximately between 1900 and 1940, everyday life became a main reference point for a critical theory that invented the relationship between art, aesthetic experience, and labor anew and fraternized with the emancipation of the working class. First and foremost, those strands of theory that were turning against a bureaucratization of politics then started to put the focus on everyday life. Here, discussions of the everyday turned into conceptualizations of revolutionary agency and of permanent revolution. Early examples of this were the writings of Leon Trotsky and Alexandra Kollontai. The former confirmed Lenin's claim that the party should shift its focus after the consolidation of power to the transformation of political work into cultural work, even if he diverged for example in the evaluation of the spontaneity of the masses or the further role of the party from the ruling conception about how such a politicization of culture should look like.[9] And the latter concentrated on the development of new kinds of social and sexual relationships, which for her could also only happen inside the domain of the everyday.[10] The argumentation of both, however, was shaped by the machino-technical imperative, which depicted a technical transformation of pre-Capitalist forms of collectivization as a result of industrialization.[11]

This focus on the everyday was carried on by two thinkers who became very influential later, especially since 1968: Antonio Gramsci and Walter Benjamin. The former, for example, developed a philosophy of praxis further using the notion of hegemony, which put an emphasis on the contradictory, plural successes and unintended linkages of the various actions carried out by diverse popular agents.[12] In parallel, Walter Benjamin described the everyday in his late writings as a site of unexpected events "filled with the presence of the now [Jetztzeit]"[13] caused by memories but also by the encounters with certain images, objects, or artistic interventions such as those fabricated by Dadaism, surrealism, or contemporary cinema. For Benjamin, such events contain a political potential, for which he also uses the notion of awakening[14]: they are able to stimulate public action.

The view that the everyday life already contained political life and simultaneously comprised the potentiality of a revolutionary critique of politics was further disseminated by the writings of Henri Lefèbvre.[15] In his later works on space and the urban revolution, he highlighted in particular the invisible charges of the everyday such as myths, ideologies, and utopias, but also passions, wishes, and disavowal, which every intervention into social space has to account for—whether from side of the institutions or from side of the popular collective wills.[16]

All these theorizations of the everyday were characterized by an identification with the working-class struggle for emancipation and consequently by adoptions of handed-down Marxist worldviews. Because of this, the everyday—however multifariously it has otherwise been characterized—here remains often (as in the case of Henri Lefèbvre) finally determined by the economic instance.

In the early 1980s, such a conceptualization of the everyday was strongly reformulated. Ernesto Laclau and Chantal Mouffe, for example, placed a "field of contingent variations as opposed to essential determination."[17] And Stuart Hall in an essay with the programmatic title "Marxism without Guarantees" starts out to replace "the notion of fixed ideological meanings and class ascribed ideologies with the concepts of ideological terrains of struggle and the task of ideological transformation."[18] The deeds of various collective agents are now depicted as together producing a political conflictual sphere where always actual hegemonic relations emerge in a purely contingent way and remain in themselves subject to further questioning.

The Art of Acting and the Celebration of the Everyday

In modern times, objects, spaces, gestures, and actions of everyday life as well as exponents of lower social classes have become a prominent object of representation in the visual arts. Dutch paintings depicting ordinary objects or the representation of pilgrims in the paintings of Caravaggio (1571–1610) as barefooted poor people with dirty feet are early indicators of this. In the twentieth century, the medium of photography became especially closely connected with common life. Susan Sontag, for instance, writes: "Photographic seeing meant an aptitude for discovering beauty in what everybody sees but neglects as too ordinary. ... The proper moment is when one can see things (especially what everyone has already seen) in a fresh way. The quest became the photographer's trademark in the popular imagination."[19]

But in parallel, in the twentieth century another transformation also took place: In live acts produced by the Dada avant-garde movement in the 1920s as well as in artistic actions associated with the student movement of the 1960s or in today's practice of using art as social intervention, the claim was and still is to transfer art into everyday life. And conversely, in the second half of the twentieth century, everyday action has been reenacted and redescribed as art.

Pivotal for the latter were subcultural styles created by groups such as the punks. On a theoretical level, Michel de Certeau's *Art du faire* (1980) was very influential, in which he set out to discover the logic of the practices of everyday life. He too chose a method that accounts for conflict and a plurality of social situations and distributions of forces. In this, he came down strongly on the side of the everyday, the everybody, the low, and the marginal, even if he pointed out that in this respect we are usually dealing with a "massive and pervasive" marginality.[20] In his approach, we find a pronounced use of pair of opposites such as "discipline—antidiscipline," "strategies—tactics," or "place—space," whereas he usually celebrates one part of the pair—the antidiscipline, the tactics, and spaces—which according to him define the essence of the practices of "everybody."

This binary division of the everyday, however, obstructs the view on the unintended linkages and crossovers between actions of different political agents. So, for example, tactics of the consumers and strategies of the institutions cannot so neatly be separated as De Certeau's theory would have us believe. Some characteristics, he mentions in respect to tactics,[21] can also be seen as being part of strategies and vice versa. For instance, not only the strategies of the institutions but also the tactics of consumers are attempts to establish a realm of something "own," and—conversely—not only are tactics calculated in order to use favorable moments but strategies, too, are directed toward the same end.

Nevertheless, De Certeau strongly directs our attention toward aspects of everyday life, which were for a long time neglected or misrepresented by cultural analysis. In investigating casual activities such as walking through the city or reading a text, he shows that consumers are not just reconstructing meanings but do reinvent, reuse, translate, and invent. He thus highlights the productivity and creativity of consumers, who until then had mainly been portrayed as passive, alienated, manipulated, or driven by "false consciousness." In this, he meets with other theoreticians such as Roland Barthes, who in his later works also focused on such a multiplicity of meaning of even the smallest details of photographs, films, or everyday appearance, and on reading practices he viewed as strongly driven by desire.[22]

Hence in these writings, the everyday became described as a field of significant encounters that exert a transforming power. This move went together with a rediscovery of the writings of Sigmund Freud,[23] who already some generations earlier saw the everyday as the happening of trauma, enigma, and the uncanny. In such a perspective, even the most customary of our actions no longer appear as controlled by a sovereign subject and by intention but as nourished by hidden powers and causing unexpected and sometimes surprising effects.

These approaches were frequently picked up for an analysis of postmodern everyday life transformed by media. Bo Reimer and John Gibbins, for example, pointed out how the media is influential in functioning as cultural forums, in assisting in a pleasurable process of sense-making, and in structuring everyday life in a new way. However, they likewise pay extraordinary attention to the "bricolage" that consumers make out of the variety of sources they became attracted to and involved in.[24] Consequently, they portray media reception no longer as a kind of withdrawal from public exchange or as an apolitical attitude such as earlier analysis of public spheres in the late twentieth century did,[25] but as important steps in the formation of expressive protest performance constituting contemporary political struggles.

The Social, the Cultural, the Political

Despite the emergence of a new political, public sphere with the French Revolution described in the beginning of this text, in modern times and especially in the late nineteenth and early twentieth century, the "social" and not the "political" ascended as the key term in the debate about the everyday. The state is depicted as an extended family, where every individual occupies an assigned place and problems are solved via strategies that secure and integrate these places. In relation to this "state-family," in this period of time no difference between "the political" and "the social" is made.[26] Since the 1970s, however, the "cultural" came to the fore and started to replace the social. Pivotal for this was a definition of culture as a "whole way of life"[27] as well as the simultaneous emergence of new social movements such as those formed by feminists, ecologists, (second or third generation) immigrants, or by homosexuals who started to struggle for cultural recognition.[28]

Consequently, the main challenge for future research on the everyday is to find ways to bring the political back into the agenda. This however implies not isolating and privileging any single one of these notions but rather relating the political, the social, and the cultural, and taking into account how their rise and fall correlates with broader historic transformation of the private and the public spheres and of how individuals make sense out of their everyday existence. A further desideratum in research on the everyday is to investigate the unintended linkages and crossovers between actions of various political wills beyond hastily classifications in "subversive" versus "dominant" ones.

Anna Schober currently directs the research project "Everybody: a transnational iconography" at Justus Liebig University in Giessen, supported by the Deutsche Forschungsgemeinschaft. In 2009 she got her postdoctoral habilitation at Vienna University. Afterwards she was Marie Curie Fellow and Visiting Professor at Verona University and Mercator Visiting Professor and Deputy Professor at Justus Liebig University Giessen. Her publications include: *Blue Jeans. Vom Leben in Stoffen und Bildern* (Frankfurt, 2001); *Ironie, Montage, Verfremdung. Ästhetische Taktiken und die politische Gestalt der Demokratie* (Munich, 2009); and *The Cinema Makers. Public Life and the Exhibition of Difference in Central and South Eastern Europe since the 1960s* (Bristol, 2013).

Notes

1. Claude Lefort, "The Image of the Body and Totalitarianism," in *The Political Forms of Modern Society: Bureaucracy, Democracy, Totalitarianism,* ed. JB Thompson (Cambridge, 1986), 292–306.
2. Hannah Arendt, *The Human Condition* (Chicago, 1958), 207*ff.*
3. On the process of symbolic restructuring following the French Revolution: Claude Lefort, *Democracy and Political Theory,* trans. D Macey (Cambridge, 1988), 216*ff.* On this notion of politicization, see Jacques Rancière, *Dis-agreement: Politics and Philosophy* (Minneapolis, MN, 1999), 36–37.
4. Nick Crossley, "Movements, Lifestyles, Identities, Bodies," presented at the Designing a New Life: Aesthetics and Lifestyles of Political and Social Protest conference of the Marie-Curie-Training-Network "European Protest Movement since the Cold War. The Rise of a Transnational Civil Society and the Transformation of a Public Sphere after 1945." Department of German, Zurich University. Zurich, March 2007.
5. Arendt, *The Human Condition,* 218.
6. On the "evidential paradigm," see Carlo Ginzburg, "Clues. Roots of an Evidential Paradigm," in *Myths, Emblems, Clues,* ed. C Ginzburg (London, 1990), 96–125.
7. Georg Simmel, "Fashion," in *On Individuality and Social Forms,* ed. D N Levine (Chicago, 1971), 294–323.
8. Anna Schober, *Blue Jeans: Vom Leben in Stoffen und Bildern* (Frankfurt, 2001), 248–49.
9. Leon Trotsky, *Problems of Everyday Life, and Other Writings on Culture and Science* (New York, 1973).
10. Alexandra Kollontai, "Marriage and Everyday Life," in *Alexandra Kollontai: Selected Writings,* ed. A Holt (London, 1977).
11. John Roberts, *Philosophizing the Everyday: Revolutionary Praxis and the Fate of Cultural Theory* (London, 2006), 22–23.
12. In his *Prison Notebooks,* he writes: "Common sense is not something rigid and immobile, but is continually transforming itself, enriching itself with scientific ideas and with philosophical opinions which have entered everyday life"; Antonio Gramsci, *Selections from the Prison Notebooks* (London, 1971), 326.

13. Walter Benjamin, "Über den Begriff der Geschichte," in *Walter Benjamin: Gesammelte Schriften in 7 Bänden,* vol. I(2), ed. R Tiedemann and H Schweppenhäuser (Frankfurt, 1999), 701.
14. Walter Benjamin, "Der Sürrealismus," in *Walter Benjamin: Gesammelte Schriften in 7 Bänden,* vol. II(1), ed. R Tiedemann and H Schweppenhäuser (Frankfurt, 1999), 297. On the reception history of this thesis of Walter Benjamin: Anna Schober, "Irony, Montage, Alienation: Aesthetic Tactics and the Invention of an Avant-Garde Tradition," *Afterimage: The Journal of Media Arts and Cultural Criticism* 37, no. 3 and 4 (2009): 15–29.
15. Henri Lefèbvre, *Critique of Everyday Life,* vol. 1 (London, 1991).
16. Henri Lefèbvre, *Writings on Cities,* ed. E Kofman (Oxford, 1996).
17. Ernesto Laclau and Chantal Mouffe, *Hegemony & Socialist Strategy: Towards a Radical Democratic Politics* (London, 1985), 99.
18. Stuart Hall, "The Problem of Ideology: Marxisms without Guarantees," in *Stuart Hall: Critical Dialogues in Cultural Studies,* ed. D Morley and K-H Chen (London, 1996), 25–46.
19. Susan Sontag, *On Photography* (London, 2002), 89.
20. Michel de Certeau, *The Practice of Everyday Life* (Berkeley, CA, 1984), xvii.
21. Ibid., 34–35.
22. Roland Barthes, *The Empire of Signs* (New York, 1983); Roland Barthes, *Camera Lucida: Reflections on Photography* (London, 1993).
23. Sigmund Freud, *Psychopathology of Everyday Life* (Harmondsworth, 1938).
24. John R Gibbins and Bo Reimer, *The Politics of Postmodernity: An Introduction to Contemporary Politics and Culture* (London, 1999), 68*ff.*
25. Richard Sennett, *The Fall of Public Man* (Cambridge, 1977), 205*ff.*
26. Arendt, *The Human Condition,* 33*ff.*
27. Raymond Williams, "Culture Is Ordinary," in *Studying Culture: An Introductory Reader,* ed. A Gray and J McGuigan (London, 2003), 5–14.
28. Michel Wieviorka, *La Différence* (Paris, 2001).

Recommended Reading

Gibbins, John R, and Bo Reimer. *The Politics of Postmodernity: An Introduction to Contemporary Politics and Culture.* London, 1999. Investigates the relation of everyday life and protest action for protest movements since the 1960s in detail.

Roberts, John. *Philosophizing the Everyday: Revolutionary Praxis and the Fate of Cultural Theory.* London, 2006. An insightful overview on critical writing focusing on the everyday.

Schober, Anna. *Blue Jeans: Vom Leben in Stoffen und Bildern.* Frankfurt, 2001. Analyzes the influence of mass media on lifestyles in the twentieth century and especially on subcultural groups.

Chapter 31

Cyberspace

Paul G Nixon and Rajash Rawal

First, following Warkentin's notion,[1] political action or protest is a human activity. Second, it follows from this that when we talk of virtual civil society, virtual groups, and so on, we are talking of protest activity that may involve technology but is fundamentally a human action. Today it is "impossible to ignore the new forms of interaction facilitated in cyberspace and the threats and opportunities that these offer."[2] Some see cyberspace as being a place where "the Internet offers a potential for direct democracy so profound that it may well transform not only our system of politics but also our very form of government."[3]

The virtual world is often viewed as either separate from or an adjunct to real life. We argue that they are one and the same. Indeed, it could be argued that given restrictions upon traditional protest demonstrations, cyberspace is one area that is left where the freedom still reigns, despite increasing attempts by governments to monitor online activities. In Western democracies, there is a discernible crisis of confidence regarding the ability of traditional political systems to live up to the increasing public aspirations as they reject leviathan-like political parties and seek other, more flexible, and varying solutions to their fluid and fragmented lifestyle issues and concerns, as identified by Beck.[4] We can see that this political disenfranchisement and detachment from traditional forms of politics,[5] as evidenced via declining party membership,[6] has opened up new and competing forms of political engagement. Moreover, as we adopt and embrace more digital options in our daily lives, e-government, e-health, and so on, it is only inevitable that e-protest emerges.

General Definitions and Applications of Online Protest

Following Habermas,[7] the diffusion of political activity, complexity, and the pace of change has rendered public spheres more complex and thus more fragmented, both qualitatively and quantitatively, and at present, one can only see that impact becoming greater.

Diani's ideas[8] on how Information Communication Technology (ICT) could serve NGOs' goals are: (a) inexpensive, (b) fast, (c) immediate, and (d) participatory; they facilitate interactions between organizations; and members/activists are equally applicable to looser, more fragmented groups who operate in cyberspace. Alkalimat and Williams see ICT use creating three types of cyber power:

1. *Individual:* empowering individuals and creating new human capital.
2. *Social:* collectives engaged in cyber organizing harnessing individual human capital.
3. *Ideological:* ideas and policy promoted by individual and social cyber power.[9] A prime example of this would be the flourishing anti-Capitalist movement and its associated organizations, for example, Indymedia.[10]

This changing scenario, facilitated by the use of new media, has impacted upon a number of elements and actors within the democratic system. Governments, private citizens, lobby groups, NGOs, and political parties have all employed new technologies as part of their normal activities and also adapted their actions, and some have found new activities, opportunities, or strategies that have been facilitated by the ICT usage. As shown below, this is not without consequences.

Without wishing to reify cyberspace, we can argue that "the Internet is a thing that changes things, more than a 'mere' object."[11] Scott and Street note that cyberspace and the Internet in general offers new opportunities for social movements, NGOs, and other groups, as it facilitates "meso-mobilisation—co-ordination between movements networks across borders and without the need for a transcending hierarchical organisational form ... for a high impact without needing major resources" and that it enables "organisations to retain editorial control over content and external communication; ... organisations to bypass state control and communicate in a safe environment."[12] Adding ICT enabled capabilities to what Tilly describes as protest groups' "repertoires of action."[13] The influence of the

Internet, in general, on social movement activity has been identified,[14] with increasing focus on protest groups that reflect nonhierarchical, diversely networked bases.[15]

Networked sociality exemplifies looseness and informality. Individuals engage in networks randomly, staying anonymous if they wish to do so, select activities to engage in and sign out, or simply cease to operate in that network when they have become disinterested or choose to move on to another cause or topic. This should not be viewed as a negative, for as Lovink writes, "loose ties are constitutional these days. We should stop reading them in terms of decline. ... Engagement comes in radically new ways. Networks are playgrounds; they are probes."[16] User-generated content as afforded by applications such as Facebook and Twitter have only further enhanced these possibilities, as depicted by Rawal and Shotton.[17]

The Development of Online Protest

The prehistory of online protest is interesting with examples such as Larry Seiler's efforts to mobilize e-mail activists to protest against the Lotus software company's attempt to gather, distribute, and sell the private information of 120 million people using Lotus MarketPlace.[18] Barlow's Declaration of Independence of Cyberspace[19] set out the more idealistic side of how people felt the Internet could be used to both protest against government activity and to change and potentially reconstruct the societies we live in. Diani notes that Internet communications blur the boundaries of traditional communication theories,[20] and such social networks must be included when examining mobilization to take part in social movement and protest activity.[21]

Other examples can be seen by the use of petitions by Moveon.org, which sought to get the U.S. congress to censure President Clinton and move on to more important issues troubling the nation; the 1994 attempts by supporters of the rave music culture to use a saturation of e-mail traffic, as a way of constituting a distributed denial of service (Distributed Denial of Service Attack, short DDoS) attack on the UK government[22] and various ICT-facilitated techniques by the Zapatista National Liberation Army party in Mexico as part of their strategy of creating the Zapatista Movement, which later allowed them to spread their message on a global scale through a network of overseas activists.[23] This mobilization potential[24] shows that, although Keck and Sikkink argued that ICTs were not an essential tool,[25] they were nevertheless a valuable tool for those seeking to advance transnational protest and advocacy, which Garner compared with the way the invention of the printing press had allowed information to spread.[26]

The prime example of online activism and protest came of age moving to a new level of public consciousness is the anti–World Trade Organization (WTO) mobilizations in Seattle in 1999.[27] A divergent conglomeration of activists, groups, and social movements took actions against the WTO summit utilizing both street level and cyber level strategies to coordinate their protest. The Internet capabilities facilitated activists to give near, real-time updates of police locations and allowed the protesters to respond to those changes and plan events accordingly.[28] It also enabled them to create an unofficial mirror web site, which lampooned the WTO's own web presence.[29]

Van Laer and Van Aelst created a typology of action putting into perspective the differing types of action as used by social movements.[30] The typology "centres around two related dimensions: ... there is the distinction between 'real' actions that are supported and facilitated by the Internet, and 'virtual' actions that are Internet-based ... [and] a classic dimension that makes a distinction between tactics with low and high thresholds."[31]

The rise of social media and the use of such platforms have provided new opportunities for protest[32] that makes it is easy to forget that protest has been alive since the early days of the net. If one takes the U.S.-based activist Mengara who created a web site Dongo Doit Partir (1998; Dongo Must Go) in order to try to spark a movement to remove the Gabonese government, one can see that there is a precedent to the events of the Middle East and North African countries. The subsequent Arab Spring revolutions of early 2011 and the occupy movements that produced much speculation about the role of Internet enabled social media tools such as Facebook and Twitter in facilitating social movement protest activity.[33]

Forms of Online Protest

Protest online takes a number of forms. It can range from attempting to attract global attention by posting blogs, videos, or online petitions to try to either overcome censorship or report a viewpoint other than that of the official line. For example, despite the expulsion of foreign media, Iranians themselves have posted extensive video footage on web sites, including YouTube.[34] In Germany, an online petition was created and has been signed by over 30,000 people to try to overturn a government decision to revise gaming laws.[35] A further example of this would be the online petition[36] against L'Exploitation documentaire et valorisation de l'information générale a highly intrusive database for use by French intelligence services and police, which stores among other items data on an individual's health and sexual orientation.

Regarding blogs, we have the case of Salam Pax, the Bagdad blogger who shot to global prominence during the Iraq war in 2003 and was subsequently hired as a journalist for the British newspaper *The Guardian*. P2P technology has facilitated communication means that are difficult to trace and monitor. This technology can be readily found in everyday items such as gaming consoles.

Seattle 1999

The protests that took place during the 1999 Seattle round of WTO Ministerial Conference are widely considered to be one of the first that used information technologies (IT) in preparing for the protest and spreading it worldwide. The methods used ranged from extensive use of e-mail and discussion boards to creation of fake web sites, virtual sit-ins, use of Internet for information and counter information, and Internet audio and video broadcasting. Many web sites were created to prepare for the event. Using the code N30 (November 30), a number of actions were organized on the Internet. For example, the site, A Global Day of Action (http://www.seattlewto.org/N30/), called for action in ten different languages and provided a directory of local contacts all over the world. The spirit of the contents of the site is clearly summarized by the slogans reported in the home page: "Resistance, and Carnival against Global Capitalist System" or "May Our Resistance Be as Transnational as Capital." It is suggested by Baldi that, "it is evident that the whole appeal was based on an extensive use of IT."[37]

Organized Interests and Web 2.0, and Their Cultural Impact

The possibilities inherent in the ongoing development and refinement of Web 2.0 technologies to facilitate protest would seem to presage a potential burgeoning of such activity in cyberspace. Though the scope of interaction and the creation of human capital can be viewed as being somewhat limited to date,[38] one would expect that situation to perhaps change in the next few years.

One quick glance at the social networking site Facebook and its groups and networks clearly shows that protest is rife on the Internet. Many groups have been quick to utilize the potential that the Internet has to offer them. One such example is GreenNet.[39] This is a "not for profit, ethical, collective Internet Service Provider"[40] Established in the late 1980s, it was seen as an effective and cost-effective way for environmental activists to communicate.

A well-documented example of Facebook politics has been the rise of Barack Obama. His admiration of the Internet is well-documented, "one of my fundamental beliefs from my days as a community organizer is that real change comes from the bottom up ... and there's no more powerful tool for grass-roots organizing than the Internet."[41] While his movement is no longer one of protest, the early days of his Facebook page, which later evolved into My.BarackObama.com, was very much based on using the web as a tool to engage and mobilize citizens in local politics and then turn them into his supporters.

Following on from this, in Dunedin, New Zealand, a Facebook group, "The DCC Has Lost the Plot," started by local citizen Chris Keogh, was established. Membership had risen from just over 1,600 to nearly 2,500 within one week, while the number of messages posted had also increased, from 130 to 230. However, council communications coordinator Rodney Bryant said there were "more effective ways" than Facebook to comment on the council's performance. The council received feedback through various traditional means of consultation, including the council's long-term council community plan (LTCCP) consultation, the residents' opinion survey, public forums, and consultation on specific issues, such as parking or curbside rubbish collection,[42] thus ignoring the clamor of public criticism that was being aired.

In Colombia, an engineer used the social networking site to organize a massive protest against the Revolutionary Armed Forces, known as FARC. In February 2008, millions of Colombians joined simultaneous marches in 27 cities throughout the country, and 104 major cities around the world shouting, "No more kidnappings! No more lies! No more deaths! No more FARC!"[43] Oscar Morales, the organizer, was somewhat surprised by the success, admitting that he thought it was going to be something less significant. However as he said, "thanks to Facebook, we have created an exponential effect."[44] Morales started a Facebook group called, One Million Voices Against FARC, as a virtual protest with his friends. There was an enormous response from other Facebook users, so Morales decided to call for a national march. Colombians living abroad also learned about the protest through Facebook. Morales was contacted by expatriates wanting to participate in the event by e-mail. After receiving hundreds of expressions of interest, Morales decided to turn the national march into an international event, which was covered by traditional media throughout the globe.

Protest or Terror?

Returning now to the assertion that the Internet is one of the few viable avenues of protest left open to protesters in modern society, it is necessary to look at how governments have attempted to deal with this phenomenon. While, as Van De Donk and colleagues note,[45] these changing developments offer opportunities to protest groups, they also pose problems. Upon examination, it would appear that the Internet is not as free as it appears at first glance, certainly post 9/11.

The UK-based Electrohipppies have suggested that legislation such as the Terrorism Act 2000 and The Regulation of Investigatory Powers Act 2000 has "whilst not affecting 'mainstream' Internet users in the UK, impact(ed) on the rights of ordinary people who wish to protest or take some form of protest action on the Internet."[46] Note that the legislative measures mentioned here predate the 9/11 attacks. It has been suggested that Internet protest has been under closer scrutiny than any other form of communication. For example, instigating an e-mail campaign that sent thousands of e-mails to a government minister, so as to cause problems with the minister's office because of the mass of public communication, would be considered a terrorist act under the current interrelation of definitions of the act. That would be potentially unlawful. However, if carried out using the postal system, so disrupting the function of the whole office, it would not. Loundy[47] further echoes these concerns and warns that governments must be wary of flexing their muscles too strongly. In the United Kingdom over recent years, antiroads protesters, animal rights protesters, countryside campaigners, and even the fuel price protests, have been difficult to police because the mode of the action, while causing disruption, was essentially legal. Many security consultants are concerned that such actions, should they be transferred to the Internet, could be equally effective. Indeed, as noted by Loader, the Internet has presented a "paradigmatic change in the constellation of power relations ..."[48] between governments and individuals. Authorities need to adjust their philosophies.

The European Union has introduced a directive that will allow police authorities to access users traffic data.[49] The directive, which was introduced in *every* member state of the European Union by deadline of July 2007, compels every telephone company and Internet service provider (ISP) to save call and Internet records for up to two years. The ISP data is comprehensive and includes, web sites visited, header information of e-mail correspondence detailing the sender, recipient, date, time, and Internet address.[50] Whereas law enforcement agencies welcomed the new legislation, privacy advocates fear for the wider implications. Our communication tools now form part of the largest surveillance system ever created, this surely causes enough reason to worry.[51]

These controls and their ensuing implications on society have left spectators lamenting the abuses of privacy and freedoms that governments can now legitimately undertake under the guise of protecting their citizens. The benefits of IT in making society more open and democratic may be undone by e-policing and e-control.

Conclusions

Protest carried out through the Internet has often left governments and international organizations at a disadvantage. This is due to their structure as hierarchies; therefore their capacity to react to these electronic attacks is rather slow. Governments and international organizations no longer underestimate the effects of electronic protest. They constantly monitor the activities and initiatives that take place online. Government's willingness to use heavy-handed restrictions will only hand the initiative to authoritarian (undemocratic) governments who may violate privacy, curb the free flow of information, and hamper freedom of expression, ironically the very core values of the society we are claiming to be trying to protect.[52]

It is now evident that a new means of disrupting the work of international organizations, if not society at large, has become visible. However, we should not forget that as is true for all technology, ICT—as it relates to political action—has a double potential: for more democracy and wider information or for disinformation and mere disruption. The Seattle protest showed how independent movements run a risk of disseminating fake information or disinformation. Through the Internet, such disinformation can be amplified and spread all over the world and become difficult to counterbalance. In order to ensure that ICTs will be put to good use, we should in any case become more aware of its characteristics and possibilities.

Despite the fact that the Internet will make it easier and cheaper to coordinate widespread protests, nothing will ever replace the effectiveness of people protesting in the streets, as the antiwar protest in 2003 illustrated. Perhaps the most important long-term contribution of ICTs to protest is that it enables people all over the world to communicate and join forces to fight a common battle. But for how long will cyberspace remain the final frontier of protest?

Paul G Nixon is principal lecturer in political science and head of research at the Academy of European Studies and Communication Management, The Hague University of Applied Sciences, The Netherlands. He has contributed chapters to many edited collections on the use of ICTs, particularly in the fields of political parties, electronic democracy, and social welfare. Among his recent publications, he coedited *Politics and the Internet in Comparative Context: Views from the Cloud* (London, 2013), with Rajash Rawal and Dan Mercea; *Understanding E Government in Europe: Issues and Challenges* (London, 2010), with Vassiliki Koutrakou and Rajash Rawal; and *E-Government in Europe* (London, 2007), with Vassiliki Koutrakou.

Rajash Rawal is principal lecturer in political science at the Academy of European Studies and Communication Management, The Hague University of Applied Sciences, The Netherlands. He is a visiting lecturer at the Fachochschule Eisenstadt, Austria, and the Department of European Studies, Budapest Business School. He has coedited *Politics and the Internet in Comparative Context: Views from the Cloud* (London, 2013), with Paul G Nixon and Dan Mercea; and *Understanding E Government in Europe: Issues and Challenges* (London 2010), with Vassiliki Koutrakou and Paul G Nixon. He specializes in the impact of media on political agents in the modern era and has written a number of papers on this theme.

Notes

1. Craig Warkentin, *Reshaping World Politics* (Lanham, MD, 2001).
2. Paul G Nixon, Antje Grebner, and Laura Suddulich, "Challengers to Traditional E-Government (Non-Governmental Actors)," in *Understanding E-Government,* ed. PG Nixon, VN Koutrakou, and R Rawal (London, 2010), 235–51.
3. Dick Morris, "Direct Democracy and the Internet," *Loyola of Los Angeles Law Review* 34, no. 3 (2001): 1033–53.
4. Ulrich Beck, *Risk Society: Towards a New Modernity* (London, 1992).
5. Nixon, Grebner, and Suddulich, "Challengers to Traditional E-Government."
6. Michael Gallagher, Michael Laver, and Peter Mair, *Representative Government in Modern Europe: Institutions, Parties, and Governments,* 3rd ed. (New York, 2001), 273.
7. Jürgen Habermas, *The Structural Transformation of the Public Sphere: An Inquiry into a Category of Bourgeois Society* (Cambridge, MA, 1989).
8. Mario Diani, "Social Movement Networks Virtual and Real," *Information, Communication & Society* 3, no. 3 (2000): 386–401.
9. Abdul Alkalimat and Kate Williams, "Social Capital and Cyberpower in the African-American Community," in *Community Informatics: Shaping Computer Mediated Social Relations,* ed. L Keeble and BD Loader (London, 2001), 203.

10. "Indymedia.org," http://www.indymedia.org/nl/index.shtml.
11. Dawn Nafus, "The Aesthetics of the Internet in St. Petersberg: Why Methaphor Matters," *The Communication Review* 6 (2003): 185–212.
12. Alan Scott and John Street, "From Media Politics to E-Protest? The Use of Popular Culture and New Media in Parties and Social Movements," in *Culture and Politics in the Information Age: A New Politics?*, ed. F Webster (London, 2001), 32–51.
13. Charles Tilly, *From Mobilisation to Revolution* (Reading, MA, 1978).
14. Diani, "Social Movement Networks Virtual and Real"; Barry Wellman, "Little Boxes, Glocalization, and Networked Individualism," *Revised Papers from the Second Kyoto Workshop on Digital Cities II, Computational and Sociological Approaches* (2002), http://homes.chass.utoronto.ca/~wellman/publications/littleboxes/littlebox.PDF; Donatella Della Porta and Lorenzo Mosca, "Global-net for Global Movements? A Network of Networks for a Movement of Movements," *Journal of Public Policy* 25, no. 1 (2005): 165–90; Dan Mercea, "Digital Prefigurative Participation: The Entwinement of Online Communication and Offline Participation in Protest Events," *New Media and Society* 14, no. 1 (2012): 153–69.
15. Manuel Castells, *The Information Age, Vol. I: The Rise of the Network Society* (Oxford, 1996); John Arquilla and David Ronfeldt, *Networks and Netwars: The Future of Terror, Crime, and Militancy* (Santa Monica, CA, 2001); Jeffrey Juris, "Networked Social Movements: Global Movements for Global Justice," in *The Network Society: A Cross-Cultural Perspective*, ed. M Castells (London, 2004), 341–62; W Lance Bennett, Christian Breunig, and Terry Givens, "Communication and Political Mobilization: Digital Media and the Organization of Anti-Iraq War Demonstrations in the U.S.," *Political Communication* 25, no. 3 (2008): 269–89.
16. Micheö Fehner, Gaelle Krikorain, and Yates McKee, eds, *NonGovernmental Politics* (New York, 2007), 302–3.
17. Rajash Rawal and Paul Shotton, "New & Social Media Use by Interest Groups: Hype? Why Onliners *and* Offliners Matter," panel presented at the IPSA World Congress of Political Science, Madrid, 2012.
18. Laura J Gurak, *Persuasion and Privacy in Cyberspace: The Online Protests over Lotus MarketPlace and the Clipper Chip* (New Haven, CT, 1997).
19. John P Barlow, "A Declaration of the Independence of Cyberspace," 1996, https://projects.eff.org/~barlow/Declaration-Final.html.
20. Diani, "Social Movement Networks Virtual and Real."
21. Barry Wellman, "Computer Networks as Social Networks," *Science* 293 (2001): 2031–34.
22. Meghan Peters, "A Brief History of Online Activism," 2011, http://mashable.com/2011/08/15/online-activism/.
23. Manuel Castells, *The Information Age. Economy, Society and Culture: The Power of Identity* (Malden, MA, 2004).
24. Stefan Walgrave et al., "Network Bridging and Multiple Engagements: Digital Media Use of Protest Participants," *Mobilization* 16, no. 3 (2012): 325–49.
25. Margaret E Keck and Kathryn Sikkink, *Activists beyond Borders: Advocacy Networks in International Politics* (Ithaca, NY, 1998).

26. Roberta T Garner, "Virtual Social Movements," presented at Zaldfest: A Conference in Honor of Mayer Zald, University of Michigan, Ann Arbor, 1999, http://deepblue.lib.umich.edu/bitstream/handle/2027.42/51343/579.pdf?sequence=1.

27. Jackie Smith, "Globalizing Resistance: The Battle of Seattle and the Future of Social Movements," *Mobilization* 6, no. 1 (2001): 1–19; Wim van der Donk, Brian D Loader, and Paul G Nixon, *CyberProtest, New Media, Citizens and Social Movements* (London, 2004).

28. Paul de Armond, "Netwar in the Emerald City: WTO Protest Strategy and Tactics," in *Networks and Netwars: The Future of Terror, Crime, and Militancy,* ed. J Arquilla and D Ronfeldt (Santa Monica, CA, 2001), 201–35.

29. Graham Meikle, *Future Active: Media Activism and the Internet* (New York, 2002).

30. Jeroen van Laer and Peter van Aelst, "Cyber Protest and Civil Society: The Internet and Action Repertoires in Social Movements," in *Handbook of Internet Crime,* ed. Y Jewkes and M Yar (New York, 2009), 230–54.

31. Ibid., 233.

32. Ibid.; Paul G Nixon, Vassiliki Koutrakou, and Rajash Rawal, eds, *Understanding E-Government* (London, 2009).

33. Ulises Mejias, "The Twitter Revolution Must Die," *International Journal of Learning and Media* 2, no. 4 (2011): 3–5.

34. Ashley Hall, "Amateur Video of Iranian Protest Broadcast on Internet," 22 June 2009, http://www.abc.net.au/am/content/2009/s2604312.htm.

35. "Massal Protest in Duitsland tegen gamerverbod," *Nu.nl,* 12 July 2009.

36. "Pour obtenir l'abandon du fichier 'EDVIGE,'" http://www.sgdg.org/nonaedvige/.

37. Stefano Baldi, "The Internet for International Political and Social Protest: The Case of Seattle," http://hostings.diplomacy.edu/baldi/articles/protest.htm.

38. A Meijer, N Burger, and W Ebbers, "Citizens4Citizens: Mapping Participatory Practices on the Internet," *Electronic Journal of e-Government* 7, no. 1 (2009): 99–112.

39. "GreenNet," http://www.gn.apc.org/about.

40. Ibid.

41. Brian Stelter, "The Facebooker Who Friended Obama," *New York Times,* 7 July 2008, http://www.nytimes.com/2008/07/07/technology/07hughes.html?pagewanted=all&_r=0.

42. "Parking Protest Taken to Internet," *Otago Daily Times,* 15 July 2008.

43. Maria Camila Pérez, "Facebook Brings Protest to Colombia," *New York Times,* 8 February 2008, http://www.nytimes.com/2008/02/08/business/worldbusiness/08iht-protest11.html.

44. Ibid.

45. Van der Donk, Loader, Nixon, *CyberProtest, New Media, Citizens and Social Movements.*

46. "Cyberlaw UK: Civil Rights and Protest on the Internet," *the electrohippie collective,* December 2000, http://www.fraw.org.uk/mei/electrohippies/archive/comm-200002.html.

47. David Loundy, "Constitution Protects All Modes of Speech," *Chicago Daily Law Bulletin,* 11 May 1995, http://www.loundy.com/CDLB/Terrorism.html.

48. Brian D Loader, "The Governance of Cyberspace," in *The Governance of Cyberspace,* ed. BD Loader (London, 1997), 1–19.
49. Wendy M Grossman, "Will Logging Your Email Combat Terrorism in Europe?," *Guardian Unlimited,* January 2006, http://www.theguardian.com/technology/2006/jan/12/newmedia.terrorism.
50. Ibid.
51. Rajash Rawal, "Responding to Cyberterror—A Failure to Firewall Freedoms?," in *Understanding E-government,* ed. PG Nixon, VN Koutrakou, and R Rawal (London, 2010), 252–68.
52. Ibid.

Recommended Reading

Castells, Manuell. *The Information Age. Vol. I: The Rise of the Network Society.* Oxford, 1996. A classic introduction to Internet and cyber worlds.
Milakovich, Michael E. *Digital Governance: New Technologies for Improving Public Service and Participation.* Abingdon, 2011. A contemporary analysis of civic cyberspace.
Van der Donk, Wim, Brian D Loader, and Paul G Nixon. *CyberProtest, New Media, Citizens and Social Movements.* London, 2004. An anthology of case studies from around the world.

Part V

Morphology of Protest

Re-Presentation of Protest

Chapter 32

Witness and Testimony

Eric G Waggoner

General Definition of the Term

Of the literary and artistic genres that have emerged from protest culture since the mid twentieth century, few have achieved the popularity and high critical regard of the witness and testimony genre. As the terms suggest, such writing and art presents, for posterity and in a public forum, either (a) personal accounts of historical traumas, or (b) firsthand statements of community mistreatment by oppressive sociopolitical systems, where such systems have attempted to silence resistant voices. Witness and testimony thus operates along three primary discursive axes: (1) offering a first-person narrative related to an extant record of historical trauma, (2) offering a counter narrative to the official (state) historical record, or (3) offering a record of personal experience of historical trauma in the absence of any official record at all. Witness and testimony thereby bears witness to traumatic communal experiences, which might otherwise be marginalized, or go unspoken and unheard.

Witness and testimony—which may appear as visual art, music, film, nonfiction/memoir, and even some fiction—proceeds from the assumption that a subjective narrative of historical trauma or sociopolitical oppression can attest to the effects of such phenomena in powerful and immediate ways that fall outside the scope of objective historiography. In this regard, witness and testimony takes the form of historical *micronarrative,* or a subjective account of one's personal experience within a specific historical moment, as opposed to a *macronarrative,* or an objective account of the facts and chronology of that same moment. While micronarrative must avail itself of some aspects of macronarrative (such as references to major events and relevant public figures) in order to situate its story socially and historically, in general, the micronarrative's power inheres in the subjective expression of the individual, or individuals, whose immediate experiences provide its dramatic center.

General Cultural Functions

The terms witness and testimony derive from the discourse of law and official documentation (and sometimes share a connotative connection with the discourse of certain religious faiths). Indeed, one obvious rhetorical model for such artistic projects is official testimony regarding oppression and brutality, for example, the transcripts of war crime and atrocity trials and hearings. Primarily, however, witness and testimony art purports to offer evidence into the court of public opinion, not a court of law. Witness and testimony art therefore offers itself as public-sphere evidence supporting a political or ideological argument. It attests to, and in so doing protests, a community's oppression, mistreatment, or even attempted extermination at the hands of the state.

A particularly significant rhetorical element of witness and testimony may be found in its narrative subject positioning, which often moves freely between the individual and communal perspectives. Testimony speaks inherently from the perspective of one who has witnessed the events and phenomena under discussion, meaning that the first-person speaker(s) found in most examples of witness and testimony speak both from within (individually), and on behalf of (communally), the communities whose experiences the text purports to represent. That is, witness and testimony presumes that the experiences of specific individuals, always and everywhere within the work, should be understood as representative of the experiences of larger communities to which those individuals belong. This representative status may operate implicitly or explicitly, as needed, and one often finds the particular narrative voice of witness and testimony shifting consciously and quite freely between the individual "I" and the communal "we." The particular form of that voice may change to adapt to the media employed for individual works of art, but the narrative voice or perspective will often provide multiple examples of this blending of individual and communal perspectives.

Communal identity may be established by ethnic, political, racial, national, or religious classification, as defined from within the community or without. They may even be partly rooted in more seemingly general categories such as age, gender, and sexuality. Often, however, witness and testimony art blends *multiple* identities together within its narrative framework. A story about political oppression might also be, to a greater or lesser degree, a story about religious or ethnic oppression. A story about ethnic oppression might particularly emphasize the effects of that oppression on an ethnic community's younger generation, or on its female or homosexual population. In all cases, however, witness and testimony art speaks *for*—which is to say on behalf of, or in defense of—a defined community, with respect to which the individual narrative voice claims either direct connection or, in some cases, direct observation of the effects of oppression.

Role in Protest Cultures

Often beginning in a private experience and moving slowly to a public forum, witness and testimony's roles in protest culture are primarily two: (1) to preserve a record of oppression of a specific community at the hands of power systems, usually the political state; and (2) to build a sense of connection and shared identity among members of that oppressed community. The former is a direct function of individual acts of witness and testimony, while the latter is largely an effect of aggregate acts.

In shifting between individual and communal subject positions as part of its resistance to oppression, witness and testimony additionally engages in a second, rather more subtle political project, one which bears special relevance in relation to its role in protest culture generally. In addition to offering a direct act of protest, witness and testimony implicitly attempts to create or reinforce a sense of shared identity among members of the community whose experiences are therein recorded. The free shifting between the individual "I" and the communal "we," referenced above, implies that the narrative voice's identity is constructed through a conscious negotiation of an individual's points of connection with a community. The narrative voice, in other words, presents itself as speaking from within the boundaries of that community, suggesting that the truth of a community's experience is implied in the narrative voice's particular articulation of its own. One widely known example of this collective dynamic is Jeanne Wakatsuki-Houston's *Farewell to Manzanar*, a memoir of her childhood years in a U.S. concentration camp between 1942 and 1945, when the United States incarcerated citizens and residents of Japanese heritage as part of its militarizing of the Pacific coast during World War II.[1] In her memoir, Wakatsuki-Houston's narrative perspective freely shifts between the "I" of Jeanne, the young narrator, and the "we" of the 11,070 Japanese and Japanese Americans incarcerated in the camps. Wakatsuki's memoir is often cited as one of the first *Nisei* (second-generation Japanese American) testimonies regarding the camp experience, and a book that helped to define and contextualize the experience for other *Nisei,* many of whom wrote their own accounts afterward.

Conversely, a piece of witness and testimony may collect and present a figurative chorus of voices, offering a series of individual stories meant to narrate a community's experience collectively. *Shoah,* director Claude Lanzmann's epic 1985 film documentary on the Holocaust, is in many ways a quintessential example of witness and testimony art.[2] Eschewing two of the standard conceits of documentary film—historical footage and reenactments of important events from the past—Lanzmann instead gives over most of the nearly nine and a half hours of the film to first-person testimonials regarding life in the Nazi concentration camps in occupied Poland. These stories are told by survivors of, witnesses to, and (in rare cases) administrators and employees of the camps. Present-day footage revisits some of the sites and locations discussed in these stories, providing geographical evidence and context for the accumulative oral history constructed by the film. In presenting itself as both a cumulative historical record and a record of multiple individuals' specific experiences, *Shoah* achieves the balance of micronarrative and macronarrative essential to any successful piece of witness and testimony art.

Theoretical and Empirical Research Perspectives

Though witness and testimony refers to expressive acts whose examples we find even in ancient records, contemporary theory and research has only recently begun to systematize the empirical study of such acts. Furthermore, as witness and testimony constitutes an act of expressive articulation by definition, most such expressions that are not a matter of legal record are to be found in literature and the arts.

As the Holocaust remains arguably the single most significant historical trauma of twentieth-century Europe, it should not surprise us that most critical studies of witness and testimony art reference that event, and the art that has emerged in response to it, as a point of departure for describing the genre's central characteristics and concerns. The earliest contemporary theory and research on witness and testimony focused on the challenges inherent in "speaking the unspeakable," taking as its central topic the seeming futility of language to encapsulate trauma. Theodor Adorno's *Negative Dialektik,* though not centered upon witness and testimony *per se,* provided contemporary theoreticians one useful formulation of these challenges,[3] in his identification of "the extremity that eludes the concept"; to think criti-cally in the contemporary age, argued Adorno, required being mindful of the tendency of language to tame extreme thoughts or subjects.

Subsequent theoreticians explored the implications of this taming effect on acts of witness and testimony, asking whether it was even possible for any expressive medium to approximate the severity of real trauma, and thus whether witness and testimony could ever approach anything like a reliable representation of the real. Michael F Bernard-Donals and Richard R Glejzer's *Between Witness and Testimony: The Holocaust and the Limits of Representation* offers an especially erudite examination of this question.[4] Bernard-Donals and Glejzer conclude, as most contemporary theoreticians have come to agree, that while notable, the limits of expressivity finally do not negate the inherent value of witness and testimony—particularly in its capacity to express what macronarrative history cannot. Following this first wave of research, most theoreticians began to focus their critical inquiry not on *whether,* but on *how* specific acts of witness and testimony can preserve instances of trauma from historical erasure. Frances Guerin and Roger Hallas's edited collection *The Image and the Witness: Trauma, Memory, and Visual Culture* offers an excellent overview of how witness and testimony—visual art, in this case—can serve as an adjunct to individual and collective memory, and also how the accelerated state of media produc-tion in the twenty-first century can raise new critical questions regarding veracity and verifiability.[5]

Most current research, then, focuses on witness and testimony's rhetori-cal structure, in both general and particular forms. For example, regarding the question of veracity, current research on witness and testimony fre-quently takes as its focus the proximity, as it were, of the narrative perspec-tive to the community experience it purports to relate. That proximity is generally direct, but need not always be so. *Shoah* points up an important structural consideration of the genre, from a theoretical standpoint, which is that a piece of literature or art need not be written or created by a *direct* survivor of historical trauma to qualify as witness and testimony. Of course art created by survivors qualifies de facto as witness and testimony, but eyewitness accounts written by persons not directly impacted by that trauma may qualify as well. As a comparative point, U.S. Ambassador Henry Morgenthau's *I Was Sent To Athens,* a first-person account of Morgenthau's direct observation of the systematic extermination of the Ottoman Empire's Armenian population in the years during and after World War I, is often cited as an early twentieth-century example of the genre.[6]

In an interesting example of witness and testimony's cultural longev-ity and aesthetic malleability, some contemporary artists adapt primary sources for their own pieces of protest art. In 2003, North American avant-garde vocalist and composer Diamanda Galás recorded the song cycle *Defixiones: Will and Testament,* based on the same historical events as narrated in Morgenthau's book, and for which she set firsthand witness and testimony poetry to original music.[7] Galás's musical work, in fact, frequently underscores the usefulness of textual interpolation for artists concerned with witness and testimony; her 1991 song cycle *Plague Mass,* written in response to the demonization of homosexual men during the AIDS epidemic of the 1980s, interpolates original text with excerpts from the Old Testament Book of Leviticus, thereby appropriating the language of religious censure and speaking back to it, in a dialogic act of protest against that demonization.[8]

The act of witnessing in individual works, then, may emerge from inside the boundaries of the oppressed community (testimony regarding personal suffering) or from outside those boundaries (testimony regarding direct observation of others' suffering). Undoubtedly, however, the accounts of historical trauma audiences often find most compelling are those that offer immediate, first-person testimony of an individual's own experiences. Yet the creative process and presentation of such testimony is often problematic, presenting challenges related to such issues as the independent data needed for historical verification of claims, the fundamentally inexpressible elements of the effects of deep trauma, the personal difficulty of reliving traumatic experiences for the teller, and the emotional difficulty of receiving such stories for the listener.

Shoshana Felman, whose extended work on witness and testimony is essential to a critical understanding of the genre, has examined these challenges in *Testimony: Crises of Witnessing in Literature, Psychoanalysis, and History.*[9] In her introductory chapter, Felman suggests that the giving of witness and testimony, far from being a simple act of storytelling, is in fact "a discursive *practice.* ... To testify, to *vow to tell,* to *promise* and *produce* one's own speech as material evidence for truth—is to accomplish a *speech act,* rather than to simply formulate a statement."[10] In Felman's formulation, widely understood as a reliable assessment of the profound challenges of this sort of creative process, giving witness and testimony is itself a revolutionary act, an act positioning both the speaker (the artist) and the text (the art itself) in resistance to systems of power and the oppressive machinery of the state. Such an act is intended to achieve, whether by itself or (more often) in concert with supportive materials and documents, a revolutionary impact upon those systems. Because of that resistant positioning, and the implication that to give witness is to challenge the state itself, the act of giving witness and testimony may itself become a secondary moment of trauma for the teller. In recent years, the critical study of witness and testimony has begun to examine this "secondary trauma" aspect of its creative and rhetorical process.

Research Gaps and Open Questions

Witness and testimony employs a form of rhetoric that is inherently contestable and, considered on a case-by-case basis, possibly even unverifiable by the standards of objective historical research. By its very nature, witness and testimony purports to offer an account of events that is deeply subjective but also communally representative, meaning that it may augment or even directly contest an official historical record. Too, and especially in the developmental stages of the literature of witness and testimony surrounding a particular historical event, individual pieces may only reach a wider audience with the passing of time, because of official acts of silencing or the private context of the initial articulation. (I think here of Anne Frank's now-canonical *The Diary of a Young Girl*[1]: written between 1942 and 1944, it was first published in the Netherlands in 1947, but did not achieve wide or critical popularity until translated into English in 1952, after which its fame grew exponentially.) It seems common, though not inevitable, that a piece of witness and testimony art may only reach an audience despite an array of factors militating quite strongly against its successful entry into public consciousness in the first place.

For these reasons, the very nature of research on witness and testimony literature will be invariably fraught with gaps and questions regarding the testimony's relation to the historical record, the verifiability of its biographical particulars, and the broader matter of whether certain historical events may have generated pieces of witness and testimony that have not yet come to light. In the twenty-first century, developments in media dissemination and recording technology (e.g., phone cameras, digital cameras, and online publication) have made opportunities to record, publish, and research documents bearing witness to oppression much more prevalent than in the twentieth century, and may also assist researchers' attempts to verify such documents through cross-referencing and direct comparison with other texts. But each act of witness and testimony begins in an individual articulation of a collective experience, and as such represents a process of negotiation among private consciousness, communal identity, and the historical record. Rarely is that process a clean or orderly one.

The production and collection of witness and testimony art is further complicated, in a very practical way, by human longevity. Eventually survivors of specific historical traumas will pass away, positioning subsequent attempts to produce and collect such art at secondhand and thirdhand removes from the actual historical experience, for example, memoirs written by children of survivors. The window for production of firsthand witness and testimony art is limited by human life span, whether death comes after the fact from natural causes, or as a direct result of the very historical trauma such art commemorates. Witness and testimony art is therefore considered a critical, precious production of persons living under extreme conditions, and its publication and dissemination a significant and important act of rescue from possible historical erasure. In essence, witness and testimony art reinserts the speaking voice of the traumatized into the silence that is, ultimately, the intended effect of official neglect, brutality, or annihilation.

Eric G Waggoner is associate professor of American literature and cultural studies at West Virginia Wesleyan in Buckhannon. His published research on political protest focuses particularly on autobiography and experimental/avant-garde writing and cultural narratives. His academic work has appeared in *Hemingway Review, a/b: Auto/Biographical Studies, Appalachian Journal,* and other journals and book collections. In addition to his critical work, his writing on American popular music and film appears in numerous newspapers and magazines.

Notes

1. Jeanne Wakatsuki-Houston and James Houston, *Farewell to Manzanar* (New York, 1973).
2. *Shoah: An Oral History of the Holocaust,* dir. Claude Lanzmann (France, 1985).
3. Theodor Adorno, *Negative Dialektik* (Frankfurt, 1966).
4. Michael F Bernard-Donals and Richard R Glejzer, *Between Witness and Testimony: The Holocaust and the Limits of Representation* (New York, 2001).
5. Frances Guerin and Roger Hallas, eds, *The Image and the Witness: Trauma, Memory, and Visual Culture* (London, 2007).
6. Henry Morgenthau, *I Was Sent To Athens* (Garden City, NY, 1929).
7. Diamanda Galás, *Defixiones: Will and Testament* (United Kingdom, 2003), compact disc.
8. Diamanda Galás, *Plague Mass* (United Kingdom, 1991), compact disc.
9. Shoshana Felman and Dori Laub, *Testimony: Crises of Witnessing in Literature, Psychoanalysis, and History* (New York, 1991).
10. Ibid., 5. Emphasis in original.
11. Anne Frank, *The Diary of a Young Girl,* ed. OH Frank and M Pressler (New York, 2010).

Recommended Reading

Bernard-Donals, Michael F, and Richard R Glejzer. *Between Witness and Testimony: The Holocaust and the Limits of Representation.* New York, 2001. Examines the problems inherent in engaging in acts of witness and testimony, and also in researching such acts, with particular focus on the idea of the unthinkable, the trauma so totalizing that it seems to resist expression or encapsulation. Uses multimedia representations of Holocaust trauma as its primary texts in an attempt to formulate an ethics of representation.

Felman, Shoshana, and Dori Laub, MD. *Testimony: Crises of Witnessing in Literature, Psychoanalysis, and History.* New York, 1991. Examines the role and function of testimony and witnessing as it relates to the acts of reading and writing, with particular emphasis on the Holocaust.

Guerin, Frances, and Roger Hallas, eds. *The Image and the Witness: Trauma, Memory, and Visual Culture.* London, 2007. An overview of critical challenges and questions surrounding visual representations of the trauma and its effects, with particular emphasis on the ethics of skepticism, the role of witness in redeeming and remembering traumatic experience, and technological advances in twenty-first century image-making that complicate the creative and theoretical processes.

Chapter 33

Media Coverage

Andy Opel

General Definition of the Term

Public protest is intimately connected to media coverage. The place-based actions of individuals gathering at a particular moment often rely on the amplification of those actions through the mass media. From print to broadcast, photojournalism to social media and the Internet, protest actions are represented through diverse media channels. As Stuart Hall suggests, representation "connects meaning and language to culture."[1] The ability to interpret images and find common meaning in representations is based on shared language and codes resulting in a set of social conventions fixed in culture.[2] In addition to the culture within which the representations are produced and circulated, media industries play a central role in selecting, amplifying, and contextualizing protest representations, introducing a political economic layer that historically has served to maintain the status quo and marginalize protests.

General Cultural Functions

When protesting bodies gather in public places, media attention often follows, resulting in spectacular images and incomplete coverage of the issues. The centuries-old tradition of public displays of dissent has recurring elements of entertainment and carnival that work to create "a place where what was important in popular culture could be expressed."[3] From the early resistance to the enclosure of the commons in fourteenth-century Europe up to the present-day puppets and street theater of the global justice movement, public displays of resistance have used a variety of techniques to attract attention and convey complex messages through visual imagery. Over the twentieth century, the rise of mass media has presented new opportunities and new challenges for protest movements. This chapter outlines the contours of those challenges and opportunities.

Media's Role in Protest Cultures: Political Economy and Institutional Routines of Commercial Media

The tensions between social movements, protest strategy, and media coverage are intimately connected to the structure of commercial media and the professional routines and practices of news production. Since World War II, there has been a steady concentration in the ownership of the major commercial media outlets across film, television, radio, and print.[4] This concentration of media ownership has increased the connections between Capitalism and the media system, "through ownership and its reliance upon advertising, a function dominated by the largest firms in the system."[5] The corporate dominance of the global media system that developed over the latter part of the twentieth century resulted in news coverage of protests that consistently marginalized groups seeking moderate and radical reform.[6] Similarly, news media coverage of protest movements functioned "primarily as guard dogs for powerful interests and mainstream values."[7] Analysis of news coverage has shown that while news media consistently provide prominent coverage of protest groups, these news stories "act as agents of social control" where "the more radical the dissent, the less impartial and objective the media."[8] The interests of the elite/corporate owners and advertisers are considered significant factors in marginalizing protest groups that seek to challenge the status quo.

News values[9] play a central role in determining what stories are covered in the press. Commercial media consistently prioritize conflict and spectacle, resulting in a pattern of "if it bleeds it leads."[10] These enduring news values have played a central role in shaping media coverage of protests, emphasizing the violent, spectacular imagery in lieu of analysis of the issues driving the protests. This attention to violence and spectacle has had both positive and negative effects for the protest movements over time. In the case of the civil rights era in the United States, when news media represented Sheriff Bull Conner's use of dogs and fire hoses on the crowd of nonviolent citizens, these images served to galvanize public opinion in support of what became the Civil Rights Act, repealing Jim Crow "separate but equal" segregation laws. In contrast, the more recent coverage of the global justice movement protests, beginning in Seattle 1999 on up through recent G20 meetings in Toronto, Canada in 2010, news media have consistently represented the protests through the use of violent images of clashes between police and the fringe element known as the black bloc. The drama of these images is consistent with commercial news values but reduces protest coverage to polarized, irrational conflict, obscuring the detailed policy alternatives being proposed by the protesters.

The presence of a conflict news frame depicting police versus protesters is a marginalizing technique used in news media coverage of protest.[11] This conflict frame or protest paradigm is often supported by visual material such as pictures and video. This frame is often accompanied by interviews with protest participants as opposed to leaders, emphasis on the protest event as opposed to the issues, and primary attention to dress/style instead of message content.[12] Research suggests that when the conflict frame is reinforced with visual media such as images of riot police and violence, viewers tend to perceive the protest organization in a more negative light.[13] Negative perceptions were found to be attenuated by "prior attitudes toward protests and protesters," suggesting a complex set of factors that influence audience reception of news media coverage of protest.[14]

News production routines and institutional values are often cited as significant forces that shape news media representations. Journalists and editors place a premium on stories that involve conflict and protests that are inherently about challenges to status quo power structures.[15] Conflict then becomes one of a series of news values that influence story selection, sources, and duration of the issue attention cycle.[16] The combination of these news media practices results in a product that has been referred to as media spectacle. Spectacular news is argued to be a significant force in the continued delegitimization of social movement organizations.[17]

Social Movement Groups Respond to Media Practices

Dramatic images of police confrontations with protesters are the most common media representation of public protest. These images embody the paradox of attracting public attention at the same time that the attention is often directed to the immediate street fight and not to the issues that prompted the protest to begin with. As commercial media became increasingly reliant on the spectacle, activists saw an opportunity to enlist media habits into the service of the movement.

One of the most significant media turns that developed in response to the spectacular conventions of commercial news production was the development of the "tactical image event."[18] Examples of image events emerged in the 1970s when Greenpeace activists in small inflatable Zodiac boats positioned themselves between Japanese whaling ships and the whales being hunted. The dramatic visual differential between the enormous whaling ships and the small boats of the activists created a visual "David and Goliath" metaphor that enlisted the media habit of promoting dramatic images while garnering public attention to the issue of commercial whaling. Similarly, the image needed little explanation and bypassed the gate-keeping processes that so often misquoted movement representatives or chose to quote uninformed activists instead of organizational leaders. Image events are said to be "crystallized philosophical fragments, mind bombs, that work to expand 'the universe of thinkable thoughts.'"[19] The strategy of staging dramatic events proliferated throughout the 1970s and 1980s, particularly among environmental groups. Other examples include Julia Butterfly Hill who sat in a redwood tree in California for over two years,[20] as well as the many direct action strategies developed by the group Earth First! in which protesters lock and chain themselves to heavy machinery such as logging equipment.

In the ever-evolving circuit of appropriation and resistance between elite dominated media and social movement organizations, new strategies were developed to intervene in the explosive potential of the image event. One response to the creation of image events has been the deployment of less-lethal technology against nonviolent civil disobedience. Most common among these are pepper spray and Tasers, both of which are not easily captured by visual media and yet inflict significant pain on the recipients. In October of 1997, police in California swabbed pepper spray into the eyes of three women who were locked together in the office of a government official. This incident marked one of the first cases where less-lethal technology was used to attain compliance from a protester, despite the absence of any security threat.[21] Two years later at the 1999 Seattle WTO protests, the Seattle police exhausted their supply of pepper spray as they indiscriminately sprayed anyone marching in the streets. In the years following Seattle, global justice protesters have gathered at international trade meeting sites around the world, and increasingly, they are met with militarized police forces deploying largely invisible less-lethal technologies. In 2003 at the Miami Free Trade Area of the Americas summit, a combination of preemptive detentions, mass arrests, and overwhelming police force was used against the protesters. This strategy became known as the "Miami Model" and is now standard operating procedure for the world over anytime global trade officials gather.[22]

The images created by pepper spray and Tasers offer a sharp distinction from pervious police actions that included dogs, fire hoses, and billy clubs. In sharp contrast to the public reaction to the police actions during the U.S. civil rights movement of the 1950s and 1960s—where images of police attacking peaceful marchers were broadcast on national television and elicited widespread sympathy for the marchers—policing tactics in the new millennium have intervened in the representation cycle, opening a space where these new pain compliance technologies can be deployed without eliciting significant public reaction. In the absence of media representations that have strong indexical bonds, public reaction to the widespread use of less-lethal technology has been muted. The result is that dissent in public spaces is increasingly met with widespread use of electrical shock and chemical agents to redirect political impulses away from the public arena, outside the view of news media.[23] The inability to capture these pain compliance tools on film or video creates significant barriers to accountability and transparency,[24] and has resulted in a growing list of fatalities associated with Tasers and other less-lethal technologies. The question of representation then becomes a struggle *over* representation, the ability *to* represent and the ability to control access to the site of protest struggle.

Research Gaps and Open Questions: New Contours of Media Representations

One significant response to the appropriation of extreme images has been the proliferation of user-generated content and an increasingly democratized politics of visibility. As urban areas are progressively monitored by state-sponsored video cameras and private surveillance systems (e.g., bank cameras, Google maps documentation), citizens are also steadily empowered to record sound and motion through the proliferation of digital imaging devices. The abundance of user-generated content coupled with networked distribution possibilities (e.g., YouTube, Facebook) has shifted the representational landscape of social movements once again. For example, when Andrew Meyer questioned former U.S. presidential candidate John Kerry at a public forum, he was Tasered by security who found his questions and ensuing resistance unacceptable. The event was captured on a series of cell phones and small video cameras, and these images were circulated around the world in a matter of hours, resulting in the phrase "Don't Taze me Bro" becoming the most memorable quote of 2007.[25]

This sort of user-generated content has been used to challenge official police accounts of Taser incidents (e.g., the 2007 Dziekanski case, Vancouver, BC[26]) and allows citizens to bring their own visual documents to substantiate claims of police brutality or civil rights violations. This dramatic change in the repertoire of representation is challenging old media models and opening new spaces for protest groups to manufacture and distribute their own media as a corrective to the commercial media products that are so often overdetermined by vested interests. As newspapers continue to face business challenges, these new digital tools are empowering citizen journalists to explore new open source media models such as the web sites that make up the Indymedia network (www.indymedia.org) and the many blogs that specialize in niche topics for communities of interest. As these participatory media models develop and become part of the social media landscape, social movement organizations will begin to have more control over—and ability to manipulate—their own representations. This social media will not replace corporate commercial media but rather exist alongside it, suggesting significant new possibilities for the future of media coverage of protest actions and movements.

At the very moment when movements are increasingly able to represent themselves as well as document events on the ground during actual protests, state actors are instituting a series of strategies to limit the impacts of citizen-generated media. Three states in the United States have passed laws outlawing the videotaping of police actions, and in the spring of 2011, Florida passed a law restricting public access to videotape of beatings or death in police custody. These legal responses reveal the power of movements to engage in the politics of self-representation and reflect an attempt to maintain the gatekeeping and framing power of the mass media. As the citizen-generated images from the Arab Spring and Occupy Wall Street protests demonstrate, citizen-generated media is challenging the regimes of representation that have marginalized social movement mobilization over the past century. While this is an ongoing struggle with state agencies working to limit the power and potential of self-representation, new opportunities have emerged and will likely continue to offer protest groups viable media alternatives to the historic limitations of mass media.

Andy Opel is professor in the School of Communication at Florida State University. His research addresses questions of protest, politics, and visibility, with a particular interest in the environmental movement. He coauthored the book *Preempting Dissent: The Politics of an Inevitable Future* (Winnipeg, MB, 2008) with Greg Elmer, and this project was expanded into an open source documentary film. He also directed the award winning documentary, "Beating Justice: The Martin Lee Anderson Story" (Filmmakers Library, 2012), a documentary that explores the power and limitations of visual media.

Notes

1. Stuart Hall, "The Work of Representation," in *Representation: Cultural Representations and Signifying Practices,* ed. S Hall (London, 1997), 15.
2. Ibid., 21–22.
3. Louise Leclair, "Carnivals Against Capital: Rooted in Resistance," in *Representing Resistance: Media, Civil Disobedience and the Global Justice Movement,* ed. A Opel and D Pompper (Westport, CT, 2003), 3–15.
4. See Ben H Bagdikian, *The New Media Monopoly* (Boston, 2004); Robert W McChesney, *The Problem of the Media* (New York, 2004).
5. Robert W McChesney, *Rich Media, Poor Democracy* (Chicago, 1999), 3.
6. Michael P Boyle et al., "The Influence of Level of Deviance and Protest Type on Coverage of Social Protest in Wisconsin from 1960 to 1999," *Mass Communication & Society* 7, no. 2 (2004): 43.
7. Charles N Olien, Phillip J Tichenor, and George A Donahue, "Media Coverage and Social Movements," in *Information Campaigns,* ed. CT Salmon (London, 1989), 160.
8. Pamela J Shoemaker, "Media Treatment of Deviant Political Groups," *Journalism Quarterly* 61, no. 4 (1984): 72.
9. Herbert J Gans, *Deciding What's News: A Study of CBS Evening News, NBC Nightly News, Newsweek and Time* (London, 1980).
10. Marshall McLuhan, *Understanding Media* (New York, 1964).
11. See Tim Baylor, "Media Framing of Movement Protest: The Case of American Indian Protest," *Social Science Journal* 33, no. 3 (1996): 241–56; Douglas M McLeod, "Communicating Deviance: The Effects of Television News Coverage of Social Protest," *Journal of Broadcasting and Electronic Media* 39, no. 4 (1995): 4–19.
12. Todd Gitlin, *The Whole World Is Watching* (Berkeley, CA, 1980), 21–31.
13. Laura M Arpan et al., "News Coverage of Social Protests and the Effects of Photographs and Prior Attitudes," *Mass Communication and Society* 2, no. 1 (2006): 1–20.
14. Ibid., 16.
15. Gitlin, *The Whole World Is Watching,* 28.
16. Gans, *Deciding What's News.*
17. Douglas Kellner, *Media Spectacle* (London, 2003), 2–27.
18. Kevin M DeLuca, *Image Politics: The New Rhetoric of Environmental Activism* (New York, 1999), 3.
19. Cristopher Manes, *Green Rage, Radical Environmentalism and the Unmaking of Civilization* (New York, 1990) quoted in DeLuca, *Image Politics,* 6.
20. Douglas Wolens, *Butterfly* (Berkeley, CA, 2000), DVD, http://www.butterflyfilm.net.
21. Andy Opel, "Punishment Before Prosecution: Pepper Spray as Postmodern Repression," in *Representing Resistance,* ed. A Opel and D Pompper (Westport, CT, 2003), 44–60.
22. Greg Elmer and Andy Opel, *Preempting Dissent: The Politics of an Inevitable Future* (Winnipeg, MB, 2008), 29–41.

23. Heidi Bogosian, *Punishing Protest: Government Tactics That Suppress Free Speech*, National Lawyers Guild report, 2007, http://www.nationallawyersguild.org/NLG_Punishing_Protest_2007.pdf.
24. Elmer and Opel, *Preempting Dissent*, 29–41.
25. University of Florida Taser Incident, http://en.wikipedia.org/wiki/University_of_Florida_Taser_incident.
26. Robert Dziekański Taser incident, http://en.wikipedia.org/wiki/Robert_Dzieka%C5%84ski.

Recommended Reading

Boykoff, Jules. *The Suppression of Dissent: How the State and Mass Media Squelch US American Social Movements*. New York, 2006. Uses social movement theory and media analysis to demonstrate a pattern of suppression of contentious protest movements.

D'Arcus, Bruce. *Boundaries of Dissent: Protest and State Power in the Media Age*. New York, 2006. Using an interdisciplinary approach, D'Arcus explores the power and limitations of new media to challenge the conventions of mass media marginalization of protest movements.

DeLuca, Kevin M. *Image Politics: The New Rhetoric of Environmental Activism*. Mahwah, NJ, 1999. DeLuca defines the term "image event" and, in the process, reveals the visual strategies environmentalists used to get media coverage of their protest actions.

Gitlin, Todd. *The Whole World Is Watching*. Berkeley, CA, 1980. Gitlin documents the power of news media discourse to either celebrate or marginalize a social movement.

Chapter 34

Archives

Hanno Balz

General Definition of the Term

"Archives and museums are mirrors of power and cosmologies," emphasized
Australian historian Greg Denian.[1] Indeed, recently it has been discussed
how the process of selection and professional neglect structures our collective memory of the past. But then—without forgetting there is no remembrance—the selection helps focusing on the significance of the filed material.
Thus archives, being sites of collective memories, of identic allocation, and of
heuristic evidence, are organized by hegemony, or the dominant (political)
view.

General Cultural Functions

In the case of protest cultures, it can repeatedly be observed "that memories
of social conflict can be a powerful force in political discourse."[2] At first all
memories are recollections and reconstructions of the past while the main
form of collective memory is narrative. Maurice Halbwachs, who developed
the concept of collective memory during the first half of the twentieth century, argued that collective memory is always social memory.[3] Memories
of the individual develop in interaction with others—they emerge from
the grounds of sociality.[4] Therefore, collective memories are less an official
canon, a story of the past that never changes, but a social practice in the
production of meaning. So collective memory has more in common with
dominant memories, which are those that are widely available in the public

sphere. "Collective memories are the stories that everyone knows about the past, even if not everyone believes the story."[5]

Methodologically, a wider concept of archive should be regarded as being a combination of material culture and historical semantics. This includes historical and present discourses.

Michel Foucault described discourse as a group of statements for which conditions of existence are definable. A discourse is also a historical agency or an archive of historical statements. Foucault describes his concept of an archive as a system that governs the appearance of statements as historical events. The archive of a society, culture, or civilization, therefore, is a system of formation or transformation of statements and is characterized by discontinuity in that it tells us what we can no longer say.[6]

Role in Protest Cultures

During recent years, a historization of the global protest movements of 1968 could be observed. Thus, researchers pointed out the difficulties with archives as they represent collective memory: "For the foreseeable future, the availability and access to source material related to the 1960s will continue to pose a serious challenge to archivists and historians."[7]

Newer archival guidelines now try to define what exactly should be preserved. Still, new criteria for the collection of primary sources will have to be developed to handle the uneven and often sketchy documentation. A self-reflective and critical evaluation of official historical tradition is still in its early stages. In recent years, there have been approaches to deal with the problematic archival situations, though. This is the case primarily with German archivists who organized two conferences on the aforementioned questions: In 2007 the Landesarchiv Baden-Würtemberg hold a colloquium on traditions, sources, and written records of 1968.[8] On the German Historikertag in 2006, a panel hosted by the German Archivist Organization focused on sources and interpretations of the antinuclear power movements of the 1970s.[9]

Official sources generally reflect the institutions' antagonistic role toward political protest and its measures of containment and suppression. Therefore, written records can primarily be found in the files of the judiciary and the political departments of the police as well as the intelligence services. It is sufficient to say that sources of the latter institutions are mostly not available to the public even after decades.

Other (semi-)institutional archives offer some potential on the research of protest movements as, for example, those institutions that have been affected by the multitude of movements from the inside, that is, universities, unions, churches, and even company archives.[10] Here, the research results heavily depend on the records management of the particular institution or company.

Although some rethinking at the official archives can be observed lately, the main archival resources for protest research are the archives of the movement itself and some specialized archives that are mostly run by academic or private institutes.[11] For the latter, the most prominent examples are the International Institute of Social History in Amsterdam with its extensive collection and a tradition that dates back until the 1920s, and for Germany, the Hamburger Institut für Sozialforschung, which collects a wide range of material from the movements and obtains numerous private inheritances. More orientated to the history of working-class movements and Communist organizations is the International Association of Labour History Institutions, which is also located in Amsterdam.[12]

The majority of the resources on protest movements offer the nearly countless numbers of movement archives. These mostly nonprofit and collective institutions are very helpful for research on the different movements. A clear distinction between archive and library can most often not be drawn here, and generally, the movement archives focus on particular issues like women's rights, internationalism, antiracism, antimilitarism, ecology, anarchism, direct action, militancy, and more. Yet most of the social movements, by contrast to political parties for example, are short-lived and often unaware of their own history. Also, these movements do not show much interest in collecting and filing their written records.[13]

Theoretical and Empirical Research Perspectives: The Media as Archives

Taking a broader approach toward archives into consideration, and therewith following Foucault, the media coverage of protest and social movements should be regarded an important part of the archive. Protest movements of the twentieth and twenty-first century heavily focused on media attention, and thus media coverage on protest represents important material for research. Todd Gitlin emphasized the role of the media for social movements, although being critical about mass media's ideological effects: "Mass media define the public significance of movement events or, by blanking them out, actively deprive them of larger significance. Media images also become implicant in a movement's self-image; media certify leaders and officially noteworthy 'personalities.'"[14]

To use, for example, newspaper coverage as sources is a necessary task in research on protest cultures. By now, a range of newspapers and weeklies offer Internet access of their archives, as for example the *New York Times, Der Spiegel,* and *The Times.* Still it is mandatory to evaluate the media's framing on events and issues.

Research Gaps and Open Questions

The evaluation of the archival problems still seems to pose a research gap as well as a challenge to an overall archival policy. Because of the tradition of a scene of various movement archives in Germany, that has been recently documented in a commented guide by Bernd Hüttner,[15] the debate on archives of protest movements seem to dominate the academic discourse.

Considering the history of social movements and protest cultures, it can be stated that official archives are lacking continuous collections of publications from nonparliamentary opposition groups. This is lamentable because this material, that usually has small circulation, represents important sources on the understanding of societal change. Furthermore, its knowledge proved to be mandatory for any critical appropriation of the history of political protest by today's activists.[16]

As it can be seen, a critical approach toward structures of hegemony in all the archival sources should be regarded as essential.

Hanno Balz is visiting assistant professor for German and European history at the Johns Hopkins University, Baltimore, Maryland. His fields of research are the history of social movements, media and discourse history, Cold War studies, history of anti-Communism, and the Shoah and Nazi rule. Recent publications include *Europäische Protestbewegungen der 1980er Jahre [European Protest Movements of the 1980s]*, edited with J-H Friedrichs (Bonn, 2012), and "Throwing Bombs in the Consciousness of the Masses. The Red Army Faction and Its Mediality," in *Media and Revolt: Strategies and Performances from the 1960s to the Present*, edited by K Fahlenbrach, E Sivertsen, and R Werenskjold (Oxford, 2014).

Notes

1. Greg Dening, "A Poetic for Histories," in *Performances,* ed. G Dening (Chicago, 1996), 35–63.

2. Jill A Edy, *Troubled Pasts. News and the Collective Memory of Social Unrest* (Philadelphia, PA, 2006), 2.
3. Maurice Halbwachs, *The Collective Memory* (New York, 1980).
4. Aleida Assmann and Jan Assmann, "Das Gestern im Heute. Medien und soziales Gedächtnis," in *Die Wirklichkeit der Medien,* ed. K Merten, SJ Schmidt, and S Weischenberg (Opladen, 1994), 114–77.
5. Edy, *Troubled Pasts,* 3.
6. Michel Foucault, *Archäologie des Wissens* (Frankfurt, 1981), 187.
7. Philipp Gassert and Pavel A Richter, *1968 in West Germany. A Guide to Sources and Literature* (Washington, DC, 1997), 5.
8. "1968—Was bleibt von einer Generation? Überlieferung und Überlieferungs-bildung zu einer nicht alltäglichen Zeit," Kolloquium des Landesarchivs Baden-Württemberg, February 2007. Documented in *"1968" und die "Anti-Atomkraft-Bewegung der 1970er Jahre": Überlieferungsbildung und Forschung im Dialog,* ed. R Kretzschmar, C Rehm, and A Pilger (Stuttgart, 2008).
9. "Dokumente und Deutungen zur Anti-Atomkraft-Bewegung der 1970er Jahre," September 2006. Documented in *"1968" und die "Anti-Atomkraft-Bewegung der 1970er Jahre"*; see also *H-Soz-u-Kult,* 9 April 2009, http://hsozkult.geschichte.hu-berlin.de/tagungsberichte/id=1181.
10. Clemens Rehm, "1968—Was bleibt von einer Generation?," in *"1968" und die "Anti-Atomkraft-Bewegung der 1970er Jahre,"* 37–61.
11. Bernd Hüttner, *Archive von Unten* (Neu-Ulm, 2003), 7.
12. Further important archives are listed.
13. Hüttner, *Archive von Unten,* 10.
14. Todd Gitlin, *The Whole World Is Watching. Mass Media in the Making & Unmaking of the New Left* (Berkeley, CA, 1980), 3.
15. Hüttner, *Archive von Unten.*
16. Ibid., 7.

Recommended Reading

Edy, Jill A. *Troubled Pasts. News and the Collective Memory of Social Unrest.* Philadelphia, PA, 2006. This book offers a fruitful approach toward using mass media as an archival source for the research on protest cultures. It also focuses on the usage of the past for today's political discourse.

Foucault, Michel. *The Archeology of Knowledge.* London, 1982. The canonical text for the understanding of how discourse resembles a system of meaning, that Foucault describes in its overall quality as being an archive.

Gitlin, Todd. *The Whole World Is Watching. Mass Media in the Making & Unmaking of the New Left.* Berkeley, CA, 1980. A modern classic for every-one studying or researching protest movements and its connection to mass media. A critical, theoretically ambitious study on the U.S. student move-ment of the 1960s.

Hüttner, Bernd. *Archive von Unten*. Neu-Ulm, 2003. Hüttner delivers a very
detailed list of nonofficial archives, mainly those run by social movement
organizations themselves. He offers a brief and critical introduction as well.

Assorted Internet Archives:

International Institute of Social History, http://www.iisg.nl.

International Association of Labour History Institutions, http://www.ialhi.org.

Hamburger Institut für Sozialforschung, http://www.his-online.de.

FrauenMediaTurm—Das feministische Archiv und Dokumentationszentrum,
http://www.frauenmediaturm.de, important collection especially on the
early feminist movements in Western Germany.

Free Speech Movement Digital Archive, http://bancroft.berkeley.edu/collections/
fsm.html.

Libraries at the University of California at Berkeley, http://www.lib.berkeley.edu.

The oral history collection at Columbia University in New York, http://library.
columbia.edu/content/libraryweb/indiv/ccoh/our_work.html.

The special collections at Harvard University, http://lib.harvard.edu/archives/
index.html.

The Hoover Institution at Stanford University, http://www.hoover.org/
library-and-archives.

Mémoires du '68, http://www.media68.net/eng/archivi/memorie.htm; see also:
Collectif et Michelle Perrot, eds, *Mémoires de 68. Guide des sources d'une
histoire à faire* (Paris 1993). Extensive and important collection of media
and recollections on 1960s and 1970s social movements in France, in collaboration with Bibliothèque de Documentation Internationale Contem-
poraine, Nanterre.

Archivio storico della Nuova sinistra "Marco Pezzi" (Bologna), http://www.
comune.bologna.it/iperbole/asnsmp/, founded in 1989 the archive holds a
collection of written and audiovisual material from the Italian radical left
from the 1960s up to today.

Guida alle fonti per la storia dei movimenti in Italia (1966–1978), http://www.
archivi.beniculturali.it/DGA-free/Strumenti/Strumenti_CLXII.pdf,
Extensive guide to all archival resources on social movements in Italy
between 1966 and 1978.

London School of Economics Archives, http://www.lse.ac.uk/library/archive. Collection of the British CND and the Hall-Carpenter archives on gay and
lesbian rights.

Part VI

Pragmatics of Protest

Protest Practices

Chapter 35

Uttering

Constanze Spiess

General Introduction to the Topic/Definition of Terms

Based on an action-oriented concept of language, the linguistic unit *utterance* or rather the speech act *uttering* can be described as an action strategy that is arranged in a certain pattern. Thus, utterances are social acts and practices that interact with other nonlinguistic practices in a certain sedimented pattern. They are sub-elements of action sequences in larger action units like different text types or communicative genres that enable establishing a communicative meaning.

Linguistic research about the action potential of linguistic utterances is quite diverse. All the more, it is astounding that so far there have been hardly any linguistic surveys about the function of linguistic utterances and linguistic action strategies in protest communication in its diverse shapes. Acts of protest that are performed in the general public are part of the political system and therefore belong to the field of politolinguistics, which deals with linguistic utterances as actions, strategies, and patterns.[1] So far there are no linguistic studies that address linguistic utterances exclusively and that systematically analyze these utterances with regard to their action potential in the wide range of protest communication. Rather, previous surveys refer to action strategies and linguistic action patterns in the context of other research questions—incidentally or implicitly. What all analyses dealing with the language of protest so far have in common is an action-theoretical concept of language in so far as the communication forms and communicative genres of protest are seen as action units and social practices.

In protest communication, utterances serve as a means to establish or to constitute common ground, group identities, or socially shared worlds. At the same time, this implies that not all utterances or rather *actions of uttering* are formulated in a solidary and integrating way. Instead they can also function as dissociation markers; in a way they have to establish dissent so that a group can be seen as a collective identity being able to articulate its interests. The fact that there are protest groups or communities that utter their protest together and that can make themselves heard by this group affiliation is central to the formulation of protest. By expressing affiliation to these groups, protest communities also establish themselves performatively and discursively in protest forums of the so-called new media, whose audience seems to be rather limited (cf. opportunities of participating in online protest actions for Greenpeace). The term "protest communication" as it is applied in the following always implies the background assumption that it is collective identities that formulate protest and that—by formulating this protest—construct or constitute themselves as a group. Identity, social and collective identity, constructions take place by language, exactly by performing protest actions together.[2] Here, identity is not treated as a fixed entity, but it is rather seen as a dynamic process of an ongoing identity formation.[3] Individual, social, or collective identities or group identities form an interdependent relationship, which is indispensable and inseparable, and therefore constitutes one another.[4] Collective identity in protest communities then means the permanent construction of collective identity with linguistic and nonlinguistic protest actions and thus the performativity of protest. Correspondingly, linguistic utterances have a decisive share in constructing collective identities.

In this context, various extremely heterogeneous characteristics of linguistic utterances become central: group orientation (self positioning and other positioning), stabilizing the "in group" by attributing to one's own group in a positive way, destabilizing the "out group" through stigmatizations, the general public as an arena for protest communication, dissent orientation and consensus orientation, dependence on the publicity in the media, recipient design.

Relevance for Protest Cultures

In democracies, the linguistic utterance of protest belongs to the stable repertoire of political modes of communication. Here, the linguistic utterance of protest manifests itself in different ways, and it can have diverse functions. Looking at the different possible expressions and communication

forms that protest protagonists use—like, for example, protest posters, banners, wall newspapers, the communicative form of the demonstration, sit-ins,
teach-ins, rallies, speeches, the communicative practice of discussion, the
workers' strike, hunger strike, student strike, flyers, stickers, and so on—the
linguistic utterance is a basic constant in the different communicative forms
of protest, the chosen communicative genre and text types. Depending on
the communicative situation, the linguistic utterance takes up a different
meaning and function. Central functions of utterances in protest communication can be captured as language strategies. There are fundamental
strategies from which one can deduce more specific action patterns or which
serve these fundamental action patterns: here, *demanding* and *criticizing*
form central strategies that are outward-oriented. The protest group turns
against predominant practices and regulations and—for a start—wants to
draw attention to its position in order to convince others of this position
eventually, in order to gain power and to implement their political ideas.
The function of protest utterances lies furthermore in articulating interests,
public relations, criticism; in advertising protest aims; or in uncovering and
denouncing deficits, attracting attention with expressive and appellative
speech acts (e.g., chants like "Ho Ho Ho Chi Minh" in the student protests of the 1960s in West Germany or the "Wir sind das Volk" chants in
the 1989 Monday demonstrations in Leipzig, former German Democratic
Republic (GDR) or using highly evaluative "stigma words" on flags, also see
Greenpeace's medial staging practices), which often come up in the context
of larger protest actions.

On the one hand, it is persuasion that matters to the protagonists of
protest on a general level; for the most part protest communication has a
persuasive language mode, which can be allocated to at least one of the two
named action patterns. On the other hand, the protesters want to express
problems and attract attention regarding these problems, and they want to
solidarize with the protest group.

Mostly, linguistic utterances of protest constitute themselves in the
public sphere. In order to be heard and seen, they rely on the media public.

Here, one has to pay special attention to the role of mass media with
their specific system-inherent logic of binary encoding (attention/non-
attention) and the principles of selection or rather new factors (conflict
value, prestige value, news value) connected with this logic.[5] In order to be
recognized by mass media, protest actions have to adhere to these principles
or rather have to aim at constructing this news factor, which—of course—
has effects on the choice of linguistic utterance strategies.[6] Uncommon,
expressive language actions are preferred because one can attract attention
with this.

Austin's speech act theory is the origin of an action-based typology of protest utterances.[7] Austin states that in social rituals, "the uttering of the sentence is, or is part of, the doing of an action, which ... would normally be described as saying something." Social reality is constituted through language.[8]

Eventually, the individual linguistic protest actions all serve the purposes of solidarization, polarization, and social change. The action patterns can be differentiated according to the communication situation (monological, dialogic-interactional, degree of publicity, participants, communication form, medium of communication, spatial proximity, spatial distance, temporal structure, political system, etc.), according to the intended aim, the topic as well as the expectations of those who are part of the action. Utterances can be formulated orally or in writing, they can emerge in or be a constitutive part of different larger linguistic units like for example texts, communicative genres, or communication forms as posters, banners, or inscriptions on clothing and things.

The factors influence the linguistic form of the protest utterances that correspondingly manifest themselves in linguistically different ways. The following are central and fundamental actions of protest communication. This list does not make a claim to be complete.

Demanding, provoking criticizing, making counterproposals, give explanations, prescribe, admonishing someone, charging, accusing, influencing political decisions, threatening, warning, evaluating (increase or decrease value), stigmatizing antagonists (by semantic specifications, e.g., negative contextualization of the lexemes *party, state machinery,* or *police machinery* in the 1968 protest movement), convincing, attracting attention, dramatizing, raising the willingness to consent, solidarizing, appealing, disturbing the institutional/ritual order, reevaluating situations and signs, legitimizing, delegitimizing, construction reality, violating norms and rules, and scandalizing (environmental protest activities, protests against nuclear power stations, etc.).

Depending on the communication situation, these actions are accomplished in different ways. Especially protest in totalitarian systems is realized with different linguistic means compared with protest in democratic systems.[9] The language actions are realized or supported linguistically by coining concepts, by negotiating meaning, by establishing a competition of terms, and by using a competition of meanings, by willful strategies of reevaluation,[10] thus through so-called semantic fights.[11] The individual utterance actions are positioned in a dense network of relationships with one another: this is how, for instance, provocative actions (cheering and cries of boo, insults) or actions of delegitimization (questioning of competence) and so on disturb the institutional order.[12]

Linguistic strategies can be formulated explicitly or implicitly, directly or indirectly, they can be applied offensively or subversively. They are oriented either internally (e.g., as an appeal for solidarity to the group) or externally (to an out group).

Historical Aspects

In the canon of linguistics, politolinguistics has emerged in the second half of the twentieth century as a subfield of sociolinguistics and has established itself as a pragmatic discipline in the canon of all subfields of linguistics. Thus, the analysis of protest communication as a repertoire of political communication has to be placed in this branch of linguistics. These protest strategies have been investigated since the second half of the twentieth century, to be more precise, since the *pragmatic turn* has taken place in linguistics.

The linguistic discourse analysis based on Foucault, which draws upon central ideas from the field of cultural studies and which has been well-established for some years now, offers an extremely productive method for analyzing public and political communication, thus including protest communication. It is distinguished by its context-sensitive procedure as far as it analyzes the linguistic actions and strategies as linguistic utterances, which are embedded in larger action contexts and texts as well as in non-linguistic social practices. A central role is ascribed to this embeddedness with reference to attributions of meaning and function or the constitution of functions.

So far, nothing can be said as to when the linguistic utterance strategies have evolved as protest strategies since there are no studies on this. Yet, one can assume that—because they are so fundamental—they have existed as long as there is protest communication. What also remains unanswered is if there have been change processes in their concrete realization; this can, however, be understood as a stimulus for further research.

State of Research in Related Social Movement Research and Interdisciplinary Perspectives for the Analysis of Protest Cultures

So far, a linguistic perspective has been followed in just a few studies in the research on protest and movements in the social sciences.[13] Studies from a media-scientific, communication-scientific, communication-historic, or from a historic angle have analyzed different aspects of the communicative practice in which linguistic utterances play a role.[14]

Protest utterances are a complex phenomenon that ideally should be analyzed from different perspectives: protests are constituted through language (linguistics), they are distributed and constructed through media (media science and communication science), they take place in the public sphere (social sciences, research on publicity), they are, among others, carried and staged by social movements (social-scientific research on movements), and they are a fundamental part of our democratic constitutional state (political science). That is why the results of the various disciplines are highly relevant for the description of the linguistic mark-up of protest communication since linguistic actions rely on extra-linguistic actions, and they can only constitute meaning with reference to one another.

Therefore, linguistic analyses of linguistic protest utterances are always already interdisciplinary as far as they use a pragmatic concept of language as their basis. Thus, a discourse-analytic approach is interdisciplinary as such and focuses on multiple research levels.[15] However, the individual disciplines could indeed collaborate to a greater extent by cross-linking to get convincing results.

Research Gaps and Open Questions

Concerning methodological and theoretical aspects, current research on political language use shows that a discourse-analytic approach to the language material can be quite fruitful; it should therefore be applied to protest communication to an even greater extent. On a methodological level, a discourse-analytic approach can be followed qualitatively as a holistic multi-level approach[16] or quantitatively as a corpus-linguistic approach.[17] Whereas the quantitative approach can describe surface phenomena in an optimal way, the qualitative approach offers the opportunity to ask for the functionality and semanticity of linguistic phenomena. With regard to the analysis of different protest movements and their action strategies, much more work has to be done from a linguistic perspective: peace movement, feminist movement, student protests, environmental movement, protest communication in the GDR, antiglobalization movement, protest movements of past centuries, and so on, are all fields of study in which linguistic utterances are of central importance. Moreover, here it becomes apparent that protest actions have to be analyzed in a wider context, that is, in the discursive context, which enables us to see them as part of complex discursive events just as analyses of the armament discourse,[18] the nuclear energy discourse,[19] the 1968 movement,[20] or—from a historical perspective—as analyses of the language use of different groups in the Mainz Republic[21] have shown. Linguistic manifestations of protest cultures on the Internet and the new communication forms connected to this have also not been considered adequately from a linguistic point of view. Future projects could therefore use discourse-analytic research methods to take into account and to describe these movements and their pragmasemiotic aspects. This opens a wide linguistic research field, which can lead to interesting results in cooperation with other disciplines.

Constanze Spiess is postdoctoral researcher at Karl-Franzens-University Graz, Austria. One of her main research topics is the analysis of political discourses. She is author of a book on theory and methodology of linguistic discourse analysis: *Diskurshandlungen. Theorie und Methode linguistischer Diskursanalyse am Beispiel der Bioethikdebatte* (Berlin, 2011). Together with Susanne Günthner and Dagmar Hüpper, she is editor of the book *Genderlinguistik. Sprachliche Konstruktionen von Geschlechtsidentität* (Berlin, 2012).

Notes

1. Joachim Scharloth, "Die Sprache der Revolte: Linke Wörter und avantgardistische Kommunikationsstile," in *1968: Handbuch zur Kultur- und Mediengeschichte der Studentenbewegung*, ed. M Klimke and J Scharloth (Bonn, 2008), 223–34; Kathrin Fahlenbrach, *Protestinszenierungen: Visuelle Kommunikation und Kollektive Identitäten in Protestbewegungen* (Opladen, 2002); Matthias Jung, *Öffentlichkeit und Sprachwandel: Zur Geschichte des Diskurses über die Atomenergie* (Opladen, 1994); Martin Wengeler, *Die Sprache der Aufrüstung: Zur Geschichte der Rüstungsdiskussion nach 1945* (Wiesbaden, 1992); Philipp Dreesen, "Zwischen herrschendem Diskurs und Gegendiskurs: Nicht-explizite Widerstandsaussagen in der DDR: Drei Thesen zur Diskurslinguistik," in *Diskurslinguistik—Systemlinguistik. Theorien—Texte—Fallstudien: Stettiner Beiträge zur Sprachwissenschaft*, vol. 3, ed. R Lipczuk et al. (Hamburg, 2010).
2. Cf. Alberto Melucci, "The Process of Collective Identity," in *Social Movements and Culture,* ed. H Johnston and B Klandermans (Minneapolis, MN, 1995), 41–63.
3. Ibid.
4. Cf. Dieter Rucht, "Kollektive Identität: Konzeptionelle Überlegungen zu einem Desiderat der Bewegungsforschung," *Neue Soziale Bewegungen. Sonderheft Soziale Bewegungen und kollektive Identität* 1 (1995): 9–23; Oliver Schmidtke, "Kollektive Identität in der politischen Mobilisierung territorialer Bewegungen: Eine Analytische Perspektive," *Neue Soziale Bewegungen: Sonderheft Soziale Bewegungen und kollektive Identität* 1 (1995): 24–31; Lutz Niethammer, *Kollektive Identität: Heimliche Quellen einer unheimlichen Konjunktur* (Reinbek, 2000).
5. Cf. Niklas Luhmann, "Öffentliche Meinung," *Politische Vierteljahresschrift* XI (1970): 2–28; Niklas Luhmann, "Veränderungen im System gesellschaftlicher Kommunikation und die Massenmedien," in *Soziologische Aufklärung*, vol. 3,

ed. N Luhmann (Opladen, 1981), 309–20; Niklas Luhmann, "Gesellschaftliche Komplexität und öffentliche Meinung," in *Soziologische Aufklärung*, vol. 5, ed. N Luhmann (Opladen, 1990), 170–82; Cf. Friedhelm Neidhardt, ed., *Öffentlichkeit, öffentliche Meinung, soziale Bewegungen: Sonderheft 34 der Kölner Zeitschrift für Soziologie und Sozialpsychologie* (1994); Friedhelm Neidhardt, "Einleitung: Öffentlichkeit, öffentliche Meinung, soziale Bewegungen," *Öffentlichkeit, öffentliche Meinung, soziale Bewegungen: Sonderheft 34 der Kölner Zeitschrift für Soziologie und Sozialpsychologie* (1994): 7–41; Cf. Kathrin Fahlenbrach, "Protest als politische Kommunikation in der Medienöffentlichkeit," in *Handbuch Politisches Marketing*, ed. VJ Kreyher (Baden-Baden, 2004),129–41.

6. Sigrid Baringhorst, "Zur Mediatisierung des politischen Protests. Von der Institutionen- zur 'Greenpeace-Demokratie'?," in *Politikvermittlung und Demokratie in der Mediengesellschaft*, ed. U Sarcinelli (Bonn, 1998), 326–42.

7. Cf. John L Austin, *How to Do Things with Words* (Oxford, 1962).

8. Peter Berger and Thomas Luckmann, *Die gesellschaftliche Konstruktion der Wirklichkeit*, 20th ed. (Frankfurt, 2004).

9. For protest in the GDR, see Dreesen, "Zwischen herrschendem Diskurs und Gegendiskurs."

10. Cf. Scharloth, "Die Sprache der Revolte."

11. Cf. Ekkehard Felder, "Semantische Kämpfe in Wissensdomänen: Eine Einführung in Benennungs-, Bedeutungs- und Sachverhaltsfixierungs-Konkurrenzen," in *Semantische Kämpfe: Macht und Sprache in den Wissenschaften*, ed. E Felder (Berlin, 2006), 13–46; Cf. Josef Klein, "Wortschatz, Wortkampf, Wortfelder in der Politik," in *Politische Semantik: Bedeutungsanalytische und sprachkritische Beiträge zur politischen Sprachverwendung*, ed. J Klein (Opladen, 1989), 3–50; Cf. Heiko Girnth, *Sprache und Sprachverwendung in der Politik* (Tübingen, 2002).

12. Cf. Scharloth, "Die Sprache der Revolte."

13. Sigrid Baringhorst, Veronika Kneip, and Johanna Niesyto, "Wandel und Kontinuität von Protestkulturen seit den 1960er Jahren: Eine Analyse ausgewählter Anti-Corporate Campaigns," in *Politik mit dem Einkaufswagen. Unternehmen und Konsumenten als Bürger in der globalen Mediengesellschaft*, ed. S Baringhorst et al. (Bielefeld, 2007), 109–36; Sveta Klimova, "Speech Act Theory and Protest Discourse: Normative Claims in the Communicative Repertoire of Three Russian Movements," in *Culture, Social Movement and Protest*, ed. H Johnston (Farnham, 2009), 105–33.

14. Cf. among others Fahlenbrach, *Protestinszenierungen*; Fahlenbrach, "Protest als politische Kommunikation in der Medienöffentlichkeit"; Scharloth, "Die Sprache der Revolte"; Joachim Scharloth, *1968: Eine Kommunikationsgeschichte* (Munich, 2011); M Klimke and J Scharloth, eds, *1968: Handbuch zur Kultur- und Mediengeschichte der Studentenbewegung* (Bonn, 2008).

15. Cf. Constanze Spiess, *Diskurshandlungen: Theorie und Methode linguistischer Diskursanalyse am Beispiel der Bioethikdebatte* (Berlin, 2011).

16. See for instance Spiess, *Diskurshandlungen*.

17. See for instance Noah Bubenhofer, *Sprachgebrauchsmuster: Korpuslinguistik als Methode der Diskurs- und Kulturanalyse* (Berlin, 2009).

18. Wengeler, *Die Sprache der Aufrüstung*.

19. Jung, *Öffentlichkeit und Sprachwandel.*
20. Scharloth, *1968: Eine Kommunikationsgeschichte.*
21. Joachim Herrgen, *Die Sprache der Mainzer Republik (1792/93): Historisch-semantische Untersuchungen zur politischen Kommunikation* (Tübingen, 2000).

Recommended Reading

Baringhorst, Sigrid, Veronika Kneip, and Johanna Niesyto. "Wandel und Kontinuität von Protestkulturen seit den 1960er Jahren. Eine Analyse ausgewählter Anti-Corporate Campaigns." In *Politik mit dem Einkaufswagen. Unternehmen und Konsumenten als Bürger in der globalen Mediengesellschaft,* edited by S Baringhorst, V Kneip, J Niesyto, and A März, 109–36. Bielefeld, 2007. Explores questions of changes in protest with regard to its content as well as to its formal aspects. In this study, the authors also refer to the linguistic characteristics of protest.

Klimova, Sveta. "Speech Act Theory and Protest Discourse: Normative Claims in the Communicative Repertoire of Three Russian Movements." In *Culture, Social Movement and Protest,* edited by H Johnston, 105–33. Farnham, 2009. Presents central linguistic actions within the protest of the Russian protest movements from 1995 to 2006 from a socioscientific perspective and with a normative claim. Her approach is informed by Searle's speech act theory.

Melucci, Alberto. "The Process of Collective Identity." In *Social Movements and Culture,* edited by H Johnston and B Klandermans, 41–63. Minneapolis, MN, 1995. Shows how the constitution of identity, which is a basic parameter of protest communication, works/operates.

Scharloth, Joachim. "Die Sprache der Revolte: Linke Wörter und avantgardistische Kommunikationsstile." In *1968. Handbuch zur Kultur- und Mediengeschichte der Studentenbewegung,* edited by M Klimke and J Scharloth, 223–34. Bonn, 2008. Emphasizes the relevance of evaluative used words as elements of communication style.

Chapter 36

Street Protest

Matthias Reiss

General Introduction to the Topic/Definition of Terms

The "street" is the generic term for all public spaces in a village, town, or city. It is the quintessential public sphere as it is open to everybody. Street protest describes any expressive manifestation of claim making in this arena. Initially deplored as mob rule, a marker of disorder or prelude to revolution, street protest began to enjoy growing legitimacy from the nineteenth century onward. It is now widely viewed as a human and democratic right (covered by the freedom of assembly) as well as an opportunity for the people to express their will and to participate in the political process.

Street protest requires few resources, is likely to create attention and publicity due to its disruptive effects on urban routines or the state's countermobilization, and strengthens the identity, cohesion, and profile of the organizations behind it. Pioneered in the industrializing countries of the West, it has now spread to all parts of the world. Even though the digital revolution has created new forums for protest, the street remains an important "mass medium" for those who feel that their voices and concerns are marginalized or that they are excluded from the political decision-making process.[1]

The two most common forms of street protest, which often appear in combination, are the march and the rally. Other patterns of street protest, such as the vigil, blockade, sit-in, human chain, torch procession, or rave can be viewed as variations of these two basic forms. Street protest is usually collective, but there are exceptions, such as the protest of Brian Haw in London's Parliament Square from 2001 to 2011 or the public self-incineration of Buddhist monks in Vietnam, Tibet, and other countries. Other variants indicate dissent without the physical presence of protesters in the street. Boycotts of official events, collective noise-making from private homes that fills the streets with sound instead of bodies, or clandestine change of urban landscapes by guerrilla gardeners, graffiti artists, or other groups belong into this category.

Relevance for Protest Cultures

Street protest uses symbolic action to influence supporters, opponents, and bystanders. It is shaped by as well as influences the political, social, and cultural context from which it emerges. Street protest serves as a way of publicly voicing a claim and soliciting support and is usually part of a sustained campaign, the social movement. Even though participants often have no expectations of having their grievances addressed immediately, street protest offers movement organizations concrete benefits. It allows them to use the street as stage to showcase themselves, their beliefs, and their ability to mobilize, control, and direct their supporters. Marches and rallies are the visible enactment of a movement's essence and a language through which they communicate with other groups in the public sphere. They are therefore highly relevant for anyone interested in protest cultures. Street protest events are influenced by previous national and international protest actions. They are by necessity innovative as organizers need to create and maintain media attention as well as react to efforts to marginalize or neutralize their actions. They are dynamic processes in which ordinary people become political actors and engage in activities that can change society or history. The use of the street symbolizes exclusion from or lack of standing in established political structures. However, it also challenges this status through the display of "worthiness, unity, numbers, and commitment."[2] Street protest therefore allows us to study how notions of legitimacy, entitlement, identity, and order are negotiated in the public sphere.

Historical Aspects

Preindustrial forms of collective public protest, such as riots, attacks on buildings, or shaming ceremonies, already included a great deal of ritual and expressive symbolism. However, they were mostly parochial in nature, particular to single communities and concerned with local issues. In the late eighteenth century, a new repertoire of protest began to emerge in reaction to the advancement of Capitalism and its impact on socioeconomic relations, the centralization of power at the national level, and the emergence of a public sphere. Pioneered in Great Britain and North America, these new forms of protest performances were national/cosmopolitan, modular, and autonomous in character and accompanied by a shift from often violent direct action designed to bring immediate results to overwhelmingly indirect and cumulative action designed to express support or opposition to a particular program.[3] Although these new forms of protest performances quickly spread and were widely disseminated by the middle of the nineteenth century, "general public meetings and street demonstrations on behalf of self-defined interests took a long time to gain acceptance."[4] The authorities' hostility frequently forced protesters to hold meetings outside of urban centers or use established and accepted forms of public assembly, such as funeral corteges, religious processions, or artisans' parades, for their purposes.

In the growing cities of the industrial era, the street became widely associated not only with vice and crime, but also with destructive "mobs" or "crowds". Street protesters tried to distance themselves from this image by emphasizing discipline, organization, and respectability. Trade unionists, for example, marched in ordered ranks and columns, dressed in their best clothes, and displayed tools or banners of their trade or emblems of working-class organizations. Women, if they participated, marched in separate blocks. In the street, the labor movement presented itself as a class in action. Order and discipline did not imitate the military, but intended to demonstrate the movement's intention and ability to create an alternative order of society.

Starting in 1890, the annual May Day demonstrations became an opportunity to practice these patterns in a celebration of international working-class solidarity on a global scale. Although national labor movements adapted the event to their respective needs and traditions, the general template remained the same and provided the model for countless other marches, for example those of the suffragettes. The latter tried to address the issue of respectability by using pageantry that stressed the femininity and virtue of the participants, and in some countries organized carriage or motorcar processions to avoid the stigma of walking in the streets. The unemployed often sought legitimacy by organizing their marches around the ancient and established right to present petitions, by placing themselves in the tradition of Christian pilgrimages and sacrifice, and/or by highlighting the marchers' previous or potential future contributions to national defense.

Especially World War I created a widespread notion of entitlement among former servicemen and war workers and instilled them with a new militancy and willingness to challenge the state's monopoly on violence. Fascist parades and rallies and Communist hunger marches were organized with military precision, discipline, and pageantry and became the signature street protests of the interwar period. Older forms continued to exist, and new forms emerged, such as Mahatma Gandhi's Salt March in 1930 or A Philip Randolph's—eventually cancelled—March on Washington, D.C. ten years later. However, the Fascist and Communist attempts to capture the streets maintained the association of street protest with political extremism and often caused authorities to react with disproportioned force. The use of tanks, cavalry, and tear gas against the unemployed war veterans of the 1932 Bonus Army in Washington, D.C. is a case in point, while the excessive force used by the British police against the hunger marchers led to the foundation of the Council for Civil Liberties in Great Britain in 1934.

The campaigns for nuclear disarmament, which started in Great Britain in the 1950s, marked the adoption of street protest by wider segments of the middle classes. Despite a continuing emphasis on respectability, some groups eventually resorted to sit-ins, blockades, and other forms of nonviolent civil disobedience. The civil rights movement in the United States employed the same methods, although with far more severe consequences for many protesters. Initially, the movement had planned to also practice civil disobedience during its 1963 March of Washington, but then turned the event into a mass rally in support of President Kennedy's Civil Rights Bill. For the first time, the participants on the ground only provided the backdrop for the much larger audience on the television screens. The 1963 march built on a long tradition of civil rights protest in Washington, D.C. and subsequently provided the model for countless other protest events. Street protest had become mainstream and respectable.

However, the tradition of civil disobedience continued. The student and antiwar movements of the 1960s and 1970s created new subversive or provocative forms of street protest, and the growing importance of television put a premium on protest performances that produced newsworthy images. Irony, pageantry, street theater, and publicity stunts experienced a revival and still feature in many protest events today. The early 1980s saw a return of mass street protest against nuclear weapons in the West, while large-scale and sustained demonstrations contributed to the downfall of the Communist regimes in the former Eastern bloc from the end of that decade onward. Massive street demonstrations also challenged the legitimacy of autocratic regime during the so-called Arab Spring and inspired the Occupy movement in the West. However, the institutionalization of street protest in Western democracies has reduced its ability to achieve radical change, and large-scale protests against social and economic reforms or military interventions have been largely unsuccessful over the last decades. Where authoritarian regimes were able to use massive force, such as in China, street protest also often proved ineffective. Since the 1990s, new communication technologies such as camera phones have made it more difficult for the police to control protest or use illegitimate force while social media networks have improved the ability of organizers to mobilize and coordinate protesters. The call to demonstrate against the WTO meeting in Seattle in late 1999 was signed by no less than 1,387 groups, and the protesters employed a whole range of different protest techniques in the streets. Subsequent demonstrations organized by the global justice movement have shown a similar pattern and mobilized a wide array of different groups in support of a host of issues under the umbrella of single protest events.

State of Research in Related Social Movement Research/Interdisciplinary Perspectives for the Analysis of Protest Cultures

Specialized studies of street protest events are still relatively rare across the different academic disciplines that constitute the field of protest studies. Social scientists treat street protest largely as a tactic and focus on collecting and analyzing data on protest actions over longer periods of time and/or across national boundaries to compare patterns and outcomes. Some of their work branches out into history, such as Charles Tilly and Lesley J. Wood's *Social Movements, 1768–2012* (2013), but Olivier Fillieule and Danielle Tartakowsky's *La Manifestation* (2008) stands out as a rare collaborative monograph of a social scientist and a historian. Following E P Thompson's path-breaking article on the "Moral Economy of the English Crowd" (1971), historians have long focused on preindustrial protest action, although this started to change in the 1990s. The works of Manfred Gailus and Thomas Lindenberger on street politics are noteworthy examples, and an international conference in London in 2005 showed how diverse the historical research on this topic had become within the following decade.[5] In the field of social psychology, the studies of Stephen Reicher, Clifford Stott, and others on the crowd offer valuable insides into the behavior of protesters and the police. Space and place are likewise central categories for street protest, and human geographers have turned out an impressive body of research on contentious actions. The *Atlas of Industrial Protest 1750–1990* (1996) has to be mentioned here, as well as Tim Cresswell's *In Place/Out of Place* (1996) or the work of Paul Routledge. Their interests often intersect with those of anthropologists and their study of protest rituals, for which Neil Jarman and Dominic Bryan's publications on parades in Northern Ireland are good examples.

Research Gaps and Open Questions

Future research needs to expand and intensify the dialogue and exchange between the different academic disciplines and especially facilitate the development of interdisciplinary theoretical models. Many significant street protest events have not yet been studied at all, and a number of questions are still not sufficiently understood, such as the extent and mechanics of transnational borrowing or the role of sound. Visual sources are also still under-utilized, as are the files and publications of the often short-lived organizations behind many protest events in the street.

Matthias Reiss is senior lecturer in history at the University of Exeter, Great Britain. He has written *Blind Workers against Charity: National League of the Blind of Great Britain and Ireland, 1893-1970* (Basingstoke, 2015), a monograph on German prisoners of war in the United States during World War II and edited two books on protest marches and unemployed protest: *The Street as Stage: Protest Marches and Public Rallies since the Nineteenth Century* (Oxford, 2007) and together with Matt Perry, *Unemployment and Protest: New Perspectives on Two Centuries of Contention* (Oxford, 2011). He has also authored numerous articles and essays on street protest and the history of unemployment

Notes

1. Bernd Jürgen Warneken, ed., *Massenmedium Straße: Zur Kulturgeschichte der Demonstration* (Frankfurt, 1991), 7.
2. Charles Tilly, and Lesley J. Wood, *Social Movements, 1768-2012* (3rd ed.; Boulder, 2013), 4.
3. Charles Tilly, *Popular Contention in Great Britain, 1758–1834* (Boulder, CO, 2005), 45–66, 352.
4. Tilly, *Popular Contention in Great Britain*, 11.
5. Manfred Gailus, *Straße und Brot: Sozialer Protest in den deutschen Staaten unter besonderer Berücksichtigung Preußens, 1847–1949* (Göttingen, 1990); Thomas Lindenberger, *Straßenpolitik: Zur Sozialgeschichte der öffentlichen Ordnung in Berlin, 1900–1914* (Bonn, 1995); Matthias Reiss, ed., *The Street as Stage: Protest Marches and Public Rallies since the Nineteenth Century* (Oxford, 2007).

Recommended Reading

Fillieule, Olivier, and Danielle Tartakowsky. *La Manifestation*. (Paris, 2008). A multidisciplinary analysis of demonstrations as a form of political participation. in English: *Demonstrations, translated by Phllis Aronoff and Howard Scott* (Halifax, Nova Scotia, 2013).

Reiss, Matthias, ed. *The Street as Stage: Protest Marches and Public Rallies since the Nineteenth Century*. (Oxford, 2007). A comparative analysis of various modern protest marches with short introductions into the ways social psychologists, geographers, and social scientists approach the topic.

Sajó, András, ed. *Free to Protest: Constituent Power and Street Demonstration*. (Utrecht, 2009). Discusses the constitutional and human rights aspects as well as the historical, political, and philosophical dimensions.

Tilly, Charles, and Lesley J. Wood, *Social Movements, 1768-2012* (3rd ed.; Boulder, 2013). A concise history of social movements and demonstrations.

Chapter 37

Insult and Devaluation

John Michael Roberts

Insult and devaluation have played a key and somewhat contentious role in social movements. After all, a phrase, description, or piece of writing might be perceived as being insulting, and as such, a contribution to the devaluation of public discourse by one party may be thought of as the reverse by another party. Of course, the degree to which, say, an act or text can be said to insult another person, group, set of beliefs and ideals, and so on, depends on a number of factors, some of which we explore below. Before this occurs, we first say a little more about why insult and devaluation are relevant areas of research for social movement studies.

Relevance for Protest Cultures

The relevance of insult and devaluation for protest cultures can be noted in at least two respects. First, and most obviously, many protest movements in both the past and present have used insults as a means to get their respective cause heard in the public sphere. These have taken a variety of forms, but what is noticeable about many such (perceived) insults is that they have been conducted in a carnivalesque manner. But what exactly is the carnivalesque, and how is it related to protest cultures?

It was the Russian social theorist Mikhail Bakhtin (1895–1975) who provided one of the most well-known definitions of the carnivalesque. In his analysis of the French Renaissance writer Francois Rabelais, Bakhtin claims that the carnivalesque is a moment when the "lower orders" manage to blur the boundaries between high culture and low culture. In particular, carnival envisages three humorous forms that mock the official and serious cultural politics: (1) ritual spectacles: carnival pageants, comic shows of the marketplace; (2) comic verbal compositions; and (3) various genres of curses, oaths, and popular blazons.[1] This also implies that carnivalesque protest chooses images and language from popular culture through which to parody, invert, and subvert what is often believed to be the more formally serious politics associated with high culture.[2] As a mechanism of protest, the carnivalesque therefore deliberately embeds itself in popular culture and tries to weave together political and social discussion with everyday emotions.

An illustration of this last point can be found in British history. In the late seventeenth century, public insults among ordinary people on London's streets had started to be replaced by insulting words appearing in a growing print media.[3] Perhaps this is not so surprising once we consider that from the English Civil War (1642–51) there emerged a whole host of new radical social movements like the Levellers. Many of the groups involved in these movements published a large number of tracts pushing the case for deep-seated reform of the political and social system of England.[4] As the eighteenth century dawned, other popular and radical media outlets came into existence that drew in part on satirical and carnivalesque humor to make their points. Some radical humor of the day for example was inspired by the traditional plebeian urban art form of sensationalist and frequently obscene street posters.[5] Later on in the eighteenth century, various radicals took their activism into formal politics. John Wilkes, the radical Member of Parliament (MP) for Middlesex, established his newspaper, *The North Briton*, in 1762 as part of his attempt to tap into growing discontent over increased bread prices, falling wages, and unpredictable employment.[6] At the same time, many of the articles published in Wilkes's newspaper made satirical jokes about the monarchy and government.

The second reason why insult and devaluation are relevant areas of interest for protest cultures is that they can tell us something about how the state reacts to protest cultures. Public officials for example often see carnivalesque utterances as devaluing civilized public discussion. This will then lead them to employ state and legal mechanisms to silence what they consider to be insulting carnivalesque words. For instance, in the English legal system, defamation is defined as a statement "which injures the reputation of another by exposing him to hatred, contempt, or ridicule (or) which tends to lower him in the esteem of right-thinking members of society."[7] Defamation can also be divided between libel, which is written defamation, and slander, which is oral defamation. In respect to social movements, the British state has frequently resorted to the use of defamation, or variants of it, in order to silence what it considers to be insulting types of popular protest toward the government. Eighteenth-century British history once again presents us with a useful illustration of this procedure.

By the time that the eighteenth century was drawing to a close, Britain was home to a number of famous radical texts, Thomas Paine's *The Rights of Man* (1791) and Mary Wollstonecraft's *A Vindication of the Rights of Woman* (1792) being two of the most famous examples, along with a number of other populist radical publications already mentioned. Given this ongoing upsurge in radical publications during this time, how did the government react? One way it had already responded was by establishing a more coherent legal definition of libel. At the forefront of this development was the English judge and Tory politician, Sir William Blackstone. In volume 4 of his landmark text, *Commentaries on the Laws of England* (1770), Blackstone argued that while a person had the freedom to print what they wished, if the said publication contained "improper, mischievous, or illegal" words, then the person in question could in fact be prosecuted for libel. Indeed, Blackstone went as far as to argue that even if the offending words were true, the person might still be punished if it could be proved that the words had led to violent revenge against somebody else.[8] In practice, this legal definition helped to give credence to the legal term "seditious libel," which was often arbitrarily used to prosecute political opponents of the state and those thought to bring the monarchy or government into public disrepute through written or spoken words.[9]

The next section shifts the discussion to the present era in order to explore how researchers analyze insult and devaluation in respect to contemporary social movement activism. We see that while carnivalesque practices have altered over the years, they still nevertheless provide robust means for political and social activism.

State of Research in Social Movement Studies

Some social movement research on insults is informed by Bakhtin's original analysis of the carnivalesque and his belief that carnivalesque rowdy laughter induces variety and change as notions of the eternal, fixed, past, and absolute are challenged by the unfinished and open character of humor. Of special importance in this respect is the ability of contemporary social movements to use such humor to invert and subvert more dominant social codes. This is noticeable in one area in social movement research concerned with *culture jamming*. Associated with various media techniques by social movements, culture jamming can be broadly defined as those protest tactics designed to disrupt corporate messages to consumers. Such disruption can occur through imitating corporate advertisements or subjecting them to parody and satire.[10] Mixing humor with protest is thus a clear aim of culture jammers, and through this mix, different emotions are released during the actual moment of culture jamming. For example, Wettergren notes how at one incident a group of culture jammers entered a Wal-Mart shop in New York and proceeded to push empty shopping carts in a Zombie-like fashion through an unbroken line up and down the shopping aisles. In this humorous way, these particular culture jammers encroached on the semi-public space of Wal-Mart through an anti-consumerist act.[11]

Protest movements therefore often combine insults with carnivalsque humor, satire, and parody. The aim of insults in this respect is not to articulate hate speech as is evident in far-right social movements.[12] Rather, the aim of maintaining insults of the sort found in culture jamming is to generate an image event in which protest action is a highly staged moment through which to publicly highlight negative corporate practices.[13] Through the humor involved in such practices, new emotional spaces are momentarily opened up, which may very well prove insulting to some but not to others taking part in the actions. Drawing on the work of Schriver and Nudd,[14] Chvasta usefully brackets such theatrics into two main groups. First, there are celebratory types of protest performance, and these relate primarily as to how a protest group elicits legitimation among its own members. "Gathering publicly in carnivalesque fashion energizes the activists while increasing public awareness of their existence and purpose."[15] Second, there are interventionist protest performances, and these relate to actions by demonstrators designed to influence the decisions made by institutional powers.

But just as there are different varieties of humor, so are there different kinds of protest that use different modes of humor. Harold (2004) observes in this respect that Bakhtin's notion of parody (which is one element of his wider theory of the carnivalesque) is a somewhat negative tactic to embrace insofar that parody reinforces binary oppositions rather than subjecting them to a more thorough deconstructive process. What Harold means here is that parody relies on the belief that a hidden political truth can be revealed beneath that which is parodied. Harold distinguishes parody in this respect from another humor tactic, which is that of pranks. Pranks are different to parodies to the extent that they eschew the idea that a hidden truth is waiting to be revealed. Instead, pranks take existing materials at hand (e.g., a brand or a customer object) and use and experiment with this material in new ways so that its original meaning is questioned irrespective of any underlying message. What is considered as being potentially insulting to others through pranks is therefore not decided beforehand but is allowed to develop through debate and discussion as the prank enfolds.[16]

Naturally, the use of insults through image events is not confined to humor, parody, or pranks. Often, protest movements will create an image event through the deliberate and careful use of violent forms of demonstration. Anarchist social movements for instance have resorted to staged acts of violence at specific protest events in order to reframe media debate about global social and political issues. This has been achieved in conjunction with alternative media forums such as anarchist web sites.[17] While such staged violence would be seen by many as a devaluation of public debate about global social and political issues, some evidence suggests that it has managed to gain some success in pushing forward an alternative anarchist perspective into public debate around particular global issues.[18] This being the case, some movement activists draw on a range of both alternative and mainstream media in order to orchestrate media events to gain publicity for their political aims and goals.

Conclusion

Research on insult and devaluation has been made from a variety of disciplines. Many researchers have been attuned as to how insults have been used to good effect by protest movements and have been integral for establishing coherent and organized political protest. In other words, insults are highly contested when employed for social and political purposes. In saying this, much of the research on insults and devaluation tends to look at these areas from the perspective of social movements themselves. This means that there is often less research conducted on how regulatory authorities such as the state aims to either incorporate or govern what is perceived to be insulting public behavior by social movements. Where regulatory mechanisms have been brought into the analytical picture, this has sometimes been through the lens of Habermasian discourse theory.[19] But such a perspective sometimes perpetuates unhelpful binary oppositions in research practice, such as the opposition between the instrumental and strategic logic of state mechanisms versus the expressive cultural forms of social movements in civil society. What is perhaps therefore required is more research on how regulatory mechanisms like the state can in fact also create expressive cultural forms in civil society that then serve to represent some activists as devaluing public debate. For example, the British state has in the past constructed some free speech activists as engaging in uncivilized and verminous public debate.[20] This then allows the state to curb what it sees as uncivilized forms of free speech in civil society. Arguably, this research is therefore useful when it demonstrates how the state regulates movement activism by creating its own insulting images of those activists it wishes to expel or devalue from the public sphere.

John Michael Roberts is senior lecturer in sociology and communications at Brunel University in London. One of his main research topics is the use of public space by social movements to promote radical spaces of free speech. He has also recently explored the relationship between public activism and new media. He has published a number of sole authored and coedited books and has written research articles for a wide variety of academic journals. His recent books include *The Competent Public Sphere: Global Political Economy, Dialogue, and the Contemporary Workplace* (Basingstoke, 2009), and *New Media and Public Activism* (forthcoming).

Notes

1. Michail Bakhtin, *Rabelais and His World,* trans. H Iswolsky (Bloomington, IN, 1994), 196.
2. See also Peter Stallybrass and Allon White, *The Politics and Poetics of Transgression* (London, 1986).
3. Robert B Shoemaker, "The Decline of Public Insult in London 1660–1800," *Past and Present* 169 (2000): 97–116.
4. David R Como, "Secret Printing, the Crisis of 1640, and the Origins of Civil War Radicalism," *Past and Present* 196 (2007): 37–82; See also David Randall, "Epistolary Rhetoric, the Newspaper, and the Public Sphere," *Past and Present* 198 (2008): 3–32.
5. Richard Hendrix, "Popular Humor and 'The Black Dwarf,'" *Journal of British Studies* 16, no. 1 (1976): 108–28; Iain McCalman, "Unrespectable Radicalism: Infidels and Pornography in Early Nineteenth-Century London," *Past and Present* 104 (1984): 74–110; Iain McCalman, "Ultra-Radicalism and Convivial Debating-Clubs in London, 1795–1838," *English Historical Review* 102 (1987): 309–33.
6. Henry L Jephson, *The Platform: Its Rise and Progress,* vol. 1 (London, 1968).
7. Basil S Markesinis and Simon F Deakin, *Tort Law,* 4th ed. (Oxford, 1999), 601.
8. Michael K Curtis, *Free Speech, "the People's Darling Privilege"* (Durham, NC, 2000), 45.
9. See also John Roberts, "The Development of Free Speech in Modern Britain," *Speakers' Corner Trust Occasional Essays,* 25 March 2011, http://www.speakerscornertrust.org/forum/occasional-essays/.
10. Vince Carducci, "Culture Jamming: A Sociological Perspective," *Journal of Consumer Culture* 6, no. 1 (2006): 116–38.
11. Asa Wettergren, "Fun and Laughter: Culture Jamming and the Emotional Regime of Late Capitalism," *Social Movement Studies* 8, no. 1 (2009): 1–15.
12. See Josh Adams and Vincent J Roscigno, "White Supremacists, Oppositional Culture and the World Wide Web," *Social Forces* 84, no. 2 (2005): 759–78.
13. John W Delicath and Kevin M Deluca, "Image Events, the Public Sphere, and Argumentative Practice: The Case of Radical Environmental Groups," *Argumentation* 17 (2003): 315–33.

14. Kristina Schriver and Donna M Nudd, "Mickee Faust Club's Performative Protest Events," *Text and Performative Quarterly* 22, no. 3 (2002): 196–216.

15. Marcyrose Chvasta, "Anger, Irony, and Protest: Confronting the Issue of Efficacy, Again," *Text and Performance Quarterly* 26, no. 1 (2006): 5–16.

16. Christine Harold, "Pranking Rhetoric: 'Culture Jamming' as Media Activism," *Critical Studies in Media Communication* 21, no. 3 (2004): 189–211.

17. Lynn Owens and L Kendall Palmer, "Making the News: Anarchist Counter-Public Relations on the World Wide Web," *Critical Studies in Media Communication* 20, no. 4 (2003): 335–61.

18. Kevin M Deluca and Jennifer Peeples, "From Public Sphere to Public Screen: Democracy, Activism, and the 'Violence' of Seattle," *Critical Studies in Media Communication* 19, no. 2 (2002): 125–51.

19. Michael Huspek, "Habermas and Oppositional Public Spheres: A Stereoscopic Analysis of Black and White Press Practices," *Political Studies* 55 (2007): 821–43.

20. John M Roberts, "Expressive Free Speech, the State and the Public Sphere: A Bakhtinian-Deleuzian Analysis of 'Public Address' at Hyde Park," *Social Movement Studies* 7, no. 2 (2008): 101–19.

Recommended Reading

Bakhtin, Michail. *Rabelais and His World*. Translated by H Iswolsky. Bloomington, IN, 1994. Bakhtin's book still remains the starting point for any serious consideration of the relationship between the carnivalesque and politics.

Carducci, Vince. "Culture Jamming: A Sociological Perspective." *Journal of Consumer Culture* 6, no. 1 (2006): 116–38. Carducci provides an extremely readable account and explanation of culture jamming.

Deluca, Kevin M, and Jennifer Peeples. "From Public Sphere to Public Screen: Democracy, Activism, and the 'Violence' of Seattle." *Critical Studies in Media Communication* 19, no. 2 (2002): 125–51. This is a very good discussion as to how social movements create media image events.

McCalman, Iain. "Ultra-Radicalism and Convivial Debating-Clubs in London, 1795–1838." *English Historical Review* 102 (1987): 309–33. McCalman's article captures the rowdy nature of social and political activism when radicalism and underground popular culture collide.

Stallybrass, Peter, and Allon White. *The Politics and Poetics of Transgression*. London, 1986. This is a very influential book that among other things applied, developed, and popularized the carnivalesque through a range of examples.

Chapter 38

Public Debating

Mary E Triece

Protest practices cover a wide range of strategies and tactics aimed at challenging dominant economic, political, and judicial systems. To explore the ways that public debate has been deployed as a protest practice, we must understand the conservative origins of debate—as an exclusive, male-dominated activity—and the ways that debate, its form, and content has been shaped over the years by an expansion of the public sphere.

The concept and practice of debate originated in ancient Greece where only free citizens—land-owning, native-born men—were sanctioned to participate in deliberation over important issues of the day. The art of public speaking and the ability to debate were prized in Athenian society particularly since a citizen could always be called on to participate in the general assembly or on a jury.

Contemporary scholarship on public debate indicates a continued interest in the ways in which a citizen expresses various perspectives, weighs alternative viewpoints and courses of actions, and makes decisions for the common good. Jürgen Habermas originally described the public sphere where private people come together, free of self-interest, to discuss and debate relevant social issues of the day.[1]

Since the publication of Habermas's *The Structural Transformation of the Public Sphere,* writers have continued to refine understandings of publics and how they operate, in part by focusing on the ways and extent to which public sphere debate plays a role in protest and social transformation.[2]

Some scholars express concern over public debate norms of decorum and civility that can potentially serve as "masks for the preservation of injustice."[3] The dilemma concerns developing a "critical rhetoric that articulates standards for good public discourse that does not exclude the already excluded" through rules, restrictions, and norms that regulate what counts as acceptable discourse.[4] Indeed, some scholars have observed that traditional argument is not always a viable form of expression for those outside of the establishment advocating radical change of the status quo. These scholars focus more readily on protest practices such as confrontation and provocation discussed in other chapters of this volume.[5]

Relevance of Public Debate for Protest Cultures

In some senses, the practice of debate sits uneasily in the context of protest, given the conservative origins of debate. The concept of "subaltern counterpublic" or counterpublic sphere provides a way to theorize the relationship between public debate and protest while taking into consideration some of the limitations noted above. Subaltern counterpublics are "parallel discursive arenas where members of subordinated social groups invent and circulate counterdiscourses to formulate oppositional interpretations of their identities, interests, and needs."[6]

Given that outsiders have established counterpublics as a means for distinguishing themselves and their goals from existing economic, political, and judicial systems, it stands to reason that protesters often emphasize argumentative strategies and goals that differ from those employed in traditional debate settings. Foss and Griffin go so far as to argue that traditional debate is inherently patriarchal and domineering. They offer invitational speaking as an antidote, which they argue emphasizes equality between participants and enables self-determination.[7] Still, vigorous debate and even confrontation continue to be defended by other scholars who note that marginalized groups lacking formal power must often rely on tactics such as strikes, sit-ins, and more recently, occupations (as in *Occupy Wall Street*), which have historically proven successfully at winning basic rights.[8]

Protesters may engage in public debate in formal settings such as congressional hearings or city council meetings while also employing direct actions. For example, in the late 1960s/early 1970s, poor black mothers testified before congress for welfare rights while utilizing welfare office sit-ins and pickets to get their voices heard.[9]

Interdisciplinary Perspectives: Protest and Debate in Media and Cyber Studies

Regardless of the aims or strategies employed, protesters must engage with mass media—whether it be online or offline, corporate or grassroots. Gitlin examined the way the Vietnam antiwar movement was, in part, made by the media, while a growing number of scholars are exploring the role the World Wide Web may play in forming an "electronic democracy."[10] Studies have focused on Internet usage in the context of specific movements or protests, while others have studied the rise of independent media centers (IMCs; e.g., Indymedia), which are interactive grassroots news web sites.[11]

Research Gaps and Open Questions

The Internet and its role in protest and debate remains a relatively new area of study that warrants continued exploration. Future studies can examine under what conditions information and communication technologies work to the betterment or detriment of sound argumentation and equal participation in public debate. And, to what extent can the Internet facilitate the formation of counterpublic spheres that can successfully bypass more traditional debate forums?[12] Additionally, in what ways can the Internet be used to increase participation on the part of social movement actors? Finally, scholars can continue to study the ways protesters have employed debate in more traditional venues—particularly in light of what such historical examples can tell us about protest and debate in an electronic age.

Mary E Triece is professor in communication studies at The University of Akron. Her research focuses on protest rhetoric from a feminist materialist perspective. She is author of *"Tell It Like It Is": Women in the National Welfare Rights Movement* (Columbia, SC, 2013), *On the Picket Line: Women's Strategies during the Depression* (Champaign, IL, 2007), and *Protest and Popular Culture: Women in the U.S. Labor Movement 1894–1917* (Boulder, CO, 2001). She has published articles in *Critical Studies in Mass Communication* (1999), and *Western Journal of Communication* (2012).

Notes

1. Jürgen Habermas, *The Structural Transformation of the Public Sphere* (Cambridge, 1989).
2. Robert Asen, "Seeking the 'Counter' in Counterpublics," *Communication Theory* 10, no. 4 (2000): 424–46; Robert Asen and Daniel C Brouwer, eds, *Counterpublics and the State* (Albany, NY, 2001); Craig Calhoun, ed., Habermas and the Public Sphere (Cambridge, 1992); Nancy Fraser, Unruly Practices: Power, Discourse and Gender in Contemporary Social Theory (Minneapolis, MN, 1989).
3. Robert L Scott and Donald K Smith, "The Rhetoric of Confrontation," *Quarterly Journal of Speech* 55, no. 1 (1969): 1–8; J Michael Hogan and Dave Tell, "Demagoguery and Democratic Deliberation: The Search For Rules of Discursive Engagement," *Rhetoric & Public Affairs* 9, no. 3 (2006): 479–87; Mari Boor Tonn, "Taking Conversation, Dialogue, and Therapy Public," *Rhetoric & Public Affairs* 8, no.3 (2005): 405–30.
4. Patricia Roberts-Miller, "Democracy, Demagoguery, and Critical Rhetoric," *Rhetoric & Public Affairs* 8, no. 3 (2005): 459–76; Hogan and Tell, "Demagoguery and Democratic Deliberation."
5. Parke G Burgess, "The Rhetoric of Black Power: A Moral Demand?," *Quarterly Journal of Speech* 54 (1968): 122–33; Scott and Smith, "The Rhetoric of Confrontation"; Herbert Simons, "Persuasion in Social Conflicts: A Critique of Prevailing Conceptions and a Framework for Future Research," *Speech Monographs* 39 (1972): 227–47; Mary E Triece, *On the Picket Line: Strategies of Working-Class Women During the Depression* (Urbana, IL, 2007). See Hogan and Tell for an overview of studies that discuss the limitations of formal debate for social movements.
6. Fraser, Unruly Practices, 123. See Rita Felski, *Beyond Feminist Aesthetics: Feminist Literature and Social Change* (Cambridge, 1989); Nancy Fraser, "Rethinking the Public Sphere," in *Habermas and the Public Sphere*, ed. C Calhoun (Cambridge, 1992), 109–42; Oskar Negt and Alexander Kluge, *Public Sphere and Experience: Toward an Analysis of the Bourgeois and Proletarian Public Sphere,* trans. P Labanyi, J Owen Daniel, and A Oksiloff (Minneapolis, MN, 1993); Daniel C Brouwer, "ACT-ing UP in Congressional Hearings," in *Counterpublics and the State,* ed. R Asen and DC Brouwer (Albany, NY, 2001), 87–109; Mark Porrovecchio, "Lost in the WTO Shuffle: Publics, Counterpublics, and the Individual," *Western Journal of Communication* 71, no.3 (2007): 235–56.
7. Sonja K Foss and Cindy L Griffin, "Beyond Persuasion: A Proposal for an Invitational Rhetoric," *Communication Monographs* 62 (1995): 2–18.
8. Mary E Triece, *On the Picket Line: Strategies of Working-Class Women During the Depression* (Urbana, IL, 2007); Nina M Lozano-Reich and Dana L Cloud, "The Uncivil Tongue: Invitational Rhetoric and the Problem of Inequality," *Western Journal of Communication* 73 (2009): 220–26; Tonn, "Taking Conversation, Dialogue, and Therapy Public."
9. Mary E Triece, *"Tell It Like It Is": Women in the National Welfare Rights Movement* (Columbia, SC, 2013).

10. Todd Gitlin, *The Whole World Is Watching: Mass Media in the Making and Unmaking of the New Left* (Berkeley, CA, 1980); Steffen Albrecht, "Whose Voice Is Heard in Online Deliberation? A Study of Participation and Representation in Political Debates on the Internet," *Information, Communication & Society* 9, no. 1 (2006): 62–82; Bart Cammaerts and Nico Carpentier, eds, *Reclaiming the Media: Communication Rights and Democratic Media Roles* (Bristol, 2007); Stephen Coleman, "The Future of the Internet and Democracy Beyond Metaphors, Towards Policy," in *Promise and Problems of E-Democracy: Challenges of Online Citizen Engagement*, ed. OECD (Paris, 2003), 143–62; Ananda Mitra, "Marginal Voices in Cyberspace," *New Media & Society* 3, no. 1 (2001): 29–48; Seungahn Nah, Aaron S Veenstra, and Dhavan V Shah, "The Internet and Anti-War Activism: A Case Study of Information, Expression, and Action," *Journal of Computer-Mediated Communication* 12 (2006): 230–47.

11. Victor W Pickard, "Assessing the Radical Democracy of Indymedia: Discursive, Technical, and Institutional Constructions," *Critical Studies in Media Communication* 23, no. 1 (2006): 19–23; W Lance Bennett, "Communicating Global Activism: Strengths and Vulnerabilities of Networked Politics," *Information, Communication & Society* 6, no. 2 (2003): 143–68; Richard Kahn and Douglas Kellner, "New Media and Internet Activism: From the 'Battle of Seattle' to Blogging," *New Media & Society* 6, no. 1 (2004): 87–95; Dorothy Kidd, "Indymedia.org: A New Communications Commons," in *Cyberactivism: Critical Theories and Practices of Online Activism*, ed. M McGaughey and M Ayers (New York, 2003), 47–70; Lynn Owens and Kendall L Palmer, "Making the News: Anarchist Counter-Public Relations on the World Wide Web," *Critical Studies in Media Communication* 20, no. 4 (2003): 335–61; Peter Van Aeist and Stefaan Walgrave, "New Media, New Movements? The Role of the Internet in Shaping the 'Anti-Globalization' Movement," *Information, Communication & Society* 5, no. 4 (2002): 465–93.

12. R Kelly Garrett, "Protest in an Information Society: A Review of Literature on Social Movements and New ICTs," *Information, Communication & Society* 9, no. 2 (2006): 202–42.

Recommended Reading

Fraser, Nancy. *Unruly Practices: Power, Discourse and Gender in Contemporary Social Theory.* Minneapolis, MN, 1989. Fraser offers an incisive feminist critique of Habermas's theory of citizenship and the public sphere.

Habermas, Jürgen. *The Structural Transformation of the Public Sphere.* Cambridge, 1989. This foundational book historicizes the development and functions of the bourgeois public sphere.

McCaughey, Martha, and Michael D Ayers, eds. *Cyberactivism: Online Activism in Theory and Practice.* New York, 2003. This anthology provides works exploring online protest including cyber protests against the World Bank, the Zapatista's use of the Internet, and Gay Media Inc.

Simons, Herbert. "Persuasion in Social Conflicts: A Critique of Prevailing Conceptions and a Framework for Future Research." *Speech Monographs* 39 (1972): 227–47. This essay critiques the establishment bias in communication scholar, which emphasizes traditional modes of persuasion at the expense of coercion and extra discursive tactics, which are often necessary for marginalized groups to get their voices heard in the context of debates marked by power differentials.

Chapter 39

Media Campaigning

Johanna Niesyto

Although this volume suggests that media campaigning can be understood as protest practice in singular, this chapter explores in what ways media campaigning not only is one protest practice but includes many practices. These various practices are connected to the protest actors themselves: to their ideological orientation, action repertoire, organizational type, resources, and last but not least to their environment. Hence, an understanding of the dynamic interplay between protest and media campaigning requires further that one considers the role that sociopolitical and technological changes have been playing in shaping media campaigning as the central instrument in gaining public visibility and resonance.

General Introduction and Definition of Terms

Protest campaigning as one form of political campaigning is etymologically rooted in the late Latin word *campania* meaning *level country* (from Latin *campus*: a field). It denoted a temporarily limited activity in the country as well as any *expiditio* understood as temporarily limited military operation. By then, armies spent their time in quarters during the winters and went to the open field to battle in summer. Until today, the military meaning is carried in the English term "campaign." Later on, the term moved into the political arena when in the mid seventeenth century the sessions of the English House of Commons were called campaigns. With the introduction of democratic elections to parliament, the strategic aspect was attached to campaigning as by then the word campaign was used to describe the efforts undertook by candidates in order to win an election.[1] So what is political protest campaigning? A comprehensive definition of protest campaigning that considers the abovementioned temporal and strategic aspects is provided by Lahusen:

> First, campaigns are action programs or maps designed by activists explicitly in terms of alter-ego interactions. Second, campaigning evolves throughout time. … Third, campaigns are issue-oriented systems of action that gather a variety of activists around a common topic or demand, making them crucial means of coalition building, networking and the structuration of social movements. Fourth, they integrate different fields of action, of which elite-campaigning (i.e., lobbying and agenda setting) and public campaigns (i.e., resource allocation, mass action or the generation of public pressure for elite-campaigning) are two core elements with their different targets and actions repertoires. Finally, campaigns organize diverse actions on the local, national and/or international level, as well as activities in diverse societal sectors (science, politics, economy, media, etc.) and blend them into an integrated, goal-directed venture.[2]

Hence one can distinguish not only according to the who to mobilize (elite or public campaigning), but also according to what to evoke. In particular, public campaigns aim to generate public pressure (action campaigns) and/or to mobilize solidarity in favor of moral issues like global justice or human rights (solidarity campaigns).[3] With regard to the change protest campaigns' aim to achieve as well as with regard to the repertoire used, other systematizations are rather specialized. For example in the context of anticorporate campaigns—understood as campaigns directed toward corporations and claiming a change in corporate behavior—the difference between production-oriented campaigns and consumption-oriented campaigns is pointed out. While production-oriented campaigns turn toward the production process, for example, by calling corporations to implement safety standards through strikes, consumption-oriented campaigns focus on buy and boycott actions as well as on discursive political consumerism[4] in order to positively or negatively criticize corporate actors in public.[5]

The shape and success of campaigns is highly influenced by so-called media opportunity structures. While discursive opportunity structures detect the influence of mass media discourse on protest communication,[6] media opportunity structures look at the rather structural question, to what extent changing constellations of media ensembles (e.g., through the introduction of new media) influence the communication and organization of protest campaigns.

Relevance for Protest Cultures

By now, protest campaigning as mobilizing format has become ubiquitous and can be linked directly to the changing social conditions of late modern, globalizing societies and their weakened group, party, and ideological bases of political organization and mobilization.[7] Considering that the term "campaign" emanated from the military, it is not surprising that some scholars speak of info wars and battles evolving around codes of information and images of representations.[8] Practitioners in public relations agencies even speak of campaign war rooms to name the communication center that coordinates messages and rapid responses directed to widen the public and media outreach of a campaign. There are examples that strictly follow the rules of mass media, foreground aspects of lifestyle within protest communication, and/or have a rather offensive approach by tackling controversial moral issues. For example, PETA's animal rights campaign, "Holocaust on Your Plate," juxtaposed pictures of men in a concentration camp with chickens in battery cages and added on the web site www.masskilling.com comments of different Jewish men, for example:

> When I see cages crammed with chickens from battery farms thrown on trucks like bundles of trash, I see, with the eyes of my soul, the Umschlagplatz [the spot in the Warsaw Ghetto where Jews were forced onto trains leaving for the death camps]. When I go to a restaurant and see people devouring meat, I feel sick. I see a holocaust on their plates. —*Georges Metanomski, Holocaust survivor who fought in the Warsaw Ghetto uprising*[9]

This comparison leads to a love–hate relationship with mass media: the campaign gained wide media coverage and societal *Anschlusskommunikation* (follow-up communication).[10] However, the growing significance of media campaigning interrelates with social transformations like the decline of membership numbers in political organizations (e.g., trade unions). At the same time, the amount of issues of why people protest has not declined but multiplied, an understanding of citizens as both a public and consumers has been developed, and media environments have been changing. For today's protest campaigns, it has become more and more difficult to develop a specific, readily identifiable, and complexity-reducing campaign language since expressive aspects of protest cultures and guerilla marketing have been integrated in commercial advertising.[11]

Historical Aspects

Most notably, the introduction of public and commercial television as well as the establishment of news values (e.g., proximity, emotions)[12] has given rise to many characteristics that are attached to media campaigning: professionalization, personalization, commercialization, visualization, symbolic compression, and audience targeting. Given that mass media are following principles of an "economy of attention" (Franck), protest actors have, to varying degrees, adopted their communication strategies and styles to mass media. Already in the media historical situation of the 1960s, student protesters of the anti-Springer campaign in Germany were following a hybrid orientation: on the one hand, they kept on addressing to their specific environment in institutionalized fora of counter publics and through alternative grassroots-oriented media; on the other hand, activists generated response in press and television through their expressive, visual forms of protest symbolizing lifestyle and habitus. Fahlenbrach's analysis even comes to the conclusion that the student movement started to use mainstream media's attention strategically both in order to enlarge the campaign's outreach and to assure the student movement of their own guide values.[13] With the spread of the visual culture into the mainstream media, producing media events with a clear, symbolical, and morally loaded language of protest frames that follow a binary schema of good and evil has become the central campaign task. The so-called prime-time activism[14] found its peak in the mid 1990s. This is best illustrated by the production of ritually dramatized "David-Goliath pictures" in the context of Greenpeace campaigns that transported the message of "Rainbow warriors in rubber boats fighting the big corporate giants."[15] Analysis of social movement campaigning in the 1990s has also revealed that social movement campaigns increasingly made use of celebrities to spread their protest demands.[16]

State of Research in Related Social Movement Research

Some scholars express concern that one should not limit the campaign concept to orchestrated action. They suggest broadening the focus with regard to actor networks, issue orientation, and time. Bennett extends the term "permanent campaign" being coined in the field of party politics[17] to protest actors. In comparison to single issue, strategic NGO campaigns, permanent campaigns are said to be conducted by polycentric direct activist networks and are characterized by inclusive diversity, a multi-issue orientation, shifting foci, and changing actors (e.g., moveon.org, campact.de).[18] Similarly, Teune introduces the idea of a "multiple campaign," which is, according to him, a protest campaign being perceived as significant by large parts of a social movement and evoking parallel mobilizations such as the mobilizations against the G8 summit in Heiligendamm in 2007.[19] Given the complexity of today's media landscape being multiplied with the introduction and establishment of the (social) web, and given also the heterogeneity of social movement actors and the differentiation of protest environments, social movement studies have also gone beyond a notion of media campaigning that unfolds in a singular relationship to mass media. Notions of "grassroots campaigning" or "peer-to-peer-campaigning" point to manifold campaign strategies and media addressing. For instance, in Germany, the platform www.greenaction.de calls everyone to set up his or her own campaign and to become part of a campaign community.

Drawing from Rucht, four ideal types of campaign strategies can be identified: adaptation, attack, alternatives, and abstention. Adoption has been already illustrated as a type of campaign adopting the mass media's rules and criteria to influence coverage positively. Attack is also directed toward the mass media by an explicit critique of and/or violence against mass media; for example, in the aforementioned anti-Springer campaign in which the German tabloid paper *Bild-Zeitung,* owned by the publishing house Springer, was verbally and physically attacked. Alternative as a form of grassroots campaigning consists of creating and/or addressing movement and independent media in order to bypass the established media. Abstention as another form of grassroots is made up primarily of inward-directed group communication.[20] Protest campaigns as mobilization format for social change can be the lowest common denominator of the various definitions and concepts. Hence, protest campaigns employing strategies of alternative and abstention still aim at public visibility and thus form a complex relationship with mass media. This complex relationship builds upon some protest actors' claims of the revitalization of a critical civil society in which the media system is one of the central actors that has to be indirectly or subversively addressed. At this juncture, it becomes obvious that decisions for or against a certain campaign strategy or tactic is not exclusively connected to resources, organizational types (e.g., vertical or horizontal), or political and discursive opportunities, but also to the ideological orientation of the actors conducting the campaign.[21]

Interdisciplinary Perspectives for the Analysis of Protest Cultures

Protest campaigns in media-saturated environments are studied by the strands of political sociology, cultural studies, and visual studies, as well as by media and communication studies. Because media campaigns bridge social movements' dynamics and public visibility, they have often been taken as a unit of analysis for interdisciplinary research interested in the contextualization of protest cultures within larger—even transnational—political processes and sociocultural transformations unfolding in the public space. From an interdisciplinary perspective, research is particularly interested in the manifold interrelations between changes in media technology and media cultures on the one hand, and changes in protest issues and cultures on the other hand. In doing so, research centers on practices and models of deliberative and participatory democracy. For example, by analyzing the democratic capacity of digital media, the *Democracy in Europe and the Mobilization of Society* (DEMOS) project looked at the variety of deliberative practices connected to protest campaigns from a transnational, in particular European perspective. Connected to questions of democracy are further questions concerning the rise of new forms of political participation. In this vein, the research project at the University of Siegen, Germany, focused for instance upon the dynamics between protest campaigns and corporations by analyzing the significance of new media for new forms of postconventional and transnational political participation (e.g., political consumerism).[22] A further interdisciplinary perspective has highlighted the aesthetic dimension of media campaigns and thus taken into account the symbolic construction of protest images, the dramatization of political conflicts, and the role of rituals within collective action. By also considering insights from visual studies, the research of Doerr and Mattoni pointed for example to the role of visual language for the construction of a mediated public space from below.[23] The analysis of power-related social conflicts and hegemonic power structures calls for another interdisciplinary approach, namely for a discourse theoretical approach. De- and reconstructing of the mediated self-presentations as well as of the protest actors' representations in (mass) media forms, for instance, the core of Marchart's research project that specifically is interested in the formation and reconfiguration of protest issues—in particular the issue of precarity—against the backdrop of a paradigm change in society.[24]

Research Gaps and Open Questions

Overall, the aim of gaining public attention in the highly competitive field of media, which is contemporarily characterized by seemingly fragmented audiences, special interest publics, and distributed users forms a dilemma. Media campaigning with its agonistic—sometimes even antagonistic—character and aesthetic stylization has evoked the critique of undermining democracy through polarization, conflict orientation, and irrationality in terms of moralization and dramatizing of discourse. Additionally, the dominance of strategic thinking over authentic subjective self-expressions in campaign communication has been problematized: "These campaigns have in many cases replaced traditional grassroots actions and social pressure with astroturf (i.e., artificial) groups and electronic publics."[25] Counterarguments brought forward point to the potential of campaigns as initiators of *Anschlusskommunikation* in terms of deliberation and/or critical debate. Also, grassroots campaigning and online peer-to-peer campaigning are depicted as potential communication spaces that open up for authentic, distributed communication.[26] Regardless of the type, media campaigns are seen by some scholars as an inherent part of a media-saturated political culture that interconnects politics "with the world of everyday experience and with the modes of 'the popular' variously to be found within work and leisure."[27] Because interconnectivity and *Anschlusskommunikation* is stressed in this debate, scholars are called to study more deeply the micro level of campaigning and its relations to the other (resonance) spaces of media campaigns.[28] By now, there is only little research tracing the flows between micro media like e-mails, meso media like campaign web sites, and mass media that tackles the question of media campaigns' success.[29] Research on digitalized protest campaigning shows so far that a varying conjunction of online and offline campaign practices can be found on local, national, and transnational levels bypassing, as well as addressing, mass media.[30] As the net is a "moving target," further research is needed, in particular with regard to the use of the World Wide Web as tactical media (hacking, local spamming, smart mobs, etc.) and with regard to so-called viral online campaigning in the social web. Also, what do practices like friending or micro blogging mean for protest campaigns?

Johanna Niesyto was a PhD student in the Department of Social Sciences at the University in Siegen. She worked as research fellow in the project "Changing Protest and Media Cultures," which was part of the Collaborative Research Centre "Media Upheavals" and funded by the German Research Foundation. Her field of research covers political cultures, political consumerism, political campaigning, and political knowledge coproduction—with a focus on the Internet in general and Wikipedia in particular. With Sigrid Baringhorst and Veronika Kneip, she has coedited the publication *Political Campaigning on the Web* (Bielefeld, 2009).

Notes

1. Sigrid Baringhorst, "Introduction: Political Campaigning in Changing Media Cultures—Typological and Historical Approaches," in *Political Campaigning on the Web,* ed. S Baringhorst, V Kneip, and J Niesyto (Bielefeld, 2009), 9–30.
2. Christian Lahusen, *The Rhetoric of Moral Protest. Public Campaigns, Celebrity, Endorsement, and Political Mobilisation* (Berlin, 1996), 17; Similarly, Dieter Rucht and Donatella Della Porta, "The Dynamics of Environmental Campaigns," *Mobilization* 7, no. 1 (2002): 1–14.
3. Sigird Baringhorst, *Politik als Kampagne. Zur medialen Erzeugung von Solidarität* (Wiesbaden, 1998).
4. Discursive political consumerism includes the communicative expression of opinions about corporate policy and practice. Michele Micheletti and Dietlind Stolle, "Fashioning Social Justice Through Political Consumerism, Capitalism, and the Internet," *Cultural Studies* 22, no. 5 (2008): 749–69.
5. Michele Micheletti, *Political Virtue and Shopping: Individuals, Consumerism, and Collective Action* (New York, 2003), 38.
6. Ruud Koopmans and Paul Statham, "Ethnic and Civic Conceptions of Nationhood and the Differential Success of the Extreme Right in Germany and Italy," in *How Social Movements Matter,* ed. M Giugni (Minneapolis, MN, 1999), 225–51.
7. Lance W Bennett, "Branded Political Communication: Lifestyle Politics, Logo Campaigns, and the Rise of Global Citizenship," in *Politics, Products and Markets. Exploring Political Consumerism Past and Present,* ed. M Micheletti, A Follesdal, and D Stolle (New Brunswick, 2004), 101–25.
8. Manuel Castells, *The Rise of the Network Society. The Information Age: Economy, Society and Culture,* vol. 1 (Oxford, 1996).
9. A mirror site of the PETA campaign is available at http://web.archive.org/web/20040613030629/www.masskilling.co.uk.
10. Karen Dawn, "Moving the Media: From Foes or Indifferent Strangers, to Friends," in *In Defense of Animals: The Second Wave,* ed. P Singer (Oxford, 2006), 196–205.
11. An example is the TV commercial of Renault's Rumanian car brand "Dacia" broadcasted in 2008 in Germany: While Mahatma Gandhi, Wladimir Lenin, and Rosa Luxemburg are playing table football, Fidel Castro, Karl Marx, and Che Guevara are hoping for a new revolution (of cars). A mirror site is available at http://web.archive.org/web/20080405215307 or http://www.dacia.de/revolution/. An analysis of this shift in commercials in provided by Ronald Bishop, "The Presbyopic Six: Exploring Marginalization of Protest and of Journalism in a Television-Online Advertising Campaign," *Popular Communication* 1, no. 3 (2003): 143–62.

12. For example, Johan Galtung and Mari H Ruge, "The Structure of Foreign News: The Presentation of the Congo, Cuba and Cyprus Crises in Four Norwegian Newspapers," *Journal of Peace Research* 2, no. 1 (1965): 64–91.

13. Kathrin Fahlenbrach, *Protestinszenierungen. Visuelle Kommunikation und kollektive Identitäten in Protestbewegungen* (Wiesbaden, 2002).

14. Charlotte Ryan, *Prime Time Activism: Media Strategies for Grassroots Organizing* (Boston, 1991).

15. Baringhorst, "Introduction: Political Campaigning in Changing Media Cultures," 18.

16. David S Meyer, "The Challenge of Cultural Elites: Celebrities and Social Movements," *Sociological Inquiry* 65, no. 2 (1995): 181–206.

17. Concerning campaigning and party politics see Pippa Norris, *A Virtuous Circle. Political Communications in Postindustrial Societies* (Cambridge, 2000).

18. Lance W Bennett, "Social Movements beyond Borders: Understanding Two Eras of Transnational Activism," in *Transnational Protest and Global Activism,* ed. S Tarrow and D Della Porta (Oxford, 2005), 213–16.

19. Simon Teune, "A Snapshot of Movements. Assessing Movement Diversity through Campaign Analysis?," paper presented at the Campaign Analysis in a Globalizing World workshop, Evangelische Akademie Tutzing, April 2007, http://protestkuriosa.files.wordpress.com/2008/05/a-snapshot-of-movements.pdf.

20. Dieter Rucht, "The Quadruple 'A'. Media Strategies of Protest Movements since the 1960s," in *Cyberprotest. New Media, Citizens and Social Movements,* ed. W van de Donk et al. (London, 2004), 29–56.

21. For an elaborated approach, see Verta Taylor and Nella van Dyke, "'Get Up, Stand Up': Tactical Repertoires of Social Movements," in *The Blackwell Companion to Social Movements,* ed. DA Snow, S Soule, and H Kriesi (Malden, MA, 2004), 262–93.

22. Research project *Changing Protest and Media Cultures. Transnational Anti-Corporate Campaigns and Digital Communication,* http://www.protest-cultures.uni-siegen.de.

23. Nicole Doerr and Alice Mattoni, "Public Spaces and Alternative Media Networks in Europe: The Case of the Euro Mayday Parade against Precarity," in *The Revolution Will Not Be Televised? Media and Protest Movement,* ed. R Werenskjold, K Fahlenbrach, and E Sivertsen (New York, forthcoming).

24. Research project *Protest als Medium—Medien des Protests,* http://www.protestmedia.net.

25. Lance W Bennett and Jarol B Manheim, "The Big Spin. Strategic Communication and the Transformation of Pluralist Democracy," in *Mediated Politics: Communication in the Future of Democracy,* ed. LW Bennett and RM Entman (Cambridge, 2001), 279–98.

26. For the broader argument of peer-to-peer-production, see Michel Bauwens, "The Political Economy of Peer Production," *CTheory* (2005), http://www.ctheory.net/articles.aspx?id=499.

27. John Corner and Dick Pels, "Introduction: The Re-Styling of Politics," in *Media and Restyling of Politics: Consumerism, Celebrity and Cynicism,* ed. J Corner and D Pels (London, 2003), 1–18.

28. By now, first insight is provided by the analysis of election campaigns in *Communication Theory* 19, no. 1 (2009).

29. An exception forms Jonah Peretti and Michele Micheletti, "The Nike Sweatshop Email. Political Consumerism, Internet, and Culture Jamming," in *Politics, Products and Markets: Exploring Political Consumerism Past and Present,* ed. M Micheletti, A Follesdal, and D Stolle (New Brunswick, 2004), 127–42.

30. Alice Mattoni, "Organization, Mobilization, and Identity: National and Transnational Grassroots Campaigns between Face-to-Face and Computer-Mediated Communication," in *Political Campaigning on the Web,* ed. S Baringhorst, V Kneip, and J Niesyto (Bielefeld, 2009), 199–230; or Veronika Kneip and Johanna Niesyto, "Interconnectivity in the 'Public of Publics'—The Example of Anti-Corporate Campaign," presented at the Changing Politics through Digital Networks conference, University of Florence, October 2007, http://www.regione.toscana.it/documents/10180/23652/Kneip%20 Niesyto/881c9105-efb5-4a18-9b88-fd9e569e117b.

Recommended Reading

Baringhorst, Sigrid, Veronika Kneip, and Johanna Niesyto, eds. *Political Campaigning on the Web.* Bielefeld, 2009. Provides an overview of political campaigning on the web.

Lahusen, Christian. *The Rhetoric of Moral Protest. Public Campaigns, Celebrity, Endorsement, and Political Mobilization.* Berlin, 1996. Provides a useful foundation for understanding protest and media campaigning.

Scammell, Margaret. "Political Marketing: Lessons for Political Science." *Political Studies* 47, no. 4 (1999): 718–39. Offers a general overview about political marketing.

Chapter 40

Theatrical Protest

Dorothea Kraus

Definition of Terms

A demonstration with just one demonstrator to fifty demonstration stewards; actors sharing their own fresh bread with the audience of each performance; a Gus Goose for president campaign at the Munich university: three examples for theatrical protest in Germany and the United States during the 1960s. What do they tell about theatrical protest practices?

For some time now, the notion of theater has been a cultural paradigm in social sciences as well as in theater studies. Coronation ceremonies, public executions, sport events, and many other situations have been described as forms of theater. This use of the term is often metaphorical, whereas the concept of theatricality is not: it focuses on the particular context and the circumstances of the theatrical act, thus allowing a more specific description and analysis of social phenomena—not in the negative sense of the word, though, implying stagy or showily. Rather, this concept draws our attention to the fact that social settings may indeed have specific features that bear resemblance to the art form we commonly associate with theater; their theatricality, however, does not depend on these qualities alone, but rather on the public perception of these settings.

Thus, following Andreas Kotte's definition of theatricality, social situations are never theatrical in themselves: they need to have a public ready and willing to accept that the primary function of the performance they follow lies in the very act of performing. If it fails to do this, a given situation would not be interpreted as theatrical. Even other characteristics of theater considered, this basic condition alone can make all the difference between a social and a theatrical act.

Theatrical performances are closely related to everyday social situations. As such, they can take place at whatever location and at any time that seems appropriate. They do not necessarily need a special setting, a stage, and costumes for the actors or seats for the spectators. Their key elements might be planned, but they retain room for improvisation. Besides, they do not have to be artistically challenging or even creative, though at times they are. Yet they always depend on the public context, the confrontation with an audience they involve in the performance—sometimes even physically. At all times, theatrical acts are acts of communication. And theatrical protest is—in a way—art without art.

Relevance for Protest Cultures

It is this indecisiveness between artistic form and sociopolitical effectiveness that renders theatrical performances so relevant for protest cultures. Theatricality can enhance the cohesion within the protest movement as well as between the actors and the audience, attracts public attention, and helps communicate and explain central ideas. As Carl Oglesby, president of the Students for a Democratic Society in the United States, wrote to Ronnie Davis: "A theater assumes a crowd; it makes a single audience out of individuals, gives them a common rhythm of reeling, reaction, insight; focus, too, sometimes even purpose; makes compact what was diffuse, gives direction to what was random and ambient."[1]

There is another important characteristic of theatrical performances. In the context of political protest, it is not always apparent if what happens is a real situation or just acting, which might be exactly what the protesters intend. On 4 April 1967, for example, members of the West Berlin Kommune 1 (Commune 1) planned to symbolically attack American Vice President Hubert Humphrey with so-called bombs made of flour, paint, and custard powder. The police stopped them before the attempt, but still insisted on having saved the vice president's life when it had become obvious that no real bombs were involved. By overreacting in this way, the West Berlin police force became, for many citizens, a laughing stock.

Although they were both attractive and effective, theatrical protest forms stayed a rather marginal phenomenon within the protest movements since 1945. This, too, might be due to their ambiguity. Quite often, the benefit and the signification of theatrical performances as protest practices were heavily discussed within the protest groups themselves. One of the central questions was whether this protest form was really appropriate to bring about any change of social categories and values. Did theatrical protest not imply that all statements were only fictional in form and content, and therefore not to be taken seriously? Could theater really be a revolutionary instrument for the mobilization and organization of mass protest?

The variety of theatrical protest forms during the 1960s can partly be seen as a result of this conflict. Two main forms are to be distinguished: agitprop street theater and happening. In spite of their potential similarities in appearance, and their many hybrid forms, they had different roots, different social conceptions, and different aesthetical means.

Historical Aspects:
Where and When Were These Protest Techniques Developed? In Which Situations Were They Applied?

Theatrical happenings can be traced back to three main roots: First, the avant-garde movement of the 1920s with its unconventional and provoking performances (for example Dadaism). Second, the international political-artistic group called "Situationist International," founded in 1957—Situationist theory played a central role in many protest activities during the 1968 uprisings, and Situationist events were commonplace, especially in West Germany and France. Third comes the tradition of performance art: during the 1950s, artists across the United States, Germany, and Japan organized multidisciplinary art performances without physical object of art or narrative; Allan Kaprow was the first to coin the term "happening" in 1957. For many of these artists, the concept of happening meant not only a radical doubt in traditional art forms, but also a genuine social statement.

Most of the happenings organized by the international protest movements in the 1960s also focused on increasing awareness of political aberrations, social injustice, and the necessity of immediate action. In this, they were often meant to be acts of emancipation for the participants as well as for the spectators. Besides, they mostly included a breach of social conventions and expectations. Like the happening as art form, they involved four basic elements: time, space, the protestant's/performer's body, and a relationship between protestant/performer and audience. They generally lacked any symbolism in the use of objects and materials. Objects used in the theatrical situations were not props, clothes not costumes, surroundings not stage settings in the literal sense—they did not signify anything apart from what they actually were.[2]

A theatrical protest happening, which got quite a lot of public attention was the demonstration in West Berlin on 13 June 1967. Taking place soon after the student Benno Ohnesorg had been shot by a police officer on

2 June 1967, it was originally meant to be a rather traditional protest march against the Berlin Senate and the local police. Plans were changed when it turned out that security requirements for the demonstration had become unduly strict following political directives: no offending or provoking banners were allowed, and there had to be a demonstration steward on fifty demonstrators. To show the arbitrariness of this requirement, the organizers decided to have instead fifty demonstration stewards marching in regular lines of ten on one single demonstrator holding a banner. In the fore of the demonstration were members of the Kommune 1 cloaked in white bed sheets performing acts of obviously feigned penitence.

In the United States, performance art was also an important inspiration for Off-Off-Broadway and guerilla theater. Troupes like Bread and Puppet Theater, Living Theater, or San Francisco Mime Troupe were looking for alternatives to the commercial orientation of Broadway productions. They focused their attention mainly on the idea of self-liberation from the confining conventions of life and society, and were often directly engaged in the American protest movement, especially in the protest against the Vietnam War. The Living Theater, for example, dedicated its plays and performances to transforming the organization of power within society, striving for cooperative and communal expression instead of competitive, hierarchical structure. To counteract complacency in the audience, they developed forms of direct spectacle seeking to involve the spectators. The name Bread and Puppet Theater even derives from the theater's practice of sharing its own fresh bread with the audience, as well as from the use of larger-than-life puppets in political spectacles and demonstrations. Both Bread and Puppet Theater and Living Theater often toured in Europe and were widely known there.[3]

Guerilla theater was a radical form of political theater in the United States that shared its origins with many forms of political protest and street theater. Troupes like the San Francisco Mime Troupe also understood themselves to be a direct answer to the population's indifference toward the Vietnam War. Although guerilla theater had much in common with agit-prop theater, it included elements of happening and Dadaistic performance tactics as well.

In contrast to these visually strong and abundant theatrical experiments, street theater troupes in West Germany such as the *Sozialistisches Straßentheater Berlin* (West; Socialist Street Theater West Berlin) or the *Kölner Straßentheater* (Cologne Street Theater) were mostly interested in a rather blunt and strident, often simplifying presentation of short realistic scenes and dialogues in the streets or other public places. They focused mainly on the information about, and the analysis of, social situations as well as on activating the audience by means of direct agitation for social and political change. On this note, these street theater groups tried to avoid forms of figurative theatrical language, concentrating instead on social analysis, rational appeals, and rhetorical forms of speech. Therefore, their performances became mostly rather static and lacking in visual appeal: the actors were standing together reciting a text, their different roles only marked by cardboard nameplates they wore around their necks.

Initially, this conception of theatrical protest did not have a lot in common with happening-like performances. Rather, it was deeply rooted in the political agitprop theater of the 1920s. In 1930, there had been more than 200 of those highly popular nonprofessional troupes in Germany. In these agitprop troupes, workers performed for other workers, rallying the people around the Communist cause. At the same time, they distanced themselves sharply from all forms of high culture or bourgeois theater that— in their eyes—did nothing but affirm the established social reality instead of fighting for social change.

Many of the street theater troupes in West Germany became increasingly skeptical about the political effectiveness of this tradition. This was due, first, to the lack of interest among the workers as the original target group. Second, the neglect of visual creativity and sensuality was now often considered an unnecessary restriction rendering performances rather dull and stale. For this reason, the troupe *Politisches Forum* (Political Forum) in Munich, for example, started to include elements of happenings in their performances. Among other things, they used Gus Goose from the Disney comics in varying contexts as a little known, but multidimensional character that finally became an important symbol for the political protest at the Munich university: during the Gus Goose for president campaign in 1969, students even erected a Gus Goose statue in front of the university.

State of Research in Related Social Movements Research

Although too significant not to be appreciated as part of protest actions, happenings and street theater performances have rarely been an actual focus of social movements research so far. In fact, theatrical protest has mostly been analyzed from a rather instrumental point of view, as one possible way of expressing new issues and thus trying to influence the political agenda. In this approach, theatrical practices have been regarded as means to an end—funny and eye-catching maybe, but above all a more or less successful way of symbolically communicating new ideas.

This functional perspective, however, ignores the fact that theatrical protest, being a political practice, has both social and expressive meaning.

It might of course provide concrete information, yet is at the same time aesthetically meaningful and effective. Therefore, to fully understand the sociopolitical implications and impacts of street theater and happenings looking at questions of content is not enough. Political or cultural meaning as well as social identity can result from the performativity of the theatrical act, too.

Interdisciplinary Perspectives for the Analysis of Protest Cultures

Therefore, an interdisciplinary approach is of paramount importance for any research in the field of theatrical protest. A well-grounded analysis that includes cultural, artistic, and aesthetical questions is impossible without referring to the concepts and theoretic framework of cultural and literary studies or art history. In dramatics, for example, the performative turn has led to abundant research results regarding analytical and interdisciplinary perspectives on theatrical protest.

Research Gaps and Open Questions

As far as the theatricality of protest movements is concerned, there remain quite a number of research gaps and open questions. A comparative history of theatrical protest practices worldwide is still to be written. This includes the question of the exchange of ideas and practices in the field of theatrical protest between international protest movements. Besides, there is still a lack in profound analyses of the connections and contacts between alternative forms of theater—like guerilla theater—and professional theater (private or subsidized) in a narrow sense of the term, which could tell us something about the influences and effects of social movements in society as a whole. Finally, there is still much to learn about forms of theatrical protest from the 1970s down to the present day, for example about the Clandestine Insurgent Rebel Clown Army, currently active in many countries with protests against war, corporate globalization, and other issues.

Dorothea Kraus is scientific staff member of the Foundation Haus der Geschichte der Bundesrepublik Deutschland in Berlin, Germany. She has published several articles on the politicization of theater and of theatrical performances in West Germany. Together with Ingrid Gilcher-Holtey and Franziska Schößler, she is editor of a book on the struggles for a redefinition of the limits and boundaries of political theater in the 1960s and 1970s, *Der Kampf ums politische Theater. Regie, Dramatik, Organisation nach 1968* (Frankfurt, 2006). She is also author of a book on political theater and performative action in the protest movement around 1968, *Theater-Proteste. Zur Politisierung von Straße und Bühne in den 1960er Jahren* (Frankfurt, 2007).

Notes

1. As cited in Michael Schmidtke, *Der Aufbruch der jungen Intelligenz: Die 68er Jahre in der Bundesrepublik und den USA* (Frankfurt, 2003), 101.
2. Cf. Erika Fischer-Lichte, "Grenzgänge und Tauschhandel: Auf dem Weg zu einer performativen Kultur," in *Theater seit den sechziger Jahren. Grenzgänge der Neo-Avantgarde,* ed. E Fischer-Lichte, F Kreuder, and I Pflug (Tübingen, 1998), 1–20.
3. For these two famous theater troupes, see *Peter Schumann's Bread and Puppet Theater,* ed. Stefan Brecht (New York, 1988); and Pierre Biner, *The Living Theater* (New York, 1972).

Recommended Reading

Fischer-Lichte, Erika. *Ästhetik des Performativen.* Frankfurt, 2004. Standard work on the aesthetics of performativity and the performative turn since the 1960s. It has to be taken into account that the relevant literature on performativity and theatricality as defined above has been published in the field of dramatics and genuinely in the German research context.

Fischer-Lichte, Erika. "Theater als kulturelles Modell." In *Germanistik. Disziplinäre Identität und kulturelle Leistung,* edited by L Jäger, 164–84. Weinheim, 1995. A specific and highly relevant article on theatricality as one of the most important cultural paradigms of the present.

Kohtes, Martin Maria. *Guerilla Theater: Theorie und Praxis des politischen Straßentheaters in den USA, 1965–1970.* Tübingen, 1990. An introductory study containing substantial information about Off-Off-Broadway, guerilla, and street theater in the United States during the 1960s.

Kotte, Andreas. "Theatralität: Ein Begriff sucht seinen Gegenstand." *Forum Modernes Theater* 132 (1998): 133–77. Brief, yet comprehensive article with important reflections on the concept of theatricality.

Kraus, Dorothea. *Theater-Proteste: Zur Politisierung von Straße und Bühne in den 1960er Jahren.* Frankfurt, 2007. A broad analysis of both theatrical happenings and street theater, especially in the West German protest movement with references to the events in other countries.

Chapter 41

Movie/Cinema

Anna Schober

Cinema and Socialization

The cinema is usually a quite standardized spatial setting: there is a huge room, which on one side is delimited by an enormous screen that can be covered behind curtains. On the opposite side—even if behind a wall and so invisible to the viewer—we find the film projection machinery and the projectionist. And in between, there are a great many numbered seats, in orderly, narrow rows, all pointing in one direction: toward the screen. Already the amplitude of the space and the closeness between the people in the seats can create an exciting effect, an impulsiveness and a sweeping-away of the public, which enhances the feeling of being part of a collective. In addition, the darkness of the cinema space creates an uncertainty of the spatial frame, which further amplifies these effects. In the cinema, we are huddled together with those next to us, and at the same time, the boundaries of the space as a whole disappear and allow fantasy to expand it toward infinite dimensions.[1]

This power cinema has, in respect to socialization, led a variety of social forces to use it to expand their sphere of action: since its inception, the cinema has been part of educational and promotional discourses of cities, nations, political parties, transnational organizations, corporations, and even religious institutions.[2] At the same time, the gatherings of consumers and citizens around cinema spaces (or other localities where films are projected) created communities too and even led to the formation of particular cinema-related political movements such as the working-class cinema movement and avant-garde cinema clubs in the 1920s, the communal cinema movement and other alternative cinema initiatives such as the Expanded Cinema in the 1960s or the Cinema Beur in the 1980s and 1990s.[3]

This socialization around cinema spaces shows that, with the break towards modernity, the community-forming process is in itself subject to historic change: people no longer unite mainly guided by traditional ways of ordering the world, such as those inherited via birth, craft, or religious affiliation, but because of shared judgements, taste, interest, or identification. Moreover, such assignments no longer exert exclusivity, but any individual participates in a variety of collective bodies and changes group affiliations more quickly and more often.[4]

At the same time, the cinema has also worked as an agent in respect to a transformation of the form of perception: in modernity, faith began to withdraw from a paradise outside the world and has been transformed into a form of belief closely connected with the appearances in the world. With this, the cinema became a place where it can become evident who someone is and where he or she stands—this who and where shows itself in images, perceptions, certain urban situations, and significant encounters. And in their self-definitions, people increasingly refer to significant events of perception too and expose identifications and dissociations in certain styles of living and dwelling and of staging themselves in public.[5]

Entertaining and/or Negotiating the Sense

In modern cities, meaning and sense have become mobile and in an enhanced way ambivalent: on the one hand, they are regarded as present, visible, and graspable inside the mundane apearances, but on the other hand, they are seen as missing or at least difficult to reach and as lying behind the words and the things.[6] In this context, the cinema functions as an important place for negotiating sense—what is one of the reasons why it has so freqently been used for protest tactics. Its role thereby is double-edged too: it acts as a shelter, a space, where a (new) sense of the world can be experienced alongside gestures, facial expressions, postures, gazes, spaces, and things brought via montage in a temporary form.[7] Here visitors enter into a plurality of viewpoints, laugh, encounter surprising cuts or images with the capacity to call forth and to affirm reality, and get involved in a bodily way. And at the same time, they digress into a conversation between the various selves accentuated in the course of the viewing process. The cinema thus has to do with a being in between—hence it is an almost private space of inter-essere, of interest.

Thereby in cinemas, such an experience of sense is usually a collective one: not in the way that there is immediately any communication happening about what a film shows but rather in the sense of a shared being together, which is interrupted with the end of the film. Afterward, however, exchange and discussion of what was experienced occur, various viewpoints are posed, and sometimes even actions or the making of further films are stimulated. In this way, cinema and film become part of a public sphere were a civil interaction between strangers as well as an expression of diversity could take place[8]—they are involved, together with spectators, cinema-programmers, and critics in constituting such a sphere.

Movie spectatorship, as well as film exhibition, did however not appear all at once but are practices that developed over decades, approximately between 1895 and 1909, when the classical mode of cinema narration emerged, and has continued to change ever since.

At the same time, cinema was soon a highly contested terrain: it was for instance judged to be a debased and dangerous amusement, and new ways of a more "educating" film exhibition and of addressing the public were promoted. These battles led already after World War I to the development of a larger mass-cultural audience where social distinction was rather submerged by middle-class values of respectability.[9]

However, despite the quite standardized presence of this classical cinema setting until today, film narration as well as exhibition in democratic societies[10] has remained subject to struggle and has been practiced in a variety of ways. In the 1920s and 1930s, there were cinema palaces as well avant-garde and explicitly political ciné clubs; in the 1950s single-hall cinemas and film societies prevailed; the 1960s and 1970s were characterized by an especially prolific emergence of protest movements using film and urban cinema situations such as the communal cinema movement and Expanded Cinema initiatives as well as by wide-screen cinemas and studios; and since the 1990s, multiplex as well as arthouse cinemas have spread as well as urban guerrilla groups such as "A Wall Is a Screen"[11] with portable projectors using city walls as temporary projection areas.

But notwithstanding the emergence of all these different types, the cinema has maintained its double role of being experienced as a space for an almost placeless deciphering of the world connected with imagination and (self-)reflection and of being part of a broader public sphere constituted out of various viewpoints, actions, and expressions. And because of this latter communal function, the cinema situation remains—even if in a transformed way as multiplex cinema, art house cinema, film festival, or cinema bar—an integral part of postmodern urban life even after technically new ways of

Figure 41.1. Kinoapparatom, Housing Estate Grünau, Zurich 2004, www.
kinoapparatom.net. © Simone Schardt and Wolf Schmelter.

digital image creation[12] have been initiated and have further changed the
regime of perception.

Film Exhibition and the (Informal) Public Sphere

Because film is a commodity that circulates nationally as well as internationally, can be reproduced on a mass scale, is connected with the idea of being
a universal art, and has a particular capacity to involve its spectators, it soon
proves to be a widely adopted means of gaining public presence and has
often been produced and/or included in political actions in ways that involve
utopian sensibilities. Already around 1913, groups started to form around
cinema spaces in quite explicit political ways and created for instance, the
Cinema du Peuple (Peoples Cinema) in Paris.[13]

Fascism as well as one-party regimes in former state-Socialist countries
mark a profound break in this respect: there is on the one hand an extraordinary pronounced use by the fascist or state-socialist regime of the potential
that cinema has in respect to socialization.[14] But on the other hand, in these

kind of societies any oppositional use of the cinema was eliminated or pushed underground because there was a denial that difference is constitutive for society—the only accepted difference is that between the people as one and its enemies.

However—despite this elimination of a conflictual public sphere—in some centers such as Belgrade or Prague in the 1960s, even in state-Socialist system activities around cinema spaces were noticeable, which took part in the construction of an informal public sphere. The groups constituted by way of these activities are for instance called Open Cinema, Novi film, Black Cinema, or New Wave. They emerged out of amateur film clubs, which were part of the official system of youth education, and—first involuntarily and later on more consciously—started to enter into a dispute with the ruling elites.[15]

Similarly, in the United States, as well as in Western Europe following the student movement of the 1960s, filmmakers, urban cinema squatters, and cineaste circles appeared in a prolific way and thereby again exploited film, a variety of urban spaces, and public film exhibition in order to open an aesthetic-political space, in which potentially everyone could then count

Figure 41.2. Xscreen, Expanded Cinema action, Cologne 1968. © Xscreen Archive Berlin, courtesy Wilhelm Hein.

him- or herself as adhering to certain ideas, convictions, and aesthetic styles.[16] Contrary to previous political cinema squats, which relied on relatively stable party organizations and the social strata related to them, these newer protest movements gave even more weight to processes of identification and a similarity in judging as well as to aesthetic tactics and spectacular styles of self-presentation. For instance, new styles of making films were developed that relied on the explicit involvement of all participants and the public into the process of filmmaking, the pronounced working with interviews and nonprofessional actors, or the search for stories in specific sociopolitical milieus. This change was also reflected in names these groups chose, such as Cinéma verité, Neorealismo, Expanded Cinema, Experimental Cinema, Free Cinema, Cinéma Lettriste, or Nouvelle Vague—whereas earlier movements for example called themselves Cinema du People.[17]

This—in itself—plural tradition was again questioned in the 1980s for example by cinema activists and filmmakers shaped by feminism[18] as well as by newly emerging discourses on migration—and on an aesthetic level by video techniques and the digital image—which started to use film and the cinema in order to negotiate (sexual or ethnic) difference in a pronounced way and to redefine their relationship with the public toward a less hierarchic interaction.[19] In parallel, in former state-Socialist countries, film and cinema was used to cope with the newly re-created national and ethnic differences as well as with the totalitarian heritage.[20]

Works on the political dimension of cinema usually do not focus on the diversity of reactions of spectators and the broader public dimension of cinema in general but still conceive the spectator as a function of formal film codes and/or ideology[21]—which also makes this public dimension a challenge for future research. Besides this, the main desideratum in researching cinema as a space for protest action is the transnational dimension of tactics involving film and cinema.

Anna Schober currently directs the research project "Everybody: a transnational iconography" at Justus Liebig University in Giessen, supported by the Deutsche Forschungsgemeinschaft. In 2009 she got her postdoctoral habilitation at Vienna University. Afterwards she was Marie Curie Fellow and Visiting Professor at Verona University and Mercator Visiting Professor and Deputy Professor at Justus Liebig University Giessen. Her publications include: *Blue Jeans. Vom Leben in Stoffen und Bildern* (Frankfurt, 2001); *Ironie, Montage, Verfremdung. Ästhetische Taktiken und die politische Gestalt der Demokratie* (Munich, 2009); and *The Cinema Makers. Public Life and the Exhibition of Difference in Central and South Eastern Europe since the 1960s* (Bristol, 2013).

Notes

1. Georg Simmel, "The Sociology of Space," in *Simmel: On Culture,* ed. D Frisby and M Featherstone (Thousand Oaks, CA, 1997), 137–70.
2. For example, Elizabeth Lebas, "The Clinic, the Street and the Garden: Municipal Film-Making in Britain Between the Wars," in *Spaces in European Cinema,* ed. M Konstantarakos (Bristol, 2000), 138–51; and Christian Kuchler, *Kirche und Kino: Katholische Filmarbeit in Bayern, 1945–1965* (Paderborn, 2006).
3. Christophe Gauthier, *La Passion Du Cinéma. Cinéphiles, ciné-clubs et salles spécialisées à Paris de 1920 à 1929* (Paris, 1999), 174*ff*; Anna Schober, *The Cinema Makers: Public Life and the Exhibition of Difference in South-Eastern and Central Europe Since the 1960s* (Bristol, 2013), 56*ff*; Peter Bloom, "Beur Cinema and the Politics of Location: French Immigration Politics and the Naming of a Film Movement," in *Transnational Cinema: The Film Reader,* ed. E Ezra and T Rowden (London, 2006), 131–41.
4. John R Gibbins and Bo Reimer, *The Politics of Postmodernity: An Introduction to Contemporary Politics and Culture* (London, 1999), 76*ff.*
5. This is investigated for the dissemination of myths connected with Blue Jeans via film and consumer practice in Anna Schober, *Blue Jeans: Vom Leben in Stoffen und Bildern* (Frankfurt, 2001).
6. Jean Luc Nancy, *L'oubli de la Philosophie* (Paris, 1986).
7. As an important institution for such a new way of negotiating sense that draws strongly on our capacity to decipher the world as well as the actions of others, the cinema enters into a strange complicity and equivalence with twentieth-century philosophy, which also dwells persistently in a quite similar way on the sense. On this, see Maurice Merleau-Ponty, "The Film and the New Psychology," in *Sense and Non-Sense* eds. H L Dreyfus and P A Dreyfus (Evanston, IL, 1964), 48–59.
8. On the public dimension of cinema activism since the 1960s, see Schober, *The Cinema Makers,* 26*ff.* On early cinema and the public sphere, see Miriam Hansen, *Babel & Babylon: Spectatorship in American Silent Film* (Cambridge, 1991), 90*ff.*
9. Hansen, *Babel & Babylon,* 96.
10. One-party societies however are defined by excluding such a struggle and try to eliminate any uncertainty and temporarity that is connected with political processes. On similarities and differences between cinema movements in democratic-pluralistic and one-party societies, see Schober, *The Cinema Makers.*
11. "A Wall Is a Screen," http://www.awallisascreen.com/.
12. Marc Hansen describes that even if the digital image is again expression as well as agent of further transformations in the regime of perception, the cinema remains an important setting for showing (digital) films. However, he does not explain this as related to the potential the cinema setting has for constituting a public sphere. See Marc Hansen, *New Philosophy for New Media* (Cambridge, 2006), 32*ff.*
13. Gauthier, *La Passion Du Cinèma,* 35.
14. Clemens Zimmermann, *Medien im Nationalsozialismus. Deutschland 1933–1945, Italien 1922–1943, Spanien 1936–1951* (Vienna, 2007).
15. Schober, *The Cinema Makers,* 107*ff.*

16. On such processes of gaining public presence, see Jacques Rancière, *Dis-Agreement: Politics and Philosophy* (Minneapolis, MN, 1999).

17. On Cinéma Vérité, Peter Graham, "Cinéma-Vérité in France," *Film Quarterly* 44, no. 1 (1964): 30–36.

18. Esther Quetting, ed., *Kino. Frauen. Experimente* (Marburg, 2007).

19. Rosanna Maule, *Beyond Auteurism: New Directions in Authorial Film Practices in France, Italy and Spain since the 1980s* (Bristol, 2008).

20. Ljiljana Filipović, "Film as an Abreaction of Totalitarianism," in *The Couch and the Silver Screen: Psychoanalytic Reflections on European Cinema,* ed. A Sabbadini (New York, 2003), 204–12.

21. For instance, Thomas Christen, "Die Entwicklung der Filmsprache in den 1960er Jahren. Offene Enden, erzählerische Lücken, Selbstthematisierung, Zufallsprinzip," in *1968. Handbuch zur Kultur- und Mediengeschichte der Studentenbewegung,* ed. M Klimke and J Scharloth (Stuttgart, 2007), 187–97.

Recommended Reading

Hansen, Miriam. *Babel & Babylon: Spectatorship in American Silent Film.* Cambridge, 1991. Gives a comprehensive introduction into methodologies conceptualizing the cinema in relation to the public sphere, especially in relation to the cinema culture of the silent era.

Maule, Rosanna. *Beyond Auteurism: New Directions in Authorial Film Practices in France, Italy and Spain since the 1980s.* Bristol, 2008. The postmodern transformation of film styles and the related political dimension of film practice since the 1980s is analyzed in detail and for various European countries in this publication.

Schober, Anna. *The Cinema Makers: Public Life and the Exhibition of Difference in South-Eastern and Central Europe Since the 1960s.* Bristol, 2013. Discusses cinema as a political space of action for transnational protest movements in central and southeastern Europe since the 1960s.

Chapter 42

Civil Disobedience

Helena Flam and Åsa Wettergren

Civil disobedience means *conscientious, nonviolent acts* of disobedience of law carried out in protest against a perceived injustice. Its early modern ideal combined a visible willingness to accept penalty with resorting to illegal action, thus underlining one's status as a law-abiding citizen, moved only by conscience to disobey law. This form of protest seeks to win sympathy by demonstrable individual and collective discipline. It is carried by the hope of positively affecting public opinion and decision makers, and so affecting social change.

Henry David Thoreau's essay *On Civil Disobedience* introduced the modern concept.[1] Expressing in a nonviolent manner an individual, principled objection to their own government's unjust policy, law, or practice, exemplaries have defied the law: Thoreau refused to pay poll taxes to object to the U.S. war against Mexico, slavery, and violations of the rights of the native Indians. Leo Tolstoy[2] opposed bearing arms. Both explained their objections in publications that justified and propagated their conscientious disagreement with the authorities of the day. Gustav Landauer, a German exemplary, and also trade unionists, Anarcho-Syndicalists, and Socialists promoted civil disobedience just as John Locke's and Etienne de La Boétie's treatises, which argued that citizens have the right to rise against the state they consider unjust or Émile Zola's *J'accuse*-campaign, which turned around the French anti-Semitic Dreyfus Affair.

More recently, a liberal political philosopher, Rawls, defined civil disobedience as openly breaking the law and showing disrespect for legitimately established democratic authority.[3] Similarly to Thoreau, he saw it as justifiable only when the duty to oppose injustice requires the breaking of the law. Civil disobedience is normally employed by minorities who see violations of values and principles higher than the rule of law, such as the *equality of liberty* (vote, property, mobility, faith) and the *equality of opportunity*. To remain legitimate and prevent a general disrespect for law and basic rights, civil disobedience must be combined with respect for the general rule of law; appeal to the sense of justice shared with the general public. Its proponents must create cooperative political alliances, keep low the overall level of dissent, and rely primarily on nonviolent means. If thus regulated, civil disobedience, along with free and regular elections and the independent judiciary, contributes to the reproduction and strengthens just institutions.

In contrast to Rawls, Cohen and Arato argue that no absolute moral principles, but instead the *normative principles of democracy* available *within* the democratic discourse itself, legitimize and navigate civil disobedience. They attribute to civil disobedience, and to the civil society in which it develops, a pivotal role in sustaining (the utopia of) a democratic and just society.[4] Social movements employing civil disobedience for the sake of such utopias, initiate societal learning processes, expand the variety and forms of participation open to private citizens, and improve the faulty and develop new democratic institutions. Cohen and Arato position civil disobedience as integral, rather than exceptional, to the democratic discourse.

Civil disobedience plays an important role in authoritarian or totalitarian regimes. In fact, the emergence of the civil society and civil disobedience protests in Central Europe in the 1970s prepared the ground for the Velvet Revolutions and the breakdown of the Soviet Empire in 1990, while reviving scholarship on the civic society.[5] The Arab Spring of 2011 has similar effects on the region and the scholarship. Research indicates that in these regimes, civil disobedience is the most effective when it entails winning over regime military or police and administrative forces, unmasking the pretentions of the opponent and building up transnational pressure on these regimes.[6]

Historical Aspects

Mahatma Gandhi advocated the adoption of principled, nonviolent, and obstructive civil disobedience costly to the opponent as the major strategy. He relied on it while opposing the oppression of Indians in South Africa in the early 1900s and after World War I while heading the nationalist Indian mass movement aiming at putting an end to the oppressive colonial British rule.[7] His followers refused to cooperate with, submit to, or obey the British rulers, ultimately driving them out. Gandhi believed that once the subjects refuse their cooperation or disobey, the rulers' power ends. Mobilizing against racist discrimination in the United States between the mid 1950s and 1960s, Martin Luther King Jr., leader of the American civil rights movement, repeatedly expressed his general respect for the rule of law.[8] He saw conscientious, disciplined, responsible direct action, entailing marches, sit-ins, and boycotts, as creating "constructive nonviolent tension" and as the last resort in a battle against injustice, after all legal means and negotiations have failed. Like Gandhi, King believed that breaking an unjust law must be done openly. He pleaded for "loving" willingness to accept penalty, and warned that protesters' minds and bodies must be prepared for hurt to make the case before the local and national community. Other historical examples of civil disobedience are the nineteenth-century Irish rent strikes, tax refusals, and boycotts against the British, and the Chinese boycotts of the American goods directed against the U.S. anti-Chinese legislation in 1905–6. British and American suffragettes early on also experimented with, inter alia, picketing, demonstrations, saloon-raiding, and individual and collective hunger strikes.[9] All these movements helped expand the general repertoire of protest action.

State of Research

Understood as rule-breaking or surpassing regular democratic channels to be heard, civil disobedience belongs to the established action repertoire of social movements. Consider, for example, boycott, picketing, sit-ins, protest disrobing, strike, stalling, obstruction, or noncooperation with conscription and deportation.[10] A recent overview discusses these and recent additions to the social movement action repertoires.[11] A few important books, asking when civil disobedience is effective, mark a recent revival of primarily academic interest in civil disobedience.[12] In contrast, Sharp[13] and his Albert Einstein Institution laid foundations for scholarly research focused solely on the history, exemplaries, and movements relying on civil disobedience with the explicit aim of promoting this type of protest. Powers and Vogele's encyclopedia of *Power, Protest and Change* and Clark's edited volume *People Power* follow his footpath.[14] With a similar agenda, a steering group led by Carol Rank and Andrew Rigby set up the Coventry Nonviolence Research Group at the University of Coventry; Stellan Vinthagen pushed for Resistance Studies of Gothenburg; and Peter Ackerman and Jack DuVall established the International Center on Nonviolent Conflict (ICNC) in Washington, D.C. The Coventry data bank gathers thousands of nonviolent resistance cases, while the ICNC's News Digest on Nonviolent Conflict keeps its online subscribers up-to-date. The aim now is go beyond collecting, cataloguing, and networking with activists all over the world by pushing for systematic theorizing.

Nonviolence and Its Limits

While the scholars in the Sharp tradition strongly believe in an exclusive use of nonviolent means of protest, discussions about whether civil disobedience constitutes a legitimate strategy took place within, for instance, the American civil rights, European pacifist, and the anti-apartheid movements, and many movements thereafter. Recently, Medearis pinpointed that the theory of deliberative democracy fails to recognize that asymmetric power relations exclude some groups from the democratic debate.[15] To expand the space of the public discourse or force their own entry, movements of the unheard or excluded must formulate a subversive message, stage drama and increase the costs of the established routines by obstruction, threats, and even violence. The initial exclusion legitimizes acts of coercive civil disobedience such as infringement on *property rights,* as in occupations or sit-ins, which do not violate democratic rights of free speech, association, or participation. Movements may also (1) endanger businesses by boycotts, upsetting production or access to financing, (2) disrupt daily routine or public peace, or (3) threaten the legitimacy of political actors.

Gandhi's and King's classic versions still called for disciplined nonviolent resistance, even at a cost to one's own body or life. They also called for accepting punishment upon legal transgressions to demonstrate one's sincerity and general respect for the rule of law. In contrast, today civil disobedience is more diversely understood. It may be legal or illegal, direct or indirect, with immediate or post-factum effects. As long as protest is motivated by unselfish, principled, compassionate concern for justice or legitimate values, such as transparency, equality, autonomy, or sustainable development, many activists still speak of civil disobedience. This is because today citizen duties are much more self-evidently defined as going beyond the obligation to follow law and observe democratic procedures and include (1) challenging prevailing views, (2) compelling majorities and governments to reassess their moral parameters, and (3) mobilizing for change and breach of the law, if the status quo impedes on the liberties, rights, and values of minorities, or the opponent is oppressive or violent.

Emotions, Culture, and the Media

Civic disobedience entails breaking not only legal, but also cultural codes. The grief-stricken mothers who over the past 30 years have protested against the disappearance, mistreatment, torture, or killings of their children by the military and political authorities in a steadily increasing number of countries, usually display pictures, cardboard silhouettes, or names of their children in public squares or online. They not only transgress their traditional gender roles, but also create a powerful emotional appeal—often harvesting first ridicule and then repression. Civil rights activists growing an Afro or movement slogans expressing movement goals, such as "black power" or "take the toys away from the boys" or the "personal is political," seem innocent. Yet they provoked aggressive and repressive responses of the authorities because of their unsettling emotional-normative charge.

The very act of protesting is generally connected to a bundle of emotions, such as fear, embarrassment, and anger.[16] Civil disobedience, because it entails literally putting one's body on the line and facing harsh treatment and legal consequences, demands specific training.[17] Numerous manuals recommend role-playing and other exercises to envision being confronted by brute force of the police or military units and to learn how to avoid violence escalation. Activists are encouraged to articulate and explore what they will feel: fear, rage, pain, and physical discomfort. Collective preparation enhances unity: knowing, trusting, and sympathizing with each other.

Martin Luther King stressed that nonviolent defiance calls for heroic, "sublime courage … willingness to suffer and … amazing discipline in the midst of the most inhuman provocation."[18] This noble dimension makes nonviolent civil disobedience a profoundly emotional nerve-racking game about moral advantage. Whereas collective action since the turn of the twentieth century has had to distance itself from the image of the uncontrolled, angry, rioting mob whose claims cannot be taken seriously, the disciplined performance of civil disobedience turns the tables. When successful, it is the state/authorities that lose control, resorting to blind rage and meaningless violence (see note 12).

In contemporary society, political protest often assumes diverse cultural expressions.[19] The mass media speed up the diffusion of innovative protest forms, including tragic or comic street performances, candlelight vigils, mass pet walking, whistling, kitchen pot banging, die-ins, reverse strikes, protest voyages, crawl-ins, church-seizure, police- or soldier-hugging, and public coming-out. Often humorous disguises become a means of reducing own fear, winning bystander sympathy, and disarming angry or violent responses from the opponent. Funny protests challenge the opponent's self-control, making a violent response seem not only abusive but also ridiculous.[20]

The electronic media makes possible such new protest forms as hacking, online sit-ins or political campaigns, e-mail floods, viruses and worms, grassroots info war—known as the *World Wide Web of political hacktivism* or *electronic civil disobedience*.[21] While enabling individuals to perform spectacular and far-reaching acts of protest, electronic civil disobedience entails groups forming for the specific purpose of creating blocking or destructive software for protest use, the best well-known being the Electronic Disturbance Theater that created FloodNet, enabling mass virtual sit-ins against the Mexican government. Global movements—the pro-Zapatista movement, *Attac,* and *World Social Forum*—are unthinkable without the Internet as a networking, campaigning, and tactical device. The electronic forms of civil disobedience seem less emotionally demanding than the older forms that put bodies and lives on the line.

Research Gaps

Civil disobedience can (1) be enacted by an individual or a collective, (2) pursue individual, group, or abstract sense of justice, (3) be enacted by objecting to practices, decisions, rules, laws, institutions, or policies, and (4) be enacted by appealing to but also challenging prevalent moral standards and authorities. It can be employed not only against the authorities or an intransigent majority but also against another minority or a foreign government or group. It emerges in democratic and nondemocratic regimes, aiming at either reforms or a revolution.

Within the area of social movement research, civil disobedience is rarely highlighted in its own right. There is great need for research on the conditions under which civil disobedience emerges and is successful in various types of regimes. Adherents of civil disobedience, often directly cooperating with nonviolent movements, have assembled a large amount of data, but are only beginning with theory-building. Yet the Velvet Revolutions, the Arab Spring, their precedents, and many contemporary nonviolent movements spread all over the world beg the question why civil disobedience emerges and when it actually works.

Helena Flam is professor of sociology at the University of Leipzig in Germany. One of her main research topics are emotions. Her recent publications on emotions include: *Mosaic of Fear* (New York, 1998) and *The Emotional "Man" and the Problem of Collective Action* (Berlin, New York, 2000). She edited and contributed to *Emotions and Social Movements* (London, 2005). Most recently, she coedited a collected volume on *Methods of Exploring Emotions* (Routledge, 2015)..

Åsa Wettergren is associate professor of sociology at the University of Gothenburg. Her main area of research is the role of emotions in organizations and social movements. She is the coeditor of *Emotionalizing Organi-*

zations and Organizing Emotions (Basingstoke, 2010) and the author of a number of book chapters and articles, among them "Managing Unlawful Feelings: The Emotional Regime of the Swedish Migration Board," *International Journal of Work Organization and Emotion* 3, no. 4 (2010), and "Fun and Laughter: Culture Jamming and the Emotional Regime of Late Capitalism," *Social Movement Studies* 8, no. 1 (2009).

Notes

1. Henry David Thoreau, "Civil Disobedience," in *Civil Disobedience in Focus,* ed. HA Bedau (London, 1991), 28–48.
2. Leo Tolstoy, ed., *Writings on Civil Disobedience and Non Violence* (Santa Cruz, CA, 1987).
3. John Rawls, "Definition and Justification of Civil Disobedience," in *Civil Disobedience in Focus,* ed. HA Bedau (London, 1991), 103–21.
4. Jean L Cohen and Andrew Arato, eds, *Civil Society and Political Theory* (Cambridge, MA, 1992).
5. See a brief overview of this literature in Helena Flam, ed., *Pink, Purple, Green* (New York, 2001), 1–3; and Zbigniew A Pelczynski, "Solidarity and 'The Rebirth of Civil Society' in Poland, 1976–81," in *Civil Society and the State,* ed. J Keane (London, 1988), 361–80.
6. Neil Stammers, ed., *Human Rights and Social Movements* (London, 2009); Håkan Thörn, ed., *Anti-Apartheid and the Emergence of a Global Civil Society* (London, 2006); Helena Flam, "Anger in Repressive Regimes: A Footnote to Domination and the Arts of Resistance by James Scott," *European Journal of Social Theory* 7, no. 2 (2004): 171–89; Helena Flam, *Soziologie der Emotionen* (Konstanz, 2002), 253–97.
7. Gene Sharp, ed., *Gandhi as a Political Strategist* (Boston, 1979).
8. Martin Luther King Jr., "Letter from Birmingham City Jail," in *Civil Disobedience in Focus,* ed. HA Bedau (London, 1991), 68–84.
9. Pam McAllister, "You Can't Kill the Spirit: Women and Nonviolent Action," in *Nonviolent Social Movements: A Geographical Perspective,* ed. S Zunes, LR Kurtz, and SB Asher (Oxford, 1999), 18–35; R Powers and W Vogele, eds, *Protest, Power, and Change: An Encyclopedia of Nonviolent Action from ACT-UP to Women's Suffrage* (New York, 1997).
10. In Powers and Vogele, *Protest, Power, and Change,* these methods are listed as nonviolent actions. With its current emphasis on citizens' actions, civil disobedience differs in its meaning from nonviolent action, which also government officials, businesses, or even the military may choose to realize a wide variety of aims, such as defeating an enemy or inducing peaceful conflict resolution. Although Powers and Vogele (pp. 326–28) rightly see civil disobedience as a subcategory of nonviolent action, devoting one single entry to it, they list 41 methods of nonviolent action and 198 methods of nonviolent protest and persuasion—taken over from Gene Sharp, ed., *The Politics of Nonviolent Action* (Boston, 1973)—*most* but not all of

which are indistinguishable from civil disobedience. This suggests that in terms of action repertoires, the contrast between civil disobedience and nonviolent action is not great.

11. Verta Taylor and Nella Van Dyke, "Tactical Repertoires, Action and Innovation," in *The Blackwell Companion to Social Movements,* ed. DA Snow, SA Soule, and H Kriesi (Oxford, 2004).

12. Tilly discusses also violence-free contentious politics Charles Tilly, ed., *The Politics of Collective Violence* (Cambridge, 2003); see also Kurt Schock, ed., *Unarmed Insurrections: People Power Movements in Nondemocracies* (Minneapolis, MN, 2005); Erica Chenoweth and Mary J Stephan, eds, *Why Civil Resistance Works: The Strategic Logic of Nonviolent Conflict* (New York, 2011); Sharon Erickson Nepstad, *Nonviolent Revolutions: Civil Resistance in the Late 20th Century* (New York, 2011); Adam Roberts and Timothy G Ash, eds, *Civil Resistance & Power Politics: The Experience of Non-violent Action from Gandhi to the Present* (Oxford, 2011); April Carter, *People, Power and Political Change: Key Issues and Concepts* (London, 2012); and the German-language Reiner Steinweg and Ulrike Laubenthal, eds, *Gewaltfreie Aktion. Erfahrungen und Analysen* (Frankfurt, 2011); Mischa Gabowitsch, "Gewaltfreier Widerstand. Vergleichende Betrachtungen zu Dynamik und Erfolgsbedingungen," *Mittelweg 36,* no. 2 (2012): 61–67.

13. Sharp, *The Politics of Nonviolent Action.*

14. Powers and Vogele, *Protest, Power, and Change*; Howard Clark, ed., *People Power: Unarmed Resistance and Global Solidarity* (London, 2009).

15. John Medearis, "Social Movements and Deliberative Democratic Theory," *British Journal of Political Science* 35, no. 1 (2005): 53–75.

16. Helena Flam, "Emotional 'Man': I. The Emotional 'Man' and the Problem of Collective Action," *International Sociology* 5, no.1 (1990): 39–56; Helena Flam, "Emotions' Map: A Research Agenda," in *Emotions and Social Movements,* ed. H Flam and D King (London, 2005), 19–40; Jeff Goodwin, Jasper James, and Francesca Polletta eds, *Passionate Politics—Emotions and Social Movements* (Chicago, 2001); Helena Flam and Debra King, eds, *Emotions and Social Movements* (London, 2005).

17. See Peter Woodrow, "A Brief History of Training for Nonviolent Action," in *Protest, Power, and Change: An Encyclopedia of Nonviolent Action from ACT-UP to Women's Suffrage,* ed. R Powers and W Vogele (New York, 1997), 530–33; Erika Summers-Effler, *Laughing Saints and Righteous Heroes: Emotional Rhythms in Social Movement Groups* (Chicago, 2010); Stellan Vinthagen, "Icekvåldsaktion—En social praktik av motstånd och konstruktion" ["Nonviolent Action—A Social Practice of Resistance and Construction"], PhD diss., Göteborg University, 2005; see also "Handbok i civil olydnad," http://ickevald.net/perherngren/handbokicivilolydnad.htm.

18. King, "Letter from Birmingham City Jail," 83.

19. Alberto Melucci, *Challenging Codes—Collective Action in the Information Age* (Cambridge, 1996).

20. Flam and King, "Emotions and Social Movements," *Social Theory in Contemporary Asia,* ed. Ann Brooks (Routledge, 2010); Åsa Wettergren, "Fun and Laughter: Culture Jamming and the Emotional Regime of Late Capitalism," *Social Movement Studies* 8, no. 1 (2009): 1–16.

21. Brett Rolfe, "Building an Electronic Repertoire of Contention," *Social Movement Studies* 4, no. 1 (2005): 65–74; Sefan Wray, "Electronic Civil Disobedience and the World Wide Web of Hacktivism: A Mapping of Extraparliamentarian Direct Action Net Politics," http://switch.sjsu.edu/web/v4n2/stefan/.

Recommended Reading

Bedau, Hugo A, ed. *Civil Disobedience in Focus*. London, 1991. A collection of classic, original texts written by the modern proponents of civil disobedience.

Medearis, John. "Social Movements and Deliberative Democratic Theory." *British Journal of Political Science* 35, no. 1 (2005): 53–75. A brilliant argument about the necessity to reflect upon the role of violent action as a means of securing entry into the arena of peaceful deliberations.

Powers, Roger, and William Vogele, eds. *Protest, Power, and Change: An Encyclopedia of Nonviolent Action from ACT-UP to Women's Suffrage*. New York, 1997. A goldmine for anybody concerned with nonviolent forms of protest. It includes definitions, shorter entries, and full-length articles on nonviolent, past and present action. It builds on the foundations laid down by Gene Sharp, including also his list of 198 nonviolent protest forms.

Chapter 43

Creating Temporary Autonomous Zones

Freia Anders

The term *temporary autonomous zones* (TAZ) took root in the 1980s combining two senses: first, a "socio-political tactic of creating temporary spaces that elude formal structures of control," and second, short-term events away from regular markets in music and arts subcultures.[1] Contemporary understanding of the term was decisively coined by the American anarchist Peter Lamborn Wilson who, unter the pseudonym of Hakim Bey, used it as the title of a libertarian-anarchist essay, first published in 1985, that advanced a critique of conventional and static concepts of revolution that relate to the future rather than the present.[2] Bey defines a temporary autonomous zone (TAZ) as "an uprising which does not engage directly with the State, a guerilla operation which liberates an area (of land, of time, of imagination) and then dissolves itself to re-form elsewhere/elsewhen, *before* the State can crush it. ... The TAZ is thus a perfect tactic for an era in which the State is omnipresent and all-powerful and yet simultaneously riddled with cracks and vacancies. And because the TAZ is a microcosm of that 'anarchist dream' of a free culture."[3] The concept aims at nonhierarchical, self-determined structures to be developed in the here and now, in which it will become possible to avoid state-run and societal control mechanisms so that the revolutionary impetus will escape being swallowed up by consumer society. In the political strategy of protest groups, this means the application of practices that allow activists to provoke situations that temporarily question the prevailing rules and power constellations and thus to create room for new social relationships and experiences.[4]

Relevance for Protest Cultures

Bey's considerations drew on the tradition of Situationism and picked up on discussions, protest practices, and strategies designed to subversively appropriate public spaces, which were rife among the autonomist groups that emerged in Western Europe since the 1970s. The present article uses the example of the autonomists in Germany to investigate this further, while stressing that their culture repertoire, despite national and regional peculiarities, was not limited by the borders of the nation-state.

Projects such as alternative magazines and squatted houses and youth centers formed crystallization points without developing a rigid organizational core. Mobilization themes were wide-ranging. Autonomous groups became active in almost every social movement. They formed the militant wing of the antinuclear movement, they were active within the squatters' movement, the antiwar or peace movement, which in their understanding, was mainly a movement against NATO. Working together with changing allies, even including church groups, they protested against U.S. intervention politics in Central America, or the International Monetary Fund and the World Bank. Well into the 1990s, new interpretations of anti-imperialism had a highly integrating effect on the autonomists, especially in Germany.[5]

Being an active part of forums and networks of the social movements, the *Autonomen* tried to push through thematic shifts of emphasis. They tried to introduce the dehierarchization of decision-making structures (grassroots democracy, rejection of proxy politics), the abolition of the separation between politics and individual living conditions (politics of the first person), and mobilization strategies using symbolic-expressive, confrontative, and also violent actions. A crucial backdrop for these demands was the consistent claim for participation in the power to define which topics should be awarded political relevance. There were several instances when the autonomists successfully realized mobilization campaigns independently from other groups, but without excluding them. Their activities within the social movements as well as their independent campaigns were accompanied by illegal clandestine actions of sabotage, reaching a quantitative peak in the early 1980s. Next to anti-Fascist activities including self-defense against neo-Nazi attacks, this also comprised cooperation with migrant groups and support for refugees and illegals.

Historical Aspects

Creating TAZ and the appropriation of liberated spaces in a material, virtual, and metaphorical sense was at the very center of autonomist politics. Here, militancy did not only become the means to push through political issues but represent the subversive strategy in itself. The militancy-promoting activities of the *Autonomen* led to a polarization within the organized left and the social movements. In a discursive struggle over the interpretation of what could be deemed legitimate means of resistance, the *Autonomen* faced several groups upholding nonviolent resistance: former protagonists of the 1968 movement and the subsequent *Sponti* movement, who increasingly became institutionalized in the Green Party. The *Autonomen* formed part of those forces within the social movements of the 1980s that partly, but not exclusively, focused on identity politics. They could not be completely excluded from the political field because again and again their actions and innovative communication strategies suceeded in forcing issues onto the political agenda. More recently, with new global protest movements emerging and social conditions deteriorating, the resurgence of political activism can be observed including the rediscovery, appropriation, and transformation of action forms pioneered by the autonomists.

The focus of autonomist activities changed over time. Until the mid 1980s, street protest prevailed. This was related to the concept of mass militancy that would find its expression in street battles, clashes with the police, and riots (especially on May Day). Extended police forces determined the limits of this concept. Subsequently, activists increasingly turned to clandestine actions (damage to property, sabotage), but this depended on individual efficiency and increasingly encountered criminalization. After initial rejection, autonomist groups accepted the New Media on a wider scale and used them for political communication.[6] This is where the concept "communication guerilla"[7] was developed. A rather defensive and aestheticized form of political practice—performed by small groups in different situations—it is accompanied by a certain loss of the capacity to build social relationships on a broader scale and to act politically. This may be responsible for making both the concept of "organized mass militancy" and clandestine sabotage action from the beginnings of autonomist mobilization appear unreal to later activists. During all these phases, strategies of material and discursive appropriation existed side by side. However, they were of varying importance to the actual political practice as the following examples may illustrate.

Squatting

Squats form an important element of autonomist politics, even after the squatter movement's breakup. They were conceived as social and political laboratories producing alternative models of life. Being part of the subcultural scene, squats contributed to the mobilization reservoir of autonomist groups. They fulfilled important functions as meeting sites, providing room for the activists' plenary as well as other political and cultural meetings. The names of neighborhoods and streets, riots, and eviction battles became emotive symbols. As squattings queries property and consequently touches upon basic principles of the law, the state and its institutions are challenged.

Concepts/Debates

In Germany, the concept "Autonome" only became common at the end of the 1970s as an initially controversial self-designation. Before that, the term "autonomous groups" was used sporadically in a pejorative way by different Communist splinter groups of the 1970s. The subversive appropriation of pejorative exonyms presents a typical pattern of autonomist communication strategies. The "Schwarze Block" (Black bloc) may serve as another example: a makeshift construction established by Frankfurt public prosecutors to subsume the militant participants in a demonstration. In the semantic battle over the concept of violence—in which both sides seek to delegitimize the opposing side—the autonomists introduced the term "militancy" in order to qualify the concept of violence in its legal meaning and to sidestep the official definition. Ultimately, it became an essential element of an autonomist identity. The concept benefits from its specific vagueness, rendering a clear distinction between legal/nonviolent and illegal/violent action impossible, which in turn gave rise to a never-ending discussion about the limits of the legitimate. The autonomists thus contributed to a further differentiation of left-wing concepts of violence by seeking to deny the ruling system the recognition that it derives from a general acceptance of its legitimacy.[8]

Virtual Spaces

Networks such as *nadir* and *indymedia* were used to build linkages on a national and international scale. In the autonomists' targeted search for a subversive communicative practice, media theory and debates over the importance of the public featured frequently. A comprehensive practice of subversive political communication made use of various forms of virtual civil disobedience (blockade of particular web sites; network sit-ins that temporarily made it impossible to reach sites), virtual graffiti (unauthorized modifying of Internet sites), and semiotic hijacking (claiming signs and symbols, use of semantic similarity to spread own contents for image spoiling, or adbusting).

There is a certain tension between the concept of TAZs and the autonomists' efforts to appropriate history. The latter found its expression in so-called movement archives that from early on emerged from the so-called infoshops. These put their documents and finding aids onto the Internet so that the construction of the movement's own history could be realized collectively. Other means of autonomist memory politics were memorials (e.g., for individuals who died during demonstrations or at the hand of neo-Nazis), repeated rituals at the occasion of holidays and memorial days (May Day, counter events against traditional commemorations), the renaming of streets and places, and the temporary establishment of physically contested memorial sites (e.g., the *Zaunkämpfe* at the fortified hoardings during the protests against the construction of the runway west at Frankfurt airport).

State of Research

Despite the availability of an extensive body of source material, research that would put the autonomists—one of the most central and innovative groups within the manifold protest movements of the 1980s—into a political, social, and cultural context remains in its infancy. There are the descriptions and analyses by the German Federal Office for the Protection of the Constitution (and by scholars related to this institution), which result from the security services' observation of the autonomists. Self-analyses accompanying the history of the *Autonomen* since the early 1980s include the reflections of an author writing under the pseudonym Geronimo, in which ample material relating to the history of the movement is compiled (1990, 1992).[9] Regarding the *Autonomen* of the Federal Republic of Germany, the political science work of Schultze/Gross (1997) concentrates on background and motives of the actors.[10] Schwarzmeier (2001) sees the *Autonomen* as a social movement in its own right and not as only a part of the new social movements. Using a framing approach, he justifies this by their unique style. At the level of political discourse, Haunss (2004) explores the impact of collective identity constructions on the activists. So far, only Katsiaficas (1997) adopts a perspective of international comparison, trying to explain the phenomenon with postmodern and post-Fordist theoretical approaches (Negri, Benhabib).

Research Gaps and Open Questions

At present, a genuine historical approach to the protest history of the 1970s onward is still lacking. It would seem promising to interpret the autonomists in the context of the period's characteristic pluralization of political ideas, marked by a growing degree of informalization, which by no means precluded a heavy reliance on different types of expert opinion alongside an increasingly self-reflective approach. This also includes the questions and debates of legitimization and delegitimization that surrounded the various action forms including militant action. While historical interest remains limited, the autonomists have become a favorite topic of extremism and terrorism research. Beyond these specialized fields, the autonomists have hardly entered the scholarly debate on social movements or more general research on political violence.[11] The same goes for questions concerning the context of the autonomists' consolidation within the youth movement of the early 1980s, or the remarkable international dimension of the diffusion of autonomist concepts.

Freia Anders, Johannes Gutenberg University Mainz, was a research fellow at the University of Bielefeld in the Special Research Programme, "The Political as Communicative Space in History." She recently completes a major project on the West German autonomous left and their attitudes to issues of violence. Her publications include: *Public Goods versus Economic Interests: Global Perspectives on the History of Squatting* (ed. with Alexander Sedlmaier), New York, 2016; "The Limits of the Legitimate: The Quarrel over 'Violence' between Autonomist Groups and the German Authorities," (with Alexander Sedlmaier), in *Writing Political History Today*, eds. W Steinmetz, H-G Haupt, and I Gilcher-Holtey, (Frankfurt, 2013), and „Wohnraum, Freiraum, Widerstand: Die Formierung der Autonomen in den Konflikten um Hausbesetzungen Anfang der achtziger Jahre," in *Das alternative Milieu. Unkonventionelle Lebensentwürfe und linke Politik in der Bundesrepublik Deutschland und Westeuropa 1968–1983*, eds. S Reichardt and D Siegfried (Göttingen, 2010).

Notes

1. Chris Gray, *Cyborg Citizen* (New York, 2001), 47.
2. Hakim Bey, *The Temporary Autonomous Zone, Ontological Anarchy, Poetic Terrorism. Anarchy and Conspiracy* (New York, 1985).
3. Ibid., 105.

4. Jeff Shantz, *Living Anarchy: Theory and Practice in Anarchist Movements* (Bethesda, MD, 2009), 105.

5. Sebastian Haunss, *Identität in Bewegung. Prozesse kollektiver Identität bei den Autonomen und in der Schwulenbewegung* (Wiesbaden 2004), 108–90.

6. Freia Anders and Alexander Sedlmaier, "The Limits of the Legitimate: The Quarrel over 'Violence' between Autonomist Groups and the German Authorities," in *Writing Political History Today*, ed. Willibald Steinmetz, Heinz-Gerhard Haupt, and Ingrid Gilcher-Holtey (Frankfurt, 2013).

7. Communication guerrilla means a discursive strategy that aims at infiltrating the dominant political discourse. The concept was defined by an autonomist group and was subsequently absorbed into experimental art. The aim is not to destroy codes used by the power, but to distort them. This demands a focus on a concrete sociopolitical environment, combining virtual with real space. It comprises a play with multiple names and meanings and is driven by the idea of building networks for the creation of a counter-public. The Handbuch der Kommunikationsguerilla [Handbook of the Communication Guerilla], which has been modified several times, draws on different forms of action and theoretical approaches of cultural avant-gardes like the Situationists. Luther Blisset, Sonja Brünzels, and Autonome a.f.r.i.k.a Gruppe, eds, *Handbuch der Kommunikationsguerilla*, 5th ed. (Berlin, 2012).

8. For the term "militancy," see Freia Anders, "Die Zeitschrift radikal und das Strafrecht," in *Herausforderungen des staatlichen Gewaltmonopols. Recht und politisch motivierte Gewalt am Ende des 20. Jahrhunderts*, ed. F Anders and Ingrid Gilcher-Holtey (Frankfurt, 2006).

9. Geronimo, *Feuer und Flamme. Zur Geschichte und Gegenwart der Autonomen* (Amsterdam, 1990); and Geronimo, Tecumseh, and Richard Proletario, eds, *Feuer und Flamme II. Kritiken, Reflexionen und Anmerkungen zur Lage der Autonomen* (Amsterdam, 1992).

10. Thomas Schultze and Almut Gross, *Die Autonomen. Ursprünge, Entwicklung und Profil der autonomen Bewegung* (Hamburg, 1997).

11. Dieter Rucht, "Gewalt und Neue Soziale Bewegungen," in *Internationales Handbuch der Gewaltforschung*, ed. Wilhelm Heitmeyer and John Hagan (Wiesbaden, 2002), 461–78.

Recommended Reading

Blisset, Luther, Sonja Brünzels, and Autonome a.f.r.i.k.a gruppe, eds. *Handbuch der Kommunikationsguerilla*, 5th ed. Berlin, 2012. This handbook provides an overview of subversive techniques, illustrated with various examples from the New Left.

Geronimo. *Feuer und Flamme. Zur Geschichte und Gegenwart der Autonomen*. Amsterdam, 1990: Analyses by movement activists, a rich source of primary material; among the first and best attempts at autonomist self-reflection in the Federal Republic of Germany.

Geronimo, Tecumseh, and Richard Proletario, eds. *Feuer und Flamme II. Kritiken, Reflexionen und Anmerkungen zur Lage der Autonomen.* Amsterdam, 1992. Analyses by movement activists, a rich source of primary material; among the first and best attempts at autonomist self-reflection in the Federal Republic of Germany.

Haunss, Sebastian. *Identität in Bewegung. Prozesse kollektiver Identität bei den Autonomen und in der Schwulenbewegung.* Wiesbaden, 2004. Following current models of identity theory in social movement research, this study provides a comprehensive overview of actions, strategies, and discourses of the German autonomists in the 1990s.

Katsiaficas, Georges. *European Autonomous Movements. Subversion of Politics.* Atlantic Highlands, NJ, 1997. Katsiaficas's account covers the period 1968–96 and pays special attention to the role of autonomist feminist movements, the influence of squatters and feminists on the movement for disarmament and the anti-nuclear movement, and the anti-Fascist movement developed in response to the neo-Nazi upsurge. In addition to providing a rare depiction of the autonomists' role in these movements, Katsiaficas develops his own concept of autonomy drawing on the statements and aspirations of the movement.

Sedlmaier, Alexander. *Consumption and Violence: Radical Protest in Cold-War West Germany* (Ann Arbor, 2014). Integrates the autonomists in a broader historical perspective since the 1960s and examines their attitudes to issues of consumption and violence.

Chapter 44

Mummery

Sebastian Haunss

General Introduction to the Topic and Relevance for Protest Cultures

Between 1839 and 1843, protesters wearing "disguise or simply blackened faces"[1] were attacking and, if possible, destroying the newly erected tollgates in Southern England. In the summer of 2007, several hundred protesters wearing hooded shirts and sunglasses and covering their faces with bandanas clashed violently with the police. The press identifies them as the "black bloc," and they dominate the news coverage of the protests of more than 60,000 using various, mostly nonviolent forms of protest, against the G8 meeting in Heiligendamm, Germany, for several days.

The two examples show that mummery has a long tradition as a repertoire of contention, and the prominence of Guy Fawkes masks in the recent worldwide occupy and Internet protests underline its ongoing relevance. Mummery comprises all practices to conceal one's identity—usually by (partially) covering the face.

Historical Aspects

Despite its long tradition, the actual history of mummery as a protest practice is not at all linear. Less than forty years ago, mummery at protests and demonstrations was very uncommon. Photos from the 1920s, 1930s, and up to the 1960s show no accounts of demonstrators or even rioters covering their faces. It is only in the early 1970s that mummery became (again) an integral part of the repertoire of contention of many social movements around the globe.

How and why did this practice become part of social movements' action repertoire? What does this practice tell us about protests and protesters? In the following pages, I explore the practice of mummery, starting with a description of its various forms, and proceeding with a discussion of its meanings, its historical roots, and the authorities' reactions to this practice.

Newspaper articles and photos from the first half of the twentieth century give generally no accounts of protesters covering their faces with scarfs or other means—with one notable exception, the Ku Klux Klan. Their white pointed masks were an integral part of the movement's insignia. They served to conceal its members' identity and to intimidate their potential victims and opponents. But otherwise, protesters did generally not try to hide their identity. Demonstrations were what Tilly has called "WUNC displays," coordinated performances to show the movement's worthiness, unity, numbers, and commitment, where participants wore neat clothes or uniforms and showed their faces.[2] The revival of mummery as an integral element of political protests started only in the early 1970s in the aftermath of the student movement and with the advent of the new life-world-oriented radical leftist movements in Europe. In battles about squatted houses and international solidarity, protesters again employed various forms of mummery.[3] Motorcycle and industrial protection helmets worn for protection against police batons were combined with bandanas for protection against identification. The Palestinian headscarf (kaffiyeh) appeared as a tool for mummery, reflecting the admiration of the revolutionary movements in the Middle East, shared by many activists of that period. In the 1970s and 1980s, mummery became more and more common and developed into a routine practice at demonstrations and protests of the antinuclear, the squatters, and the *Autonomen* movement. The latter elevated the black ski mask or baclava to an iconic status that soon became the symbol of the movement.

Today, manifold forms of mummery are practiced. The preferred form of the black bloc is the hooded shirt combined with sunglasses and a bandana. Other forms are white masks, masks printed with faces of politicians, carnivalesque attire, and clown masks.

To understand why this protest practice arose in the 1970s, and why it has become a part of the current protest repertoire, essentially two aspects have to be considered—practical and performative reasons.

On the practical level, mummery is used when protesters are threatened with negative sanctions for their activities. If protesters are determined or at least willing to break the law, and if they do not want to be arrested for doing so, then mummery is a logical choice. On this level, the last decades show a constant seesaw between protesters and authorities. The introduction of video surveillance equipment by the police was one reason why protesters started to cover their faces in the 1970s. The growing practice of mummery then has prompted the introduction of more sophisticated video surveillance and led to the introduction of antimummery laws in some countries. These laws that make mummery an offense have then in turn influenced the practice of mummery—not by preventing it but by changing its form. The current form of concealing one's face by wearing hooded shirts and sunglasses is one that is legally more ambiguous than helmets and ski masks, but not less efficient.

But practical reasons alone certainly do not explain the use and forms of mummery. Mummery is always also—and possibly often even in the first place—an expressive form. Showing or hiding one's face is not just a question of avoiding repression, but a symbolic political statement. As a collective practice during a demonstration, mummery is an expression of the willingness to disrespect the legal constraints and to use violence.[4] Paris has called this symbolic aspect of mummery "militancy without militancy"[5] because the promise of violence does not have to be realized immediately— even though at some time it has to, or would otherwise loose its power. The uniformed black bloc is the prime example of this practice.

Individually, the form of mummery can be read as an identity statement. The black ski mask stands for the "urban street fighter," the Palestinian scarf for the "freedom fighter." Other forms of mummery are more immediate political statements. Masks printed with the faces of politicians are used to protest against policies attributed to them. White masks worn by peace or antinuclear activists symbolize death associated with nuclear technology and weapons. More recently, protesters wearing clowns masks[6] and costumes are reviving the older traditions of carnival and mockery, which can be traced back to the Renaissance and the Middle Ages.[7] During the carnival, "all hierarchical rank, privileges, norms, and prohibitions"[8] were suspended. Disguised with masks and presented in the form of ridicule and mockery, political attacks against the authorities were possible that would otherwise have had severe consequences for those who uttered them.[9] The black bloc type of mummery and the identical white or printed masks let the individual fade into the crowd. They are a uniform, an identity statement that puts the collective before the individual.

The carnival type mummery functions differently. Concealing one's true identity behind a mask allows the individual to slip into another role. It gives its bearer visibility and authority that he or she would otherwise not have. The use of superhero costumes by Superbarrio,[10] who was campaigning for the rights of Mexico's poor or the "precarious super heroes"[11] who were redistributing stolen fancy food among Hamburg's poor are possibly the most visible examples of this use of mummery that guarantees media attention but nevertheless hides the activists' true identity.

Certainly the most iconic figure using mummery as a political tool is Subcomandante Marcos, the spokesman of the Mexican EZLN. The black ski mask that may originally guaranteed him some anonymity soon became—together with the pipe—his hallmark. The mask functioned in a curious way as at the same time inciting a cult around his persona and proclaiming that his individual identity would not matter at all.

As we see from this cursory review, the practice of mummery can serve to hide one's identity as well as create an identity. The mask conceals its bearer and marks her at the same time, and this dual character makes it an important ingredient of processes of collective identity in social movements.

Research Gaps and Open Questions

Despite its prominence in press reports about protests, the practice of mummery has so far been largely neglected in the scientific literature. The one exception is Rainer Paris's article on the psychology and symbolism of mummery where he discusses mummery as a method of self-empowerment, orchestration of heroism, and as a flight from identity.[12] Other studies of protest practices are either completely silent on the practice of mummery or mention it only fleetingly.

The gap between the importance of mummery in the public perception of protest and its negligence in the literature on social movements and protest leaves many questions unanswered. Further research might explore the relationship between prefigurative politics and mummery, between surveillance technology and mummery, or the transnational travel of various forms of mummery between movements.

Sebastian Haunss is leading the research group social conflicts at the Research Center on Inequality and Social Policy (SOCIUM) at the University of Bremen. His research interests are social conflicts and political mobilizations in the knowledge society, political and economic legitimacy, social networks and social movements. Recent publications are: *Conflicts in the Knowledge Society. The Contentious Politics of Intellectual Property* (Cambridge 2013); "Promise and Practice in Studies of Social Media and Movements," in *Critical Perspectives on Social Media and Protest*, ed. Lina Dencik und Oliver Leistert, (Lanham, MD, 2015); and "Internationalization and the Discursive Legitimation of the Democratic Nation State," in

State Transformations in OECD Countries: Dimensions, Driving Forces and Trajectories, ed. Heinz Rothgang und Steffen Schneider (with Henning Schmidtke and Steffen Schneider; Basingstoke 2015).

Notes

1. George Rudé, *The Crowd in History: A Study of Popular Disturbances in France and England 1730–1848* (New York, 1964), 159.
2. Charles Tilly, *Social Movements, 1768–2004* (Boulder, CO, 2004), 4.
3. Nikolaus Jungwirth, *Demo. Eine Bildergeschichte des Protests in der Bundesrepublik* (Weinheim, 1986).
4. John Holloway and Vittorio Sergi, "Of Stones and Flowers—Dialogue between John Holloway and Vittorio Sergi," http://turbulence.org.uk/turbulence-1/heiligendamm-2007/of-stones-and-flowers/.
5. Rainer Paris, "Vermummung," *Leviathan* 1 (1991): 117–29.
6. For the mission statement of the "Clandestine Insurgent Rebel Clown Army," see http://www.clownarmy.org/about/about.html.
7. Marc Amann, ed., *go.stop.act! Die Kust des kreativen Straßenprotests,* 2nd ed. (Grafenau, 2007).
8. Mikhail M Bakhtin, *Rabelais and His World* (Cambridge, MA, 1968), 10.
9. Herbert Carl and Doris Kessler, "Eine Revolution ohne Gaudi ist keine Revolution," in *Wilde Masken. Ein anderer Blick auf die Fasnacht,* ed. Tübinger Vereinigung für Volkskunde (Tübingen, 1989), 181–97.
10. Berta Jottar, "Superbarrio Gomez for US President: Global Citizenship and the 'Politics of the Possible,'" *e-misférica, Performance and Politics in the Americas* 1, no. 1 (2004), http://hemi.nyu.edu/journal/1_1/sb_intro.html.
11. Luke Harding, "A Merry Band," *The Guardian,* 17 May 2006, http://www.guardian.co.uk/world/2006/may/17/germany.lukeharding.
12. Paris, "Vermummung."

Recommended Reading

Amann, Marc. *go.stop.act! Die Kust des kreativen Straßenprotests.* 2nd ed. Grafenau, 2007. A rich source of descriptions and interpretations of current protest tactics, including the carnivalesque forms of mummery as clowns.
Holloway, John, and Vittorio Sergi. "Of Stones and Flowers—Dialogue between John Holloway and Vittorio Sergi." http://turbulence.org.uk/turbulence-1/heiligendamm-2007/of-stones-and-flowers/. A conversation between the sociologist John Holloway and the Black Bloc activist Vittorio Sergi in which Holloway questions the practice of mummery and violence during the G8 protests in 2007 in Heiligendamm, whereas Sergi interprets the Black Bloc as an authentic, antagonistic, and prefigurative practice.

Paris, Rainer. "Vermummung." *Leviathan* 1 (1991): 117–29. A rare in-depth treatment of mummery in relation to protest and social movements in which Paris discusses mummery as a thick symbolic practice of identity construction, resulting in a double movement of self-stigmatization and self-elevation.

Chapter 45

Recontextualization of Signs and Fakes

David Eugster

To recontextualize a sign means to take a sign, once already connected to a specific meaning, and reuse it in a different context.[1] Literary collage, for example, may use fragments by other authors in order to condense them into a new work.

Producing a fake works the other way round. The fake takes certain attributes of contextualization of a given statement in order to lend persuasiveness to a false statement. The faker may use, for example, a letterhead, a typeface, belonging to a different writer, but he may also use—depending on his level of expertise—stylistic attributes to imitate the writer for whom he wants to be mistaken.

Relevance for Protest Cultures

At the beginning of the twentieth century, the Dadaists introduced a new form of protest, by means of the collage, but also, for example, by use of fake newspaper announcements: they (re-)used their adversaries' signs and styles to delegitimize them. Thereby, they operated akin to the parody. But in the focus of the parodist message is the information that the criticized subject is a ridiculous one. The strategy emerging with the Dadaists is no longer about the transmission of information, but about the attack on information itself. The alleged aim is to directly disturb or even destroy communicative systems as well as sign systems, to irritate, to disrupt one's habits of seeing and reading. The spectator's change of mind is no longer achieved via informational elucidation—as in the self-understanding of *alternative* information—but by experiencing inconsistence between message and reality. In the twentieth century, the notion that a clean recontextualization and a confrontation of signs, images, and also fakes can immediately subvert entire discursive systems made its career in protest movements, and still keeps going.[2]

Generally speaking, the protesters' strategies of recontextualization follow three central aims:

1. *They should help subvert, change, or at least disturb socially dominant constructions of meaning.* By disarranging signs, the order of the social world should be disarranged, too. Judith Butler's argumentation, that travesty has the power to blur the essentialism of the order of sexuality in a heterosexually dominated society[3] or Dick Hebdidges position, that the *bricolage* in youth cultures has subversive effects, may serve as examples for this theorem.[4] Through these strategies, the daily order of signs should become confused and denaturalized, and the daily order of uttering should become suspicious.

2. *These strategies often serve as selective attacks against discursively authorized positions of uttering.* Faked newspapers or official bulletins should either spread confusing information to cause different, possibly chaotic behavior among their trusting readers, or have an educational effect of mistrust. Protesting via fake tries, for example, to raise critical awareness against the utterances of some speakers or media.

3. *The recontextualization of stylistic elements or arguments is also used to mock the attitude of the criticized speakers.* In Zurich, Switzerland, during the youth revolt, two invited protesters sabotaged a TV discussion between officials and protesters, in 1980, just by pretending to be even more strictly against the youth movement than their opponents, using, as its representatives only the most violent arguments against the movement, provoking their discussion partners to react harshly themselves, and prove therefore the interpretation of the protesters' mimicry.[5] This strategy has been called overidentification. Whereas the imitation in this case is obvious, in other cases, the imitation is used to talk illegitimately for an institution, either to provoke a denial from the institution's part or to criticize the institution via its own means, for example, in faked advertisements or propaganda. This has been called "image correction."[6]

Historical Aspects: Where and When Were These Protesting Techniques Developed? In Which Situations Were They Applied?

Of course, a complete overview of these techniques cannot be given. The following overview shall expose concise implementations of those strategies, which are still points of reference—in a tradition of protest upheld via Internet or specific books—for present-day use.

The artistic output of the Dada movement after 1915 can be understood, in large parts, as a protest against a bourgeois culture of language and signs, which in the perspective of the Dadaists lost all its legitimation, as it had supported the machinery of war during World War I. Thus, one aim of the Dadaist collage technique was the "decomposition of the bourgeois system of terms" by usage of its own signs. Dada should use "all forms and measures to decompose the moral-Pharisaic bourgeoisie with its own means."[7] Through their confusion in the collages, the signs should lose any effect of persuasion. Propaganda should be confused with advertisement, and glorification of war heroes should be confused with embroidery patterns,[8] the arrangement of the misused letters be disarranged. The irritating effect of the newly composed signs should disintegrate the criticized ideologies. Also, the forgeries of newspaper announcements and news imagery—placed in Zurich and Berlin by Dadaists—should reveal the manipulation effectuated through the news.[9]

In 1956, heavily influenced by Dadaism and Surrealism, the lettrists and future Situationists, Guy Debord and Gil Wolman, published a manifesto, which would often be referred to in the protest tradition of recontextualization: *Mode d'emploi du détournement*.[10] In this manifesto, they propagated the abolition of personal ownership in the realm of art and literature and postulated a disrespect toward the original work. Same as the surrealists, they recommended letting opposites collide, to employ sensually charged elements. One of their aims was the destruction of authorship, a "literary communism," and an attack on "social and legal convention."[11] This technique, which ultimately adopts the Dadaists' collage, saw implementation with the Situationists in various media. The influence of the *Situationiste Internationale* on the European New Left in the 1960s was considerable. In Germany, the Munich-based *SPUR* group, acting as a part of the *Situationistische Internationale* (SI), can be considered a group, which early adopted the Situationists' technique of the *détournement* transnational. They influenced the *Sozialistischer Deutscher Studentenbund* and the *Kommune 1*. One of its communards, Fritz Teufel, for example, sent fake letters of dismissal to unpopular professors.[12]

In the late 1970s, as a reaction to the disappointment about the so-called historical compromise of the *Partito Communisto Italiano*, Italy saw an emergence of several new forms of resistance, which had their stronghold in Bologna. The collective *A/Traverso* worked with the slogan *Informare non basta*.[13] They called themselves "Mao-Dadaists" and "information guerilla,"[14] their writing and their speech should *attraverse*[15] the "dictatorship of meaning" and the "separated organizations of discourse."[16] They supported their hopes via reference to current semiotic and poststructural theories. Their techniques included prank calls to politicians, broadcast on *Radio Alice*.[17] In the streets, *Indiani Metropolitiani* (protesters dressed as Indians)[18] distorted political posters and ads.[19] The satirical newspaper *Il Male* was established in the same contextual environment. Starting from 1978, it published a couple of editions, imitating—on its cover pages—the typographic design of leading national newspapers. But it also distributed faked *Prawda* editions in the former USSR.[20]

In the early 1980s, a highly complex play with political signs was conducted by the industrial band *Laibach* in Slovenia.[21] *Laibach* used a diverse, German-based, mock Fascist rhetoric both in speech and in imagery. From the Slovenian government's Socialist point of view, this was regarded as an abasement of the workers on their history.[22] Already the band's name was a provocation, *Laibach* being the German name of the capital Ljubilinjas, imposed before 1918 and also with the German occupation during the Third Reich. But Laibach did not constrain themselves to totalitarian ready-mades, but they also mashed up partisan songs, Latin church chorales, folklore songs, and pop music in their songs, always underlying them with a stomping, militaristic industrial beat.[23] Their strong relation to Dadaism shows especially in the graphic design of their posters and booklets.[24] *Laibach*'s tactic can be read as overidentification,[25] as an attempt to be more totalitarian than totalitarism and to thereby imply a critique on the semi-totalitarian situation in Slovenia that, for example, came to the fore with the cult of partisans.[26] This is not a matter of irony, parody, or satire, but an attempt to allow for an experience of the power of totalitarian signs.[27] Finally, *Laibach* was greatly supported by the new social movements in Slovenia. The struggle against a national ban on *Laibach*'s totalitarian rhetoric served, only seeming paradoxically, as struggle for a more pluralistic society.[28]

Since the 1980s, the techniques of faking and of recontextualization take a firm position in the so-called communication guerrilla of the autonomous left scene.[29] The often smaller actions, which range from modified advertising slogans to faked public announcements, can hardly be depicted here; rich material can be found in the "Handbuch für Kommunikationsguerilla," which was first published in 1994 by activists.[30]

The technical developments of the Internet further allow for activists to criticize the self-representation of corporations by use of fakes. The *Yes Men* are one prominently successful instance of this principle. They built several fake web sites that they explicitly established as online bait.[31] This led to media requests to the alleged corporations and to productive misunderstandings. For instance, the BBC interviewed a *Yes Man* in 2004 as alleged company spokesman. He, the fake spokesman, claimed full responsibility of his corporation for the chemical catastrophe in Bhopal, a responsibility that was always rejected by the real Dow Chemical Company.[32]

State of Research

With its strong roots in modern avant-garde art such as Dadaism and Situationism, the techniques have also a strong aesthetic appeal. Most researchers are interested in the execution of the described strategies and their effects in place or in the media. The strategies and their short-term impact are scientifically covered. A discussion of the long-term consequences for the surrounding or executing social movements is especially to be found in Anna Schober and Alexei Monroe's work.[33]

Research Gaps and Open Questions

The use of the described strategies draws on a widely common lay semiotics. It needed to be investigated, which knowledge within activist groups is active, and how this knowledge disseminates. The focus should be on the effects of specific actions for the groups, as well as the effects on other involved persons. The range of success that these practices have still needs investigation.

David Eugster is assistant at the German Institute at Zurich University, Switzerland. His main interest lies in the connection between change of economist thought and communication. In his PhD in cultural analysis, he focuses on the interrelations between the culture of the Cold War, political criticism toward advertising, and the public relations effort of the advertising industry. His recent publications include: "Heimliche Verführer im Kalten Krieg: Ernest Dichter Motivforschung in der Kritik," in *Transatlantische Verwerfungen—Transatlantische Verdichtungen. Kulturtransfer in Literatur und Wissenschaft, 1945–1989,* ed. G Gerber, R Leucht, and K Wagner (Göttingen, 2012), and "Gegen-Bilder zur Vermassung: Die Kampagne 'Inserate erschliessen den Markt' der Schweizer Werbeindustrie um 1966," in *Hegemonie und die Kraft der Bilder,* ed. A Pechriggl and A Schober (Cologne, 2013).

Notes

1. I thank Simon Brühlmann for his help with the translation of the text.
2. Anna Schober, *Ironie, Montage, Verfremdung. Ästhetische Taktiken und die politische Gestalt der Demokratie* (Munich, 2009), 103–210.
3. See Judith Butler, *Gender Trouble. Feminism and the Subversion of Identity* (New York, 1990).
4. See Dick Hebdige, *Subculture. The Meaning of Style* (London, 1979).
5. Luther Blisset, Sonja Brü^{n}zels, and Autonome a.f.r.i.k.a Gruppe, eds, *Handbuch der Kommunikationsguerilla*, 4th ed. (Berlin, 2001), 156.
6. Ibid., 54 and 149.
7. Anonymous, "15 Minuten für Dada täglich," *Der Dada* 3, no. 1 (1920): 6–7, cited in Anna Schober, *Ironie, Montage, Verfremdung*, 213.
8. Harriette Watts, "Dada and the Press: Introduction," in *Dada and the Press*, ed. H Watts (New Haven, CT, 2004), 3.
9. Hanne Bergius, "Dada-Berlin and Its Aesthetic of Effect: Playing the Press," in *Dada and the Press*, ed. H Watts (New Haven, CT, 2004), 69.
10. First published in *Les Levres Nues*, no. 4 (1956). English version in *Situationist International Anthology*, ed. K Knabb (Berkeley, CA, 2007), 8–13.
11. Astrid Vicas, "Reusing Culture: The Import of Detournement," *The Yale Journal of Criticism* 11, no. 2 (1998): 381–406.
12. Joachim Scharloth, "Kommunikationsguerilla 1968—Strategien der Subversion symbolischer Ordnung in der Studentenbewegung," in *Musikkulturen in der Revolte. Studien zu Rock, Avantgarde und Klassik im Umfeld von, 1968*, ed. B Kutschke (Stuttgart, 2008), 192; Simon Teune, "Humour as a Guerrilla Tactic: The West German Student Movement's Mockery of the Establishment," *International Review of Social History* 52, Supplement S15 (2007): 115–32.
13. "To inform is not enough." Klemens Gruber, *Die zerstreute Avantgarde : strategische Kommunikation im Italien der 70er Jahre* (Vienna, 1989), 8.
14. Nanni Balestrini and Primo Moroni, *Die goldene Horde: Arbeiterautonomie, Jugendrevolte und bewaffneter Kampf in Italien,* trans. C Fröhlich (Berlin, 1994), 402.
15. "To foil."
16. Balestrini and Moroni, *Die goldene Horde*, 402.
17. Gruber, *Die zerstreute Avantgarde*, 135–36.
18. Giorgi Mariani, "'Was Anybody More of an Indian than Karl Marx?' The Indiani Metropolitani and the 1977 Movement," in *Indians and Europe*, ed. CF Feest (Aachen, 1987), 588.
19. Gruber, *Die zerstreute Avantgarde*, 106.
20. Ibid., 139; Balestrini and Moroni, *Die goldene Horde*, 398; Klemens Gruber, "Parodie, Fälschung, Simulation. Die getürkten Zeitungen der 'Kommunikationsguerilla' il male," *zibaldone. zeitschrift für italienische kultur der gegenwart* 12 (1991): 32–42.
21. Später eng assoziert mit *Neue Slowenische Kunst* (NSK).
22. Inke Arns, *Neue Slowenische Kunst—Eine Analyse ihrer künstlerischen Strategien im Kontext der 1980er Jahre in Jugoslawien* (Regensburg, 2002), 24.
23. Ibid., 26.

24. Comparisons in ibid., 27.
25. Blisset, Brünzels, and Gruppe, *Handbuch der Kommunikationsguerilla, 47.*
26. Alexei Monroe, *Interrogation Machine. Laibach und NSK* (Cambridge, MA, 2005), 171.
27. Inke Arns, *Neue Slowenische Kunst,* 163.
28. Alexei Monroe, *Interrogation Machine,* 173.
29. Simon Teune, "Wie ein Fisch im Wasser der Zeichenwelt. Spassguerilla seit den 1960er Jahren," in *Politischer Protest und Öffentlichkeit im 20. Jahrhundert. Studien zur Steuerung und Resonanz politischer Proteste in Deutschland,* ed. D Rucht and S Reichardt (forthcoming, 2009).
30. Blisset, Brünzels, and Gruppe, *Handbuch der Kommunikationsguerilla*; a very concise analysis of the philosophical and theoretical background of the "Kommunikationsguerilla" can be found in Markus S Kleiner, "Semiotischer Widerstand. Zur Gesellschafts- und Medienkritik der Kommunikationsguerilla," in *Neue Kritik der Medienkritik,* ed. G Hallenberger and J-U Nieland (Köthen, 2005), 314–66.
31. "Dow—A Chemical Company on the Global Playground," http://www.dowethics.com.
32. Klaus Schoenberger, "How False Information Creates 'True Events.' Persistent and Recombined Forms of Activist Communication through Internet Fakes and Hoaxes," *East Bound Journal* 4, no. 1 (2006): 285–95; Benedikt Sarreiter, "Die Yes Men. Identitätskorrekturen," in *Und jetzt? Politik, Protest und Propaganda,* ed. H Geiselberger (Frankfurt, 2007), 323–33.
33. Anna Schober, *Ironie, Montage, Verfremdung*; Alexei Monroe, *Interrogation Machine.*

Recommended Reading

Blisset, Luther, Sonja Brünzels, and Autonome a.f.r.i.k.a Gruppe, eds. *Handbuch der Kommunikationsguerilla,* 4th ed. Berlin, 2001. Published by activists, the "Handbuch der Kommunikationsguerrilla," offers a historical overview over exemplary activist groups, but also includes a service section in which diverse semiotic techniques are presented and contextualized in an extensive theoretical framework.

Schober, Anna. *Ironie, Montage, Verfremdung. Ästhetische Taktiken und die politische Gestalt der Demokratie.* Munich, 2009. Schober focuses on the effects of recontextualization of signs within techniques such as the collage. Challenging the activists' belief in success of those subversive strategies, Schober explains with the examples of Dadaism, the Austrian Expanded Cinema, and the protest movement in former Yugoslavia during the 1990s which (unexpected) impact those techniques can have.

Chapter 46

Clandestinity

Gilda Zwerman

General Definition of the Term

In his seminal essay "The Sociology of Secrecy and of Secret Societies," Georg Simmel[1] identified and demystified a distinctive collective process which, in its very nature, aims at creating mystery. The secret society as defined by Simmel is an interactional unit concerned with distributing information in ways that protect ideas, objects, activities, and sentiments of a group from a perceived external threat. They appear in two forms: those in which the secret incorporates information about all aspects of the group including its very existence and those in which only some aspects of the group such as rituals, goals, or the identity of members, remain secret. In both cases, Simmel argues that secrecy enhances collective solidarity and commitment to the group while at the same time legitimizing a power hierarchy based on differential access to coveted information. By separating the *form* of the secret society from its *content,* Simmel laid the groundwork for analyzing secrecy as a dynamic sui generis, as a microsociological process and normal feature of human intercourse. "If human interaction is conditioned by the capacity to speak, it is shaped by the capacity to be silent."

Of course, Simmel was writing at the dawn of the twentieth century when the small secret societies that informed his analysis, including outlaw bands, craft guilds, religious sects, and fraternal organizations, were on the decline and the rule of law, so central to the development of the new industrializing nation-states, promised a future where big politics—international relations, government policy, and legislation—would be guided by rational imperatives. What Simmel did not foresee—although his contemporary

Max Weber did—was the extent to which the industrializing nation-states would rationalize the use of secrecy in their efforts to secure the emerging global order.

General Cultural Context

For decades, little attention was paid to Simmel's initial contribution to the topic of secrecy. It was not until the start of the Cold War when, according to political theorist Edward Shils, secrecy appeared as an obsessive over-riding feature of political life inside the administrations of the two most powerful states to emerge in the post World War II period, the United States and the USSR.[2] The Soviets, according to Shils, had been marching in the direction of a closed system ever since Lenin and the Bolsheviks seized control of the Revolution in October 1917. With the establishment of the KGB in 1954, the USSR had arrived at her final destination—a totalitarian state. In the United States, the turn to secrecy was framed as a response to Soviet aggression and the paranoid fantasies of a single government official (Joseph McCarthy), who was convinced that political subversives and Com-munist sympathizers were embedded inside American institutions and that their influence had to be contained by extraordinary means. The result was a lapse in America's commitment to constitutional liberties on which, as Shils points out, the real security of America's open democratic system is based. However, even as the obsession receded, the secrecy remained. The CIA was established in 1947. That was followed by the proliferation of covert opera-tions inside key governmental agencies. In 1956, a secret counterintelligence program (COINTELPRO) was created within the FBI. COINTELPRO possessed the power to monitor, surreptitiously intrude on, and even disrupt dissident activity deemed threatening or potentially threatening to the social order. So despite divergent economic systems and the antagonism between them, the United States and the Soviets were conjoined by a set of common trends—toward authoritarianism and a commitment to maintaining hege-mony over increasingly divergent and distant populations, all of it dependent on clandestine operations that ranged from the functional to the nefarious.

Into the equation of the Cold War between the super powers entered the Third World guerrilla—a new type of activist who, by virtue of an unwavering commitment to social justice, initiates a *guerra chiquita* (little war) aimed at the overthrow of the military dictatorships, colonial govern-ments, and emergent imperialist regimes that are exploiting the labor of the impoverished masses and plundering the resources of underdeveloped nations.[3] The guerrilla does not operate in public view nor does she or he aspire to build a mass political movement, for such forms are easily repressed or co-opted by the dominant regime. Alternatively, she or he joins with 30 or 40 others to form a *foco*—a secretive cell. The foco is the basic combat unit in guerrilla war—a war of the flea fighting against a well-trained, conventional, mechanized military. In jungles and mountains and forests, they hop, hide, and bite, "nimbly avoiding the foot that would crush them." Their weapons are the weapons of the weak—dynamite, determination, and deception. Their goal is to attack, survive, and attack again. Survival is the proof—and inspiration—to the masses that even the most powerful military is not invincible. Over time, the determined and devious flea can wear out a beast.

In 1949, Mao Tse Tung had waged and won a war of the flea, thereby converting a nation of 600 million Chinese to Communism. A decade later, Fidel Castro and Che Guevara wiped out the corrupt Cuban dictator, Batista, by the same means. In Latin America, Africa, and the Middle East, guerrilla warriors stepped up their clandestine attacks. Significantly, both Mao and Che had made it clear that guerrilla warfare was effective only under specific conditions—in rural, agrarian societies, where guerrilla activists were spawned from among the oppressed, connected by birth, through familial ties and occupation to the people they were defending and intimate with the territories in which they hid. However, by the mid 1960s, as social protest movements in the United States, Western Europe, and Japan reached the limits of reform, and the war in Vietnam raged on, activists in these New Left movements began to flirt with possibilities of waging guerrilla war in the belly of the beast (within the imperialist nation itself). Government efforts to repress even public protest through overt and covert measures provided activists with further motivation to turn to dynamite and deception, and disappear into the urban bush.

Historical Aspects: Clandestine Organizations and Political Protest Movements in Western Europe, the United States, and Japan during the 1960s and 1970s

Clandestine organizations that appeared in the context of New Left protest movements in democratic societies emerged gradually as a result of a radicalization process from within the movement. In most cases, the activists' decision to go underground was the result of either a chain of events that culminated in increased state repression or specific moments of sustained conflict between dissidents and the state. Texts detailing—and glorifying—

Table 46.1. Clandestine Organizations Studied[4]

Germany: Red Army Fraction
Movement of the Second of June
Revolutionary Cells
Italy: Red Brigades
Communist Fighting Formation
Front Line
Japan: Red Army Faction
Revolutionary Left Faction
United Red Army
Japanese Red Army
East Asia Anti-Japanese Armed Front
United States: Weather Underground
Black Liberation Army
Fuerzas Armadas de Liberacion Nacional
United Freedom Front

the strategies of guerrilla warfare in the Third World were widely circulated and used by Western activists to justify clandestinity as a central feature of the escalation process.

The clandestine foco did not draw recruits from among the oppressed communities for whom they were seeking justice but neither were they completely isolated. Typically, the members of a foco were part of a radical faction that formed inside a public social movement organization. Thus, even after disappearing, activists could rely on a network of former compatriots and sympathizers, with whom they had preexisting friendship and libidinal ties, to provide support: to supply funds, transport materials and messages, and help the foco coordinate their armed actions with the goals of the public movement. Although some members of the foco were fugitives and were forced to stay underground, most led double lives: they changed their names, disguised their appearance, moved from one safe house to another, and moved vigilantly, but they also had jobs, raised children, shopped, and went to the movies.

As was the case in all guerrilla movements, clandestine organizations in Western societies relied on a division of labor in order to sustain stability and solidarity. Individual members were permitted to negotiate their proximity to the violence and participate in only the actions that they felt able to handle, physically and emotionally. Emphasis on fluidity of roles and loosely structured relationships—a significant difference from the tight, hierarchical structures found in nonpolitical secret societies—allowed clandestine organizations to survive years longer than most of the public social movement organizations from which they emerged.

However, longevity had its price. Clandestine organizations did not form until the late 1960s, as the overall cycle of protest was declining. The new social movements, which appeared in the 1970s—feminism, gay rights, environmentalism—were committed to reform and nonviolence, and wanted nothing to do with the dynamite and deception so central to the strategies of urban guerrilla. Members of clandestine organizations became isolated and impervious to changing external realities. Their goals seemed unrealistic and abstract to most others. The strategy of attack-survival-attack became more difficult to implement in a way that distinguished the guerrilla from a common criminal. Yet for those determined to remain a revolutionary in the absence of a revolutionary movement, the foco was the perfect structure in which to persist—an hermetically-sealed environment that infused the lives of those who remained underground with meaning and noble intentions invisible to others.

For as Simmel pointed out, secrecy elevates the knowledge it conceals and protects the anointed from criticism.

Clandestinity and Social Movement Theory

How do social movement scholars understand the trajectories and logic of activists who use secrecy or go underground in the name of a social justice cause? Prior to 1970, the field of social movements, then known as "collective behavior," was characterized by an array of theoretical paradigms informed by functionalist assumptions of social structure that warned of the dangers of rapid and radical social change.[5] Movements that formed outside the boundaries of mainstream institutions were read as irrational expressions of discontent. Participants were viewed as individuals who could not manage the balance between egoism and altruism (in functionalist terms) or the id and the ego (in psychoanalytic terms) that is required by complex, democratic societies. Consequently, activism was seen as motivated by psychological need—a longing to abandon the self through participation in the more primitive, unregulated environment of an *ersatzgemeinschaft*—an alternative community in which unstable people gather together and imagine a future where all the complications and imperfections of modern life are eradicated. Use of secrecy and/or violence by activists served only to accentuate their deviance.

However, to a new generation of sociologists trained in the late 1960s and 1970s, the dynamics of the many popular and transformative social movements of that period—the marches and sit-ins against segregation in the South or protests against the war in Vietnam—seemed poorly explained by models that pathologized collective behavior. The principal, new, theoretical perspectives that developed—resource mobilization and political process theories—shifted the focus of research away from investigation of the psychological traits of individual participants to analysis of the strategic aspects of the protest process. These theories posited a fundamental continuity between institutional politics and protest politics, and examined the ways social movements mobilize, strategize, and succeed in achieving social reforms. No longer was protest seen as a fringe activity. Rather, the new paradigms sought to explain protest as rational, goal-oriented political action.

The shift reinvigorated the field of social movements, but it also created a new set of biases. The scholarship focused almost exclusively on the legal, public, and popular elements of protest, ignoring or explicitly excluding activists who engaged in tactics considered extreme including secrecy and violence. Covert action, concealment, and cover-ups were seen as the domain of states—slimy tactics used by unjust authorities seeking to repress movements.

Then in the 1980s, the overall political climate of Western democratic states shifted dramatically to the right. Activists who had gone underground in the late 1960s and 1970s—and stayed—became targets of a new counterterrorism initiative.[6] A rash of arrests, lengthy public trials, and long-term prison sentences offered an opportunity for researchers to obtain access to former members of clandestine groups. By employing the conceptual tools that scholars were using to analyze public movement organizations including framing, political opportunity structure, network analysis, emotion, and culture, these researchers broke new ground in the effort to fit the subject of armed, clandestine activity into the dominant frames of social movement research.[7]

Research Gaps: Clandestinity as Strategy in Nonviolent Political Protest

Research on guerrilla war in the Third World and on New Left activists who experimented with waging guerrilla war within the context of constitutional democracies has provided a detailed analysis of the dynamics that take place in clandestine organizations. But in all of these cases, clandestinity was associated with violence. Alternative contexts—cases in which activists go underground but do not adopt violent strategies; cases where a clandestine organization predates a mass mobilization or acts in tandem with a public political mobilization; and cases where clandestinity serves an effective buffer against repression—need to be identified and studied.

Of course the one shining example that meets all the above criteria is the Underground Railroad, a nonviolent clandestine network of safe houses and couriers, which operated in the nineteenth century in tandem with the aboveground abolitionist movement and enabled fugitive slaves to escape from plantations in the South. More recent and noteworthy examples include the clandestine wing of the African National Congress, the Umkhonto we Sizwe (MK), which formed in 1961. After a brief try at guerrilla warfare, the group changed course, limiting itself to armed propaganda aimed at raising black South Africans' morale, rather than waging a full-scale war.[8] Anna Brava's research on civilian resistance during the Nazi occupation in Europe[9] provides another interesting illustration. Brava found that clandestine networks established by ordinary people, mainly women, were quite effective in undermining the genocidal practices of the Fascist regimes. And perhaps the most amusing form of clandestinity to date are the attacks (on stilts) waged by *clownbattants* of the Clandestine Insurgent Rebel Clown Army (CIRCA). Operating under the high command of the Clown Provision Army, these activists first appeared at anti-Iraq war demonstrations in 2003. They used costumes, trickery, and antics of carnival in order to diffuse confrontation between dissidents and police.[10]

These examples suggest that clandestinity is a highly fluid, strategic tool. It does not have to be linked to violence, devolve into a closed secret society, nor end in isolation and defeat. When used creatively, clandestine activity can take its place among the arts of resistance and open up new spaces for dissident subcultures to grow.

Gilda Zwerman is professor of sociology at the State University of New York, Old Westbury. Her research interests include social movements, political violence, and African American protest history. Writings on these subjects have been published in *Social Justice* (1988, 1989), *Feminist Review* (1994), *Mobilization* (2000, 2012), *Qualitative Sociology* (2008), and *Cultures and Conflicts* (2013).

Notes

1. Georg Simmel, "The Sociology of Secrecy and of Secret Societies," *American Journal of Sociology* 11, no. 4 (1906): 441–98.
2. Edward Shils, *The Torment of Secrecy: The Background and Consequences of American Security Policies* (Glencoe, 1956).

3. Robert Tabor, *War of the Flea* (New York, 1965).
4. Reprinted from Gilda Zwerman, Patricia G Steinhoff, and Donatella Della Porta, "Disappearing Social Movements: Clandestinity in the Cycle of New Left Protest in the U.S., Japan, Germany and Italy," *Mobilization: An International Journal* 5, no. 1 (2000): 85-104, 87.
5. Doug McAdam, John McCarthy, and Mayer Zald, "Social Movements," in *Handbook of Sociology,* ed. N Smelser (Los Angeles, 1988), 695–738.
6. Gilda Zwerman, "Domestic Counter-Terrorism: U.S. Government Responses to Political Violence on the Left in the Reagan Era," *Social Justice* 16, no. 2 (1989): 31–63.
7. Alberto Melucci, *Nomads of the Present* (Philadelphia, PA, 1988); Donatella Della Porta, *Social Movements, Political Violence and the State* (New York, 1996); Patricia Steinhoff, "Hijackers, Bombers and Bank Robbers: Managerial Style in the Japanese Red Army," *Journal of Asian Studies* 48, no. 4 (1989): 727–40; Zwerman, Steinhoff, Della Porta, "Disappearing Social Movements".
8. Jeff Goodwin, "The Struggle Made Me a Nonracialist: Why There Was So Little Terrorism in the Antiapartheid Struggle," *Mobilization: An International Quarterly Review* 12, no. 2 (2006): 193–203.
9. Anna Brava, "Armed and Unarmed: Struggles Without Weapons in Europe and Italy," *Journal of Modern Italian Studies* 10, no. 4 (2005): 468–84.
10. Kolonel Klepto, "Making War with Love: The Clandestine Insurgent Rebel Clown Army," *City* 8, no. 3 (2004): 403–11.

Recommended Reading

Brava, Anna. "Armed and Unarmed: Struggles Without Weapons in Europe and Italy." *Journal of Modern Italian Studies* 10, no. 4 (2005): 468–84. A study of women in the anti-Fascist resistance in Italy, which demonstrates how clandestine activity permitted the women to make contributions to the movement without becoming involved in the risks and armed activity of the partisans.

Crossley, Nick, Gemma Edwards, Ellen Harries, and Rachel Stevenson. "Covert Social Movement Networks and the Secrecy-Efficiency Trade-Off: The Case of the UK Suffragettes (1906–1914)." *Social Networks* 34, no. 4 (2012): 643–44. Empirically based research about the limitations on political mobilization imposed by activists' use of secrecy and clandestine networks in the early British women's suffrage movement.

Klepto, Kolonel. "Making War with Love: The Clandestine Insurgent Rebel Clown Army." *City* 8, no. 3 (2004): 403–11. A discussion of clowning as a resource in recent anti-Capitalist protests. The rebel clown opens space at demonstration sites by bringing in elements of camouflage, creativity, and confusion.

Zwerman, Gilda. "Mothering on the Lam." *Feminist Review* 47 (1994): 33–56. Psychoanalytically oriented interviews with fourteen female members of 1960 era insurgent organizations in the United States that focus on subjective experiences of living underground with children.

Zwerman, Gilda, Patricia Steinhoff, and Donatella Della Porta. "Disappearing Social Movements: Clandestinity in the Cycle of New Left Protest in the U.S., Japan, Germany and Italy." *Mobilization: An International Journal* 5, no. 1 (2000): 85–104. A study of sixteen New Left clandestine groups in Germany, Italy, Japan, and the United States that centralizes the role of state repression in the activists' decision to go underground and remain committed to building an armed resistance movement.

Chapter 47

Violence/Destruction

Peter Sitzer and Wilhelm Heitmeyer

General Introduction to the Topic and Definition of Terms

Violence is a complex construct.[1] In the context of social and political protests, it means "intentionally caused or carelessly accepted damage to/ destruction of property or injuring/killing people."[2] Beneath the threshold of violence are confrontational forms of protest, intentional breaches of rules that, unlike protest meetings, picketing, or hunger strikes, interfere in other people's freedom of action or disrupt due process, but are not intended to cause physical harm to persons or property.[3] Although civil disobedience is defined as nonviolent protest, rule breaches such as sit-in protests or squats are sometimes classified as violence.[4] This highlights the tactical and strategic roles played by definitions of violence. If one party to a conflict succeeds in defining as violence something previously characterized more innocuously, it can present a situation as scandalous, discredit its opponents, and legitimize counterviolence.[5] Violence is an ambivalent concept. On the one hand, it can be aimed at destroying the existing order and causing injury to persons, on the other it may serve to establish order and protect individuals. If labeled illegitimate, it is seen as destructive and proscribed, but if the use of violence is made to appear legitimate, it is seen as a necessary means of creating order.[6]

Relevance for Protest Cultures

Though media reports suggest a rising incidence of violent protests, a glance at sixteenth-century peasant revolts or seventeenth-century civil wars will show that "nowadays most internal conflicts, in Western democracies at least, are conducted in a comparatively peaceable manner."[7] Nonetheless, in Europe the proportion of protests involving confrontation and violence varies considerably from country to country. According to Kriesi et al., in the period from 1975 to 1989, confrontational protests accounted for more than 13 percent of protests in Switzerland, more than 19 percent in West Germany, more than 24 percent in France, and 35 percent in the Netherlands. France had the highest proportion of violent protests, at roughly 31 percent, followed by the Netherlands with around 15 percent, Switzerland with more than 12 percent, and West Germany with around 11 percent. The proportion of protests involving serious violence was also considerably higher in France, where it was 25 percent, as against 9 percent in West Germany, 6 percent in the Netherlands, and just under 5 percent in Switzerland.[8]

Violence is not a constitutive element of social movements. Some social movements expressly reject violence, some use the threat of violence as a tactic, and some use violence as a matter of course.[9] Even terrorist movements do not define themselves through acts of violence as an end in themselves, but through political goals pursued by violent means. Protest violence derives its significance as a symbolic form of communication from the taboo on violence and from the reasons given to justify it. It attracts public attention by breaking the taboo, and the given justification places a topic on the public agenda. Insofar as protest violence is aimed at changing power and authority structures, it is also political violence.

Violence is the outcome of conflict escalation. Conflict has been described as any kind of relation between elements that is characterized by objective or subjective contradictions.[10] Thus, conflicts originate not only in objective problems such as an unequal distribution of life opportunities, but can also be the result of reciprocally defined norms, values, and identities. Escalation has been described as the intentional or unintentional intensification of a conflict as regards to the type and extent of instruments used.[11] In addition to key events, it is mainly processes of interaction within and between protest groups and other societal groups such as the general public, politicians, and the police, that cause conflicts to escalate. New collective interpretations and normative revisions may engender a new readiness to act and raise a conflict to a new level of escalation. Although conflicts are characterized by their process of escalation, the existence of typical development processes that recur in different conflicts is debatable.[12]

Historical Aspects

One characteristic feature of physical violence is that it is largely independent of preconditions. Heinrich Popitz sees the anthropological roots of physical violence on the one hand in humans' relative freedom from instinct and the associated far-reaching liberation from compulsions and inhibitions, and on the other in the power of human imagination: "a person is never obliged to act violently, but always able to … because there are no bounds we cannot imagine breaking."[13] The use of violence presupposes neither superior long-term strength nor symbolic communication, "because its power stems from the elemental vulnerability of the human body."[14] Violence is therefore an option available to anyone at any time, almost universally deployable, and effective without cultural preconditions. "The essence of the special nature of physical violence is that its effects are more reliable, more direct, and more general than those of other means of coercion; when the chips are down, physical violence is superior to any other tool of social control or instrument of political power."[15] Given this background, an explicit renunciation of violence as a means of protest would appear to be much more innovative than its use.[16]

Related Social Movement Research

The connection between protest and violence and the conditions of the transition from the former to the latter have been examined from various theoretical perspectives.[17] The individual explanatory theories should be treated as complementary rather than competing.[18] Macrostructural explanations interpret the origin and progression of violent protests against the background of developments and structures in society as a whole. Ted Gurr's theory of political violence[19] is based on the frustration-aggression theory, first proposed by Dollard and colleagues[20] in the 1930s and later refined by Berkowitz,[21] according to which frustration tends to produce a series of behavioral responses that under specific conditions will manifest as aggression. Building on this individual-level psychological approach, Gurr understands political violence as "a specific kind of response to specific conditions of social existence."[22] While Gurr does not entirely disregard the issues of state legitimacy, state coercive potential, and societal tradition, he locates the main cause of political violence in the subjective discrepancy between value expectation and value fulfillment, which is experienced as disappointment and can lead to dissatisfaction with the social system. Increasing dissatisfaction generates frustration, which can lead to aggression. Although many of those affected would express their dissatisfaction in other ways, every society contains victims of unfavorable socialization processes who, while poorly equipped to instigate a full-scale struggle, can be mobilized for political violence.

According to Peter Waldmann, the meticulous definitions of terms, the explicit formulation of hypotheses, and the broad empirical data that has been cited as confirmation are largely responsible for the prestige of this approach despite its obvious weaknesses.[23] First, protest is a relatively rare phenomenon even though dissatisfaction with the social system is widespread. Moreover, the extent of relative disadvantage among protesters may be smaller than among nonprotesters.[24] Second, it draws on individual psychology to explain a collective phenomenon. Third, from the behavioral perspective, political violence appears inescapably irrational. And fourth, the role of intra- and intergroup dynamics in the escalation of violence is largely ignored.

Resource mobilization approaches emphasize the rational nature of political violence.[25] From this theoretical perspective, sociostructural problems are neither a necessary nor a sufficient condition for the genesis of violent political movements. Instead, protest must be organized, which means mobilizing material and immaterial resources and deploying them rationally. This is why military coups have a greater success rate than revolutionary mass assaults: insubordinate generals are better able to coordinate and deploy their resources.[26] Alongside financial and military resources, organized political violence presupposes the mobilization of ideological resources that allow the use of violence to appear legitimate both internally and externally. Reference to social grievances of political origin can legitimize violence against persons and property representing the political system. Nonetheless, societies where the taboo on violence is deeply rooted are more likely to experience peaceful protest movements than violent protests.[27] In democratically constituted societies, violence at protests is rarely planned and is more likely to be triggered by uncontrolled subgroups or heavy-handed policing: most participants in mass protests are, like state authorities, concerned to contain violence,[28] even if the chosen means are not always suited to the purpose. Insurmountable differences concerning the choice of means of protest can lead militant subgroups to split from peaceful protest movements.[29] But the choice of means also depends on the available resources: some protest groups resort to the everybody's resource of violence because they lack other means to pursue their demands.[30]

Admittedly, there are holes in the resource mobilization approach that can only be closed using elements from other theories. For example, it cannot explain why massive clashes between demonstrators and police causing many deaths are inconceivable in certain countries. A further weakness lies in its inadequate consideration of the symbolic and discursive aspects of protest organization. The broader political circumstances and the associated opportunity structures for organizing protest are also largely neglected.

Political process and political opportunity approaches can be understood as complementary to the resource mobilization approach. Both start from the necessity of organization and mobilization. Political process approaches focus on the dynamics of interaction between the protest movement and relevant outside groups to explain the ebb and flow of mobilization and the radicalization or deradicalization of actions.[31] Political opportunity approaches focus above all on the political structures for articulating protest and mobilizing protest actors.[32] To the extent that both approaches examine both fixed opportunities and those that the movement can influence, there is little difference between the two.[33]

In his comparison of Great Britain, France, Germany, the Netherlands, and Switzerland, Koopmans shows that relevant political opportunity structures explain extreme right-wing protest violence in the 1990s better than grievances related to the presence of migrants or economic strains.[34] Radicalization of the right-wing extremist movement occurred especially in countries where the political space was narrow but the discursive opportunities great. Using the example of the Northern Ireland conflict, Bosi shows how closing political opportunities withdrew the basis for the inclusive and reformist mobilizing messages of the 1960s Northern Irish civil rights movement and gave rise to a situation where police repression, lack of political responsiveness, and countermobilization advantages fostered the exclusivist Nationalist message of the 1970s.[35] Altogether, empirical investigations show that exclusion from the political system and unstable political conditions in particular can encourage radicalization of political protest and escalation of violence.[36] But the example of terrorist movements also demonstrates that political opportunity structures can transcend the borders of the nation-state. The globalization of conflict diminishes the relevance of the nation-state as the unit of analysis.[37]

Alongside the openness and stability of the system, the strength of violent state repression influences the mobilization of political violence. Here both the deterrence theory (violent repression reduces protest violence) and the escalation theory (violent repression provokes protest violence) fail to do justice to the complexity of the situation. Combining both these theories, Friedhelm Neidhardt identifies an S-shaped curve representing the relationship between violent state repression and protest violence.[38] If there is no threat of repression, a high level of violence can be expected, because there are always reasons for violence, and no sanctions need be feared. If the state applies the means of repression at its disposal appropriately, violence by citizens initially decreases, "because at this level of repression the costs of using violence rise without generating the indignation required to provoke a sustained collective desire for resistance."[39] But if the deployed means of repression are perceived to be disproportionate, the violence curve may rise again. Here even "a small dose of repression can trigger great indignation and vigorous resistance if it is felt to be unprovoked and arbitrary. Conversely, harsh repression may be accepted by the victims if it is legitimated according to accepted standards of justice."[40] The curve of escalation ends when rising levels of repression replace the initial feelings of outrage with fear of losing life and limb. At this turning point, violent resistance recedes and is replaced by the "deathly tranquility of totalitarianism."[41]

Alongside political opportunity structures, consideration of cultural and other opportunity structures could contribute to our understanding of the genesis and development of protest violence.[42]

Despite their theoretical autonomy, framing and collective identity approaches exhibit areas of overlap. Building on the work of Erving Goffman, the frame is the scheme of interpretation with which a protest movement generates legitimacy for its actions and justifies the reasons for the protest to society.[43] First, a convincing interpretation of the problem must be generated: one that signalizes social relevance and names those responsible (diagnostic frame). Second, practicable solutions must be offered, for without the possibility of success protest would be superfluous (prognostic frame). And third, those affected must be motivated to engage for the cause (motivational frame).[44]

This analytical perspective offers an understanding of why violent protest may be unlikely even where social grievances and personal violence are ubiquitous. A suitable frame not only mobilizes potential members, but also can demobilize political adversaries by credibly challenging the legitimacy of their actions.[45] In this sense, the myth that the violence monopoly of the constitutional state guarantees intrasocietal peace can be understood as the "master frame,"[46] dialectically and reciprocally binding the state and protest actors to one another: "on the one hand, the myth serves the state as a means of demobilizing the resources of social movements and mobilizing legitimization of its own actions; on the other, it prevents social movements from engaging in discursive mobilization efforts with the topos of violence."[47] Thus, social movements tend to be overwhelmingly peaceful and nonviolent,[48] while those that refuse to reject violence quickly become revolutionary, terrorist, or simply criminal.

On the other hand, state violence can mobilize social protest movements and legitimize counterviolence if repression is perceived to be disproportionate.[49] Accordingly, protest movements that are willing to use violence challenge either the legitimacy of the regime or the appropriateness of violent repression. Their own violence then appears justified as counterviolence.

One important component of framing is the construction of collective identity and its internal and external communication.[50] Here the collective self-representation of a protest movement has internal self-policing and mobilizing functions. Generally, collective identity is constructed in opposition to the political adversary. Especially where the outgroup is regarded as a threat to the ingroup's substantial identity, justifying rituals of self-preservation can be invoked that allow violence to appear as a necessary form of political action.[51]

From this theoretical perspective, the violence of fundamentalist left-wing or right-wing extremist groups (including so-called autonomist groups) can be interpreted as identity-building: the outgroup is perceived as threat to the substantial identity of the ingroup, and a justifying ritual of self-preservation is set in motion. "This ritual can be cultural, social, economic, or existential and makes the use of violence appear a normal form of political action."[52]

To the extent that a movement's collective identity is the outcome of an ongoing construction process, radicalization and secession processes are also of interest. For example, the Italian New Left that emerged from the 1960s student movement was radicalized in its intellectual struggle with the traditional left, counterposing its urgency of action to their capitulation and preferring the principle of "everything now!" to a revolution postponed.[53] The Italian Red Brigades and Prima Linea[54] and the German Red Army Faction[55] all arose through splits caused by tensions within radical groups.

Interdisciplinary Perspectives for the Analysis of Protest Cultures

As shown above, one can only explain the escalation of social protests toward collective violence by drawing on the perspectives of different approaches. Accordingly, hardly any studies have tried to explain social movements from a theoretical perspective alone. To reach a comprehensive understanding of social movements and collective violence, especially the interdisciplinary approaches must be developed. For this, the competitively oriented approaches of social movement research must first be elaborated into a stage theory. This will involve testing their relevance for explaining the course of protest campaigns. Second, approaches taken in research on violence must be adopted, especially as regards to the destructive transformation of collective protests, that is how biographical conditions, social situations, and ideological legitimization of violence lurk behind peaceful protest intentions, and so on. Multilayer models that bring together the macro-, meso-, and microlevels should therefore be expanded in research on protest. This will only succeed if connectable concepts from different scientific disciplines are included.

Research Gaps and Open Questions

Future research will need to combine different research perspectives more closely in order to describe more fully the complex of conditions leading to radicalization of protest movements and escalation of violence. Admittedly, there is a problem with wanting to do so. Research findings are meant to have a certain degree of general applicability, but as a rule, contradictory findings can only be explained by specific circumstances. A promising approach could therefore be to develop empirically substantiated protest types that both cater for diverse conditional factors and reveal regularities within this variance.

At the same time, approaches endogenous and exogenous to movements must be integrated more strongly by analyzing the overall conflict system. Interaction models that view violent protest as the outcome of interaction between at least two parties without losing sight of the historical, political, legal, social, and structural framework within which conflict takes place can satisfy this requirement.

Peter Sitzer is member of the Institute for Interdisciplinary Research on Conflict and Violence at Bielefeld University. His main research interests are theories of socialization, youth violence, right-wing extremism, media and violence, and cyberbullying. Together with Nils Böckler, Thorsten Seeger, and Wilhelm Heitmeyer, he is editor of the book School Shootings. International Research, Case Studies, and Concepts for Prevention (New York, 2013).

Wilhelm Heitmeyer is senior research professor at the Faculty of Educational Science at Bielefeld University. From 1996 to 2013, he was director of the Institute for Interdisciplinary Research on Conflict and Violence at Bielefeld University. His research interests concentrate on violence, social disintegration, right-wing extremism, and ethnic-cultural conflicts. Together with John Hagan, he edited the *International Handbook of Violence Research* at Kluwer Academic Publishers (Dordrecht, 2003), and is editor-in-chief of the *International Journal of Conflict and Violence*.

Notes

1. Peter Imbusch, "The Concept of Violence," in *International Handbook of Violence Research,* ed. W Heitmeyer and J Hagan (Dordrecht, 2003), 1–39.
2. Dieter Rucht, "Violence and New Social Movements," in *International Handbook of Violence Research,* ed. W Heitmeyer and J Hagan (Dordrecht, 2003), 369–82.
3. Rucht, "Violence and New Social Movements," 369.
4. Otto Backes and Peter Reichenbach, "Freedom to Demonstrate and the Use of Force," in *International Handbook of Violence Research,* ed. W Heitmeyer and J Hagan (Dordrecht, 2003), 1079–96.
5. Friedhelm Neidhardt, "Gewalt. Soziale Bedeutung und sozialwissenschaftliche Bestimmung des Begriffs," in *Probleme der Nötigung mit Gewalt (Was ist Gewalt?),* ed. V Krey (Wiesbaden, 1986), 109–47.
6. Wilhelm Heitmeyer, "Gewalt," in *Handbuch der politischen Philosophie und Sozialphilosophie. Band I,* ed. S Gosepath, W Hinsch, and B Rössler (Berlin, 2008), 421–25.
7. Dieter Rucht, "Konfrontation und Gewalt. Verlauf, Struktur und Bedingungen unfriedlicher politischer Proteste in der Bundesrepublik," in *Die Eigenwilligkeit sozialer Prozesse. Festschrift zum 65. Geburtstag von Friedhelm Neidhardt,* ed. J Gerhards and R Hitzler (Opladen, 1999), 352–78; Jürgen Kocka and Ralph Jessen, "Die abnehmende Gewaltsamkeit sozialer Proteste. Vom 18. zum 20. Jahrhundert," in *Verdeckte Gewalt. Plädoyers für eine Innere Abrüstung,* ed. G Albrecht and O Backes (Frankfurt, 1990), 33–57.
8. Hanspeter Kriesi et al., *New Social Movements in Western Europe: A Comparative Analysis* (Minneapolis, MN, 1995), 50.
9. Rucht, "Violence and New Social Movements," 370; Marilena Simiti, "The Volatility of Urban Riots," in *Violent Protest, Contentious Politics, and the Neoliberal State,* ed. by S Seferiades and H Johnston (Burlington, VT, 2012), 133–45.
10. Ralf Dahrendorf, *Gesellschaft und Freiheit. Zur soziologischen Analyse der Gegenwart* (Munich, 1961), 201.
11. Dean G Pruitt and Jeffrey Z Rubin, *Social Conflict. Escalation, Stalemate and Settlement* (New York, 1986).
12. Roland Eckert and Helmut Willems, "Escalation and De-Escalation of Social Conflicts: The Road to Violence," in *International Handbook of Violence Research,* ed. W Heitmeyer and J Hagan (Dordrecht, 2003), 1181–99.
13. Translated from Heinrich Popitz, *Phänomene der Macht* (Tübingen, 1992).
14. Imbusch, "The Concept of Violence," 23.
15. Translated from Neidhardt, "Gewalt. Soziale Bedeutung und sozialwissenschaftliche Bestimmung des Begriffs," 134.
16. Roland Eckert, *Wiederkehr des "Volksgeistes"? Ethnizität, Konflikt und politische Bewältigung* (Opladen, 1998).
17. Michael Hasse and Kai-Uwe Hellmann, "Protest und Gewalt. Paradigmen auf dem Prüfstand," *Forschungsjournal Neue Soziale Bewegungen* 11, no. 4 (1998).
18. Rucht, "Violence and New Social Movements," 374.
19. Ted Robert Gurr, *Why Men Rebel* (Princeton, NJ, 1970).

20. John Dollard et al., *Frustration and Aggression* (New Haven, CT, 1939).
21. Leonard Berkowitz, *Aggression: A Social Psychological Analysis* (New York, 1962).
22. Gurr, "Why Men Rebel," 317.
23. Peter Waldmann, "Politik und Gewalt," in *Politische Theorien. Band 1 des Lexikon der Politik*, ed. D Nohlen and R-O Schultze (Munich, 1995), 430–35.
24. Joan N Gurney and Kathleen J Tierney, "Relative Deprivation and Social Movements: A Critical Look at Twenty Years of Theory and Research," *Sociological Quarterly* 23, no. 1 (1982): 33–47.
25. Charles Tilly, *From Mobilization to Revolution* (Reading, MA, 1978).
26. Erich Weede and Edward N Muller, "Rebellion, Violence and Revolution: A Rational Choice Perspective," *Journal of Peace Research* 35, no. 1 (1998): 43–59.
27. Ekkart Zimmermann, "Ressourcenmobilisierung und Gewalt," *Forschungsjournal Neue Soziale Bewegungen* 11, no. 4 (1998): 59.
28. Ekkart Zimmermann, "Protest- und Gewaltbereitschaft in Ostdeutschland," *Politische Vierteljahresschrift* 38, no. 1 (1997): 79–113.
29. Gilda Zwerman, Patricia G Steinhoff, and Donatella Della Porta, "Disappearing Social Movements: Clandestinity in the Cycle of New Left Protest in the U.S., Japan, Germany and Italy," *Mobilization: An International Quarterly* 5, no. 1 (2000): 83–100; Cynthia L Irvin, *Militant Nationalism: Between Movement and Party in Ireland and the Basque Country* (Minneapolis, MN, 1999); Gregory M Maney, "From Civil War to Civil Rights and Back Again: The Interrelation of Rebellion and Protest in Northern Ireland 1955–1972," *Research in Social Movements, Conflict, and Change* 27 (2007): 3–35.
30. Waldmann, "Politik und Gewalt," 432–33.
31. Doug McAdam, *Political Process and the Development of Black Insurgency 1930–1970* (Chicago, 1982).
32. Sidney Tarrow, "Kollektives Handeln und politische Gelegenheitsstruktur in Mobilisierungswellen: Theoretische Perspektiven," *Kölner Zeitschrift für Soziologie und Sozialpsychologie* 43 (1991); Dieter Rucht, *Modernisierung und neue soziale Bewegungen. Deutschland, Frankreich und USA im Vergleich* (Frankfurt, 1994).
33. Rucht, "Violence and New Social Movements," 373.
34. Ruud Koopmans, "The Extreme Right: Ethnic Competition or Political Space?," in *Contested Citizenship: Immigration and Cultural Diversity in Europe*, ed. R Koopmans et al. (Minneapolis, MN, 2005), 180–204.
35. Lorenzo Bosi, "The Dynamics of Social Movement Development: Northern Ireland's Civil Rights Movement in the 1960s," *Mobilization* 11, no. 1 (2006): 81–100.
36. Donatella Della Porta, "Research on Social Movements and Political Violence," *Qualitative Sociology* 31 (2008): 221–30.
37. Della Porta, "Research on Social Movements and Political Violence," 224–25.
38. Friedhelm Neidhardt, "Gewalt und Gegengewalt. Steigt die Bereitschaft zu Gewaltaktionen mit zunehmender staatlicher Kontrolle und Repression?," in *Jugend—Staat—Gewalt. Politische Sozialisation von Jugendlichen, Jugendpolitik und politische Bildung*, ed. W Heitmeyer, K Möller, and H Sünker (Weinheim, 1989), 233–43.
39. Translated from ibid., 238.
40. Translated from ibid., 239.
41. Translated from ibid., 240.

42. Karl-Werner Brand, "Vergleichendes Resümee," in *Neue soziale Bewegungen in Westeuropa und den USA,* ed. K-W Brand (Frankfurt, 1985), 306–34.

43. Erving Goffman, *Frame Analysis. An Essay on the Organization of Experience* (Cambridge, 1974).

44. David A Snow and Robert D Benford, "Ideology, Frame Resonance and Participant Mobilization," in *International Social Movement Research,* ed. B Klandermans, H Kriesi, and S Tarrow (Greenwich, 1988), 197–218.

45. Snow and Benford, "Ideology, Frame Resonance and Participant Mobilization," 198.

46. Jürgen Gerhards and Dieter Rucht, "Mesomobilization: Organizing and Framing in Two Protest Campaigns in West Germany," *American Journal of Sociology* 98, no. 3 (1992): 555–96.

47. Translated from Reinhard Kreissl and Fritz Sack, "Framing. Die kognitiv-soziale Dimension von sozialem Protest," *Forschungsjournal Neue Soziale Bewegungen* 11, no. 4 (1998): 41–54.

48. William A Gramson, *The Strategy of Social Protest* (Homewood, 1975).

49. Neidhardt, "Gewalt und Gegengewalt," 239.

50. Alain Touraine, *Production de la société* (Paris, 1973); Alberto Melucci, "Getting Involved, Identity and Mobilization in Social Movements," in *From Structure to Action: Comparing Social Movement Participation across Cultures,* ed. B Klandermans, H Kriesi, and S Tarrow (Greenwich, 1988), 329–48; Verta Taylor and Nancy Whittier, "Collective Identity in Social Movements Communities," in *Frontiers in Social Movement Theory,* ed. AD Morris and C McClurg Mueller (New Haven, CT, 1992), 104–29.

51. Thomas Meyer, "Political Culture and Violence," in *International Handbook of Violence Research,* ed. W Heitmeyer and J Hagan (Dordrecht, 2003), 957–72; Seraphim Seferiades and Hank Johnston, "The Dynamics of Violent Protest: Emotions, Repression and Disruptive Deficit," in *Violent Protest, Contentious Politics, and the Neoliberal State,* ed. S Seferiades and H Johnston (Burlington, VT, 2012), 3–19.

52. Meyer, "Political Culture and Violence," 965ff.

53. Donatella Della Porta, "Violence and the New Left," in *International Handbook of Violence Research,* ed. W Heitmeyer and J Hagan (Dordrecht, 2003), 392.

54. Donatella Della Porta, *Il Terrorismo di Sinistra in Italia* (Bologna, 1990); Donatella Della Porta, *Social Movements, Political Violence and the State* (New York, 1995).

55. Della Porta, *Social Movements, Political Violence and the State*; Friedhelm Neidhardt, "Über Zufall, Eigendynamik und Institutionalisierbarkeit absurder Prozesse. Notizen am Beispiel der Entstehung und Einrichtung einer terroristischen Gruppe," in *Soziologie in weltbürgerlicher Absicht,* ed. H Alemann and HP Thurn (Opladen, 1981).

Recommended Reading

Imbusch, Peter. "The Concept of Violence." In *International Handbook of Violence Research*, edited by W Heitmeyer and J Hagan, 13–39. Dordrecht, 2003. In this article, Imbusch explores the breadth of interpretations, indicators, subcategories, forms, and dimensions of violence on the micro-, meso-, and macrolevels.

Rucht, Dieter. "Violence and the New Social Movements." In *International Handbook of Violence Research*, edited by W Heitmeyer and J Hagan, 369–82. Dordrecht, 2003. Rucht analyzes the diverse approaches of protest movements and argues that the various concepts are compatible rather than competing because they played out on several levels (micro, meso, macro).

Seferiades, Seraphim, and Hank Johnston. "The Dynamics of Violent Protest: Emotions, Repression and Disruptive Deficit." In *Violent Protest, Contentious Politics, and the Neoliberal State*, edited by S Seferiades and H Johnston, 3–19. Burlington, VT, 2012. Seferiades and Johnston stress the relevance of collective protest, the central role of emotions, and the place of strategic violence in relation to the police.

Simiti, Marilena. "The Volatility of Urban Riots." In *Violent Protest, Contentious Politics, and the Neoliberal State*, edited by S Seferiades and H Johnston, 133–45. Burlington, VT, 2012. Simiti investigates cases of riot and identifies important differences distinguishing them from social movements.

Part VII

Pragmatics of Protest

Reactions to Protest Actions

Chapter 48

Political and Institutional Confrontation

Lorenzo Bosi and Katrin Uba

Definition of Political and Institutional Response to Protest

Protest for its same nature is intended to invite political and institutional confrontation. If it does not happen, the protest has failed one of its tasks, that of gaining responses from one or more political actors. Although states and state agents are the most common targets of protest, there are also other recipients of demands from collective action (for instance a private enterprise). Sometimes protest can even express its concerns indirectly, through targeting one institution but aiming to affect another—"a proxy target."[1] For instance, French farmers tend to target the government in Paris with demands that actually regard the agricultural policy of the European Union.[2] The social movement literature has focused on the state as the main target of protesting since the hegemony of the political opportunity approach.[3] But elites, pressure groups, political parties, and countermovements can confront protest similarly to state institutions—with concessions, repression, co-optation, or with a combination of these. The following introduces these forms of responses in more detail. Social movements' targets means any recipient of demands from collective actors.

First, the concession can be understood in terms of responsiveness of the target. It refers to "the relationship between the manifest or explicitly articulated demands of a protest group and the corresponding actions of the political system which is the target of the protest-group demands."[4]

Concessions can be made at different levels of policy making: (1) providing protesters access to policy making and listening to them; (2) taking the issue of the protest into the agenda; (3) adopting a policy congruent to protest group demands; (4) implementing the adopted policy; and (5) in practice alleviating the grievances of protest groups.[5] While the majority of literature focuses on political responsiveness, that is, adopting or changing the legislation,[6] recent studies show that the degree of concession varies across the policy-making process.[7] Even nonstate targets, like large corporations, might sometimes concede to protesters' demands.[8]

Second, the response to protest can take the form of physical repression, ultimately mass killings by government agents, suppression via censorship, or economic penalties. Tilly notes that repression refers to obstacles of state (or its agents) to individual or collective action by challengers.[9] Repression has also a contented meaning: activists consider protest policing as a form of repression, but state authorities see it as a mean to guarantee social order.[10] We should keep in mind that repression is a complex process in which not only the state but also mass media, countermovements, civil society, political parties, and individual citizens are involved. For example, political parties can expel radical groups that challenge the party line from within, and large corporations can easily fire workers demanding the right for unionization.[11]

Third, protests can be responded by political and institutional efforts of co-opting the mobilizing group.[12] The moderate activists are integrated into the mainstream politics with a hope that radicals will demobilize soon enough.[13] The issues are often co-opted by establishing new institutions—official trade unions for dampening labor protest, committees to discuss women's rights, or new political parties for dealing with the environmental movement.[14] The antinuclear power mobilization in the 1970s of Western Europe was responded by the emergence of green political parties that incorporated the issue to the mainstream politics.[15] Co-optation involves some level of concession as activists get access to policy making or their demands are taken on the agenda, but does not guarantee full success. For instance, McAdam and Su show how the U.S. peace movement affected the pace of congressional voting over the Vietnam War, but did not influence the final result of the voting.[16]

Protest targets are strategic and dynamic political actors. They "constantly seek to strategically ameliorate or defend their position of power over material and ideological resources."[17] Confronting protest in one way or another could either dampen or encourage further mobilization. Repression, for instance, is either lethal for mobilization or leads to further escalation of contention.[18] The variation could be explained by the fact that different protest groups vary in their reaction to repression.[19] Thus, protest and repression, but also concession and co-optation, are closely interrelated via reciprocal relationship.[20] There are not magic responses able to dampen protest, as there are not specific protest strategies able to achieve social movement goals. The impact of political and institutional responses should be understood in their context.

Who Reacts and What Conditions Shape Their Reactions?

The political and institutional confrontation emerges between protesters and a state, or state agents, private enterprises, elites, pressure groups, political parties, and groups that directly oppose challengers' demands, that is, countermovements.[21]

Scholars have mostly been interested in the strategies of concession and repression, and the confrontation between protesters and state.[22] The reason why the target selects a particular strategy of confrontation could be explained with the cost-benefit framework.[23] State authorities weigh the costs and benefits of continued protests and their own response.[24] The same accounts for nonstate targets, as for corporations, protests bring negative publicity and they would like to settle the issue before further escalation.[25] Calculating costs and benefits is shown to be dependent on many factors, mostly on protest and state characteristics, as well as the general political, socioeconomic, and cultural factors.[26] In a detail, the reaction to protest is affected by protest size and degree of disruptiveness, presence of political allies, public support of challengers' demands, and the characteristics of political system.

First, protest tactics and size have long been considered to be one of the most important factors for explaining state's response to political contention.[27] However, empirical evidence of the relationship is inconsistent. Some studies show that protests must cause some disruption to achieve concession,[28] while others demonstrate that violent protests are often responded by repression.[29] Tarrow argues that intermediate degree of contention is the most beneficial for challengers, as violence could fire back, and conventional tactics of demonstrations could be easily ignored.[30] Even the size, duration, and connectedness to larger political campaigns might lead to concession from the state.[31] The demands stated via protest are also important, as moderate ones are more often responded to by concession.[32]

Second, protest characteristics alone do not explain why some targets choose repression over concession, but the response is contingent on political and institutional circumstances. Social movement literature emphasizes that political allies[33] and public support to challengers' demands[34] are also important. Allies and public opinion could also be seen as the noninstitutional targets that mediate the impact of protest mobilization on policy making.[35]

It is widely agreed that political institutions, especially the regime type, shape state agents' response to protests. A democratic regime is less likely to use repression than a nondemocratic regime, and it even dampens the probability of repressing the large violent actions.[36] Concessions are more likely in a democratic regime,[37] but can be found even in nondemocracies if protests are large and disruptive enough.[38] Both of the choices are path-dependent; the more a country avoids repression, the less likely it is that repression will be used again.

Other structural factors like the degree of centralization, strength of the central government, electoral rules, and party system also affect the confrontation invited by protests.[39] Even the degree of protest policing relates to the distribution of power between different societal coalitions.[40] The same accounts for noninstitutional actors like elite or political parties.

The ideological position of the executive power has also importance for repression and concession. Left-wing governments accommodate environmental protests or those concerning the civil and labor rights more often than right-wing governments.[41] Police tend to respond to protests with violence under the right-wing government in France, but antiglobalization protests in a social democratic Sweden faced the same fate.[42]

In addition to state agents, protests are also responded by counter-mobilization, particularly if the state does not repress the protests.[43] For example, the marching of the Northern Ireland civil rights movement in nationalist and unionist streets during the late 1960s was violently confronted by a Loyalist countermovement.[44] Andrews shows that the degree and character of counter-mobilization to civil rights protest in the United States had historical roots, but was also related to protest characteristics.[45] In sum, we would emphasize that the way targets respond to protest are shaped simultaneously by multiple factors, and these interactions vary over time.[46]

Historical Traditions

The political and institutional confrontation between protester and its target has long historical roots.[47] Responding to protests with some combination of concession and repression is an old phenomenon with well-examined examples from Europe[48] and elsewhere.[49] The responses to tax and food riots of seventeenth- and eighteenth-century Europe were rarely concessions, but one could see the subsequent successful revolutions as a form of it.[50] Historical confrontations that have been studied were mainly in forms of revolution or rebellion, and depending whether they led to institutional change (challengers seized the power), these have been labeled as success or failure.[51] The terms are contested today, and some of the institutional responses cannot be clearly defined as concession or repression.[52] For instance, Stanley Palmer describes how the police forces of late eighteenth-century England and Ireland were created as a result of working-class and peasant protests.[53]

Authorities have over the centuries broadened the set of groups who have access to decision making, and this could be seen as a concession to movement fighting for the rights of these groups (e.g., poor, women, ethnic and sexual minorities, immigrants). Another option is that political parties co-opt the issues promoted via protests, for example, the responses to protests in Western Europe during the 1960s and 1970s.[54]

State of Research in Related Social Movement Research

The political and institutional confrontation with protesters is well studied in social movement research, although for long, the attention was more on the factors influencing the mobilization of protest rather than the response to protest.[55] Contemporary research on social movement outcomes focuses mainly on the political responsiveness to movements, and the conditions that impact the concession to social movement mobilization in general tend to be the same that shape state agents' response to protesting. Still, social movements can combine protest strategies with other actions (e.g., lobbying), and therefore, one should not fully equalize the response to movements and protesting. Moreover, social movement outcomes could be those other than political and institutional confrontation, as mobilization affects a broader cultural setting,[56] as well as the participants in the movement.[57]

Interdisciplinary Methods and Approaches for the Analysis of Reactions to Protest

As noted, the studies of protest response are similar to the ones of social movement outcomes, which are dominated by disciplines like sociology and political science. This also affects the applied methodology—many quantitative protest event analysis and qualitative case studies based on historical archive and newspaper data.[58] As the field on social movement outcomes studies, which deal with political and institutional responses, suffers a combination of theoretical and methodological obstacles: "goal adaptation, time reference and effect stability, interrelated effects, unintended and perverse effects, as well as causal attribution."[59] Protest response studies, especially the ones focusing on repression, aim to follow the dynamics of the process and often apply quantitative methods like time series or event-history analysis.[60]

Recent studies also combine qualitative case studies with systematic multicase analysis, as well as use the qualitative comparative analysis.[61] Although a few studies have paid attention on cultural aspects of confrontation, particularly framing,[62] very few studies combine political, historical, anthropological, and cultural approaches of political contention.[63]

Research Gaps and Open Questions

We have demonstrated that there is a broad literature on political and institutional responses to protests, but there are also a few gaps. Existing research focuses mainly on the reactions from state and its agents, but often neglects the responses from countermovements, other members of civil society, economic actors, and public opinion.[64] Considering the increasing attention to the antiglobalization protests, it is curious that we have little systematic research on the ways international organizations like the World Bank or International Monetary Fund respond to these actions.[65] Similarly, the reaction of the EU institutions to different protest groups would also be an important task for future research.

Finally, there seems to be some methodological gaps, particularly the lack of interdisciplinary analysis in the studies of political and institutional contention. The use of linguistic, literary, or other cultural methods would benefit our future understanding on the ways different actors respond to protesting.

Lorenzo Bosi is assistant professor at the Institute of Humanities and Social Sciences at the Scuola Normale Superiore, Italy. He is a political sociologist pursuing comparative analysis into the cross-disciplinary fields of social movements and political violence. Since January 2014 he is the principal investigator for the Italian team on a project titled, "Living with Hard Times: How European Citizens Deal with Economic Crises and Their Social and Political Consequences." He is also convener of the European Consortium of Political Research (ECPR) Standing Group on Political Violence, and head of the "Moveout-network." He has published in several journals of political and sociological studies. He is co-editor of *Dynamics of Political Violence* (Ashgate, 2014), of *Political Violence in Context* (ECPR Press, 2015), of *The Dynamics of Radicalization: A Relational Comparative*

Perspective (Oxford University Press, 2015), and of *The Consequences of Social Movements* (Cambridge University Press, 2016).

Katrin Uba is researcher at the Department of Government, Uppsala University, Sweden. Her main research interests are social movements and protest events, particularly the political outcomes of citizens' participation in noninstitutional actions. She is author of a meta-analysis of articles analyzing the impact of protest and public opinion on policy process, "The Contextual Dependence of Movement Outcomes: A Simplified Meta-Analysis," *Mobilization: An International Quarterly* 14, no. 4 (2009). Together with Fredrik Uggla, she has also written about patterns of protests mobilized against the European Union, "Protest Actions against the European Union, 1992–2007," *West European Politics* 34, no. 2 (2011).

Notes

1. Edward Walker, Andrew Martin, and John McCarthy, "Confronting the State, the Corporation, and the Academy: The Influence of Institutional Targets on Social Movement Repertoires," *American Journal of Sociology* 114, no. 1 (2008): 35–76.
2. Doug R Imig and Sidney Tarrow, eds, *Contentious Europeans: Protest and Politics in an Emerging Polity* (Oxford, 2001).
3. Jeff Goodwin and James Jasper, "Caught in a Winding, Snarling Vine: The Structural Bias of Political Process Theory," *Sociological Forum* 14, no. 1 (1999): 27–54.
4. Paul Schumaker, "Policy Responsiveness to Protest-Group Demands," *Journal of Politics* 37 (1975): 488–521.
5. Ibid., 495.
6. Marco Giugni, "Was It Worth the Effort? The Outcomes and Consequences of Social Movements," *Annual Review of Sociology* 24 (1998): 371–93.
7. Bryan King, KG Bentele, and Sarah Soule, "Protest and Policymaking: Explaining Fluctuation in Congressional Attention to Rights Issues, 1960–1986," *Social Forces* 86 (2007): 137–63.
8. Bryan King, "A Political Mediation Model of Corporate Response to Social Movement Activism," *Administrative Science Quarterly* 53, no. 3 (2008): 395–421.
9. Charles Tilly, *Popular Contention in Great Britain, 1758–1834* (Cambridge, MA, 1995), 136.
10. Donatella Della Porta and Herbert Reiter, *Policing Protest: The Control of Mass Demonstrations in Western Democracies* (Minneapolis, MN, 1998); Jennifer Earl, "Tanks, Tear Gas, and Taxes: Toward a Theory of Movement Repression," *Sociological Theory* 21, no. 1 (2003): 44–68.
11. See also Walker, Martin, and McCarthy, "Confronting the State, the Corporation, and the Academy."
12. Doowon Suh, "Institutionalizing Social Movements: The Dual Strategy of the Korean Women's Movement," *The Sociological Quarterly* 52 (2011): 442–71.

13. Alexa Trumpy, "Subject to Negotiation: The Mechanisms Behind Co-Optation and Corporate Reform," *Social Problems* 55, no. 4 (2008): 480–500.

14. Chris Rootes, *Environmental Protest in Western Europe* (Oxford, 2007).

15. Benoit Rihoux and Wolfgang Rüdig, "Analyzing Greens in Power: Setting the Agenda," *European Journal of Political Research* 45 (2006): 1–33.

16. Doug McAdam and Yang Su, "The War at Home: Antiwar Protests and Congressional Voting, 1965 to 1973," *American Sociological Review* 67, no. 5 (2002): 696–721.

17. Lorenzo Bosi, "Explaining the Emergence Process of the Civil Rights Protest in Northern Ireland (1945–1968): Insights from a Relational Social Movement Approach," *Journal of Historical Sociology* 2 (2008): 243–71.

18. Charles Tilly, *From Mobilization to Revolution* (Boston, 1978); Karen Rasler, "Concessions, Repression, and Political Protest in the Iranian Revolution," *American Sociological Review* 61, no. 1 (1996): 132–52.

19. David Meyer and S Staggenborg, "Movements, Countermovements, and the Structure of Political Opportunity," *American Journal of Sociology* 101, no. 6 (1996): 1628–60; Jennifer Earl and Sarah A Soule, "Seeing Blue: A Police-Centered Explanation of Protest Policing," *Mobilization: An International Journal* 11 (2006): 145–64; Paul Almeida, *Waves of Protest: Popular Struggle in El Salvador, 1925–2005* (Minneapolis, MN, 2008); Lorenzo Bosi, "Social Movement Participation and the 'Timing' of Involvement: The Case of the Northern Ireland Civil Rights Movement," *Research in Social Movements, Conflicts, and Change* 27 (2007): 37–61.

20. C McPhail and J McCarthy, "Protest Mobilization, Protest Repression, and Their Interactions," in *Repression and Mobilization,* ed. C Davenport, H Johnston, and CM Mueller (Minneapolis, MN, 2004), 3–33.

21. Goldstone, Jack. *States, Parties and Social Movements* (Cambridge, 2003.).

22. Christian Davenport, "State Repression and Political Order," *American Review of Political Science* 10 (2007): 1–23.

23. Joseph Luders, *The Civil Rights Movement and the Logic of Social Change* (Cambridge, 2010).

24. Jack A Goldstone and Charles Tilly, "Threat (and Opportunity): Popular Action and State Response in the Dynamics of Contentious Action," in *Silence and Voice in the Study of Contentious Politics,* ed. RR Aminzade et al. (Cambridge, 2001), 179–94.

25. Dennis Garrett et al., "Issues Management and Organizational Accounts: An Analysis of Corporate Responses to Accusations of Unethical Business Practices," *Journal of Business Ethics* 8 (1989): 507–20.

26. Giugni, "Was It Worth the Effort?"; D Cress and D Snow, "The Outcomes of Homeless Mobilization: The Influence of Organization, Disruption, Political Mediation, and Framing," *American Journal of Sociology* 105 (2000): 1063–1104; and David Meyer, "Protest and Political Opportunities," *Annual Review of Sociology* 30 (2004): 125–45.

27. For example, Schumaker, "Policy Responsiveness to Protest-Group Demands"; William A Gamson, *The Strategy of Social Protest,* 2nd ed. (Belmont, CA, 1990).

28. Fox Piven and Richard Cloward, *Poor People's Movements: Why They Succeed, How They Fail* (New York, 2012); Gamson, *The Strategy of Social Protest*; McAdam and Su, "The War at Home."

29. Davenport, "State Repression and Political Order."
30. Sidney Tarrow, *Power in Movement: Social Movements and Contentious Politics* (Cambridge, 1998).
31. For example, Katrin Uba, "Political Protest and Policy Change: The Direct Impacts of Indian Antiprivatization Mobilizations, 1990–2003," *Mobilization: An International Journal* 10 (2005): 383–96.
32. Gamson, *The Strategy of Social Protest.*
33. Martin Lipsky, "Protest as Political Resource," *American Political Science Review* 62 (1968): 1144–58.
34. Jon Agnone, "Amplifying Public Opinion: The Policy Impact of the U.S. Environmental Movement," *Social Forces* 85 (2007): 1593–1620; W Santoro, "The Civil Rights Movement's Struggle for Fair Employment: A 'Dramatic Events–Conventional Politics' Model," *Social Forces* 81 (2002): 177–206.
35. Edwin Amenta, Neal Caren, and Sheera J Olasky, "Age for Leisure? Political Mediation and the Impact of the Pension Movement on US Old-Age Policy," *American Sociological Review* 70 (2005): 516–38.
36. Davenport, "State Repression and Political Order."
37. Amenta, Caren, and Olasky, "Age for Leisure?"
38. David Kowalewski and P Schumaker, "Protest Outcomes in Soviet Union," *Sociological Quarterly* 22 (1981): 57–68.
39. Herbert Kitschelt, "Political Opportunity Structures and Political Protest: Anti-Nuclear Movement in Four Democracies," *British Journal of Political Science* 16 (1986): 57–85; Tarrow, *Power in Movement*; and Amenta, Caren, and Olasky, "Age for Leisure?"
40. Dominique Wisler and Hanspeter Kriesi, "Public Oder, Protest Cycles, and Political Process: Two Swiss Cities Compared," in *Policing Protest: The Control of Mass Demonstrations in Western Democracies,* ed. D Della Porta and H Reiter (Minneapolis, MN, 1998), 91–116.
41. David Meyer and DC Minkoff, "Conceptualizing Political Opportunity," *Social Forces* 82 (2004): 1457–92.
42. Donatella Della Porta and Olivier Fillieule, "Protest Policing: An Introduction," in *The Blackwell Companion to Social Movements,* ed. D Snow, S Soule, and H Kriesi (Malden, MA, 2008), 217–41.
43. Meyer and Staggenborg, "Movements, Countermovements, and the Structure of Political Opportunity."
44. Bosi, "Explaining the Emergence Process of the Civil Rights Protest in Northern Ireland."
45. K Andrews, "Movement—Countermovement Dynamics and the Emergence of New Institutions: The Case of 'White Flight' Schools in Mississippi," *Social Forces* 80 (2002): 911–36.
46. Richard Fording, "The Conditional Effect of Violence as a Political Tactic: Mass Insurgency, Welfare Generosity, and Electoral Context in the American States," *American Journal of Political Science* 41, no. 1 (1997): 1–29; D Cress and D Snow, "The Outcomes of Homeless Mobilization"; Marco Giugni, *Social Protest and Policy Change: Ecology, Antinuclear, and Peace Movements in Comparative Perspective* (Oxford, 2004); Sarah Soule and Susan Olzak, "When Do Movements

Matter? The Politics of Contingency and the Equal Rights Amendment," *American Sociological Review* 69 (2004): 473–97; JD McCarthy, A Martin, and C McPhail, "Policing Disorderly Campus Protests and Convivial Gatherings: The Interaction of Threat, Social Organization, and First Amendment Guarantees," *Social Problems* 54 (2007): 274–96.

47. Davenport, "State Repression and Political Order."
48. For example, Charles Tilly, *Contention and Democracy in Europe, 1650–2000* (Cambridge, 2004).
49. For example, Almeida, *Waves of Protest.*
50. Tilly, *From Mobilization to Revolution.*
51. Gamson, *The Strategy of Social Protest.*
52. Edwin Amenta and Neal Caren, "The Legislative, Organizational, and Beneficiary Consequences of State Oriented Challengers," in *The Blackwell Companion to Social Movements,* ed. D Snow, S Soule, and H Kriesi (Malden, MA, 2008), 461–89.
53. Stanley Palmer, *Police and Protest in England and Ireland, 1780–1850* (Cambridge, 1988).
54. Martin Klimke and Joachim Scharloth, *1968 in Europe: A Handbook on National Perspectives and Transnational Dimensions of 1960/70s Protest Movements* (London, 2008).
55. Giugni, "Was It Worth the Effort?"; Meyer, "Protest and Political Opportunities"; and Amenta and Caren, "The Legislative, Organizational, and Beneficiary Consequences of State Oriented Challengers."
56. Jennifer Earl, "The Cultural Consequences of Social Movements," in *The Blackwell Companion to Social Movements,* ed. D Snow, S Soule, and H Kriesi (Malden, MA, 2008), 508–30.
57. Giugni, *Social Protest and Policy Change.*
58. Bert Klandermans and Suzanne Staggenborg, eds, *Methods of Social Movement Research* (Minneapolis, MN, 2002).
59. Marco Giugni and Lorenzo Bosi, "The Effect of Protest Movements: Theoretical and Methodological Issues," in *The "Establishment" Responds,* ed. K Fahlenbrach et al. (Oxford, 2011), 17–28.
60. For example, Rasler, "Concessions, Repression, and Political Protest in the Iranian Revolution."
61. For example, Amenta, Caren, and Olasky, "Age for Leisure?"; R McVeigh, C Neblett, and S Shafiq, "Explaining Social Movement Outcomes: Multiorganizational Fields and Hate Crime Reporting," *Mobilization: An International Quarterly* 11 (2006): 23–49.
62. For example, D Cress and D Snow, "The Outcomes of Homeless Mobilization."
63. Bert Klandermans and Conny Roggeband, eds, *Handbook of Social Movements across Disciplines* (New York, 2007).
64. Lorenzo Bosi and Katrin Uba, "The Outcomes of Social Movement Action: An Introduction," *Mobilization: An International Journal* 14, no. 4 (2009): 405–11.
65. Walker, Martin, and McCarthy, "Confronting the State, the Corporation, and the Academy."

Recommended Reading

Banaszak, Lee Ann. *Why Movements Succeed or Fail.* Princeton, NJ, 1996. Argues that movement tactics, beliefs, and values are critical in understanding why political movements succeed or fail. By looking at the cultural determinants of the varying success of pro-suffrage activists in Switzerland and the United States, Banaszak addresses both policy adoption and broader structural outcomes.

Bosi, Lorenzo, Marco Giugni, and Katrin Uba. *The Consequences of Social Movements: Policies, People and Institutions.* Cambridge, 2016. This book examines the consequences of social movements, covering such issues as the impact of social movements on the life course of participants and the population in general, on political elites and markets, and on political parties and processes of social movement institutionalization.

Gamson, William A. *The Strategy of Social Protest,* 2nd ed. Belmont, CA, 1990. Originally published in 1975 and based on a random sample of challenging groups active in the United States between 1800 and 1945, this seminal book provides evidence for the role of organizational and movement-controlled variables for their success—probably the most systematic treatment of the effects of social movements to date.

Giugni, Marco. *Social Protest and Policy Change: Ecology, Antinuclear, and Peace Movements in Comparative Perspective.* Oxford, 2004. A comparative study showing that social movements seldom affect political outcomes directly, and that the joint effect of protest, public opinion, and favorable political opportunities are more likely to lead to policy outcomes.

Luders, Joseph. *The Civil Rights Movement and the Logic of Social Change.* Cambridge, 2010. A useful addition to the literature that brings an analysis of targets' responses to movement mobilization. Provides a general explanation of movement success by examining the responses of targets and third parties to the mobilization of the American civil rights movement.

Chapter 49

Suppression of Protest

Brian Martin

General Introduction and Definition of Terms

Protesters—especially when they are dramatic, colorful, or innovative—are a magnet for attention. But there are others to be aware of: opponents of the protesters. Individuals and groups that disagree with the aims or methods of protest sometimes ignore protest activity, hoping it will fade away, and sometimes compete with it by more vigorously advocating their own positions and values. Other options for opponents are to attack protest or to co-opt it, incorporating less-threatening components, modifying its demands, and isolating radical elements. A social movement during its life cycle may experience all of these responses, sometimes simultaneously by different opposing forces. The focus here is on one particular response: attack.

It is useful to distinguish several types of active efforts against protest. *Suppression* refers to methods for hindering, undermining, and disrupting without using force. *Censorship,* the withholding or hiding of information, is one type of suppression. *Repression* refers to use of force against challenging groups, including arrests, imprisonment, beatings, torture, and killing. *Oppression* is the systematic domination of subject groups through social arrangements such as economic inequality, political exclusion, and racial domination.

Who Reacts and What Conditions Shape Their Reactions?

Repression is used primarily by authoritarian regimes, or by liberal democracies, against armed movements. Western protest movements that use peaceful methods may encounter little serious repression, though following a military takeover or during wartime, the use of repression is more likely. Oppression is a structural feature in most societies. It can hinder protest but is not an active response. The focus here is on suppression, with some attention to milder forms of repression.

Protest can be suppressed in a variety of ways. *Cover-up* includes any method to hide information that might be helpful to movements. For example, environmental campaigners thrive on information about pollution, impending disasters, and the effectiveness of alternatives. Governments and corporations may refuse to collect such information, prevent scientists from reporting their results, or put pressure on media to curtail reporting. Campaigners also suffer from cover-up of their own activities: public protest movements may experience a virtual media blackout, sometimes due to news values—peaceful protests often are not considered newsworthy—and sometimes because media are directly or indirectly influenced by powerful groups to use industry-friendly perspectives.

Devaluation includes any method to discredit protesters, including labeling (terrorists, loonies, rabble), circulation of damaging stories—often irrelevant or distorted—about movement leaders, or trivializing important issues. Some protesters are stereotyped as mindless, emotional, or unscientific. Others are tarred by making them appear associated with fringe elements, extreme policies, or enemies of the state.

Protest movements usually devote a lot of effort to mustering evidence and arguments for their views, making a logical case. Opponents commonly challenge the evidence and arguments, but this on its own is not suppression: it is part of legitimate public debate. However, argument is often accompanied by *misrepresentation,* the use of claims and arguments in an unfair fashion. This includes lies about a movement's positions and methods, blaming activists for things they are not responsible for, and deceptively describing the consequences of movement positions. This is a form of rhetorical attack aimed at the credibility of the movement's arguments. Whether misrepresentation counts as a form of suppression depends on prevailing norms of public debate and on opportunities for responding. In any case, when public debate is open and robust, misrepresentation is less likely to be damaging.

Official-channel attack is the use of laws, regulations, and official processes to restrain and stifle protest. For example, governments may change or interpret tax regulations so that contributions to movement groups do not receive tax benefits. When groups seek to rent office space or buy equipment, governments may impose onerous requirements. Unnecessary tax audits can be a form of harassment. Governments and corporations sometimes sue activists, for example for defamation or restraint of trade, often as a form of harassment. In the United States, such legal actions are called Strategic Lawsuits Against Public Participation (SLAPPs).[1] Governments sometimes impose regulations on protest actions, for example requirements to notify police of rallies, to keep out of specific areas, to pay for the cost of policing, or to pay for insurance for possible consequences of actions. Such regulations lay the groundwork for arrests and subsequent legal actions against protesters, which can sap energy through protracted and expensive involvement in court proceedings.

Disruption aims to undermine the solidarity of a group or movement. It can involve the use of infiltrators—sometimes members of the police, sometimes group members paid or advised by government agencies—to cause members to become suspicious of each other, for example by spreading rumors. Sometimes government agencies send false letters or produce fake leaflets to produce tensions between rival movement organizations. Infiltrators who are *agent provocateurs* urge members to take rash actions, for example to use violence, and sometimes initiate such actions. This can split the movement through disagreements about tactics and can also discredit the movement in the eyes of wider audiences and provide a pretext for government crackdowns.

Intimidation includes threats and physical attacks, including arrests and beatings, and threats to an individual's livelihood or opportunities. Many citizens are easily scared even when no physical violence is involved. Protesters may be harassed at work, lose their jobs, or be shunned by coworkers (who are afraid for their own jobs). Sometimes their possessions, such as their cars or homes, are damaged or destroyed. Police surveillance of protest—tapping telephones, photographing demonstrators, infiltrating meetings—can lay the basis for arrests and itself can be intimidating to protesters. Attacks on just a few protesters can scare others: intimidation can have a chilling effect on protest.

The media play a key role in supporting or opposing protest. Suppression is easiest when mass media take the side of movement opponents. Sometimes media assist in cover-up by ignoring protest activities; they can assist in devaluation by focusing on negative aspects of protest, for example isolated incidents of violence or alleged links with stigmatized groups; they can assist in misrepresentation through biased coverage.

At a surface level, attacks on protest are targeted at individuals and organizations. This is relatively easy to see. At a deeper level, elements vital to the survival and success of movements can be targeted.

Resources such as money, equipment, and meeting places are essential to many protest activities, as recognized by the resource mobilization perspective in social movement studies. Several of the methods of attack, such as manipulation of tax regulations, target resources.

Communication is vital to movements. They need to communicate with current members to plan activities and with wider audiences to recruit new members and spread their message. Some communication occurs in face-to-face discussions and meetings, some via communication technology such as telephone and e-mail, and some via reporting on movement actions such as petitions, public meetings, and rallies. Suppression can prevent or discourage any of these forms of communication.

Credibility enables a movement to maintain and gain support; credibility is closely related to legitimacy and appeal. If a movement is seen as honest, committed, exciting, and concerned with important issues, it will be attractive to a wider public. Suppression against a popular, highly credible movement is seen as more unfair than against a disreputable fringe group. Therefore, undermining credibility enables other attacks.

Morale is what keeps activists going. It is linked to solidarity, which is the commitment of participants to each other and to the cause. Morale does not necessarily relate closely to movement success. According to Bill Moyer's Movement Action Plan,[2] morale often dips just as a movement is gaining widespread support, whereas morale sometimes can remain high in the face of adversity. By undermining morale, opponents can hinder even a powerful movement.

Activists use a wide variety of methods to promote their goals. Within groups, there are meetings and electronic communication. In soliciting support from the public, groups circulate information, organize petitions, and hold public meetings and rallies. Activists may use direct action to support their goals. Many of these methods serve as countertactics to suppression.

The countertactic to cover-up is exposure. Activists collect and disseminate information that supports their positions, sometimes by their own efforts and sometimes by drawing on the work of researchers, investigative journalists, or whistle-blowers. Activists usually seek publicity for their own activities, which serves to expose their very existence. That is one of the goals of public protests.

Table 49.1. Some Links between Methods of Suppression and Vital Features of Movements

	Resources	Communication	Credibility	Morale
Cover-up		Reduced contact with audiences	Less public awareness of strengths and contributions	Reduced public validation
Devaluation	Less credibility can mean less support		Lower reputation	Reduced public validation
Misrepresentation			Public misunderstanding	Reduced public validation
Official-channel attack	Access to resources reduced	Means of communication restricted		Reduced public validation
Disruption		Mistrust reduces useful communication		Trust undermined
Intimidation	Resources damaged	Mistrust reduces useful communication		Fear can reduce motivation

For a more detailed explanation of repertoires of action applied by protest campaigns and targeted corporations see Veronika Kneip, "Protest Campaigns and Corporations: Cooperative Conflicts?" *Journal of Business Ethics* 118, no. 1 (2013): 189–202.

The countertactic to devaluation is validation, namely building the credibility of the movement. Movements often try to recruit prominent respected individuals either as spokespeople or for endorsements. Another technique is to behave contrary to stereotypes, for example dressing in formal clothes for protests. Protesters may make commitments to nonviolence both for principled reasons and to counter attempts to discredit them as violent or criminal.

To challenge misrepresentation, protesters need to keep presenting their message, using a variety of methods, such as logical argument, metaphors, cartoons, and videos. Perhaps the most obvious aspect of movement efforts is a continual effort to explain what activists are trying to achieve and how they are going about it.

There are several ways to respond to official-channel attacks that burden a movement with regulations. One is to expose and argue against the bureaucratic obstacles, highlighting their unfairness. Another is to openly challenge restrictive regulations, using this defiance as a way of generating greater support. Yet another is to sidestep obstacles by organizing through networks and more spontaneous actions, obtaining resources as needed, for example relying on volunteers rather than paid staff and relying more on resources such as free e-mail accounts and photocopying at workplaces of supporters.

The countertactic to disruption is solidarity. Building solidarity can be achieved by opening and maintaining communication; building trust through sharing ideas, feelings, and actions; and putting in place processes to deal with internal disputes. Being aware of the possibility of disruption is important in being able to counter it.

The countertactic to intimidation is resistance. This means continuing in the face of threats and attacks, exposing the intimidation, and using it to discredit the movement's opponents.

Methods of suppression and activist countertactics may evolve in response to each other. For example, suppose police assault protesters at a rally, but graphic photos of police brutality actually generate more support for the protesters. The government may respond by using more subtle and less visible means of harassment or by trying to provoke movement violence, using agent provocateurs, or perhaps by turning to official-channel methods, banning taking photos of police. The result is that suppression dynamics can change over time, though there are some recurring patterns as new cohorts of people join campaigns and new opponents respond. The lessons of earlier campaigns are sometimes written down, but there are no required training courses for either activists or opponents, so processes of trying out tactics and learning from mistakes tend to recur.

Protesters, in responding to suppression, can take one of three general approaches: defending, counterattacking, and sidestepping. For example, if the government tries to discredit protesters by calling them rabble, criminals, or terrorists, protesters can defend by appearing and behaving respectably. They can counterattack by pointing out how government leaders are disreputable, even criminal, or terrorist. And they can sidestep the attack by adopting a low profile, using quiet, private methods of promoting change that do not provide an obvious target.

Historical Traditions

Dominant groups have always used their power against challengers. The precise ways in which this occurs depend on the context.

Consider for example the movement against nuclear power. In early years, there was little media coverage of problems in the nuclear industry, a sort of de facto cover-up. But after the movement gained momentum in the 1970s, reactor accidents became newsworthy, and the 1979 Three Mile Island accident received worldwide coverage. The Soviet government initially tried to hide details about the 1986 Chernobyl accident, but foreign scientists detected radiation from it. A key focus of struggle was publicity about problems in the nuclear industry.

Antinuclear-power activists were criticized for being uninformed and unscientific. This sort of devaluation was linked to misrepresentation of antinuclear arguments, for example the claim that nuclear power critics had no solution for society's energy needs.

Official channels were used in some countries to constrain protesters. For example, laws against trespass were used to prevent or remove blockades against nuclear plants. Some scientists and engineers who spoke out against nuclear power lost their jobs.

Other movements have had somewhat different experiences. For example, left-wing revolutionary groups—especially those that consider violence to be a legitimate tactic—are much more likely to be met with disruption and intimidation.

The feminist movement has had a different trajectory because so much of its efforts have been oriented to changing ways of thinking and behaving. Few feminists have ever advocated armed struggle, so disruption and intimidation of movement organizations are rare, though many individual feminists have been harassed and assaulted. Beliefs and interpersonal behaviors have been key arenas of struggle for feminism, so suppression has more commonly been through cover-up, devaluation, and misrepresentation.

Efforts at suppression can occur at any stage in the life of a movement. When a movement is in the early stages of development, with interested individuals formulating ideas and organizing a few actions, attacks can be especially damaging, because there is little capacity for mobilizing resistance. Early-stage attack is more likely in repressive regimes where there is pervasive monitoring, infiltration, and disruption of any sign of dissent. In more open societies, a more common response to movements in formation is either neglect or derisive dismissal. Active suppression is often a signal that the movement has become a threat to vested interests or prevailing values.

At the height of a movement's visibility and strength, open attempts at suppression may be attempted but usually have the least chance of success, because the movement can use the attacks to mobilize greater support. Movements in decline are more vulnerable.

State of Research in Related Social Movement Research

Social movement research has given considerable attention to repression, for example analyzing the effects of repression on social movement mobilization: in some cases, repression stymies movements whereas in others it can stimulate greater resistance.[3] A different entry point to studying repression and social movements is via nonviolent action (also known as people power or civil resistance). A key finding is that nonviolent action used against regimes is effective independently of the level of repression: the key to movement success is strategic acuity and the level of mobilization.[4]

In contrast to the study of repression, suppression has received relatively little attention in studies of social movements. Instances of suppression can be found in numerous accounts of social movement struggles, but suppression is seldom studied as a separate topic.

Interdisciplinary Methods and Approaches for the Analysis of Reactions to Protest

The predominant approach to studying suppression of protest has been case studies. Usually, suppression is addressed as one aspect of what happens to a movement, rather than suppression being the focus of attention. As a result, there is no established method for studying suppression.

There have been few attempts to systematize the study of suppression. One useful approach is to identify different types of suppression, providing examples of each.[5]

Research Gaps and Open Questions

Activists regularly deal with suppression, sometimes effectively and sometimes not, but the wealth of practical experience has not been matched by equivalent depth of research. From the point of view of movements, suppression is a practical matter involving choices between methods of avoidance and resistance, but researchers have seldom investigated tactics as a primary focus.[6] To fill the central research gap in the area, the obvious path is to study suppression as a phenomenon in its own right, drawing on activists' experiences to provide and test frameworks.

There are many open questions in this endeavor. One is whether to focus on methods of suppression—for example documenting and classifying them—or to look for broader frameworks that may be able to provide strategic insight by being applied to particular circumstances. Another is whether scholarly research into suppression has the same agenda as activist interest, or whether these could or should diverge.

Suppression of protest can be seen as a facet of protest or, alternatively, as a facet of multifaceted ways of exercising power, for example bullying, censorship, exploitation of workers, suppression of minority groups, environmental destruction, and genocide. It remains to be seen whether suppression of protest is best understood by paying closer attention to the methods used against protesters or by examining power struggles in diverse domains and applying resulting insights to the study of protest.

The academic study of protest can be used reflexively to better understand suppression of dissent in academia itself. Dissident intellectuals and ideas regularly come under attack using many of the same methods used against social movements.[7] These attacks, and the cautious intellectual climate created by attacks, can lead to research gaps—areas that few scholars dare to study—and may be one reason for the paucity of investigations of practical relevance to activists. The study of suppression of protest thus has the potential for synergy between academics and activists.

Brian Martin is professor of social sciences at the University of Wollongong, Australia. He is the author of fifteen books and hundreds of articles on dissent, nonviolent action, scientific controversies, and other topics. His recent publications include: *Nonviolence Unbound* (Sparsnäs, Sweden, 2015); *The Controversy Manual* (Sparsnäs, Sweden, 2014); and *Whistleblowing: A Practical Guide* (Sparsnäs, Sweden, 2013)

Notes

I thank Jules Boykoff and Steve Wright for valuable comments.

1. George W Pring and Penelope Canan, *SLAPPs: Getting Sued for Speaking Out* (Philadelphia, PA, 1996).
2. Bill Moyer, JoAnn McAllister, Mary Lou Finley, and Steven Soifer, *Doing Democracy: The MAP Model for Organizing Social Movements* (Gabriola Island, BC, 2001).
3. Christian Davenport, Hank Johnston, and Carol Mueller, eds, *Repression and Mobilization* (Minneapolis, MN, 2005).
4. Erica Chenoweth and Maria J Stephan, *Why Civil Resistance Works: The Strategic Logic of Nonviolent Conflict* (New York, 2011).
5. Jules Boykoff, *The Suppression of Dissent: How the State and Mass Media Squelch US-American Social Movements* (New York, 2006).

6. James M Jasper, *Getting Your Way: Strategic Dilemmas in the Real World* (Chicago, 2006).
7. Anthony J Nocella II, Steven Best, and Peter McLaren, eds, *Academic Repression: Reflections from the Academic-Industrial Complex* (Oakland, CA, 2010).

Recommended Reading

Boykoff, Jules. *The Suppression of Dissent: How the State and Mass Media Squelch US American Social Movements.* New York, 2006. This comprehensive analysis classifies suppression into eight modes by the state and four by the mass media.

Bunyan, Tony, ed. *Statewatching the New Europe: A Handbook on the European State.* London, 1993. This covers suppression of protest in Europe and can be supplemented by the magazine *Statewatch.*

Glick, Brian. *The War at Home: Covert Action Against U.S. Activists and What We Can Do about It.* Boston, 1989. This is a valuable treatment of how protesters can resist suppression.

Chapter 50

Cultural Conflicts in the Discursive Field

Nick Crossley

General Introduction

The dominant image of protest during much of the twentieth century was centered upon conflict over material interests, particularly that between Marx's proletariat and their Capitalist adversaries. Whether it was ever true that such conflicts could be reduced entirely to a material foundation is questionable. Human beings are symbol producing and using. We have needs and desires that transcend the requirements of our immediate material reproduction. As such, protest and social movement activity always has a symbolic dimension. We suffer symbolic injuries (e.g., when we are not recognized as we believe we should be), form our protests in discourse (from the child's "no!" to such complex philosophical tracts as Marx's *Capital*), and take exception to the symbolic activities (e.g., the categories and labels) developed and deployed by others.

Discursive Reactions to Protest:
Discourses on Crisis and Risks

As Western societies have developed, however, protest has arguably become more symbolic and discursive than in the past, not least because our productive activities are increasingly focused upon ideas, information, and symbols, and because our inhabitation of the world is increasingly symbolically mediated. The expert and her expertise have risen to the fore, assuming a political role and provoking challenges that are also necessarily therefore political. And the threats to which we expect political solutions, most obviously from pollution and contamination of various kinds, exist to an extent in a realm beyond our own immediate (empirical) experience; a realm only accessible to us, to the extent that it is, by way of expert discourse and knowledge. The two most obvious sociological explorations of this new political figuration are Beck's account of the "risk society"[1] and Foucault's critique of modern configurations of "power/knowledge."[2] In what follows, this chapter focuses primarily upon these accounts.

The collective discourses of modern societies, according to Beck, are increasingly focused upon risk.[3] Our newspapers, television media, and now the World Wide Web too are replete with accounts of risks to our health and happiness. Threats, it would seem, surround us on all sides: from what we eat and drink, through invisible toxins and radiation that penetrate our being in other ways, to crisis possibilities in the complex ecological and economic systems to which we belong and upon which we depend. Risks, in this account, are not identical to threats. There is no reason to believe that the threats we face now are any greater than they were in the past, even if the nature of threats has changed, but we are more aware of such threats and that makes a difference. We seek to calibrate and manage them, often having to play one off against another and, since some level of threat is unavoidable, defining for ourselves an acceptable level of it. This is risk in Beck's terms: a threat we know about, seek to measure, and manage. It is mediated, in many cases, through science, because many modern threats are neither immediate nor immediately visible: pollution may have visible, aesthetic effects, for example, but much of what troubles us most about it occurs over protracted periods of time, obscuring its visibility to ordinary consciousness and/or in ways that are not immediately given to our senses.

Risk provokes anxiety, and the anxiety it provokes is amplified when scientists disagree or appear to change their mind at regular intervals about what is safe and what is dangerous—an appearance that no doubt owes as much to media reporting of scientific work as to that work itself. This anxiety, in turn, fuels a new form of politics. New knowledge generates new risks that become a focus for mobilization. Moreover, the new knowledge is often tentative and uncertain, open to critiques which, insofar as claims enter the public sphere, become political in their own right. Indeed, a range of scientific domains have been politicized in the late twentieth and early twenty-first centuries, and these domains have become areas of social movement struggle. Environmentalism and the politics of global warming are obvious examples.

In addition to this, scientific advances raise and illuminate new ethical dilemmas which, likewise, generate further political controversy. Stem cell research, for example, generates new ethical dilemmas regarding the use of fetal tissue, which would have been unimaginable as recently as twenty years ago. Likewise, new knowledge about the activities of the fetus, combined with new technologies that help to sustain the life of premature babies, all raise debates about when a fetus becomes viable or conscious and therefore, according to the moral calculus of certain campaigners in abortion politics, has a right to life.

Research Perspectives on Discursive Reactions to Protest

Building upon Beck's account, and also upon similar work by Touraine and Melucci,[4] Anthony Giddens argues (somewhat prematurely in retrospect[5]) that the "emancipatory politics" characteristic of early modern societies, exemplified by the labor movement in particular, has been displaced by what he calls "life politics."[6] Life politics is essentially the political activity that forms within the moral discourse provoked by new scientific and technological capacities. Social movement discourse in late modernity, according to Giddens, is a reflexive discourse about the kinds of beings we want to be and also a moral discourse about how far and in what ways we are prepared to pursue these ideals.

Very similar themes can be found in the work of Foucault.[7] He points, for example, to what he calls "bio-politics," a form of politics that stems from a transformation of the governmental discourse of the state.[8] The state's power over death, its power to take life and send citizens to their death (e.g., in wars), he claims, while still in evidence (very much so at my time of writing), has been eclipsed by its "power over life." The state seeks to cultivate life and takes responsibility for the health and vitality of the population; an aim that both raises contentious issues and provokes conflict. Likewise, Foucault traces certain forms of expertise (chiefly medical, psychiatric, and social) that have taken root in the course of modernity and, in effect, created an infrastructure upon which the modern state, with its biopolitical agenda, can rest.[9] Modern life is regulated by experts, and this is contested and resisted.

Where Foucault's work differs from Beck and Giddens is that he focuses less upon the issues provoked by new forms of knowledge, more upon the claim to knowledge and expertise itself, and upon the political dynamics of knowledge and truth. Any society, Foucault argues, has what he calls its "regime of truth."[10] Claims to truth and knowledge play a regulatory role in society. Norms and rules are legitimated by reference to and are often derived from authoritative bodies of discourse. But at the same time, society validates certain forms of knowledge and certain forms/procedures of knowledge production over others. The contrast between religiously dominated societies and contemporary, secular, and scientific societies illustrates this point. Where religious truths prevail in one, scientific truths prevail in the other. Where knowledge is produced through exegesis of sacred texts in one, it is produced by rational argument and experiment in the other.

In addition, politics extends further into knowledge production in at least two ways for Foucault. First, at least as far as knowledge of human beings is concerned, the techniques that make knowledge possible also often function as instruments of control. The prisons and madhouses of early modern Europe were simultaneously observatories and laboratories for studying the human condition, for example, and also mechanisms for sequestering unruly elements within the population. Likewise, census surveys made populations both knowable and more amenable to strategies of regulation.

Second, Foucault explores the politics of the dominance of particular paradigms or discourses within science and, indeed, the dominance of particular discourses, such as science itself (as opposed to religion, for example) within wider society. Like Kuhn,[11] he argues that scientific knowledge and practice rest upon background assumptions, which, if not arbitrary, are at least untested, largely unnoticed, and historically variable. Moreover, again like Kuhn, he recognizes the potential for conflict between advocates of competing paradigms, particularly in the early history of a given science but also then at moments in the history of a science where its dominant paradigm or discourse shifts. Where Foucault differs from Kuhn is that he is more explicit about the politics of paradigms and paradigmatic dominance. The dominance of the dominant paradigm is, in some part, a reflection of the politics of scientific and wider communities and the play of power therein. Epistemic dominance is both a cause and an effect of social dominance within the scientific community—and, indeed, beyond the scientific community within the wider machinery of social power. Conflicts between competing discourses, Foucault believes, are often decided on the basis of their practical, political value rather than any claim they may have to greater scientific or philosophical veracity. Thus, for example, Nikolas Rose has shown how competition between competing discourses in early British psychology was resolved when one proved more useful for purposes of policy and administration.[12] Paradigms, which are socially and/or politically useful, are often favored over others even if they have no greater claim to purely scientific value or validity.

However, and significantly for our purposes, the power invested in knowledge inevitably meets with resistance. Foucault writes, for example, of the marginalized and disallowed discourses of modernity, suppressed by regimes of truth, which periodically find expression and serve to challenge the dominant discourse: for example, the discourse of the madman, the child, and the ill.

Quite how marginal such discourses are in contemporary society is an open question. They are undoubtedly subordinated to expert discourses, but considerable efforts have been made in recent years to, for example, listen to and improve the experience of those on the receiving end of medicine. And though this is no doubt partly an effect of the dominance of neoliberal forms of economic governance, which frame this in terms of the consumer, it is also partly an effect of *bottom up* struggles by social movements representing those whom Foucault deems marginalized and excluded. Some once marginal discourses are arguably less so today than at Foucault's time of writing and perhaps play a role, albeit a subordinate and subordinated role, within dominant discourses. They are no longer simply silenced or excluded (a point which Foucault himself makes, to some extent, in later work which focuses upon confession[13]). In the context of British psychiatry, for example, there have been successive waves of movement activism challenging medical expertise and championing the voice and, indeed, expertise of the patient.[14] Early manifestations of this, in particular the so-called antipsychiatry movement, were led by doctors who sought to challenge the medical paradigm in psychiatry and to replace it with models that were variously social and existential. From the early 1970s onward, however, with the formation of the "Mental Patients Union" and the many organizations and networks that followed in its wake, the challenge has been led by patients themselves—or rather, since the language of patients (along with other medical terms) has been subject to considerable critique within the movement, by users or survivors of the psychiatric system.

The efforts of survivor groups within psychiatry and medicine, to have their voices heard and accepted as legitimate forms of expertise, constitutes one example of the counterexpertise that Eyerman and Jamison deem central to much contemporary social movement activism.[15] To understand contemporary movements, they argue, we must understand the *cognitive praxes* through which they generate new and challenging forms of and claims to knowledge. And central to this is the claim to a counterexpertise that challenges those forms of expertise that tend to support the status quo. Counterexpertise might work within the broad parameters of established expertise as, for example, when certain environmental scientists (sometimes employed by major environmental lobby groups, such as Greenpeace) challenge the established orthodoxy in environmental science on basic scientific grounds. Equally, however, as with expert survivors in psychiatry, they might challenge the very criteria by which claims to truth and the good are defined. They might, for example, challenge the idea that certain behaviors or experiences are problematic or indicative of illness and in need of curing.

Nick Crossley is professor of sociology at the University of Manchester, United Kingdom. He has a particular interest in the role of social networks in the mobilization of protest and other forms of collective action. He published a book on social movements, *Making Sense of Social Movements* (New York, 2002), with the Open University Press, and his most recent book is *Towards Relational Sociology* (London, 2012).

Notes

1. Ulrich Beck, *Risk Society* (London, 1992).
2. Michel Foucault, *Discipline and Punish* (Harmondsworth, 1979); Michel Foucault, *Power/Knowledge* (Brighton, 1980); and Michel Foucault, *The History of Sexuality* (Harmondsworth, 1984).
3. Beck, *Risk Society*.
4. Alain Touraine, *The Voice and the Eye* (New York, 1981); Alberto Melucci, *Nomads of the Present* (London, 1989).
5. The emergence of the anticorporate or altermondialization movement, which is replete with emancipatory and materialist claims, challenges Giddens's claims and, indeed, the claims of many writers who at least implied that such matters were no longer important to social movement agendas. We should also be mindful that the increased prominence of the politics of Islamic fundamentalism and the response to it have also somewhat altered the social movements' landscape in a way that departs from the characterizations of the 1980s and 1990s.
6. Anthony Giddens, *Consequences of Modernity* (Cambridge, 1990); Anthony Giddens, *Modernity and Self-Identity* (Cambridge, 1991).
7. Foucault, *Discipline and Punish*; Foucault, *Power/Knowledge*; and Foucault, *The History of Sexuality*.
8. Foucault, *The History of Sexuality*.
9. Foucault, *Power/Knowledge*; Michel Foucault, *Madness and Civilization* (London, 1965); and Michel Foucault, *Mental Illness and Psychology* (Berkeley, CA, 1987).
10. Foucault, *Power/Knowledge*.
11. Thomas Kuhn, *Structure of Scientific Revolutions* (Chicago, 1970).
12. Rose Nikolas, *The Psychological Complex* (London, 1985).
13. Foucault, *The History of Sexuality*.
14. See Nick Crossley, *Contesting Psychiatry* (London, 2006).
15. Ron Eyerman and Andrew Jamison, *Social Movements* (Cambridge, 1991).

Recommended Reading

Beck, Ulrich. *The Risk Society*. London, 1992. A very influential and important book. It is easy to read and set the agenda for many important debates in social sciences during the years following its publication. It is still very relevant.

Crossley, Nick. *Contesting Psychiatry*. London, 2006. Offers an extended and clear illustration of political contention surrounding one discourse (psychiatry) over a period of more than fifty years.

Foucault, Michel. *Power/Knowledge*. Brighton, 1980. Many of the chapters of this book comprise interviews with Foucault. As such, they tend to cut to the chase regarding his key theoretical ideas and discuss them in a clear and accessible manner. The down side of this is that the empirical/historical analysis that informs Foucault's theory is sometimes not present—although in several important cases it is.

Giddens, Anthony. *Modernity and Self-Identity*. Cambridge, 1991. Like Beck's, this is a classic text, still insightful and provocative many years after its publication. It is light on empirical engagement and sometimes rather loose in its theoretical formulation, but it has a very clear thesis that remains important in key debates in this area.

Chapter 51

Assimilation of Protest Codes

Advertisement and Mainstream Culture

Rudi Maier

General Introduction

Mainstream is another word for dominant culture and left-coded, and for decades, alternative protests against this dominant culture found expression on two levels. There were organized forms; here people were mobilized by parties, trade unions, or left political movements, and more unorganized, personal forms of subcultures, which always also were expressions of what George Melly called a "revolt into style." Today, this clear distinction is not valid anymore. Protest codes have found their way in mainstream media and mainstream culture in various forms. Both mainstream and protest cultures share the task of catching public attention, and therefore, they use the strategy of communicative disruption. For some years now, shocking and disturbing pictures of protests can not only be found in mainstream media and especially in commercial advertising; they have become a concept of *cognitive Capitalism*.[1]

Reaction to Protest Codes in Advertising

Flipping through lifestyle magazines, watching pop videos on MTV, or doing some window shopping, slogans like: "Viva la libertad!," "Power to the people!," "I have a dream ...," and "Radicalize life!" are not just frequently encountered. They are almost unavoidable. Even though these expressions have their origins in different social and political movements and became well-known from these contexts, they were all utilized within the last decade as advertisements for products and services like cigars, laptops, web communication, or a TV music channel for young people. The appearance of the signs, symbols, slogans, and icons of left and alternative protest movements in commercial mass media evidences that protest codes and countercultural symbols have found their way into mainstream culture. By using the dynamic and affective images of raised fists, burning barricades, rallying crowds, red stars and red flags, punk fashion and haircuts, and well-known icons like Che Guevara, Karl Marx, or Lenin, these ads try to grasp the consumer's attention. The assimilation of protest codes into mainstream culture shows a complex situation that raises questions about power, culture, sub/counterculture, media, and resistance. This relationship has found special focus in the emerging field of cultural studies. In order to illustrate a development that started in the 1950s, this article will discuss the connections between protest codes and mainstream culture, using examples of this type of advertising.

The list of corporations using the described marketing strategy is extensive. Car companies (Audi, Porsche, Daimler) refer to the wild days of 1968, of those who have made their way and careers inside the institutions or aim currently at environmentally conscious consumers with green mainstreaming campaigns. Big fashion brands (Nike, Diesel, Levi's) use the motif of being different, a theme that can be found in nearly every form of advertising intended for young pop culture and fashion-oriented audiences. Computer manufacturers and software designers (Apple, SuperOffice) illustrate their new products with revolutionary gestures. Once in a while, forms of real protest can be found in commercial campaigns in public space, in marketing language labeled as guerilla advertising. The Italian fashion company Diesel paid for illegal graffiti making in its 2002 campaign, "Action—protest, support and act."[2] Reversed graffiti was used in public space by Adidas in 2006, where dirty house walls were cleaned up by the use of a brand stencil, this of course leaving an ad on the wall. A commercial flash mob, an action form rooted in the idea of critical mass, was reported in spring 2009 as organized in London's Liverpool Street Station for T-Mobile. Other marketing strategies seek to establish public places with a branded aura of subculture. In her description of the campaign "Berlin City Attack," Cordelia Polinna showed how the lifestyle company Nike turned public places into branded spaces and therefore consequently attained street credibility.[3] All these commercial interventions have the common aim of attracting public attention by doing the unexpected and the surprising, by jamming everyday communication routines within the economy of aestheticization and culturalization.

Since the end of the 1990s, new advertising strategies appeared in which revolutionary iconography pointed toward the autonomous self. "Think different" is the name of a campaign started by computer producer

Figure 51.1. You, too, can move great things, 2002 (Europcar Campaign 2002).

Apple, which began in 1997, using pictures of John Lennon and Yoko Ono, Mahatma Gandhi, and other different thinkers. They devoted this campaign to "the misfits, the rebels, the troublemakers" because "they change things."[4] The rise of *difference Capitalism* saw being different become the normative task and departure from the norm turning into the new norm.[5] The use of leftist or liberal iconography often appears to visualize this task. The Italian communication company Tiscali used the incident of shot protester Carlo Giuliani in the Genoa G8 protests in 2001 to illustrate its advertisement in Benetton's magazine *Colors* and with the caption "Disconnect."[6] Compared with the 1960s and 1970s, where the repression of the signs and symbols of protest was the hegemonic order of the day, the signs of protest today are staged as a permanent promise of personal freedom by aiming at the production of an aestheticized/stylized subjectivity.

This shift represented in expressions like the aforementioned television music station Viva2, which in the year 2002 came out with its keynote slogan, "Radicalize life!" Slogans like this and leftist iconography try to activate and mobilize the subject for the sole purpose of fulfilling his or her role as a subject. According to Michel Foucault, this is a new form of self-governance, one he analytically termed the "technology of the self."[7] In other words, and to borrow from yet another ad, "Be all that you can be!" (U.S. Army), the "affective work"[8] the advertising industry is doing here is actually "cognitive work," and their method, also understood as guidelines for becoming a subject, is described in nearly any marketing handbook these days: learn the rules and then break them.

Starting in the 1950s, a period of growing wealth in Western Europe, the idea of a rebellious lifestyle, embodied by the bohemian figure of the beatnik, made its way from the United States to Europe through music, fashion, and the media. The market discovered counterculture and youthful consumers both as an important source of new products and as a booming business trend. Film actors like James Dean and Marlon Brando became idols for young males, ones mostly from the working class, like the British Teddy Boys or the German *Halbstarke*. Habits, in fashion and physically, also changed with rock 'n' roll reaching Europe with the U.S.-American GIs. The first commercial advertisements that used explicitly left-wing iconography (in Germany) was published later. It was no coincidence that this occurred in 1967, the year students worldwide protested against the war in Vietnam, protested against outdated university structures, and fought for new collective approaches to housing, education, and work. In the German news magazine, *Der Spiegel,* a full-page ad showed Karl Marx twice: once bearing his famous beard, once freshly shaved.[9] The producer, a razor manufacturer, most likely intended to show in an ironic way the real face of Marx.

This premise is supported by the fact that this company was also reported to be the main supporter of the *Deutsche National- und Soldatenzeitung,* an extremely right-wing, anti-Semitic newspaper of the 1960s (see Roehler/ Born 1966). Around thirty of these advertisements can be found in the years 1967 to 1980 in the magazine *Der Spiegel.* They all show the icons, symbols, and carriers of leftist protests as a diverting spectacle and can therefore be identified as a symbolic maneuver in the battle for cultural hegemony.[10] Hebdige comments on interventions like these, where oppositional, subcultural, or threatening ideas are turned into goods able to be consumed, as a process that converts protest into a commodity and therefore sees it lose its dangerousness. The consumer lifestyle offered by the industry found its way in the large shopping malls in the 1980s, where punk fashion and accessories were sold not only to a subcultural scene, but to any suburban kid with a desire to buy them. The ads of those years are small in number and refer mostly to an increasingly differentiated society, displaying manifold different lifestyle orientations.

With the fall of the Berlin Wall in 1989, leftist icons appear again in mainstream culture. Yet this time, they are shown as examples of symbolic destruction of the icons of existent Socialist societies, which for the most part crumbled after 1990. Illustrating this point is the full-page ad placed in the *Wall Street Journal* by the Wall Street-based brokerage firm Solomon Brothers on 12 July 1990, featuring a huge portrait of Karl Marx with the caption: "We're helping Eastern Europe trade Marx for Dollars."

Research Perspectives and Research Gaps

The interdependence of protest and counterculture, lifestyles, and mainstream culture has been described from many different perspectives. An early and noteworthy criticism was made by Adorno and Horkheimer in their essay "The Culture Industry: Enlightenment as Mass Deception."[11] Founded in the mid 1960s, the Centre for Contemporary Cultural Studies (CCCS) in Birmingham became one of the most important research institutes, where a lot of studies on the relationship of protest, media, everyday life, and class cultures were made. Dick Hebdige pointed in his work "Subculture: The Meaning of Style" to the important role of signs, subculture and counterculture, and the meanings of style as answer to the society.[12] Paul Willis showed that *profane culture* must be understood as an interaction of protest, (group) identity, and society as well.[13] Angela McRobbie and Jenny Garber criticized the absence of attention to feminist issues in these early works.[14] American sociologist Thomas Frank showed in "The Conquest of Cool" the role and relationship of how counterculture became mainstream business culture.[15] By taking a closer look at advertisements produced in the 1950s in the United States, he terms those years as the starting point of the "rise of hip consumerism." The commercial adaptions of performative breaches of rules in the years 1968 and later are described by Stephan Malinowski and Alexander Sedlmaier.[16] A Marxist criticism of this development was made in the book *Kritik der Warenästhetik* by Wolfgang Fritz Haug[17] and renewed in his essay "Warenästhetik als Globalisierungsmotor," in which he focuses on the growing meaning of immaterial production and points out that criticizing post-Fordist Capitalism had grown more complicated.[18] In his study "Das Gefühl von Freiheit und Abenteuer," Rolf Lindner took a close look on the ideology and practices of the advertising industry.[19] He argued for a research environment that does not focus on the advertising itself, but the social structures of the consumers in order to find the various meanings that the promises advertising promotes might have for people from different classes, genders, races, and age groups. Robert Goldman and Steven Papson examined the rise and the media presence of Nike's "Swoosh" as a "core cultural icon."[20] A more theoretical perspective on the questions of norm and difference is edited by Marion von Osten, where various models of the idea of being different are laid out and where the topic of creativity is analyzed as current imperative in the field of the world of work.[21] Naomi Klein's book *No Logo: Taking Aim at the Brand Bullies* brings together the questions on marketing and culturalized good production, and asks for political alternatives and new forms of resistance in a globalized economy.[22] With a more moral, less academic, attitude, Kalle Lasn's *Culture Jam: The Uncooling of America*[23] and Joseph Heath and Andrew Potter's *Nation of Rebels*[24] also show the complex interaction of protest and mainstream culture.

All these different patterns show the transformation of (Western) societies in the last fifty years from Fordist Capitalism to current cognitive Capitalism, where knowledge became a new and important productive force. This new productive force, that can be seen in the "immaterial knots of the production of language, communication and the symbolic" both shows and produces a new form of what Michael Hardt and Antoni Negri called the "biopolitical fabrication of the order."[25]

This issue finds its expression also both in arts and in literature. The intervention "Nikeground" in Vienna in 2003[26] was where a fake announcement of Nike buying a square and renaming it into "Nikeground" caused some image trouble for the corporation. The rubber sculpture, "Big Sneaker" from Olaf Nicolai (2001), a huge nine-meter long, three-meter high, and four-meter wide sneaker, stands as a synonym for and criticism of the cultural and financial power of this company. In his postmodern novel *Pattern*

Figure 51.2. What are you fighting for? 2006
(40WEFT, in Unknown Italian Magazine, dated 30 September 2006).

Recognition, William Gibson invented Cayce Pollard, a brand allergic marketing consultant.[27] Meanwhile, author Max Barry gave "Jennifer Government" the opportunity to fight against the every day life impertinences in a totally liberated and culturalized market.[28] The collection, "this is how revolution looks" (German: "*so geht revolution*"), run by the *Mediologische*

Vereinigung Ludwigsburg, contains around 2,500 different pieces of protest ads published from 1967 up to now.[29] Around one hundred of them were (and are still) shown in a traveling exhibition since 2003 in more than 40 cities in Europe.

All these different perspectives show the broad framing of the topic, where consumption, lifestyle, media, communication, (youth) identity, and power are bound together in a well-described complex system. This requires first of all being researched in empirical case studies.

Rudi Maier is a cultural anthropologist and works as lecturer at the University of Applied Sciences in St. Gallen, Switzerland. His research topics are the world of work, subjectivity and society, political iconography, protest movements, and consumption. With Christoph Haug and Berit Schröder, he is coeditor of *Kampf um Teilhabe. Akteure, Orte, Strategien* (Hamburg, 2008) and is still collecting commercials dealing with left and alternative protest topics.

Notes

1. Yann Moulier Boutang, "Neue Grenzziehungen in der Politischen Ökonomie," in *Norm der Abweichung,* ed. Marion von Osten (Zürich, 2003), 251–80.
2. *Stuttgarter Zeitung,* 26 April 2003.
3. Cordelia Polinna, "Berlin City Attack. Die Marketingstrategien des Sportartikelherstellers Nike," *Derive. Zeitschrift für Stadtforschung* 13 (2003).
4. Wikipedia Contributors, *Think different,* http://en.wikipedia.org/w/index.php?title=Think_Different&oldid=276829499.
5. Marion von Osten, ed., *Norm der Abweichung* (Zürich, 2003).
6. *Colors,* 55/2003.
7. Michel Foucault, *Technologien des Selbst* (Frankfurt, 1993).
8. Michael Hardt, "Affektive Arbeit," in *Norm der Abweichung,* ed. Marion von Osten (Zürich, 2003), 211–24.
9. *Der Spiegel,* 45, 30.10.1967, 209.
10. Dick Hebdige, *Subculture—The Meaning of Style* (London, 1979).
11. Theodor W Adorno and Max Horkheimer, "The Culture Industry: Enlightenment as Mass Deception," in *Dialectic of Enlightenment* (Stanford, CA, 2002).
12. Hebdige, *Subculture.*
13. Paul Willis, *Profane Culture* (London, 1978).
14. Angela McRobbie and Jenny Garber, "Mädchen in Jugendkulturen," in *Jugendkultur als Widerstand,* ed. John Clarke (Frankfurt, 1981), 217–37.
15. Thomas Frank, *The Conquest of Cool: Business Culture, Counterculture, and the Rise of Hip Consumerism* (Chicago, 1998).

16. Stephan Malinowski and Alexander Sedlmaier, "'1968' als Katalysator der Konsum-gesellschaft. Performative Regelverstöße, kommerzielle Adaptionen und ihre gegenseitige Durchdringung," *Geschichte und Gesellschaft. Zeitschrift für historische Sozialwissenschaften* 32 (2006): 238–67.

17. Wolfgang Fritz Haug, *Kritik der Warenästhetik* (Frankfurt, 1971).

18. Wolfgang Fritz Haug, "Warenästhetik als Globalisierungsmotor," in *Politisch richtig oder richtig politisch: Linke Politik im transnationalen High-Tech-Kapitalismus,* Wolfgang Fritz Haug (Hamburg, 1999), 33–43.

19. Rolf Lindner, *Das Gefühl von Freiheit und Abenteuer: Ideologie und Praxis der Werbung* (Frankfurt, 1977).

20. Robert Goldman and Stephen Papson, *Nike Culture: The Sign of the Swoosh* (London, 1998).

21. von Osten, *Norm der Abweichung.*

22. Naomi Klein, *No Logo: Taking Aim at the Brand Bullies* (Vancouver, 2000).

23. Kalle Lasn, *Culture Jam—The Uncooling of America* (New York, 1999).

24. Joseph Heath and Andrew Potter, *Nation of Rebels: Why Counterculture Became Consumer Culture* (New York, 2005).

25. Michael Hardt and Antonio Negri, *Empire: Die neue Weltordnung* (Frankfurt, 2002), 47.

26. See Rudi Maier, "Image. Imagine. Imagineering. Intervenieren im kognitiven Kapitalismus," in *Kampf um Teilhabe. Akteure, Orte, Strategien,* ed. C Haug, R Maier, and B Schröder (Hamburg, 2008), 44–57.

27. William Gibson, *Pattern Recognition* (New York, 2003).

28. Max Barry, *Jennifer Government* (New York, 2003).

29. Mediologische Vereinigung Ludwigsburg, *so geht revolution,* http://home.bawue.de/~mauss/monat.html.

Recommended Reading

Adorno, Theodor W, and Max Horkheimer. "The Culture Industry: Enlightenment as Mass Deception." In *Dialectic of Enlightenment.* Stanford, CA, 2002.

Frank, Thomas. *The Conquest of Cool: Business Culture, Counterculture, and the Rise of Hip Consumerism.* Chicago, 1998. Aims at a central tenet of present society, the aestheticization of life itself.

Chapter 52

Corporate Reactions

Veronika Kneip

Introduction: Corporations under Attack

Besides reactions in the realms of political institutions or mainstream culture, implications of protest cultures have to be considered with regard to confrontation in the economic sphere. Protest campaigns address not only political institutions but the business world as well, mainly in the shape of multinational corporations. Within so-called anticorporate campaigns, single NGOs or broad coalitions of civil society actors target corporations or industries with the intention to influence corporate policy or institutional structures.

Multinational corporations (MNCs) are identified as the origin of deficiencies such as bad labor conditions or environmental damage, as they are said to profit from processes of economic globalization at the expense of others. Against the backdrop of lacking transnational regulation and unintended side effects with global impacts resulting from corporate action, Palazzo and Scherer refer to companies as "quasi-public actors."[1] However, despite their economic and political power, MNCs, too, find themselves in a state of dependence. Credibility has become a key asset for corporations because globalizing marketplaces come along with converging product qualities and require the trust of consumers as well as the general public.[2] Hence, anticorporate campaigns mainly tackle their attacks by aiming at a corporation's reputation or brand image. Thwarting consumer trust and mobilizing consumers as political actors has become a starting point for anticorporate campaigns.

Corporate Reaction to Anticorporate Campaigns

Of course corporations respond to changing societal demands and public protest. However, corporate behavior and corporate change cannot directly be ascribed to anticorporate protest as conflicts between corporate and campaign actors are not separated from their environment. With regard to the problem of identifying social movement outcomes in view of effects of outside events and actions, Tilly constitutes: "multiple causal chains lead to a plethora of possible effects in a situation where influences other than social movement activity necessarily contribute to the effects."[3] As corporations are well aware of their environment and try to identify potential threats through issues management and cause-related marketing, their strategies may also be employed in a proactive manner. Hence, changes must be examined against the backdrop of a broad interplay between civil society demands, economic structures and logics, and political frameworks. Nevertheless, systematizing specifications of corporate behavior in the light of protest action provides an insight into the dynamics of conflict and the scope of corporate reactions.

Empirical analysis on anticorporate campaigns and corporate (re)action has been conducted by the research project "Changing Protest and Media Cultures" at the University of Siegen, Germany. Between 2005 and 2010, the project identified 109 transnational anticorporate campaigns that are (partially) conducted by German-speaking civil society actors or address German-speaking publics and target corporations or industries.[4] Based on a frame analysis of documents and web sites as well as interviews with targeted corporations, corporate behavior could be systematized along the comprehensive dimensions of *confrontation, concealed counteraction,* and *cooperation* (see Table 52.1).

Confrontational corporate policies can be expressed through the *defiance* of campaign demands, as corporations ignoring anticorporate protest take a confrontational position even if they are not actively reacting to the demands of their critics. For instance, campaigns targeting the arms industry are widely confronted with strategies of defiance as they are questioning the industry's very right of existence. For campaign actors, a (non)reaction such as this is not easy to manage because public awareness and public

	Confrontation	Concealed counteraction	Cooperation
Corporations	Ignoring	Social campaigning	Public acknowledgement
	Public denial	Intraorganizational	Bargaining
	Intensification	reconstruction	Accommodating
	Legal action	Exclusive coalitions	Inclusive coalitions

Table 52.1. Corporate Reactions to Anticorporate Campaigns[5]

pressure—core tasks of campaign politics—are largely dependent on the dynamics of a conflict situation shaped by both protagonistic and antagonistic action. Besides, confrontational action to anticorporate campaigns may occur through active *denial* or even through an *intensification* of the scandalized behavior. This strategy can be seen as an attempt to frame corporate action as legitimate and campaign claims as inappropriate and superfluous. Moreover, such a reaction may signify the importance of the scandalized pattern for the organizational structure of the corporation. Maintaining certain behavior and asserting it even more rigidly may be of greater relevance than the potential threat through growing public pressure (e.g., in the case of corporations producing genetically modified crops). Finally, confrontational corporate action finds expression in measures to *prevent* or cut off corporate protest—mainly through legal proceedings like injunction, action for trademark infringement, or libel suits. Corporate legal action may have different consequences for protest actors. On the one hand, lawsuits increase public attention and are in many cases connected with a loss of corporate reputation, as the media often sides with the underdog. Nevertheless, legal proceedings and even the possibility of legal consequences must be seen as a serious threat for NGOs or social movement actors lacking financial resources to endure a long-standing court case.

Cooperative corporate policies include *official statements* within which corporations assert their awareness of the problems broached by the campaign and confirm their efforts for remedy. Moreover, cooperative approaches comprise *direct communicative exchange* between campaign actors and targeted corporations in order to compare perceptions and to search for options that are suitable for both parties. Within our empirical research, such dialogues were particularly prevailing between campaigns dealing with labor conditions in textile industry and their corporate counterparts. Garment producers have been targeted by anticorporate campaigns for many years, which may be one reason for wide willingness to engage in dialogue. The acceptance and appreciation of campaign demands and campaign actors may set the course for *inclusive coalitions* like joint monitoring projects or the development of common industry norms. Beyond, corporations may agree to campaign demands without directly interconnecting with the campaign. Such reactions can be characterized as *accommodating* and are mainly connected with product changes due to health and safety or ecological issues (e.g., product bans on noncertified tropical wood).

In addition to confrontational and cooperative responses, corporations react to anticorporate protest through concealed counteraction. This type of reaction can neither be described as completely confrontational nor entirely cooperative. Concealed counteraction can rather be understood as a mixture between cooperation and confrontation (often concealing confrontation behind a cooperative surface). Characteristic of concealed counteraction is a subtle reframing of the counterpart's behavior in terms of the other party's own interpretation. In this way, corporations make use of their opponent's strategy in order to further develop their own repertoires. Concealed counteraction becomes apparent through the framing of corporate communication in general or through larger *social campaigns*. For instance, the German discounters tried to reframe the employment issue, which has been put forward by several civil society organizations with respect to unionization and labor conditions. By promoting apprenticeship positions through public campaigns, the companies pointed to the protest issue, though not in terms of bad labor conditions but rather with regard to opening perspectives for young people. Hence, concealed counteraction can be characterized by the general acknowledgement of certain protest issues linked with attempts to turn them to good account for the corporation. Measures taken in this context do not seek for cooperation with campaign actors but are enforced by *intraorganizational reconstruction* or in *exclusive coalitions* with either different civil society organizations or other economic actors. Intraorganizational reconstruction, for example, became apparent through the establishment of special departments for corporate responsibility or the introduction of new eco or fair trade product lines. Likewise, exclusive coalitions between the corporation and civil society organizations outside the campaign picked up campaign claims. However, they did not involve campaign actors. Rather, NGOs that were less oppositional were chosen in order to enact social and environmental projects or certification programs.

The different types of corporate reaction are not isolated from each other but interact in various ways. For instance, confrontational instruments like ignoring or denying may be followed by decisions to relent if a campaign succeeds in increasing public pressure on a corporation. Likewise, public announcements to cooperate with protest actors may not be put into action but rather result in exclusive coalition building.

Historical Background of Anticorporate Protest

Criticizing corporations in public, holding them accountable for their actions, and empowering consumers to enter the political arena is not a new idea in Europe and across the world. For instance, some historians refer to the American war of independence as "consumer revolution" because they connect the emerging American identity to boycotts on English products.[6]

Furthermore, the eighteenth century gave rise to anticorporate action in Europe. In 1787, a group of men gathered around Thomas Clarkson founded a society to prohibit British companies from participating in the slave trade. Four years later, mobilized by calls for boycott, about 400,000 British men boycotted slave-grown sugar.[7] While most of these early consumer protests were connected to the mobilization of certain religious, national, and ethnic identities, contemporary anticorporate protest often transcends the borders of the nation-state and focuses on the transnational dimension of problems, for example, in the realm of human rights, environmental, or health and safety issues. Here, complex processes of production and corporate gain of power in the course of economic globalization take center stage: "consumer critique exposes the potential power of consumers as citizens and provides incentives to businesses, which regulation increasingly does not, to mind corporate responsibility to and dependence on democracy."[8]

State of Research on Corporate Reaction to Anticorporate Protest

Research on corporate reaction to anticorporate protest is widely embedded into more general topics of organizational change and corporate reactions to public demands. For instance, Zald et al. analyzed the impacts of movements on formally hierarchical organizations. In doing so, they differentiate between organizations that adopt policies demanded by movement leaders and activists and organizations that resist movement imperatives.[9] Moreover, the authors identify the strategy of "symbolic conformity" by referring to organizations that articulate policies in accordance with movement goals, and even establish "programs and offices that suggest concern with changing the organization consonant with movement demands"[10] but do not implement substantial changes of their policy directives. Like Zald et al., other scholars refer to symbolic or evasive dimensions of organizational behavior as well. For instance, Fiss and Zajac[11] or Oliver[12] concentrates on the symbolic management of strategic change or strategies of avoidance and manipulation. In doing so, they refer to organizations that attempt to escape external pressure by symbolic compliance.

With regards to cooperative relationships, Yaziji and Doh list five primary benefits for corporations partnering with NGOs: (1) heading off trouble, that is, engaging in dialogue to find shared standpoints; (2) accelerating innovation, that is, improving processes or products; (3) foreseeing shifts in demand, that is, detecting new norms and values; (4) shaping legislation, that is, brokering interests by searching coalitions with NGOs;

and (5) setting industry standards, that is, establishing new technology.[13] By contrast, Schepers refers to problems corporations face when responding to external demands and interacting with NGOs. He argues that multinational corporations, in particular, are usually confronted with diverse demands, for example, in the realm of environmental performance, labor conditions or local investing programs. Even if they are generally open to stakeholder dialogue and cooperation, they run the risk of being stigmatized for under-delivering on certain issues. Moreover, international NGO networks may face ideological conflicts between their northern and southern parts; hence, their political tactics may be aimed at the interests of their northern donors (e.g., environmental protection) and neglect local needs (e.g., employment, indigenous rights), which makes it even more difficult for corporations to find the right way to cooperate.[14]

Methods and Approaches for the Analysis of Corporate Reactions to Protest

Both the systematization of corporate reactions to anticorporate campaigns and the arguments brought forward in current literature on corporate behavior can be used as a starting point for in-depth research on the analysis of corporate reactions to anticorporate protest. Here, interdisciplinary approaches are needed to grasp the complexity of the subject that features divergent actors and logics of action. First, instruments of communication studies and linguistic methods are required to analyze protest communication and corporate communication regarding the structure of arguments, the development of discourses, and the arenas wherein corporate and anticorporate statements are brought forward. Moreover, economic ideas should be taken into account in order to consider corporate reactions against the backdrop of logics inherent to the economic system. The mentioned approaches should be tied up to the perspectives and methods of social science like organizational theory or the analysis of policies and regulation cycles.

Research Gaps and Open Questions

By adopting interdisciplinary methods and approaches for the analysis of anticorporate protest and corporate reaction to protest, the interplay of corporate and anticorporate strategies can be further evaluated in terms of its possible contribution to processes of societal self-regulation as well as regarding their connection to political opportunity structures. Civil society actors—although they can be considered a driving force in holding corporations accountable for societal impacts of their economic decisions—rely to a great extent on the support of national or international political institutions. Further research is needed on these interrelations between public campaigning and legal regulations. In this regard, country specific aspects should be taken into account. Are there relevant differences in protest repertoires and corporate reaction dependent on national institutional contexts? In doing so, further research could identify universal patterns and country-specific differences in conflicts between social movement actors and corporations.

Veronika Kneip is lecturer for business ethics at the Frankfurt School of Finance & Management, Germany. Her areas of research are sustainability, corporate responsibility, and consumer citizenship. Her most recent publications on those topics are "Protest Campaigns and Corporations: Cooperative Conflicts?" in *Journal of Business Ethics* (2013) and "Corporate Reaction to Anticorporate Protest: Multinational Corporations and Anticorporate Campaigns" in *The 'Establishment' Responds: Power, Politics and Protest since 1945*, eds. K Fahlenbrach, M Klimke, J Scharloth, and L Wong (New York, 2012).

Notes

1. Guido Palazzo and Andreas G Scherer, "Corporate Legitimacy as Deliberation: A Communicative Framework," *Journal of Business Ethics* 66 (2006): 71–88.
2. Sigrid Baringhorst, "Political Empowerment of Citizen Consumers—Chances and Problems of Anti-Corporate Campaigning on the Net," in *Net Working/Networking: Citizen Initiated Internet Politics,* ed. T Häythtis and J Rinne (Tampere, 2008), 281–309; Margaret Scammell, "Citizen Consumers. Towards a New Marketing of Politics?," in *Media and the Restyling of Politics,* ed. J Corner and D Pels (London, 2003), 117–36.
3. Charles Tilly, "Conclusion. From Interactions to Outcomes in Social Movements," in *How Social Movements Matter,* ed. M Giugni, D McAdam, and C Tilly (Minneapolis, MN, 1999), 253–70.
4. Sigrid Baringhorst, Veronika Kneip, Annegret März, and Johanna Niesyto, *Unternehmenskritische Kampagnen. Politischer Protest im Zeichen digitaler Kommunikation* (Wiesbaden, 2010).
5. For a more detailed explanation of repertoires of action applied by protest campaigns and targeted corporations see Veronika Kneip, "Protest Campaigns and Corporations: Cooperative Conflicts?," *Journal of Business Ethics* 118, no. 1 (2013): 189–202.
6. Timothy H Breen, "'Baubles of Britain': The American and Consumer Revolutions of the Eighteenth Century," *Past and Present* 119, no. 1 (1988): 73–104.

7. Melanie B Oliviero and Adele Simmons, "Who's Minding the Store? Global Civil Society and Corporate Responsibility," in *Global Civil Society 2002*, ed. M Glasius, M Kaldor, and H Anheier (Oxford, 2002), 77–107.

8. Margaret Scammell, "The Internet and Civic Engagement: The Age of the Citizen Consumer," *Political Communication* 17, no. 4 (2000): 351–55.

9. Mayer N Zald, Calvin Morill, and Hayagreeva Rao, "The Impact of Social Movements on Organizations," in *Social Movements and Organization Theory*, ed. GF Davis et al. (Cambridge, 2005), 245–80.

10. Ibid.

11. Peer Fiss and Edward Zajac, "The Symbolic Management of Strategic Change: Sensegiving via Framing and Decoupling," *Academy of Management Journal* 49, no. 6 (2006): 1173–93, http://aom.pace.edu/amjnew/unassigned/fiss.pdf.

12. Christine Oliver, "Strategic Responses to Institutional Processes," *The Academy of Management Review* 16, no. 1 (1991): 145–79.

13. Michael Yaziji and Jonathan Doh, *NGOs and Corporations: Conflict and Collaboration* (Cambridge, 2009), 129–34.

14. Donald H Schepers, "The Impact of NGO Network Conflict on the Corporate Social Responsibility Strategies of Multinational Corporations," *Business & Society* 45, no. 3 (2006): 282–99.

Recommended Reading

Kneip, Veronika. "Corporate Reaction to Anti-Corporate Protest—Multinational Corporations and Anti-Corporate Campaigns." In *The Establishment Responds—Power and Protest During and After the Cold War*, edited by K Fahlenbrach, M Klimke, J Scharloth, L Wong, 211–27. New York, 2012. The article provides a detailed analysis of corporate repertoires in dealing with anticorporate protest.

Oliver, Christine. "Strategic Responses to Institutional Processes." *The Academy of Management Review* 16, no. 1 (1991): 145–79. Oliver deals with organizational change due to institutional pressure and highlights the strategic character of responses to external demands.

Yaziji, Michael, and Jonathan Doh. *NGOs and Corporations. Conflict and Collaboration.* Cambridge, 2009. The monograph weighs the pros and cons of cooperation both from a NGO and a corporate perspective.

Part VIII

Pragmatics of Protest

Long-Term Consequences

Chapter 53

Biographical Impact

Marco Giugni

The Role of Biography in Protest Cultures

As any other action, protest activities have a number of consequences, both internal and external. Such consequences are often marginal and short-lived, but sometimes they are profound and long-lasting. The focus of this essay is on internal and durable effects of individual participation in social movements. We can refer to them as biographical impact. Biographical consequences of social movements are effects on the life course of individuals who have participated in movement activities, effects that are at least in part due to involvement in those activities.[1] This kind of impact can be distinguished from two other main types of impact, which have been the object of research by students of social movements and contentious politics: political consequences[2] and cultural consequences.[3]

The analysis of the biographical impact of social movements lies at the crossroad of two major fields in the social sciences: studies of life course and the life cycle[4] on one hand, and work on processes of political socialization and participation[5] on the other. In an attempt to locate the study of the biographical consequences of social movements within a broader literature on demography, life course, and contention, Goldstone and McAdam distinguish between four discrete literatures according to their thematic focus (movement emergence/development or decline/outcomes) and their analytic focus (macro or micro levels of analysis): macro-level studies of the origin of contention (for example, on the impact of demographic pressures for the emergence of contention, on the relationship between land pressures and peasant rebellion, or on the role of migration processes for the rise of ethnic competition); micro-level studies of the biographical availability or other life-course factors mediating entrance into activism; macro-level studies of contention as a force for aggregate change in life-course patterns; and micro-level studies of the biographical consequences of individual activism.[6] The third and, above all, the fourth group of works can be considered as dealing with the biographical impact in a broader meaning.

Research on the consequences of social movements and protest activities have overwhelmingly focused on political and, even more narrowly, policy effects. These are often related to the movement's goals. Cultural and biographical effects have not been completely ignored, but lag far behind in scholarly work. Yet sometimes, perhaps even most often, the major effects of social movements have little or nothing to do with their stated goals[7] or are only indirectly related to them. In other words, social movements often have unintended consequences (either positive or negative) that lie out of their control. Individual participation in social movements and protest activities, in particular, most often has unintended consequences. These can be limited to changing in a durable fashion the personal life of those who have participated (biographical impact narrowly defined), but may also have much broader implications by producing changes in life-course patterns at the aggregate level (biographical impact broadly defined). Research on the biographical impact has mostly focused on the former aspect, but more recent studies have started to tackle the latter, thus providing new insights into the origin of social and political change.

State of Research

The study of the biographical impact of activism was boosted by the protest wave of the 1960s, which spurred a series of follow-up studies of former participants in that protest wave. These studies, however, have a limited scope. Most, if not all of them, have examined the impact of the involvement of former activists in movements of the New Left. Furthermore, many of them have focused on participants in the U.S. civil rights movement.

In spite of, or perhaps due to, their narrower focus, these follow-up studies of New Left activists provide quite a consistent picture, pointing in general to a strong and durable impact of involvement in movement activities.[8] They suggest in particular that activism has a strong effect both on the political and personal lives of the subjects. Concerning the political life, former activists had continued to espouse leftist political attitudes,[9] had continued to define themselves as liberal or radical in political orientation,[10] and had remained active in contemporary movements or other forms of political activity.[11] Concerning the personal life, former activists had been concentrated in teaching or other helping professions[12]; had lower incomes than their age peers; were more likely than their age peers to have divorced, married later, or remained single[13]; and were more likely than their age peers to have experienced an episodic or nontraditional work history.[14] Furthermore, some have compared longstanding personal and biographical consequences of both people on the left and people on the right of the political spectrum.[15]

In addition to research on New Left activists, other studies examine the consequences of the involvement of strongly committed activists, finding an important biographical impact.[16] More recently, a number of authors have inquired into the individual-level effects of involvement in social movements by not-so-committed participants using survey data,[17] showing that more routine, low-risk forms of participation in social movements also have a strong biographical impact. These studies, in particular thanks to the use of survey data, offer a better ground for generalizations and show that people who have been involved in social movement activities, even at a lower level of commitment, carry the consequences of that involvement throughout their life.

Furthermore, these studies open up new perspectives for a broader understanding of the impact of individual participation in social movements on the aggregate-level change in life-course patterns. Research conducted by McAdam and collaborators[18] suggests that participation in the movements of the 1960s has contributed to the broader cultural shift associated with the baby boomers born after World War II. This impact of the movements of the 1960s and 1970s on changes in life-course patterns associated with the baby boomer cohorts, would go through a three-stage process[19]: in the first stage, activists in the political and countercultural movements of the period rejected normal life-course trajectories in favor of newer alternatives; in the second stage, these alternatives to traditional patterns became embedded in a number of geographic and subcultural locations that were the principal centers of the 1960s experience and of New Left activism, thus leading upper-middle-class suburbs to embody the new alternatives through socialization processes; in the third and final stage, these alternative life-course patterns spread to increasingly heterogeneous strata of young Americans through processes of diffusion and adaptation, and were largely stripped of their original political or countercultural content to be experienced simply as new life-course norms. Thus, involvement of a few people in social movements has broad consequences on society at large.

Research Gaps

In their overview of the literature on demography, life course, and contention, Goldstone and McAdam identify two major shortcomings: first, the lack of a sustained demographic/life-course perspective on contention in favor of a piecemeal approach to the topic, and second, a general asymmetry whereby "most work by social movement scholars is pitched at the *micro level* and concerned with life-course outcomes, while students of revolutions reverse the two emphases, focusing on the *macro determinants* of contention."[20]

Generally speaking, studies of the biographical impact of New Left activism share two kinds of methodological problems: one related to timing and the cause–effect nexus, the other to sampling and the generalization of empirical findings. There are noteworthy exceptions, of course, but the scope of most of the existing studies is often limited on either one or both of these counts. At least four problems can be noted related to timing, which make the attribution of causality from empirical data difficult. The first and perhaps most important one is the lack of before/after data on activists. Researchers have often inferred the effects of movement participation from information gathered after the fact.[21] This is problematic to the extent that one must rely on retrospective data, that is, on people's recollection of previous attitudes or opinions. Second, most work has focused on the 1960s cycle of contention, which is a period of particularly intense noninstitutional mobilization and participation in social movements. In such a context, it becomes difficult to ascertain whether changes in life-course result from individual involvement in political activities or more generally from the special era forming the background of the research and prevents empirical generalizations. Third, one should consider the time span separating activism from its consequences. If the follow-up investigation is too close in time to the moment when the subjects were active in the movement, one cannot ascertain whether activism has had a durable influence on life course.[22] Fourth, prior activism has often been measured at a single point in time, which does not allow for distinguishing between durable and ephemeral activism and commitment. This can be avoided through repeated measures of the consequences of activism that would strengthen the explanation, for example with a panel design.

Four further problems related to sampling and the generalization of findings can also be mentioned. First and foremost, most of the follow-up studies of New Left activists drew their subjects from nonrepresentative samples of the population, either focusing on a specific type of activists[23] or on those who are most strongly involved.[24] This of course seriously undermines the possibility to make empirical generalizations beyond the specific groups studied. Second, the lack of a control group made of people who did not participate in movement activities is a further major weakness of certain follow-up studies of former activists.[25] Without comparing the subjects under study with a control group of nonactivists, one lacks a baseline against which to judge the impact of participation. Third, many of the existing studies suffer from a small number of subjects, often less than forty, sometimes even close to ten.[26] This, of course, is not a problem in itself (qualitative research often is done on a small number of subjects), but it is a major obstacle to generalization. Using survey data stemming from larger samples is a solution to this problem. Finally, researchers often drew their subjects from narrow geographical areas, sometimes even from a single city.[27] Selecting the subjects from different locations or at least from a larger area might in part, but not completely, counter this problem.

All these methodological shortcomings related to timing and sampling issues make it problematic to establish causal relationships on one hand, and to generalize the empirical findings beyond the specific group under investigation on the other. Further work on the biographical impact of individual participation in social movements should try to avoid as much as possible these problems and set up a research design allowing researchers to check and possibly rule out plausible rival hypotheses. Ideally, such a design should have the following features: before/after measures of the dependent variable, experimental and control conditions, multiple groups for both experimental and control conditions, time sampling of the variables under study, and time series of the before/after measures.[28] The use of survey data, when implemented correctly, is a good start to reach this goal.

Conclusion

The literature on the biographical impact of social movements or, to say it more accurately, on the biographical consequences of participation in social movements, offers a number of important insights about protest cultures. To begin with, in spite of the methodological shortcomings of some of them, follow-up studies of New Left activists as well as works on other movements, periods, and participants suggest that taking part in social movements does matter for one's personal life. Being part of a movement as an activist has an impact on both one's attitudes and behaviors. In particular, it reinforces political commitment over time and leads to important changes in the life course, including in the work and family spheres. What is less clear is whether this also applies to people who get involved on a lower degree of intensity in social movement activities, that is, those whom we may call run-of-the-mill participants. Yet, recent works that go beyond a specific focus on New Left activism provide evidence allowing us to conclude, if only tentatively, that even such more ordinary engagement has profound consequences on one's own life.

However, being involved in social movements not only has an impact at the individual level, but may also and more fundamentally bring about broader changes in society. This is what suggests the still sparse scholarship on the aggregate-level effects of participation in social movements. By looking, as done most notably by McAdam and collaborators, at the ways in which individual participation in social movements and protest activities might result in broader changes through a number of mechanisms that still need to be disentangled, we are able to connect the micro-level processes at work in individual commitment to social movements with the macro-level processes underlying social and cultural change. The study of protest culture cannot but be enriched by such a perspective.

Marco Giugni is professor in the Department of Political Science and International Relations and director of the Institute of Citizenship Studies (InCite) at the University of Geneva, Switzerland. His research interests include social movements and collective action, immigration and ethnic relations, unemployment, and social exclusion. He is the author of *Social Protest ad Policy Change* (Lanham, MA, 2004), and he wrote a chapter on personal and the biographical consequences in the *Blackwell Companion to Social Movements,* ed. by DA Snow, SA Soule, and H Kriesi (Oxford, 2004).

Notes

1. For reviews, see Marco Giugni, "Personal and Biographical Consequences," in *The Blackwell Companion to Social Movements,* ed. DA Snow, SA Soule, and H Kriesi (Oxford, 2004), 489–507; Jack Goldstone and Doug McAdam, "Contention in Demographic and Life-Course Context," in *Silence and Voice in the Study of Contentious Politics,* ed. RR Aminzade et al. (Cambridge, 2001), 195–221; and Doug McAdam, "The Biographical Consequences of Activism," *American Sociological Review* 54 (1989): 744–60.
2. For a review, see Edwin Amenta and Neal Caren, "The Legislative, Organizational, and Beneficiary Consequences of State-Oriented Challenges," in *The Blackwell Companion to Social Movements,* ed. DA Snow, SA Soule, and H Kriesi (Oxford, 2004), 462–88.

3. For a review, see Jennifer Earl, "The Cultural Consequences of Social Movements," in *The Blackwell Companion to Social Movements,* ed. DA Snow, SA Soule, and H Kriesi (Oxford, 2004), 508–30.

4. For a review, see Tamara K Hareven, "Aging and Generational Relations: A Historical and Life Course Perspective," *Annual Review of Sociology* 20 (1994): 437–61.

5. For reviews, see Pamela Johnston Conover, "Political Socialization: Where's the Politics?," in *Political Science: Looking to the Future,* vol. 3, ed. W Crotty (Evanston, IL, 1991), 125–52.

6. Goldstone and McAdam, "Contention"; see also Doug McAdam, "The Biographical Impact of Social Movements," in *How Social Movements Matter,* ed. M Giugni, D McAdam, and C Tilly (Minneapolis, MN, 1999), 117–46.

7. Charles Tilly, "From Interactions to Outcomes of Social Movements," in *How Social Movements Matter,* ed. M Giugni, D McAdam, and C Tilly (Minneapolis, MN, 1999), 253–70.

8. For reviews, see Giugni, "Personal and Biographical Consequences"; McAdam, "The Biographical Consequences of Activism"; and McAdam, "The Biographical Impact of Social Movements."

9. For example, NJ Demerath III, Gerald Marwell, and Michael T Aiken, *Dynamics of Idealism* (San Francisco, CA, 1971); James M Fendrich and Alison T Tarleau, "Marching to a Different Drummer: Occupational and Political Correlates of Former Student Activists," *Social Forces* 52 (1973): 245–53; Gerald Marwell, Michael T Aiken, and NJ Demerath III, "The Persistence of Political Attitudes among 1960s Civil Rights Activists," *Public Opinion Quarterly* 51 (1987): 359–75; McAdam, "The Biographical Consequences of Activism"; and Jack Whalen and Richard Flacks, *Beyond the Barricades* (Philadelphia, PA, 1989).

10. For example, Fendrich and Tarleau, "Marching to a Different Drummer."

11. For example, James M Fendrich and Ellis M Krauss, "Student Activism and Adult Left-Wing Politics: A Causal Model of Political Socialization for Black, White and Japanese Students of the 1960s Generation," *Research in Social Movements, Conflict and Change* 1 (1978): 231–56; James M Fendrich and Kenneth L Lovoy, "Back to the Future: Adult Political Behavior of Former Political Activists," *American Sociological Review* 53 (1988): 780–84; M Kent Jennings and Richard G Niemi, *Generations and Politics* (Princeton, NJ, 1981); McAdam, "The Biographical Consequences of Activism."

12. For example, James M Fendrich, "Activists Ten Years Later: A Test of Generational Unit Continuity," *Journal of Social Issues* 30 (1974): 95–118; Michael Maidenberg and Philip Meyer, "The Berkeley Rebels Five Years Later: Has Age Mellowed the Pioneer Radicals?," *Public Opinion Quarterly* 24 (1970): 477–78; and McAdam, "The Biographical Consequences of Activism."

13. For example, Doug McAdam, *Freedom Summer: The Idealists Revisited* (New York, 1988); McAdam, "The Biographical Consequences of Activism."

14. For example, McAdam, *Freedom Summer*; McAdam, "The Biographical Consequences of Activism." Other relevant works on New Left activism include Stephen I Abramowitz and Alberta J Nassi, "Keeping the Faith: Psychological Correlates of Activism Persistence into Middle Adulthood," *Journal of Youth and Adolescence*

10 (1981): 507–23; James M Fendrich, "Keeping the Faith or Pursuing the Good Life: A Study of the Consequences of Participation in the Civil Rights Movement," *American Sociological Review* 42 (1977): 144–57; James M Fendrich, *Ideal Citizens* (Albany, NY, 1993); M Kent Jennings, "Residues of a Movement: The Aging of the American Protest Generation," *American Political Science Review* 81 (1987): 367–82; Alberta J Nassi and Stephen I Abramowitz, "Transition or Transformation? Personal and Political Development of Former Berkeley Free Speech Movement Activists," *Journal of Youth and Adolescence* 8 (1979): 21–35; Jack Whalen and Richard Flacks, "Echoes of Rebellion: The Liberated Generation Grows Up," *Journal of Political and Military Sociology* 12 (1984): 61–78; and Whalen and Flacks, *Beyond the Barricades*.

15. Rebecca Klatch, *A Generation Divided: The New Left, The New Right, and the 1960s* (Berkeley, CA, 1999).

16. For example, Joane Nagel, "American Indian Ethnic Renewal: Politics and the Resurgence of Identity," *American Sociological Review* 60 (1995): 947–65; Nancy Whittier, *Feminist Generations* (Philadelphia, PA, 1995); and Verta Taylor and Nicole C Raeburn, "Identity Politics as High-Risk Activism: Career Consequences for Lesbian, Gay, and Bisexual Sociologists," *Social Problems* 42 (1995): 252–73.

17. For example, McAdam, "The Biographical Impact of Social Movements"; Doug McAdam et al., "Social Movements and the Life-Course," unpublished paper, University of Arizona, 1998; Darren E Sherkat and T Jean Blocker, "Explaining the Political and Personal Consequences of Protest," *Social Forces* 75 (1997): 1049–70; Nella Van Dyke, Doug McAdam, and Brenda Wilhelm, "Gendered Outcomes: Gender Differences in the Biographical Consequences of Activism," *Mobilization* 5 (2000): 161–77; Brenda Wilhelm, "Changes in Cohabitation across Cohorts: The Influence of Political Activism," *Social Forces* 77 (1998): 289–310.

18. McAdam, "The Biographical Impact of Social Movements"; McAdam et al., "Social Movements and the Life-Course"; Van Dyke, McAdam, and Wilhelm, "Gendered Outcomes"; and Wilhelm, "Changes in Cohabitation across Cohorts."

19. McAdam, "The Biographical Impact of Social Movements"; furthermore, see Jack Goldstone and Doug McAdam, "Contention in Demographic and Life-Course Context," in *Silence and Voice in the Study of Contentious Politics,* ed. RR Aminzade et al. (Cambridge, 2001), 195–221.

20. Goldstone and McAdam, "Contention in Demographic and Life-Course Context," 196–97.

21. But see Demerath, Marwell, and Aiken, *Dynamics of Idealism*; Jennings, "Residues of a Movement"; Jennings and Niemi, *Generations and Politics*; Marwell, Aiken, and Demerath, "The Persistence of Political Attitudes among 1960s Civil Rights Activists"; McAdam, *Freedom Summer*; and McAdam, "The Biographical Consequences of Activism."

22. But see Fendrich, *Ideal Citizens*; Fendrich and Lovoy, "Back to the Future"; Marwell, Aiken, and Demerath, "The Persistence of Political Attitudes among 1960s Civil Rights Activists"; McAdam, *Freedom Summer*; and McAdam, "The Biographical Consequences of Activism."

23. New Left activists, precisely; but see Klatch, *A Generation Divided.*

24. But see McAdam, "The Biographical Impact of Social Movements"; McAdam et al., "Social Movements and the Life-Course"; Sherkat and Blocker, "Explaining the Political and Personal Consequences of Protest"; Van Dyke, McAdam, and Wilhelm, "Gendered Outcomes"; and Wilhelm, "Changes in Cohabitation across Cohorts."

25. But see Fendrich, "Activists Ten Years Later"; Fendrich, "Keeping the Faith or Pursuing the Good Life"; Fendrich, *Ideal Citizens*; Fendrich and Krauss, "Student Activism and Adult Left-Wing Politics"; Fendrich, and Tarleau, "Marching to a Different Drummer"; Fendrich and Lovoy, "Back to the Future"; Jennings, "Residues of a Movement"; Jennings and Niemi, *Generations and Politics*; McAdam, *Freedom Summer*; and McAdam, "The Biographical Consequences of Activism."

26. For example, Jack Whalen and Richards Flacks, "The Isla Vista 'Bank Burners' Ten Years Later: Notes on the Fate of Student Activists," *Sociological Focus* 13 (1980): 215–36; Whalen and Flacks, "Echoes of Rebellion"; and Whalen and Flacks, *Beyond the Barricades*.

27. For example, Whalen and Flacks, "The Isla Vista 'Bank Burners' Ten Years Later."

28. Thomas F Pettigrew, *How to Think Like a Social Scientist* (New York, 1996), chapter 3.

Recommended Reading

Fendrich, James M, and Kenneth L Lovoy. "Back to the Future: Adult Political Behavior of Former Political Activists." *American Sociological Review* 53 (1988): 780–84. One of a number of publications based on Fendrich's study of former civil rights activists, showing that they had remained active in contemporary movements or other forms of political activity.

Giugni, Marco. "Personal and Biographical Consequences." In *The Blackwell Companion to Social Movements,* edited by DA Snow, SA Soule, and H Kriesi, 489–507. Oxford, 2004. A review of works on the biographical outcomes of social movements, which also discusses methodological issues relating to the study of biographical outcomes.

Jennings, M Kent, and Richard G Niemi. *Generations and Politics: A Panel Study of Young Adults and Their Parents.* Princeton, NJ, 1981. One of the most thorough and methodologically sound follow-up studies of New Left activists, showing that former activists had remained active in contemporary movements or other forms of political activity.

McAdam, Doug. "The Biographical Consequences of Activism." *American Sociological Review* 54 (1989): 744–60. A study of biographical outcomes based on an important research on participants in the 1964 Mississippi Freedom Summer project, showing that participants were more likely than their age peers to have experienced an episodic or nontraditional work history.

Sherkat, Darren E, and T Jean Blocker. "Explaining the Political and Personal Consequences of Protest." *Social Forces* 75 (1997): 1049–70. Examines the political and personal consequences of more routine, low-risk forms of participation in antiwar and student protests of the late 1960s using survey data, showing that ordinary involvement in these movements had an impact on the lives of those who had participated.

Chapter 54

Changing Gender Roles

Kristina Schulz

In modern history, ideas of gender roles and power relations between men and women have remained markedly constant. The early nineteenth century witnessed ideals of separation between, on the one hand, gainful employment, attributed to the male sphere, and, on the other hand, family and household, proper to women. This ideal flourished initially among the bourgeoisie, but rapidly had an impact on other social groups. Neither World Wars, nor the economic crises of the late 1920s, or even that of the mid 1960s could shake these gender-specific attributions. However, female resistance has a long tradition, especially when it comes to individual cultural practices such as reading and writing, or to everyday practices (e.g., sexual denial). Furthermore, Bonnie S Anderson and Karen Offen have, among others, shown that transatlantic and European feminist networks between well-educated women existed already in the first half of the nineteenth century and saw a second heyday around the turn of the century.[1] What is striking for the 1970s women's liberation movement (WLM) is its successful attempt to raise a collective consciousness among women from very different backgrounds. For a period of about a decade, it formed a dynamic, diverse social movement spanning many countries.

When this chapter talks about long-term consequences of protest, we have to bear in mind that the history of 1970s WLM is only forty years old. Furthermore, some of the more recent achievements in terms of gender equality cannot exclusively be attributed to the social movement of the 1970s but also to previous and parallel feminist efforts, and broader societal developments.

Characteristics of the Long-Term Consequences

Before assessing actual impacts, it is helpful to examine the outcome *poten-tiality* of the WLMs in Europe. For many countries, it seems useful to distinguish between two conceptions of feminism, *symbolic feminism* and *social feminism*.

Symbolic feminism took as point of departure human patterns of perception, cognitions, and categorizations. From this point of view, the symbolic preceded the social, and change in social structures therefore had to start with a change in mental structures. Known as representatives of *écriture feminine,* a couple of French thinkers with an intellectual background in literature, philosophy, and psychoanalyses were perceived as the literary feminist avant-garde,[2] and their works were highly influential in many countries.[3] But female writing became also a literary practice outside academia. It was central for collective identity and network building processes around women's journals, women's bookshops, women's libraries, and so on. All those emerging projects assumed that the very heart of women's oppression was to be identified in a symbolic system (patriarchy), cemented in linguistic expression that was developed by and principally addressed to men. Changing the symbolic order by the means of literary expression and everyday language seemed the most productive means to proceed. Furthermore, symbolic feminism developed methods of individual and collective liberation through consciousness-raising groups, therapy, and other creative activities.

Social feminism focused on matters of material redistribution. The aim was less to valorize femininity and rather to overcome gender difference as such. Social feminism sought to influence directly the political decision-making process, centering, in the first place, on social institutions and on social rather than on individual mental change. Protest activities, from this point of view, were addressed to a larger public. Social feminists sought to raise consciousness not so much by encounter groups but by public provocation. Collective action created a feeling of solidarity among women and addressed at the same time political decision makers. The logic of social feminist activism put pressure on the governing institutions of many countries. Grievances especially focused on two aspects: women's protection and women's promotion. Although it was a constant source of conflict within the women's movement, the dual transformation strategy had positive effects as well. It led to a broad diversity of feminist claims and ensured that women's concerns were put on the agenda in such different domains as public health, the academy, and labor markets.

The WLM outcome potential was defined not only by different transformation strategies of social and symbolic feminism but also by different degrees of proximity or distance to the state. The WLM self-defined as radical, revolutionary, and autonomous, sometimes Socialist. However, it formed partnerships with established groups and institutions and made claims that stipulated collaboration with the legislator. Both dimensions, the attitude toward public institutions (close, distanced) and the dualistic strategy (social or symbolic feminism) marked different settings of feminist grievances that addressed different persons and institutions and corresponded with distinct protest activities. Table 54.1 summarizes the areas of influence of the new women's movement in a schematic way. Against this background, three different—yet linked—features characterize the long-term consequences:

1. *The coexistence of officially recognized institutions and counterinstitutional self-organization.* The women's movement started its march through the institutions in the second half of the 1970s. Its strategy created specific claims on the agenda of institutions such as universities or public administrations. At the same time, independent small groups and networks appeared, preferring grassroots politics and seeking to stay rather independent from established institutions external to the women's movement. This was not always possible as, for instance, women's centers and refuges for battered women were in the need of public subsidies. Therefore, they had to compromise their autonomy and to render an account of their activities. But generally, the women's centers and projects stayed relatively independent and defined the structures of decision making as well as the main topics of their work without intrusion from the outside.

2. *The coexistence of power- and identity-related modes of operation.* Scholars of new social movements have identified two ideal typical logics of action, each leading to a distinct movement strategy: on the one hand, a power-oriented strategy corresponding with an instrumental logic of action; on the other hand, an identity-oriented strategy implying an expressive logic of action.[4] According to this, a power-oriented movement is more likely to draw on specific strategies of political participation, bargaining, and political confrontation. Identity-oriented movements, on the other hand, seek to

	Symbolic feminism	Social feminism
Proximity to the state	Encouragement of the female Countercultural Retreat	Legislative reform Measures to ensure equal treatment
Distance to the state	Symbolic revolution Cultural subversion	Social revolution Counterinstitutions Strike (of reproduction)

Table 54.1. Areas of Influence of the New Women's Movement

reassure themselves constantly by reformist divergence, subcultural retreat, and countercultural challenge. In the women's movement, both strategies existed simultaneously. Legislation reform, initially the abortion legislation, but also antisexism laws and maternity protection, were center stage, as was the creation of feminist consciousness with its manifold forms of expression. The wide range of theoretical approaches of feminism reflects the space opened up by the double mode of operation: women's liberation varied from political to linguistic analysis and psychoanalysis. Similarly broad too were the services offered by feminist organizations and institutions: they ranged from self-help groups, houses for battered women, and emergency services to information centers, women's libraries, and bookshops, not to mention belly dance, pottery, and theater groups.

3. *The coexistence of modern and postmodern elements.* The social movements after 1968 (new social movements) are generally considered postmodern movements. Their common feature is to have themselves distanced from a teleological vision of ongoing progress proper to former movements, including parts of the 1968 protest movement and the New Left. New social movements have adopted a critical, reflexive standpoint toward modernity. They represent particular interests rather than universal aspirations. They adopt postmaterial values and focus on issues such as life quality and sustainability.

Many scholars perceive the women's movement as such a *new* social movement, aiming primarily at the recognition of a specific group: women.[5] But the women's movement also defended universal values, the demand of equality being one of them. The women's movements of the 1970s struggled for both recognition of women's needs in the name of particularity *and* for a universal redistribution of material resources.[6]

General Cultural Functions of the Impact of WLM

The cultural functions of the aspects of movement outcomes are diverse. They express themselves, among other things, in facets of lifestyle and aesthetic dispositions, and cannot be observed in the same way in different social milieus. In the higher segments of society—artistic bohemia and the urban middle class, which served as recruitment bases to WLM—female full-time employment, homosexual relationships, male part-time work, and shared responsibilities for child care became no longer exceptional. In these privileged sectors of Western societies, gender roles have become less rigid, and the idea of changing from one sex to another has at least become thinkable, in exceptional cases even practicable. From here to suggest a broader societal change remains problematic, especially if one takes into consideration empirical evidence about ongoing salary discrimination and the double burden of women who work to earn money but also have the responsibility for domestic labor. At least one can say that gender discrimination, alongside discrimination due to sexual orientation, has become illegitimate in the elite culture of most of European countries and beyond.

Roles of WLM Impact in Protest Cultures

In retrospect, the coexistence of different strategies was key to successful mobilization and institutionalization of WLM. But in the 1970s, feminist activists hardly perceived those divergent positions as a condition for successful mobilization; instead, they seemed a sign of conflict and decline. When, in Italy, Austria, Germany, France, Sweden, and many other countries, legislation reforms (or, as in Switzerland, its refusal) with respect to the regulation of abortion put a (temporary) end to the struggle for free abortion in the second half of the 1970s, divergent ideas and attitudes within women's liberation reemerged and clashed. The collective actors that had emerged during the abortion struggles disintegrated and left different groups and individuals with divergent aims. From today's point of view, ex-activists look back to that "time of contradiction"[7] with certain bitterness. They have experienced this moment as a deep blow that put an end to the euphoric atmosphere and feeling of togetherness that prevailed in the first half of the 1970s. Of course, feminist activism did not vanish traceless. The boundaries between feminist protest culture and general culture have become permeable.

State of Research

An analysis of the effects and outcomes of the WLM is still in its beginnings. Scholars have worked on some specific aspects of the effects and outcomes of women's liberation, like for example on feminist interventions against violence[8] or in favor of affirmative action and quotas.[9] A big effort has been made to assess, from a comparative point of view, the influence of the WLM on abortion legislation.[10] Scholars become also interested in the local[11] and the international dimension of feminism, as it raises the question of the relation between women's movements and globalization.[12] Christine Thon's interview-based case study of the West German women's movement analyzes the role that the women's movement plays in the biographical self-constructions of ex-activists belonging to different generations of protest.[13] She convincingly argues that the ideas of the women's movements had positive effects on the growing legitimacy of gender-specific discrimination in the following generation.

Research Gaps and Open Questions

The development of feminist history after World War II is heterogeneous with regard to different themes and national contexts. This is all the more true for a study of feminism's effects and outcomes. Yet the following questions seem fundamental: did participating in the WLM change women's life course patterns (family, partnership, qualifications, career) in a durable way? Have women's (movement's) representatives been included in decision-making processes regarding the rights and life chances of women? Did mediators—intermediary organizations, parties, unions, or, in the case of direct democracies, initiative groups—translate the claims of the WLM into politically enforceable demands, and did the original objectives change in this process of mediation? Has feminist subculture become part of mainstream culture?

Each of these questions needs to be studied as part of a complex constellation of social change, and so far, our conclusions concerning the WLM's outcomes must be speculative. What can be said is that, unlike some other new social movements, it sustained successful and ongoing institutionalization. This development was one of the reasons for the decline of feminism as a social movement at the end of the 1970s, but conversely, it was a hopeful beginning of a process of agenda setting of feminist concerns on a broader societal level.

Kristina Schulz is senior lecturer for contemporary history and migration history at Bern University, Switzerland. She is a specialist of Western feminist history in comparative perspective. Her recent publications include: *"Der lange Atem der Provokation." Die Frauenbewegung in der Bundesrepublik und in Frankreich, 1968–1976* (Frankfurt on the Main, 2002) and "Politics of Reproduction in a Divided Europe: Abortion, Protest Movements and State Intervention after the Second World War," in *The 'Establishment' Responds—Power and Protest During and After the Cold War,* ed. K Fahlenbrach et al. (New York, 2012), with Lorena Anton and Yoshi Mitobe. She also edited a special issue on Swiss women's liberation of *Schweizerische Zeitschrift für Geschichte* 57 (2007).

Notes

1. Bonnie S Anderson, *Joyous Greetings. The First International Women's Movement 1830–1860* (New York, 2000); Karen Offen, *European Feminism, 1700–1950. A Political History* (Stanford, CA, 2000). See also Lucy Delap, *The Feminist Avant-Garde. Transnational Encounters of the Early Twentieth Century* (Cambridge, 2007).
2. That was despite of the fact that most of these intellectuals refused the term "feminist" as self-description.
3. Elaine Mark and Isabelle de Courtivron, *New French Feminism. An Anthology* (New York, 1981).
4. Cf. Dieter Rucht, "The Strategies and Action Repertoires of New Movements," in *Challenging the Political Order: New Social and Political Movements in Western Democracies,* ed. JR Dalton and M Kuecheler (Cambridge, 1990), 156–75.
5. Cf. for example Dieter Rucht, *Modernisierung und neue soziale Bewegungen. Deutschland, Frankreich und USA im Vergleich* (Frankfurt, 1994).
6. Cf. Axel Honneth and Nancy Fraser, *Redistribution or Recognition? A Political-Philosophical Exchange* (New York, 2003).
7. Francoise Picq, *Libération des femmes: Les années-mouvement* (Paris, 1993), 181.
8. Reinhild Schäfer, *Demokratisierung der Geschlechterverhältnisse. Die politischen Strategien der Neuen Frauenbewegung gegen Gewalt* (Bielefeld, 2001).
9. Joan W Scott, *Parité! Sexual Equality and the Crisis of French Universalism* (Chicago, 2005); Stefanie Ehmsen, *Der Marsch der Frauenbewegung durch die Institutionen: die Vereinigten Staaten und die Bundesrepublik im Vergleich* (Münster, 2008).
10. Dorothy Stetson McBride, ed., *Abortion Politics, Women's Movements, and the Democratic State: A Comparative Study of State Feminism* (Oxford, 2001).
11. Amrita Basu, *The Challenge of Local Feminisms* (Boulder, CO, 1995).
12. Peggy Antrobus, *The Global Women's Movement—Origins, Issues and Strategies* (London, 2004); Ilse Lenz, Charlotte Ullrich, and Barbara Fersch, *Gender Orders Unbound: Globalisation, Restructuring, Reciprocity* (Leverkusen, 2007).
13. Christine Thon, *Frauenbewegung im Wandel der Generationen: Eine Studie über Geschlechterkonstruktionen in autobiografischen Erzählungen* (Bielefeld, 2008).

Recommended Reading

McBride Stetson, Dorothy, ed. *Abortion Politics, Women's Movements, and the Democratic State: A Comparative Study of State Feminism*. Oxford, 2001. The volume compares processes of legislative liberalization of abortion in Western countries by especially focusing on the impact of the WLM and other feminist actors.

Scott, Joan W. *Parité! Sexual Equality and the Crisis of French Universalism*. Chicago, 2005. The author reconstructs debates about the inclusion of women in elective office in the 1990s in France and analyzes feminist positions between universalistic and particularistic aspirations.

Smith, Bonnie G. *Global Feminisms since 1945.* New York, 2000. The anthology gives a wide overview about the development of feminist movements in the second half of the twentieth century in the world.

Zellmer, Elisabeth. *Töchter der Revolte. Frauenbewegung und Feminismus der 1970er Jahre in München.* Munich, 2011. This case study centers on the interplay between the WLM and intermediary groups and organizations, such as parties and policy makers, on a local level.

Chapter 55

Founding of Milieus

Michael Vester

Definition of Terms and Characteristic Features of the Long-Term Impact

The network of groups rising with protest movements since the 1960s is often described as "the alternative milieu." In social sciences, the concept of *milieu* was revitalized also since the 1960s to explain new changes of advanced societies. It goes back to the classical sociology of Durkheim and Weber,[1] regarding social differentiations in two ways.

First, the authors give *social milieus* a dual definition. For Durkheim, milieus are social groups organizing internal cohesion and external distinction (a) by *practical interaction* and (b) by a *moral identity*, that is, when individuals have ideas, interests, feelings, and occupations in common, which others do not share, they tend to unite in groups developing a moral life and a set of moral rules that is internalized in the individual *moral habitus*. Milieus describe the "fact of association," that is, the "fundamental elements" of societies as a whole: "family milieus" organized by kinship relations, "territorial milieus" organized by political relations, and "occupational milieus" organized by the division of labor.

Second, explicated by Weber, society is no monolithic structure but a complex field of action combining the *three* relatively autonomous *field levels* of *economic, social,* and *political* relations. These relations imply an unequal distribution of power, which is produced by unequal economic positions and by social closure through mechanisms of moral conventions of behavior and of juridical institutionalization of privileges. This divides society into positively privileged, middle, and negatively privileged classes.

Combining these definitions (further developed by Geiger and Bour-dieu[2]), individuals are located in social space by three aspects: (a) by *employment classes* (or occupational milieus); (b) by *social classes* (or class milieus, differing by external situation, everyday life conduct, and habitus); and (c) by *political camps* (or political parties with different organizations, networks, and ideologies). With these classical concepts, according to von Oertzen and Vester,[3] alternative milieus can be located socially:

1. *Sociocultural:* Research described the protest cultures on the practical and the symbolic level, noting that these cultures were heterogeneous by class, gender, and ethnicity. Two concepts of milieus were used.

a. Organizational activities are studied by movement researchers like Rucht and Roth since the end of the 1970s.[4] The *movement milieus* were integrated by infrastructures (associations, shops, pubs, cultural centers, meetings, etc.), which allowed internal communication, mutual support, and organizing projects and actions of people of similar views, but also by open infrastructures (work places, schools, universities, sports, exhibitions, public spaces, etc.), which allowed the widening of the original alternative milieus to the new social movements (including the mainstream left) toward the end of the 1970s. This acceptance prepared the reintegration of the alternative milieus into society as elements of a pluralized everyday culture (new social milieus) and political culture (entrenchment in the institutional, media, and political party landscape).

b. A recent rediscovery of the earlier changes of youth culture and political culture was organized by historians like Siegfried and Reichardt.[5] They studied the *subcultural milieus* originating in the protesting youth leisure and music cultures since the 1950s and in the "Sponti" student culture, which since the end of the 1960s, became the mass base of the New Left politics of changing everyday life. They studied the symbolic level of a culture and habitus based on alternative values of emancipation: authenticity (vs. alienation), self-determination (vs. authoritarianism); equality by gender, ethnicity and so on (vs. discrimination); respect for nature and humanity (vs. ecological and war risks); direct democratic participation (vs. oligarchic domination). This included an external *alternative habitus,* shown in clothing, gestures, language, symbols, ways of consumption, and rules of interaction.

2. *Sociopolitical:* Political and cultural sociologists studied how everyday and political levels of milieus were connected in East and West Germany.[6] Representative data confirmed that the alternative movements and milieus were *not* homogeneous by class, but a coalition across vertical class differ-

ences kept together by the practical experience of a deep conflict in society as a whole, a kind of *horizontal class conflict* between the *traditional* and the *modernizing factions* on each vertical class level.

These findings concurred with new research on political party history,[7] revealing that also the old political party camps (conservative, liberal, socialist, etc.) had never been mere reflections of vertical class differences. Instead, they formed a special kind of political camp, which Lepsius called "social-moral milieu"[8] because it linked the field of everyday milieus (occupational, regional, and confessional cultures, institutions, and infrastructures) with the political field (political representation, organization, communication media, and ideology). They were hierarchic coalitions between parts of the popular and of the higher classes (dominant because more experienced in professional politics) brought together by big historic struggles. This mostly led to oligarchic leaderships, a problem that also accompanied the transformation of the alternative movements into institutions. But, as political party research confirms in international scope,[9] the establishment of a new camp cleavage between green issues and traditional politics remains a lasting effect of the alternative movements.

3. *Socioeconomic level:* The alternative and new milieus were also related to the dynamics of social structure as a whole. These were studied since the 1990s for seven countries. The studies registered a persistence of class divisions in the vertical power dimension but important differentiations in the horizontal competence dimension. Here, new and younger class factions have been rising, with increased educational capital related to a shift toward service and knowledge occupations[10] and with increasing emancipative elements of habitus and of everyday practices.[11] Following Bourdieu's methodology, Vester et al. combined both levels and related them to the movement milieus,[12] stating the development toward a "pluralized class society" in which these new factions of the higher middle and lower classes, the "new social milieus," had already grown to 28 percent in 1991. They represented a less idealistic version of the alternative values while the movement milieus were their politically mobilized, most idealistic parts.

The long-term impacts sum up to a horizontal shift and conflict on all three levels: (a) the establishment of a persistent new green political camp cleavage dividing all political parties, (b) the respective institutionalized structures of increased parliamentarian and civic participation and infrastructures, and (c) the stable intergenerational development of the new social milieus as the seedbed of emancipatory forms of everyday culture and political participation.

General Cultural Functions

Durkheim[13] understood milieus as agencies of historical change, a "vital force" and "decisive factor of common development" that creates and changes structures (institutions, law, monuments of arts, and literature) by active practice. Considering the historic movements of the Roman plebeians and the modern working classes, Durkheim saw two historical functions of milieus: (a) developing the potentials of emancipation, as the occupational division of labor increases the striving for education, intellectual competences, cooperation, individuality, and democratic participation; (b) working against tendencies of social disintegration and anomie related to uncurbed Capitalism.

Similarly, the alternative milieus promoted innovation on the cultural, social, and political levels of advanced societies. Originating from rebellious youth cultures, they tried to correct the cultural lag of inherited everyday morals and institutions according to values of human emancipation. Although idealistic aims could only partly be realized, they initiated a piecemeal change of everyday and political culture.

Role in Protest Cultures

The enormous growth of the alternative milieu was owed to the coincidence of fundamental changes of everyday culture, political culture, and economic structures of advanced Capitalist societies reinforcing each other.[14]

1. *Formation of new everyday and political milieus.* The spectacular 1968 protests were the top of a huge iceberg produced by parallel developments (a) in everyday culture and (b) in political culture that had begun earlier.

a. The new prepolitical *everyday mass youth culture* rooted in the changes of social structures and everyday life since the 1950s.[15] The younger generations experienced widening material and cultural possibilities against which the restrictive morals of older generations appeared obsolete. The desire for liberation was expressed in rebellious music and lifestyles leading to constant conflicts. This leisure culture transformed into the permanent Sponti milieus since 1967.[16] In Germany, the growth of student numbers from 242,000 (1961) to 393,000 (1970) was accompanied by expanding student household communities, with 68,600 members already in 1973. In these communities, the rising educational opportunities for women and the popular classes were reflected in an increased social mixing.

b. The new *antiauthoritarian political culture* rose with the protests against rearmament and political oppression in the Eastern and Western blocs, against racism, and the relics of Fascism. This was mainly organized by young intellectuals, that is, youth and educational activists in labor unions, social-democratic, ex-communist, protestant, catholic, and scout organizations and the high school and university student press. Through conflicts with the established powers, they increasingly turned left, formed own intellectual milieu networks, and opened to the new youth culture and to the antiauthoritarian and nondogmatic New Left spreading first from England (and then from Frankfurt). They developed the new politics of the unspectacular everyday. The New Left tried to overcome political apathy by "linking private troubles to public issues" (Mills, Thompson, Hayden[17]) and became popular through nonviolent and participatory protest forms. Echoed by the Sponti milieus, the Socialist Student Federation (SDS) after 1966 transformed into a large movement with campaigns, countless local groups, and actions for sexual and feminist liberation, nonauthoritarian kindergartens and schools, and organizing apprentices and pupils. They were called Sponti milieus, as their culture expressed emancipative and spontaneous lifestyles, by which they distinguished themselves from the authoritarian old left, especially the Social Democratic and Communist parties, and also the new rigid Marxist-Leninist and underground groups that attracted media attention until they collapsed after 1977.

Already in 1970, these Sponti communities were the seedbed of a broad scene of alternative milieus, projects, infrastructures, and protests.[18] Growth continued into the 1980s.[19] The number of West Berlin projects rose from about 300 (1978) to about 900 (1989). For Federal Germany in 1980, there were counted about 80,000 activists in 11,500 projects, which rose to 200,000 activists in about 18,000 projects in 1986. It was estimated that in West Berlin in 1978, 4 percent of the projects were agrarian, 8 percent engaged in craft production, 9 percent in circulation, 9 percent in leisure infrastructures, 17 percent in intellectual and informational activities, 5 percent in administrative services, 22 percent in social work, 8 percent in culture, and 18 percent in political work. This scene included manifold groups of self-help, alternative living, feminists, gays, and practical international solidarity. Most remained transitional. But parts also changed into the field of sociopolitical reforms, for example, the autonomous youth centers, which boomed since 1971 with about 1,000 initiatives (even in small towns); about 300 later reached stabilization with professional staffs and public financing. The manifold infrastructures included numerous self-made journals (in 1980 about 390 with up to 1.6 million copies) and, since 1979, a national daily that survived successfully (*die tageszeitung*). In 1981, sympathizers of alternative culture were estimated at about 30 percent of all youth between 18 and 23 years, and about 49 percent of all university students.

2. *A new political camp.* This expansion was—also internationally—encouraged by political openings following electoral victories of the mainstream left (Kennedy 1960, Brandt 1969) and including a mobilization of intellectuals and of a young left wing inside Social Democracy. Brandt's governments translated movement aims into legislation: ending the cold war and extending the welfare state, civil rights, women's rights, educational chances, and the participatory rights of pupils, students, apprentices, and employees. (Similar developments were observed in other countries.) Mainstream left and alternative politics even more joined forces when, after the 1973 oil crisis, rising civic mobilizations were caused by the ecological and social risks of modernization and growth, recurring unemployment, insufficient civic rights and participation, urban and infrastructural problems, and nuclear armament and energy.

This alliance was facilitated by the fact that the hegemony of participatory, nonviolent, and non-Communist political groups, led by the original New Left (after the dissolution of SDS mainly coordinated by the Socialist Bureau), was no more contested. After the collapse of dogmatic and of terrorist groups around 1977, project and protest mobilizations were larger than before, including also a second youth revolt.

This progress provoked countermobilizations of the right wings in all political parties, which after 1980 gradually tipped the scales to the neoconservative and neoliberal side. In these confrontations, the movements formed their own political camp, separated by deep cleavages from the old party majorities, giving rise to the Green party and to green wings in the other parties. Simultaneously, civic participation was professionalized and institutionalized. Mainstream acceptance implied an increase of political realism, of institutionalization, and of adapting utopian idealism to practical everyday ways of life. After 1989, with the fall of the iron curtain and with deregulated international competition, new problems became urgent. Alternative forces lost their hegemony in political culture but, with its large milieu basis, retained its role as one factor among a plurality of camps.

3. *Formation of new class milieus.* Research based on the multidimensional concept of classical sociology allowed new sights on the general transformations of advanced societies like Germany and their relation to protest cultures.[20] Combining qualitative studies with representative surveys, the study allowed to produce a comprehensive portrait of complex social differentiations and dynamics which was constructed and summed up in a map according to Bourdieu's three levels of social space:

a. *Class habitus.* The movement members were divided into five submilieus still following the different parent class cultures, however, modified by emancipatory and participatory elements. These movement submilieus could be located in the larger social structure as the most radical parts of four large *new class milieus,* which represented the youngest, best educated, and most modern factions of the upper, the middle, and the lower milieus, and added up to almost 30 percent of the total population.

Of these, only the *Original Alternative Milieu,* a milieu of the academic intelligentsia, still represented idealistic alternative political and lifestyle commitment. Its majority consisted of higher urban service and knowledge professionals and continued the elitist leadership values of their upper and middle class parents. Until 1991, this milieu melted down to 2.3 percent. But inside the younger factions of the popular milieus, there has grown a large and more egalitarian milieu of the *practical intelligentsia,* the *Modern Employee Milieu* (11.7 percent). As children of the skilled employee middle, its members took part in the big shifts toward higher education and modernized industrial and service occupations and a culture of good professional work, autonomy, democratic participation, gender equality, and solidarity. The two other modernized factions of the popular classes were less ambitious. The members of the *Hedonist Youth Milieu* (12.0 percent), children of the average skilled employee middle, wanted participation in hedonist lifestyles and widened cultural and material chances, but also showed average union memberships and above average red-green voting. The *Modern Underprivileged Milieu* (2.2 percent) shared their parents' low skills and insecure situation but tried to at least symbolically participate in modern lifestyles including skepticism toward state, church, and educational authorities and male domination.

b. *Economic class.* Milieu growth was related to two relatively autonomous though related transformations: the change of everyday culture and the shifts from industrial toward service and knowledge occupations, which need higher professional specialization, educational capital, and autonomy at the workplace. Movement members often found occupation in the expanding welfare sectors (education, culture, health, science, social work, urban infrastructures, etc.), technical professions, and semi-professions. In these new occupations, the sympathizers of the new milieus formed a majority, but there were also members of the more conservative older milieus

c. *Political protest potentials.* Studies of movement milieus revealed that the sense of belonging to an alternative political camp had mainly been acquired through severe and mainly local conflicts. The experience of social and political cleavages fostered the cohesion of the alternative political milieus despite of their occupational and habitus heterogeneities. But this political cohesion relaxed after alternative issues were accepted in the mainstream, and since 1990s, the original alternative milieu lost its vanguard role in society to the postmodern milieu, which consisted of neoliberal upstarts.

However, the neoliberal restoration of social inequalities and authoritarian control was not a one-way road. In the prepolitical everyday milieus, nonauthoritarian and participatory dispositions are still expanding. There are still large New Left reservoirs in certain occupational groups. Under the pressure of the international crisis of the economy and of democracy, many countries experience a slow recovery of young movements, which challenge the old oligarchies and demand genuine, participatory democracy and a self-determined life.

State of Research in Related Social Movement Research

Since the late 1970s, there has been abundant research on alternative projects and infrastructures and their institutionalization, which in Germany is carried on especially by movement researchers like Roth and Rucht and in the magazine *Forschungsjournal (Neue) Soziale Bewegungen*. There has been also much research on the practical and symbolic side of alternative and youth lifestyles and political identities[21]; this has recently been resumed on a broader scale by historians like Siegfried and Reichardt.

Research Gaps and Open Questions

There are still the following research gaps: formation of New Left milieus since the end of the 1950s, especially inside the labor movement, church, scout, and high school youth and educational structures; the key role of the SDS since the early 1960s and of the Socialist Bureau in the 1970s; the post-movement milieu developments since the early 1990s. The gap concerning the apprentices' movements and youth centers is going to be closed.[22] International case studies and comparative studies based on such milieu approaches are in their beginnings.

Michael Vester is professor emeritus of political science at Leibniz Universität Hannover, Germany. His main research fields are the political sociology, history and theory of social structures, mentalities, and movements. Publications include studies on the early labor and emancipatory movements and their theory, *Die Frühsozialisten 1798–1848*, 2 vols. (Reinbek, 1970/1971); on cooperatives and self-help in European regions, *Unterentwicklung und Selbsthilfe in europäischen Regionen* (Hannover, 1993); and on the rise of new social structures, milieus, and movements in Germany, *Soziale Milieus* *im gesellschaftlichen Strukturwandel,* with P von Oertzen et al. (Frankfurt, 2001) and their international comparison.

Notes

1. Emile Durkheim, *La Divison du Travail Social* (Paris, 1967), part I (chapters 6–7), part III (chapters 1–2); Emile Durkheim, *Les Règles de la Méthode Sociologique* (Paris, 1950), chapter 5 (iii); Max Weber, *Economy and Society* (London, 1978), part I (chapter iv), part II (chapter viii).

2. Theodor Geiger, *Die soziale Schichtung des deutschen Volkes* (Stuttgart, 1932); Pierre Bourdieu, *Distinction* (London, 1984).

3. Peter von Oertzen, "Klasse und Milieu als Bedingungen gesellschaftlichen Handelns," in *Soziale Milieus und Wandel der Sozialstruktur,* ed. H Bremer and A Lange-Vester (Wiesbaden, 2006), 37–69; Michael Vester, "Alternativbewegungen und neue soziale Milieus," in *Das Alternative Milieu,* ed. S Reichardt and D Siegfried (Göttingen, 2010), 27–60.

4. Dieter Rucht, "Das alternative Milieu in der Bundesrepublik: Ursprünge, Infrastruktur und Nachwirkungen," in *Das Alternative Milieu: antibürgerlicher Lebensstil und linke Politik in der Bundesrepublik Deutschland und Europa, 1968–1983,* ed. S Reichardt and D Siegfried (Göttingen, 2010), 61–86; Roland Roth and Dieter Rucht, eds, *Die sozialen Bewegungen in Deutschland seit 1945. Ein Handbuch* (Frankfurt, 2008).

5. Detlef Siegfried, *Time Is on My Side. Konsum und Politik in der westdeutschen Jugendkultur der 60er Jahre* (Göttingen, 2006); Sven Reichardt, *Authentizität und Gemeinschaft. Linksalternatives Leben in den siebziger und frühen achtziger Jahren* (Berlin, 2014).

6. Michael Vester et al., *Soziale Milieus im gesellschaftlichen Strukturwandel* (Frankfurt, 2001); Michael Vester, Michael Hofmann, and Irene Zieke, eds, *Soziale Milieus in Ostdeutschland* (Cologne, 1995).

7. von Oertzen, "Klasse und Milieu als Bedingungen gesellschaftlichen Handelns," 37–69.

8. Mario Rainer Lepsius, "Parteiensystem und Sozialstruktur," in *Demokratie in Deutschland,* ed. MR Lepsius (Göttingen, 1993), 25–50; for the concept of multidimensional cleavages see: Stein Rokkan, "Zur entwicklungssoziologischen Analyse von Parteisystemen," *Kölner Zeitschrift für Soziologie und Sozialpsychologie* 17 (1965): 675–702.

9. Ulrich Eith and Gerd Mielke, eds, *Gesellschaftliche Konflikte und Parteiensysteme. Länder- und Regionalstudien* (Wiesbaden, 2001).

10. Walter Müller, "Klassenstruktur und Parteiensystem," *Kölner Zeitschrift für Soziologie und Sozialpsychologie* 50 (1998): 3–46; Jan CC Rupp, "Rethinking Cultural and Economic Capital," in *Reworking Class,* ed. JR Hall (Ithaca, NY, 1997), 221–41; Lennart Rosenlund, *Exploring the City with Bourdieu* (Saarbrücken, 2009); Mike Savage, James Barlow, Peter Dickens, and Tony Fielding, *Property, Bureaucracy and*

Culture: Middle-Class Formation in Contemporary Britain (London, 1992); Vester, von Oertzen, Geiling, Hermann, and Müller, *Soziale Milieus im gesellschaftlichen Strukturwandel.*

11. Dieter Karrer, *Die Last des Unterschieds. Biographie, Lebensführung und Habitus von Arbeitern und Angestellten im Vergleich* (Opladen, 1998); Michèle Lamont, *Money, Morals and Manners: The Culture of French and American Upper Class* (Chicago, 1992); Vester, von Oertzen, Geiling, Hermann, and Müller, *Soziale Milieus im gesellschaftlichen Strukturwandel.*

12. Vester, von Oertzen, Geiling, Hermann, and Müller, *Soziale Milieus im gesellschaftlichen Strukturwandel*; Vester, "Alternativbewegungen und neue soziale Milieus."

13. Durkheim, *La Divison du Travail Social*; Durkheim, *Les Règles de la Méthode Sociologique.*

14. For a comprehensive analysis see Roth and Rucht, *Die sozialen Bewegungen in Deutschland seit 1945.*

15. Siegfried, *Time Is on My Side.*

16. Reichardt, *Authentizität und Gemeinschaft. Linksalternatives Leben in den siebziger und frühen achtziger Jahren.*

17. Influential New Left founding texts: EP Thompson, ed., *Out of Apathy* (London, 1960); C Wright Mills, *Power, Politics and People: Collected Essays* (New York, 1963); Thomas Hayden, *The Port Huron Statement* (New York, 2005).

18. See Roth and Rucht, *Die sozialen Bewegungen in Deutschland seit 1945*; Siegfried, *Time Is on My Side*; Reichardt, *Authentizität und Gemeinschaft. Linksalternatives Leben in den siebziger und frühen achtziger Jahren.*

19. Rucht, "Das alternative Milieu in der Bundesrepublik. Ursprünge, Infrastruktur und Nachwirkungen."

20. Vester, "Alternativbewegungen und neue soziale Milieus"; Vester, von Oertzen, Geiling, Hermann, and Müller, *Soziale Milieus im gesellschaftlichen Strukturwandel*; Michael Vester, "Class and Culture in Germany," in *Rethinking Class,* ed. F Devine, M Savage, J Scott, and R Crompton (Basingstoke, 2005), 69–94.

21. Including: Heiko Geiling, *Das andere Hannover. Jugendkultur zwischen Rebellion und Integration in der Großstadt* (Hannover, 1996); Claudia Ritter, *Lebensstile und Politik* (Opladen, 1997).

22. David Templin, *Freizeit ohne Kontrollen. Die Jugendzentrumsbewegung in der Bundesrepublik der 1970er Jahre* (Göttingen, 2015).

Recommended Reading

Baumann, Cordia, Sebastian Gehrig, and Nicolas Büchse, eds. *Linksalternative Milieus und Neue Soziale Bewegungen in den 1970er Jahren.* Heidelberg, 2011. A handbook on central fields of movement groups, actions, institutions, and everyday social relations, including milieu-analysis in movement research (Rucht), selected international comparisons and the role of media.

Precht, Richard David. *Lenin kam nur bis Lüdenscheid. Meine kleine deutsche Revolution.* Berlin, 2011. A rare example of a convincing and lively history of the emergence, flourishing, and dissolving of the left-alternative social and political milieu in a medium city (Solingen) on a high literary, autobiographical, and sociological level of narrative and reflection.

Reichardt, Sven. *Authentizität und Gemeinschaft. Linksalternatives Leben in den siebziger und frühen achtziger Jahren.* Berlin, 2014. A comprehensive cultural and social history about life practice in the left alternative milieus to the early 1980s in Germany, regarding especially the striving for a nonalienated way of life and culture in the Sponti communities, projects, institutions, press, and protest actions.

Reichardt, Sven, and Detlef Siegfried, eds. *Das alternative Milieu. Antibürgerlicher Lebensstil und linke Politik in der Bundesrepublik Deutschland und Europa 1968–1983.* Göttingen, 2010. A handbook on central fields of movement groups, actions and institutions, subculture, and everyday social relations, including representative milieu analyses (by Rucht and by Vester) and selected international aspects.

Siegfried, Detlef. *Time Is on My Side: Konsum und Politik in der westdeutschen Jugendkultur der 60er Jahre.* Göttingen, 2006. A comprehensive study on the change of everyday and political culture and their influence on the emerging left-alternative milieus, movements, and currents until the early 1970s.

Vester, Michael, Peter von Oertzen, Heiko Geiling, Thomas Hermann, and Dagmar Müller. *Soziale Milieus im gesellschaftlichen Strukturwandel.* Frankfurt, 2001. A comprehensive study of the emergence of the alternative and new social milieus in the fields of everyday political cultures and conflict embedded in representative empirical analyses of the change of socioeconomic and political structures from 1950 to 1990 following the theoretical and methodological approaches of the early Cultural Studies and of Bourdieu.

Chapter 56

Diffusion of Symbolic Forms

Dieter Rucht

Every human communication, hence also public protest, has an expressive dimension. Protesters exhibit emotions such as anger or frustration; they use metaphors and slogans, carry flags and banners, wear balaclavas or go naked, sing songs, play street theater, encircle targets, gather at historical sites, engage in a silent march, light candles or torches, commemorate their heroes or victims, provoke the police by clowneries, or carry a coffin at a bogus funeral. They may also burn puppets, flags, and official documents; destroy infrastructure; or undertake an arson attack on a shelter for asylum seekers.

Obviously, the shapes and contexts in which symbolic forms emerge vary greatly. Whether or not the symbols are understood by the target groups and/or diffused to other places depends on a number of factors which, at the more general level, have been specified by diffusion theory. Therefore, it is useful to take a brief look at this theory before discussing the kinds of symbolic forms and their diffusion in more detail.

Characteristic Features in the Diffusion of Symbolic Forms from a Long-Term Perspective

Diffusion theory spells out under which conditions certain phenomena, ranging from diseases to revolutions, are likely to travel. With regard to social phenomena, early theorists have concentrated on explaining the speed, rate, and course of diffusion[1] by using examples from variegated fields such as languages, consumer behavior, church attendance, and medical technology.[2] Other scholars have criticized these approaches for being overly mechanistic and deterministic. Instead, more emphasis has been put on the social and cultural conditions under which diffusion is likely to occur and the adaptation processes that come into play.[3] These conditions are of particular importance when not only simple icons but more complex phenomena are considered, for example, organizational models, institutional procedures, public relations strategies, or protests tactics. In order to make diffusion of such phenomena happen, a number of conditions have to be met.

First and foremost, there must be an observation and recognition of the phenomenon on the side of the potential receiver or adopter. The more similar the (perceived) properties or situation of the emitter and the receiver, the more likely diffusion will occur. This is why the model of trade unions could quickly spread within a relatively homogenous society.[4] This is why, for example, the collective act of self-accusation of French (feminist) women to have performed an abortion could be easily copied by their German counterparts in the early 1970s.

Second, the more the receiver is under pressure of a problem for which diffusion promises some relief, the more likely is adoption. Again, this has been observed in campaigns to liberalize abortion in France and Germany. At the time, the still existing penalization of abortion contrasted sharply with the widespread practice of abortion and the beliefs of major parts of the population that it should not be criminalized. Moreover, there existed a so-called abortion tourism to the Netherlands and Great Britain, where a liberal policy on abortion was already in place.

Third, the properties of the diffused object have an impact. As a rule, diffused items or ideas are more likely to travel when they are easy to understand and apply. Especially the punchy symbols of protest are spreading quickly. When, for instance, war resisters in a country publicly burned their conscription orders, this invited similar-minded people in other countries to follow this example.

Fourth, the channels of diffusion matter. Direct channels, that is, transfer on the basis of firsthand experience or personal observation, tend to be more credible and convincing to the adopter than vague reports from unclear sources. In the case of the self-accusation campaign to liberalize abortion, a German feminist who happened to witness the action in France in 1971 was crucial to initiate a similar campaign in Germany shortly after. On the other hand, direct channels usually reach lower numbers of potential adopters than institutionalized and/or mediated channels. In some cases, similar to public relations firms that help to introduce new products, special protest groups are created to facilitate diffusion by providing arguments, advice, and tools, as exemplified by the United States-based Ruckus Society that teaches protesters to perform and legitimize acts of civil disobedience.

The diffusion of protest symbols is greatly facilitated by the increased mobility of protesters within and across nations, the spread of transnational organizations and campaigns, the ease of audio and visual documentation, and, above all, the omnipresence of modern mass media, especially television and, most recently, the Internet. These technical means allow to exhibit and transport protest symbols at an unprecedented speed and scope as probably best illustrated by the case of contemporary global justice movements.

Forms of Protest Symbols

There are numerous examples of successful diffusion of protest symbols in the past and present. Protest symbols are understood broadly here, including not only icons but also more complex phenomena such as elaborated frames and tactics.

Looking back in history, many protest groups developed and displayed their own symbols. Examples range from the rebellious peasants in the late Middle Ages (with the icon of a peasant's boot) to the German Nazi movement (with the icon of the swastika) to feminists (adopting the biologists' icon for female). Another widely known example is the peace symbol, the reversed Y arranged in a circle, which can be found in almost every protest against war and armament. It was created by Gerald Holtom, a designer and artist, as the logo for the first Aldermaston march initiated by the British Direct Action Committee against nuclear war in 1958. Shortly after, the British Campaign for Nuclear Disarmament adopted the symbol. Together with the cross-national diffusion of what became known as the Easter March, the logo was also used beyond the marches and the focus on nuclear weapons. This diffusion occurred irrespective of whether or not the adopters were aware of the symbol's reference point, namely the combination of the letters "N" and "D" (for nuclear disarmament) visualized by the flag semaphore alphabet.

A similar success story is the multicolored flag, also known as the rainbow flag that can be observed in many contemporary protests of progressive movements around the globe. It was originally designed with horizontal stripes in seven colors as an icon for the gay movement, symbolizing the variety of lifestyles and the need to tolerate these. Later on, the number of colors was reduced to five. At the same time, the meaning of the symbol was broadened. It became an icon for peace (sometimes in combination with the word "peace"—in Europe often carrying the Italian word "pace"). Eventually, the flag could be seen in the context of the global justice movements, underlining their multinational and multi-issue character.

Figure 56.1. Berlin, Germany, 5 April 2010. Protesters with a "peace" flag at the annual Easter march. © Photo by Stefan Boness.

Figure 56.2. Berlin, Germany, 26 March 2011. Antinuclear demonstrator taking part in a large protest march in Berlin in the aftermath of the nuclear accident in Fukushima (Japan). © Photo by Stefan Boness.

A third internationally known icon is used by the antinuclear power movement, displaying the "laughing sun" in combination with the slogan "nuclear power—no thanks" (available in many languages). This logo, created in Denmark in the 1970s, was especially widespread in the late 1970s and early 1980s. It could be seen not only at demonstrations but was also used as a button in everyday life or a tag attached to many items, ranging from a baby buggy to an automobile. Interestingly, when the debate on nuclear power, after a period of doldrums, reemerged in some countries in the 2000s, the antinuclear icon could be seen again, though in a modified form. In Germany, for example, the design of the sun remained unchanged, but the slogan was now: "Nuclear power, please not again." In this version, it was a reminder to both a past conflict and a signal to reengage in the same kind of struggle.

Protest symbols may reach beyond simple graphical icons. A key element, sometimes combined with a visual symbol, is the use of slogans, metaphors, and frames in the context of collective protest ("Workers of the world, unite!," "Never again Fascism," "Venceremos"). These slogans evoke associations with historical movements and related struggles. "Another world is possible" is a more recent slogan that emerged in reaction to neoliberal globalization in the early 2000s. It was introduced in the context of the first World Social Forum in Brazil in 2001. Similar to the diffusion of the peace symbol, the slogan quickly spread across the globe thanks to the rapid rise of these movements that needed a denominator on which all activists could agree. A more specific slogan, for example, one with a clear anti-Capitalist message, would have been contested among the activists and therefore not served the purpose of expressing a shared idea. Frames can be used, extended and further specified by protest songs (e.g., the "International" in the context of the workers movement) or street theater. In a similar vein, the use of drums or the performances of samba bands can be part of protest activities by sending out signals of excitement and, by their sheer acoustic volume, dominate a scene.

Finally, particular forms or tactics, based on their symbolic function, are suited for easy diffusion. The long march to capital, whether undertaken by hungry workers in the United States, the Fascist movement in Italy, or the Zapatistas in Mexico, is an obtrusive message to the political power holders to take notice of a challenger movement willing to sacrifice time and energy, and eventually fight for its cause. On an individual or collective level, also self-inflicted harm, ranging from modest bodily injuries to a hunger strike to self-immolation, can be interpreted as a powerful symbol of the powerless, a signal of seriousness, drama, and despair.

Functions in Protest Cultures: Symbolic and Instrumental Aspects of Protest Action

The symbolic component of such activities may have a different weight relative to their instrumental dimension. In some cases, when protest is an immediate expression of emotions, the behavior transgresses the logic of means and ends. It is not, or not primarily, intended to convey a message to outsiders but rather driven by a psychic tension triggering a bodily expression. Very likely, such behavior is not influenced by diffusion. In other cases, symbolic elements of protest are inherently bound to an essentially purposive and instrumental action. In an act of civil disobedience, protesters engage in deliberate disruption, but at the same time express their commitment to nonviolence, for example, by sitting on the ground, singing a song, and avoiding aggressive language. In still other cases, the symbolic element of a protest action is not only a result of careful planning but crystallizes in tangible objects. For example, activists occupying the site for a planned nuclear reactor may engage in building a wooden meeting house to symbolize their willingness to stay as long as possible. In these kinds of instrumental actions, diffusion may play an important role, as exemplified by spread of the idea and practice of civil disobedience from North America to South Africa to India to Europe and back to North America.[5]

Considering these and other examples, one can conclude that the use of symbols in protest activities can have different aims or functions: (1) to express the protesters emotions and moods such as hope, anger, fear, or humor; (2) to motivate their own constituency; (3) to demonstrate collective identity, unity, and determination both internally and externally; (4) to frame, visualize, and even dramatize a problem; (5) to discourage or threaten an opponent; and (6) to attract the attention of the bystander public and mass media, and possibly, win their sympathy and support.

The Cultural Role of Context in the Diffusion of Protest Symbols

By definition, protest symbols as cultural codes do not imply physical power. Whether and to which degree these codes resonate and ultimately yield the intended consequences of affecting the minds and hearts of target groups depends on a number of factors. First and foremost, the content of the symbols must be deciphered and thus understood by the addressees. This requires some background knowledge about the values and norms in a given society. In addition, understanding may also presuppose a more specific contextual knowledge, particularly when symbols are quite subtle or make allegations that become meaningful only when being familiar with a certain situation or problem. This is why an ethnologist studying a remote native tribe has to live quite some time with its members in order to make sense of their activities and especially rituals. Further, even when symbols are correctly interpreted by the addressees, they do not necessarily result in the mental and behavioral changes that the protesters are aiming at. After all, vested interests on the side of the addressees can outweigh the appeal of clear and strong symbolic messages. Also, because of their repetitive character, some symbolic protests activities may loose their attractiveness and eventually become boring.

The importance of cultural preconditions for making protest symbols intelligible and powerful becomes obvious when the message remains arbitrary or is completely misunderstood. For example, a network of self-help groups of unemployed in contemporary Germany chose a rhinoceros as a logo. While the activists intended to symbolize force, most outsiders associated this animal with inertness or even laziness, thus evoking an already existing prejudice with regard to the unemployed. Another case of misunderstanding was the so-called guerrilla gardening in the city of London on May Day 2000.[6] When some dozens of environmentalists began to remove the lawn in a public park to plant flowers and vegetables, most bystanders, concerned about the rare greenery in midst of their city, interpreted the removal of the lawn as an act of vandalism.

Correct interpretation is especially crucial in subversive and/or ironic protests. Sometimes the irony is all too obvious to most observers. Consider the case of leftist (peace) demonstrators who hailed U.S. President George W Bush during his visit in Berlin in 2002 by shouting "We want more weapons, we want a big war!" A seemingly clear but in fact highly arbitrary message was sent out by the Berlin-based "Happy Unemployed." At various occasions, group members installed hammocks in public places to take, or rather simulate, a nap. On the one hand, the visual message that unemployment equals leisure time was meant as a provocation. As expected, some spectators aggressively addressed the activists, blaming the unemployed for enjoying their parasite status on the back of the taxpayers. The ensuing debates allowed the activists to question prejudices about unemployed people and make clear that, under the given circumstances, they considered unemployment as an evil, especially for those without a job. On the other hand, the activists articulated another message: unemployment is only an evil in a society that—financially and otherwise—puts formal occupation at the center of life and social esteem, thereby marginalizing those without a job. If, however, a basic income, granted by the state and completely detached from formal and paid occupation, was introduced, then unemployment would no longer be perceived as a burden. Rather, it could liberate individuals from the pressure to look for (mostly unwanted) gainful occupation, thereby allowing them to engage in unpaid activities for which there exists a societal need. While the Happy Unemployed were successful in unveiling prejudice and drawing people into a discussion, they could certainly not convince everybody in the debate. The worst case, however, is when an ironic protest is taken literally by the target group. Then, of course, the whole point of irony, and thus the critical intention of the protesters, is completely missed. This occurred with regard to the before mentioned fake "pro-war demonstration" in Berlin in 2002 when a few spectators took the activists' slogans at face value.

These examples demonstrate that context matters. In some cases, symbols that are created in a particular context remain bound to that context: either in the narrow sense that they are considered so unique and specific that they seem not to be applicable somewhere else. More often, symbols travel from one context to another provided that the cause and/or the groups are similar. The burning of bras, undertaken by U.S. feminists in the 1970s, may be copied by feminists in other countries. But the same action would not make sense in the context of, say, protesters for animal rights or against nuclear reactors. In still other cases, tactics are diffused because the contexts, and probably the broader themes as well, are considered to be structurally akin, notwithstanding differences in specific content, time, and space. This might apply, for example, to grain seizures, machine breaking, or the refusal to pay taxes. Finally, there are examples when particular elements of protest, be they visual images, pieces of cloth, or forms of action, become completely modular. In other words, they are decontextualized. Despite of their original context that is bound to a particular ideological position, symbols can be even adopted by the opponents of the initial users. For example, in recent years, the portrait of Che Guevara could be found on T-shirts of right extremists. Another stunning example is the practise of antiabortion activists who used tactics (such as the sit-in) and sang songs (such as "We shall overcome") that stem from a liberal-progressive background.

Conclusion

Symbols, whatever their degree of complexity and specific design, are widely used in the realm of protest politics. They are valuable in strengthening internal cohesion and collective identity, making a group or claim visible,

Figure 56.3. Berlin, Germany, 11 February 2012. A protester wearing a tape Acta over her mouth during a demonstration against the Anti-Counterfeiting Trade Agreement (ACTA). © Photo by Stefan Boness.

and expressing motives and reasons for protest to the opponents, third parties ranging from passersby to the mass public, and eventually political decision makers. It appears that the expressive and orienting function of symbols is especially important in the field of social movements and protest politics—a field which, by its very nature, is very dynamic, has a low degree of structuration and institutionalization, and therefore is difficult to overview.

In most cases, protest symbols are not created by their actual users but are part of a known cultural reservoir or adopted from outside. They have been diffused either directly, from person to person, or indirectly via some sort of medium. In this regard, audiovisual documentation, and more recently the use of the Internet, are of crucial importance. In the process of adoption, however, protest symbols may be submitted to changes in form and content. Depending on their versatility as well as the needs and specific context of the adopters, protest symbols can be modified. In a historical perspective, it seems that protest symbols become more moldable and modular. In rare cases, they may even completely lose their original meaning and become adopted by their creators' opponents.

Dieter Rucht is professor emeritus of sociology at the Free University of Berlin. He was codirector of the research group "Civil Society, Citizenship and Political Mobilization in Europe" at the Social Science Research Center Berlin. His research interests include political participation, social movements, political protest, and public discourse. Among his recent books in English are: *The World Says No to War: Demonstrations against the War on Iraq* (Minneapolis, MN, 2010), coedited with Stefaan Walgrave; and *Meeting Democracy: Power and Deliberation in Global Justice Movements* (Cambridge, 2013), coedited with Donatella Della Porta.

Notes

1. According to Rogers, diffusion typically evolves in a S-shaped curve: initially, diffusion starts at a low pace followed by a period of significant increase in which the great mass of the adopters is reached. Finally, there is a phase of rapid deceleration and probably even halt of further diffusion. See Everett M Rogers, *Diffusion of Innovations* (New York, 1983).
2. Rogers, *Diffusion of Innovations*; David Strang and John W Meyer, "Institutional Conditions for Diffusion," *Theory and Society* 22 (1993): 487–511.
3. For an application of these ideas to social movements, see Doug McAdam and Dieter Rucht, "Cross-National Diffusion of Social Movement Ideas and Tactics," in *Citizens, Protest, and Democracy. The Annals of the American Academy of Political*

and Social Sciences, vol. 528, ed. R Dalton (New York, 1993), 56–74; Sean Chabot, "Transnational Diffusion and the African Reinvention of the Ghandian Repertoire," *Mobilization* 5, no. 2 (2000): 201–16; Conny Roggeband, "Immediately I Thought We Should Do the Same Thing. International Inspiration and Exchange in Feminist Action against Sexual Violence," *European Journal of Women's Studies* 11, no. 2 (2004): 159–75; Sarah A Soule, "Diffusion Processes Within and Across Movements," in *The Blackwell Companion to Social Movements,* ed. DA Snow, SA Soule, and H Kriesi (Malden, MA, 2008), 294–310; David Strang and Sarah A Soule, "Diffusion in Organizations and Social Movements: From Hybrid Corn to Poison Pills," *Annual Review of Sociology* (1998): 265–90.

4. See, for example, Anthony Oberschall, "The 1960 Sit-Ins: Protest Diffusion and Movement Take-Off," *Research in Social Movements, Conflict and Change* 11 (1989): 31–53; Peter Hedstrom, "Contagious Collectivities: On the Spatial Diffusion of Swedish Trade Unions, 1890–1940," *American Journal of Sociology* 99 (1994): 1157–79; John D McCarthy, Clark McPhail, and John Crist, "The Emergence and Diffusion of Public Order Management Systems," in *Social Movements in a Globalizing World,* ed. D Della Porta, H Kriesi, and D Rucht (New York, 1995), 71–94; Daniel J Myers, "The Diffusion of Collective Violence: Infectiousness, Susceptibility, and Mass Media Networks," *American Journal of Sociology* 106 (2000): 173–208.

5. Chabot, "Transnational Diffusion and the African Reinvention of the Ghandian Repertoire."

6. Dieter Rucht, "Appeal, Threat, and Press Resonance: Comparing Mayday Protests in London and Berlin," *Mobilization* 10, no. 1 (2005): 163–81.

Recommended Reading

McAdam, Doug, and Dieter Rucht. "Cross-National Diffusion of Social Movement Ideas and Tactics." In *Citizens, Protest, and Democracy. The Annals of the American Academy of Political and Social Science,* vol. 528, edited by R Dalton, 56–74. New York, 1993. An early attempt to apply the general concept of diffusion to social movement phenomena with a focus on left-wing groups in the United States and Germany in the 1960s and 1970s.

Soule, Sarah A. "Diffusion Processes Within and Across Movements." In *The Blackwell Companion to Social Movements,* edited by DA Snow, SA Soule, and H Kriesi, 294–310. Malden, MA, 2008. A dense overview on the state of the art of applying the concept of diffusion to the area of social movements and political protest.

Strang, David, and John W Meyer. "Institutional Conditions for Diffusion." *Theory and Society* 22 (1993): 487–511. This is an influential conceptual article on structural conditions that are likely to foster processes of diffusion.

Chapter 57

Political Correctness

Sabine Elsner-Petri

Characteristic Features of Long-Term Impact

"The closer you examine the argument over political correctness, the more it begins to look like one of Paul de Man's literary interpretations, where everything is a puzzle without a solution. ... Every participant carries around his own definitions ... The debate is unintelligible."[1] In an exaggerated fashion, Paul Berman hits the crux of political correctness, which covers a multitude of different subjects and discourses. In order to understand this phenomenon and its adaptation in Europe, it is necessary to look first at the history of its origins, which leads us beyond Europe into the United States.

The debate on political correctness arose in the United States between the end of the 1980s and the beginning of the 1990s. However, the adjectival phrase "politically correct" can be noted in a 1793 ruling of the Supreme Court, long before the emergence of the actual term that gave the debate its name.[2] The term politically correct is still used here as a neutral, spontaneous construction without connotations. Furthermore, this passage shows that the idea of categorizing certain opinions as correct or incorrect also belongs to an old tradition.[3] It is not until one hundred years later that politically correct becomes an established lexical term.

The origin of politically correct is still unclear, although it is commonly placed within left-wing groups and other social movements of the twentieth century. There is evidence inter alia from Communist, Leninist and Marxist,[4] Stalinist, and feminist movements and the Black Power[5] movement. Many texts show an ironical, self-critical use to mark distinct political orthodoxy. First, indications of this come from Communist ranks and date back to the 1930s.[6] Even in this early phase of the term's use, some authors assume an almost exclusively ironic slant.[7] Use of the term in a serious sense can be found occasionally within the Black Power or the women's liberation movement.[8] Dinesh D'Souza, a particularly active political correctness opponent, denies any self-critical, ironic character of the term during that phase.[9]

The English translation of Mao Tse-tung's "Quotations from Chairman Mao Tse-tung" is often regarded as having significantly influenced the concept of political correctness.[10] During the late 1960s and early 1970s, politically correct was increasingly becoming a lexical unit, thus gaining more contextual independence in its meaning[11] and increasingly used by social movement activists.[12] The various ironic, satirical, or serious uses of politically correct, which also can have dogmatic and rigid connotations, have one thing in common: they are all self-descriptions within a particular group and a means of determining how the group defines itself.[13] Up to this point, politically correct denoted a particular behavior, not a movement—as the nominalization of the term later did.

During the 1980s, the collocation politically correct spread beyond the left wing to other political camps.[14] In research literature, there is agreement that the nominalization political correctness and the debate on political correctness at American universities arose as a reaction to local restructuring processes.[15] Unfortunately, there is a lack of textual evidence, and so the exact history of the origin of the term remains vague. Contemporary witnesses are cited instead.[16] It is assumed that political correctness has arisen among conservative students, journalists, and academics who did not form a homogenous or organized group. For the first time, it became a term to categorize the members of a group from an outside perspective[17] and an instrument to undermine left-wing political positions.[18] John K Wilson notes that the self-critical aspect of the adjectival phrase was thus deliberately ignored, and its range of meaning expanded so as to cover any and every radical attitude. Therefore, political correctness can be seen as a blanket concept from the very beginning.[19] At the same time, the nominalization implies a unified movement that can be made responsible en bloc for certain trends. The term was used to criticize changes that occurred at some American universities to accord equal rights to various social groups.

The response to gender and race discrimination was affirmative action, a quota system for disadvantaged groups such as Afro-Americans. Also, the content of curricula was supposed to reflect the multicultural society by no longer being Eurocentric.[20] Discriminatory behavior was to be prevented by codes of conduct including so-called speech codes, since a significant part of discrimination takes place verbally. Speech codes have assumed a central role within political correctness. These changes were preceded by various processes that can be seen as results of the 1960s, including human rights movements such as the civil rights movement, the women's liberation movement, the homosexual movement, and others as well as influential philosophical theories.[21] All this could easily be subsumed under the new label political correctness and discredited by negative connotations.

General Cultural Functions

Political correctness first reached the general public via the media, which finally took up the topic and showcased it.[22] Newspapers and magazines became the main scene of the debate that reached a climax in the 1990s. Its polemical character becomes obvious within the articles' headlines: "Watch What You Say: Thought Police,"[23] "The Tyranny of Political Correctness."[24]

The discourse is dominated by political correctness opponents; counter-arguments are scattered and rather weak and mainly endeavor to relativize the phenomenon.[25] The political correctness opponents' many different definitions of political correctness resemble each other in associating it with totalitarianism, radicalism, extremism, and political persecution (thus following McCarthyism).[26] By using military metaphors and drastic examples, they brand political correctness as a peril to freedom and an enemy of democracy.[27] This line of argument essentially addresses linguistic criticism such as the speech codes.[28] The two main lines of criticism are in diametrical opposition, revealing the internal inconsistencies of the debate: on the one hand, political correctness is blamed for linguistic euphemism and, in that connection, for the unnecessary, ineffective, and ridiculous quality of its (allegedly) politically correct personal descriptions. For this purpose, absurd substitutes such as "vertically challenged" or "small person" are adduced, but very often, it is not possible to tell whether these terms are serious suggestions or mere inventions.[29] On the other hand, political correctness is played up as a serious peril that threatens freedom of speech.[30]

Whereas political correctness opponents are easily identified, the proponents are not. In oppositional texts, various groups are defined as political correctness proponents, as for example homosexuals, disabled persons, women, African Americans, liberals, left-wing intellectuals, scholars in the humanities, literary scholars, Marxists, and multiculturalists. These groups, however, neither defined nor saw themselves as political correctness proponents, and their rare replies were merely reactions to attacks by the conservatives. The latter had long won the discourse and had forged political correctness into a pejorative term[31]: "The end result of all this was that the label political correctness had turned into a powerful rhetorical stick to beat your political opponents with; [...] an effective strategy to short-circuit serious debate."[32]

Role in Protest Cultures

The response to the American debate brought political correctness to Europe, where it took on individual forms in accordance with the given societal structure. It would require extra studies to describe the prevailing development of political correctness in every single European country.[33] The German debate on political correctness may thus serve here as an example: the linguistic criticism consists of feminist linguistic criticism, linguistic criticism influenced by the environmental and peace movements (ecolinguistics), and linguistic criticism based on Germany's Nazi history. It is precisely the German way of coming to terms with the past that shows how the origin of what is later called political correctness derives from an old tradition in Germany.[34] Moreover, politically correct is there used to label behavior, situations, or language in an ironical way as inappropriate or absurd.

State of Research in Related Social Movement Studies

It is not possible to describe *the* state of political correctness research. Therefore, it seems appropriate in conclusion to sum up the American and the German state of research: the studies made so far in the two countries primarily deal with individual aspects of political correctness; the desirable thing here would be a comprehensive study explaining the phenomenon in its entirety and determining what aspects, measures, and supporters may be assigned to political correctness. A fairly comprehensive survey is attempted only by two German studies, namely Schenz on the subject of political correctness in the United States[35] and Wierlemann with regard to the United States and Germany.[36]

In the United States, there exist many historico-cultural treatments, for example those by Aufderheide,[37] Berman,[38] Dunant,[39] Newfield and Strickland,[40] Richer and Weir,[41] and Wilson.[42] Janicki[43] and Lakoff[44] have done research on sociolinguistic aspects.

In the German language area, Manske[45] and Hildebrandt[46] have worked on the subject from a historico-cultural perspective. Hoffmann[47] and Kapitzky[48] focus on linguistic criticism with regard to the German language, and Greil with regard to the English language.[49] Mayer[50] and

Germann[51] analyze the effects of political correctness on language usage and semantic change. Behrens and Rimscha do research on the German *Politische Korrektheit*.[52]

Research Gaps and Open Questions

There is a fairly surveyable quantity of corpus-based studies that could lead to valuable insights with regard to usage and history as well as to the reception of the term. Furthermore, it would be interesting to analyze if and to what extent political correctness has actually had an influence on individual languages. From the historic-cultural point of view, comparative studies on the various manifestations of political correctness in different countries might be revealing.

Sabine Elsner-Petri is a member of the research staff of the "Goethe-Wörterbuch" (dictionary of the lexicon of Goethe) of the Göttingen Academy of Science and Letters in Hamburg. One of her research topics is how discourses and social movements affect language and dictionaries. She wrote her dissertation about political correctness in monolingual dictionaries of German. Her book *Political Correctness im Duden-Universalwörterbuch: Eine diskurslinguistische Analyse.* (Greifswalder Beiträge zur Linguistik, Volume 9, Bremen) was published in 2015.

Notes

1. Paul Berman, "The Debate and Its Origins," in *Debating P.C. The Controversy over Political Correctness on College Campuses,* ed. P Berman (New York, 1992), 1–26.
2. Keith Allan and Kate Burridge, *Forbidden Words. Taboo and Censoring of Language* (Cambridge, 2006), 91.
3. Allan and Burridge, *Forbidden Words,* 91.
4. Berman, "The Debate and Its Origins," 5.
5. A mid to late 1960s movement.
6. John K Wilson, *The Myth of Political Correctness. The Conservative Attack on Higher Education* (Durham, NC, 1995), 4.
7. Mary Talbot, "Political Correctness and Freedom of Speech," in *Handbook of Language and Communication: Diversity and Change,* ed. M Hellinger and A Pauwels (Berlin, 2007), 751–63.
8. Ruth Perry, "A Short History of the Term 'Politically Correct,'" in *Beyond PC. Toward a Politics of Understanding,* ed. P Aufderheide (Saint Paul, MN, 1992), 71–79.

9. Ariane Manske, *Political Correctness und Normalität. Die amerikanische PC-Kontroverse im kulturgeschichtlichen Kontext* (Heidelberg, 2002), 30.

10. Perry, "A Short History of the Term 'Politically Correct,'" 72–73. As the movements of an epoch do not stand side by side in an isolated way but mutually influence each other conceptually, it is difficult to clearly discover the prevailing origin.

11. Tanja Greil, *Political Correctness und die englische Sprache. Studien zu (nicht-) diskriminierendem Sprachgebrauch unter besonderer Berücksichtigung des Social Labeling* (Hamburg, 1998), 9.

12. Lorna Weir, "PC Then and Now: Resignifying Political Correctness," in *Beyond Political Correctness: Toward the Inclusive University*, ed. S Richer and L Weir (Toronto, 1995), 51–87.

13. Manske, *Political Correctness und Normalität*, 32–33.

14. Mathias Hildebrandt, *Multikulturalismus und Political Correctness in den USA* (Wiesbaden, 2005), 74.

15. John Annette, "The Culture War and the Politics of Higher Education in America," in *The War of the Words: The Political Correctness Debate*, ed. S Dunant (London, 1994), 1–14.

16. Wilson, *The Myth of Political Correctness*, 4. Kelner's opinion might explain the inadequate situation of research because according to him, political correctness was a word from student language and therefore not likely to be found in written language.

17. Hildebrandt, *Multikulturalismus und Political Correctness in den USA*, 75.

18. Manske, *Political Correctness und Normalität*, 33.

19. Wilson, *The Myth of Political Correctness*, 4.

20. Berman, "The Debate and Its Origins," 15–19.

21. Just to give a few names: Herbert Marcuse, Martin Heidegger, Roland Barthes, Michel Foucault, and Jaques Derrida. Berman describes a part of this social-philosophical context. Berman, "The Debate and Its Origins."

22. Deborah Cameron, "'Words, Words, Words': The Power of Language," in *The War of the Words: The Political Correctness Debate*, ed. S Dunant (London, 1994), 15–34.

23. (Jerry Adler, *Newsweek*, 1990) cf. Manske, *Political Correctness und Normalität*, 19.

24. (Joan Beck, *Chicago Tribune*, 1990) cf. Manske, *Political Correctness und Normalität*, 19. After that, monographs such as Dinesh D'Souza's "Illiberal Education: The Politics of Race and Sex on Campus" made it to the bestseller lists.

25. Manske, *Political Correctness und Normalität*, 20.

26. Annette, "The Culture War and the Politics of Higher Education in America," 4.

27. Weir, "PC Then and Now," 71.

28. These are often put on the same level with the so-called Orwell "Newspeak" (George Orwell, *Nineteen Eighty-Four*), Kersten Sven Roth, *Politische Sprachberatung als Symbiose von Linguistik und Sprachkritik. Zu Theorie und Praxis einer kooperativ-kritischen Sprachwissenschaft* (Tübingen, 2004), 240.

29. Sibylle Germann, *Vom Greis zum Senior. Bezeichnungs- und Bedeutungswandel vor dem Hintergrund der "Political Correctness"* (Hildesheim, 2007), 2.

30. A famous example of that position is George Bush's speech: George Bush, "Remarks at the University of Michigan Commencement Ceremony in Ann Arbor," in *Weekly Compilation of Presidential Documents: Administration of George Bush 27*,

no. 19 (1991): 557–96. Very often, this has been considered as the inspiration for the reporting on the debate on American TV. (Hildebrandt, *Multikulturalismus und Political Correctness in den USA,* 77).

31. Manske, *Political Correctness und Normalität,* 26–29.

32. Allan and Burridge, *Forbidden Words,* 94.

33. In France, however, it seems as if there has been created a different opinion on political correctness. It seems as if *politiquement correct* is never used within political contexts—and if so, refers to conditions in foreign countries. It turns up only in cultural and sociological fields and on the whole seems to be ideologically less at a disadvantage, as a survey of the newspaper *Le Monde* by Michael Toolan shows: Michael Toolan, "Le politiquement correct dans le monde français," *Discourse and Society* 14, no. 1 (2003): 69–86.

34. Sally Johnson and Stephanie Suhr, "From 'Political Correctness' to 'Politische Korrektheit.' Discourses of 'PC' in the German newspaper *Die Welt,*" *Discourse and Society* 14, no. 1 (2003): 49–68.

35. Viola Schenz, *Political Correctness: Eine Bewegung erobert Amerika* (Frankfurt, 1994).

36. Sabine Wierlemann, *Political Correctness in den USA und in Deutschland* (Berlin, 2002).

37. P Aufderheide, ed., *Beyond PC Toward a Politics of Understanding* (Saint Paul, MN, 1992).

38. P Berman, ed., *Debating P.C. The Controversy over Political Correctness on College Campuses* (New York, 1992).

39. Sarah Dunant, ed., *The War of the Words: The Political Correctness Debate* (London, 1994).

40. Christopher Newfield and Ronald Strickland, eds, *After Political Correctness. The Humanities and Society in the 1990s* (Boulder, CO, 1995).

41. S Richer and L Weir, eds, *Beyond Political Correctness: Toward the Inclusive University* (Toronto, 1995).

42. Wilson, *The Myth of Political Correctness.*

43. Karol Janicki, "Political Correctness: Conflict-Ridden Language, Language-Ridden Conflict or Both?," *Belgian Journal of Linguistics* 11 (1997): 297–312.

44. Robin Tolmach Lakoff, *The Language War* (Berkeley, CA, 2000).

45. Manske, *Political Correctness und Normalität.*

46. Hildebrandt, *Multikulturalismus und Political Correctness in den USA.*

47. Arne Hoffmann, *Political Correctness. Zwischen Sprachzensur und Minderheitenschutz* (Marburg, 1996).

48. Jens Kapitzky, *Sprachkritik und Political Correctness in der Bundesrepublik* (Aachen, 2000).

49. Greil, *Political Correctness und die englische Sprache..*

50. Caroline Mayer, *Öffentlicher Sprachgebrauch und Political Correctness. Eine Analyse sprachreflexiver Argumente im politischen Wortstreit* (Hamburg, 2002).

51. Sibylle Germann, *Vom Greis zum Senior. Bezeichnungs- und Bedeutungswandel vor dem Hintergrund der "Political Correctness"* (Hildesheim, 2007).

52. Michael Behrens and Robert von Rimscha, *"Politische Korrektheit" in Deutschland. Eine Gefahr für die Demokratie,* 2nd ed. (Bonn, 1995).

Recommended Reading

Allan, Keith, and Kate Burridge. *Forbidden Words: Taboo and Censoring of Language*. Cambridge, 2006. This book is about the use of language taboos in everyday conversation. It examines the role of taboos in everyday life and offers a lot of examples.

Dunant, Sarah, ed. *The War of the Words: The Political Correctness Debate*. London, 1994. An accumulation of essays that discusses the political correctness debate of the 1990s from different points of view. The authors do not only focus on the U.S. debate, they are also concerned with the political correctness movement in France or England, for example.

Hildebrandt, Mathias. *Multikulturalismus und Political Correctness in den USA*. Wiesbaden, 2005. The author reveals the main topics, concepts, and terms of the debate of multiculturalism and political correctness in the United States.

Hölscher, Lucian, ed. *Political Correctness: der sprachpolitische Streit um die nationalsozialistischen Verbrechen*. Göttingen, 2008. The authors examine the development of political correctness in Germany and its connection with the dispute over the crime of the National Socialists.

Manske, Ariane. *Political Correctness und Normalität: Die amerikanische PC-Kontroverse im kulturgeschichtlichen Kontext*. Heidelberg, 2002. The author shows the interrelation between historico-cultural aspects and political correctness in the United States.

Index